lonely planet

Georgia
Armenia &
Azerbaijan

Georgia
(p40)

Armenia
(p144)

Azerbaijan
(p227)

Nagorno-
Karabakh
(p306)

Azerbaijan
(p227)

Tom Masters, Joel Balsam, Jenny Smith

Contents

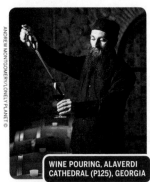

WINE POURING, ALAVERDI
CATHEDRAL (P125), GEORGIA

ANDREW MONTGOMERY/LONELY PLANET ©

NORAVANK MONASTERY
(P201), ARMENIA

JUSTIN FOULKES/LONELY PLANET ©

Contents

ALEKSANDAR TODOROVIC/SHUTTERSTOCK ©

FLAME TOWERS (P238),
BAKU, AZERBAIJAN

Welcome to Georgia, Armenia & Azerbaijan

This thrillingly mountainous, scenically spectacular and culturally diverse region is where Asia and Europe rub up against each other, with often unpredictable and fascinating results.

The Great Caucasus

The vast mountain range forming a natural border between the South Caucasus and Russia, the Great Caucasus runs from the Black Sea to the Caspian and provides the most astonishing scenery in the region, its sequence of dramatic peaks fronted by green river valleys and unbelievably picturesque villages. The mountain regions are strung with spectacular walking and riding trails where ruined fortresses, watchtowers and ancient churches are often perched in achingly lovely locations. Each country has superb day-hike potential, but high in the Great Caucasus, Georgia's Svaneti, Kazbegi and Tusheti regions are particularly ideal for longer-distance village-to-village treks.

Exhilarating Landscapes

At lower altitudes in the region you'll find idyllic farms, vineyards and woodland as well as arid semi-deserts, rocky gorges and even some alluring beaches. Each of the three nations has modern ski resorts, while rafting and paragliding are possible in Georgia, where climbers can also scale Mt Kazbek and several other 5000m peaks. Delve underground in Armenia's many caves, or explore Azerbaijan's Caspian hinterland, where natural curiosities include mud volcanoes and even water that catches fire.

Asia Meets Europe

While the South Caucasus is a relatively small region, it's made up of three highly diverse countries, features three ethnically distinct breakaway republics, one isolated exclave and at least 16 different languages, all within an area smaller than the UK. This is a cultural crossroads where Europe meets Asia and where influences from Russia, Iran, Turkey and Central Asia have been absorbed over the centuries into proudly distinctive local cultures. Here social attitudes remain traditional and family networks rule supreme despite three decades of fast-paced change since the end of the Soviet Union.

Multifaceted Cultures

Antique forts, monasteries, churches and ruins pepper the region, and the bigger cities boast some excellent museums, splendid galleries and a rich theatrical heritage. Savour all this with deep-rooted hospitality, varied food made from some of the best natural ingredients on earth and reinvigorated wines from the original home of viniculture. The ever-improving tourism infrastructure in the South Caucasus may seem modest by European standards, but come here soon, before these ancient lands lose their rough edges, and you'll discover what's been keeping visitors coming for centuries.

Why I Love Georgia, Armenia & Azerbaijan

By Tom Masters, Writer

In 20 years of travelling in this incredible region, I've gained enough experiences for a life-time, and despite the monumental changes I've witnessed in all three countries, the things I most love have barely changed. The mountains, despite their shrinking glaciers, remain just as majestic and mysterious, even if the roads to reach them are dramatically improved. The food, in all its carb-laden, spicy glory, hasn't changed once you leave the culinary oases of the three capitals, and perhaps above all, the people of the South Caucasus remain as kind, curious, good-humoured and contradictory as ever.

For more about our writers, see p352

Above: Zvartnots Cathedral (p172), Armenia

Georgia, Armenia & Azerbaijan

Svaneti
Spectacular mountain walks,
175 ancient towers (p106)

Stepantsminda
Great outdoor activities, majesti
Caucasus scenery (p100)

Tbilisi
Contemporary style in a
crucible of history (p42)

Dilijan National Park
Wildflower valleys and
thick forests (p194)

Yerevan
Cafe culture, fancy fashions,
fast cars (p146)

Noravank Monastery
Stunning 13th-century
churches (p201)

ELEVATION

5000m
4000m
3000m
2000m
1500m
1000m
500m
0

0
0
200 km
100 miles

RUSSIA

○ Grozny

● Khasavyurt

Davit Gareja
Otherworldly cave monasteries
and landscape (p130)

● Makhachkala

Xınalıq
Remote shepherds' settlement
in the Caucasus (p262)

Mt Tebulos
(4492m)

CHECHNYA

▲ Mt Diklos
(4285m)

USHETI

CASPIAN SEA

Şəki
Caravanserai town that's now
Unesco-recognised (p272)

● Derbent

**Baku's 21st-Century
Architecture**
Extraordinary oil-boom
skyscrapers (p230)

Lagodekhi
Protected
Areas

○ Telavi

AKHETI ○ Gurjaani

Lagodekhi ○

† Davit
Gareja

● Balakən

BALAKƏN

○ Tsnori

ZAQATALA ○ Qax

Zaqatala ○

Bazardüzü
Dağ
(4467m) ▲ Laza ○

○ Xaçmaz

Quba ○

● Şabran

Vashlovani
Protected
Areas

Şəki ○

Xaçmaz ○

▲ Şahdağ
(4243m)

○ Xınalıq

○ Siyəzən

azax

Qəbələ ○

Babadağ
(3629m) ▲

XIZI

○ Tovuz

*Mingəçevir
Reservoir*

● Mingəçevir

Göyçay ●

○ Şamaxı

Sumqayıt ●

Mastağa ○

AVUSH

Şəmkir ○

Gəncə ●

Ağdaş ○

Dzhangichay

*Abşeron
Peninsula*

○ Saratovka

Goranboy ●

Yevlax ○

Ağsu ○

AZERBAIJAN

Zirə ○

LESSER

Ücar ○

Kürdəmir ○

BAKI

★ BAKU

*Lake
Sevan*

CAUCASUS

● Bərdə

Zərdab ●

Sabirabad ○

Haciqabul ○

EGARKUNIK

○ Vardenis

Ağdərə ○

Kür

Ağcabədi ○

Şirvan ○

○ Ələt

AYOTS

NAGORNO-

Ağdam ○

İmişli ○

Araz

DZOR ○ Jermuk

KARABAKH

Karkar River

Salyan ○

Yeghegnadzor

Laçin
(Berdzor) ◎

**Stepanakert
(Xankəndi)**

● Parsabad

○ Neftçala

Mt Mets
Ishkhanasar ▲
(3548m)

AXÇIVAN

SYUNIK

○ Goris

● Bilesevar

ZERBAIJAN

○ Naxçıvan
City

Kapan ○

IRAN

Cəlilabad ○

Zharskiy ○

Mt Kaputjugh
(3904m) ▲

⊗ Culfa

Ordubad

Masallı ○

Jolfa ○

Meghri ○

Yardımlı ○

Agarak ○

Lerik ○

TALIS MOUNTAINS

○ Lənkəran

Toradı ○

Hirkan National Park

● Astara (Azerbaijan)
⊗ Astara (Iran)

Marand ○

○ Ahar

Meshgin
Shahr ●

Mt Sabalan
(4811m) ▲

○ Ardabil

◎ Tabriz

Georgia, Armenia & Azerbaijan's
Top 10

Tbilisi

1 Nowhere blends the romance of Georgia's past with its exciting future better than its magical and chaotic capital, Tbilisi (p42). Its Old Town, in parts gloriously restored and in others still totally dilapidated, is a wonderfully atmospheric place of winding lanes, ancient stone churches and shady squares. The rest of the city is relentlessly fast-paced and a showcase for all that contemporary Georgia has to offer: world-class dining, fabulous natural wine bars, local fashion brands, a thriving techno scene and a slew of architectural gems from the ancient to the modern. Above: Old Town (p42)

Svaneti

2 The mysterious mountain valleys of Georgia's Svaneti (p106) sit high in the Caucasus, surrounded by spectacular snowy peaks, alpine meadows and thick forests – a paradise for walkers in summer. Long isolated and insulated from the outside world, Svaneti has its own language and a strongly traditional culture, symbolised by the centuries-old 175 *koshkebi* (ancient stone defensive towers) that stand proudly in its villages, and the 1000-year-old frescoes in its churches. Accessible only by a long road trip until relatively recently, Svaneti can now be reached by plane from Tbilisi.

Baku's 21st-Century Architecture

3 Hot on the heels of Dubai, Azerbaijan's capital Baku (p230) has transformed its skyline with some of the world's most audacious new architecture. Counterpointed with the city's medieval Old City core is a trio of 190m skyscrapers shaped like glass flames that really appear to burn at night once the remarkable light show comes on. The white curves of Zaha Hadid's Heydar Aliyev Center form a similarly thrilling spectacle, and along the Caspian Sea waterfront an otherworldly hotel complex shaped like a crescent moon is being built. Top: Heydar Aliyev Center (p238)

Dilijan National Park

4 Roughly 90km northeast of Yerevan is Dilijan National Park (p194), an oasis of wildflower-speckled valleys and dense forests which form the backdrop for derelict medieval churches and picturesque herds of roaming cattle and sheep. Plenty of hikes have been mapped in the area thanks to the ever-expanding Transcaucasian Trail, which aims to connect the Black Sea to the Caspian Sea, and the HIKEArmenia app. In the friendly town of Dilijan, you'll find some of Armenia's best restaurants outside of Yerevan and a smattering of excellent B&Bs.

Stepantsminda

5 Just a couple of hours' drive from Tbilisi, the small town of Stepantsminda (p100) is the hub of one of the South Caucasus' most spectacular, yet easily accessed, high-mountain zones. The sight of Tsminda Sameba Church silhouetted on its hilltop against the massive snow-covered cone of Mt Kazbek is perhaps Georgia's most iconic image. Numerous walking, horse and mountain-bike routes lead along steep-sided valleys and up to glaciers, waterfalls, mountain passes and isolated villages – ideal for getting a first taste of the high Caucasus. Top: Tsminda Sameba Church (p100)

Yerevan

6 Grab a *soorch* (Armenian-style coffee), a beer from the city's most buzzworthy craft brewery or a glass of local wine and breathe in one of the region's most endearing cities. The Armenian capital (p146) has been booming with construction and activity in recent years, with hip new bars and restaurants opening next to Soviet-era shops. Slip into a *dalan* (archway) and enter a portal into a new world – you may find a charming 19th-century balcony, a cobbler who's been working the same tiny shop for decades or a restaurant serving grandmother-to-table Armenian cuisine.

JUSTIN FOULKES/LONELY PLANET ©

Noravank Monastery

7 As the world's oldest Christian nation, Armenia is dotted with spectacular churches, but none outshine the 13th-century Noravank Monastery (p201). Stand in front of one of its three medieval churches at sunset and you'll see them ablaze in gorgeous shades of red and gold, the surrounding cliffs providing a breathtaking backdrop to one of the South Caucasus' finest sights. The sun-drenched area around the monastery is dotted with caves, including Areni-1, where archaeologists recently found the world's oldest winery, dating back 6100 years.

Davit Gareja

8 Set in remote, arid lands near Georgia's border with Azerbaijan, these much-revered cave monasteries were carved out of a lonely cliff-face by 6th-century missionaries. They became a cradle of medieval monastic culture and fresco painting. Saints' tombs, vivid 1000-year-old murals, an otherworldly landscape and the very idea that people voluntarily chose – and still choose – to live in desert caves all combine to make visiting Davit Gareja (p130) a startling experience today. Though remote, the site makes an easy day trip from Tbilisi, Telavi or Sighnaghi.
Above right: frescoes (p130)

Şəki

9 The small Azerbaijani city of Şəki (Sheki; p272) sits amid lushly wooded hills behind which rise majestic snow-dusted peaks. Recognised as a Unesco World Heritage Site since 2019, its antique core features heavy fortress bastions, two mural-walled palaces of former khans and several historic brick mosques. The town is famed for its pastries, the laconic humour of its population, and the chance to sleep in a range of boutique hotels, one of which offers basic but bargain rooms in a genuine caravanserai dating back to the Silk Route days. Top right: Xan Sarayı (p273)

Xınalıq

10 Behind the peaceable country town of Quba, woodland glades and sheep-nibbled hillsides lead up into the foothills of the Great Caucasus. Here, separated by dramatic canyons and wild river valleys, lie a scattering of remote shepherds' villages, some speaking their own unique languages. The best known of these is Xınalıq (p262), with its stacked, grey-stone houses, middle-of-nowhere vibe and authentic homestays allowing an inside glimpse of shepherd life in Azerbaijan. Even if you don't stay, the sheer scenic variety of a journey here is well worth the trip.

Need to Know

For more information, see Survival Guide (p321)

Currency

Armenia: dram (AMD)
Azerbaijan: manat (AZN)
Georgia: lari (GEL)

Languages
Armenian, Azerbaijani, Georgian

Visas

Simple or unnecessary for visitors to Georgia and for many to Armenia. Essential but generally painless for most visiting Azerbaijan; allow at least 24 hours.

Money

ATMs, Western Union transfer offices and money-changing facilities are widely available. Credit-card use remains limited outside big cities, so carry enough cash.

Mobile Phones

All three countries use the GSM standard. If your mobile is unlocked for international use, it's often worth buying an inexpensive local SIM card.

Time

Four hours ahead of GMT/UTC. Daylight saving is not observed.

When to Go

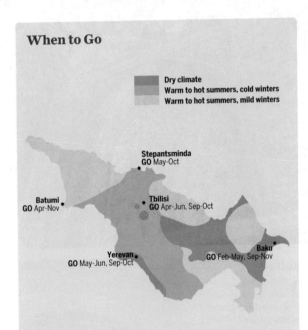

Dry climate
Warm to hot summers, cold winters
Warm to hot summers, mild winters

Stepantsminda GO May-Oct

Batumi GO Apr-Nov

Tbilisi GO Apr-Jun, Sep-Oct

Baku GO Feb-May, Sep-Nov

Yerevan GO May-Jun, Sep-Oct

High Season
(Jul & Aug)

➡ Locals' holiday time; tourist accommodation is crowded.

➡ Visit mountain areas; temperatures are warm and paths are dry in the high Caucasus.

➡ Capitals and other lowland areas unpleasantly hot and humid.

Shoulder (May, Jun, Sep & Oct)

➡ May and October offer the most pleasant temperatures in the lowlands.

➡ Upland areas can be snowbound from late September to early June.

➡ May is rainy but between showers the flowers are magical.

Low Season
(Nov–Apr)

➡ Winter sports January to March; most non-ski mountain lodgings close.

➡ Inland often below freezing December to February.

➡ Tbilisi: wet and slushy; Yerevan: icy; Baku: cold till March.

➡ Wintry weather often lasts into April.

Useful Websites

Armenia Travel (www.armenia.travel) Official site.

Azerbaijan Travel (www.azerbaijan.travel) Official site.

Caravanistan (www.caravanistan.com) Visa and border-crossing tales collated.

Caucasian Knot (www.eng.kavkaz-uzel.eu) News from North and South Caucasus.

Eurasianet (www.eurasianet.org) Regional news features.

Georgia Starts Here (www.georgiastartshere.com) Travel information by locals.

Georgia Travel (www.georgia.travel) Official site.

Hike Armenia (www.hikearmenia.org) Extensive guide to trails and hiking in Armenia.

Thorn Tree (www.lonelyplanet.com/thorntree/forums/europe-eastern-europe-the-caucasus) Lonely Planet travellers' forum.

Visions of Azerbaijan (www.visions.az) History and culture.

Important Numbers

Armenia's country code	☑ 374
Azerbaijan's country code	☑ 994
Georgia's country code	☑ 995
International access code	☑ 00
Emergency	☑ 103 (Georgia ☑ 112)

Daily Costs

Budget:
Less than US$50

➡ Hostel bed: US$5–20

➡ Simple snack meals: from US$2.50

➡ Museum entry: US$2–10

➡ Cheap draught beer: US$0.50–3

➡ Long-distance bus/train ride: US$5

Midrange:
US$50–100

➡ Midrange hotel double room: per person US$25–60

➡ Midrange restaurant meal: US$6–15

➡ Drink and pastry at a coffee shop: US$3–6

➡ Long-distance shared-taxi ride: US$10

Top End:
More than US$100

➡ Luxury hotel double room: per person from US$100

➡ High-quality dinner: US$15–35

➡ Beer in an expat pub: US$3–6

➡ Rental car per day: from US$50

Opening Hours

Museums 10am–5pm or longer; many close Monday

Offices 9am or 10am–5pm or 6pm Monday to Friday; lunch breaks last an hour or more

Restaurants 8am–9pm in rural locations, 11am–11pm in big cities or even longer

Shops 10am–7pm, often much longer

Theatres Shows often start around 6pm; many close for the season from June to early September

Arriving in the Region

David the Builder Kutaisi International Airport Prebook minibus seats (georgianbus.com) to Kutaisi (5 GEL, 30 minutes), Tbilisi (20 GEL, four hours) or Batumi (15 GEL, two hours).

Heydar Əliyev International Airport Bus (aeroexpress.az) runs all day/night to Baku train station once or twice hourly (AZN1.30, 40 minutes). No booking required. Taxis cost from AZN25.

Tbilisi International Airport Bus 37 runs 24 hourly, typically half-hourly (0.50 GEL), taking around an hour to reach the terminus in Station Sq via Freedom Sq and Rustaveli gamziri. Bargain hard for reasonable taxi fares (from 50 GEL).

Zvartnots Airport (Yerevan) Minibus 18 (AMD300, thrice hourly, 8am to 8pm) runs to Abovyan St via Sasuntsi Davit metro station and Rossiya Mall. Save money on taxis (20 minutes) by using apps Yandex or GG (from AMD2000).

Etiquette

Local homes When visiting someone's home, take a gift, and offer to remove your shoes.

Feasting Local hospitality can be almost overwhelming: don't be ashamed to say you can't eat or drink any more.

Contributions If invited to a dinner or an overnight stay, tactfully offer some money, but don't insist. If it's a wedding, you will be expected to pay a (fairly hefty) contribution.

Greetings A handshake is the normal greeting between men. Women generally don't shake hands, though if foreigners don't follow this it won't be an insult. Friends (of whatever sex) normally peck each other on the cheek.

For much more on **getting around**, see p331

What's New

It's all change in the South Caucasus. Georgia has expanded its traveller offerings hugely with superb new hotels, hostels and nightlife options, while Azerbaijan has added Şəki to its Unesco World Heritage Sites and Armenia continues its expansion of walking trails and tourism activities, as well as stellar wine production.

Tbilisi Nightlife

With the opening of some world-class nightlife spaces in recent years, Tbilisi (p61) has well and truly found its calling as the South Caucasus' coolest city and its undisputed epicentre of techno.

Şəki Heritage

The remarkable charms of Şəki's historic Old City core (p272) gained Unesco World Heritage status in 2019 and a new tourist shuttle service from Azerbaijan House in central Tbilisi will put the city ever more firmly on the traveller circuit.

Areni-1 Cave Opens

In 2007, archaeologists discovered remnants of a 6100-year-old winery at the Areni-1 Cave (p200). The next year they found a 5500-year-old leather shoe in the same cave. Areni-1 is finally open to visitors, who can see some of the ancient winemaking tools.

Gəncə Filarmoniya

Azerbaijan's second city continues its reinvention with this remarkably ornate neoclassical music venue (p283), pimpled with spires and statues and contrasting with a very contemporary shopping mall on the central square.

Black Rocks Lake Trek

This superb three-day hike to the Shavi Kldeebis Tba (Black Rocks Lake; p132) on the Georgian–Russian border in the

---

LOCAL KNOWLEDGE

WHAT'S HAPPENING IN GEORGIA, ARMENIA & AZERBAIJAN

Tom Masters, Lonely Planet Writer

The three South Caucasus nations have travelled radically different roads since gaining their unexpected independence during the disintegration of the Soviet Union. In 2016 the simmering conflict between Azerbaijan and Armenia flared up again with a four-day series of battles along the ceasefire line of the disputed Nagorno-Karabakh region. Some 350 people died, with Azerbaijan recovering three formerly occupied villages in what many world observers believed to be an exercise in probing Nagorno-Karabakh's defence capabilities for a possible future attack.

However, since then, tensions have cooled as the focus turned to reviving the economy. In 2018 Armenia underwent its own Velvet Revolution, as President Serzh Sargsyan was booted out of power by popular demand in favour of Nikol Pashinyan. The following year it was Georgia's turn, with massive protests in Tbilisi during the summer of 2019 against both the country's own government and Russia, which most Georgians consider an occupying force due to its military presence in Abkhazia and South Ossetia.

Lagodekhi Protected Areas is now circular, thanks to the completion of a new return trail and the construction of a second mountain shelter.

Transcaucasian Trail

Trailblazers have been hard at work building what will eventually become a walking trail (p100) network connecting all three countries in the region. Recently completed trails include one through Armenia's Dilijan National Park.

Rafting the Debed Canyon

Debed Canyon (p186) is now home to white-water rafting outfit Rafting in Armenia, which takes eight-person rafts along the Debed River. There's no better way to see the canyon.

Easy Azerbaijani Visas

Azerbaijan has ripped up the visa rule book and now offers visas (p305) effortlessly in 24 hours if you apply online. Just don't forget to print out the confirmation before you reach the border.

Welcome to Naxçivan (Finally)

For years, the disconnected Azerbaijani exclave of Naxçivan (p294) looked rather suspiciously at tourists, but the region is suddenly changing tack, and today there's a swathe of restored monuments and even a small ski resort under construction.

PLAN YOUR TRIP WHAT'S NEW

LISTEN, WATCH & FOLLOW

For inspiration visit www.lonelyplanet.com/georgia, www.lonelyplanet.com/armenia and www.lonelyplanet.com/azerbaijan.

Insta @armeniatravelofficial Official tourism account of Armenia.

Insta @experienceazerbaijan Azerbaijan's official tourism account.

Insta @georgiatravel Georgia's official instagram account.

FAST FACTS

Population 16.6 million

Languages spoken Armenian, Azerbaijani, Georgian

Largest cities Baku, Tbilisi, Yerevan

GAA   UK   GERMANY

≈ 90 people per sq km

Natural Wine

Natural wine is having a moment all over the region, with dozens of natural wine bars and independent vineyards in both Georgia and Armenia producing some excellent vintages. Cheers!

Getting Around

For more information, see Transport (p328)

Travelling by Car

Car Hire

Driving in the capital cities can be very tough due to convoluted one-way systems, rush-hour traffic jams and uncertain parking conditions. Elsewhere parking is usually uncomplicated and traffic is light, though it can prove challenging to adapt to sometimes-anarchic local driving styles.

The capital cities have branches of major international car-rental companies as well as local outfits that are typically far cheaper (from around US$20 per day), but generally, hired cars cannot be taken across borders (except Georgia–Armenia in some cases). Hiring a local driver is worth considering for inter-city trips or excursions. A cost-effective way to do this is to find the shared taxi stand for your proposed destination and then offer to pay four times the regular fare plus a little extra for diversions and photo stops. Hostels can also arrange a driver at prices that can prove more favourable than finding a taxi on the street.

Driving Conditions

Less-used mountain roads are often very poorly surfaced and can get blocked or washed away by landslides or flash floods. These need a 4WD, for which car-rental agents usually charge at least US$80 a day. If self-driving in such areas, it's safest to travel in a convoy of at least two vehicles with winches and tow cables for mud patches. You'll often do better finding a local driver with an old Niva or UAZ at the starting village of any off-

RESOURCES

Automobile Federation of Armenia (https://faa.am) News and information for drivers in Armenia, with content in English.

Azerbaijan Automobile Federation (www.mys.gov.az) Information for drivers of all types in Azerbaijan.

Caravanistan (www.caravanistan.com) An excellent travel website about the Caucasus and Central Asia, with good driving sections devoted to all three countries in the region.

Georgian National Automobile Federation (www.gaf.ge) News, links and information about driving in Georgia.

Thorntree (www.lonelyplanet.com/thorntree) Lonely Planet's travel forum has lots of information about getting around all three countries in the South Caucasus.

road adventure; but without speaking local languages (or Russian), organising things can be tough.

Roundabout priority is typically reversed from European norms (give way to oncoming vehicles). It is usually acceptable to drive using a driving licence from most Western countries, but it is wise to also get an International Driving Permit before departure, especially if your licence does not have a photo. Filling stations are fairly common along main roads, but if you are going into remote areas, fill up beforehand.

No Car?

Bus

Almost every town and village has some sort of bus or minibus service, the latter being known widely as a *marshrutka* (plural *marshrutky*). Services can run hourly between larger towns, but rural villages often have just one minibus that departs for the regional centre in the morning, then returns from the bazaar after lunch.

Domestic fares average around US$1.50 per hour of travel. Standards can vary considerably. Local vehicles can get loaded up with freight (sacks of potatoes, crates of drinks), as well as people. It's rarely necessary (and often not possible) to book ahead except for a few international services.

Marshrutky usually have a destination sign inside the windscreen but it will use the local alphabet. To hail a *marshrutka* on the road, stick out your arm and wave. When you want to get off, say 'stop' in the local language (*kangnek* in Armenia, *sakhla* in Azerbaijan or *gaacheret* in Georgia).

Train

Trains are slower and less frequent than road transport. However, tickets are cheap, and on overnight routes sleeper berths are included in the price.

You need your passport both for buying tickets and for boarding an overnight night train whether domestic or international, but not for a suburban/local day train (known as an *elektrichka*), nor for other domestic trains in Armenia.

Bicycle

Cycling in the South Caucasus is becoming popular as a leg of a cross-Asia trip. Driving styles are somewhat less predictable than in Western countries, with hilly terrain and some poor road surfaces. However, traffic is relatively light (except for the few busy highways) and scenery is mostly picturesque.

DRIVING FAST FACTS

➡ Driving is on the right-hand side of the road.

➡ The legal maximum blood-alcohol level for driving in all three countries is zero.

➡ Legal driving age is 17 in Georgia and 18 in Azerbaijan and Armenia.

➡ Top speeds are 90km/h in Armenia and 110km/h in Azerbaijan and Georgia.

ROAD DISTANCES (KMS)

	Tbilisi	Batumi	Baku	Yerevan
Batumi	374			
Baku	578	948		
Yerevan	275	445	663	
Kutaisi	230	151	804	456

If You Like...

Walking & Horse Riding

Svaneti Many varied trails cross this spectacular region of green valleys, snowy peaks and picturesque villages. (p106)

Stepantsminda Quick climbs, longer glacier hikes and lovely valley walks or treks over high passes to remote Khevsur villages. (p100)

Dilijan With verdant hills and millions of summer wildflowers, the park surrounding the town of Dilijan offers terrific hiking. (p191)

Quba hinterland Hike between some of Azerbaijan's loveliest mountain villages, but plan well ahead for the Shahdag National Park. (p256)

Tusheti Beautiful mountain area with fine village-to-village walking and the region's best longer trek. (p117)

Kasagh Gorge A 7.5km trail alongside the Kasagh River links the spectacularly sited monasteries of Hovhannavank and Saghmosavank. (p172)

Views & Landscapes

Laza The natural amphitheatre of peaks and waterfalls behind this village is perhaps the South Caucasus' most impressive vista. (p266)

Stepantsminda Tsminda Sameba Church silhouetted against the towering, snow-covered Mt Kazbek is an unforgettable sight. (p100)

Voratan Pass Spectacular views over snow-capped mountains and wildflower-strewn pastures. (p199)

Ananuri Lake, fortress and church in perfect rural harmony. (p98)

Khor Virap The monastery that houses St Gregory's former prison cell also has an epic view of Mt Ararat in the distance. (p167)

Şahdağ Enjoy the panorama from Park Qusar. (p266)

Ushguli Snow-streaked Mt Shkhara towers above around a dozen traditional Svan watch-towers here. (p111)

Selim Pass Look down on the picturesque Yeghegis Valley from a 14th-century stone caravanserai. (p206)

Citadels & Fortresses

Baku Old City Photogenic crenellated walls enclose an inner city with a mysterious tower, 15th-century palace and medieval minarets. (p230)

Shatili Unique agglomeration of defensive towers forming a single fortress-like whole. (p116)

Rabati Castle Night-time floodlights make this giant citadel glow and highlight the golden dome of the mosque within. (p80)

Alinja Castle Crag-top ruins that have been dubbed the Machu Picchu of the Caucasus. (p298)

Amberd Fortress Lonely ruin worth the two-hour hike. (p173)

Şəki A mural-decorated khan's palace lies inside sturdy fortress walls. (p272)

Svaneti Mountain villages bristling with defensive refuge towers. (p106)

Religious Sites

Geghard Monastery Chapels and churches hewn from the rock, plus remarkable *khachkars* (carved stone crosses). (p168)

Mtskheta The beating heart of Georgian Orthodox Christianity, centred on magnificent Svetitskhoveli Cathedral. (p68)

İmamzadə Gəncə's most memorable sight, featuring a historic dome within a modern one. (p284)

Noravank Monastery A 13th-century reddish-gold monastery,

surrounded by towering red cliffs, which illuminates when the sun sets. (p201)

Şamaxı Grand Mosque The Caucasus' second-oldest mosque, magnificently rebuilt with a dazzling interior. (p267)

Tatev Great fortified monastery on a fairy-tale natural rock fortress. (p211)

Vardzia Fascinating remnants of a cave city that was the spiritual heart of medieval Georgian Christianity. (p81)

Mir Mövsüm Ağa Ziyarətgahı Folk superstition meets Islam at this shrine where locals believe wishes will come true. (p253)

Ateşgah Suraxanı's fire temple still burns, though it's now a museum. (p252)

Modern Architecture

While there's plenty of new building, the region's most jaw-dropping contemporary architecture is concentrated in three cities: Baku, Batumi and Tbilisi.

Heydar Aliyev Center The smooth white curves of what could be an alien spacecraft morphing into a gigantic snail. (p238)

Flame Towers Three 190m flame-shaped skyscrapers dominate Baku's skyline. (p238)

Bridge of Peace Glass filigree footbridge that, along with the Presidential Palace, creates a startling contrast with the rest of old Tbilisi. (p51)

Stamba Hotel Enjoy this fabulous recent conversion of a Soviet-era Tbilisi publishing house into one of the South Caucasus' leading hotels. (p57)

PLAN YOUR TRIP IF YOU LIKE...

JUSTIN FOULKES/LONELY PLANET ©

Top: Tatev Monastery (p211), Armenia
Bottom: Hikers in Svaneti (p106), Georgia

Art

All three countries have a solid artistic heritage. Baku's Old City has a particular wealth of small private galleries.

Yarat, Baku Azerbaijan's latest Contemporary Art Centre in a reclaimed ex-naval warehouse. (p237)

National Gallery, Tbilisi Houses a large number of works by Niko Pirosmani, Georgia's beloved primitivist painter. (p47)

National Gallery of Armenia, Yerevan Remarkable collection of Armenian art, including stunning paintings by Vardges Surenyants. (p153)

Sergei Parajanov Museum, Yerevan Eccentric house museum of artist-cum-film director. (p149)

Mayak 13, Baku Designed by one of Azerbaijan's foremost modern artists, this restaurant is more artwork than eatery. (p244)

Svaneti History & Ethnography Museum, Mestia This excellent museum has a remarkable collection of beautiful old icons. (p107)

Soviet Throwbacks

Lenin statues may have long since disappeared from public plinths, but some notable reminders of the 70-year period of Soviet rule remain.

Stalin Museum Still going strong in Gori, the town where Uncle Joe was born. (p71)

Republic Square Soviet triumphalist architecture reclaimed in Yerevan. (p149)

Parliament Building Tbilisi's Soviet-era legislature is a striking example of 1950s Stalinist architecture. (p47)

Mother Armenia Military Museum Originally a statue of Stalin, the gigantic *Mother Armenia* statue towers above Yerevan. (p154)

Düzdağ A Soviet-era salt mine now used as an asthma treatment centre. (p298)

City Hall Multi-arched archetype of Stalinist neoclassicism in Gəncə. (p287)

Offbeat Curiosities

Yanar Dağ A hillside in Azerbaijan that never stops burning. (p254)

Sataplia Nature Reserve Fossilised dinosaur footprints and a 300m-long cave. (p88)

Mud Volcanoes Small but fascinating hills that burp forth cold bubbling mud. (p251)

World's Oldest Shoe This curio, found in the Areni-1 Cave, is now in the History Museum of Armenia. (p148)

Yanar Bulağ A stand pipe of spring water that catches fire due to its high methane content. (p294)

Levon's Divine Underground An intricate cave network carved by one man over 23 years. And to think, all his wife wanted was a potato cellar. (p153)

Winter Sports

The best snow is in January and February, though heli-skiing is available at Gudauri much later into the season.

Gudauri The South Caucasus' largest and most established ski area, set in spectacular high mountains. (p98)

Shahdag This 17km piste network has a sumptuous setting and glitzy hotels that appeal to well-heeled weekenders. (p266)

Tsaghkadzor Armenia's best-known ski centre, with 27km of pistes, mostly red and black runs. (p180)

Laza Ice climbing is possible on the frozen waterfalls, but you'll need to organise everything yourself. (p266)

Qəbələ Easily accessible resort whose network of 21st-century ropeways operates year-round. (p269)

Bakuriani This budget-friendly skiing and tobogganing resort is expanding rapidly and bringing in top-end hotels too. (p78)

Village Getaways

Pretty mountain villages, where homestays or other basic tourist infrastructure let you experience rural lifestyles.

Shenaqo Summer-only delight in Tusheti. (p120)

Xınalıq Fascinating highland village with its own language. (p262)

Juta Summer-only accommodation beneath the rocky candelabra of Mt Chaukhi. (p103)

Odzun Plateau-perched village overlooking Debed Canyon. (p186)

Tatev Tiny village known for its 9th-century fortified monastery and for having the world's longest double-track cable car. (p211)

Month by Month

January

The coldest month. Expect snow and below-freezing temperatures over much of the region. Winter sports get going. Georgians and Armenians celebrate Christmas, with the devout going on fasts of varying rigour for days or weeks beforehand.

New Year

Cities are prettily decorated, with fireworks launching the year. Georgians may gather for post-midnight feasts. In Armenia children receive gifts from Dzmer Papik (Santa Claus/Grandpa Winter) on New Year's Eve; families and friends visit and exchange gifts over several days until Orthodox Christmas (6 January).

Armenian Christmas (Surb Tsnund)

Hymns and psalms ring out from churches, where part of the ritual is the blessing of water to mark Epiphany (Jesus' baptism), with which Christmas is combined. Families gather for Christmas Eve dinners, where the traditional main dish is fish and rice (6 January).

Georgian Christmas (Shoba)

On 7 January, flag-carrying, carol-singing crowds make Alilo (Alleluia) walks through the streets, with children wearing white robes. For some, the festive season continues to 14 January, 'Old New Year', the year's start on the Julian calendar used by the Georgian Orthodox Church.

Martyrs' Day

A national day of mourning held on 20 January in Azerbaijan, commemorating the 1990 massacre of Baku civilians by Soviet troops. Bakuvians head up to Şahidlər Xiyabani (Martyr's Lane) in a major commemoration.

February

It is very cold, albeit somewhat less so on the Caspian coast. The winter sports season is in full swing.

Skiing

The season runs from about late December to the end of March, but February generally has the best snow conditions. The top resorts are Gudauri, Bakuriani and Mestia in Georgia; Shahdag and Qəbələ in Azerbaijan; Jermuk and Tsaghkadzor in Armenia.

Surp Sargis Don

The Day of St Sargis, a handsome warrior saint, is popular among unmarried Armenians: tradition tells that the person who gives them water in their dreams this night will be their spouse. It falls nine weeks before Easter (between 18 January and 23 February).

Trndez

This Armenian religious festival of the Purification falls on 14 February. Bonfires are lit and people leap over them for protection from the evil eye, illness and poisons. Trndez also signals the approach of spring.

March

It's starting to get a little less cold, but don't expect anything above 10°C except perhaps on the coasts. Across Azerbaijan shops sell emerald-green fresh wheatgrass (*səməni*) as signs of the coming spring.

📅 Women's Day

Celebrated on 8 March throughout the region with flowers and presents given to female colleagues and friends, and lots of flower stalls on the streets. It's a public holiday in Georgia and Armenia.

Noruz Bayramı

Azerbaijan's biggest celebration lasts many days but focuses on the equinox (night of 20 March) marking the Persian solar New Year and the coming of spring. Traditions include preparing special rice dishes and cleansing the spirit by jumping over bonfires on the four Tuesday nights before the equinox.

International Muğam Festival

In mid-March, Baku celebrates Azerbaijan's Unesco-protected traditional musical heritage with this festival, inviting artists from similar genres to a series of concerts and discussions.

April

Temperatures may climb to 25°C in lowland areas. Spring rains and melting snows bring bigger, faster rivers and the start of the main white-water rafting season in Georgia (until July).

Armenian Easter (Zatik)

Happens on the same variable date as Roman Catholic and Protestant Easter. On Palm Sunday (Tsaghkazard), a week earlier, trees are brought into churches and hung with fruit. Easter tables in homes are laid with red-painted eggs on beds of lentil shoots grown during the Lenten fast.

Georgian Easter (Aghdgoma)

The Eastern Orthodox Easter can happen up to five weeks after the Western one. Churches hold special services on Passion Thursday (with Last Supper ceremonies) and Good Friday, notably at Svetitskhoveli Cathedral (p70) in Mtskheta.

📅 Genocide Memorial Day

On 24 April, thousands of Armenians make a procession to Yerevan's memorial, Tsitsernakaberd. The date is the anniversary of the arrest of Armenian leaders in İstanbul in 1915, generally considered to mark the start of the massacres.

Azerbaijan Grand Prix

One of F1's most distinctive races tears around the Baku city streets, showcasing the city's charms to a global audience but causing traffic chaos and high hotel prices for much of late April.

📅 Ramazan

The Islamic fasting month of Ramazan (Ramadan) starts around 10 days earlier each year, on 12 April 2021, 2 April 2022 and 22 March 2023. In Azerbaijan, Ramazan does not impact greatly on travellers: some devout Muslims refrain from eating, drinking and smoking during daylight, but most restaurants remain open. A few stop serving alcohol.

May

Spring rains are interspersed with bright sunshine, while fields are covered in canopies of wildflowers. Temperatures become warm and walking trails in mountain foothill areas start to open up. Generally one of the best times to visit the region.

📅 Victory Day

The anniversary of the Nazi surrender to the USSR on 9 May 1945 is still commemorated throughout the region, although without the urgency it enjoyed during the Soviet era. You can expect military displays and events for veterans.

☆ 4GB Music Festival

This nonprofit underground electronic music festival held over two nonconsecutive weekends at an incredible venue north of Tbilisi commemorates Georgian techno pioneer Gio Bakanidze with Georgian and international DJs. (p53)

June

One of the best months to visit. Temperatures get up to 30°C in most areas; spring

rains have eased off. Walking season in the mountains gets into its stride, although some high passes only become accessible in July and August.

📅 Abano Pass Opens

The only road into the beautiful Georgian mountain region of Tusheti, via the nerve-jangling 2900m Abano Pass, normally opens from June to October, though exact dates depend on the weather.

☆ Tbilisi Open Air

This music festival held over three days at a former theme park on the outskirts of the Georgian capital is one of the Caucasus' most inclusive and friendly events. International acts such as Franz Ferdinand and Mogwai have headlined in recent years. (p53)

☆ Baku Summer Jazz Days

The Azerbaijani capital's eclectic music festival is held in a range of city venues and is one of the best chances to see live jazz performed in Baku.

📅 Caspian Oil & Gas Show

Baku's biggest trade show is hardly a draw for tourists but beware that business-standard hotels can be heavily booked for these few days in early June.

July

It can get oppressively hot in the cities and lowlands but this is a great time to head to the mountains or the seaside.

Top: Gudauri Ski Resort (p98), Georgia
Bottom: Performer at Tbilisoba (p53), Georgia

☆ Golden Apricot Yerevan International Film Festival

Yerevan hosts the region's biggest international film fest (www.gaiff.am), under the theme Crossroads of Cultures and Civilisations. Lasts a week in early or mid-July. (p157)

☆ Art Gene Festival

This very popular folk festival tours Georgia and culminates with several days of music, cooking, arts and crafts in Tbilisi's Open-Air Museum of Ethnography. (p56)

☆ Black Sea Jazz Festival

International jazz artists gather in Georgia's second city and main holiday resort, Batumi, for a week of rhythm, improvisation and fun at this popular festival in late July. (p94)

☆ Kvirikoba

Georgian countryside festivals usually combine Christian devotion with merrymaking and pagan roots. Kvirikoba, one of Svaneti's biggest gatherings, is no exception. Liturgy, blessings, bell-ringing, animal sacrifice and a boulder-tossing contest are followed by feasting and song. It's held on 28 July in the Kala community.

☆ Vardavar (Transfiguration)

The big summer holiday in Armenia, 14 weeks after Easter. In a throwback to the legendary love-spreading technique of pre-Christian goddess Astghik, kids and teenagers throw water on everyone, and no one takes offence (much).

It's hilarious but don't carry anything that can't survive a soaking.

☆ Gabala International Music Festival

This top-class international festival of mainly classical music rings out at Qəbələ in Azerbaijan for a week in late July and early August. (p271)

August

The weather is airlessly hot and it's the big local holiday month, with people flocking to coasts, lakes and mountains. Accommodation in these areas, and transport to them, are at their busiest.

☆ Batumi Season

Georgia's Las Vegas–wannabe coastal resort fills up with holidaymakers from Georgia, Armenia and beyond in July and, especially, August. Much of Tbilisi's nightlife migrates here for the season, adding to the party atmosphere.

☆ Tushetoba

A part-traditional, part-touristic Georgian mountain festival at Omalo, Tusheti, on the first Saturday in August (or last in July). It features folk music and dancing, traditional sports like horse racing and archery, and the chance to shear your own sheep. (p119)

☆ Astvatsatsin

This Armenian festival devoted to the Virgin Mary is celebrated on the Sunday nearest to 15 August. It

marks the beginning of the harvest season, with priests blessing grapes in churches.

☆ Mariamoba (Assumption)

One of the biggest holidays in Georgia, especially eastern Georgia, celebrating the Assumption of the Virgin Mary into heaven (28 August by the Julian calendar). People attend church services and light candles, then gather for family picnics. Sheep may be slaughtered at churches, and then eaten at the gatherings.

September

Temperatures subside a little from their August heights, making for excellent weather. The main local holiday season is over. This is the last month of the walking season in many mountain areas.

☆ Alaverdoba

These late-September religious-cum-social festivities around Alaverdi Cathedral in Kakheti celebrate the harvest, especially of grapes. People come from remote mountain villages to worship. (p125)

October

Autumn is here, with temperatures ranging between 10°C and 20°C in most areas. This is the season of harvest festivals and still a nice time to be here. It's usually still warm and pleasant on the Caspian and Black Sea coasts.

✨ Kakheti Grape Harvest

The picking and pressing of grapes in Georgia's main wine-producing region, Kakheti, lasts from about 20 September to 20 October. Feasts, musical events and other celebrations go hand-in-hand with the harvest, and it's easy for visitors to join in both the harvest and the partying. (p121)

☆ High Fest

The region's top international theatre festival (www.highfest.am) brings a broad range of dramatic companies from around 30 countries to Yerevan, during the first week of October.

✨ Armenian Harvest Festivals

Almost every village and small town in Armenia holds a harvest festival. You'll see singing, dancing and plenty of fresh fruits and vegetables, and the preparation of traditional dishes. In the wine-growing village of Areni (Vayots Dzor) the festivities focus on wine. (p199)

✨ Svetitskhovloba (Mtskhetoba)

The Day of Svetitskhoveli Cathedral, 14 October, sees the town of Mtskheta and its people returning to the Middle Ages with medieval dress, decorations and re-enactments. The Catholicos-Patriarch of the Georgian Church prays for the 12 Orthodox Apostles to give their protection to Georgia.

✨ Gurban Bayramı

The Muslim Festival of Sacrifice commemorates Abraham's test of faith when God ordered him to sacrifice his son Isaac. Azerbaijanis visit family and friends, and the head of the household traditionally slaughters a sheep, which forms the basis of a grand feast.

☆ Baku Jazz Festival

Baku's late October jazz festival varies in stature year by year but has drawn some top-notch artists in past years and takes place in venues around the city. (p239)

✨ Tbilisoba

Tbilisi's biggest festivity sees the whole city coming out to party for a weekend in October. Amid music and dance events, food stands abound and the wine flows celebrating the autumn harvest. (p53)

November

Winter is closing in. The days are rapidly shortening and inland city temperatures drop from the high teens to single digits. Snow begins to fall in the mountains.

📷 Giorgoba (St George's Day)

Georgia celebrates two days of its patron saint, St George, on 6 May and 23 November. Both see people attending church and family feasts; 23 November is the more widely celebrated, particularly in eastern Georgia. The president pardons some lucky convicts and concerts are held in Tbilisi.

December

Winter is well and truly here. Temperatures are down to around 0°C in most places.

☆ Tbilisi International Film Festival

Georgian, regional and European movies are showcased at this excellent film festival held over a week at the start of December. (p53)

Itineraries

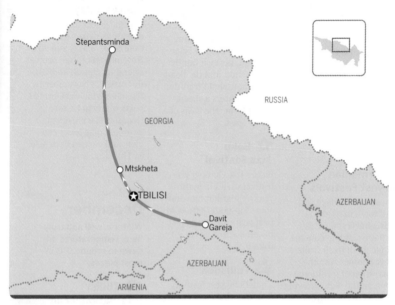

 **A Taste of Georgia**

This short but sweet one-week itinerary is a great introduction to Georgia.

Fly into **Tbilisi** and base yourself there for the first three nights of your stay. This gives you some time to explore the throbbing heart of Georgia. Don't miss the opportunity to take a sulphur bath, journey by cable car to Narikala Fortress, enjoy amazing views of the city from Mtatsminda Park or see the excellent National Museum.

On day four, head north via **Mtskheta** – the historic former capital of Georgia and home to two of its most important churches – to the town of **Stepantsminda**. Two nights here will allow you to visit Tsminda Sameba Church and do a day hike in the Truso Valley, a magnificent walk through a sulphurous landscape that includes a mineral lake and abandoned villages.

Head back to Tbilisi and then do a day trip to **Davit Gareja**, the extraordinarily located complex of cave monasteries right on the Azerbaijan border. Head back to Tbilisi via the charming Oasis Club for a late lunch and spend your last night checking out Tbilisi's club scene.

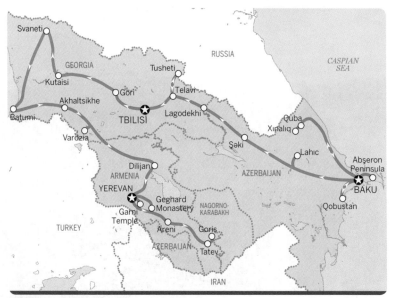

8 WEEKS Ultimate South Caucasus

This mega itinerary takes you through all three countries over two fascinating months of contrasts and surprises. Begin in **Baku**, contrasting its world-beating 21st-century architecture with the medieval charm of its Unesco-listed Old City. As well as **Qobustan**, explore the offbeat **Abşeron Peninsula**, with its fire phenomena and haunting oil-industry debris. Then head to the mountain village of **Xınalıq** via the carpet-making town of **Quba**. Return to Baku and strike out northwest to quaint **Lahıc**, a good village base for summer walks and local encounters. Continue to lovely **Şəki** with its murralled khan's palace and caravanserai hotel.

Enter Georgia at **Lagodekhi** and explore the classic wine region of Kakheti from **Telavi**, including the Chavchavadze Estate and the spectacular Alaverdi Cathedral. Take the rough summer-only road to Omalo in remote **Tusheti** for some wonderful horse riding and day hikes. Recharge for a few days in fabulous **Tbilisi**, before heading west to **Gori**, Stalin's home town, and historic **Kutaisi**, from which you have a huge choice of great day trips. From here, fly to Mestia for another summer-only fix of mountains, spectacular valleys and fortified villages in remote **Svaneti**. Return by bus to the lowlands and enjoy some relaxed seaside fun at the quirky Black Sea town of **Batumi**. Continue by bus through the gorgeous mountainous scenery of inland Adjara to **Akhaltsikhe**, where you can explore majestic Rabati Castle and take a day trip to the cave city of **Vardzia** before entering Armenia.

In Armenia, head first to the adorable resort town of **Dilijan** and hike past millions of wildflowers if it's June or July. Then continue to the capital and enjoy the cafe culture and buzzing nightlife of **Yerevan**. After taking in the city's fascinating museums, including the sobering Armenian Genocide Museum, take day trips to **Geghard Monastery** and **Garni Temple** as well as to Armenia's very own version of the Vatican, Mother See of Holy Etchmiadzin, before heading south. In around four days you could visit the **Areni** area (monasteries, lovely walks and wineries), spectacular **Tatev** and slow-paced **Goris**. Goris is also notably next to Old Khndzoresk, an abandoned cave city carved out of soft volcanic rocks. Return to Yerevan for one last hurrah at one of the city's many delicious restaurants and atmospheric bars.

Above: Tsminda Sameba Church (p100), with the backdrop of Mt Kazbek, Georgia

Left: Petroglyphs in Qobustan Petroglyph Reserve (p251), Azerbaijan

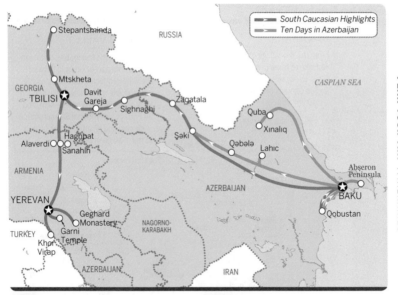

Legend:
- South Caucasian Highlights
- Ten Days in Azerbaijan

South Caucasian Highlights
2 WEEKS

You can get an introductory flavour of all three countries in the South Caucasus in two weeks, though it will be rather a busy trip. Arrive in **Baku**, the ever-more glitzy Azerbaijani capital. Spend a couple of days exploring the art galleries and Old City core, plus make an excursion to **Qobustan** and the mud volcanoes. Take the night train to lovely **Şəki**, then hop west via **Zaqatala** into Georgia's wine region, Kakheti.

Stop overnight in hilltop **Sighnaghi** and drive on to the Georgian capital via the **Davit Gareja** cave monasteries. Spend three days in **Tbilisi**, where you can explore the Old Town, the restaurants and nightlife before heading to the old Georgian capital **Mtskheta** en route to **Stepantsminda** for a couple of days' walking in the Great Caucasus. Return to Tbilisi and head south into Armenia, hopping to the border via Marneuli and Sadakhlo then taking a taxi to the monasteries of **Haghpat** and **Sanahin**. Continue from **Alaverdi** to the capital **Yerevan** with its wine bars and museums. Add excursions to **Garni Temple** and to the monasteries of **Geghard** and **Khor Virap**, and you'll complete a short taster of what this incredible region has to offer.

Ten Days in Azerbaijan
10 DAYS

In 10 days you can see the highlights of Azerbaijan, taking in its lively capital and various traditional mountain towns.

Begin with a few nights in mind-blowing **Baku**, the once-sleepy Soviet city that has transformed itself over the past two decades into an oil-boom town with a skyline and moneyed classes to match. Explore its Unesco-listed Old City and take day trips to the mud volcanoes and petroglyphs of **Qobustan**, and the offbeat **Abşeron Peninsula**.

On day four, head north to the carpet-making town of **Quba** for one night, before continuing to the village of **Xınalıq**, with its old stone houses, unique language and access route through a gloriously varied canyon-land road. Head back to Baku for the night and then continue the next day to the mountain town of **Lahıc**, a good village base for summer hikes. Continue to **Qəbələ**, an upmarket country resort town where year-round cable-cars whisk visitors onto foothill peaks, and then spend your last few nights in lovely **Şəki**, another Unesco site with two mural-festooned little palaces, fortress ramparts and a caravanserai hotel.

Off the Beaten Track

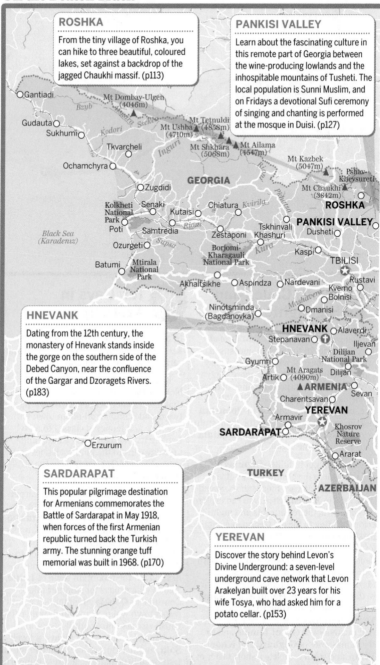

ROSHKA

From the tiny village of Roshka, you can hike to three beautiful, coloured lakes, set against a backdrop of the jagged Chaukhi massif. (p113)

PANKISI VALLEY

Learn about the fascinating culture in this remote part of Georgia between the wine-producing lowlands and the inhospitable mountains of Tusheti. The local population is Sunni Muslim, and on Fridays a devotional Sufi ceremony of singing and chanting is performed at the mosque in Duisi. (p127)

HNEVANK

Dating from the 12th century, the monastery of Hnevank stands inside the gorge on the southern side of the Debed Canyon, near the confluence of the Gargar and Dzoragets Rivers. (p183)

SARDARAPAT

This popular pilgrimage destination for Armenians commemorates the Battle of Sardarapat in May 1918, when forces of the first Armenian republic turned back the Turkish army. The stunning orange tuff memorial was built in 1968. (p170)

YEREVAN

Discover the story behind Levon's Divine Underground: a seven-level underground cave network that Levon Arakelyan built over 23 years for his wife Tosya, who had asked him for a potato cellar. (p153)

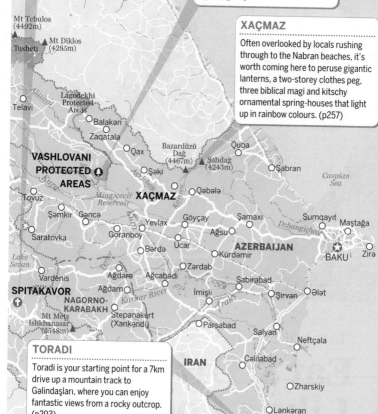

SPITAKAVOR

Hike along a walking path to 14th-century Spitakavor Monastery, built on the site of a 5th-century basilica and featuring a church and bell tower. (p203)

VASHLOVANI PROTECTED AREAS

Tucked away on Georgia's remote border with Azerbaijan, this nature reserve set amid semi-desert badlands and steppe grasslands teems with wildlife, including more than 130 bird species and 30 types of reptile. (p131)

XAÇMAZ

Often overlooked by locals rushing through to the Nabran beaches, it's worth coming here to peruse gigantic lanterns, a two-storey clothes peg, three biblical magi and kitschy ornamental spring-houses that light up in rainbow colours. (p257)

TORADI

Toradi is your starting point for a 7km drive up a mountain track to Gəlindaşları, where you can enjoy fantastic views from a rocky outcrop. (p293)

SIM

Hike through the shaggy forests of the Hirkan National Park between Astara Istisu and the fabled village of Sım and attempt to spot Azerbaijan's last Persian leopards. (p293)

Map labels:

0 200 km
0 100 miles

Mt Tebulos (4492m)
Mt Diklos (4285m)
Tusheti
Telavi
Lagodekhi Protected Areas
Balakən
Zaqatala
Qax
Bazardüzü Dağ (4467m)
Şahdağ (4243m)
Quba
Şabran
VASHLOVANI PROTECTED AREAS
Şəki
Qəbələ
Caspian Sea
Tovuz
Mingəçevir Reservoir
XAÇMAZ
Şəmkir
Gəncə
Yevlax
Göyçay
Şamaxı
Sumqayıt
Maştağa
Saratovka
Goranboy
Ağsu
Zirə
Bərdə
Ucar
AZERBAIJAN
BAKU
Lake Sevan
Vardenis
Ağdərə
Ağcabədi
Zərdab
Kürdəmir
SPITAKAVOR
Ağdam
İmişli
Sabirabad
Şirvan
Ələt
NAGORNO-KARABAKH
Karkar River
Mt Mets Ishkhanasar (3548m)
Stepanakert (Xankəndi)
Pərşabad
Salyan
Neftçala
IRAN
Cəlilabad
Zharskiy
Lənkəran
TORADI
SIM
Hirkan National Park
Astara (Azerbaijan)
Astara (Iran)
Ardabil

Churchkh◄

Plan Your Trip
Eat & Drink
Like a Local

The South Caucasus is blessed with extraordinarily strong culinary traditions. There's a huge amount of regional variation, but across Georgia, Armenia and Azerbaijan you'll find a consistent focus on fresh vegetables, herbs and fruits, grilled meats and calorific combinations of pastry and dairy.

The Year in Food

Spring (Mar–May)

Sour plums and tarragon are in season in Georgia, making *chakapuli* (lamb in a tarragon and sour plum sauce) the perfect spring dish for visitors to try.

Summer (Jun–Aug)

The entire region enjoys the most perfect tomatoes, aubergines and cucumbers. Fruit harvests bring superb apricots, nectarines, peaches, pomegranates, plums, watermelons and figs.

Autumn (Sep–Nov)

It's the annual grape harvest in Armenia and Georgia, a wonderful time to visit the wine-producing regions of both countries and join in the hard work and festivities. In Azerbaijan, there's a long-running pomegranate festival in Göyçay.

Winter (Dec–Feb)

In December, orange persimmons make the otherwise bald trees around Balakən in Azerbaijan look like surreal sculptures, and the fruit can be found in huge quantities at markets.

Khachapuri

a handful of greens, which is often eaten as a wrap with a dash of lemon. The popular snack is called *lahmajoon* in Armenia.

Ponchki For something sugary, try a *ponchik* or its plural *ponchki*. These Russian-introduced stuffed doughnuts are usually filled with sweet cream and are found in all three countries.

Qutab A kind of thick pancake folded in half with a small filling of herbs or pumpkin. Available across Azerbaijan, particularly in Baku.

Food Experiences

Cheap Treats

Churchkhela This popular Georgian snack of nuts strung together and dipped in grape resin is a chewy and sweet energy boost at any time of day. Similar is sweet *sujukh,* the Armenian equivalent.

Khachapuri This Georgian cheese-stuffed pastry or pie can be found at stalls all over the country in almost infinite varieties.

Lahmajun In both Armenia and Azerbaijan this is a very thin pizza topped with minced lamb and

Dare to Try

Khash Boiled sheep or cow parts often including the animal's head, feet and stomach. Versions with similar names can be found in all three countries and are popular hangover cures. Try it yourself at Culinarium Khasheria (p59) in Tbilisi.

Quyrq Kebab generally eaten as one of several other kebabs rather than a meal in itself, this Azerbaijani shish kebab is essentially all tail fat from a sheep. Can be ordered in almost any rural kebab restaurant in Azerbaijan.

Tvini Baked sheep or cow brains are a popular delicacy in Georgia, though increasingly rare these days.

GEORGIAN WINE

Georgians have been making and drinking wine (*ghvino*) for at least 8000 years. Wine may well have been invented here, but perhaps more importantly, Georgians have continued to make wine by basically the same method ever since they started – fermenting it along with grape skins, pips and often stalks, in large clay amphorae known as *qvevri*, buried in the earth. This 'skin contact' is why traditionally made Georgian whites have a more amber/orangey tint than other white wines. European-style winemaking – fermenting the grape juice without the pulp – has also been around in Georgia since the 19th century, but the basic local method practised by tens of thousands of families throughout Georgia has remained unchanged. It also yields the potent, grappa-like, firewater *chacha*, distilled from the pulp left after the wine is eventually drawn off.

Qvevri wine (also sometimes called 'unfiltered' wine) is beloved by followers of the fashion for 'natural wine' because it contains little or none of the additives (such as yeast, sugar or sulphites) commonly put into wine today. *Qvevri* wines certainly taste different from the wines most of the world is accustomed to, but there are now some spectacular ones, and prices remain affordable throughout the country.

In Soviet times, larger-scale winemaking in Georgia was geared to the Russian taste for strong wine with lots of sugar, resulting in a decline in quality. Since the Soviet collapse Georgian commercial winemakers have been steadily upgrading their operations. The result is a wider and much better range of European-style wines, many of which are exported to the West and Asia. Today many winemakers produce both European-style and *qvevri* wines.

Wine is made all over Georgia, but more than half of it comes from the eastern Kakheti region (p121). Over 500 of the world's 2000 grape varieties are Georgian. Most commonly used for wine today are the white Rkatsiteli, Mtsvane and Kisi, and the red Saperavi.

Bottles of good commercially produced Georgian wine start at around 10 GEL in Georgian shops. You'll find further helpful information at Georgian Wine Association (www.gwa.ge) and National Wine Agency (http://georgianwine.gov.ge).

Best Places to Eat

Barbarestan (p61) High-end contemporary takes on rediscovered 19th-century Georgian recipes.

Lavash (p160) Everything at this eastern Armenian restaurant in Yerevan is excellent: try hard to land a table.

Cherkezi Dzor (p178) This Gyumri fish restaurant with on-site ponds attracts Russians who fly over just for a meal.

Keto and Kote (p60) Superb Georgian cooking served up at a fabulously revamped old mansion overlooking Tbilisi.

Calğalıq Restoranı (p282) Rustic eatery full of ethnographic knickknacks that's hidden away at the end of a rural lane.

Şirvanşah Muzey-Restoran (p244) A veritable museum of a place in a historic bathhouse building.

How to Eat & Drink

Where to Eat

Food is a highlight of any visit to the South Caucasus, and in most cases you never have to worry about reserving a table in advance. However, if you want to eat at the very best places in any of the three capitals, you'll often be better booking a few days in advance, especially in the summer months.

Restaurants The region's restaurants run from traditional local to contemporary international cuisine, and are best in the three capitals.

Guesthouses Enjoying a home-cooked meal is best done in a local guesthouse.

Hotels You'll often find some excellent eating options in the region's hotels.

Price Ranges

The following price ranges refer to a main course.

$ under US$5

$$ US$5–10

$$$ over US$10

Countries at a Glance

Wherever you go in the South Caucasus, two of your strongest impressions will be the epic mountain scenery and the wonderfully hospitable people. The spectacular Great Caucasus makes for memorable hiking in Georgia and Azerbaijan, while Armenia is a crinkled jigsaw of mountains, valleys, plateaus and gorges, with good day walks.

Georgia is the most visited country, with a relatively good tourism infrastructure and rather more English spoken than in the other countries, though some Russian will still serve you in good stead. Travel is easy enough in Armenia, though fellow travellers are likely to be fewer. Azerbaijan is the least touristed by Westerners, though this is changing now it's easier for travellers to get a visa.

Georgia

Scenery
Hospitality
Outdoor Activities

Scenery

The Great Caucasus mountains will take your breath away with snowy peaks, green valleys and stone villages. The lowlands are strewn with vineyards, rivers, forests and rocky canyons, while the Georgian habit of building churches and fortifications on picturesque perches only enhances the glories of the land's natural beauty.

Hospitality

Georgians believe guests are gifts from on high, so providing hospitality is both customary and a pleasure. You'll often be delighted by the warmth of your welcome, at its best when you share locals' food and unfeasible quantities of their beloved homemade wine.

Outdoor Activities

Long-distance trails abound, some linking isolated mountain hamlets where time seems to stand still. Villagers offer homestays and can supply horses should you tire of carrying a backpack. Rafting, paragliding and skiing are also popular.

p40

Armenia

Sacred Sites
Hiking
Self-Driving Tours

Sacred Sites

More than 1700 years of Christian heritage has left Armenia with a rich collection of ancient churches and monasteries, many still active places of worship. Most sacred is the heart of Armenian Christianity at Etchmiadzin, west of Yerevan.

Hiking

Armenia may not have alpine summits to challenge Georgia's, but it offers plenty of scope for light hiking and backpacking trips. There are good walks around Dilijan, the Yeghegis Valley and Tatev, and a more strenuous hike to the top of Mt Aragats.

Self-Driving Tours

Hiring a car will allow you to visit isolated monasteries and mountain villages. Roads wend through wildflower-strewn meadows, over magnificent passes, past thousands of four-legged livestock and alongside rivers offering photo opportunities and picnic sites galore. Some rental deals allow you to drop off the car in Georgia.

p144

Azerbaijan

Scenery
Earth & Fire
Architecture

Scenery

With dizzy Caucasian peaks, bald sheep-mown highlands, Caspian beaches, bucolic woodland meadows and craggy desert badlands, Azerbaijan packs an astonishing variety of landscapes into a remarkably small space.

Earth & Fire

If you're looking for off-beat curiosities, seek out Azerbaijan's gurgling mud volcanoes at Qobustan or investigate the unusual selection of fire phenomena, including 'inflammable' rivers, fire springs, burning hillsides and a classic fire temple that seems designed for a movie set.

Architecture

Baku's rash of dazzling 21st-century constructions contrast boldly with the city's stately century-old original oil-boom mansions, some grand Stalinist constructions and a Unesco-protected medieval Old City still enclosed within crenellated stone walls.

p227

On the Road

Georgia
(p40)

Armenia
(p144)

Azerbaijan
(p227)

Nagorno-
Karabakh
(p306)

Azerbaijan
(p227)

Georgia

📞 995 / POP 3.7 MILLION

Why Go?

Having gone from backpacker secret to mainstream darling in just a decade, Georgia today is by far the most visited country in the South Caucasus, and it's easy to see why: its rich culture and astonishingly diverse landscapes make it an ideal destination for anyone loving history and nature on the grandest of scales.

From its green valleys spread with vineyards to its old churches and watchtowers perched in fantastic mountain scenery, Georgia (Saqartvelo) never disappoints. In recent years Tbilisi has emerged as one of the coolest cities in Europe, with a burgeoning club scene, world-class restaurants and a selection of natural wine bars that easily make it the hippest spot in the region. Equally special are its proud, high-spirited people: Georgia claims to be the birthplace of wine, and this is a place where guests are considered blessings and hospitality is the very stuff of life. *Gaumarjos!*

Best Places to Eat

➡ Barbarestan (p61)

➡ Cafe Littera (p60)

➡ Keto and Kote (p60)

➡ Pheasant's Tears (p129)

➡ Alubali (p59)

Best Places to Stay

➡ Stamba Hotel (p57)

➡ Back2Me Hostel (p94)

➡ Zeta Camp (p106)

➡ Rooms Hotel (p102)

➡ Maia's Guesthouse (p110)

When to Go

➡ The ideal seasons in most of the country are from mid-April to early July, and early September to mid-October, when it's generally very warm and sunny.

➡ July and August can be uncomfortably humid in the lowlands, with temperatures sometimes reaching 40°C. On the other hand, this is an excellent time to be in the mountains, and it's high season on the Black Sea.

➡ The best months for hiking in the Great Caucasus are June to September.

➡ Early autumn brings the festive wine harvest in Kakheti, from about 20 September to 20 October.

➡ The eastern half of Georgia often suffers below-freezing temperatures between December and February.

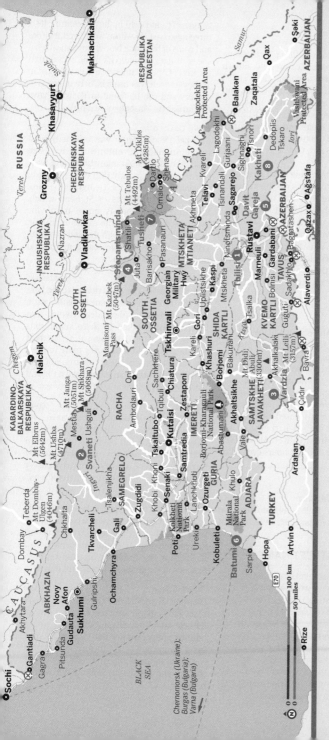

Georgia Highlights

1 Tbilisi (p42) Taking in amazing restaurants, superb museums and a thriving club culture.

2 Svaneti (p106) Discovering unique Svan culture, ancient defensive towers and wonderful hiking amid Georgia's finest alpine scenery.

3 Vardzia (p81) Exploring an entire medieval city carved out of a cliff face.

4 Stepantsminda (p100) Catching the breathtaking sight of Tsminda Sameba Cathedral silhouetted against Mt Kazbek.

5 Davit Gareja (p130) Visiting Georgia's most ancient cave monastery in its unique lunar setting.

6 Batumi (p91) Soaking up the party atmosphere and wandering the charming Old Town.

7 Tusheti (p117) Hiking in this spectacular, pristine, high-mountain region.

8 Kakheti (p121) Spending days tasting the produce of Georgian wine country.

TBILISI

🎵 32 / POP 1.5 MILLION

With its dramatic valley setting, picturesque Old Town, eclectic architecture and superb eating and drinking opportunities, Tbilisi is the vibrant, beating heart of Georgia and home to more than one in three of its citizens. Add to that the pull of the city's hipster culture, its techno scene and general air of cool, and Tbilisi is confidently sealing its reputation as the South Caucasus' most cosmopolitan city.

While at first glance Tbilisi can seem both crowded and chaotic, many neighbourhoods retain a village-like feel with their narrow streets and small shops, while the Old Town is still redolent of an ancient Eurasian crossroads, with its winding lanes, balconied houses and leafy squares, all overlooked by the 17-centuries-old Narikala Fortress. Whichever side of the city you're looking for, you'll discover both on any exploration of Georgia's capital.

◉ Sights

The Old Town is the obvious place to start exploring Tbilisi, though since a total revamp a decade ago, it has become extraordinarily crowded, and walking down its streets on a summer day can be challenging, with big tour groups, touts and souvenir sellers at every turn. There's also plenty to see in the 19th-century city focused on Rustavelis gamziri and in the Avlabari area on the left bank of the Mtkvari River. Most of the churches are open daylight hours every day.

◉ Old Town

★ **Anchiskhati Basilica**   CHURCH
(Map p46; Shavteli) Tbilisi's oldest surviving church is perhaps its loveliest. Built by King

---

GEORGIAN STREET NAMES
· ·

The spelling of Georgian street names varies depending on whether words such as *qucha* (street), *gamziri* (avenue) or *moedani* (square) are present. In Georgian, Rustaveli Ave is Rustavelis gamziri, but is normally just referred to as Rustaveli. To simplify matters, we use noninflected names in addresses – eg, Rustaveli rather than Rustavelis gamziri – but we use the whole street name when referring to it in text elsewhere.

Gorgasali's son Dachi in the 6th century, it's a three-nave basilica whose weathered frescoes and walls of big stone blocks emphatically bespeak its age. The church's name comes from the icon of Anchi Cathedral in Klarjeti (now in Turkey), which was brought here in the 17th century and can be found in Tbilisi's Shalva Amiranashvili Museum of Art (p50).

Sioni Cathedral   CATHEDRAL
(Map p46; Sioni 6) Sioni was originally built in the 6th and 7th centuries, but has been destroyed and rebuilt many times, and what you see today is mainly 13th century. It is of special significance for Georgians because it's home to the cross of St Nino which, according to legend, is made from vine branches bound with the saint's own hair. A replica of the cross sits behind a bronze grille to the left of the icon screen. The real thing is kept safe inside.

Abanotubani   ARCHITECTURE
(Map p46; Abano) The brick domes rising here are the roofs of subterranean bathhouses, the Abanotubani. Alexanders Dumas and Pushkin both bathed in these sulphurous waters, the latter describing it as the best bath he'd ever had. Outwardly more impressive than the others, the above-ground Chreli Abano (p53) thermal baths have a Central Asian feel to their blue-tile facade.

Meidan   SQUARE
(Map p46) In tsarist times Meidan was the site of Tbilisi's bustling main bazaar. Today it's busy with traffic but opens to the Metekhi Bridge over the Mtkvari – all overlooked by Narikala Fortress. There's a touristy market in the tunnel running under the main road.

Jvaris Mama Church   CHURCH
(Map p46; cnr Kote Abkhazi & Ierusalimi) Little Jvaris Mama stands on a site where a church has stood since the 5th century. The current incarnation dates from the 16th century and its interior is covered in recently restored frescoes in striking reds, golds and blues.

Clock Tower   TOWER
(Map p46; Shavteli 13; 🎭) One of old Tbilisi's most emblematic structures is also one of its newest, a higgledy-piggledy clock tower, built by puppet master Rezo Gabriadze during a renovation of his theatre in 2010. On the hour an angel pops out of a door near the top and strikes the bell outside with a hammer.

Armenian Cathedral of St George
CATHEDRAL

(Map p46; Samghebro) This large cathedral just above Meidan was founded in 1251, though the current structure dates mainly from the 18th century. Its interior has colourful 18th-century frescoes, and was restored by the Armenian diaspora in 2012–15. King Erekle II's famed Armenian court poet Sayat Nova was killed here during the Persian invasion of 1795. His tomb is just outside the main door.

Mosque
MOSQUE

(Map p46; Botanikuri) On the short walk up to the Botanical Gardens you pass the only mosque in Tbilisi that survived Lavrenty Beria's purges of the 1930s. It's a red-brick building dating from 1895 and, unusually, Shia and Sunni Muslims pray together here. The interior is prettily frescoed and visitors are welcome to enter after removing their shoes.

Tbilisi History Museum
MUSEUM

(Map p46; Sioni 8; 5 GEL; ⊙10am-6pm Tue-Sun) The eclectic exhibits here, housed in an old caravanserai, range from models and photos to high-society and folk costumes from the 19th century, and realistic mock-ups of period craft workshops and a small restaurant. It's rather lacking in context or narrative, with no story told, but some of the displays give you a real sense of Tbilisi's past.

⊙ Narikala Fortress & Around

★ Narikala Fortress
FORTRESS

(Map p46; Orpiri; ⊙9am-9pm) **FREE** Dominating the Old Town skyline, Narikala dates right back to the 4th century, when it was a Persian citadel. Most of the walls were built in the 8th century by the Arab emirs, whose palace was inside the fortress. Subsequently Georgians, Turks and Persians captured and patched up Narikala, but in 1827 a huge explosion of Russian munitions stored here wrecked the whole thing, and today it's a rather picturesque ruin, with only its walls largely intact.

The **Church of St Nicholas**, inside the fortress, was rebuilt in the 1990s. The choice way to reach Narikala is by cable car (p51) from Rike Park. Or you can walk from Meidan or via the Betlemi St Stairs, which lead off Lado Asatiani qucha in Sololaki. The views over Tbilisi from the top of the fortress are superb.

★ Kartlis Deda
MONUMENT

(Mother Georgia; Map p46) This 20m-tall aluminium symbol of Tbilisi holds a sword in one hand and a cup of wine in the other – a classic metaphor for the Georgian character, warmly welcoming guests and passionately fighting off enemies. It's a short walk along the ridge from Narikala Fortress and the cable-car station.

FAST FACTS

Currency
Lari (GEL)

Language
Georgian

Emergencies
☑112

Visas
Generally not required for stays of up to one year. Those who need visas can apply online at www.evisa.gov.ge.

Resources

Civil.ge (www.civil.ge)

Georgia (www.georgia.travel)

Georgia Starts Here (www.georgia startshere.com)

Georgian Journal (www.georgian journal.ge)

Georgian Wanderers (www.facebook. com/groups/Georgianwanderers)

Exchange Rates

Australia	A$1	1.98 GEL
Canada	C$1	2.20 GEL
Euro zone	€1	3.26 GEL
Japan	¥100	2.73 GEL
NZ	NZ$1	1.88 GEL
UK	UK£1	3.51 GEL
USA	US$1	2.91 GEL

For current exchange rates, see www. xe.com.

Daily Costs

➡ Budget accommodation per person: 10–40 GEL

➡ Two-course meal: 15–20 GEL

➡ Museum admission: 5 GEL

➡ Beer per bottle: 3 GEL

➡ Daily car hire: from 100 GEL

Tbilisi

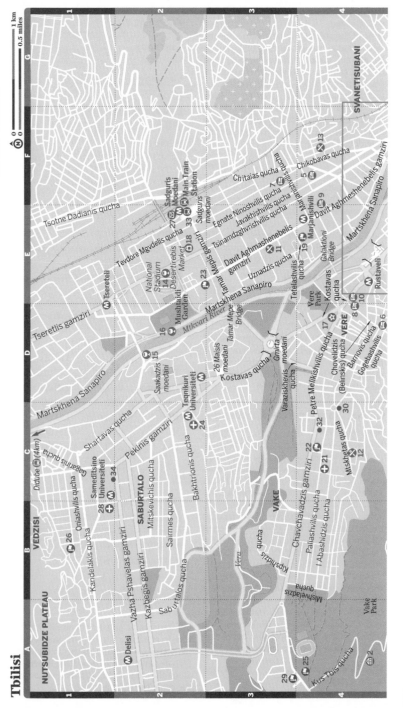

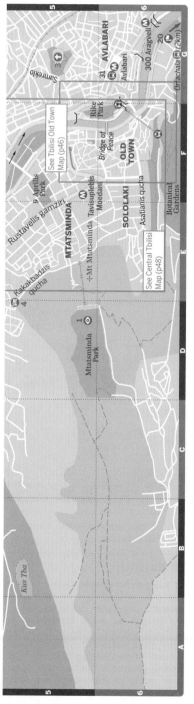

Tbilisi

Botanical Gardens   GARDENS
(Map p46; Botanikuri; adult/student 4/1 GEL;
⊙9am-6pm Mar, to 8pm Apr-Aug, to 7pm Sep, to
5pm Oct-Feb) It's easy to wander for a couple of
hours in these tree-filled and waterfall-dotted
gardens, which stretch more than a kilometre

Tbilisi Old Town

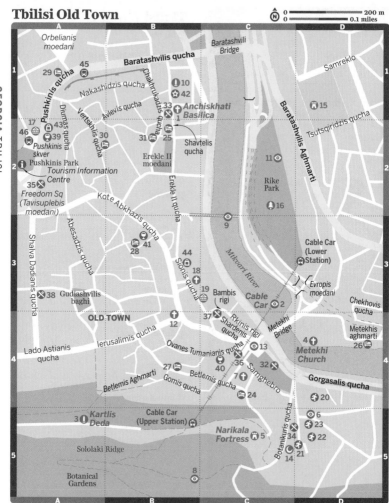

up the valley behind the cliffs of Narikala Fortress. They were opened in 1845 on what had earlier been royal gardens and are today beautifully kept, with a river running through them and some wonderful views.

Residence of Bidzina Ivanishvili PALACE
(Map p48) The monstrous residence of Bidzina Ivanishvili, Georgia's richest man, former prime minister and éminence grise on the political scene, looms over the city from the west end of the Sololaki ridge. You can't see much of the palatial private residence up close (the road discreetly passes beneath it) but from a distance the complex looks a bit like a regional airport terminal, which is fitting given its heliport.

◉ Rustaveli

★**Georgian National Museum** MUSEUM
(Map p48; ☎ 32-2998022; www.museum.ge; Rustaveli 3; adult/student 15/0.50 GEL; ⊙10am-6pm Tue-Sun) The major highlight of the impressive national museum is the basement Archaeological Treasury, displaying a wealth of pre-Christian gold, silver and precious-stone work from burials in Georgia going back to the 3rd millennium BC. Most

Tbilisi Old Town

stunning are the fabulously detailed gold adornments from Colchis (western Georgia). On the top floor, the Museum of Soviet Occupation has copious detail on Soviet repression and local resistance to it.

On the ground floor are exhibits from Dmanisi, the archaeological site in southern Georgia whose 1.8 million-year-old hominid skulls are rewriting the study of early European humanity.

★**National Gallery**   GALLERY
(Map p48; Rustaveli 11; adult/student 12/0.50 GEL; ⊙10am-6pm Tue-Sun) For most visitors the highlight here is the hall of wonderful canvases by Georgia's best-known painter Niko Pirosmani (1862–1918), ranging from his celebrated animal and feast scenes to lesser-known portraits and rural-life canvases. There's also a good selection of work by other top 20th-century Georgian artists Lado Gudiashvili and David Kakabadze. Enter from the park beside Kashveti Church (p50).

MOMA Tbilisi   MUSEUM
(Museum of Modern Art Tbilisi; Map p48; www.tbilisimoma.ge; Rustaveli 27; 10 GEL; ⊙11am-6.30pm Wed-Mon) This beautiful conversion of the former Tbilisi Cadet Corps building has been given over to displays of work by the museum's founder, Zurab Tsereteli, the Moscow-based Georgian who is one of Vladimir Putin's favourite artists. The sculptures and paintings here are characteristic of his grandiose, larger-than-life work found in many countries, though this space also hosts very good temporary exhibits, which are arguably worth more of your time than the permanent collection.

Parliament Building   HISTORIC BUILDING
(Map p48; Rustaveli 8) The impressive high-arched Parliament building has seen many momentous events, including the deaths of 19 Georgian hunger strikers at the hands of Soviet troops on 9 April 1989, and the Rose Revolution on 22 November 2003, which

Central Tbilisi

0   0.2 miles
0   400 m

See Tbilisi Old Town Map (p46)

SVANETISUBANI

Mosi Toidze qucha

Nino Chkheidze qucha

Ketevan Tsamebuli qucha

Elene Akhvlediani Khevi qucha
10

Kosta Khetagurovi qucha

Noe Jordania Sanapiro

Mtkvari River

Arnold Chikobava qucha

Ivane Javakhishvili qucha

Saarbrücken Sq

Marjvena (Gamsakhurdias) Sanapiro

Atonelis qucha

36

Putseladzis qucha

Mikheil Tsinamdzghvrishvili qucha

Chughureti (Saarbrücken) Bridge

24

34

9 Aprilis Park

Davit Aghmeshenebelis gamziri

17

22

National Gallery
3   5

Uznadzis qucha

Martskhena Sanapiro

Mtkvari River

25

Tabukashvili qucha

G Chanturia qucha

33   29
39   40
42

Besikis qucha

Lesia Ukrainkas qucha

Marjvena (Gamsakhurdias) Sanapiro

R Lagnidzis qucha

32

11

Zurab Zhvanias qucha

Vardebis Revolutsis moedani

9

Rustavelis gamziri

37

A Chanchavadzis qucha

Zubalashvilebi qucha

Arsenas qucha

41

Griboedovis qucha

Javakhishvili qucha

Klachelis qucha

Akhvledianis qucha
27   14

28
30

Kostavas qucha

18

Rustaveli M

Rustavelis moedani

Dzmebi Kakhadzeebi qucha

Zandukelis qucha

Saralishvilis qucha

20
23

26

Kakabadzis qucha

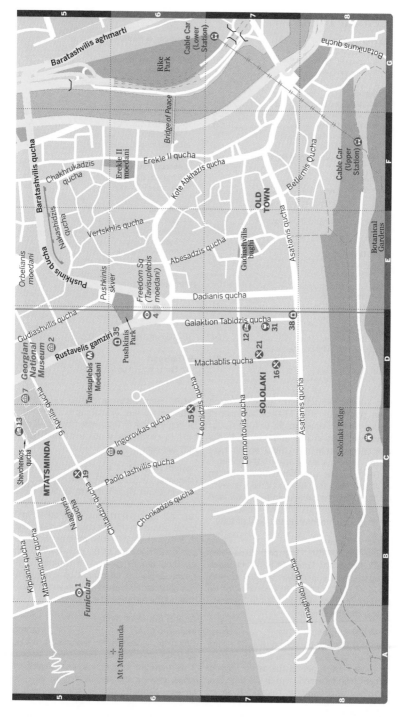

Baratashvilis aghmarti

Cable Car (Lower Station)

Rike Park

Botanikuris qucha

Bridge of Peace

Chakhrukadzis qucha

Erekle II moedani

Erekle II qucha

kote Abkhazis qucha

Cable Car (Upper Station)

Betlemis Qucha

OLD TOWN

Botanical Gardens

Baratashvilis qucha

Nakashidzis qucha

Vertskhlis qucha

Abesadzis qucha

Gudiashvilis baghi

Asatianis qucha

Orbelianis moedani

Pushkinis qucha

Freedom Sq (Tavisuplebis moedani)

Dadianis qucha

🅿 4

Galaktion Tabidzis qucha

✖ 12 31

🅿 38

Gudiashvilis qucha

Georgian National Museum

🏛 2

Rustavelis gamziri Ⓜ

🅿 35

Pushkinis Park

✖ 21

Machablis qucha

✖ 16

SOLOLAKI

Asatianis qucha

🏛 7

Tavisuplebis Moedani Ⓜ

9 Aprilis qucha

Ingorovkas qucha

Leonidzis qucha

✖ 15

Lermontovis qucha

Asatianis qucha

Sololaki Ridge

🏨 13

Shevchenkos qucha

MTATSMINDA

🏛 8

Paolo Iashvilis qucha

🏨 9

Niaghvris qucha

Chitadzis qucha

✖ 19

Chonkadzis qucha

Kipianis qucha

Mtatsmindis qucha

Amaghlebis qucha

🚡 1 Funicular

Mt Mtatsminda

Central Tbilisi

saw Eduard Shevardnadze abruptly forced from power. In 2012 Mikheil Saakashvili moved Georgia's parliament to Kutaisi, but it returned here in 2019 and this building is now once again home to the Georgian legislature. As such it is not open to the public.

The building was constructed between 1938 and 1953 for Georgia's Soviet government. A small monument in front of it, and paving stones and glass panels set at irregular angles, commemorate the dead of 1989.

Freedom Square   SQUARE
(Tavisuplebis moedani; Map p48) This busy traffic nexus was Lenin Sq in Soviet times. Georgia's last Lenin statue, toppled in 1990, stood where the golden St George (a gift to the city from its sculptor, Zurab Tsereteli) now spears his dragon.

Kashveti Church   CHURCH
(Map p48) The first church on this site is supposed to have been built in the 6th century by Davit Gareja, one of the ascetic 'Syrian fathers' who returned from the Middle East to spread Christianity in Georgia. Kashveti

means 'Stone Birth': according to legend, a nun accused him of making her pregnant. He replied that if that were true, she'd give birth to a baby, and if not, to a stone, which duly happened.

Project ArtBeat   GALLERY
(Map p48; ☎32-2996403; www.projectartbeat. com; Ingorovka 14; ⊙11am-7pm Tue-Sun) FREE This gallery is Georgia's leading contemporary art space, nurturing local talent and giving shows to up-and-coming artists. Pop in to see what's currently exciting the curators on the local art scene, and also look out for their mobile gallery – a shipping container displaying an exhibit by a regularly changing individual artist – on your travels around the country.

Shalva Amiranashvili
Museum of Art   MUSEUM
(Map p46; ☎32-2988246; Gudiashvili 1; 3 GEL, guide per group 45 GEL; ⊙10am-6pm Tue-Sun) This museum contains a vast wealth of icons, crosses and jewellery from all over Georgia. Sadly, it can only be entered with a

guide (English available, call ahead to book), and unless you're in a group the expense is significant. Many of Georgia's most sacred objects are here, such as the little pectoral cross of Queen Tamar, set with four emeralds, five rubies and six pearls – the only known personal relic of the great 12th-century monarch.

◉ Avlabari

★ Cable Car   CABLE CAR
(Map p46; one-way ride 1 GEL; ⊘11am-11pm) Tbilisi's most exhilarating ride is its massively popular cable car, which swings from the south end of Rike Park high over the Mtkvari River and the Old Town up to Narikala Fortress. To ride it, you need a Metromoney card (p68), available at the ticket offices if you don't have one. Expect to wait in the summer months, though the line moves fairly quickly.

★ Metekhi Church   CHURCH
(Map p46; Metekhis aghmarti) The landmark Metekhi Church, and the 1960s equestrian statue of King Vakhtang Gorgasali beside it, occupy the strategic rocky outcrop above the Metekhi Bridge. This is where Vakhtang Gorgasali built his palace, and the site's first church, when he made Tbilisi his capital in the 5th century. The existing church was built by King Demetre Tavdadebuli (the Self-Sacrificing) between 1278 and 1289, and has been reconstructed many times since.

Tsminda Sameba Cathedral   CATHEDRAL
(Holy Trinity Cathedral; Map p44; Samreklo) The biggest symbol of the Georgian Orthodox Church's post-Soviet revival towers on Elia Hill above Avlabari. Tsminda Sameba, unmissable by night and day, was consecrated in 2004 after a decade of building. A massive and lavish expression of traditional Georgian architectural forms in concrete, brick, granite and marble, it rises a staggering 84m to the top of the gold-covered cross above its gold-covered central dome. While largely bare inside, it does, however, contain many of Georgia's most important icons.

Rike Park   PARK
(Map p46; 🚼) This green expanse along the eastern riverbank, with its winding paths, pools and fountains, is joined to the west side of the Mtkvari by the Bridge of Peace. It's also where the lower station of the cable car takes you to Narikala Fortress.

Bridge of Peace   BRIDGE
(Mshvidobis Khidi; Map p46) The Bridge of Peace, a rather incongruously modern glass-and-steel footbridge over the Mtkvari with a totally unnecessary roof, was designed by Italian Michele De Lucchi and opened in 2010. It's definitely one of the most eye-catching of the love-it-or-hate-it avant-garde structures that went up around Georgia during the Saakashvili years.

Concert Hall & Exhibition Centre   ARCHITECTURE
(Map p46) The two large tubular metallic structures at the north end of Rike Park were commissioned from Italian architect Massimiliano Fuksas during the Saakashvili era as a concert hall and an exhibition centre. After Mikheil Saakashvili lost power, funding dried up and the project remains unfinished today, though the collective behind famous techno club Bassiani (p62) managed to hold its first party here in 2013.

Presidential Palace   PALACE
(Map p46; Tsutsqiridze) Georgia's presidential palace, which is not open to visitors, was a Saakashvili-era prestige project that opened in 2009. Its ultraclassical portico is surmounted by a large, egg-shaped, glass dome, and the overall impression is one of architectural poverty. Georgia's current president, Salome Zurabishvili, lives elsewhere, however, and the palace is used just for ceremonies.

◉ Mtatsminda

★ Funicular   FUNICULAR
(Map p48; Chonkadze; one-way ride 3 GEL; ⊘9am-4am) The ride up Mt Mtatsminda on the city's funicular is spectacular, as are the views from the top – and there are a couple of great places to eat or drink, as well as dozens of funfair rides too. It's also several degrees cooler up here than in the city below, which can be very welcome in the heat of summer.

To ride the funicular you need a 2 GEL plastic card (sold at the ticket office) on which you then add credit for your rides (and any rides in Mtatsminda Park).

Mtatsminda Park   AMUSEMENT PARK
(Map p44; http://park.ge; rides 1-5 GEL; ⊘9am-11pm; 🚼) The amusement park on top of Mt Mtatsminda will interest children, but can also be a lot of fun for adults (check out the enormous Ferris wheel) and the views over

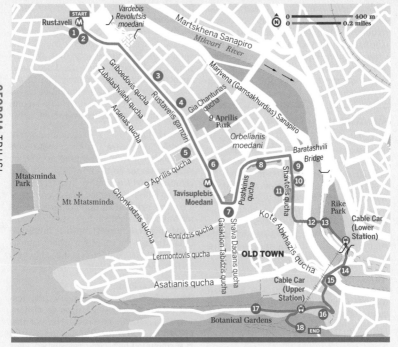

Neighbourhood Walk
Tbilisi New & Old

START RUSTAVELI METRO STATION
END BOTANICAL GARDENS
LENGTH 3.5KM; THREE HOURS

Start at the **1 monument to Shota Rustaveli** outside Rustaveli metro station. Pass the Stalinist **2 Academy of Sciences** at Rustaveli 52, with an informal souvenir market outside, then walk along Rustavelis gamziri to imbibe the busy atmosphere of Tbilisi's main artery. The street is strung with handsome and important buildings such as the Moorish-style **3 Opera & Ballet Theatre** (p64), built in 1896; the baroque-cum-rococo 1901 **4 Rustaveli Theatre** (p64); the **5 Parliament building** (p47); and the **6 Georgian National Museum** (p46). Rustavelis gamziri ends at wide **7 Freedom Square** (p50) with its landmark St George and Dragon monument.

Head to the left down Pushkinis qucha, skirting the old **8 city walls**. At the bottom turn right into traffic-free Shavtelis qucha to Tbilisi's quirkiest building, the Gabriadze Theatre's rakishly crooked **9 Clock Tower**

(p42). Continue to the city's oldest and one of its prettiest churches, **10 Anchiskhati Basilica** (p42). **11 Cafe Leila** (p59) across the street here is one of Tbilisi's most charming cafes and a perfect drinks stop. Continue south then turn left on to the most emblematic of Tbilisi's new structures, the elegant **12 Bridge of Peace** (p51) over the Mtkvari River, taking in the views of the Presidential Palace and the massive, golden-domed Tsminda Sameba Cathedral up on the east side of the river.

Walk through charming **13 Rike Park** (p51) and pay a visit to the hilltop **14 Metekhi Church** (p51) for some fabulous views before crossing back into the Old Town at busy **15 Meidan square** (p42). From here, make your way up the hillside to **16 Narikala Fortress** (p43), which you can clamber around before wandering along the top of the ridge to **17 Kartlis Deda** (p43), the Soviet-era statue of Mother Georgia that overlooks the city. From here you can walk down the hill through the **18 Botanical Gardens** (p45), the perfect shady respite from the sun.

the city are nothing short of spectacular. Get here from the city centre by using the funicular.

Vake

Open-Air Museum of Ethnography
MUSEUM

(Map p44; Kus Tbis qucha 1; adult/child 5/0.50 GEL; ◷10am-6pm Tue-Sun) This collection of traditional, mostly wooden houses, from all around Georgia, is spread over a wooded hillside with good views, and makes for an enjoyable visit. The most interesting exhibits are in the lower section (near the entrance), where the buildings are kitted out with traditional furnishings, rugs and utensils, and the attendants can often explain things in English.

You can walk up to the museum through large, verdant Vake Park (reachable by bus 61 from Freedom Sq or northbound on Rustaveli), or stay on the bus until the petrol station 200m past the large Iranian embassy, then walk or take a taxi 1.4km up the road opposite.

Activities

While in Tbilisi don't miss the chance to visit one of the city's traditional sulphur baths, all of which can be found packed in tightly along one Old Town street.

Chreli Abano
THERMAL BATHS

(Orbeliani Baths; Map p46; ☎32-2930093; www.chreli-abano.ge; Abano; private rooms per hour from 50 GEL; ◷8am–midnight) The popular Chreli Abano boasts an impressive Persian-style facade and has been comprehensively renovated in recent years. Although it now looks inside much like any sauna in the world, this is probably the most comfortable place to enjoy a sulphur bath in Tbilisi. Booking ahead online is advisable.

Don't miss the traditional skin-peeling massage (20 GEL).

Abano No 5
THERMAL BATHS

(Map p46; public baths per hour male/female 5/4 GEL, private rooms per hour 60-110 GEL; ◷public baths 7am-9pm, private baths 24hr) Tbilisi's main public baths are divided by sex and have showers, pools and mosaic domes. They also have a couple of decent-value private rooms, and massages cost 10 GEL.

Royal Bath
THERMAL BATHS

(Map p46; Grishashvili 1; rooms 70-140 GEL, scrub or massage 10 GEL; ◷8am-11pm) The Royal Bath has private rooms only, with mosaic domes, and friendly Russian-speaking attendants. Tea and beer available too.

Gulo's Thermal Spa
THERMAL BATHS

(Map p46; ☎599-588122; www.thermal.ge; Grishashvili 5; private room per hour 40-220 GEL; ◷7am-2am) This lavish marble bathhouse offers private rooms only and is one of the fanciest places in town. At the top end, rooms come with huge pools, and can accommodate up to a dozen people. Massages cost 10 GEL.

Festivals & Events

Tbilisi Open Air
FESTIVAL

(www.tbilisiopenair.ge; Lisi Wonderland, Beritashvili; ◷late Jun) This annual three-day music festival held on woodland at the edge of the city is the best of its kind in the Caucasus, with three stages, a small camping area (most people come up from Tbilisi for the day) and an inclusive, hippyish vibe. Big international performers headline.

Tbilisi Jazz Festival
MUSIC

(www.tbilisijazz.com; ◷late Feb-eary Mar) Since 1978 Tbilisi's annual jazz festival brings local and international jazz stars to various venues in the capital during early spring.

4GB Music Festival
MUSIC

(www.4gb.ge; Institute of Space Structures, Saguramo; per day 100 GEL; ◷last 2 weekends late May) Georgia's biggest electronic music festival kicks off the summer party season in an amazing venue just north of Tbilisi. Running since 2011, the nonprofit festival commemorates Georgian techno pioneer Gio Bakanidze with Georgian and international DJs invited to perform over two weekends in late May.

Tbilisoba
FOOD & DRINK

(◷Oct; ⊞) Tbilisi comes out to party for this festival of the autumn harvest and the city's founding, centred around the Old Town and Rike Park, over a weekend in October. There are *mtsvadi* (shish kebabs), *khinkali* (meat dumplings) and wine stalls everywhere, music and dance events, cheese, fruit and craft stalls and plenty more.

Tbilisi International Film Festival
FILM

(☎32-2356760; www.tbilisifilmfestival.ge; David Aghmashenebeli 164; ◷Nov/Dec) Showcases recent Georgian and international movies, over a week usually in November or December.

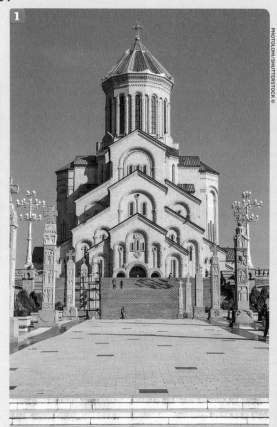

TANATAT PONGPIBOOL/500PX ©

1. Tsminda Sameba Cathedral (p51)

Tbilisi's Holy Trinity Cathedral is a spectacular expression of traditional Georgian architectural forms.

2. Tbilisi (p42)

Take in incredible views of this riverside city, with its ancient fortress and eclectic architecture.

3. Bridge of Peace (p51)

Adding a modern touch to the capital, this glass-and-steel footbridge opened in 2010.

4. Nightlife in Tbilisi (p61)

Enjoy the city's buzzing after-dark scene, at places such as the bar at Fabrika (p57).

3

BADAHOS/SHUTTERSTOCK ©

Art Gene Festival MUSIC
(www.artgeni.ge; ⊘ early Jul) This popular Georgian folk festival visits the regions, then culminates with several days of music, dance, cooking, arts and crafts at Tbilisi's Open-Air Museum of Ethnography (p53).

🛌 Sleeping

Tbilisi enjoys a good range of accommodation options, particularly in the Old Town and around Rustavelis gamziri, including dozens of Western-style hostels that have replaced the guesthouses that were previously budget travellers' best bet. A well-developed range of top-end hotels have been built too, with international chains along with home-grown luxury hotels such as Stamba Hotel and Rooms Hotel Tbilisi.

🛌 Old Town

Envoy Hostel HOSTEL $
(Map p46; ☑ 32-2920111; www.envoyhostel.com/tbilisi; Betlemi 45; dm 32-38 GEL, d/tr 95/100 GEL, all incl breakfast; ❄ 🛜) Envoy has a great location just above Meidan and is one of Tbilisi's best hostels. It's an old parquet-floored house, with six dorms, four private rooms, a wonderful roof terrace with superb Old Town views, a good modern kitchen-dining area, and an adequate number of showers and toilets. Do try to avoid the one double room with no windows, though.

Guests get a free two-hour Old Town walking tour, and on Saturdays it runs a minibus to its Yerevan hostel (p157) with stops at several of northern Armenia's main sights (140 GEL for guests, 11 hours).

Namaste Hostel HOSTEL $
(Map p46; ☑ 32-2753446; www.facebook.com/pages/Namaste-Hostel-Tbilisi/585674301453197; Betlemi 26; dm 30-35 GEL, q 150 GEL; 🛜) This friendly, well-kept hostel has a great location with expansive views over the Old Town. Its good facilities include panoramic terraces and a colourful, quirkily decorated lounge area with a fireplace. There's just one private room, but it has its own terrace. The two dorms sleep six and 12 people respectively.

Hostel Anchi & Old Wall HOSTEL $
(Map p46; ☑ 557-998874, 555-554527; Shavteli 12; dm/s/d/tr/q incl breakfast 25/57/70/90/100 GEL; 🛜) This merger of what was once two separate hostels in the same building is as amicable as it sounds, featuring one seven-bed dorm and several private rooms, which all share three bathrooms and a kitchen. Its Old Town location is super, and rooms are fan-cooled and clean.

Skadaveli Guesthouse GUESTHOUSE $$
(Map p46; ☑ 595-417333; www.ska.ge; Vertskhli 27; s 50 GEL, d 70-100 GEL, tr 100 GEL; ❄ 🛜) This Old Town hideaway has four very attractive, good-value rooms with contemporary furnishings and comfy beds – plus a lovely wood-columned verandah for sitting out, and a super-helpful English-speaking host. It's all in amazing contrast to the quaintly dilapidated exterior of this 1860s building. All but one room share bathrooms, and there's a simple kitchen for guests to use.

An extra 10 GEL per room is charged for one-night stays; no children under 14 years.

Villa Mtiebi BOUTIQUE HOTEL $$
(Map p46; ☑ 32-2920340; www.hotelmtiebi.ge; Chakhrukhadze 10; s/d/tr incl breakfast 180/210/270 GEL; ❄ 🛜) This rather charming bolthole is hidden in a quiet and almost tourist-free part of the Old Town and has maintained its building's original art-nouveau elegance, with a lovely atmospheric atrium where breakfast is served by charming staff. Rooms are modern, clean and soundproofed.

Iota Hotel BOUTIQUE HOTEL $$$
(Map p48; ☑ 32-2403010; www.ioatahotels.com; Lermontovi 10; s/d from 320/365 GEL; ❄ 🛜) This very welcome boutique addition to the charming Sololaki district is a superb and vaguely futuristic conversion of a 1970s building that uses space cleverly to create some very sleek quarters, the best of which are the terrace rooms, which enjoy large walk-outs overlooking a terrific wall of plants. The rooftop Ghumeli restaurant also has fantastic views and excellent food.

No12 Boutique Hotel BOUTIQUE HOTEL $$$
(Map p46; ☑ 32-2552212; www.no12hotel.com; Vakhtang Beridze 12; s/d incl breakfast 280/345 GEL; ❄ 🛜) On a quiet lane right in the heart of the Old Town, No12 offers attractive if smallish rooms with exposed brick panels, pretty tile-surrounded mirrors and coloured-glass lampshades. Staff are amiable and there's a pleasant upstairs terrace.

🛌 Rustaveli Area

Pushkin 10 Hostel HOSTEL $
(Map p46; ☑ 577-651156, 599-095155; www.pushkin10.ge; Pushkin 10; dm/d incl breakfast 35/100 GEL; ❄ 🛜) This mini hostel is perfectly lo-

cated between the Old Town and Rustavelis gamziri, and has just a couple of dorms and one double room all sharing three bathrooms and a kitchen. The hostel's best feature is its large living room complete with a fireplace, a piano and a balcony, the perfect place to unwind after a day of sightseeing.

Hotel Boombully HOTEL **$$**

(Map p48; ☑ 32-2999008, 599-991771; www.boombully.com; Rustaveli 22; s/d/f 150/235/350 GEL; ✲ ☎) Boombully has a fantastic location, a sociable atmosphere and friendly young management. Rooms are brightly and stylishly decorated and share a pine-panelled kitchen and a spacious sitting area with a balcony overlooking Rustavelis gamziri. Guests staying more than five nights get free airport transfers.

★**Stamba Hotel** BOUTIQUE HOTEL **$$$**

(Map p44; ☑ 32-2021199; www.stambahotel.com; Kostava 14; r from 985 GEL; 🅿 ✲ ☎) Tbilisi's best hotel is currently unsurpassable, and Stamba has won new devotees – as well as awards – aplenty since its doors opened in 2018, when the crew behind the adjoining Rooms Hotel Tbilisi unveiled their highly ambitious conversion of a Soviet-era publishing house. Everything about this hotel is on the grandest scale imaginable and will delight the discerning and demanding traveller.

From the moment you enter Stamba's labyrinthine lobby, where bookshelves form the walls and vertical gardens rise to the ceiling, you find yourself in an oasis of subdued calm despite being on Tbilisi's main avenue. The rooms upstairs are enormous booklined exercises in indulgence, complete with high ceilings, vast open-plan bathrooms, gold-plated claw-footed bathtubs that somehow look contemporary rather than Trumpian, fluffy carpets, modernist pull-down armoires, La Marzocco espresso machines (and yes, even a grinder), a maxi bar and electronic blinds. The entire place is exceptional, if you're lucky enough to be able to afford its significant price tag. If not, you can always enjoy a drink or a meal at its excellent bistro-style restaurant (p59) downstairs.

★**Rooms Hotel Tbilisi** BOUTIQUE HOTEL **$$$**

(Map p44; ☑ 32-2020099; http://roomshotels.com/tbilisi; Kostava 14; s/d incl breakfast from 658/710 GEL; 🅿 ✲ ☎) Revolutionising Tbilisi's hotel scene when it opened a few years ago and now spawning imitators all over Georgia, Rooms was Tbilisi's first top-end

boutique hotel and remains one of the most stylish places to stay in the country. The plush rooms feature lavish wallpapering, leather headboards on the large beds, chandeliers and gorgeous bathrooms stuffed with luxurious toiletries.

★**Shota @Rustaveli Boutique Hotel** BOUTIQUE HOTEL **$$$**

(Map p48; ☑ 32-2192021; www.shotahotels.com; Shevchenko 1; r from 342 GEL; ✲ ☎) A very stylish option just seconds from Rustavelis gamziri, this 52-room boutique hotel gets points for its charming staff, sleekly discreet public areas and stylish, airy rooms with contemporary but understated furnishings. The relaxation rooms are particularly fancy, with glass-walled bathrooms and huge designer bathtubs for two. Shota Rustaveli's most iconic characters look down on you from the wall, Warhol-style.

🛏 Vere & Mtatsminda

Betsy's Hotel HOTEL **$$$**

(Map p44; ☑ 32-2931404; www.betsyshotel.com; Makashvili 32-34; s/d incl breakfast 294/343 GEL; ✲ ☎ ✲) An American-owned oasis of unpretentious comfort and good service, Betsy's has a panoramic location on the slopes of Mt Mtatsminda, and is the hotel of choice for generations of Tbilisi visitors for whom international chains are anathema. The rooms are bright, with attractive Georgian carpets, appealing art choices and, of course, superb views over the city from most of them. The bar (especially its Friday happy hour from 6pm to last customer) and restaurant are both highly recommended, and there's also a small outdoor pool.

Hotel British House BOUTIQUE HOTEL **$$$**

(Map p44; ☑ 558-235572; www.british-house.ge; Chovelidze 32; s/d incl breakfast from €45/65; ✲ ☎) This elegant little hotel in a quiet, leafy part of Vere has a welcoming, homelike atmosphere, with antiques and original art abounding. Staff are obliging and the rooms are attractive and well equipped, with carpets and quality furnishings including king-size beds.

🛏 East of the River

★**Fabrika Hostel & Suites** HOSTEL **$**

(Map p44; ☑ 577-313116; www.hostelfabrika.com; Egnate Ninoshvili 8; dm 40 GEL, s/tw/d 235/205/255 GEL; ✲ ☎) This enormous mould-breaking hostel in a converted Soviet sewing factory has raised the bar for local hostels to an almost embarrassing extent. Escape the crumbling Old Town and instead enjoy the huge spaces, muted tones and spotless bathrooms of Fabrika's 94 rooms (half dorms and half private rooms), as well as its five highly popular top-floor apartments with huge terraces.

The concept is brought to you by the savvy team behind Rooms and Stamba, Tbilisi's two most fabulous hotels, and offers a chance at glamour on a budget. This place blows the competition out of the water. As well as its vast ground-floor lounge bar and restaurant, there's a huge roof terrace that's used for everything from free yoga and cinema screenings to barbecues and block parties, not to mention a backyard playground full of bars, restaurants and concept stores.

Sky Guest House GUESTHOUSE **$**
(Map p44; ☑ 551-080205; www.facebook.com/skyguesthousetbilisi; Davit Aghmashenebelis 77; s/d/tr from 50/55/70 GEL; ☞) This welcoming place has four plain but bright and well-kept rooms sharing two bathrooms. There are no dorms but it has a kind of hostel feel thanks to its friendly hostess and shared kitchen-sitting room. It's the pink building at the far end of the Davit Aghmashenebelis gamziri 77 courtyard.

★ Marina Guest House GUESTHOUSE **$$**
(Map p44; ☑ 592-920769, 32-2952959; www.marina-guest-house.com; Chubinashvili 20; per person incl breakfast US$25; Ⓟ☞) Oozing old Tbilisi atmosphere, Marina's 19th-century house has a huge 1st-floor terrace with blue painted woodwork that simply couldn't be more picturesque. The rooms, which sleep between two and five people and share bathrooms, are stuffed full of knick-knacks and have more than a hint of Central Asia about them. Breakfasts are good, and your hostess is welcoming and helpful.

Green House Hostel HOSTEL **$$**
(Map p48; ☑ 32-958377, 599-265432; www.facebook.com/pages/Tbilisi-Green-House/119849388174351; Akhvlediani khevi 13; dm 25 GEL, d 70-80 GEL, tr 100 GEL; ☀☞) A lovely, spacious house in a quiet lane, Green House appeals to travellers in search of a quiet hideaway not too far from the centre of things. It has a spacious kitchen, a leafy front yard, a large upstairs terrace and a piano in the sitting room. It's run by a friendly couple full of helpful knowledge about Georgia's mountains.

Hotel Old Metekhi HOTEL **$$**
(Map p46; ☑ 32-2747404; www.ometekhi.com; Metekhis aghmarti 3; r from 180 GEL; ☀☞) Perched on a rocky cliff above the Mtkvari, this delightfully renovated hotel offers contemporary carpeted rooms with well-equipped bathrooms. About half the 21 rooms have spectacular views over the river, and this is the main reason to stay here, even if the rooms themselves aren't particularly atmospheric.

✖ Eating

Tbilisi has the best restaurants in Georgia and you'll eat superbly here, whether it's traditional cooking, modern Georgian with an international twist or various other non-native cuisines. Dive in and enjoy, but in general make reservations for the evening whenever possible, as the very best places are nearly always full in the summer months.

✖ Old Town

It can be challenging to eat well in the Old Town these days, with lots of touristy places and huge crowds. But there are a few excellent options all the same.

Cafe Alani OSSETIAN **$**
(Map p46; Gorgasali 1; mains 7-18 GEL; ◷11am-11pm; ☞) This simple little restaurant with clean, modern design serves Ossetian food, which is similar to Georgian, and it's some of the best-value fare in town. Try the very tasty *chakapuli* (lamb with tarragon and plums), *shkmeruli* (sizzling chicken in garlic sauce) or a *khabidzgina,* a filling Ossetian *khachapuri* (cheese pie). The house beer, Alani, slips down very nicely.

Machakhela-Samikitno GEORGIAN **$**
(Map p46; ☑ 577-710788; Meidan; mains 5-20 GEL; ◷10am-11pm; ☞) There are branches of this well-known Georgian chain all over the city, but the outlet on Meidan is probably the most useful for visitors seeking an inexpensive place to try *khachapuri*. It also serves salads, soups and meat dishes as well as delicious fried *khinkali.* Every pie is freshly made and there's a helpful picture menu for beginners.

There's another useful branch (Map p46; Pushkin 5/7; mains 5-20 GEL; ◷24hr; ☞) on Freedom Sq.

Racha GEORGIAN **$**
(Map p46; Lermontov 6; mains 5-11 GEL; ◷9am-10.30pm) One of Tbilisi's last *duqani* (cheap

and traditional basement eateries), Racha serves tasty home-style staples such as *khinkali, mtsvadi, khachapuri* and *badrijani nigvzit* (aubergine slices with walnut-and-garlic paste) at great prices. Go to the counter to order and pay for your dishes in advance. You can bring your own wine.

★**Culinarium Khasheria** GEORGIAN $$
(Map p46; ☑ 32-2721157; Abano 23; mains 10-20 GEL; ⊙ 11am-1am; ☎🖉) Yes, it's slap bang in the middle of Abanotubani and gets more than its fair share of tour groups, but Culinarium remains an excellent place to eat. Named after a famous hangover cure, *khash,* you don't need to be nursing a headache to dine here, though its six hangover cures, from chicken soup to *bozbashi* (beef broth with meatballs), are sorely tempting.

Cafe Leila GEORGIAN $$
(Map p46; Shavteli 20; mains 10-35 GEL; ⊙ 11am-midnight; ☎🖉) Leila is a lovely place to relax with a mint lemonade, a coffee and a light dish such as hummus, soup or a salad. In a century-old building, it has delightful decor of interlaced stucco work inset with cute little Persian-style paintings.

Organique Josper Bar INTERNATIONAL $$$
(Map p46; ☑ 593-735083; www.restorganique. com; Bambis rigi 12; mains 22-35 GEL; ⊙ 11am-11pm; ☎) The narrow Old Town streets Shardenis qucha and Bambis rigi are lined with so-so, fairly touristic restaurants, but Organique Josper stands out for its excellent charcoal-grilled steaks and burgers, natural wines and good salads, all sourced from organic ingredients. Decor is quite 'organique' too.

Café Gabriadze GEORGIAN $$$
(Map p46; Shavteli 13; mains 18-31 GEL; ⊙ 10.30am-midnight; ☎) Quirkily attractive little Café Gabriadze, under the same management as the neighbouring Gabriadze puppet theatre, offers friendly service and good Georgian food with original twists. Its *ponchki* (doughnuts) with cream are rightly famous. Decor is on theatrical themes, full of intriguing details.

🍴 Rustaveli & Around

Tbilisi's massive central avenue and its charming side streets have a plethora of eating options suitable for all budgets.

Pasanauri GEORGIAN $
(Map p48; Griboedov 37; khinkali 0.75-0.95 GEL, mains 8-25 GEL; ⊙ noon-11pm; 🖉) This modest place with around 10 wood-boothed tables is frequently packed thanks to its *khinkali,* which are among the best in town. Top choice is the meaty 'Pasanauri special', but there are vegetable *khinkali* too, including cheese, mushroom and potatoes, which can be livened up by ordering the fabulous homemade *adjika* (Georgian spicy sauce) or a plate of sour cream.

★**Alubali** GEORGIAN $$
(Map p48; ☑ 555-459539; Giorgi Akhvlediani 5; mains 10-45 GEL; ⊙ noon-midnight; ☎🖉) Totally unmarked from the street and behind a slightly anonymous door cage, this delightful courtyard spot has a deceptively simple and relatively short menu, but its dishes are delectable regional Georgian treats. Don't miss the Megrelian *elarji* (cornmeal mixed with *sulguni* cheese, creating a fabulously playful and addictive putty) or the mozzarella-like *gebzhalia* (cottage cheesein a minty yoghurt sauce).

★**Café Stamba** INTERNATIONAL $$
(Map p44; ☑ 32-2021199; www.stambahotel. com; Kostava 14; mains 11-36 GEL; ⊙ 7-11am & noon-midnight Mon-Fri, 8am-noon & 1pm-midnight Sat & Sun; ☎🖉) This super-stylish all-day bar-cafe-restaurant serves as the current meeting point for Tbilisi's various cultural elites, and is equally suited to a relaxed breakfast, a blow-out *supra* (traditional feast; literally 'tablecloth') or just top-notch cocktails prepared by the iconic Pink Bar. The menu skews Italian, with dishes such as black spaghetti with shrimp or mushroom risotto, but there's also an innovative Georgian menu.

Sofia Melnikova's Fantastic Douqan INTERNATIONAL $$
(Map p48; ☑ 592-681166; Gia Chantuira 8; mains 8-27 GEL; ⊙ noon-2am Mon-Sat, to midnight Sun; ☎🖉) This animated courtyard restaurant is a convivial and charming place for a meal on a summer evening, when it buzzes with just the right mix of locals and visitors. Choose between a table under the grapevine trellis, the trees of the yard or in the rather lovely dining room, and enjoy Sofia's eclectic menu combining Georgian and international dishes.

It's a little tricky to find and totally unsigned – look for the souvenir shop calling itself the Sarcho Museum on Tabukashvilis qucha and then walk up the small street going off from here, and the restaurant is in one of the courtyards on your left.

Lolita
EUROPEAN **$$**

(Map p44; ☑ 32-2020299; https://roomshotels.com/lolita; Tamar Chovelidze 7; mains 12-25 GEL; ☉11am-1am; ☎🏶) Easily the best place in town for a smart breakfast (served weekdays/weekends until 1pm/2pm), Lolita is the informal, hipster-heavy lounge-cafe-bar of your dreams. Its clever inside-outside design keeps it airy, the open kitchen looks like something you'd find in Manhattan and the cocktails are sublime. Most importantly: where else in Tbilisi can you find avocado toast?

Dzveli Sakhli
GEORGIAN **$$**

(Old House; Map p48; ☑ 591-711771; Marjvena Sanapiro 3; mains 10-52 GEL; ☉noon-midnight; ☎🏶) The rambling 'Old House' serves authentic dishes from all over Georgia and has an open-air section right above the river, with fantastic performances of Georgian music and dance at 8pm nightly. It also has dozens of private rooms popular with local diners, and overflows with atmosphere. Try a smoked-veal *mtsvadi* in red wine, or the trout in currant sauce.

★ Keto and Kote
GEORGIAN **$$$**

(Map p48; ☑ 555-530126; Zandukheli 3; mains 16-27 GEL; ☉11am-1am; ☎🏶) Reservations are usually essential at this sumptuous Georgian restaurant serving extraordinarily good food at the top of a small hill overlooking the city. Choose between a table in the garden, on the terrace under an awning or in the fabulous dining room, which is beautifully lit and glows in red accents from the painted beams on the ceiling.

The menu is exceptional, with a few dishes really standing out. We love the beef cooked in Roquefort and *adjika*, the mini meat *khinkali* in butter sauce and the wonderfully tender *dolma* (stuffed vine leaves), but you are unlikely to be disappointed by anything here. The wine list is exceptional, with extensive choice and some excellent vintages.

✖ Sololaki & Mtatsminda

These two hillside neighbourhoods have a villagey feel to them and are home to a handful of Tbilisi's lesser known culinary treats.

★ Klike's Khinkali
GEORGIAN **$**

(Map p48; ☑ 555-411991; Chitadze 1; khinkali 1 GEL; ☉11am-11pm; ☎🏶) You have to know about this rather hidden boho brick-lined basement on the Mtatsminda hillside, but once you've been here you're likely to keep coming back, as for our money its *khinkali* are Tbilisi's best. The thin dough and delicious fillings are super simple but utterly mouth-watering, and there's good-quality beer and wine by the glass too.

Salobie Bia
GEORGIAN **$$**

(Map p48; ☑ 32-2997977; Machabeli 14; mains 7-23 GEL; ☉11am-11pm; ☎🏶) This unassuming lower-ground-floor restaurant decked out in Soviet Georgian posters is always full, so it's a good idea to reserve at any time of day. The handwritten menu revisits Georgian classics with a twist and takes you on a delicious tour through the country's regional cooking, not least its *lobio* (bean stew), after which the place is named.

★ Cafe Littera
GEORGIAN **$$$**

(Map p48; ☑ 599-988308; Machabeli 13; mains 28-38 GEL; ☉noon-midnight; ☎🏶) A real treat, Littera serves simply superb 'nouveau Georgian' dishes in the lovely rear garden of the Georgian Writers' Union building. Don't miss trying the assorted *pkhali* (pastes combining vegetables with walnuts, garlic and herbs) as an appetiser. The frequently changing menu might include mains of fried quail with wheat berry risotto, or mussels *chakapuli*. It's advisable to book for dinner, although lunchtime is normally fine for walk-ins. In winter it moves indoors.

Azarphesha
GEORGIAN **$$$**

(Map p48; ☑ 32-2982346; www.azarphesha.com; Ingorovka 2; mains 18-35 GEL; ☉11am-11pm; ☎🏶) Azarphesha takes its food very seriously indeed and its knowledgeable English-speaking staff set it apart from many of its rivals. Wine glasses hanging from the ceiling underline its focus on natural Georgian wines, while the seasonally changing menu features dishes such as pork marinated in beer with wild mushrooms, catfish ceviche, and stinging nettle and lemon and cheese dumplings.

✖ Vake

Residential and well-heeled Vake is mainly notable for a good brunch spot.

Kikliko BREAKFAST **$$**
(Map p44; ☑551-137112; Mtskheta 28; mains 7-15 GEL; ⊙8am-3pm Mon-Fri, 9am-4pm Sat & Sun; 🛜🍴) Amazingly, this is just one of a few quality breakfast joints you'll find in Tbilisi, and it's well worth making the trip to Vake to sample the excellent eggs Benedict, cottage cheese pancakes or its signature dish, Kikliko, which is made from fried bread and eggs and comes in various delicious varieties.

🍴 East of the River

Away from the Old Town crowds you'll find a couple of excellent choices on the left bank of the Mtkvari.

Shavi Lomi GEORGIAN **$$**
(Black Lion; Map p44; ☑32-2960956; Zurab Kvlividze 28; mains 10-25 GEL; ⊙noon-midnight; 🛜🍴) Shavi Lomi is the eponymous restaurant of Georgia's best-known craft brewery, and has been instrumental in transforming Tbilisi's culinary scene in the past decade. Now housed in a large mansion with a garden some way from the normal traveller haunts, it's worth a trip for its interesting menu with dishes such as lemon shrimp couscous or chicken in a walnut-pomegranate sauce.

★Barbarestan GEORGIAN **$$$**
(Map p44; ☑32-2943779; reservation@barbarestan.ge; Davit Aghmeshenebeli 132; mains 30-60 GEL; ⊙10.30am–11.30pm; 🛜🍴) The extraordinary and elaborate meals served here are based on an antique cookbook discovered at Tbilisi's Dry Bridge Market in 2015. Of the 900 'forgotten' Georgian dishes described, featuring rarely used ingredients such as rabbit, duck and crayfish, to date 230 have been recreated by chef Giorgi Sarajishvili and his team, who present a frequently changing menu of obscure delights.

This is probably Tbilisi's most innovative fine dining restaurant and an absolute must for anyone curious to try new takes on Georgia's amazing culinary wealth. Reservations for the evening are essential, but you can often get a table at lunchtime without one. Staff are charming, speak good English and are delighted to explain various details of the cooking process.

🍷 Drinking & Nightlife

Tbilisi's nightlife scene was revolutionised with the opening of techno club Bassiani (p62) in 2014, an event that put the city's small but influential electronic music scene on the map. Now there are dozens of clubs where you can hear contemporary Georgian DJs, but there are also some wonderful venues running from cool artist collectives to cocktail lounges and wine bars.

🍷 Old Town & Sololaki

★Wine Buffet WINE BAR
(Map p46; Ovanes Tumaniani 15; ⊙1pm-1am) This somewhat hidden 2nd-floor wine bar is one of the best of scores of places in the Old Town to try Georgian natural wines. The selection is superb, and the staff, though barely speaking a word of English, are super kind and friendly. Order a plate of cheese, honey and nuts and enjoy a varied tasting of fantastic wines.

Vino Underground WINE BAR
(Map p48; www.vinounderground.ge; Tabidze 15; glass of wine 8-15 GEL, bottles 30-100 GEL; ⊙11am-11pm; 🛜) Vino Underground is Tbilisi's brick-vaulted temple to natural wine, so you can be sure to get the authentic tastes of traditional Georgian wine here. It has a mind-boggling array to choose from: ask the staff for some suggestions.

Valiko Bar COCKTAIL BAR
(Map p48; Galaktion Tabidze 24; ⊙noon-1am Sun-Thu, to 2am Fri & Sat; 🛜) This fabulous cocktail bar in a crumbling building is one of the most atmospheric places to have a drink in Tbilisi. We love the precarious balconies, the superb cocktail list and the excellent playlists. Valiko was a Georgian film director, dramatist and actor who owned the building until he was purged by Stalin; his films are projected onto the walls.

Warszawa BAR
(Map p46; Pushkin 19; ⊙10am-4am; 🛜) A tiny, brightly lit Polish cafe-bar almost on Freedom Sq, Warszawa has the most affordable drinks in town, and, at GEL 5, quite possibly the world's cheapest steak tartare. A late-night favourite, it's an ideal place to meet fellow travellers. There is a comfier wine-bar style section in the basement.

Zoestan BAR
(Map p46; Vakhtang Beridze 5; ⊙5pm-2am) This cosy basement bar is run by the eponymous Zoe, a Frenchwoman with an encyclopedic knowledge of Georgian folk music and a voice to match. Hosting concerts most Sundays, it's a place to get into Georgian traditional music in a relaxed environment.

GEORGIA TBILISI

Rustaveli Area

★ Drama Bar
BAR

(Map p48; www.facebook.com/dramatbilisi; Rustaveli 37; ☺9am-3am Thu-Sun) Fiendishly cool Drama Bar is in a residential building with no sign. Go up to the 3rd floor and you'll find a bouncer – door policy is tough and you may be rejected if they don't know you, but you may also be welcomed warmly: it's unpredictable. Inside there's a bar-cum-dance floor and several chill-out rooms stuffed with Tbilisi's elegantly wasted youth.

Dedaena Bar
BAR

(Map p48; Dedaena Park; ☺6pm-3am) One of Tbilisi's most popular hipster bars, gay-friendly Dedaena attracts a skater crowd due to its location by the skate park, as well as their friends and admirers. It's a lovely spot, overlooking the river and with a large terrace that gets completely rammed on summer evenings. Inside there are DJs normally playing techno and house.

Rooms Hotel Bar
COCKTAIL BAR

(Map p44; www.roomshotels.com; Kostava 14; ☺9am-2am; 🔊) For a bit of luxury, and some of the best cocktails in the Caucasus, head to the gorgeous bar at Rooms Hotel. Impeccable service, great interiors and good music, plus, in summer, a great garden bar: Rooms is the place to get a bit of Manhattan in Tbilisi.

Skola Coffee & Wine Bar
COFFEE

(Map p48; ☑551-533335; Rustaveli 17; ☺8am-10pm Mon-Fri, 9am-11pm Sat & Sun; 🔊) This minimalist temple to coffee (the wine is a bit of an afterthought to be honest) is hands down the best in Tbilisi, and offers a full range of hot and iced coffees, vegan milk options, fabulous beans roasted by Moscow roastery Camera Obscura for sale, and a small but decent selection of wine, cake and pastries.

Mozaika
BAR

(Map p48; Vashlovani 8; ☺7pm-3am; 🔊) This friendly and hip bar is a favourite for locals looking for a pre-club hang-out and is a popular place to meet up with friends. There's a small balcony overlooking the street that accommodates smokers, while inside the charming two-floor space is decorated with mosaics and is a lovely space to interact with a cool and open-minded crowd.

Success Bar
GAY & LESBIAN

(Map p48; www.facebook.com/successbar2017; Vashlovani 3; ☺10.30pm-4am Tue-Sun) Despite the impressive queering of Tbilisi in recent years, this small two-room basement bar is the city's only officially gay establishment, rescued by local photographer Nia Gvatua and given a desperately needed new lease on life after years of neglect. Now it's packed at weekends, with a pre-clubbing crowd who love the kitschy decor, tiny dance floor and safe-space atmosphere.

Dive Bar
BAR

(Map p48; Revaz Laghidze 12; ☺6pm-2am; 🔊) Founded by a group of Georgians and American Peace Corps volunteers, Dive has become a Tbilisi institution, and is the best place to go for cheap beer and good times. With two beer pong tables, live music on Wednesdays and a large outdoor area, it's popular with locals and expats alike. Find it in the yard. Expect the bar staff to speak any language from Persian to German, and to politely tell you they don't do music requests.

Café Gallery
CLUB

(Map p48; Griboedov 34; ☺10.30am-8am Tue & Fri, noon-8am Sat; 🔊) A laid-back cafe and art gallery by day, three nights a week Café Gallery clears away its tables and becomes a small but excellent club playing minimal techno and house. Weekends see its two storeys packed out and local and international DJs on the decks. Tuesday is a popular gay night.

Dublin
PUB

(Map p48; Akhvlediani 8; ☺11am-3am) A heady mix of young Georgians, raucous expats and live cover bands, Dublin has been keeping its neighbours awake since 1990. It has also given birth to dozens of clone bars on this section of Akhvledianis qucha, so check which has the most going on.

East of the River

★ Bassiani
CLUB

(Map p44; ☑599-880888; www.bassiani.com; Akaki Tsereteli Ave 2; ☺around midnight-8am) Fêted as one of the best techno clubs in the world and mentioned breathlessly in a thousand magazine articles, Bassiani is the Berghain of the Caucasus and an absolute highlight of Tbilisi's famous nightlife. Housed in a former swimming pool under the Dinamo Stadium, the incredibly lit space features a Funktion-One sound system, two dance floors and numerous chill-out areas.

Bassiani is run by a politically active collective that has nurtured tonnes of local talent and even led Georgian clubbers in a series of protests against heavy-handed

WE DANCE TOGETHER, WE FIGHT TOGETHER

Underground, political and queer, Bassiani was a breath of fresh air and unlike any club in the former Soviet Union – let alone Georgia – when it opened its doors under the Dinamo Stadium in 2014. Taking up a cavernous, concrete space that could have been designed to become a club, Bassiani can accommodate 1200 guests over two dance floors (including the main one in the basin of a disused swimming pool), multiple chill-out areas and warrens of dark corridors.

When Bassiani and Café Gallery were raided by Georgian special forces in 2018 and hundreds of clubbers enjoying a night out were detained in an ostensible search for drugs, Tbilisi's youth rallied round and staged a two-day demonstration the following day, which quickly became the stuff of legend. Under the slogan 'We Dance Together, We Fight Together', thousands of clubbers hoping for a more liberal future for this former Soviet republic danced to techno on Rustavelis gamziri, backed by messages of support from DJs and musicians from around the world. As well as protesting against Georgia's draconian drug laws, and particularly against the random drug testing often carried out by police on the streets, the demonstration served to unite a previously fairly disparate part of Georgian society around the ideas of freedom of expression and progressive international values.

Today Bassiani is an obligatory stop for any techno lover visiting the city, and for some, the club is even *the* reason to visit Georgia itself. Anyone wanting to take the temperature of Tbilisi's now-famous techno culture will find a visit to the incredible space a fascinating experience.

policing in Georgia following a number of club raids in 2018. The club has also been a vocal advocate of gay rights in a country where the subject remains virtually taboo, and hosts Georgia's best queer party, Horoom Nights, approximately once a month. Normally you can just turn up and buy tickets for Bassiani at the door, though for security reasons you need to be a registered and verified guest to attend Horoom Nights; register online with your ID number and Facebook URL (yes, really). It pays to register with Bassiani anyway, as it entitles you to discounted entry and will help you get past the tough door staff if you're a first-timer.

Mtkvarze CLUB

(Map p44; www.mtkvarze.com; Nikoloz Baratashvili, Left Bank; ⊙11pm-11am Fri & Sat, closed Aug) This former Soviet-era fish restaurant with a wraparound balcony overhanging the east bank of the Mtkvari River is a great space for a nightclub. Mtkvarze (literally, 'on the Mtkvari') often hosts well-known international DJs playing that Georgian favourite: minimal techno. There's all-night food, too, and once you're past the door, it's a super-friendly and welcoming place.

🍷 Northern Tbilisi

★**KHIDI** CLUB

(Map p44; www.khidi.ge; Vakhushti Bagrationi Bridge, Right Bank; ⊙11pm-9am Fri & Sat) Mean-ing 'the Bridge' in Georgian, KHIDI is quite literally built into the hillside under one of the main bridges across the Mtkvari, and is an extraordinary concrete bunker space ideal for housing one of Tbilisi's best clubs. The main floor plays techno, while the smaller dance floor is more varied in its musical direction, with dance, ambient, electro and experimental nights.

You'll need to register online with a Facebook URL and your passport number to get approval to enter, but it's well worth the hassle. The monthly queer party, Kiki (register for this at www.khidi.ge/kiki), is massively popular, while at other times the space holds art exhibits, dance and other artistic performances and workshops. This is one of Tbilisi's most progressive and interesting spaces and a vital stop for anyone exploring the local club scene.

☆ Entertainment

Tbilisi's entertainment options for non-Georgian speakers are somewhat limited, but you can still enjoy musical performances, which are common in many restaurants as well as bars and specific entertainment venues. The 2016-reopened Opera & Ballet Theatre is looking spectacular and is well worth getting tickets for.

★**Gabriadze Theatre** THEATRE

(Tbilisi Marionette Theatre; Map p46; 📞32-2986590; www.gabriadze.com; Shavteli 13; 10-30

GEL; ◉ box office 11am-7pm, closed Jul-Aug) If you think puppets aren't your thing, think again. The shows at this quaint little theatre, directed by maestro Rezo Gabriadze, are awe-inspiringly original and moving, and come with English subtitles. If they're on during your stay, *Stalingrad* or *Ramona* are both highly recommended. Book ahead either by email or by going to the box office in person.

★ **Opera & Ballet Theatre** PERFORMING ARTS
(Map p48; ☑ 32-2004466; www.opera.ge; Rustaveli 25) Tbilisi's beautiful opera house, in a 19th-century neo-Moorish building, finally reopened after years of renovation in 2016 and is looking gorgeous. Opera, ballet and classical concerts play to full houses here, but in the summer months you may find that there are more people filming performances than watching them. The box office is rather hidden around the right-hand side.

Tbilisi Concert Hall CONCERT VENUE
(Map p44; ☑ 32-2990599; www.tbilisiconcerthall. com; Petre Melikishvili 1) Seating 2300 people, Tbilisi Concert Hall is Georgia's biggest musical venue and hosts many of the country's most prestigious music events, including the annual Tbilisi Jazz Festival (p53) each spring.

Rustaveli Theatre THEATRE
(Map p48; ☑ 32-2726868; www.rustavelitheatre. ge; Rustaveli 17; ◉ closed Aug) The Rustaveli is internationally famed for the Shakespeare productions of Robert Sturua, who has directed here almost uninterruptedly since 1980. It occasionally does shows with simultaneous English translation: check at the box office.

🛍 Shopping

Tbilisi has become a very good place to shop in the past few years, with dozens of unique stores crowding the Old Town and Sololaki, while markets, malls, souvenir shops, wine merchants, carpet specialists and local fashion brands compete for your custom elsewhere.

★ **Dry Bridge Market** ANTIQUES
(Map p48; 9 Martis Park; ◉ 10am-5pm Mon-Fri, 9am-6pm Sat & Sun) You'll find all kinds of knick-knacks and intriguing miscellanea at Tbilisi's best and most popular open-air flea market – original art, shaggy shepherds' hats, accordions, jewellery, silver, glass, daggers and Soviet memorabilia. It's best at weekends when there's an almost carnivalesque atmosphere.

Galleria SHOPPING CENTRE
(Map p48; ☑ 32-2500040; www.galleria.ge; Rustaveli 2/4; ◉ 10am-10pm) Central Tbilisi's biggest and fanciest mall, Galleria is the kind of place you find yourself going to for convenience (it's just off Freedom Sq and above Tavisuplebis moedani metro station of the same name). Here you'll find everything from a basement supermarket to dozens of stores selling fashion, electronics and homewares, and a popular top-floor food court.

Termitti FASHION & ACCESSORIES
(Map p48; ☑ 558-444648; www.facebook.com/pg/termitti; Galaktion Tabidze 23; ◉ 10am-7pm) This charming Sololaki studio produces much sought-after leather goods, including beautiful backpacks, handbags, wallets, bumbags and various other stylish accessories. Prices are very reasonable and the goods are made right here in-house. Pleather items are also available.

Aristaeus FOOD
(Map p46; Pushkin 19; ◉ 10am-11pm) A great selection of Georgian cheeses, plus jars of artisanal jams, honey and sauces.

Caucasian and Oriental Carpets Gallery CARPETS
(Map p46; ☑ 577-405311; www.carpetsintbilisi.com; Erekle II 8/10; ◉ 10am-8pm) In business for 30 years, this shop has the best selection of carpets in the Old Town, with colourful rugs from Georgia, Azerbaijan, Iran and Central Asia.

Geoland MAPS
(Map p48; ☑ 32-2922553; info@geoland.ge; Telegrapis chikhi 3; ◉ 10am-7pm Mon-Fri year-round, 11am-6pm Sat Jun-Sep) Georgia's best mapmaker, Geoland sells its own excellent 1:50,000 trekking maps (nine maps covering the Svaneti, Racha, Kazbegi, Tusheti and Borjomi areas), travel maps (six regional maps covering the country at 1:200,000), country map and Tbilisi city map, for 12 GEL each. It also prints off 1:50,000 sheets of all parts of Georgia, based on Soviet military maps, for 22 GEL each. It sells camping gas and Garmin hand-held and automotive GPSs too.

Prospero's Books BOOKS, MAPS
(Map p48; ☑ 32-2923592; www.prosperosbookshop.com; Rustaveli 34; ◉ 9.30am-8pm) This English-language bookshop has a great selection of Georgia and South Caucasus titles, plus maps, travel guides, novels and the lovely Caliban's Coffeehouse in the same building. There's also a shelf of secondhand books and a good history section.

Desertirebis Bazari MARKET
(Deserters' Market; Map p44; cnr Tsinamdzghvrish-vili & Abastumani; ⊙7am-7pm) This sprawling conglomeration near the train station is Tbilisi's main central market and a wander around it will probably reveal every food that Georgians eat. There's a relatively handsome modern building at its centre, but many traders prefer to open lots on the streets outside. The market is named after deserting soldiers who sold their weapons here in the early 1920s.

ⓘ Information

MEDICAL SERVICES
CITO (Map p44; ☑ 32-2290671; www.cito.ge; Paliashvili 40, Vake; ⊙9am-6pm Mon-Fri, to 3pm Sat) One of the city's best private medical centres. Has a GP, specialists and a good laboratory.

IMSS (Map p44; ☑ 599-100311, 599-266669; www.imss.ge; 5th fl, Neoclinic Bldg, Bakhtrioni 10a, Saburtalo; ⊙24hr) Consultations and 24-hour inpatient care available with EU- or US-trained doctors. Has 24-hour emergency service.

MediClub Georgia (Map p44; ☑ 32-2251991; www.mcg.ge; Tashkent 22a, Saburtalo) Has 24-hour emergency and ambulance service, and a good inpatient clinic.

POST
Main Post Office (Map p44; ☑ 32-2240909; www.gpost.ge; Station Sq; ⊙9am-5pm Mon-Fri, 10am-2pm Sat) The main post office in Tbilisi can be found right next to the train station.

TELEPHONE
Get a local SIM card at one of the three main mobile phone providers **Beeline** (Bilaini; Map p48; www.beeline.ge; Rustaveli 14; ⊙10am-7pm Mon-Fri, to 5pm Sat & Sun), **Magti** (Map p48; www.magticom.ge; Rustaveli 22; ⊙9am-9pm Mon-Fri, to 6pm Sat & Sun) or **Silknet-Geocell** (Map p48; www.geocell.ge; Rustaveli 40; ⊙10am-8pm Mon-Sat). Bring your passport.

TOURIST INFORMATION
Tourism Information Centre (Map p46; ☑ 32-2158697; www.gnta.ge; Freedom Sq; ⊙9am-9pm or later) This small glass booth on one side of Freedom Sq (Tavisuplebis moedani) has very helpful staff who can find the answers to most questions you throw at them. The airport desk is open 24 hours.

ⓘ Getting There & Away

Marshrutky (minibuses) are the main transport around Georgia. Along with some buses and minivans (smaller and more comfortable than *marshrutky*), they depart from various terminals around the city.

Trains are mostly slower and less frequent than road transport, though they can also be very good value and a lot more enjoyable.

GEORGIA TBILISI

INTERNATIONAL MARSHRUTKY, BUSES & MINIBUSES FROM TBILISI

DESTINATION	DEPARTURE	COST (GEL)	TIME (HR)	FREQUENCY
Athens	Ortachala	230	42	1 bus daily, times vary
Baku (via Tsiteli Khidi & Gǝncǝ)	Ortachala	30	10	5pm & 6.30pm buses daily
İstanbul (via Trabzon)	Ortachala	85	26	5 or more buses daily
Moscow	Ortachala	150-200	32	2 or more buses daily
Qax	Ortachala	10	4-5	*marshrutky* 8.40am, 11am, 1pm
Vanadzor (via Alaverdi)	Ortachala	20	3½	1 bus daily at 9am
Vladikavkaz	Ortachala	60	4	1 bus daily at noon
Vladikavkaz	Didube	70	4	minivans leave when full
Yerevan (via Ijevan, Dilijan, Sevan)	Avlabari	40	6	minivans every 2hr 9am-5pm (reservations ☑ 593-229554)
Yerevan (via Alaverdi, Vanadzor)	Ortachala	40	6	*marshrutky* 8.20am, 9.10am, 10am, then afterwards when bus gets full (reservations ☑ 577-411044)
Yerevan (via Alaverdi, Vanadzor)	Sadguris Moedani	40	6	*marshrutky* every 2hr 9am-5pm
Zaqatala	Ortachala	12	3-4	*marshrutky* 8.30am & 5pm

Flying or travelling by train are overall the best options for getting direct to Baku; AZAL and Buta Airways fly direct daily, while there is also an overnight train departing every evening.

For northwest Azerbaijan you'll need *marshrutky,* although at research time a new tourist shuttle bus service to Şəki was planned to begin by summer 2020 by the **Azerbaijan Tourist Board** (Map p48; www.tourismboard.az; Rustaveli 16).

For Armenia, minivans from Avlabari metro station to Yerevan are a comfortable, convenient option, as are the minibuses run by Envoy Hostel (p56) every Saturday. Alternatively, **Georgian Airways** (Map p48; ☑ 32-2111220; www.geor gian-airways.com; Rustaveli 12; ☺10am-6pm Mon-Fri) flies direct daily.

AIR

Tbilisi International Airport (☑ 32-2310421, 32-2511511; www.airport-tbilisi.com) is 15km east of the city centre. Direct flights head to/ from more than 40 international destinations. Many flights arrive and depart at unholy early-morning hours.

Within the South Caucasus, Georgian Airways flies to Yerevan, and domestically to Batumi. **AZAL** (Azerbaijan Airlines; Map p44; ☑ 32- 2558888; www.azal.az; Chavchavadze 28; ☺10am-7pm Mon-Fri, to 3pm Sat & Sun) and Buta Airways fly to Baku.

The airport terminal has ATMs, multiple 24-hour bank branches offering currency exchange, mobile-phone providers and car-rental offices.

From **Natakhtari Airfield** (☑ 599-452525, 32-2428428; www.vanillasky.ge; 7 Bambis Rigi), 25km north of Tbilisi, domestic airline **Vanilla Sky** (Map p44; ☑ 32-2427427, 599-659099; www.vanillasky.ge; Vazha Pshavela 5, Saburtalo; ☺10am-6pm Mon-Fri, 11am-1pm Sat) runs twin props that depart for Mestia and Batumi.

BUS & MARSHRUTKA

Marshrutky may leave after or before scheduled times, depending on how quickly they fill up, and all schedules are subject to change – it's all part of the fun. Buses tend to leave as timetabled, but make up a far smaller proportion of public transport services.

Marshrutky and buses depart from the following bus stations:

Didube (p71) The sprawling main hub for national services. Areas close to the metro exit have *marshrutky* to Akhaltsikhe, Bakuriani, Batumi, Borjomi, Stepantsminda, Kutaisi, Mtskheta and Vardzia. Along a road to the right you'll find the Okriba bus station on your left,

DOMESTIC MARSHRUTKY & BUSES FROM TBILISI

DESTINATION	DEPARTURE	COST (GEL)	TIME (HR)	FREQUENCY
Akhaltsikhe	Didube	8	4	hourly 8am-7pm
Bakuriani	Didube	10	4	9am, 10am, 11am
Batumi	Ortachala	35	6	6 Metro Georgia buses daily
Batumi	Didube	20	6	hourly 8am-8pm
Borjomi	Didube	8	2½	hourly 8am-7pm
Dedoplis Tskaro	Ortachala	8	3	every 2hr 8.30am-5pm
Gori	Didube	4	1¼	every 40min 8.15am-6pm
Kutaisi	Didube	10	4	every 30min 8am-2pm, hourly 2-8pm
Lagodekhi	Isani	8	2½	every 40min 8.40am-6.30pm
Mestia	Sadguris Moedani	30	9	7am reservation ☑ 557-130529
Mestia	Navtlughis Avtosadguri	30	9	7am reservation ☑ 591-663663
Mtskheta	Didube	1	30min	every 20min 8am-8pm
Sighnaghi	Navtlughis Avtosadguri	7	2	every 2hr 9am-6pm
Stepantsminda	Didube	10	3	hourly 9am-6pm
Telavi	Ortachala	8	2	every 45min 8am-4pm
Telavi	Navtlughis Avtosadguri	8	2	hourly 9.20am-4.10pm
Vardzia	Didube	15	4½	10am
Zugdidi	Sadguris Moedani	15	5½	hourly 8am-9.30pm
Zugdidi	Didube	15	5½	every 1½hr 8am-7pm

with more Batumi and Kutaisi *marshrutky* plus Zugdidi services, and a yard opposite with Gori *marshrutky*.

Ortachala (🚗 32-2753433; Gulia 1) Ortachala, 2.5km southeast of the Old Town, has services for Kakheti, Armenia, Azerbaijan, Turkey, Greece and Russia. *Marshrutky* to destinations in Kakheti, and Zaqatala and Qax in Azerbaijan, leave from out the front; other services, including comfortable **Metro Georgia** (🚗 577-159415, 32-2750595; www.metrogeorgia.ge) buses to Batumi, depart from inside. You can reach Ortachala on bus 50, 55 or 71 from Baratashvili (Map p46) in central Tbilisi. Heading into town from Ortachala, catch these going to the left on the street outside. *Marshrutky* 108 and 150 run between Ortachala and Didube.

Sadguris Moedani (Map p44) The main train station has two bus stations attached to it: the first one at the front on the square and a second one on the 2nd floor out the back. You'll find buses to Mestia out the front, and buses to much of the rest of the country on the 2nd floor out the back.

Avlabari (Map p44; Avlabaris moedani) Outside Avlabari metro station. Buses to Yerevan leave from here.

Navtlughis Avtosadguri (Samgori; Ketevan Dedopalis gamziri; Ⓜ Samgori) About 300m west of Samgori metro station. Buses go to various destinations in Kakheti as well as to Mestia.

Isani (Atskuri; Ⓜ Isani) In the street behind the State Audit Office building behind Isani metro station. Buses to Lagodekhi leave from here.

Georgian Bus & Gareji Line Minibus Stop (Map p46) On one side of Freedom Sq, this is where daily buses in summer leave for Davit Gareja, as well as year-round buses to Kutaisi's airport.

TRAIN

Tbilisi's **main train station** (Sadguris moedani) is the railway hub of Georgia. Ticket counters, open 7am to 11pm, are on level 3 (the top floor) – there's usually someone who speaks English. You can buy tickets here for train trips starting anywhere in Georgia. Always bring your passport when buying tickets. Platforms are on level 2.

Schedules change often: some information is given in English on the Georgian Railway website (www.railway.ge).

Tickets go on sale 60 days in advance of the journey. Buying tickets online can be a real struggle. If you want to book in advance, contact a travel agency such as **Advantour** (Map p44; 🚗 32-2323000; www.advantour.com; Zakaria Paliashvili 98; ⏱10am-7pm Mon-Fri) to book your ticket for you. Train information is available in English on 🚗1331.

For trains to Baku, Yerevan, Batumi and Zugdidi, it's advisable to book tickets several days ahead, and as far ahead as possible for July and August, when trains are always sold out.

Tbilisi Metro

International Trains

The only international trains are the sleepers to Baku and Yerevan, though this should change when a line to Kars in Turkey opens; at research time this was planned for 2020. There are no trains north into Russia, as the only train line going there passes through Abkhazia.

The Baku train (3rd/2nd/1st class 45/60/100 GEL, 12 hours) leaves Tbilisi at 8.35pm daily, and arrives in Baku at 8.50am the following morning.

The Yerevan train (3rd/2nd/1st class 45/60/100 GEL, 11 hours), via Vanadzor and Gyumri, departs from 15 June to 30 September daily at 10.15pm, arriving in Yerevan at 7.25am the following morning. During the rest of the year trains only run on odd dates, leaving Tbilisi at 8.20pm and arriving in Yerevan at 6.55am the next morning.

Fares can fluctuate with exchange rates and how far ahead you book, and timetables change often, so always double-check the information above before planning your trip.

Domestic Trains

Overnight services depart Tbilisi daily at 9.45pm to Zugdidi (seat/2nd/1st class 7/21/30 GEL, nine hours), and at 12.35am to Batumi (2nd/1st class 30/70 GEL, six hours), arriving the following morning at dawn.

Morning departures (between about 8am and 10am) head to Batumi (2nd/1st class 23/40 GEL, 5½ hours), Kutaisi (seat 7.50 GEL, 5½ hours) and Zugdidi (2nd class 15 GEL, 6½ hours). Extra trains to Batumi run during the summer holiday season.

Elektrichky (slow trains with seating only) run to Borjomi (2 GEL, 4½ hours) in the morning and afternoon, and to Kutaisi (4 GEL, six hours) in the afternoon. For these, pay on the train.

GETTING AROUND

Bus & Marshrutka

Yellow city buses and *marshrutky* provide an above-ground complement to the metro. Electronic boards at most bus stops list the destinations of approaching buses in English as well as Georgian. Buses only stop at predetermined stops, but you can get on and off *marshrutky* anywhere along their route. To get the driver to stop, shout '*Gaacheret!*' ('Stop!').

Bus routes and schedules are listed and mapped, partly in English, at http://ttc.com.ge.

Cable Car

Tbilisi has two cable cars, with three more planned. For visitors the most useful service runs from the south end of Rike Park high over the Mtkvari and the Old Town up to Narikala Fortress. A second cable car runs from Vake Park to Turtle Lake in the west of the city. Purchase a Metromoney card to ride either service; these are available at the ticket offices if you don't have one.

Metro

The efficient Tbilisi metro operates from 6am to midnight, and the two lines reach the most important parts of the city, meeting at Sadguris Moedani (Station Sq). Signage and announcements are in English as well as Georgian.

METROMONEY CARDS

Metromoney cards, sold for 2 GEL at metro-station ticket offices, are essential for riding the metro, and also good for Tbilisi city buses and *marshrutky* (minivans). You tap the card on a reader when you enter the metro or when you board buses and *marshrutky*. Fares are 0.50 GEL per metro or bus ride and 0.80 GEL for *marshrutky*. You can also pay with cash on buses (exact fare only) and *marshrutky*. Further metro or bus rides within 1½ hours of tapping on are not charged.

You can put credit on the card with cash at metro-station ticket offices or in ubiquitous orange Express Pay machines, which have easy-to-follow instructions in English.

Taxi

Official taxis are almost always unmetered. Agree on the fare before getting in, or just hand over the standard fare with confidence on arrival. The standard cost for a shortish ride (up to about 2km) is 3 GEL, medium rides (up to about 4km) cost 5 GEL and longer rides up to 10 GEL. The latter should definitely be agreed in advance.

Ride hailing apps popular in Tbilisi include Bolt and Yandex. Unhelpfully, taxis rarely turn off their lights when they're busy, so you'll just have to have your arm out at all passing vehicles until one stops.

SOUTHERN GEORGIA

Georgia's southern flank is a diverse and highly scenic region whose biggest attractions are the spectacular cave city of Vardzia, the important religious centre of Mtskheta and the stunning mountain landscapes of the Borjomi-Kharagauli National Park. Historically much of the region was part of Tao-Klarjeti, a cradle of medieval Georgian culture that extended well into what's now northeast Turkey. Tao-Klarjeti fell under Ottoman rule from the 1550s to the 1870s, was briefly part of independent Georgia after the Russian Revolution, and was then divided between Turkey and Bolshevik Georgia in 1921. This is in many ways Georgia's heartland: St Nino passed through on her way to bring Christianity to Georgia and national bard Shota Rustaveli was born here. More recently, the town of Gori was the birthplace of one Joseph Stalin, who also did his bit to put the area on the map.

Mtskheta

♪ 32 / POP 8000

Mtskheta has been Georgia's spiritual heart since Christianity was established here in about 327, and holds a near-mystical significance in Georgian culture. It had already been capital of most of eastern Georgia from about the 3rd century BC, and remained so to the 5th century AD, when King Vakhtang Gorgasali switched his base to nearby Tbilisi. Mtskheta has always kept its status as Georgia's spiritual capital, and its Svetitskhoveli Cathedral is still the setting for important ceremonies of the Georgian Orthodox Church. With an alluring setting where the Mtkvari and Aragvi Rivers meet, Mtskheta makes an easy and enjoyable day trip from Tbilisi.

Southern Georgia

GEORGIA

N 0 · 0 — 20 km — 10 miles

KAKHETI

National Park of Tbilisi

Martkopi
Rustavi
Gardabani
AZERBAIJAN
Böyük / Kəsik
Kəsalo
İkinci Şıxlı
Noyemberyan

Dusheti
Bazaleti
Mukhrani
Natakhtari Airfield
MTSKHETA MTIANETI
Mtskheta
Tbilisi Airport
TBILISI
TBILISI
Koda
Marneuli
Tsiteli Khidi (Krasny Most)
Kachagoni
Bagratashen
Ayrum
Akhtala

Kaspi
SOUTH OSSETIA
Uplistsikhe
SHIDA KARTLI
Orbeti
Didi Toneti
Tsintskaro
KVEMO KARTLI
Shulaveri
Fakhralo
Sadakhlo
Jiliza
Vratsbious Range
Tashir

Gori
Didi Ateni
Ateni Sioni
Mt Arjevani (2750m)
Manglisi
Tetritskaro
Beshtasheni
Tsalka
Khrami
Bolnisi
Kvemo Bolnisi
Patara Dmanisi
Guguti
Gogavan
Metsavan
ARMENIA
Dmanisi

Agara
Kareli
Mtkvari River
Tana River
Tsalka Reservoir
Nardevani
Ktsia
Mashavera
Mt Leili (3157m)
Bavra

Khashuri
Kura
Bakuriani
Lake Tabatskuri
SAMTSKHE JAVAKHETI
Mt Didi Abuli (3300m)
Akhalkalaki
Lake Saghamo
Ozero Khanchali
Kartsakhi

National Park Visitors Centre
Marelisi Guesthouse
Mt Lomis Mta (2199m)
Kharagauli
Borjomi
National Park Visitors Centre
Tskhratskaro Pass (2454m)
Aspindza
Khertvisi Fortress
Vardzia
Ninotsminda (Bagdanovka)
Ozero Zros
Kartsakhi Lake
Çıldır

IMERETI
Mt Sametskhvario (2643m)
Borjomi-Kharagauli National Park
Meskheti Range
Nick & George Guesthouse
Akhaltsikhe
Sapara Monastery
Vale
Vale–Posof border crossing
Posof
TURKEY
Çamlıçatak
Abastumani
Baghdati
Kvabliani

◉ Sights

★**Svetitskhoveli Cathedral** CATHEDRAL
(Arsukidze; ⊘8am-10pm, no entry 5-8pm Sat or 8am-1pm Sun) This extraordinary (and for its time, enormous) building dates from the 11th century, early in the golden age of Georgian church architecture. It has an elongated cross plan and is adorned with beautiful stone carving outside and in. Christ's robe is believed to lie beneath the central nave, un-

Mtskheta

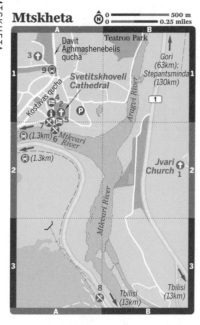

der a square pillar decorated with colourful if faded frescoes of the conversion of Kartli.

The story goes that a Mtskheta Jew, Elioz, was in Jerusalem at the time of Jesus' crucifixion and returned with the robe to Mtskheta. His sister Sidonia took it from him and immediately died in a passion of faith. The robe was buried with her and as years passed, people forgot the exact site. When King Mirian built the first church at Mtskheta in the 4th century, the wooden column designed to stand in its centre could not be raised from the ground. But after an all-night prayer vigil by St Nino, the column miraculously moved of its own accord to the robe's burial site. The column subsequently worked many miracles and Svetitskhoveli means 'Life-Giving Column'.

In the 5th century Vakhtang Gorgasali replaced Mirian's church with a stone one, and the present building was constructed between 1010 and 1029 under Patriarch Melqisedek. Now a millennium old, it's still one of the most beautiful churches in the country.

Several Georgian monarchs are buried here. The tomb of Erekle II, king of Kartli and Kakheti from 1762 to 1798, lies before the icon screen (marked with his birth and death dates, 1720 and 1798). Vakhtang Gorgasali's tomb is behind this, with his sword-holding image carved on a raised flagstone.

★**Jvari Church** CHURCH
(Holy Cross; ⊘8am-7pm) Visible for kilometres around on its hilltop overlooking Mtskheta from the east, Jvari is, to many Georgians, the holiest of holies. It stands where King Mirian erected his famous wooden cross soon after being converted by St Nino in the 4th century. Between 585 and 604 Stepanoz I, the *eristavi* (duke) of Kartli, constructed the church over the cross.

Jvari is a beautifully symmetrical little building and a classic of early Georgian tetraconch design. It has a cross-shaped plan with four equal arms, rounded on the inside (with the angles between them filled in by corner rooms), and a low dome sitting on a squat, octagonal drum. The interior is bare, ancient stone, except for a carved wooden cross on the central plinth.

The site provides spectacular views over Mtskheta and the confluence of the Aragvi and Mtkvari. The road up here from Mtskheta takes a highly circuitous 11km route; a taxi should cost 20 GEL for a return trip, including waiting time.

Samtavro Church · CHURCH
(Davit Aghmashenebelis qucha; ⊙ 9am-7pm) This large church, now part of a nunnery, was built in the 1130s. King Mirian and Queen Nana are buried in its southwest corner, under a stone canopy. The little church in the grounds, Tsminda Nino, dates back to the 4th century.

🛏 Sleeping & Eating

Hotel Tamarindi · HOTEL $
(☑ 32-2512764, 579-037772; www.hoteltamarindi. com; Arsukidze 23; s 50 GEL, d 50-80 GEL, f 100 GEL; ❋ 🛜) This small hotel literally facing Svetitskhoveli Cathedral has five very comfy, large rooms and a good terrace looking across the street. Host Jemal speaks a little English and has a comfortable 4WD for outings.

Hotel Old Capital · HOTEL $$
(☑ 593-631786; giorgi.zurabishvili.73@mail.ru; Erekle II 7; dm 20 GEL, d 60-90 GEL, apt for 3-8 130-200 GEL, breakfast 5 GEL; ❋ 🛜) Just across the street from Svetitskhoveli Cathedral, this friendly place has five neat, clean rooms and two two-bedroom apartments upstairs, all with private bathroom. There's a small hostel section at the side with a dormitory.

Salobie · GEORGIAN $
(☑ 555-671977; Tbilisi Rd; mains 5-13 GEL; ⊙ 10am-10pm; 🛜) Mtskheta's best-value and most popular restaurant is 5km out of town along the road towards Tbilisi (the *marshrutky* pass the door). It's a rambling place with multiple rooms and terraces serving all of Georgia's favourite basic dishes – *khachapuri, mtsvadi, khinkali* and, of course, *lobio* and *lobiani* (bean pie). Order at the bar and food will arrive with incredible speed.

⭐ Ada Cafe · GEORGIAN $$
(☑ 568-952402; Sanapiro 5; mains 6.50-18 GEL; ⊙ 9.30am-11pm Mon-Thu, to midnight Fri-Sun; 🛜☑) This innovative place run by two Turkish women and one local is a real delight, not least for its large terrace that overlooks the fast-flowing river and enjoys fabulous views of the hills on the other side. Delicious, freshly prepared dishes with more than a little Turkish flavour come streaming from the kitchen, while the welcome is outstanding and utterly genuine.

Old Taverna · GEORGIAN $$
(Arsukidze; mains 10-22 GEL; ⊙ 10am-11pm; 🛜) This little tavern serves decent Georgian fare such as *ostri* (spicy meat in a tomato-based sauce), *khachapuri* and mushroom dishes. In good weather it's lovely to sit outside facing Svetitskhoveli Cathedral.

ℹ Information

Tourism Information Centre (☑ 32-2512128; ticmtskheta@gnta.ge; Arsukidze 3; ⊙ 9am-6pm; 🛜) Has helpful English-speaking staff and free wi-fi. Can arrange English-speaking guides for Svetiskhoveli Cathedral (20 GEL for up to four people) and taxis to Jvari Church (20 GEL).

ℹ Getting There & Away

From Tbilisi buses leave **Didube bus station** (Tsereteli; Ⓜ Didube) around every 20 minutes (1 GEL, 20 minutes).

Marshrutky to Tbilisi leave about every 20 minutes, 8am to 8pm, from the bus stop next to the TBC Bank ATM on the town square.

Trains from Tbilisi to Gori (1 GEL to 6 GEL, one hour) stop at Mtskheta train station, on the south side of the Mtkvari River, 2km west of the town centre, at 6am, 8.30am, 11am, 4.40pm and 8.30pm.

Gori
☑ 370 / POP 49,000

Gori has long been synonymous with Joseph Stalin, who was born and went to school here. During his rule of the Soviet Union the town's centre was rebuilt to his neoclassical tastes, and even today much of the downtown area is defined by its Stalinist architecture. The large Stalin Museum is the town's best-known attraction, but there are also some fascinating older sights nearby, most notably the cave city of Uplistsikhe.

In the 2008 war over South Ossetia (whose border is just 13km north of town), Gori was bombed by Russia, with at least 20 civilians killed, and the town fell under Russian control for 10 days. Predictably, anti-Russian feeling still runs high today.

◉ Sights

⭐ Stalin Museum · MUSEUM
(☑ 370-225398; Stalinis gamziri 32; adult/student 15/10 GEL; ⊙ 10am-6pm Apr-Oct, to 5pm Nov-Mar) This impressively designed museum makes no serious attempt to present a balanced account of Stalin's career or deeds. It remains, much as when it opened in 1957, a reverent homage to the Gori boy who became a key figure of 20th-century history – although displays do now at least refer to the purges, the Gulag and

his 1939 pact with Hitler. The Dzhugashvili family's wood-and-mud-brick house where Stalin lived for the first four years of his life is reverentially preserved outside.

The museum charts Stalin's journey from the Gori church school to leadership of the USSR, the Yalta Conference at the end of WWII and his death in 1953. The first hall upstairs covers his childhood and adolescence, including his rather cringeworthy pastoral poetry, and then his early revolutionary activities in Georgia, his seven jail terms under the tsarist authorities (six of them in Siberia), the revolution of 1917 and Lenin's death in 1924. The text of Lenin's 1922 political testament that described Stalin as too coarse and power-hungry, advising Communist Party members to remove him from post of General Secretary, is on display.

One room is devoted to a bronze copy of Stalin's eerie death mask, lying in state. The next has a large collection of gifts from world leaders and other Bolsheviks. Off the staircase is a reconstruction of his first office in the Kremlin, plus personal memorabilia such as his pipes, glasses, cigars and slide rule. One small two-room section beside the foot of the stairs deals with political repression under Stalin.

To one side of the museum is Stalin's train carriage, in which he travelled to Yalta in 1945 (he didn't like flying). Apparently bulletproof, its elegant interior includes a bathtub and a primitive air-conditioning system.

★**Uplistsikhe** ARCHAEOLOGICAL SITE
(adult/student 7/1 GEL, audio guide/guided tour in English 10/25 GEL; ◷10am-7pm Apr-Oct, to 6pm Nov-Mar; P) This once enormous cave city sits 10km east of Gori above the north side of the Mtkvari River. Between the 6th century BC and 1st century AD, Uplistsikhe developed into one of the chief political and religious centres of pre-Christian Kartli, with temples dedicated principally to the sun goddess. After the Arabs occupied Tbilisi in AD 645, Uplistsikhe became the residence of the Christian kings of Kartli and an important trade centre on a main caravan road from Asia to Europe.

At its peak it housed 20,000 people. Its importance declined after King David the Builder retook Tbilisi in 1122 and it was irrevocably destroyed by the Mongols in 1240. What you visit today is the 40,000-sq-metre Shida Qalaqi (Inner City), less than half of the original whole. It's one of the oldest places of settlement in the Caucasus and almost everything here has been uncovered by archaeologists since 1957.

To enter Uplistsikhe by its old main access track, go about 5m up the rocks opposite the cafe at the entrance, and follow the rock-cut path to the left. Metal-railed steps lead up through what was the main gate, with the excavated main tower of the Shida Qalaqi's defensive walls to the right. Uplistsikhe's old main street winds up to the right after you've passed through the main gate, with several important cave structures either side of it.

Ahead from the main gate you'll find a cave overlooking the river with a pointed arch carved in the rock above it. Known as the **Theatre**, this is probably a temple from the 1st or 2nd century AD, where religious mystery plays may have been performed.

Gori

26 May Embankment	Mejuda	Tourism Information Centre
	Tskhinvali Hwy	
Gori Bus Station	Stalin Museum 1	Kutaisi
Shida Kartli	Rustaveli	Stalin Park 4
Akhalbagi	Chavchavadzis gamziri	
	Stalinis gamziri	Antonovis qucha
	Tamar Mepe (800m)	Aghmashenebelis gamziri

0 — 500 m
0 — 0.25 miles

Gori

SOUTH OSSETIA

Ethnically and linguistically distinct from the rest of Georgia, the breakaway region of South Ossetia stretches up to the main Caucasus ridge north of the Georgian town of Gori, and was the subject of a short war between Russia and Georgia in 2008. Russian forces currently guarantee the borders of the territory, an act that Georgia vehemently condemns as an illegal occupation. At research time, South Ossetia was not letting any foreigners in from Georgia and this looked unlikely to change soon. It may be possible to enter South Ossetia from Vladikavkaz in North Ossetia (part of Russia), although Georgia considers this illegal, and the British Foreign Office (www.fco.gov.uk) and US State Department (http://travel.state.gov) advise against travel to both South and North Ossetia. In the meantime, you can peer at the region any time you travel between Tbilisi and Gori, as the boundary comes to within 400m of the highway just west of Karapila village.

Down to the right is the large pre-Christian **Temple of Makvliani**, with an inner recess behind an arched portico. A little further up on the left is the big hall known as **Tamaris Darbazi** (Hall of Queen Tamar), where an ancient stone seat sits behind two columns cut from the rock, and the stone ceiling is carved to look like wooden beams. This was almost certainly a pre-Christian temple. To its left is an area with stone niches, thought to have been a pharmacy or dovecote.

A large cave building to the right of the Tamaris Darbazi was probably a sun temple used for animal sacrifices, later converted into a Christian basilica.

Uplistsulis Eklesia, the triple-church basilica near the top of the hill, was built in the 10th century over what was probably Uplistsikhe's most important pagan temple.

On your way back out of the cave city, don't miss the long **tunnel** running down to the Mtkvari, an emergency escape route that could also be used for carrying water up to the city. Its entrance is behind a reconstructed wall beside the old main gate.

A return taxi from Gori, including one hour's waiting time, normally costs around 30 GEL. *Marshrutky* leave Gori bus station a few times daily for the village of Kvakhvreli (1 GEL, 20 minutes), a 2km walk from Uplistsikhe, while a new direct service to Uplistsikhe is planned but was not yet operational at the time of research.

Ateni Sioni   CHURCH

(Didi Ateni; ☉ 8am-6pm) This impressively ancient church has a beautiful setting above a bend of the pretty, grapevine-strewn Tana valley, 12km south of Gori. Ateni Sioni was built in the 7th century and modelled on Mtskheta's Jvari Church. Beautiful reliefs of stags, a hunting scene and a knight were carved into the exterior walls later. Inside,

the 11th-century frescoes, depicting biblical scenes and Georgian rulers, are among the finest medieval art in the country.

At the time of writing the frescoes were under restoration but you could still see them through a forest of scaffolding.

A return taxi from Gori to the church should cost about 20 GEL, or 30 GEL to 40 GEL if combined with Uplistsikhe. Alternatively, buses and *marshrutky* run from Gori bus station to Ateni Sioni (1 GEL, 30 minutes) once or twice hourly until 6pm.

Gori Fortress   FORTRESS

(☉ 24hr) **FREE** This partially reconstructed oval citadel stands on the hill at the heart of Gori. It dates mostly from the Middle Ages, with 17th-century additions. With fine views, it's a good place to be around sunset. At its northeast foot, a circle of eight mutilated metal warriors forms an eerie memorial to those lost in the 2008 war with Russia over South Ossetia.

🛏 Sleeping

Guesthouses are the way to go here, with the smattering of hotels being pretty drab, and the new Royal House being a notable exception.

Guesthouse Svetlana   GUESTHOUSE **$**

(☏ 599-583001; kasatik56@mail.ru; Abashidze 8; dm/s/d 15/35/50 GEL, breakfast 7 GEL; ❋ 🛜) Good-size rooms with comfy beds in a large, well-kept house with parquet floors and modern furnishings, this is one of the best guesthouses in town. English-speaking hostess Svetlana is warm and welcoming, and is also a doctor who offers medical massages. Dinner is available on request, but guests can use the kitchen and enjoy the pleasant terrace area with a barbecue.

Guesthouse Nitsa
GUESTHOUSE $

(☏599-142488; liazauta@gmail.com; Kutaisi 58; s/d/tr/q 35/50/75/100 GEL, breakfast 7.50 GEL; ❄🛜) Charming English-speaking Lia provides four cosy rooms in her spacious house with its sweeping staircase and large lounge-dining room. The rooms share two spotless bathrooms, and two rooms have air-con. You'll be invited to try all manner of village produce, including natural wines, homemade jams and juices. It's 200m east of the Stalin Museum.

Guesthouse Levani
GUESTHOUSE $

(☏577-397123; www.facebook.com/guesthouse-levani; Aghmeshenebelis gamziri 29; d/tr/q 45/56/65 GEL, breakfast 10 GEL; 🛜) The few rooms at this ramshackle house are relatively modest, but the warmth of your host, who speaks some French and a little English, makes up for that. The bathrooms are good, too. It's 400m southeast from the south end of Stalinis moedani, on the corner at the end of Zurab Antonov.

Hostel Kalifornia
HOSTEL $

(☏551-300802; okalifornia@mail.ru; Rustaveli 79; dm/d without bathroom 17/50 GEL, breakfast 5 GEL; ❄🛜) You can sleep very cheap in the bunk dorm at this family-run hostel a few steps north off Chavchavadze. It has two colourful mansard private rooms too – plus a kitchen, free tea and coffee, and a washing machine (5 GEL per load). All rooms share bathrooms.

Royal House
HOTEL $$

(☏599-909129; Samepo 45; r from 100 GEL; ❄🛜) This new option is a welcome addition to Gori's poor selection of hotels. It has a wide range of rooms including bigger apartment-style suites with their own kitchen and balconies in the main building, and smaller and simpler ones in the yard behind. All rooms are spotless and well appointed, and the welcome is warm.

✖ Eating

Gori is no culinary destination, with a number of perfectly passable but unexciting eating options in the town centre. Most guesthouses will provide traditional dinners with advance notice.

Shin Da Gori
GEORGIAN $$

(☏557-767576; Rusudan Kurdadze 1; mains 6-25 GEL; ⊙10am-midnight; 🛜) This place is popular with tour groups and has expanded to quite a size in recent years. While its terribly translated menu makes choosing a challenge, the food is actually pretty good, served either in a pleasant tree-shaded courtyard or a rather more formal dining room inside. The signature Shin Da Gori (60 GEL) is a tray of grilled meats.

Resto-Bar Black Stars
GEORGIAN $$

(Tsereteli 39; mains 10-25 GEL; ⊙10am-midnight; 🛜🍴) This sprawling indoor-outdoor complex below Gori Fortress offers all manner of menus and cuisines, from Georgian to European and vegetarian to halal. A smart upstairs dining room makes a great choice for a meal, while the convivial atmosphere outside also makes this the best place in Gori to come for drinks of an evening.

Cafe 22
GEORGIAN $$

(Stalinis gamziri 22; mains 8-25 GEL; ⊙10am-midnight; 🛜🍴) A rattan-chaired cafe on one side of Stalinis moedani, Cafe 22 has a large menu taking in everything from Georgian classics to pasta and pizza, gooey cakes, Turkish coffee and draught beer.

ℹ Information

Tourism Information Centre (☏370-270776; ticgori@gmail.com; Kutaisi 23a; ⊙10am-6pm) Behind the Stalin Museum.

ℹ Getting There & Away

Gori is well connected to other towns in Georgia by both bus and train.

BUS

Marshrutky leave from the bus station near the base of the fortress to Tbilisi (3 GEL, one hour) about every 15 minutes from 7am to 6pm. There is just one daily *marshrutka* to Borjomi (5 GEL, 1½ hours) that continues to Akhaltsikhe at 12.30pm; one direct service to Akhaltsikhe (7 GEL, 2½ hours) at 8.30am; and one to Batumi (17 GEL, five hours) at 9.30am, which also stops in Kutaisi (8 GEL, 2½ hours). Otherwise for Kutaisi, common practice is to take a taxi to the highway for 5 GEL and flag down a Kutaisi-bound *marshrutka* (7 GEL, three hours). A new direct service from Gori to Uplistsikhe was planned at research time; enquire at the Tourism Information Centre to find out if this has begun yet.

TRAIN

About 10 daily trains head east to Tbilisi (4 GEL to 32 GEL, one to 1¼ hours) from **Gori train station** (Gorijvari), across the Mtkvari from the south end of Stalinis gamziri. Westbound, only slow trains call at Gori, meaning journeys are very long, but there are trains to Borjomi (1 GEL, three hours, 8.20am and 5.50pm), Kutaisi (1 GEL, five hours, 10.10am and 4.30pm), Zugdidi and Batumi (23 GEL, 9.45am).

Borjomi

📞 367 / POP 15,000

Famous throughout the former Soviet Union for its salty-sour, love-it-or-hate-it fizzy mineral water, Borjomi is a tranquil resort town surrounded by thickly forested hills in all directions. The 19th-century Russian governor of Georgia, Count Vorontsov, developed Borjomi as a resort after his soldiers discovered a health-giving mineral spring here in 1810, and it became a particularly fashionable one when Grand Duke Mikhail Romanov (brother to Tsar Alexander II) built a palace at nearby Likani in the 1890s.

Today the town of Borjomi is spread out along the the north of the river, while to the south is the resort area, home to Borjomi Central Park, which includes warm sulphur baths. Popular with Georgian and Russian holidaymakers and people visiting Borjomi-Kharagauli National Park, Borjomi is also a good jumping-off point for the cave city of Vardzia.

◉ Sights & Activities

Borjomi Central Park   PARK

(Tsentraluri Parki; 9 Aprili; adult/student 2/1 GEL; ⏱10am-11pm; 🚻) Borjomi's mineral water park, dating back to 1850, occupies a narrow wooded valley and includes the town's original mineral water source, Ekaterina Spring, which is straight ahead of the entrance. Most of the park is full of rather naff rides and entertainments, but if you walk about 3km upstream, you'll find several small, spring-fed swimming pools (5 GEL) with a constant temperature of about 27°C. Bring your own swimming costume and flip-flops; towels are provided.

Borjomi Plateau   WALKING

A cable car (one-way 5 GEL; ⏱10am-8pm; 🚻) just inside the entrance to Borjomi Central Park runs up to a hilltop Ferris wheel and the pine woods of the Borjomi Plateau, a lovely spot for some easy walking and with spectacular views over the town. About 2km south along the road from the Ferris wheel, a trail

GEORGIA BORJOMI

DON'T MISS

BORJOMI-KHARAGAULI NATIONAL PARK

The ranges of the Lesser Caucasus in southern Georgia are less well known and much lower than the Great Caucasus, but they still contain some very beautiful and wild country. Borjomi-Kharagauli National Park provides the perfect chance to get out into this landscape. The park spreads over 851 sq km of forested hills and alpine meadows up to 2642m high.

The park is crisscrossed by 11 marked walking trails of various lengths, some suitable for horses as well as hikers. Trail marking is mostly by paint marks on trees. Most trails are accessible from May to October or November.

All visitors must obtain a permit beforehand from either the National Park Visitors Centre (p77) in Borjomi or the National Park Visitors Centre (p77) in Kharagauli. These are also very helpful for information and equipment rental. Several trails start at the Likani ranger station, 5km from the Borjomi National Park Visitors Centre (about 6 GEL by taxi from Borjomi town). A good day hike of 13km, with an ascent and descent of 800m, is Trail 6, which comes out on the Akhaltsikhe road at Qvabiskhevi. Trail 1 (Likani ranger station to Marelisi ranger station) is a 43km, three-day route crossing the park from south to north via Mt Lomis Mta (2198m). The longest and hardest route is Trail 2 (Atskuri to Marelisi), a 54km north–south route taking three or four days.

Four basic wooden tourist shelters provide accommodation inside the park. They have spring water, but you need to carry a sleeping bag, food and cooking gear. You can also sleep at one of 10 ranger stations (per person 10 GEL; though they have no water), and there are 10 campsites (per person 5 GEL).

Some villages around the park's fringes have guesthouses, convenient for the beginning or end of some trails. They include **Marelisi Guesthouse** (📞599-951421; per person 25 GEL; 🛜) at Marelisi on the north side of the park, and **Nick & George Guesthouse** (📞597-982007, 555-259355; maiaaitsuradze@gmx.com; per person 30 GEL, breakfast/lunch/dinner 10/15/20 GEL; 🛜) at Atskuri.

Marshrutky running between Borjomi and Akhaltsikhe will drop you off or pick you up at Likani, Qvabiskhevi or Atskuri, near where several trails begin or end.

leads down to the hot pools at the end of the park and you can return to town that way.

🛏 Sleeping

Borjomi has dozens of hotels, and more than 100 guesthouses and homestays, so there'll be no problem finding a place to stay.

★**Marina's Guesthouse**   GUESTHOUSE **$**
(📞598-184550, 367-222323; marinasguesthouse@gmail.com; Ketevan Tsamebuli 2; per person with/without breakfast 30/25 GEL; 🛜) Charming hostess Marina keeps one of Borjomi's best-value guesthouses, in a welcoming, cosy home with four upstairs guestrooms, all of which have their own balconies. The house itself is stuffed full of knick-knacks and local art, and Marina speaks English and Russian.

RiverSide Hostel   HOSTEL **$**
(📞595-445585, 558-116502; hostelborjomi@gmail.com; Rustaveli 20; dm/d/q 20/50/100 GEL; 🛜) Borjomi's only real hostel, this friendly and relaxed place on the main road into town has everything a backpacker needs and is a good place to meet other travellers. There are three dorms with six to eight bunks each, a double room and a quad, all of which share bathrooms. There's also a kitchen for guests and a social area.

Guest House Besarioni   GUESTHOUSE **$**
(📞599-779055; besikilursmanashvili@yahoo.com; Pirosmani 32; s/d/tr 40/50/65 GEL, breakfast 10 GEL; 🅿🛜) The friendly family here speaks some English and offers guests the choice of three rooms, one with private bathroom.

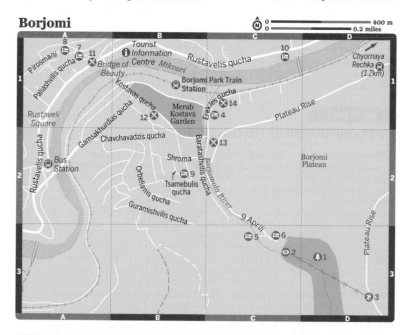

Borjomi

Borjomi

Everything is new and spotlessly clean and you'll really experience the atmosphere of a Georgian home. Guests can use the kitchen and there's a pleasant garden to hang out in.

Green Rose Guest House GUESTHOUSE $$
(☑599-901117; Pirosmani 13; r 70-130 GEL, breakfast 10 GEL; P 🛜) One of many guesthouses in the streets up above the north side of Rustaveli, this is a solidly comfy option with clean, medium-size rooms (some have private bathroom) and a sizeable garden. The owner speaks a little English and there's a kitchen for guests to use, as well as meals available. No green roses, though!

Borjomi Park Guest House GUESTHOUSE $$
(☑555-572330, 555-572557; Erekle 7; d/q from 80/120 GEL; 🛜) More like a small hotel than a guesthouse, the Borjomi Park is something of a study in beige, but remains a good midrange option with clean, cosy rooms with pine floors. Its owners are friendly and the location is central.

★ **Crowne Plaza Borjomi** LUXURY HOTEL $$$
(☑322-221221; www.crowneplaza.com; Baratashvili 9; r/ste from 270/430 GEL; P ✳🛜♨) The rather kitschy exterior of this 2016-opened luxury hotel takes up a large chunk of Borjomi's resort area and is definitely the fanciest option in town. It's a full-service, sophisticated place with glamorous and spacious rooms with fantastic views, marble bathrooms and superbly comfortable beds draped in expensive sheets. The breakfast buffet is excellent and staff members are supremely professional.

Golden Tulip Borjomi BOUTIQUE HOTEL $$$
(☑322-880202; www.goldentulipborjomipalace.com; 9 Aprili 48; s/d incl breakfast from 245/375 GEL; ✳🛜) For sheer magnificence, check into this impressive renovation of a palace once owned by a 19th-century Iranian ambassador to Tbilisi. It sits right outside the entrance to Borjomi Central Park and has some jaw-droppingly elaborate decor, particularly in its spacious public areas. Rooms themselves are a little on the small side, but impressively designed all the same.

✕ Eating

Borjomi has a generally rather average range of eating options, but you'll eat perfectly decently, especially in guesthouses and on the resort side of town.

Bergi GEORGIAN $
(☑599-223816; Rustaveli 121; mains 6-15 GEL; ⊙10am-midnight; 🛜) This simple but welcoming restaurant on the main road through town is a good place for a tasty meal and has a number of tables outside from where you can watch the world go by.

Pesvebi GEORGIAN $$
(☑367-221702; Erekle 3; mains 10-25 GEL; ⊙11am-11pm; 🛜✎) Perhaps Borjomi's most charming restaurant, Pesvebi has a cosy chalet-style dining room and a large outside dining area, both of which are packed on busy summer nights. Good kebabs, *khinkali* and local beer on tap make this a winner. Dinner reservations are a good idea during summer.

Cafe Old Borjomi GEORGIAN $$
(Kostava 17; mains 7-20 GEL; ⊙11am-11pm; 🛜) Very popular for its well-prepared *mtsvadi, khachapuri, shkmeruli* and trout in walnut sauce, in a vaguely tavernish, wood-walled space, Old Borjomi also manages friendly service. There are only eight or 10 tables and you may have to wait for one on summer evenings.

Inka Cafe CAFE $$
(9 Aprili 2; dishes 9-18 GEL; ⊙10am-10pm; 🛜) A smart, wood-panelled cafe, with sepia-tint photos of tsarist-era Borjomi, Inka does real coffee and reasonable *khachapuri,* omelettes, salads and cakes.

ℹ Information

National Park Visitors Centre (☑577-640480, 577-640444; borjomikharagauli@gmail.com; Meskheti 23; ⊙9am-6pm Mon-Fri, to 4pm Sat & Sun) The park's visitors centre is 1km west of Borjomi bus station. It sells a good trail map (5 GEL), issues the free permits everyone must obtain for visiting the park (bring your passport or ID card), and can furnish all the information you need, including on horse rentals (60 GEL per day including guide) and drinking water sources. You can pay here for your nights in the park, and rent tents (10 GEL per night) and sleeping bags (5 GEL per night). Permits are also available at the other **National Park Visitors Centre** (☑577-101894; borjomikharagauli@gmail.com; Solomon Mepe 19; ⊙9am-6pm Mon-Fri, to 4pm Sat & Sun) in Kharagauli.

Tourist Information Centre (☑558-694919, 367-221397; ticborjomi@gmail.com; Rustaveli 16; ⊙10am-6pm Mon-Fri) In a glass pavilion near the north side of the suspension bridge.

ℹ Getting There & Away

Marshrutka departures from Borjomi's **bus station** (Meskheti 8) include the following:

Akhaltsikhe (4 GEL, one hour, 8.45am) More buses leave throughout the day from the bus stop across the road from the bus station in front of the Municipality.

Bakuriani (3 GEL, one hour, six daily)

Batumi (17 GEL, five hours, 9am) Arrive at least 30 minutes in advance, as this service is very popular. Extra services are laid on between June and August.

Gori (5 GEL, 1½ hours, 10.40am and 1.45pm)

Khashuri (2 GEL, 30 minutes, half-hourly 9.30am to 5.30pm)

Tbilisi (7 GEL, three hours, hourly 7am to 6pm)

There are no direct services to Kutaisi or Zugdidi; you'll need to change at Khashuri, 32km northeast of Borjomi, for those.

Borjomi taxi drivers offer day trips to Vardzia, with stops including Akhaltsikhe's Rabati Castle and two other forts, for 150 GEL for four people. The Tourist Information Centre (p77) can book this for you with English-speaking drivers.

Slow *elektrichka* trains leave Borjomi Park train station, just east of the suspension bridge, for Gori (2 GEL, four hours) and Tbilisi (2 GEL, five hours) at 7am and 4.40pm.

The famously scenic narrow gauge Kukushka (Cuckoo) train runs from Borjomi's Chyornaya Rechka station to Bakuriani (1 GEL to 2 GEL, 2½ hours) at 7.15am and 10.55am daily.

Bakuriani

📱 367 / POP 2000 / ELEV 1700M

Thirty kilometres up a winding road through pine-clad hills southeast of Borjomi, Bakuriani is the cheaper and more family-oriented of Georgia's two main ski resorts. The area is also good for mountain walks in summer, with ski lifts operating in July and August. Georgia's wholesale conversion to the religion of tourism has led to an extraordinary building boom here, and scores of hotels were being built at research time, rather eroding Bakuriani's rustic mountain-village vibe. Outside the skiing season and July to August, much of the town closes down.

🏃 Activities

The ski season lasts from about mid-December to the end of March. Taxis to the lifts (10 GEL from the town centre) have ski racks.

Kokhta Gora SKIING

(www.bakuriani.ski; ski pass per day adult/child 40/25 GEL, per ride Jul-Aug 7 GEL; ⊘ lifts 10am-9.30pm mid-Dec–Mar, 11am-6pm Jul-Aug) The Kokhta Gora zone, on the slopes of 2157m Mt Kokhta on the east side of town, was reopened in 2016 after a full renovation that saw the construction of a brand-new ski lift. In total there are 3.1km of pistes here. The Otsdakhutiani beginners' slopes, with toboggan as well as ski runs, are located between here and the town centre.

Didveli SKIING

(www.bakuriani.ski; ski pass per day adult/child 40/25 GEL, per ride Jul-Aug 7 GEL; ⊘ lifts 10am-9.30pm mid-Dec–Mar, 11am-6pm Jul-Aug) The expanded and upgraded Didveli ski zone has 16km of blue, red and black runs, and a combination of cable car, chairlift, draglift and funicular rising from 1800m to 2700m. The lifts start 4km south of the town centre.

🛏 Sleeping

In the ski season almost every house in Bakuriani has rooms to let, some for as little as 20 GEL per person. Many guesthouses and small and large hotels are scattered around the town centre and along the roads towards the ski slopes. Some close outside the ski season, though plenty are open in July and August.

Edelweiss Guest House GUESTHOUSE $$

(📞599-506349; Mta 19; per person full board ski season 90-100 GEL, summer 80 GEL; 🅿 🛜 🕿) In the town centre, Edelweiss is a family-run enterprise with welcoming hosts. Rooms are spacious and cosy wood-panelled affairs, and there's a small summer pool and a winter sauna. Open year-round.

Crystal Hotel & Spa HOTEL $$$

(📞595-461461; www.hotelcrystal.ge; Didveli; r full board ski season from US$200, summer from US$120; 🅿 🛜 🕿) One of the most luxurious hotels in Bakuriani, this is also one of the closest to the Didveli ski lifts (1km away), with a free shuttle service). The clean-lined, contemporary rooms are all equipped with tea and coffee makers, rain showerheads, writing desks and balconies. And it boasts Bakuriani's only spa, with a pool.

Hotel Apollon HOTEL $$$

(📞599-334499; www.apollon.ge; Aghmashenebeli 21; per person full board from 225 GEL; 🅿 🛜)

Apollon provides good, pine-floored rooms with balconies and comfortable wooden beds, satisfying meals in a cosy dining room, friendly staff, and billiards and table tennis for your spare moments. It's 800m up the Didveli road from the town centre, and open year-round.

✖ Eating

There are dozens of restaurants in Bakuriani, and most hotels have their own restaurant too. Outside of the ski season and the height of summer, you may find that hotel restaurants are your only choice. Restaurant Anga is a useful year-round option.

Restaurant Anga GEORGIAN $
(Davit Aghmeshenebelis 88; mains 6-15 GEL; ⊙24hr; 🐾) On Bakuriani's main street, this small but cosy bar-restaurant is not only open year-round, but 24 hours a day. It's a great option if you're in town out of season, when almost every other restaurant is closed. The pictorial menu offers Georgian staples and draught local beer is also served.

Mimino GEORGIAN $$
(Tsakadze 3; mains 10-20 GEL; ⊙10am-11pm; 🐾) This cosy chalet-style restaurant serving large portions of Georgian food is popular for an evening meal and some après-ski, and it can get very crowded in the season. The kebabs here receive particularly rave reviews.

ℹ Information

Tourism Information Centre (☑367-240036; mari.m@bk.ru; Davit Aghmeshenebelis 1; ⊙10am-5pm Mon-Fri) On the main street; sells a good map (5 GEL) showing day walks.

ℹ Getting There & Away

From the bus station on Tamar Mepe in the town centre, *marshrutky* run to Borjomi (3 GEL, one hour) five times daily between 10am and 5pm, and to Tbilisi (10 GEL, four hours) at least six times daily. There is also a daily service to both Batumi (20 GEL, five hours, 10am) and Kutaisi (11 GEL, three hours, 3.10pm). A taxi to or from Borjomi costs 30 GEL.

Slow but scenic trains run to Bakuriani's train station (1 GEL to 2 GEL, 2½ hours) from Borjomi's Chyornaya Rechka station (2km east of Borjomi centre) at 7.15am and 10.55am, returning at 10am and 2.15pm.

Bakuriani

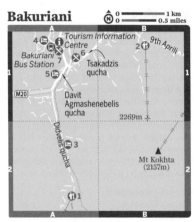

Bakuriani

Akhaltsikhe

📋 365 / POP 18,000

The capital and biggest town of the region of Samtskhe-Javakheti, Akhaltsikhe means 'New Castle' in Georgian. The castle dominating the town from the north side of the Potskhovi River hasn't been new since the 12th century, but it's been lavishly restored, helping to turn a town that was previously a sad case of post-Soviet decline into a reasonably attractive stop and jumping-off point for Vardzia.

Until the 19th century the Rabati area around the castle was all there was of Akhaltsikhe. It was celebrated for its ethnic and religious diversity and tolerance, in a frontier area where different empires, kingdoms and peoples met. Rabati today still has Georgian Orthodox, Armenian Apostolic and Catholic churches, a synagogue and a mosque, and the town still has a large Armenian population.

⊙ Sights

Rabati Castle   CASTLE
(Kharischirashvili 1; adult/student 6/3 GEL, guide 20 GEL; ⊙9am-8pm; 🅿) Rabati Castle has been comprehensively renovated from the perilous, semi-ruined state it was left in a decade ago, and while it was a much-needed investment, sadly what greets you today feels a bit Disneyfied. You'll enter through the eastern, lower part of the complex, which doesn't require a ticket but is where you should buy one for the upper castle with its mosque, citadel and museum. A tour is a good idea to bring things alive.

Samtskhe-Javakheti
History Museum   MUSEUM
(adult/student 3/1 GEL; ⊙10am-6pm Tue-Sun) This museum has well-displayed exhibits ranging from archaeological finds from the 4th-millennium-BC Kura-Araxes culture to Christian stone carvings, Ottoman and Georgian weaponry, and regional costumes from the 18th and 19th centuries.

Sapara Monastery   MONASTERY
(🅿) Sapara has a dramatic position clinging to a cliff edge about 12km southeast of Akhaltsikhe, and rivals Vardzia as one of the most important sights in the region (and receives a fraction of Vardzia's visitors). In existence since at least the 9th century, it became the residence of the local ruling family, the Jakelis, in the 13th century. The largest of Sapara's 12 churches, St Saba's, with outstanding frescoes, dates from that time. Taxis charge around 20 GEL return trip from Akhaltsikhe (or 70 GEL if combined with Vardzia).

Akhaltsikhe   ⊙ₙ 0 ▬▬▬▬ 200 m
                          0 ▬▬▬▬ 0.1 miles

🛌 Sleeping

The choice of hotels and guesthouses in Akhaltsikhe is plentiful, with most concentrated in and around the Rabati area, but also a few smarter options across the river.

Hotel Old Rabati   HOTEL $
(☑599-853085; old.rabati@yahoo.com; Tsikhisdziris 6; r incl breakfast 50-70 GEL; 🅿❄🛜) A likeable historic hotel on the street leading up to Rabati Castle, the Old Rabati has 16th-century vaults downstairs where there's now a restaurant. One of the eight rooms has no natural light, but otherwise they all have good bathrooms and beds, and the front terrace is a sociable spot. English is spoken and the welcome is extremely warm.

Hotel New Star   HOTEL $
(☑599-937331, 571-003150; Tsikhisdziris 21; d 40-50 GEL; ❄🛜) This small hotel has a magnificent location with the castle looming right on the doorstep. Rooms, which can sleep three people and all have a private bathroom and a fridge, are comfy and clean, while staff members are friendly.

Lomsia Hotel   HOTEL $$$
(☑365-222001; www.lomsiahotel.ge; Kostava 10; s/d/ste incl breakfast 180/300/360 GEL; 🅿❄🛜) A very good town-centre hotel with large, carpeted rooms equipped with bedside lights and tea and coffee makers. Everything is sparkling clean, staff are professional and speak English, and it also has Akhaltsikhe's best restaurant. It's definitely a little overpriced, but presumably it's still paying off the golden lift.

🍴 Eating

There are a few decent eating options in town, although you may want to avoid the rather touristy places inside Rabati Castle itself.

Mimino   GEORGIAN $
(☑568-660608; Tsikhisdziris 1; mains 6-15 GEL; ⊙9am-11pm; 🛜) Named after a Soviet comedy about an amiable Georgian pilot, Mimino is a charming and friendly place with good home cooking, English-speaking staff and a small outside terrace.

Hotel Lomsia Restaurant   GEORGIAN $$
(www.lomsiahotel.ge; Kostava 10; mains 7-16 GEL; ⊙8am-11pm; 🛜) The most polished restaurant in town, with a pleasant streetside terrace as well as the bright indoor dining room.

ℹ Information

Tourism Information Centre (☎365-225028; Kharischirashvili 1; ⊘9am-8pm May-Oct, to 6pm Nov-Apr) In the lower part of Rabati Castle, this helpful tourist information centre gives out local information and also sells tickets to the castle.

ℹ Getting There & Away

Marshrutka departures from the busy **bus station** (Tamarashvili), on the north side of the river near the foot of Rabati, include the following:

Batumi (via Khashuri; 25 GEL, six hours, 8.30am and 11.30am)

Borjomi (5 GEL, one hour, 30 daily, 6am to 7pm)

Khulo (15 GEL, 3½ hours, 10am, about April to October)

Kutaisi (10 GEL, 3½ hours, 10.40am, 3pm, 6.10pm)

Tbilisi (10 GEL, four hours, at least hourly 6am to 7pm)

Vardzia (3 GEL, 1½ hours, 10.20am, 12.20pm and 5.30pm)

Yerevan (25 GEL, seven hours, 8am approximately every other day)

Vardzia

The 60km drive into the wilderness from Akhaltsikhe to the fascinating cave city of Vardzia is as dramatic as any in Georgia outside the Great Caucasus. The road follows the upper Mtkvari River, passing through narrow canyons and then veering south at Aspindza along a particularly beautiful valley cutting like a green ribbon between arid, rocky hillsides. There are several places of interest along the way: taxi drivers are often happy to stop at one or two of them for no extra charge. The star of the show is Vardzia itself, however, with its scores of caves and tunnels, impressive church and dozens of extraordinary frescoes. You can see Vardzia in a day trip from Akhaltsikhe or Borjomi, but the river valley area is a magical one, and an overnight stay is very worthwhile.

◎ Sights

★**Vardzia**   MONASTERY, CAVE
(adult/student 7/1 GEL, guide 25 GEL, audio guide 10 GEL, transfer to the cave city entrance 1 GEL; ⊘10am-7pm) The remarkable cave city of Vardzia is both a cultural symbol and a spectacular natural phenomenon with a special place in Georgian hearts. King Giorgi III built a fortification here in the 12th century, and his daughter, Queen Tamar, established a cave monastery that grew into a holy city housing perhaps 2000 monks, renowned as a spiritual bastion of Christendom's eastern frontier. Altogether there are over 400 rooms, 13 churches and 25 wine cellars, with many more still being discovered today.

Its inhabitants lived in rock-hewn dwellings ranging over 13 floors, a scale almost impossible to imagine at the time. A major earthquake in 1283 shook away the outer walls of many caves and the cave city began its long decline. In 1551 the Georgians were defeated by the Persians in a battle in the caves themselves, and Vardzia was looted. Since the end of Soviet rule Vardzia has again become a working monastery, with some caves inhabited by monks (and cordoned off to protect their privacy).

Guides, available at the ticket office, don't speak English but they have keys to some passages and caves that you can't otherwise enter.

At the heart of the cave complex is the **Church of the Assumption**, with its two-arched, bell-hung portico. The church's facade has gone, but the inside is beautiful. Frescoes painted at the time of its construction (1184–86) portray many New Testament scenes and, on the north wall, Giorgi III and Tamar before she married (shown by the fact that she is not wearing a wimple). To be allowed in the church, women must wear long skirts and a head covering, and men must wear long trousers. The door to the left of the church door leads into a long tunnel (perhaps 150m), which climbs up steps inside the rock and emerges well above the church, a claustrophobic but rather exciting experience.You can't really get lost despite the size of the complex, and once you have explored various different levels, you'll find yourself led back down the hillside in a large loop.

Vanis Kvabebi   MONASTERY
(Vani Caves) FREE About 4km south of Tmogvi village and 2km before Vardzia, a track heads 600m up from the road to this cave monastery that predated Vardzia by four centuries. It's almost as intriguing as Vardzia itself and far less visited. A handful of monks have reoccupied the caves at the bottom left of the complex, after centuries of abandonment. You can climb up to the little white domed church, high up in the cliff, by a series of wooden ladders inside the rock.

Khertvisi Fortress
FORTRESS

FREE This impressive 10th- to 14th-century fortress perches on a rocky crag above the meeting of the Paravani and Mtkvari Rivers, 45km southeast of Akhaltsikhe where the Vardzia road diverges from the main road to Akhalkalaki and Armenia.

Tmogvi Castle
FORTRESS

FREE Eleven kilometres past Khertvisi Fortress towards Vardzia, atop a high rocky hill across the river (which flows far below in a gorge), the remains of the once near-impregnable Tmogvi Castle date back at least a millennium. You can walk to it in an hour or so (4km) up the west side of the valley from Vardzia – and continue north to Khertvisi, on off-road trails most of the way, if you want.

🛏 Sleeping & Eating

There are a few options at and near Vardzia, including the new upmarket Vardzia Resort. There are also a few informal guesthouses at Tmogvi.

Hotel Taoskari HOTEL **$**
(📞599-543540, 577-749996; www.facebook.com/pages/vardzia-taoskari/237963042894724; dm/s/d/tr 20/35/70/120 GEL; breakfast 10 GEL; 🅿🛜❄) Taoskari may be rather lacking in atmosphere, but it's a reliable and great-value place to lay your head, just across the bridge from Vardzia. A brand-new dorm sleeps 12 people and makes for the cheapest option in the area. The private rooms are a little dated, but clean. Breakfast is served upstairs in the huge banquet hall.

Valodia's Cottage HOTEL **$$**
(📞595-642346; www.accommodationvardzia.ge; Koriskhevi; s/d/tr/f 78/115/140/140 GEL; breakfast 15 GEL; 🕓Apr-Nov; 🅿🛜) In a beautiful riverside setting 2.5km south from Vardzia, Valodia's offers comfy rooms, some with a balcony or a terrace, in new pine or stone buildings. There's good Georgian food, much of it home-grown, and a lovely garden to eat in – a fine place for lunch even if you're not staying.

Vardzia Resort HOTEL **$$$**
(📞591-321515; www.vardziaresort.com; d/tr/ste incl breakfast 324/419/461 GEL; 🅿❄🛜❄) With a gorgeous setting facing the cave city across the river, this newly built and very contemporary resort is upmarket and caters mainly to tour groups. Each stylish room has a large balcony and the gardens are beautifully

kept with waterfalls and streams cascading through the property. The on-site restaurant is also the best in the area.

ℹ Getting There & Away

The first *marshrutka* leaving Akhaltsikhe, at 10.20am, reaches Vardzia around noon, giving you just enough time to see the cave city and catch the last *marshrutka* back at 3pm (5 GEL, 1½ hours). Earlier ones are at 9.30am (from the opposite side of the bridge from the cave city), 10.30am and 12.50pm (both from outside the cave city). But a day trip is more comfortable by taxi, for 50 GEL return trip from Akhaltsikhe, or 120 GEL from Borjomi, with a few stops en route.

WESTERN GEORGIA

Famous as the destination of Jason and the Argonauts in their search for the Golden Fleece, western Georgia is home to Georgia's third-largest city, Kutaisi, and is full of easily accessible historical, architectural and natural riches. The region has always acted as a conduit for influences from the west, from the Ancient Greeks to St Nino to the Ottoman Turks. It was for long periods ruled separately from eastern Georgia, but was also where the great united Georgian kingdom of the 11th and 12th centuries made its start.

Today the region attracts huge numbers of visitors, primarily as many of its sights are within a relatively short distance of each other, and their accessibility has been dramatically improved in recent years. However, it's not hard to get off the beaten track and discover areas as yet untouched by Georgia's tourism miracle.

Kutaisi

📞431 / POP 147,000

Once the capital of several historical kingdoms within Georgia, Kutaisi is today something of a charming backwater. Now the country's third city – Batumi eclipsed it as second city in 2014 – most people know Kutaisi for its airport, which has become Georgia's main hub for low-cost airlines. But it would be a mistake to skip this lovely town, which makes a great base for exploring the region of Imereti and has a smattering of worthwhile sights and restaurants to enjoy.

Western Georgia

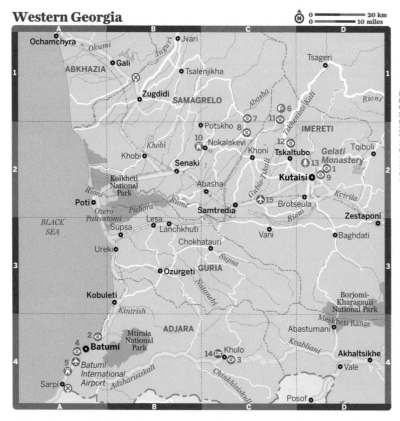

Western Georgia

◎ Sights

The Bagrati Cathedral is one of Georgia's most beautiful churches, and the attractively renovated central area around Kutaisis bulvari park and Pushkinis qucha is well worth exploring, with its colourful market, good museum, cafes and the grand Colchis Fountain.

Bagrati Cathedral   CATHEDRAL
(Bagrati; ⊙9am-8pm) Kutaisi's cathedral was built in 1003 by Bagrat III, with a tall drum and pointed dome resting on four freestanding pillars. In 1692 a Turkish explosion brought down drum, dome and ceiling to leave the cathedral in a ruined state. It

was fully renovated between 2009 and 2012, with a mix of old and new stone and a few steel sections.

The cathedral gained Unesco World Heritage listing in 1994 following intermittent restoration efforts through the 20th century.

Ironically, the 21st-century renovation put it on Unesco's World Heritage in Danger list, due to threats to the 'integrity and authenticity of the site', a status that has been removed with the redrawing of the boundaries of the heritage site, which now exclude the

Kutaisi

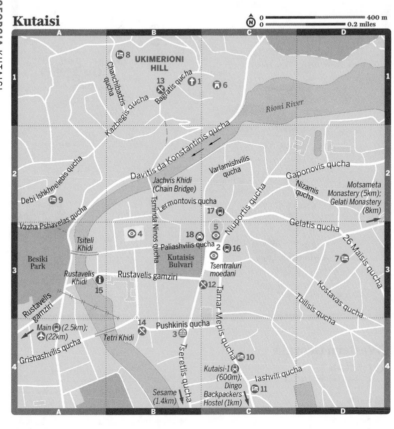

Kutaisi

cathedral itself, and include only the Gelati Monastery (p87), 8km outside the city.

The **palace-citadel** `FREE` immediately east of the cathedral dates back to the 6th century. It was wrecked in 1769 during Georgian-Russo-Turkish wars, but you can discern remains of wine cellars and a church.

Kutaisi Historical Museum   MUSEUM
(☑ 431-245691; Pushkin 18; adult/student 3/2 GEL, tour English, German, Russian or Georgian 10 GEL; ☺ 10am-6pm) The history museum has superb collections from all around western Georgia, but a guided tour is a good idea as labelling is poor. The highlight is the Golden Fund section, with a marvellous exhibition of icons and crosses in precious metals and jewels, including a large, reputedly miracle-working icon that used to reside in the Bagrati Cathedral.

Colchis Fountain   FOUNTAIN
The central square, Tsentraluri moedani, focuses on the large ornamental Colchis Fountain, adorned with large-scale copies of the famous gold jewellery discovered at the nearby archaeological site of Vani.

Market   MARKET
(btwn Paliashvili & Lermontov; ☺ 7am-5pm or later) Kutaisi's indoor produce market is one of the largest, liveliest and most colourful in Georgia, full of cheese, walnuts, spices, herbs, fruit, vegetables, meat, *churchkhela* (strings of walnuts coated in grape-juice caramel), beans, wine, pickles and plenty more.

🛏 Sleeping

Kutaisi's accommodation options have expanded hugely and you can expect new hostels, guesthouses and hotels to continue popping up, with the competition keeping prices low.

★ Dingo Backpackers Hostel   HOSTEL $
(☑ 568-823427, 571-197317; Kupradze 18; dm 20-25 GEL, d 100 GEL; ☎) Probably overall the best hostel in town, mainly due to the infectious enthusiasm of the two Italian friends who run it, Dingo Backpackers is in a traditional house full of local character, and enjoys a large garden with a camping area and its own well, several dorms and private rooms that share two bathrooms and a large balcony.

★ Giorgi's Homestay   HOMESTAY $
(☑ 431-243720, 595-591511; giorgihomestay14@ yahoo.com; Chanchibadze 14; d 80 GEL, without

bathroom 60 GEL, q 100 GEL; ℗☎☺☻) Giorgi Giorgadze and his family provide clean, pleasant and sizeable rooms in their ample house on Ukimerioni Hill. They have been hosting travellers a lot longer than most local guesthouses and understand what their guests need, offering plenty of travel tips and help, substantial breakfasts, sparkling bathrooms, and free tea and coffee. Giorgi also offers tours of the region.

Hostel Mandaria   HOSTEL $
(☑ 599-677677; Chachavadze 33; dm 10 GEL, d/tr/ apt 50/70/100 GEL, d/tr without bathroom 25/27 GEL; ☎) In a huge old Soviet building that was once a printing company, Mandaria is a hostel on a grand scale that is perfect for groups. There's a huge communal kitchen that is superbly equipped, lots of showers and toilets, and a vast lounge-dining space ideal for hanging out. It's a bit of a schlep from the city centre, but otherwise excellent.

Star Hostel   HOSTEL $
(☑ 431-251425, 599-988804; starhostel.ge@gmail. com; Tamar Mepe 37; dm 10 GEL, r from 25 GEL; ☻☎) A decent and clean Georgian-run hostel 500m south of Tsentraluri moedani. Bunk dorms hold four to eight people and there are three doubles with private bathroom. Breakfast costs 5 GEL extra and there's a very bare-bones kitchen. It offers reasonably priced taxi outings and rents bicycles (20 GEL per day).

Gelati Guest House   GUESTHOUSE $
(Hotel Gelati; ☑ 597-986222, 597-965326; www.ge lati1.narod.ru; 26 Maisi 2nd Lane 4; s/d/tr 40/60/80 GEL; ☻☎) Original art, moulded ceilings and other pretty touches give this English-speaking guesthouse a little something extra. All but one of the seven rooms have a private bathroom, and there's a small garden, a dining room and a kitchen for guests.

Hotel Elegant   HOTEL $$
(☑ 591-697570, 431-245830; dula50@mail.ru; Debi Ishknelebi 24; s/d 35/70 GEL; ℗☻☎) One of several small or medium-sized hotels on a hilltop street overlooking the city centre from the northwest, the welcoming, family-run Elegant offers 10 pleasant, comfy, parquet-floored rooms in assorted colours. There's a lovely terrace for sitting out over a coffee or just enjoying the view. Breakfast is an extra 10 GEL.

Kiev-Kutaisi Hotel   HOTEL $$
(☑ 431-245867, 598-307078; kiev.kutaisi@gmail. com; Tamar Mepe 25; d/q incl breakfast 70/100 GEL;

P ✳ 🛜) This 14-room hotel has the feel of a family home and is handily located just south of Tsentraluri moedani. The welcome is friendly and English-speaking, and the rooms spotless and feature parquet flooring, lots of natural light and Georgian antiques scattered about the place. Breakfast costs 10 GEL.

 Eating

The city centre has a decent selection of appealing cafes and small restaurants, but it's a far cry from the choice of Tbilisi.

★**Palaty** GEORGIAN $$
(🖉 431-243380; Pushkin 2; mains 10-25 GEL; ⏱ 9am-midnight; 🛜) Live piano music, pleasant low lighting and a semi-bohemian ambience make Palaty a top spot in Kutaisi. The menu includes several departures from the norm, such as the huge board (90 GEL) featuring a dozen different local specialities. If you don't fancy regional Georgian dishes, there are also pizzas and pasta available.

Our Garden GEORGIAN $$
(Bagrati 23; mains 10-20 GEL; ⏱ 11am-1am; 🛜) An ideal spot for a drink or a snack after visiting next-door Bagrati Cathedral, Our Garden is a real charmer, with a gorgeous terrace giving great views of the city below, a tasty menu of Georgian home cooking and a rather stylish dining room stuffed full of local paintings.

Agerari GEORGIAN $$
(Tsereteli 2; mains 10-15 GEL; ⏱ 24hr; 🛜) This pleasant two-floor space with an open kitchen on the ground floor serves a varied and tasty range of Georgian dishes just off Kutaisi's central square. The *khinkali* and kebabs are excellent, as is the *chikhirtma* (chicken and garlic soup) and the local beer on tap.

Sesame INTERNATIONAL $$
(Tsereteli 163/165; mains 12-25 GEL; ⏱ noon-1am; 🛜🖉) With its exposed brick, tiled bar and filament bulbs, Sesame is about as hip as Kutaisi gets. The menu is refreshingly original too, with lots of non-Georgian choice including dishes such as fajitas, chicken Kiev and beef steak with pesto, and a decent wine list. Service is swift and efficient.

★**Toma's Wine Cellar** GEORGIAN $$$
(🖉 555-445140; Sergo Kldiashvili 34; per person incl wine 40 GEL; ⏱ 3-11pm Wed-Mon; 🛜🖉) Becoming a Kutaisi essential in just a couple of years, Toma's offers you the chance to dine on traditional home-cooked foods that you'll be unlikely to find in most restaurants. The set meal is enormous, and includes Toma's delicious homemade wine and dishes such as *jonjoli* (pickled wildflowers) and *gebzhalia*. Reservations essential.

ℹ️ **Information**

Tourism Information Centre (🖉 431-241107; tickutaisi@gmail.com; Rustaveli 9a; ⏱ 9am-7pm Apr-Oct, to 6pm Nov-Mar) Georgia's largest tourist office occupies a recently converted house overlooking the river. Multilingual staff are extremely helpful. There's also a desk at the airport.

ℹ️ **Getting There & Away**

AIR

David the Builder Kutaisi International Airport (🖉 431-237000; www.kutaisi.aero) at Kopitnari, 22km west of central Kutaisi, is a popular budget-airline entry point to Georgia. **Wizz Air** (🖉 706-777483; www.wizzair.com) flies here directly from around 25 cities all over Europe, Ukrainian International Airlines flies to Kyiv and Kharkov, Ural Airlines flies to Moscow, and SCAT flies to Aktau in Kazakhstan. Domestically, Vanilla Sky (p66) connects Kutaisi to Mestia in Svaneti.

MARSHRUTKA

Marshrutky from Kutaisi's **main bus station** (Chavchavadze 67), 3km southwest of the city centre, include the following services:

Akhaltsikhe (13 GEL, 3½ hours, four daily)
Batumi (10 GEL, two hours, hourly 9am to 6pm)
Borjomi (13 GEL, three hours, four daily)
Mestia (25 GEL, 4½ hours, 9am)
Tbilisi (10 GEL, four hours, hourly 7am to 5pm)
Zugdidi (7 GEL, 1½ hours, hourly 6am to 5pm)

To get to Gori from Kutaisi, take any *marshrutka* to Tbilisi and ask to be let off at Gori. You'll be dropped 5km from the city centre; a taxi into town will cost 10 GEL.

Marshrutky to the main bus station leave from outside McDonald's on Tsentraluri moedani, and Marshrutky to Gelati leave from behind the Meskhishvili Drama Theatre on Tsentraluri moedani.

TRAIN

Kutaisi-1 station (Tamar Mepe), 1km south of the city centre, has slow trains to Tbilisi at 4.55am (4 GEL, 5½ hours) and 12.25pm (9 GEL, 5½ hours); Batumi (2 GEL, four hours) at 5.50pm; and Zugdidi (2 GEL, 3½ hours) at 1.45pm.

❶ Getting Around

FROM THE AIRPORT

Georgian Bus (☐ 555-397387; www.georgian
bus.com; David the Builder Kutaisi International Airport) runs minibuses between Kutaisi
airport and several destinations around Georgia, including Kutaisi city (5 GEL, 30 minutes),
Tbilisi (20 GEL, four hours) and Batumi (15
GEL, two hours), timed to fit in with flight
arrivals and departures. You can book and pay
online, or at its airport desk – or, for trips to the
airport, when you board the minibus. Minimum
passenger numbers may be required for some
destinations. The arrival and departure point in
Tbilisi is Pushkinis skver, just off the north side
of Tavisuplebis moedani.

Taxis between the airport and city centre cost
25 GEL.

BUS, MARSHRUTKA & TAXI

Marshrutky 1 and 200 run from the main bus
station to Rustavelis gamziri in the city centre.
Catch them across the road (Chavchavadzis
gamziri) from the bus station, going to the
left. From the city centre, the quickest public
transport to the bus station is with *marshrutka*
1, which leaves from outside McDonald's. Taxis
charge around 6 GEL from the bus station to the
city centre.

Around Kutaisi

The rolling countryside around Kutaisi is
full of natural beauty, churches, canyons and
historic fortresses. It's perfect for day trips
from the city, many of which can be covered
easily in one day if you have your own transport or hire a driver.

★ Gelati Monastery   MONASTERY
(☉ 8am-8pm; P) This Unesco World
Heritage-listed monastery complex, on a
wooded hillside 8km northeast of Kutaisi,
is an outstanding example of Golden Age
architecture and one of Georgia's most
important churches. Gelati was a cultural hub of Georgia's medieval renaissance,
and many Georgian rulers were buried
here, including the great 12th-century
king, David the Builder. The interior of the
main Cathedral of the Virgin is among the
brightest and most colourful in Georgia,
with fascinating frescoes.

King David founded Gelati in 1106 as a
centre for Christian culture and Neoplatonist learning. Medieval chroniclers described
its academy as a 'second Jerusalem' and a
'new Athens'. In 1510 the Ottoman Turks set
fire to the complex, but Bagrat III of Imereti

subsequently restored it. The monks were
cast out by the communists in 1922, but the
churches were reconsecrated in 1988.

The first building you come to as you enter the complex is the **Church of St George**,
which contains multiple colourful frescoes.
Outside the cathedral's west door is the
smaller Church of St Nicholas, built on an
unusual arcaded base, and beyond that, the
recently rebuilt Academy, where philosophy,
theology, sciences and painting were studied, and important chronicles and transla-
tions written. David the Builder's grave lies
inside the south gate: David wanted all who
entered the monastery to step on his tomb, a
notably humble gesture for such a powerful
man. Ironically, reverent visitors today take
great care not to step on it.

The frescoes in the main **Cathedral of
the Virgin** were painted between the 12th
and 18th centuries: the line of six noble figures on the wall to your left as you face the
altar includes David the Builder (holding
the church) and Bagrat III of Georgia (with
a cross over his left shoulder). A famous
1120s mosaic of the Virgin and Child, with
Archangels Michael and Gabriel to the left
and right respectively, looks down from the
apse ceiling. If you visit during the Sunday-
morning service from around 10am, you'll
be treated to beautiful Georgian chants.

Marshrutky to Gelati (1 GEL, 30 minutes)
leave from outside the Dinmart Supermarket behind the Drama Theatre on Tsentraluri moedani in Kutaisi hourly from 8am
to 6pm, passing the Motsameta turn-off
en route. The last one back from Gelati is
at 4.30pm. If you're visiting both places, it's
a mostly downhill road-walk of about one
hour from Gelati to Motsameta, should the
return *marshrutka* schedules not suit: you
can cut 800m off the distance by heading to
the left along the railway after 3.5km.

A taxi round-trip from Kutaisi to Gelati
typically costs 25 GEL, or 30 GEL with Motsameta too.

Okatse Canyon   CANYON
(Zeda Gordi; adult/child 17.50/5.50 GEL; ☉ 10am-
6pm Tue-Sun; P) An exciting 700m-long
walkway projects from the edge of this
100m-deep canyon and culminates in a
viewing platform that hangs right out over
the middle. It's a 2.5km hike from the visitors centre near Zeda Gordi village, 42km
northwest of Kutaisi. A jeep back to the visitors centre afterwards costs 15 GEL for five
or six people.

Kinchkha Waterfall   WATERFALL

(adult/child 17.50/5.50 GEL; ⊙9am-6pm) This impressive waterfall cascades 88m down the side of a huge limestone cliff, runs through a narrow gorge and then crashes down again to a pool below and on into the Okatse River. It's a gorgeous spot, made totally accessible by the construction of a metal walkway through the gorge allowing for stellar views of the site, even if it rather detracts from the natural wonder itself. It's usually combined with a visit to the Okatse Canyon.

Martvili Canyon   CANYON

(☑595-805455; adult/child 17.25/5.50 GEL; ⊙10am-6pm Tue-Sun; P⛲) The attractive Martvili Canyon has been comprehensively adapted to the needs of tourists and now contains multiple walkways and bridges giving lovely views, although between the crowds and the built environment, it feels far from natural. Rides up the Abasha River through the 40m- to 70m-deep canyon itself are pretty, though not an overwhelmingly exciting ride: the price per small inflatable boat (five or six passengers) is 15 GEL to go 350m up the canyon and back, or 30 GEL for 700m.

Martvili Monastery   MONASTERY

Martvili's monastery, a medieval Georgian cultural centre, sits on a serene hilltop overlooking the town and the surrounding valleys and hills. Its church dates from the 7th century, with its original design based on the Jvari Church near Mtskheta. The interesting frescoes inside include portraits of the Dadiani royal house of Megrelia (Samegrelo), and a famous 17th-century Virgin on the apse ceiling.

Nokalakevi Fortress   FORTRESS

(adult/student 5/1 GEL, tour in English 15 GEL; ⊙10am-2pm & 3-6pm Tue-Sun) Nokalakevi is an ancient Colchian fortress built on the banks of the Tekhuri River. It's been mooted as one of the (many) places to have housed the Golden Fleece, and is well worth a detour to explore, not least for the impressively engineered tunnel on the far side of the complex leading down to the river. Admission includes an interesting archaeological museum, a new building for which was under construction at research time. Excavations are ongoing (see www.nokalakevi.org).

About 1km upstream along the Tekhura you can take a dip in soothing thermal pools.

Motsameta Monastery   MONASTERY

(P) Little Motsameta sits on a spectacular clifftop promontory above a bend of the Tskhaltsitela River, 5km from Kutaisi, 1.8km off the Gelati road. The river's name, 'Red Water', derives from an 8th-century Arab massacre. Among the victims were the brothers Davit and Konstantin Mkheidze, dukes of Argveti. Their bodies were thrown in the river but, the story goes, they were then miraculously brought up to the monastery site (by lions, in one common version).

Prometheus Cave   CAVE

(☑577-101417; www.prometheus.ge; Kumistavi; adult/child 23/5.50 GEL, boat ride per person 17.50 GEL; ⊙10am-6pm Tue-Sun; P) This 1.4km-long cave at Kumistavi, 20km northwest of Kutaisi, is a succession of six large chambers followed by a 400m-long underground lake. Sections are truly impressive, and the guided visits along a well-made concrete path are enhanced by discreet coloured lighting and a little background classical music. Children under six years are not allowed in the cave.

Marshrutka 30 runs from the west end of Kutaisi's Tsiteli Khidi (Red Bridge) to the spa town of Tskaltubo (1 GEL, 30 minutes), where *marshrutka* 42 continues 8km to Prometheus Cave (1.50 GEL, 20 minutes) every hour or two.

Sataplia Nature Reserve   NATURE RESERVE

(☑577-101417; adult/child 17.25/5.50 GEL; ⊙10am-6pm Tue-Sun; P⛲) The star features of the 3.3-sq-km reserve, 9km northwest of Kutaisi, are a couple of dozen 120-million-year-old, fossilised dinosaur footprints (well displayed in a protective building), and an attractively lit 300m-long cave with a small underground river. The reserve is covered in thick, subtropical Colchic forest and has a couple of panoramic lookout points. It takes about an hour to walk around the main visitor route.

A taxi round-trip from Kutaisi combining Sataplia with Prometheus Cave costs 35 GEL to 40 GEL. Public transport is awkward: *marshrutka* 35 (0.40 GEL) goes from the west end of Paliashvili to the end of Javakhishvili on Kutaisi's western edge, where *marshrutka* 45 leaves for the remaining 5km to Sataplia when the driver considers he has enough passengers (four is usually sufficient).

VISITING ABKHAZIA

Abkhazia boasts the best beaches in the Caucasus, stunning semi-tropical landscapes of mountains, lakes and valleys, and an attractive capital in Sukhumi. As little has changed in the region since the end of the war in the early 1990s, there are many relics of the Soviet Union to explore, including some fascinating abandoned train stations, sanatoria and hotels. It's also possible to visit several *dachas* (country cottages) once favoured by Stalin, and the country's most famous religious complex, Novy Afon Monastery.

It's perfectly possible and safe for non-Georgians to visit Abkhazia from Georgia, though most governments advise against this, as your embassy in Tbilisi will not be able to offer you consular assistance once you enter the region.

The first step to visiting Abkhazia is to obtain a clearance letter. Instructions are on the website of the Abkhazian Foreign Ministry: you fill in a form and email it to the foreign ministry's consular service along with a copy of your passport's photo page. Within seven working days you should receive your clearance letter (in Russian) by email.

Having entered Abkhazia with your clearance letter, you must then go within three working days to the **Abkhazian Foreign Ministry** (✆840-2267069; http://mfaapsny.org; ulitsa Sakharova 33; ◷9am-6pm Mon-Fri) in Sukhumi to obtain your visa. Abkhazian visas are single pieces of paper, not stuck into your passport, which you'll surrender on exiting the country. A 10-day single-entry visa costs R400 (around US$7). For more information about what to do in Abkhazia see www.lonelyplanet.com/georgia/western-georgia/abkhazia.

❶ Getting There & Away

All of the sights around Kutaisi can be visited on day trips from the city. Having your own wheels or hiring a driver is optimal here, although it's possible to reach many of the places by *marshrutka* if you're not in a hurry and don't mind some long journeys.

Zugdidi

☑ 415 / POP 43,000

The bustling main city of Samegrelo (Megrelia), Zugdidi is the nearest city to the Abkhazian border and has absorbed a high number of refugees since the war there in the early 1990s. While it's a stepping stone for getting to Svaneti or Abkhazia, and a good base for exploring the lesser-known attractions of Samegrelo, in itself it has little to offer travellers save some decent sleeping and eating options and a rather quirky museum in the town's old palace.

◉ Sights

Dadiani Museum MUSEUM
(adult/student 5/1 GEL, treasury adult/student 5/1 GEL, tour English, German, Georgian or Russian 5 GEL; ◷10am-6pm Tue-Sun, treasury section 11am-4pm Tue-Sun) The castle-like palace of the Dadiani family (old lords of Samegrelo) is now a museum set in beautifully maintained grounds. As well as interesting 19th-century paintings of the Caucasus

and a fine collection of icons and crosses from the 10th to 20th centuries (in the Treasury section, which can only be visited on a guided tour), it contains one of Napoleon's four bronze death masks, acquired through marriage between Princess Salome Dadiani and Achille Murat, Napoleon's nephew.

The wooded botanical gardens beside the park are worth a stroll too.

⛌ Sleeping

As a popular traveller stopover, Zugdidi has dozens of hotels, hostels and guesthouses, so you'll have no problem finding a room even in the height of summer.

My Moon Hostel HOSTEL $
(☑571-444530, 595-901590; Rustaveli 61; dm/s/d 20/25/50 GEL; ☜) You'll find Jim and Bob on the walls, a garden scattered with chairs and lots of creative knick-knacks all over this rather ramshackle but very characterful house. There are a number of different-sized rooms – all sharing bathrooms and showers – and a large communal kitchen and hang-out area downstairs. My Moon also offers day trips around the region.

Art Hostel HOSTEL $
(☑568-535663; Rustaveli 31; dm/d 20/50 GEL; ☜) Owner Tamara speaks no English, but is a lively and enthusiastic communicator and warmly welcomes travellers to her

large house and playfully decorated garden. There's a 10-bed dorm downstairs and four private rooms upstairs, all sharing two bathrooms. There's a communal kitchen, a washing machine and fans in each room, and a further bathroom is planned.

★ **Leto Boutique Hotel** BOUTIQUE HOTEL **$$**
(☑ 415-255555; www.letohotel.ge; Gamsakhurdia 31; r/ste incl breakfast from 199/319 GEL; P ✳ 🕿 ☒) Zugdidi's best hotel is this brand-new, highly impressive boutique property on the town's main avenue. Its rooms are sleek and minimalist, many boasting superb views and balconies overlooking the city centre. The showstopper is definitely the rooftop infinity pool, however, which looks more like something you'd find in LA than a small regional capital of Georgia.

 Eating

There are several good places to eat scattered around the city centre, and plenty of local specialities to try.

Diaroni GEORGIAN **$$**
(☑ 415-221122; www.diaroni.ge; Gamsakhurdia 9; mains 12-55 GEL; ☉ 10am-11pm; 🕿) Zugdidi's best-known restaurant is certainly one of its smartest, with a large dark-wood and brick interior and a shaded street-side terrace where you can watch the world go by. The food is excellent, with an extensive menu featuring many Megrelian speciali-

---

THE ABKHAZIA CONFLICT

The Abkhaz are linguistically distinct from the Georgians, their language being one of the northwestern Caucasus family (although Russian is now the most common language in Abkhazia). During the Middle Ages, Abkhazia was an important component of Christian Georgia. It came under Ottoman rule in the 15th century. Russian conquest in the 19th century resulted in many thousands of Muslim Abkhaz fleeing to the Ottoman Empire, and there is a big Abkhaz diaspora in Turkey today.

Under Soviet rule in 1921, Abkhazia signed a treaty of union with Georgia, but in 1931 it was downgraded to an autonomous region within Georgia. The number of ethnic Georgians in Abkhazia increased to the point where by 1989 Abkhazia's population was 46% Georgian and only 18% Abkhaz. The Abkhaz began to agitate for more rights in the late 1970s, and in 1990 Abkhazia's Abkhaz-dominated Supreme Soviet unilaterally declared Abkhazia a separate Soviet republic.

Real conflict broke out in August 1992 when the Georgian National Guard occupied Sukhumi, driving out most of its Abkhaz inhabitants. Abkhazia was plunged into a year of fighting, in which about 8000 people died. The Abkhaz were aided by fighters from the Russian Caucasus, and on some occasions by Russian armed forces. Both sides committed appalling atrocities. In September 1993 the Abkhaz attacked Sukhumi in violation of a truce and drove the Georgian forces and almost all of Abkhazia's Georgian population (about 230,000 people) out of Abkhazia. Only in the southern Gali district have significant numbers of Georgians (around 40,000) since returned.

After the 1992–93 war, Russia imposed trade sanctions on Abkhazia, but Vladimir Putin changed Russia's stance when he entered the Kremlin in 2000. Abkhazians were offered Russian passports from 2001, and in 2008 Russia removed trade sanctions. During the 2008 South Ossetia War, Russian forces came from Abkhazia to attack Georgian military installations in western Georgia. Soon afterwards, Russia recognised Abkhazia as an independent nation, and since then only Venezuela, Nicaragua, Syria and Nauru have followed Russia's lead. Russia stepped up aid and investment and stationed anti-aircraft missiles and several thousand troops in the territory, a source of immense bitterness in Georgia, which considers this to be an illegal occupation. In 2014 Abkhazia and Russia signed an Agreement on Alliance & Strategic Partnership, under which Abkhazia's defence, law enforcement, border control and economic management were integrated with Russia's and Russian financial support to the region was doubled.

Ethnic Abkhaz now constitute about half of Abkhazia's much-reduced population. Most do not appear to want Russian rule (their ideal is genuine independence). They have, however, little choice but to obey Russia's will.

ties. A *diaroni* is a Megrelian *supra,* and the place is well named.

El Barco
GEORGIAN **$$**

(☑ 555-199798; Rustaveli 77; mains 7-25 GEL; ☺ noon-midnight; 🤙📶) 🅿 Friendly, cosy and low-key, El Barco was set up to help refugees from Abkhazia and is a charming place for a meal of local Megrelian specialities such as *gebzhalia* and *mchadi* (cornmeal flatbread). Service can be hit and miss, but the overall experience tends to be a good one.

ℹ Information

Tourism Information Centre (☑ 595-630577; ticzugdidi@gmail.com; Rustaveli 87; ☺ 9am-6pm Mon-Fri Jul-Oct, from 10am Mon-Fri Nov-Jun) The small but helpful tourist office offers maps of the city and up-to-date transport timetables.

ℹ Getting There & Away

Zugdidi has two *marshrutka* hubs, one outside the train station, and a second, known as the Bridge bus station, just off Rustavelis qucha by an old stone watchtower in a busy market area. Most services depart from the train station, however. Departures include the following:

Batumi (12 GEL, three hours, eight daily)

Borjomi (15 GEL, four hours, 10am daily)

Kutaisi (7 GEL, 1½ hours, every 30 minutes, 7am and 7pm)

Mestia (20 GEL, three hours, leave when full between 6.30am and 3pm)

Tbilisi (15 GEL, 5½ hours, about hourly, 7am to midnight)

Extra *marshrutky* to Mestia usually meet the trains arriving from Tbilisi, though they may not leave until they are full: Zugdidi's hostels can usually arrange for Mestia *marshrutky* to come and pick you up. There is no public transport to the Abkhazian border post, so you'll need to take a taxi (10 GEL, 15 minutes).

A night train to Tbilisi (seat/2nd/1st class 7.50/17/30 GEL, nine hours) departs from Zugdidi's train station at 9.45pm. There's also a faster day train to Tbilisi (2nd class 13 GEL, 5½ hours) departing 6.15pm daily.

ADJARA

Adjara has taken on the mantle of Georgia's holiday coast since the loss of Abkhazia, Soviet Georgia's traditional summer destination. Centred on the boom town of Batumi, Adjara is the destination of choice for most Georgians – and many others – in search of summer fun, with a real party atmosphere in August. Travellers entering Georgia at the busy Sarpi border post with Turkey will find that this alluring region is their introduction to the country, and it's not a bad one at all.

Though Adjara's beaches are mostly stony, the subtropical climate is fantastic and the scenery gorgeous, with lush hills rising behind the coast, and peaks topping 3000m inland, giving a dramatic backdrop of snow-capped mountains. Indeed, a drive through the region's largely Muslim hinterland is very rewarding, offering superb scenery scattered with picturesque mountain villages.

Batumi
☑ 422 / POP 155,000

With a backdrop of mist-wrapped hills and soaring snow-capped peaks, Georgia's second city is a charismatic place with a charming Old Town. Fronted by the calm waters of the Black Sea, Georgia's main summer resort boasts a long beach and a vast and beautifully maintained corniche.

Batumi is also undergoing a construction boom, with new hotels and tower blocks transforming its skyline in recent years, even if the renovated charm of its original belle-époque architecture from a century ago is hard to beat. July and August are supremely busy here, but the town has atmosphere year-round, with May, June and September also excellent times to visit.

⊙ Sights

Batumi is stuffed full of sights, many of which were built to entertain the summer crowds, such as the curious Batumi Tower, the Alphabet Tower and the Dancing Fountains. Rather more cerebral sights can be found away from the seafront, such as the excellent Batumi Archeological Museum and the Adjara Arts Museum.

★ Batumi Boulevard
PARK

(www.boulevard.ge; 📶) Everyone soon finds themselves strolling along Batumis bulvari, the park strip fronting the main beach, originally laid out in 1884 and now stretching 7km along the coast. With its trees, paths, fountains, cafes, beach bars and a few quirky attractions, this is the life and soul of Batumi. The beach itself is fine, though stony – extremely busy in July and August, but kept very clean.

GEORGIA BATUMI

Batumi

Archeological Museum MUSEUM

(📞 422-276564; Chavchavadze 77; adult/student 3/1 GEL; ⊙10am-6pm) This excellent museum showcases some of the many valuable archaeological discoveries made in Adjara, particularly at the Gonio Apsaros Fortress (p94). The main room upstairs starts with the remains of hominids from between 1.7 and 1.8 million years ago and moves through impressive Bronze Age daggers, Iron Age jewellery, Hellenistic pottery and Roman artefacts. Downstairs is an impressive display of Byzantine gold.

Cable Car CABLE CAR

(Gogebashvili; return trip adult/child 15/5 GEL; ⊙11am-10pm; 🚠) This 2.6km-long cable car carries you up to a shopping-cafe-restaurant complex on Anuria Hill, 2586m above Batumi, for panoramic views over the city. It's especially pretty after dark.

Ali & Nino SCULPTURE

(Batumis bulvari) The 7m-high, ethereally moving, metal sculpture *Woman and Man,* by Tamar Kvesitadze, is universally known as Ali & Nino after the protagonists of Kurban Said's marvellous novel of that name (see it after dark).

Batumi Botanical Garden GARDENS

(📞 422-270033; www.bbg.ge; 15 GEL; ⊙10am-8pm Tue-Sun) Batumi's Botanical Garden, 8km northeast of town, was founded in 1912 by Russian botanist Andrei Krasnov. With many subtropical and foreign species, it extends just over 1 sq km over a hillside rising straight out of the sea, and takes about 1½ hours to walk the main path at a leisurely pace.

You can get there by *marshrutka* 15, from Rustavelis qucha and Gogebashvilis qucha, or *marshrutka* 31 from Gogebashvilis qucha east of Chavchavadzis qucha.

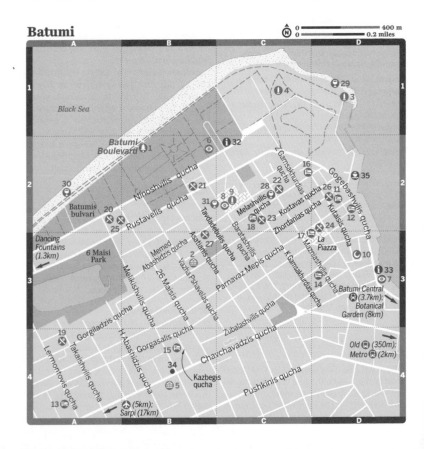

Batumi

Dancing Fountains
FOUNTAIN

(☉9pm-midnight Jun-Sep; 🚹) FREE On the southern part of the boulevard, known as the New Boulevard, an ornamental lake hosts the Dancing Fountains, an entertaining laser, music and water show. There are some other fountains at the northern end of the boulevard too.

Batumi Tower
ARCHITECTURE

(Ninoshvili) Georgia's tallest building (even if much of it is its needle), the 200m-high Batumi Tower boasts a mini Ferris wheel of deeply questionable aesthetic merit implanted in its side. Constructed under the Saakashvili government to be a technological university, it was sold off by his successors to be a Le Meridien hotel.

Alphabet Tower
TOWER

(Batumis bulvari; adult/child 10/2 GEL; ☉10.30am–midnight) This 145m-high monument to Georgian script and culture stands near the northeast tip of Batumis bulvari and can be climbed for stellar views.

Evropas Moedani
SQUARE

(🚹) Broad Europe Sq is surrounded by beautiful belle-époque buildings – renovated survivors from Batumi's original heyday, plus new buildings in a similar style. The square's musical fountains are a magnet for kids on hot summer evenings.

Medea Monument
MONUMENT

Towering over Evropas moedani is this striking portrayal of Medea, the local princess who would help her future husband Jason obtain the Golden Fleece. A monument to 'the person who brought Georgia closer to Europe', according to Batumi's mayor when it was unveiled in 2007, it was sculpted by Davit Khmaladze, and controversially cost over one million GEL.

Ortajame Mosque
MOSQUE

(Chkalov 6) Batumi's only surviving mosque, built in the 1860s, is finely painted in pinks, greens and blues, with Quranic calligraphy on the walls – but is no longer big enough to accommodate the faithful who overflow on to the streets during Friday prayers. Batumi's Muslims have been seeking permission to build a second mosque for years, but it has still not been granted, largely due to objections from the Georgian Orthodox Church.

Adjara Arts Museum
MUSEUM

(Gorgiladze 8; 3 GEL; ☉10am-6pm) Well displayed and well lit in an attractive neoclassical Soviet building, the small permanent collection upstairs covers Georgian art from the late 19th and 20th century. Downstairs you'll find temporary exhibits of local painters.

GEORGIA BATUMI

Batumi

WORTH A TRIP

GONIO APSAROS FORTRESS

Gonio's atmospheric and superbly preserved **fortress** (adult/student 3/1 GEL, audio guide 5 GEL; ⊘ 10am-6pm Jun-Sep, 11am-5pm Oct-May), 11km south of Batumi, is an impressive piece of Roman-Byzantine military architecture covering 47,000 sq metres within a rectangle of high stone walls with 18 towers. Built by the Romans in the 1st century AD, it was occupied by the Byzantines in the 6th century and by the Ottomans in the 16th century. An interesting museum sits in the middle of the site with a cross outside marking what's believed to be the grave of the Apostle Matthias.

Any bus to the Turkish border at Sarpi will be able to drop you here, or alternatively a taxi should be 40 GEL for a return trip with waiting time. There are also some good beaches nearby, making this a great escape from the crowds in Batumi.

🎊 Festivals & Events

Black Sea Jazz Festival   MUSIC
(http://blackseajazz.ge; ⊘ late Jul) Brings international stars and lots of music lovers to Batumi for several days in late July.

🛏 Sleeping

There's a large and growing range of accommodation in Batumi, from dozens of charismatic hostels and guesthouses to five-star luxury hotels along the seafront. Booking ahead is essential in the height of summer.

★ Back2Me Hostel   HOSTEL $
(☑ 422-223302; www.back2me.ge; Otar Chiladze 4; dm/q 45/150 GEL; ❄ 🛜) Brand new in mid-2019, this fabulously contemporary conversion of an Old Town building now houses Batumi's most stylish boutique hostel. Each of the five dorms (including two female-only ones) have eight high-quality wooden bunks and share plentiful showers and toilets, while the two en-suite family rooms, each of which have a bunk bed and a double, are a steal.

There's a fully equipped kitchen for guests to use, as well as a social area you have to climb up a ladder to reach. Best of all, staff are super-friendly and you're in the heart of the Old Town.

Surf Hostel   HOSTEL $
(☑ 422-223303; www.ba2me.ge; Melashvili 33/35; dm 35 GEL, s/d/tr 105/107/110 GEL; ❄ 🛜) From the folks who brought you Back2Me Hostel, Surf Hostel is an excellent addition to the hostel scene, with a brand-new and beautifully renovated ground-floor courtyard space with a private back garden, brightly painted dorms each with their own lockers, and a private triple with its own bathroom. There's a small but well-equipped kitchen and a washing machine.

Boutique Hotel & Hostel Medusa   BOUTIQUE HOTEL $
(☑ 422-275635; medusabatumi@gmail.com; Saitnova 4; dm 35 GEL, s/d/tr/q from 125/131/182/202 GEL; ❄ 🛜) A rather odd combination perhaps – hostel and boutique hotel rolled into one – Medusa nevertheless gets it right with an excellent location, spotless dorms (one female, one male) and four private rooms, including a huge luxe with a full kitchen. Breakfast is available for an extra 10 GEL in the downstairs restaurant.

Hostel Batumi Globus   HOSTEL $
(☑ 422-276721, 593-596096; www.hostelbatumi-globus.com; Mazniashvili 54; dm from 15 GEL, d 100 GEL; ❄ 🛜) A largish hostel with a warm welcome, a good kitchen, pleasant if basic dorms (including one for women only) and four private rooms with pallet beds. The big plus is the spacious, sociable courtyard out the back with a barbeque. Free laundry service is also available.

Gulnasi's Guesthouse   GUESTHOUSE $
(☑ 599-797224, 557-965859; homestay@mail.ru; Lermontov 24a; d/tr 60/80 GEL, without bathroom 40/60 GEL; ❄ 🛜) Gulnasi Mikeladze and her welcoming family run what's effectively a great-value budget hotel. The 18 rooms, on three floors, are spotless, spacious and fully renovated in 2019. There's free tea, coffee and wine tasting, a big guest kitchen and generous breakfasts for 10 GEL. They also offer free pick-ups anywhere in Batumi on arrival. Gulnasi's daughter speaks good English and the family also offers day trips into rural Adjara (100 GEL for up to four people, including picnic).

My Warm Guest House   GUESTHOUSE $
(☑ 558-176418; mywarmhouse@mail.ru; Melashvili 2; d 50-100 GEL; ❄ 🛜) Hidden away in a residential building, this welcoming, spotlessly clean guesthouse in the Old Town is a little tricky to find, but has eight good-

sized rooms (three share bathrooms) sporting original touches such as coloured-glass wash basins. Some have balconies or their own kitchen and a washing machine. Prices plummet in winter.

Light House Hotel HOTEL $$
(☑ 555-155558, 422-278218; dimaadamia868@gmail.com; Kazbegi 4; s 120 GEL, d 130-180 GEL, all incl breakfast; ❈ 🖲) A stylish hotel on a quiet street, the Light House has 15 rooms in eye-catching, modish styles and colours, making it a comfortable and friendly place to stay. Some rooms have balconies, while the junior suites have a mezzanine.

Piazza Boutique Hotel BOUTIQUE HOTEL $$$
(☑ 591-005615; www.piazza.ge; Parnavaz Mepe 25; s/d incl breakfast from 235/260 GEL; ❈ 🖲) For a treat, check into this hotel with 16 luxurious-themed rooms (from shabby chic to art deco and English) in a 13-storey clock tower over a lively square with cafes, restaurants and nightly live music in summer (the hotel has soundproofing).

🍴 Eating

Batumi has a generally good food scene, although there's little that really stands out here, despite plenty of choice. The seafront is full of lively cafes and restaurants that open in the summer only, although their quality is often patchy.

Kafe Literaturuli CAFE $
(☑ 422-272013; K Gamsakhurdia 18; cakes 3-10 GEL; ⊙ 10am-midnight; 🖲) The Literary Cafe is a great stop for hot drinks and indulgent cakes and pastries, with a mildly artsy ambience.

★**Guests** EUROPEAN $$
(☑ 577-614955; Melashvili 16/5; mains 5-15 GEL; ⊙ 3pm-midnight Mon-Sat) Owner Alexander decamped to Batumi from his native St Petersburg for the climate, and in doing so has gifted this rather charmingly bohemian place to the local populace. Meals are simple and hearty (the chicken pelmeni are wonderful) and the wine pours freely as friends drop by to play impromptu concerts, read poetry or just hang out.

★**Grill Town** GEORGIAN $$
(Rustaveli 26-28; mains 8-35 GEL; ⊙ 10am-1am; 🖲🌿) This big, buzzing, contemporary place, with large windows and a terrace facing the park over the street, is hugely popular with just about everybody. It serves

very nicely done *mtsvadi, khachapuri, khinkali,* sausages, chicken dishes and other Georgian classics.

★**Old Boulevard** GEORGIAN, EUROPEAN $$
(☑ 577-242006; Ninoshvili 23a; mains 10-45 GEL; ⊙ 9am-midnight or later; 🖲) The Old Boulevard has a refined atmosphere with deep sofas, floor-to-ceiling shelves of sculpture, and live classical guitar and piano in the evening. It cooks up great grills, seafood, Georgian classics and the odd international dish, such as fried duck fillet in berry sauce, king prawns in garlic or foie gras. There's also an excellent wine list.

Uncle Feng's CHINESE $$
(☑ 557-779112; Zhordania 3; mains 10-20 GEL; ⊙ 2-11pm Sun-Fri; 🖲) A welcome break from Georgian standards can be had at this straightforward and friendly noodle bar with a large menu that runs from *kung pao* chicken to boiled dumplings, buckwheat noodles and fried aubergine with garlic and pork.

Uolli GEORGIAN $$
(☑ 593-059955; Memed Abashidze 43; mains 12-30 GEL; ⊙ 9am-2am; 🖲🌿) With its stylish bar, lovely staff, plant-filled backyard hung with fairy lights and various attractive dining areas, Uolli is a notable addition to Batumi's eating scene. What's more, on the menu you'll find plenty of vegetarian choices and a wide range of nontypical Georgian dishes, such as mussels cooked in a number of different ways.

Fanfan GEORGIAN $$
(Ninoshvili 27; mains 15-30 GEL; ⊙ 10am-midnight; 🖲🍽) Shabby chic in decor and favoured by cool, arty folk (though not exclusive to them), Fanfan also prepares delicious food – especially the seafood and the lemon tart. In case you're travelling with your dog or cat, you'll be glad to know there's a menu section for them too.

La Brioche INTERNATIONAL $$
(Parnavaz Mepe 25; mains 10-25 GEL; ⊙ 9am-2am; 🖲) One of several cafes and restaurants around the Italian-style La Piazza, Brioche is a particularly choice spot for breakfast, pancakes, desserts and good coffee. It also has a library-style cafe in the adjoining tower.

Cafe Retro GEORGIAN $$
(☑ 599-511722; Takaishvili 10; khachapuri 6-15 GEL; ⊙ 9am-11pm; 🖲) There's no better place to decide whether you like *khachapuri Acharuli,* Adjara's large boat-shaped variety of

INLAND ADJARA

Mountainous inland Adjara is a different world from the coast. The heartland of Adjaran tradition, it's a region of beautiful old arched stone bridges, waterfalls, remnants of ruined castles, and wooden village houses clinging to steep slopes with the minarets of small mosques rising above them. The majority of Adjara's Muslims live here, principally in the Khulo district. A road runs 80km from Batumi up to the small town of Khulo, then continues unpaved for 50km (rough in parts) over the 2025m-high Goderdzi Pass (snowbound from about November to March) to Zarzma in Samtskhe-Javakheti, from where it's 30km (paved) on to Akhaltsikhe. This is a lovely drive, and a more scenic (and far slower) alternative than taking the main highway between Batumi and Tbilisi.

Sights & Activities

You'll get the most out of the region with your own 4WD vehicle, enabling you to get off the main road and up to the picturesque, remote villages. Along the main road there are typically lovely stone bridges at Makhuntseti and Dandalo. At Khulo a tiny podlike **cable car** (return trip 5 GEL; ⊙8am-8pm) of indeterminate Soviet vintage swings you across the yawning valley to the village of Tago high on the opposite slope. It's a spectacular ride that should be undertaken only by those not easily spooked by ancient machinery.

One spectacular and remote destination worth journeying to is the ruined 13th-century **Khikhani Fortress** (Bako) on a 2200m hilltop 33km southeast from Zamleti, which is on the main road 8km west of Khulo. The last kilometre to the fortress is a steep uphill walk.

A good time to visit is the first weekend of August, for the Shuamtoba festival at Beshumi, a few kilometres south of the Goderdzi Pass. This classic Georgian mountain festival features horse racing, folk music, fire jumping and wrestling, and also happens to be a favourite occasion for couples to get married!

Sleeping & Eating

Khulo has several small hotels of which the most appealing is **Hotel Toma** (☑595-582378; d/tr 50/75 GEL; ☑☎). You'll get more of a feel for local life in a village guesthouse, of which there are a couple in Kedlebi, about 5km northwest of Khulo, and several in Nigazeuli, 10km west along the main road then about 6km up to the north. They charge around 50 GEL per person with three meals.

Information

Batumi's Tourism Information Centres (p97) have information on inland Adjara, including its guesthouses, and good maps of walking or driving routes. Khulo's **Tourism Information Centre** (☑577-909015; ⊙10am-6pm) also has maps.

Getting There & Away

Marshrutky run every 20 or 30 minutes from Batumi's Old Bus Station to Khulo (5 GEL, two hours) and back, the last one leaving Khulo about 6pm (5pm in winter). From about April to October, a *marshrutka* departs Khulo for Akhaltsikhe (15 GEL, 3½ hours) at 10am.

Georgia's national fast food with a lightly fried egg on top, than this local institution widely considered to make the best in town. It even serves mini-*khachapuri* for those not entirely sold on the delicacy!

🍷 Drinking & Nightlife

During summer Batumi Boulevard (p91) is the party capital of Georgia, with an annually changing assortment of beachside clubs and bars where thousands of people party till dawn each night. The clubs start to fill from 11pm, with admission typically from 10 GEL for women and 20 GEL for men.

Sector 26　　　　　　　　　CLUB
(www.facebook.com/batumisector26; Batumis bulvari) A top venue on the Batumi summer club circuit and a beachside lounge with a pool during the day, Sector 26 can get super crowded when big DJs are in town.

Vinyl Bar　　　　　　　　　BAR
(Dumbadze 12; ⊙1.30pm-2am) A much-needed touch of alterno indie stylings in brash Batumi can be found at this intimate bar hid-

ing in plain sight just a few steps from the main square. There's quality beer on tap and plenty of vinyl displayed for the low-key and cool muso crowd.

Garage Artisan Wine & Cheese WINE BAR
(☑599-776035; Mazniashvili 8; ⊘1pm-2am) Run by a friendly and knowledgeable team of English-speaking oenophiles, this bar is a great spot to try Georgian natural wines and some excellent locally produced cheeses. On summer evenings the crowd spills out onto the pavement creating a magical atmosphere.

Iveria Beach CLUB
(☑422-299991; www.facebook.com/iveriabeach; Batumis bulvari; ⊘7am-3am) Stalwart of the Batumi beach–club scene going strong since 2013, Iveria Beach serves as a pleasant lounge bar during the day and becomes progressively busier from sundown, culminating in dancing until the early hours.

❶ Information

Tourism Information Centre (☑577-909091; www.gobatumi.com) The well-informed and helpful branches on **Batumis bulvari** (☑577-909091; Ninoshvili 2; ⊘9am-9pm Jul-Sep, to 7pm Oct-Jun) and beside the **cable-car station** (☑422-294410; Gogebashvili; ⊘24hr) do their best to answer any local queries about Batumi and the rest of Adjara.

❶ Getting There & Away

AIR
Batumi International Airport (☑422-235100; www.batumiairport.com), 5km south of town, has flights to/from Baku, İstanbul, Kiev, Minsk, Odessa, Riyadh, Tbilisi, Tel Aviv and Yerevan. Bus 10 (0.80 GEL) runs to/from Rustavelis qucha in central Batumi. Taxis into town are normally 20 GEL.

LAND
Bus, Marshrutka & Taxi

Taxis to or from the Turkish border at Sarpi, 17km south of Batumi, should cost 20 GEL. Bus 16 (0.80 GEL) and *marshrutka* 142 (1 GEL) run between the border and Batumi's **Old bus station** (☑422-278547; Maiakovski 1), via Chavchavadzis qucha. The border is open 24 hours a day.

Going from Batumi into Turkey, there are bus services crossing the border from **Metro bus station** (Batumi International & Intercity bus station; ☑422-242244; Gogoli 1), but you will often save time without adding expense by taking local transport to the border, crossing it on foot, then catching a waiting Turkish minivan to Hopa, about 20km south, where there are frequent departures to many points around Turkey.

Train
Batumi Central station (☑enquiries 1331) is about 4km northeast of the city centre on the coast road. *Marshrutky* 20 and 28 run there, heading northeast on Chavchavadzis qucha. It's best to book ahead for trains (essential in summer): you can buy tickets in town at **Adjara Tour** (☑422-228778; www.adjaratour.com; Chavchavadze 48; ⊘9.30am-7pm Mon-Fri, to 6pm Sat & Sun).

To Tbilisi (2nd/1st class 24/60 GEL, 5½ to 6½ hours) there are two day trains, and a night train departing at 12.45am every two days, plus an extra day train from about mid-June to September. You'll need to change in Tbilisi to reach Yerevan or Baku. There is also a service to Kutaisi (2 GEL, four hours) leaving Batumi at 8.15am daily.

BUSES, MARSHRUTKY & MINIVANS FROM BATUMI

DESTINATION	BUS STATION	COST (GEL)	TIME (HR)	DAILY FREQUENCY
Akhaltsikhe	Old	20	6	2 (8.30am & 10.30am, both continue to Borjomi)
İstanbul	Metro	75	22	5.30pm daily
Kutaisi	Old	10	2	hourly *marshrutky*, 7am-2am
Mestia	TIC	30	6	3pm daily Jun-Sep
Rize, Turkey	Old & Metro	15-30	4	Various departures from both bus stations throughout the day.
Tbilisi	Metro	30	6	9 Metro Georgia buses
Tbilisi	Old	25	6	hourly *marshrutky*, 8am-10pm
Trabzon, Turkey	Metro	30	4	minivans 8.30am & hourly 10am-6pm
Trabzon, Turkey	Old	20	4	7 buses, 11am-1am
Yerevan, Armenia	Old	60	10	5.30pm daily
Zugdidi	Metro	15	3	11am & 3pm daily Jun-Sep only

SEA

Weather and politics permitting, a hydrofoil operated by **Express Batumi** (📞 Batumi 593-333966, Sochi 7-918-409-12-96; Baku 3; adult/under 12yr 270/135 GEL; 🚢) departs between early June and late September for the Russian port of Sochi (270 GEL, five hours) at 11am Monday, returning from Sochi the same time on Tuesday and arriving in Batumi at 4pm. In peak seasons a second weekly sailing is sometimes added. In most cases, a Russian visa is needed to do this trip.

GREAT CAUCASUS

A trip into the Great Caucasus along Georgia's northern border is a must for anyone who wants to experience the best of the country. Spectacular mountain scenery, wonderful walks and picturesque old villages with strange defensive towers are all part of a trip to the southern side of Europe's highest mountain range.

Georgia's very identity hinges on this mighty range that rises in Abkhazia, runs the length of Georgia's border with Russia and continues into Azerbaijan. The most accessible destination is Stepantsminda (also known as Kazbegi), reached by the dramatic Georgian Military Hwy from Tbilisi, but other areas are more than worth the effort to travel to – including enigmatic, mysterious Svaneti and beautiful, pristine Tusheti.

Georgian Military Highway

This ancient passage across the mountains towards Vladikavkaz in Russia provides the quickest and most scenic access from Tbilisi to the Great Caucasus, leading from the capital along the Zhinvali Reservoir, past the Ananuri Fortress to the ski resort of Gudauri and over the 2379m Jvari Pass down into the Tergi valley. The road then continues to the town of Stepantsminda, unofficial capital of the spectacular Kazbegi Area, and a superb base for walking, climbing and birdwatching.

Ananuri

This **fortress** (🕙 9am–8pm) FREE 66km north of Tbilisi is a classic example of Georgian architecture, enhanced by its superb location overlooking the Zhinvali Reservoir. The fortress historically belonged to the *eristavis* of Aragvi, who ruled as far as the Tergi valley from the 13th to 18th centuries, and is today a (very) popular stop on the Georgian Military Hwy. Within the fortress are two 17th-century churches, the larger of which, the Assumption Church, is covered with wonderful stone carvings on its exterior walls, including a large cross on each and various ancient scripts from all over the region, some of which have now totally disappeared. Inside the Assumption Church are a few vivid 17th- and 18th-century frescoes, including a Last Judgement on the south wall, although much of the church is bare due to a 19th-century fire. You can climb the tallest of the fortress towers for fine views, as well as walk along the battlements: it was here that the last defenders were killed in 1739 when a rival duke set fire to Ananuri and murdered the Aragvi *eristavi's* family.

Gudauri

POP 2000 / ELEV 2196M

Georgia's most popular ski resort, Gudauri is the highest town on the Georgian Military Hwy and at present a rather scruffy place undergoing a massive construction boom. Its recently improved and expanded facilities are highly rated by foreigners who come here for cheap skiing, though the town itself is far from charming: a long meandering road without any obvious centre or much planning.

Normally the ski season lasts from shortly before Christmas to April, with the best snow in January and February.

💿 Sights

Soviet-Georgian Friendship Monument VIEWPOINT
(Georgian Military Hwy) This highly unusual concrete monument a short distance from the main Georgian Military Hwy and some 4km north of Gudauri is also known as the Gudauri View Point. While relations been Georgia and its northern neighbour may have soured since its construction in 1983, it remains worth wandering down to for its fabulous tiled murals and amazing valley views.

🏃 Activities

Gudauri Ski Resort SKIING
(www.gudauri.ski) The bare hillsides here make for excellent skiing and snowboarding. With recently improved and expanded facilities, this is Georgia's best and most

Georgian Military Highway

0   20 km
0   10 miles

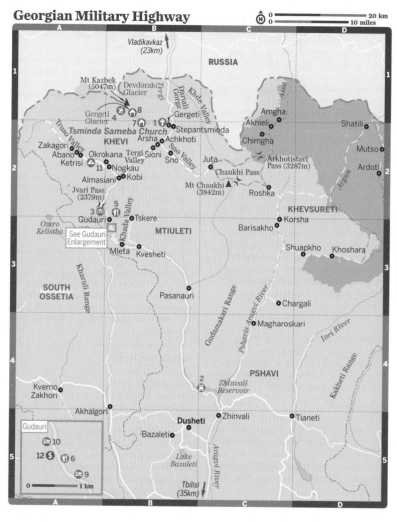

Georgian Military Highway

THE TRANSCAUCASIAN TRAIL

It sounds an improbable dream: a way-marked walking trail running the whole 700km length of the Caucasus, from the Black Sea to the Caspian Sea. But it's a dream that is taking steps towards reality with a bold project, initiated by two former US Peace Corps volunteers in Georgia, to establish the Transcaucasian Trail (www.transcaucasiantrail.org).

This is a long-term project to map, mark and, where necessary build, the trail; provide maps and guides for hikers; bring sustainable tourism to remote regions; raise the profile of protected areas; and promote connections between communities along the way.

The first steps were taken in 2015 with the mapping of the route across Svaneti and from the Kazbegi region to Tusheti. Since then they've been busy building trails in both Georgia and Armenia, while initial work on trails in Azerbaijan is due to start in 2020.

popular ski station, and is highly rated by many foreign visitors too. The 57km of pistes (black, red, blue and green) are served by five chairlifts, rising from 1990m to 3285m, and one cable car.

Fly Caucasus　　　　　　　　PARAGLIDING
(☑ 568-114453; www.flycaucasus.com; flight 10/25min €279/379) The mountainous scenery around Gudauri is a paraglider's dream and you can do tandem flights year-round with this experienced English-speaking, Ukrainian-run outfit based at the Happy Yeti Hostel.

Heliksir　　　　　　　　　　　　　SKIING
(☑ 595-404606; https://heliski.travel; ☉ Jan-Mar) This highly reputed Georgian-French company offers heliskiing and ski touring at Gudauri, based at the Hotel Gudauri Marco Polo on Gudauri Hotel Lane.

🛏 Sleeping

Gudauri has a vast number of hotels, aparthotels and hostels, plus rental apartments. Most can help with ski rental and instruction, and transfers from Tbilisi.

★ Happy Yeti Hostel　　　　HOSTEL **$$**
(☑ 571-268800; www.happyyetihostel.com; Qumlistsikhe 77; dm/d incl breakfast & dinner 25/80

GEL; ℗ 🛜) Ukrainian- and Polish-run and dedicated to everybody having a good time, the Yeti revolves happily around its sociable bar-restaurant. It's 500m back down the road towards Tbilisi from the Smart supermarket, and frustratingly not signed at all. However, once you find it you'll be in one of the best-value and most enjoyable places in town. Prices drop in summer.

Hotel Gudauri Hut　　　　　　HOTEL **$$**
(☑ 595-939911; www.gudaurihut.com; s/d incl breakfast from 180/240 GEL; ℗ 🛜) A friendly, medium-sized hotel a short distance up the road from the resort centre, Gudauri Hut offers pleasant, clean, yellow-painted rooms with good views, plus three bars, a restaurant and a sauna.

❶ Getting There & Away

Public *marshrutky* from Tbilisi to Stepantsminda will drop you in Gudauri (10 GEL, two hours) but you may have trouble finding one with free seats going down to Tbilisi. The central point of Gudauri is marked by the roadside **Smart supermarket** (☉ 24hr), which has an ATM, and this is where buses and taxis stop when passing through town.

Stepantsminda

☑ 345 / POP 2500 / ELEV 1750M

This is most people's destination on the Georgian Military Hwy: a valley town with the famous hilltop silhouette of Tsminda Sameba Church and the towering snowy cone of Mt Kazbek looking down from the west. Now officially named Stepantsminda, but still commonly known as Kazbegi, it's a base for some wonderful walking and mountain biking. What 20 years ago was just a big village has now grown into a sprawling town, with guesthouses and hotels everywhere and tourists arriving by the busload in the summer months. While this may not have added to Stepantsminda's charm, the town's location remains absolutely stunning and it's still very easy to escape the crowds and explore the surrounding mountains and valleys in peace.

◎ Sights

★ Tsminda Sameba Church　　　CHURCH
(Holy Trinity Church; Gergeti) This 14th-century church 2200m above Stepantsminda has become almost a symbol of Georgia for its incomparably photogenic hilltop setting with mighty Mt Kazbek rising behind it,

and for the fierce determination involved in building it on such a lofty, isolated perch. A circuitous new road leads up to the church (return trip by taxi 40 GEL to 60 GEL), but you can walk up to the church in one to 1½ hours from Stepantsminda. The views back over Stepantsminda are incredible.

Vakhushti Batonishvili wrote in the 18th century that in times of danger the treasures from Mtskheta, as well as St Nino's cross, were kept at Tsminda Sameba for safety. In 1988 the Soviet authorities constructed a cable-car line to the church, with one station right next to Tsminda Sameba. The people of Stepantsminda felt it defiled their sacred place and soon destroyed it.

The beautifully weathered stone church is decorated with intriguing carvings, one on the bell tower appearing to show two dinosaurs.

There are several ways of walking up from Stepantsminda. For the best distance-gradient compromise, walk up through Gergeti village to a T-junction 1.25km from the main road (80m after signs indicating the car track to the right). Go left at the T-junction, out past the last village buildings, and up beside a stream. About 120m past the last building, fork up to the right, passing to the right of a ruined stone tower; 200m after the tower take an initially lesser path diverging up to the right. This curves up round the hillside to reach the church in 1km. The new road has meant that the church is crowded these days with tour buses arriving with regularity. Come early or after 5pm to enjoy the church at its quietest.

🏃 Activities

There are many wonderful walks and riding routes in the valleys and mountains around Stepantsminda. The walking and climbing season is from May or June to October or November, depending on the weather. If you plan to come early or late in the season, call the Kazbegi National Park Visitor Centre (p103) first and check for updates on snow in the region.

★ Mountain Freaks HIKING
(📞 593-583596; www.mountainfreaks.ge; Kazbegi 44; ⊙9am-7pm Apr-Oct) The young, passionate and professional team behind Mountain Freaks have breathed some much-needed competition into the local tourism market and offer an enviable range of services that stretch from full-on Mt Kazbek and Elbrus expeditions to equipment hire, daily buses

to three important local hiking destinations and even skiing during the winter months, when they work out of Gudauri.

Mountain Travel Agency ADVENTURE SPORTS
(📞 599-269291; www.mtainfogeo.com; Kazbegi 29; ⊙May-Nov) A one-stop shop for your mountaineering and camping needs, MTA rents mountain bikes (25 GEL per day) and equipment, including crampons, ice axes and harnesses (each 10 GEL per day), climbing ropes (20 GEL), three-person tents (20 GEL), sleeping bags (10 GEL) and mats (6 GEL), and it sells cooking gas and trekking maps.

It also arranges mountain guides, including English speakers – from €580 per person for a Mt Kazbek ascent – plus packhorses, transport and accommodation bookings.

Gergeti Glacier Hike HIKING
If you're up for another 1000m of ascent after climbing to the famous Tsminda Sameba Church above Stepantsminda, this walk

Stepantsminda

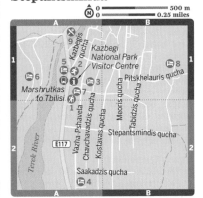

Stepantsminda

rewards with spectacular views, especially of Mt Kazbek. The path heads straight up the ridge behind the church. Allow up to eight hours from the church to the glacier and down again.

🛏 Sleeping

Stepantsminda is very well supplied with long-running guesthouses, all providing meals, as well as dozens of hotels that have opened to cater for the large number of week-enders coming up from Tbilisi and seeking some creature comforts in the mountains.

HQ of Nove Sujashvili HOSTEL $
(☑599-376339, 595-177079; Khevisberi 27, Kvemo Gergeti; dm 17-22 GEL, breakfast/dinner 10/20 GEL; 🛜) A friendly, English-speaking brother-and-sister team run this popular little hostel, 250m along the second street on the left as you walk up the Gergeti road. The two dorms each have their own bathroom, and the centre of the house is a darling dining room with stone walls, wooden furniture and lots of light.

★ Anano Guesthouse GUESTHOUSE $$
(☑595-099449; ananoqushashvili@yahoo.com; Vazha Pshavela 7; d/q 70/80 GEL, s/d 60/70 GEL, breakfast per person 15 GEL; 🛜) Six bright, spic-and-span rooms with polished pine floors, good breakfasts and helpful English-speaking owners add up to one of Stepants-minda's best guesthouses. From Kazbegis moedani take the uphill street passing Nunu's Guesthouse, turn left at the top and take the entry to the right after 30m.

Diana's Guesthouse GUESTHOUSE $$
(☑599-570313; Vazha Pshavela 90; per person with/without breakfast 60/50 GEL; P🛜) Terrific meals, a welcoming hostess and bright, clean rooms (some with private bathroom) in modern buildings make this one of the best picks. From Kazbegis moedani take the uphill street passing Nunu's Guesthouse, then go 750m to the right. It's on the left at the end of the street.

Nunu's Guesthouse GUESTHOUSE $$
(☑599-570915, 591-963335; gvanci9191@gmail.com; Kazbegis shesakhvevi 1; s/d/tr 25/50/75 GEL, breakfast/dinner 15/20 GEL; 🛜) A good option just 50m along the uphill street from the *marshrutka* stand, with a friendly hostess, good meals and lovely mountain views from the balcony. Daughter Gvantsa speaks good English and works at the Kazbegi National Park Visitor Centre. It has vehicles for outings.

★ Rooms Hotel DESIGN HOTEL $$$
(☑32-2710099; www.roomshotels.com; Gorgasali 1; s/d incl breakfast from €162/178; P🛜☒) Rooms is a massive, inspired conversion of a former Soviet sanatorium. The once-spartan building is now clad almost entirely in appealing dark wood and makes brilliant use of its elevated position looking across the valley, with a vast terrace that is packed in the late afternoon with well-heeled visitors enjoying sundowners with perfect views of Mt Kazbek and Stepantsminda Church.

Hotel Stancia Kazbegi HOTEL $$$
(☑551-948800; stanciakazbegi@gmail.com; Kazbegis moedani 25; s/d/ste/f incl breakfast 240/265/340/425 GEL; 🛜) This stylish new addition to Stepantsminda's accommodation scene is right on Kazbegis moedani and has some great views of Mt Kazbek from its rooms at the back. Rooms are design conscious, in muted greys with wooden floorboards and large balconies, while staff are charming and the downstairs bar-restaurant-terrace combination is a cosy winner.

🍴 Eating

Stepantsminda's restaurants have not caught up with its diverse hotels, and there's little of note in town. That said, you'll eat perfectly well here, especially if you're in a guesthouse or staying at the excellent Rooms Hotel. Otherwise most choices boil down to a handful of cafes around Kazbegis moedani.

Cozy Corner GEORGIAN $$
(☑593-787745; Georgian Military Hwy; mains 8.50-25 GEL; ☉10am-10pm; 🛜🍴) Based around a large enclosed garden by the river, Cozy Corner is just that, with an exceptionally cosy wooden-chalet interior that hums with hungry diners throughout the day. Don't be put off by the karaoke sign, as this only happens after 10pm once the kitchen is closed, and only then if there's demand.

★ Rooms Hotel Restaurant EUROPEAN $$$
(☑32-2710099; www.roomshotels.com; mains 12-45 GEL; ☉8am-midnight; 🛜🍴) 🖋 Hands down the best restaurant in town, the vast lounge bar of Rooms Hotel prepares gourmet Georgian, European and fusion dishes – the likes of local trout with walnut pesto, free-range chicken with Dijon sauce and spinach, couscous and pasta dishes, perfectly done *mtsvadi* and a load of other enticing concoctions, all with an emphasis on sustainably grown local ingredients.

MT KAZBEK

This 5047m extinct volcano (also called Mkinvartsveri or Mt Kazbegi), towering west of Stepantsminda, has much folk history. The Greek Prometheus was supposedly chained up here for stealing fire from the gods, as was the Georgian Amirani, for challenging God's omnipotence. The Betlemi (Bethlehem) cave, 4000m above sea level, was believed to be the abode of many very sacred objects – Christ's manger, Abraham's tent and a dove-rocked golden cradle whose sight would blind a human being. There were taboos against hunting on the mountain and climbing it. Not surprisingly, the first to conquer Kazbek's peak were foreigners: Freshfield, Tucker and Moore of the London Alpine Club in 1868.

Today many thousands of people attempt to reach Kazbek's summit each year (it's especially popular with Poles), but this is a serious mountaineering challenge that requires fitness and acclimatisation to altitude: perhaps half of those who try do not reach the top. Unless you're suitably experienced, it's highly advisable to take a guide, which you can organise through agencies in Tbilisi or locally, including Mountain Freaks (p101) and Mountain Travel Agency (p101). Climbers should register at the Emergency Management Department building at the bottom of the Gergeti road, on their way up to the mountain.

The ascent is technically straightforward, though there is some danger in crevasses. It takes three or four days from Stepantsminda, with the first day hiking up from Stepantsminda and over the Gergeti Glacier to the **Bethlemi Hut** (Betlemi Meteo Station; ☑ 32-2143939, 32-2922553; www.facebook.com/bethlemihut; dm 50 GEL, camping per tent 18 GEL; ⊗ May-Nov), a former weather station at 3650m altitude where you can sleep.

The second day is usually spent acclimatising, often with a climb to the Maili Plateau (4500m). On day three you start for the summit from Bethlemi Hut around 2am. The ascent takes up to six hours, with the final 150m involving about three rope lengths of 35° to 40° ice. The descent to Bethlemi Hut for the third night takes up to another six hours.

Packhorses can reach the Bethlemi Hut from about July to mid-September. One alternative is to sleep at the much more comfortable and far pricier **AltiHut 3.14** (☑ 595-578282; www.altihut.ge; Sabertse; dm incl breakfast 300 GEL) ✐.

ℹ Information

Kazbegi National Park Visitor Centre
(Tourist Information Centre; ☑ 591-963335; www.nationalparks.ge; Kazbegis shesakhvevi 1; ⊗ 10am-6pm; 🕾) This modern tourist office is a sleek space with well-informed English-speaking staff, lots of maps and other useful information available to help plan your time in the area. Staff can organise guides for the national park, provide bus timetables and arrange taxis for day trips.

ℹ Getting There & Away

Marshrutky to Tbilisi (Kazbegis moedani; 10 GEL, 2½ hours) are timetabled hourly from 7am to noon and at 1.30pm, 2pm, 3.30pm, 5pm and 6pm. A taxi to/from Tbilisi can cost anywhere from 100 GEL to 150 GEL. Taxis waiting at the north end of the Tergi bridge often ask lower fares than those on Kazbegis moedani. Shared taxis usually charge 15 GEL per seat to Tbilisi's Didube bus station (p71).

Vladikavkaz (Russia) is 45km north through the Dariali Gorge. To go through the **Larsi border point** (Verkhny Lars; ⊗ 24hr Jun-Sep, 7am-7pm Oct-May), 15km from Stepantsminda, you must be in a vehicle, or at least on a bicycle – no pedestrians. Taxis from Stepantsminda to Vladikavkaz cost around 100 GEL. Driving time is under an hour, but the border itself can take anywhere from 20 minutes to a few hours depending on traffic and how slow/fast the Russians are processing people.

Sno Valley

The Sno Valley runs southeast off the Georgian Military Hwy from Achkhoti, 4km south of Stepantsminda. The road ends in the dramatically sited village, however, with the only way to continue into the mountains on foot or on horseback.

◉ Sights

Juta   VILLAGE
The small village of Juta (2150m), an outpost of the Khevsur people from over the mountains to the east, is about 15km along the mostly unpaved Sno Valley road and a starting point for some great hikes. A taxi from

continued on p106

HIKING IN THE GREAT CAUCASUS

TRUSO VALLEY

START OKROKANA
END ZAKAGORI FORTRESS
LENGTH 22KM; FIVE HOURS
DIFFICULTY EASY TO MODERATE

Majestic views and a number of interesting sights in the Truso valley await you on this gorgeous day hike, including snow-capped mountains on all sides, mineral springs, melting glaciers and abandoned villages. The hike can only be done from early May to late September, but in May and September before heading out you should check with the Kazbegi National Park Visitor Centre (p103) in Stepantsminda that the roads are open. You'll need good hiking shoes, waterproofs, high-factor sunscreen and a water bottle, though a small one is fine, as there are plenty of clean mountain streams where you can refill your bottle. Bringing a packed lunch is also a good idea, though there are a couple of places serving snacks and drinks towards the end of the hike.

While the walk is a significant distance, the elevation climb is only 600m in total, and for the most part you'll be walking along the valley floor. To get to Okrokana you can either take a taxi or one of the daily buses laid on by Mountain Freaks (p101) or Mountain Travel Agency (p101) in Stepantsminda, though these should normally be booked several days in advance. You can also easily drive here yourself, though once you turn off the main road at the village of Kobi, the road to the village of Okrokana is unsurfaced and can be tough going after heavy rain.

From the village of **Okrokana**, cross the bridge to begin the hike. Head left up the hillside and follow the unsurfaced road along the river. The river curves around to the left with extraordinary rocky cliffs on the opposite side; you'll then cross a bridge over a stream before crossing over the river itself, after which the **Truso valley** widens and im-

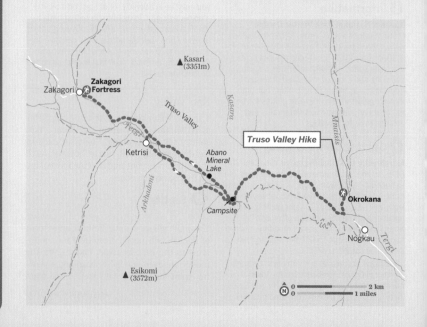

This hike is one of the Kazbegi region's most accessible and enjoyable, taking you from the semi-abandoned village of Okrokana along the fast-flowing Tergi River to the sulphurous Truso valley.

pressive snow-capped peaks come into view on all sides.

When you reach the small footbridge crossing the river to a small **campsite** (☑ 598-090801; tent/mattress in a hut per person 10/30 GEL; ⊘ 1 Jun-30 Sep), cross that and continue up the side of the hill (the campsite has built a helpful staircase made from disused tyres) and walk along the ridge before descending to the famous **Abano Mineral Lake**, something of a misnomer for what is a large pond at best, but it's a gorgeous geological wonder, where carbon dioxide bubbles gently rise from the depths and the clear, lifeless water flows down into the river below.

Continue along this side of the river (you may find yourself having to navigate your way through some bogs and lots of curious cows early in summer) until you reach the village of **Ketrisi**, with its notably pristine watchtower and dozens of collapsing houses, most of which are abandoned these days.

Beyond Ketrisi you'll continue along the middle of the valley and pass two **monasteries** (one for monks, one for nuns) and a few truly remote houses. As you approach the end of the valley, you'll see your end point at the top of a hillside to your right. These are the atmospheric ruins of the **Zakagori Fortress**, which towers above the valley floor and can be climbed easily if you're not too exhausted. There is a Georgian army post at the base of the fortress, and it's not possible to go beyond this point unless you have a permit, as the breakaway republic of South Ossetia begins in the next valley, and so the area is militarily sensitive. Be sure to have your passport with you, as you may be asked to identify yourself by soldiers on patrol here. However, it's normally no problem to climb the fortress before heading back.

On the way back, cross the small bridge at Ketrisi and return along the other side of the river. This gives you some very different perspectives of the gorgeous landscapes and lets you see the base of melting glaciers during the summer months, as well as various sulphur springs running over rock that create unusual visual effects. You'll rejoin the original path into the valley at the campsite, from where it's an easy walk back along the river to Okrokana.

continued from p103

Stepantsminda to Juta costs about 80 GEL; for the same price the driver will often wait and take you back again after a few hours if you want.

Activities

★ Chaukhi Pass   HIKING

In a long, spectacular day of nine or 10 hours you can go up to and over the 3338m Chaukhi Pass (passable from about July to mid-October) and down to Roshka in Khevsureti via the stunning Abudelauri lakes. The trail over the pass itself and down to the lakes is not particularly obvious: a guide with a packhorse costs 150 GEL from Juta to the pass or 300 GEL to Roshka.

🛏 Sleeping

Juta has several places to stay, most only open from mid-May to late September, although there are a couple of guesthouses in the village that open year-round.

★ Zeta Camp   HOSTEL $

(☑ 555-701057; www.zeta.ge; Juta; per person BYO tent/rented tent/dm 30/35/50 GEL, tr/q 180/240 GEL, all incl breakfast; ⊘ Jun-Sep) A 10-minute trudge uphill from Juta with fabulous views up the valley to Mt Chaukhi, Zeta provides good tents with sleeping bags and mats, multiple rooms in a wooden building, outside toilets and hot-water showers, and good food in its popular cafe (dishes 7 GEL to 15 GEL). It's a fun and sociable place to stay with young English-speaking staff.

B&B Jago Arabuli   GUESTHOUSE $$

(☑ 593-422951; arabuli@gmx.de; Juta; per person half board 70 GEL; ⊘ mid-May–late Oct) Signposted from the bridge at Juta, this house has two four-bed rooms and a bathroom with a hot shower in the main house, as well as two cosier new rooms in an alpine-style hut on the hillside above. The lady of the house, Maia, speaks great English and it's worth calling ahead as it's sometimes fully booked.

Juta House   HOTEL $$

(☑ 557-601881, 555-700008; www.jutahouse.ge; Juta; r per person 65 GEL; ⊘ Jun-Sep; 🛜⛱) This hard-to-miss structure at the entrance to the village is Juta's only full hotel, and it boasts very spacious rooms, a sauna, a swimming pool and a pool table, making it popular with those seeking creature comforts and activities. The on-site restaurant is the best in town, too.

❶ Getting There & Away

There is no public transport to Juta – your best option is taking the bus services laid on by Mountain Freaks (p101) and Mountain Travel Agency (p101) from Stepantsminda to Juta at 9.30am or 11am each morning (30 GEL per person), for which it's usually a good idea to book ahead.

A taxi from Stepantsminda to Juta costs about 100 GEL one-way. It's also easy to drive to Juta yourself, but you should have a 4WD.

Svaneti

Breathtakingly wild and mysterious, Svaneti is an ancient land locked in the Caucasus, so remote that it was never tamed by any ruler. Uniquely picturesque villages and snow-covered, 4000m-plus peaks rising above flower-strewn alpine meadows provide a superb backdrop to the many walking trails. Svaneti's emblem is the *koshki* (defensive stone tower), designed to house villagers at times of invasion and local strife (until recently Svaneti was renowned for its murderous blood feuds). Around 175 *koshkebi,* most originally built between the 9th and 13th centuries, survive here today.

Not so long ago Svaneti was still pretty well off the beaten track, but recent tourism development has brought ski resorts, flights from Tbilisi, a paved road from Zugdidi and a huge increase in accommodation options, to the point where Mestia, Svaneti's only town, can get pretty busy in summer. Svaneti's mystique and beauty, however, are in no danger of wearing thin.

Mestia

☑ 410 / POP 10,000 / ELEV 1400M

The 'capital' of Upper Svaneti, Mestia is a sprawling conglomeration of at least 10 hamlets, dotted with picturesque Svan towers. The oldest of the hamlets, with most of the towers, are above the river on the northern side of town: Lekhtagi in the northwest, and Lanchvali and Lagami to the northeast. Government-sponsored tourism development has seen Mestia's central square, Setis moedani, rebuilt, a rush of new hotels, and the construction of ski resorts and a small airport. While you'll no longer really feel you're exploring the remote Svaneti of legend here, it's a great base for hiking and other activities that do take you into the rest of the region, where in so many places time really has stood still.

◉ Sights

★ Svaneti History & Ethnography Museum
MUSEUM

(www.museum.ge; Ioselani 7; adult/student 10/0.50 GEL; ⊙10am-6pm Tue-Sun) Mestia's excellent main museum is one of Georgia's best, with fascinating displays of church treasures, manuscripts, weaponry, jewellery, coins and historical photos, all labelled in English. The highlight is the room of wonderful 10th- to 14th-century icons from Svaneti's churches, fashioned in silver or painted in tempera on wood. The best of these have a uniquely human and touching quality, and some, unusually, depict St George spearing emperor Diocletian instead of his normal dragon.

Activities

Many beautiful walks start from Mestia itself. Some routes are well signposted; others aren't. Your accommodation or Mestia's Tourism Information Centre (p111), which gives out hiking maps, can help you find a guide if you want one. In the winter months, Mestia is a growing winter sports destination, with two modern ski stations nearby.

Chalaadi Glacier
WALKING

This enjoyable route of six or seven hours return trip (11km each way) takes you out past Mestia's airport and up the Mestiachala valley. The last 1.5km or so, from a footbridge over the river, is uphill through woods to the foot of the glacier. Watch out for rocks falling off the glacier in summer.

You can also get to the footbridge by taxi (return 50 GEL including waiting time) or horse (40 GEL, plus 50 GEL for the guide and 40 GEL for the guide's horse).

Mazeri via Guli Pass
WALKING

From about mid-June you can walk from Mestia to Mazeri in about 10 hours via the 2900m-high Guli Pass, with spectacular views of Mt Ushba (4700m). It's a demanding hike with 1500m of ascent then 1300m of descent: the route diverges from the Koruldi Lakes route at the Lamaaja ridge.

Cross
WALKING

A moderately demanding half-day walk goes up to the cross that's visible 900m above Mestia on the north side of the valley. From the cross you can see the spectacular twin peaks of Mt Ushba.

From Setis moedani, walk 450m east along the main street then take the street up to the left (Beqnu Khergiani). Take the up-

---

SVAN COOKING

Svans eat many of the same dishes as other Georgians, but have their own specialities too. Typical dishes include *kubdari* (meat pies), *chvishdari* (cheese cooked inside maize bread) and *tashmujabi* (mashed potatoes with cheese). The renowned 'Svaneti salt' is a blend of herbs, pepper and garlic frequently used to flavour meat dishes and often sold to travellers as a souvenir.

---

hill option at all junctions, and after about 600m, on the edge of the village, the street becomes a footpath. Follow this up and after some 700m it bends to the right across the hillside, eventually meeting a 4WD track. You can follow the 4WD track, shortcutting some bends, all the way to the cross. The return trip from Mestia takes about five hours. With good weather and enough daylight, you can continue to the small, pristine **Koruldi Lakes**, about two hours beyond the cross and some 400m higher. A return trip by 4WD from Mestia to the cross, with waiting time while you go to the lakes and back, normally costs around 100 GEL.

Hatsvali Ski Station
SKIING

(☑322-051221; www.mrg.gov.ge; ski pass per day 40 GEL; ⊙late Dec-early Apr) This small ski station, just south of Mestia and clearly visible from the town, works from late December to about early April, with a 300m beginners' slope, a 2600m blue run, a 1900m red run and one chairlift (lift passes and equipment rental both 30 GEL per day). You can catch the lift from just beyond the museum in Mestia.

Tetnuldi Ski Resort
SKIING

(http://tetnuldi.com; lift pass per day 40 GEL; ⊙mid-Dec–mid-May) On the slopes of Mt Tetnuldi about 20km east of Mestia, Tetnuldi is hoping to become western Georgia's equivalent of the country's premier ski resort Gudauri. Open since 2017, Tetnuldi now has 25km of runs between 2260m and 3040m altitude and three French chairlifts. At research time further runs and lifts, plus hotels, were in the works.

🛏 Sleeping

Mestia has dozens of good hotels and guesthouses, and competition is fierce, with most places renovating in the past few years to

Svaneti

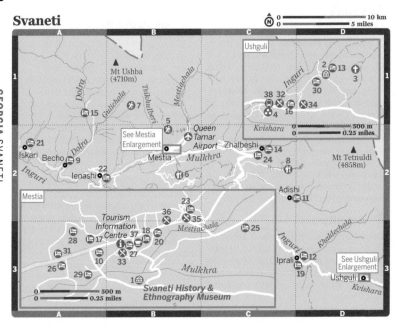

Svaneti

include private bathrooms. Nearly all hotels and guesthouses can also arrange vehicles and/or guides for out-of-town trips and can help organise any activities you'd like to do locally.

★**Villa Gabliani** GUESTHOUSE **$**
(☑ 595-513553; tsiurigab@gmail.com; I Gabliani 20; per person bed only/half board 25/45 GEL; 🛜🍽) These teacher sisters speak good English and German, and their house has five big, carpeted rooms that just ooze Soviet Georgian character. Each room shares a bathroom and a lovely verandah overlooking a garden of wildflowers and fruit trees. It's a good choice if you'd like a Georgian homestay minus the screaming children, and it's also superb value.

Guesthouse Ushba HOTEL **$**
(☑ 599-555217; www.svanetistay.com; Tamar Mepe 7; dm/r incl breakfast 35/50 GEL; 🅿🛜) This pleasant, clean and central budget-leaning place has a wide range of rooms of varied sizes and outlook. Most share bathrooms, plus there's a big terrace and a bright sitting room with great views over the rushing river below. It's just 200m east of Setis moedani along the main street, and the on-site Cafe Ushba (p111) is recommended too.

Guest House Eka GUESTHOUSE **$**
(☑ 599-726719; echartolani@yahoo.com; Vittorio Sella 8; per person incl breakfast with/without bathroom 80/35 GEL; 🛜) Hospitable, English-speaking Eka Chartolani, the archaeology curator at Mestia's museum, has six large rooms for up to four people (three of which share bathrooms) and serves delicious Svan/Georgian meals using a lot of homegrown produce. Vittorio Sella runs uphill off the main street about 60m west of Setis moedani, and the house has nice views.

Nino Ratiani's Guesthouse GUESTHOUSE **$**
(☑ 599-183555; www.facebook.com/ninoratianis guesthouse; J Khaftani 1; per person half board with/without bathroom 60/45 GEL, camping per person 5 GEL; 🅿🛜) Particularly good Svan food, a hospitable welcome and a variety of renovated rooms (nearly all with bathroom) in two buildings make Nino's one of the best and busiest budget stays in town. There's also a pleasant courtyard and lots of balcony space. It's 400m along the street towards Zugdidi from Setis moedani.

Manoni's Guesthouse GUESTHOUSE **$**
(☑ 599-568417, 577-568417; manonisvaneti@ yahoo.com; Kakhiani 25; r 100 GEL, without bath-

room 30-40 GEL, camping per person 10 GEL; 🅿🛜) A good-value guesthouse spread over three houses, Manoni offers comfy pine-panelled rooms of various sizes, and five shared bathrooms. Camping in the grassy garden includes hot shower and kitchen use. It's 1km east from Setis moedani, up a lane beside Kakhiani 31. Meals cost 10 GEL to 15 GEL, and the extended family is welcoming.

★**Roza Shukvani's Guesthouse** GUESTHOUSE **$$**
(☑ 599-641455; www.roza-mestia.com; Parjiani I Alley 9; s/d/tr 60/70/80 GEL, r without bathroom 40 GEL, all incl breakfast; 🅿🛜) Terrific Svan meals and a warm welcome from the ever-helpful, English-speaking Roza and her family make this one of Mestia's best places to stay, all the more so now it's moved to brand-new premises. The 17 spotless, spacious rooms have a mix of private and shared bathrooms, and valley views from the terrace and garden are superb.

★**Guesthouse Davit Zhorzholiani** GUESTHOUSE **$$**
(☑ 599-344948; www.svanetistay.com; Setis III chikhi 1; per person half board 50-65 GEL; 🛜) This friendly family establishment is annoyingly unsigned and hidden in a lane just by Erti Kava coffee shop. However, with its own Svan tower, 20 comfortable rooms with private bathroom and a lovely courtyard setting, it's a real winner. There's a panoramic roof terrace and meals are plentiful and tasty. Amiable host Davit is an experienced mountain-hiking guide.

Chalet Mestia BOUTIQUE HOTEL **$$**
(☑ 577-014224, 551-931717; info@chaletmes tia.com; Betlemi 47; s/d/tr/q incl breakfast 150/200/260/300 GEL; 🛜) This midrange hotel on Mestia's main street makes a good stab at boutique hotel offerings, with smart furnishings, polished wooden floorboards, crisp linens, filament bulbs and other small designer touches in its otherwise fairly normal but clean and comfortable 15 rooms. It's certainly a step up from most hotels in town, and appeals to an international crowd seeking affordable comfort.

Hotel Svan House HOTEL **$$**
(☑ 591-407020, 595-151589; svanhouse@gmail. com; Vakhtang Goshteliani 15; s/d incl breakfast 80/100 GEL; 🛜) A welcoming and smart conversion of an old stone house, with eight good, clean and well-sized rooms along two wooden verandahs. There's a pretty garden

MESTIA–USHGULI TREK

The most popular longer trek from Mestia is the scenic four-day, 50km hike east to Ush-guli, with village guesthouses for accommodation. Each of the first three days takes you up over a ridge, with an ascent of between 400m and 800m, followed by a descent to your destination, as you head across the lower folds of the main Caucasus ridge. This is perhaps Georgia's most famous multiday hike and the tiny villages can get surprisingly crowded in summer. There's always accommodation available, but do book ahead if you'd like to stay in the better options in each place. The stages:

Mestia–Zhabeshi (14km, about seven hours) Takes you east up the gorgeous Mulkhura valley to Zhabeshi, which has half a dozen guesthouses including **Guesthouse Gogia** (599-323678, 599-577542; per person half board 50 GEL) and **Givi Kakhiani's Guest-house** (599-519089; iakakhiani@gmail.com; per person incl 3 meals 50 GEL; P). As an alternative, you can also stay in the nearby village of Mulakhi (confusingly also known as Chvabiani), a couple of kilometres nearer to Mestia, where you can stay at the excellent **Maia's Guesthouse** (591-281362, 598-450043; gogagigani@yahoo.com); r per person full board 60-70 GEL, camping per person 10 GEL; 🛜).

Zhabeshi–Adishi (10km, about seven hours) A tough 800m ascent from Zhabeshi is eventually followed by a hugely impressive 400m descent, with some extraordinary views. Seriously fit hikers can take the high route to Adishi, which is tougher but you'll almost certainly find yourself alone. In Adishi, there is a wide choice of lodging including **Gunter Guesthouse** (598-933381, 598-477180; dm full board 70 GEL, r per person full board 100 GEL) and **Elizabeth Kaldani** (595-449584; kaldanielizabeth@yahoo.com; per person 70 GEL, full board 100 GEL; 🛜).

Adishi–Iprali (15km, about seven hours) The third day of this trek is its most impressive, and involves a gorgeous walk through the River Adishi valley to the Adishi glacier, a river crossing (locals charge 10 GEL per person to take you across by horse) and then a tough but stunning ascent to the Chkhunderi Pass (2655m) before a steep descent down into the next valley and then along the river to Iprali. In Iprali the best sleeping options are **Family Hotel Ucha** (598-790225, 595-557470; per person incl breakfast, dinner & lunch box 65 GEL; 🛜) and **Guesthouse Betegi** (598-790551; per person half board 60 GEL; 🛜). If these are both full, as is often the case, continue to the next village of Lalkhori and try the **Guesthouse Sweet Home** (599-982150, 595-412401; per person full board 60 GEL).

Iprali–Ushguli (10km, four to five hours) The easiest stage: on day four you'll descend from Iprali to the village of Lalkhori, from where you follow the rushing river through a steep valley before ascending to Ushguli. You're walking along a 4WD road for much of this day, and vehicle traffic can be surprisingly heavy. If you'd like to shorten the route, skip the last day between Iprali and Ushguli, which is definitely the least spectacular of the four, and take a taxi or *marshrutka* on to Ushguli.

to hang out in and good meals available. It's 600m east of Setis moedani, up the hill a bit off the main road.

Villa Mestia HOTEL $$
(551-001133; villamestia@gmail.com; Erekle Pharjiani 7; s/d/tr/q incl breakfast 70/120/150/180 GEL; 🛜) This attractive three-storey house with a lovely tree-shaded garden (where you can take meals or drinks) has a degree of traditional charm thanks to its wooden doors, windows and furnishings, and stone-walled dining room. Its nine rooms are comfy, all with private bathroom and a bal-

cony, and English is spoken. It's 500m from Setis moedani along the road to Zugdidi.

Posta Hotel BOUTIQUE HOTEL $$$
(577-323220; www.hotelposta.ge; Setis moedani; r US$130-160, ste US$180, all incl breakfast; 🛜) Opened in 2019 on Mestia's main square, the Posta is a splash of boutique fabulousness in a town still struggling to build rooms with bathrooms. Studiedly minimalist in style, rooms have their own balconies, wooden floorboards and feature luxuries such as rain showers. The downstairs lobby-lounge and restaurant is also one of the best places for drinks in town.

✖ Eating & Drinking

Many guesthouses offer good half-board packages, but there are also now dozens of restaurants in Mestia, though quality is generally fairly average.

★ Cafe Laila   GEORGIAN $
(Setis moedani; mains 5-18 GEL; ⊘8am-midnight; 🛜🅿) A hugely popular gathering place on the central square where it can be hard to get a table on summer evenings when local musicians often perform. The food is a respectable mix of Svan specialities and Georgia-wide favourites, service is generally efficient (if not charming), and evenings here – which often end in dancing – can be a lot of fun.

REA Cafe Bar   GEORGIAN $
(Tamar Mepe 32; mains 5-15 GEL; ⊘9am-11pm; 🛜🅿) This pint-sized cafe is perfect for a relaxing meal. Its handwritten menu offers Georgian treats such as *shkmeruli* and *chishdvari* (a Svan pastry made from cornflour) and the service here is quick and friendly.

Cafe Ushba   GEORGIAN $
(Tamar Mepe 7; mains 6-15 GEL; ⊘11am-midnight; 🛜🅿) Favoured for its good kebabs, this friendly guesthouse has all the main Georgian favourites including delicious *khinkali* and plenty of vegetarian choice. There's also Georgian beer on tap, as well as bottled craft beer. Choose between the cosy downstairs, the upstairs private dining rooms or the oddly disconnected terrace.

★ Lushnu Qor   GEORGIAN $$
(Tamar Mepe 44; mains 8-18 GEL; ⊘10am-midnight; 🛜🅿) Definitely one of Mestia's more interesting restaurants, this German-owned spot stands out from the crowd with its friendly service and good food. Its *kubdari* (spicy Svanetian meat pie) are excellent, and it even offers aperol spritz with fresh mint from the garden, which makes for a refreshing post-hike cocktail. There's a large courtyard and a cosy main dining room.

Erti Kava   COFFEE
(www.facebook.com/pg/ertikava; Setis moedani; ⊘7.30am-10.30pm; 🛜) This speciality coffee shop does superb coffee and is frankly an astonishing find in Mestia. It's run by the lovely team behind Hotel Makhe in Latali and is the perfect place to start the day.

ⓘ Information

Tourism Information Centre (📞551-080894; Setis moedani 7; ⊘9am-6pm Jun-Sep) This small tourist office handles the entire Svaneti region and is often very busy. English-speaking staff give out free hiking maps (when they're in stock) including one map for each day of the Mestia–Ushguli trek, and can give advice about various other day trips in the area. Office hours are not always kept to, however.

ⓘ Getting There & Away

AIR
Vanilla Sky (p66) flies a twin prop from Natakhtari airfield, 25km north of Tbilisi, to Queen Tamar Airport in Mestia and back twice daily in summer, weather permitting. The spectacular one-hour flight costs 90 GEL one-way, including transfers between Rustaveli metro station and Natakhtari airfield. You can buy tickets online. Vanilla Sky also flies to Kutaisi on Mondays and Fridays (50 GEL).

MARSHRUTKA & TAXI
Marshrutky run to Mestia from Tbilisi, Kutaisi, Zugdidi and, between June and September, from Batumi. From Tbilisi you can also take a day or night train to Zugdidi and then a *marshrutka* from there. The road up from Zugdidi is normally kept open year-round and traverses increasingly spectacular scenery as it heads up the Enguri and Mulkhura valleys.

Heading down from Mestia, *marshrutky* leave from one of half-a-dozen makeshift bus stations scattered around town. The most obvious is at Setis moedani, from where buses leave at 8am for Zugdidi (20 GEL, three hours), Kutaisi (25 GEL, 4½ hours), Tbilisi (30 GEL, nine hours) and, in summer, Batumi (30 GEL, six hours). Further *marshrutky* leave throughout the day when full; make enquiries at the various offices selling tickets around town.

Marshrutky to Ushguli cost a flat 40 GEL (two hours) for a day return and leave from Setis moedani at 10am, returning from Ushguli at 3pm. The price is the same if you only want to go one-way.

Getting around Svaneti from Mestia usually means taxis. Your accommodation can arrange these, or negotiate with drivers hanging around the town centre.

Ushguli

POP 290 / ELEV 2050M

Set in the topmost reaches of the Enguri valley beneath the snow-covered massif of Mt Shkhara (5193m), Georgia's highest peak, Ushguli is an unbelievably atmospheric place. With more than 40 ancient Svan towers, it has been on the Unesco World Heritage List since 1996, and even though it's now awash with tourists, nothing can dim its enduring magic.

Made up of four villages, Ushguli is a combination of ancient slate homesteads, muddy streets full of livestock and people who look like they've just stepped from the pages of a particularly compelling issue of *National Geographic*. Most visitors come from Mestia just for the day, but stay here for a night or two if you can to experience more of the town's day-to-day life, and to enjoy some of the wonderful nearby hikes.

Sights

Lamaria Church CHURCH
This tiny 12th-century church with its own watchtower stands proudly on a hilltop looking back over the town and marks the end of Ushguli. Inside there are some wonderful icons and frescoes, albeit rather faded, devoted to Lamaria, a Svan pagan goddess of fertility, who has gradually become identified with St Mary in the Christian faith.

Ethnographic Museum MUSEUM
(Zhibiani; 5 GEL; ☉8am-8pm Jun-Sep) Ushguli's Ethnographic Museum is located in a 12th-century building that once housed both people and livestock in the winter months, all huddled together under one crowded, smelly roof. You'll be shown the ingenious devices used by locals over the centuries, and will possibly experience a wave of gratitude at being born in the modern era.

Queen Tamar's Castle RUINS
(Chazhashi) These atmospheric ruins on top of a hill in Chazhashi were once made up of four defensive towers and a church, though just one tower and the ruins of the church can be seen today.

Activities

There's some wonderful walking around Ushguli: it takes about six hours to walk 8km up the valley to the foot of the Shkhara glacier and back, while the town is also the end point of the hugely popular four-day Mestia–Ushguli trek (p110).

Sleeping

Ushguli has experienced an accommodation explosion and now has scores of guesthouses and small hotels. Most are in the two upper villages, Chvibiani and Zhibiani,

and there are also many guesthouses along the road up from the bridge at Chvibiani.

Gamarjoba Guesthouse GUESTHOUSE $
(Temraz Nijaradze; ☑599-209719, 595-229814; www.gamarjoba-ushguli.com; Zhibiani; per person incl half board 50 GEL) Temraz has four good, clean, wood-floored rooms, and serves awesomely delicious local food. His brother Fridon's paintings decorate the communal areas of the house, giving it a rather bohemian feel, and there's a pleasant garden for relaxing. You may recognise the house as a location used in the local film *Dede*. Temraz' son speaks English.

Guest House Caucasus GUESTHOUSE $
(Tariel Nijaradze; ☑591-447665; Chvibiani; per person incl half board 55 GEL; 🛜) Amiable Tariel's lovely old stone house is the first on the right as you walk up through Chvibiani. Of the six plain, clean rooms, two face north with great Shkhara views. Son Bakar speaks English, but the house is signed only with 'Hotel' – look for the blue timber over the front door.

Villa Lileo GUESTHOUSE $$
(☑557-290550, 599-912256; Zhibiani; per person incl half board with/without bathroom 100/80 GEL; 🛜) One of Ushguli's largest and most professional establishments, with some 19 rooms in various wings of a sprawling building, Villa Lileo offers excellent Svan cooking and a charming open-plan dining-bar area perfect for relaxing in the evening. There's also a large terrace, and camping is available for free in the garden.

Eating

There are only a handful of dedicated restaurants in Ushguli, but nearly every guesthouse and hotel offers meals, so you'll have no trouble finding something to eat.

Kafe Koshki GEORGIAN $
(Chvibiani; mains 5-15 GEL; ☉9am-10pm Jun-Sep) This neat wooden cafe overlooking the town from its large terrace serves good basic fare such as *mtsvadi, khachapuri* and salads. Check out its spectacular traditional Svan man's chair, hand-carved with the Nijaradze family's history and all sorts of related motifs. Food is good, but service is slow and there's no English spoken.

★Cafe Bar Enguri GEORGIAN $$
(Chvibiani; mains 10-25 GEL; ☉10am-midnight; 🛜☑) The best option in town, this mod-

OFF THE BEATEN TRACK

ROSHKA

Nine kilometres past Barisakho, a side road climbs 7km west up to the tiny village of Roshka. A wonderful walk from Roshka takes you up to the three small, but very beautiful, coloured **Abudelauri lakes** with their backdrop of the jagged Chaukhi massif. It's about 2½ hours (5km) up to the first (green) lake, then 10 minutes on to the stunning turquoise lake, and a further hour (with no real path most of the way) up to the white lake, below a glacier coming down from the Chaukhi massif.

The excellent **Shota Tsiklauri's Guesthouse** (☑599-399789; per person incl breakfast & dinner 60 GEL; ☉approximately May-Oct), at the very top of Roshka, provides four comfy guestrooms and fine food. It's possible to continue from here to the village of Juta, on the other side of the 3338m Chaukhi Pass (passable from about July to mid-October), though you'll normally need to camp en route as completing the hike in one day is a real challenge.

ern chalet-style cafe by the river has the most interesting menu in town, including pork medallions in onion sauce, various delicious kebabs and grilled trout. English-speaking staff, real coffee and a pleasant garden to while away the time complete the picture.

❶ Getting There & Away

Marshrutky connect Mestia with Ushguli and generally leave Mestia at 10am, arriving by noon in Ushguli, leaving Ushguli at 3pm and getting back by 5pm. Return tickets cost 40 GEL whether you come back the same day or not, but if you return another day, you'll normally have to buy a second ticket. From Ushguli, *marshrutky* to Mestia depart from alongside the bridge in Chazhashi.

A taxi or 4WD day trip for up to four people from Mestia costs 200 GEL; one-way trips are only a little less. The road is now paved for most of the way, but still in poor condition for the last 30km. It's normally open year-round except after heavy snow or landslides, but non-4WD vehicles can only manage it from June to October (and they need high clearance). The rough track on from Ushguli to Lentekhi in Lower Svaneti (75km; via the 2623m Zagar Pass) is passable from about May to September. Four-wheel drives charge 300 GEL for the three- to four-hour trip.

Becho

Becho, the community of small villages strung up the Dolra valley west of Mestia, is a very beautiful and relatively little-visited area with some wonderful walks. The spectacular, twin-peaked **Ushba** (4700m), Georgia's toughest and most dangerous mountaineering challenge, towers at the

head of the valley. The highest village in the valley, Mazeri, is the best base.

🛏 Sleeping & Eating

Becho House   GUESTHOUSE **$**
(☑599-311850; bechohouse@gmail.com; Becho; per person half board 65 GEL; ☎) This very friendly, modern family home on the hillside above the main road through the valley makes for an excellent base for hiking in the area. Its seven rooms are all spotless and comfortable, and share a large terrace and a big garden suitable for kids. The younger members of the family speak good English.

Hanmer Guest House   GUESTHOUSE **$**
(☑595-791419, 599-629789; www.facebook.com/hanmer.house.svaneti; Iskari village, Etseri; per person half board 75 GEL, camping per person 10 GEL; ☎) A hospitable Canadian-and-Georgian-run guesthouse about 1km up from the main road in Etseri, this guesthouse has several bright, medium-sized rooms for up to four people, and five shared bathrooms. There's also a guest kitchen and one bedroom with private facilities. Downstairs you'll find one of the best-stocked shops in Svaneti outside Mestia.

★Grand Hotel Ushba   HOTEL **$$**
(☑592-124724; www.grandhotelushba.com; Tvebishi; s/d incl breakfast €94/104, without bathroom €59/69; ℗☎) A comfortable mountain lodge in a gorgeous setting just past Mazeri, with a **restaurant** (mains 10-15 GEL; ☉6am-late; ☎) serving good Georgian dishes, salads and desserts. Rooms are attractive in combinations of pine, stone and white paint, though not as luxurious as you might expect for the prices. Still, it's one of the best places to stay in Svaneti and a great base for walking.

MAYA KARKALICHEVA/GETTY IMAGES ©

JOHN GRUMMITT/SHUTTERSTOCK ©

EFESENKO/SHUTTERSTOCK ©

RADIOKAFKA/SHUTTERSTOCK ©

1. Ushguli (p111)
Set in the Enguri valley, this Unesco World Heritage–listed area is home to more than 40 ancient Svan towers.

2. Tusheti (p117)
Mountain goats graze in this high-mountain region located in Georgia's far northeast.

3. Georgian wineries (p36)
Sample world-class wine on a tour, such as at underground Winery Khareba (p126; pictured) in Kvareli.

4. Vardzia (p81)
This ancient, rock-hewn monastery overlooking the Mtkvari River once housed around 2000 monks.

ⓘ Getting There & Away

Marshrutky to Mestia from elsewhere in Georgia proper pass through the villages of Becho and Ienashi on the main road, and very near to Iskari too. For Mazeri get off at Becho, from where you'll need to continue by taxi.

Khevsureti

Sparsely populated Khevsureti, bordering Chechnya (Russia), is home to some fantastic defensive architecture, a part-animist religion, and spectacular scenery of steep, forested valleys and blooming mountain pastures. Men in this remote area were still wearing chain mail well into the 20th century.

Today few villages have permanent inhabitants. There's no road access to most people's main destination, Shatili, 150km from Tbilisi, from about December to May when the Datvisjvari Pass (2676m) is closed. Shepherds bring their flocks up from Kakheti from about June to September, when tourism also provides an income for some families.

Shatili

POP 22 / ELEV 1400M

Shatili's Old Town, built between the 7th and 13th centuries, is a unique agglomeration of tall *koshkebi* (defensive watchtowers) clinging together on a rocky outcrop to form a single fortress-like whole. It was abandoned in the 1980s, and the new village, of about 20 houses, has grown up around it, but the sheer sight of this place is quite an extraordinary thing to behold. Today some towers have been restored as guesthouses, but for the most part the Old Town is a charismatic slate ruin that is perfect for exploring on foot.

Shatili is an increasingly popular weekend destination for Georgians. If you come here in late summer, you might run into the

Khevsureti & Tusheti

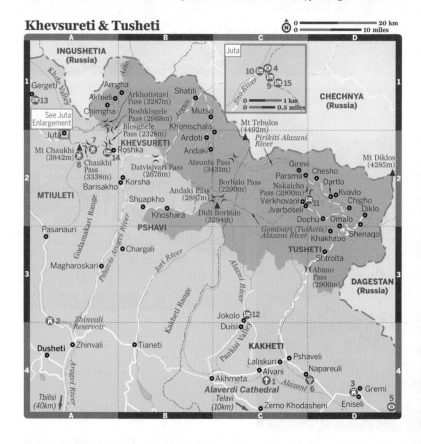

Shatiloba (⊙ Aug/Sep, dates vary) festival, with folk music and dance, horse races and Georgian wrestling.

◎ Sights

★ Shatili Old Town   OLD TOWN
This magnificent agglomeration of *koshkebi* and atmospheric slate houses packed tightly together on a steep hillside to create one sprawling fortress is an incredible sight. Most of the houses are abandoned and are slowly collapsing, but you can still clamber around them easily enough, and most of the time you'll be totally alone here.

Anatori Crypts   CEMETERY
These medieval communal tombs feature still-visible human bones and sit on a promontory above the gorge: in times of plague, infected villagers would voluntarily enter these tombs and wait for death. It's a haunting place even today, with a spectacular setting 3km north of Shatili.

⊨ Sleeping

Two of Shatili's old towers have been converted into guesthouses and sleeping there is a unique experience. Some of the houses along the village's one street and down near the river below also take guests.

Green House Shatili   GUESTHOUSE $
(☑ 599-017740, 595-850746; tamar.avazash vili@gmail.com; per person half board 60 GEL) Russian-speaking Fiso's charming guesthouse faces Shatili's extraordinary Old Town across the river and is a cosy and inviting place to stay. The five rooms share two bathrooms, and two extra shower blocks were being built during our last visit. There's a large garden and delicious food available as well.

Imeda's Koshki   GUESTHOUSE $$
(Front Castle; ☑ 598-370317, 598-225411; shorenalikokeli@gmail.com; per person half board 70 GEL; ⊙ approximately mid-May–Oct) A very atmospheric guesthouse built into a watchtower near the foot of the Old Town, Imeda's has nine rooms (some windowless) for up to seven people. There are three bathrooms with hot water downstairs, and a terrace where good meals are served. There's no English spoken, but it's hard to imagine anywhere more fascinating to spend the night.

Dato Jalabauri's
Guesthouse   GUESTHOUSE $$
(☑ 599-533379; www.facebook.com/Jalabauri; per person 30 GEL, half board 60 GEL; ⊙ approximately mid-May–Oct) An atmospheric *koshki*-guesthouse with 19 beds in small rooms reached by wooden staircases, plus a scenic balcony and a good hot shower. The family's own house is the nearest to the tiny church in the new part of Shatili.

⊕ Getting There & Away

A 20-seat *marshrutka* to Shatili (20 GEL, six to seven hours) leaves Tbilisi's Didube bus station (same area as the Stepantsminda *marshrutky*) at 9am Wednesday and Saturday, returning from Shatili at noon Thursday and Sunday from about June to October.

Tusheti

Tucked away in Georgia's far northeast corner bordering Chechnya and Dagestan in neighbouring Russia, Tusheti is one of Georgia's most picturesque and pristine high-mountain regions. The single unpaved (and often terrifying) road to get here from Kakheti passes over the nerve-jangling

2900m Abano Pass and can only be done in a 4WD from around late May to mid-October.

Centuries-old *koshkebi* still stand in many villages, and evidence of Tusheti's old animist religion is plentiful in the form of stone shrines called *khatebi* (singular: *khati*) decked with the horns of sacrificed goats or sheep.

Today most Tusheti folk only go up to Tusheti in summer, to graze their flocks, participate in festivals, cater for tourists and generally reconnect with their roots. Many have winter homes around the villages of Akhmeta and Alvani in Kakheti. Welcome to one of Georgia's least explored and most mysterious regions.

Omalo

POP 60

Tusheti's biggest settlement, Omalo is itself little more than a village, which is neatly divided into two parts, some distance from each other, Zemo (Upper) Omalo and Kvemo (Lower) Omalo. Zemo Omalo is the oldest part, and includes Keselo, a group of several ancient towers on a hillside that have recently been restored.

Both parts of Omalo are full of guesthouses that open between June and September, when the local population moves up from their winter homes in Akhmeta and Alvani. Zemo Omalo is the more picturesque of the two, with more historic buildings and the feel of a traditional village, while Kvemo Omalo is the bigger and more modern part, where you'll find two brand-new hotels, the first of their kind in Tusheti, the Tusheti Protected Areas Visitors Centre, and the few services and shops that are available in the entire region.

◉ Sights

Keselo FORTRESS

(Zemo Omalo) Constructed during the Mongol invasions during the 1230s, these five towers form a protective fortress on the hilltop above Zemo Omalo where locals would flee during raids from outsiders. Lovingly restored in the 21st century after centuries of neglect, today one of the towers hosts an interesting ethnographic museum (5 GEL – ask at Hotel Tusheti Tower if you want to visit), while in another tower the Shalva Alkhanaidze Photography Museum is planned, displaying a collection of local photographs from the 1950s to 1970s.

🛏 Sleeping & Eating

Most people stay in the older Zemo (Upper) Omalo, where those picturesque towers are situated, but there are also plenty of options in Kvemo (Lower) Omalo, 1.5km down the hill, including two new hotels, which were nearing completion in 2019.

Hostel Tishe GUESTHOUSE $

(☑ 599-905337; inga.chvritidze@gmail.com; Kvemo Omalo; per person with/without half board 65/30 GEL; 🛜) This fairly basic guesthouse in the middle of Kvemo Omalo offers some of the best-value rooms in the village. The four rooms have chipboard walls and share one bathroom, but they also have access to a pleasant terrace with good views, which also functions as a popular 'outdoor bedroom' during warmer weather. Downstairs you'll find one of Tusheti's better-stocked shops.

Keselo Guesthouse GUESTHOUSE $

(☑ 598-941270, 557-611430; arshaulidze@gmail.com; Kvemo Omalo; per person incl half board 50 GEL; P🛜) Green-fenced Keselo, scenically placed at the top of Kvemo Omalo, has comfy beds in half a dozen rooms that share bathrooms. There's lots of communal space, a big garden and tasty home-cooked food on offer.

Guesthouse Lasharai GUESTHOUSE $$

(☑ 555-645254, 551-440007; guesthouselasharai@yahoo.com; Zemo Omalo; per person half board 80 GEL; 🛜) This two-floor slate and wood house with a pleasant balcony and terrace overlooking the village square is a comfortable place to stay. There's a restaurant here too, and it's the only spot in Tusheti that serves chilled beer (the erratic electricity supply makes fridges rather unpopular).

Hotel Tusheti Tower GUESTHOUSE $$

(☑ 599-272265, 599-110879; tushetitower@gmail.com; Zemo Omalo; per person incl breakfast & dinner 70 GEL; 🛜) A small 17th-century tower on Zemo Omalo's village square has been extended vertically to house four small stone-walled rooms with private bathrooms. Meals here are good and plentiful, and the owner looks after the museum in Keselo, where he's happy to accompany you by arrangement.

Guesthouse Mgzavri GUESTHOUSE $$

(☑ 593-958515; Zemo Omalo; per person with/without half board 70/40 GEL; 🛜) This new family-run guesthouse has some charming English-speaking children running around and a pleasant restaurant on a small raised terrace. The rooms all have their own bathroom, even if their chipboard walls might not overwhelm you. It's just below the Keselo in the centre of the village.

Guesthouse Shina   GUESTHOUSE **$$**
(☑ 597-170707, 595-262046; www.shina.ge; Zemo Omalo; s/d incl breakfast & dinner 90/130 GEL; 🅿 🛜) This attractive stone-and-wood house has rooms with private bathroom, plus a nice front garden and a dedicated restaurant area serving good meals. Very limited English is spoken, and the bedroom walls are paper thin, but the spacious balcony with views of the village makes up for it and service is friendly.

❶ Information

Tusheti Protected Areas Visitors Centre
(☑ 577-101892, 577-101891; www.apa.gov.ge; ☉ 9am-6pm approximately late May–mid-Oct; 🛜) This large and helpful centre just south of Kvemo Omalo off the main jeep track into town has plentiful displays on Tusheti, provides a walking/riding route and accommodation information, and can help arrange guides, horses and vehicles. There's also a small cafeteria on-site that makes for a good lunch stop.

❶ Getting There & Away

When the Abano Pass is open, 4WDs will carry three or four passengers from Telavi or Alvani (22km northwest of Telavi) to Omalo for 200 GEL (or 50 GEL per person) – a spectacular four-hour drive (3½ hours from Alvani).

Four-wheel drives also wait for passengers at the central crossroads in Alvani; you may be able to share with others. It's best to be at Alvani by 9am; taxis there from Telavi cost 15 GEL.

The road to Tusheti has been improved, but the asphalt still ends a few kilometres past Alvani, and the road still has all the same vertiginous precipices and steep switchbacks – so it should only be undertaken by confident drivers with reliable 4WD vehicles. There are no petrol stations in Tusheti, so ensure your tank is full when you leave Alvani, and bring a full jerry can with you if you plan to do a lot of driving in Tusheti.

All transport coming up from Kakheti to Tusheti comes to Omalo. As there is no public transport here, there is no bus station or even a place to find drivers heading down again. Your best bet to arrange transport is to organise it in advance when you come up, or talk to the Tusheti Protected Areas Visitors Centre, which can often assist with finding drivers.

TUSHETI FESTIVALS

Atnigenoba, an end-of-summer festival starting about 100 days after Georgian Easter, is a non-touristic event bound up with Tusheti's ancient animist religion. It involves, among other things, ram sacrifices at the ancient shrines known as *khatebi*, separate-sex feasting, the drinking of sacred rye beer (specially brewed by men using large cauldrons) and more sports.

Tushetoba, held at Omalo on a variable Saturday in August (sometimes late July), is a semi-touristic festival featuring folk music and dancing, traditional Tusheti foods like *guda* sheep's cheese and *khinkali* (meat dumplings), and mountain sports like wrestling, archery and horse races (with riders no more than 15 years old for speed).

Around Omalo

Beyond Omalo, Tusheti is as wild and spectacular as anywhere in Georgia, with ancient villages scattered among its dramatic wilderness, soaring peaks, rushing rivers and thick forests in every direction. This is superb horse-riding and hiking country.

⊙ Sights

★**Dartlo**   OLD TOWN
Dartlo, 12km northwest of Omalo in the Pirikiti Alazani valley, is an extraordinarily picturesque village crowned by an impressive tower grouping, overlooked by the single tall tower of Kvavlo 350m above the village itself. In summer Dartlo can be almost overgrown with wildflowers, which all but close off its narrow pebble streets, and make for a spectacular sight. There has been much investment in restoring the village's ancient slate and wood houses in recent years.

Dzveli Diklo   FORTRESS
(Old Diklo) About 2km past Diklo, which is 4km northeast of Shenaqo, the Dzveli Diklo fortress perches on a spectacular rock promontory looking east to Dagestan (Russia). It's a 40-minute hike one-way from Diklo, and the jeep track does not extend beyond Diklo village.

> ### TUSHETI DOGS
>
> The dogs guarding Tusheti's sheep, goats and cattle are often fierce and sometimes dangerous. If you give the livestock as wide a berth as possible, the dogs are less likely to threaten you.

Shenaqo
OLD TOWN

Shenaqo, a few kilometres east of Omalo, is one of the prettiest villages in Tusheti, with houses of stone, slate and rickety wooden balconies grouped below one of Tusheti's very few churches. The village is also famous as one of the main locations in the Soviet film *Mimino,* a charming 1977 comedy about a Georgian bush pilot serving these remote communities.

 Activities

Omalo–Shatili
HIKING

The track up the Pirikiti Alazani valley beyond Chesho, via Parsma and Girevi, eventually leads to the 3431m Atsunta Pass, a very steep and demanding route over into Khevsureti. It's a trek of four or five days all the way from Omalo to Shatili in Khevsureti, with at least one night's camping required at the base of the Atsunta.

The pass is normally open for walkers and packhorses from about mid-June to mid-September. There is a potentially dangerous river crossing before the ascent to the pass, so a guide and horse are advisable, and it's less hazardous late in the season, though horses and guides can be in short supply after the end of August.

Omalo–Nakaicho Pass–Omalo
HIKING

A popular four- or five-day route starts in Omalo, runs up the Pirikiti Alazani valley to Dartlo, Chesho and Parsma, then crosses the steep 2900m Nakaicho Pass over to Verkhovani, and returns to Omalo down the Gomtsari Alazani valley.

The basic route does, however, involve quite a lot of road walking (not that traffic is heavy). Non-road alternatives are to approach Dartlo from Diklo via Chigho, and to take the panoramic Gonta ridge route between the Nakaicho Pass and Gele (about 6km northwest of Omalo), instead of either of the two valley roads.

Omalo–Shuapkho
HIKING

This long westward route leads all the way up the Gomtsari Alazani valley to the Bor-balo Pass (2990m), from where trails head west down to Shuapkho village in Pshavi, north down to Ardoti and Mutso in Khevsureti, and northwest to the Datvisjvari Pass (2676m).

Omalo–Shuapkho should take four days on foot: you could spend the first night in a guesthouse (such as at Verkhovani), the second in the 12-person shelter on the way up to the pass, and the third camping.

🛏 Sleeping & Eating

Tusheti's many guesthouses operate only when the road is open and some don't get going until July. Many have shared bathrooms, but increasingly guesthouses are renovating to ensure each room has private facilities.

🛏 Dartlo

★ Hotel Samtsikhe
HOTEL $$

(☏ 599-118993; beselanidze@yahoo.com; per person room only/half board 25/70 GEL) By far the most appealing sleeping option in Dartlo, the Hotel Samtsikhe – whose name means 'three watchtowers' – comprises six stone-and-wood houses, with 14 rooms in all, just above the ruined church at the foot of the village. Beds are comfy and there's a full restaurant here too (mains 2 GEL to 12 GEL).

🛏 Shenaqo

★ Guesthouse Your Home
GUESTHOUSE $

(Darejan's Guesthouse; ☏ 599-102944, 555-5859010; per person half board 65 GEL; 🛜) Beside the church at the top of Shenaqo, delightfully eccentric matriarch Darejan (Daro) offers seven bright, wood-floored and -walled rooms, all with multiple beds and most with private bathrooms. The food is a highlight here, with delicious home cooking and huge portions. Daro's daughter Irma speaks English, but Daro is a master communicator nonetheless. Ask to see Daro's small 'musuem' of old Tushetian implements in her other house nearby.

Old Tusheti
GUESTHOUSE $

(☏ 558-272006; per person incl 3 meals 70 GEL; 🛜) Host Eldar Buqvaidze provides good, plentiful meals, plays the balalaika and maintains a curious museum of traditional Tusheti artefacts. Ask about the magic rope for scaring off sheep. Cosy rooms hold up to four people each, and following a refurbishment all now have their own bathrooms.

🛏 Other Villages

Dzveli Galavani
Guest House   GUESTHOUSE **$**
(☎598-680580, 571-511711; Diklo; per person half board 60 GEL) This was the only guesthouse at research time in the village of Diklo, and it's a fun, family-run, rustic place that offers three simple rooms sharing a bathroom and a pleasant terrace. The family speaks no English but is very warm and welcoming. It's pretty much immediately on your left when you arrive in the village from Omalo.

Lamata   GUESTHOUSE **$**
(☎599-700378; tushetiguesthouselamata@mail. ru; Verkhovani; per person room only/half board 15/50 GEL; ☺20 Jun-20 Sep) Your chance to sleep in a *koshki*. Three of the seven rooms are in the tower in front of the main house (but those in the main house are actually a bit comfier, and that's where the shower is). The family is friendly and the teenagers speak some English.

Kakheti

The eastern region of Kakheti is Georgia's premier wine-producing area. Almost everywhere you go, you'll be invited to drink a glass of traditional *qvevri* brew, and it's easy to find yourself wandering around in a semipermanent mellow haze. Kakheti is also rich in history: here you'll find the incredible monastery cave complex of Davit Gareja in a desolate spot overlooking the Azerbaijan border; the vaguely Tuscan-looking hilltop town of Sighnaghi; and many extraordinarily located churches and castles – both ruined and restored – around the charming regional capital, Telavi.

Telavi
☑ 350 / POP 20,000
The largest town in Kakheti, Telavi is set in the vineyard-strewn Alazani valley, between the Gombori Mountains and the Great Caucasus (visible to the northeast). It's the perfect base for exploring the region's viticultural, historical and architectural riches, and has a number of good guesthouses, hotels and restaurants, as well as a fascinating castle and museum complex.

◉ Sights

⭐**Batonistsikhe Castle**   CASTLE
(Erekle meoris gamziri; 5 GEL; ☺10am-6pm Tue-Sun) Batonistsikhe was the residence of the Kakhetian kings in the 17th and 18th centuries and remains today a superbly preserved old castle right in the middle of Telavi. The complex includes a renovated Persian-style palace where Erekle II was born and died, two small churches, the royal baths, and a state-of-the-art combined history and art museum. Enter from the western side of the fortress walls.

Bazari   MARKET
(cnr Chavchavadze & Alazanis gamziri; ☺7am-6pm) Telavi's busy market bursts with fresh produce from the area's villages and is a chaotic visual feast to wander through.

KAKHETI WINERIES

Visiting a few of Kakheti's wineries should not be missed while you're here. With about 60% of Georgia's vineyards (225 sq km), making wine by both the traditional *qvevri* method (p133) and modern European-style techniques, this is a region where wine plays a big part in daily life. The renaissance in the Georgian wine industry in the past decade has been nothing short of phenomenal and the region is now producing some of Georgia's most interesting wine.

Kakheti's five main appellations of origin are Tsinandali (dry whites from Rkatsiteli grapes mixed with 15% to 20% Mtsvane); Mukuzani (quality dry reds from the Saperavi grape); Kindzmarauli (dry and semisweet Saperavi reds); Akhasheni (dry Saperavi reds); and Napareuli (whites and Saperavi reds).

Many wineries welcome visitors for tours and tastings. Some have restaurants and even hotels. The Kakheti Wine Guild (p125) in Telavi can help organise visits; it also sells over 100 types of wine direct. There are several wineries within easy reach of Telavi that require no reservations for tastings and tours, and will happily welcome as little as two people for a wine tasting. These include Shumi (p126), Rostomaant Marani (p124) and Teliani Valley (p123).

Kakheti

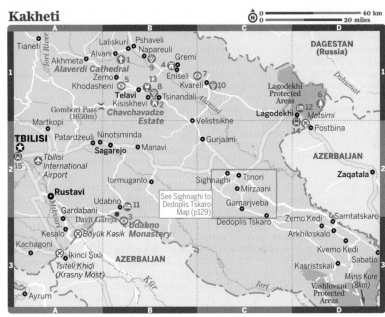

🛏 Sleeping

Telavi has enjoyed a small hotel boom in recent years, and you're now spoilt for choice with a range of boutique hotels and guesthouses that range from the simple to the elaborate.

G&G Guesthouse GUESTHOUSE $
(☑ 574-339677; gelashviliguram@mail.ru; Lionidze 6; tr 100 GEL, d/q without bathroom 60/120 GEL, all incl breakfast; 🛜) This fantastically located traditional house just under Telavi's castle has tonnes of character and four comfortable, recently renovated rooms that overlook a garden. The triple has its own bathroom, but the others share theirs. Owners speak limited English but the welcome is warm.

Marinella Guest House GUESTHOUSE $
(☑ 577-516001; maria.marinella@mail.ru; Chavchavadze 131; d 60 GEL, s/d without bathroom 40/55 GEL; P 🛜) Has six cheerful, modern and good-sized rooms, plus a nice breezy terrace and garden. English and German are spoken, and guests are free to use the kitchen.

Eto's Guesthouse GUESTHOUSE $
(☑ 599-782050, 350-277070; eto.neka@yahoo.com; Akhvlediani 27; r per person 30 GEL, breakfast/dinner 10/15 GEL; 🛜) This friendly place has four bright, clean rooms all with private bathroom, and a lovely flower-filled garden where you can sit out under a big apricot tree. Meals are made from fresh local produce and guests can use the kitchen. There's air-con in one room, and also an apartment that sleeps four people (100 GEL) in one bedroom.

Tushishvili Guesthouse GUESTHOUSE $
(☑ 350-271909, 577-756625; Nadikvari 15; per person with/without breakfast 35/30 GEL, dinner 20 GEL; P 🛜) This welcoming house is a long-time travellers' favourite and justly so. English-speaking Svetlana serves fabulous dinners and is more than helpful in organising local taxi trips and providing transport information. Rooms are comfy, share bathrooms and surround a large garden. It's totally unsigned; ask around to find the entrance.

Hotel Neli Telavi GUESTHOUSE $
(☑ 599-581820; www.facebook.com/hotelneli; Chonqadze 11; per person incl breakfast 40 GEL; P 🛜) Five of the eight big, bright rooms at Neli's charming family home have private bathrooms. Best of all is the slightly more expensive top-floor 'lux' room with great panoramas. Neli cooks excellent Georgian meals with fresh, local ingredients, and the natural wine flows.

Kakheti

Milorava's Guest House GUESTHOUSE $
(📞551-505550, 350-271257; www.miloravagh.ge;
Akhvlediani 67; r per person 30 GEL, breakfast 15
GEL; 🛜) Can accommodate six or seven people in rooms with comfy beds in a cottage
beside the garden. Each room has its own
bathroom and there's a pleasant bar area
for socialising. Good meals are available
and the amiable, helpful host has his own
wine cellar and offers tastings for 25 GEL.

Hotel Erekle II BOUTIQUE HOTEL $$
(📞596-377377; www.hotelerekle.ge; Lionidze 1;
s/d/ste incl breakfast 170/230/280 GEL; ❄🛜)
The rooms at this boutique hotel under-
neath the castle ramparts are something
else, like a Persian fantasy with elaborately
patterned tile walls, luxurious velvet sofas,
gorgeous wooden floors and large balconies
with carved arabesque details. It's probably
the fanciest place in town and certainly the
most design conscious.

Eating

Despite its importance as capital of Georgia's
biggest wine-producing region, Telavi's res-
taurants are still lagging behind somewhat,
although they are slowly improving. In local
guesthouses you'll usually eat excellently.

★Kapiloni GEORGIAN $$
(📞350-278767; Barnovi 10; mains 10-35 GEL;
⊙9am-midnight; 🛜🍴) The most appealing of
Telavi's restaurants is this spot in the town
centre with a large terrace that's perfect for
a long lunch or a big dinner. There's also a
bar area and an upstairs dining room with

a second terrace, so you're spoilt for choice.
The menu is huge and photographic – try the
pelmeni/dumplings with pastry topping.

Mala's Garden GEORGIAN $$
(📞592-030131; Rustaveli 4; mains 10-25 GEL;
⊙noon-11pm; 🛜) This is a delightful spot to
sit among the trees and bushes in a relaxed
(sometimes rather too relaxed) atmosphere,
and munch on kebabs, which are cooked
using the traditional Georgian hairdryer-on-
grill method right there, or salads, soups and
other traditional dishes from the kitchen.

Bravo GEORGIAN $$
(Nadikvari 11; mains 7-20 GEL; ⊙10am-midnight;
🛜🍴) Bravo does a decent job on a wide
range of Georgian favourites, and has a pictorial menu which makes the process of ordering slightly less like guesswork. There's a
good terrace where you can enjoy your meal,
though it fills up early. There is also a range
of pizzas and pastas if you fancy a break
from Georgian cuisine.

🍷 Drinking & Nightlife

Telavi has a smattering of wine bars where
you can enjoy drinks in the evening, but it
would be inaccurate to say that nightlife is
a draw. There are, however, some excellent
nearby wineries that welcome visitors to do
wine tastings.

Teliani Valley WINERY
(📞32-2313245; www.telianivalley.com; Tbilisi Hwy
3) Located on the outskirts of Telavi, this
excellent winery has won many international
awards and is one of Georgia's most famous

Telavi

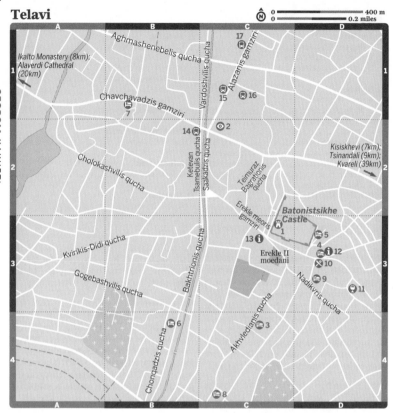

Telavi

wine producers. It welcomes drop-in visitors for wine tastings (15 GEL to 40 GEL per person, depending on number of people and wines) and vineyard tours. You can also stay overnight at its guesthouse.

Rostomaant Marani　　　　　　　WINERY
(📱599-929505; www.rmarani.com; Rcheulishvili 9; ☺11am-7pm) This family-run winery welcomes guests to its central Telavi premises for two-hour wine tastings (20 GEL to 35

GEL per person), which include snacks and grilled meats in the more expensive version.

❶ Information

Kakheti Wine Guild (☑ 350-279090; Rustaveli 1; ⊙10am-7pm) The helpful Kakheti Wine Guild has information on many of the region's wineries and can organise tours, tastings and meals; it also sells over 100 types of wine direct, though the staff don't always speak much English.

Tourism Information Centre (☑ 350-275317; Erekle II 9; ⊙9am-6pm Mon-Fri, 10am-5pm Sat & Sun) Helpful office upstairs in a verandaed building on the main square. It can arrange shared jeeps to Tusheti, among other things.

❶ Getting There & Away

Telavi has several *marshrutka* and taxi departure points:

New bus station (☑ 350-272083; Alazanis gamziri)
Old bus station (☑ 350-271619; Alazanis gamziri)
Roki bus station (☑ 350-274390; Alazanis gamziri)

Shared taxis to Tbilisi (10 GEL, 1¾ hours) wait at the top of Alazanis gamziri. *Marshrutky* to Ikalto (0.50 GEL) go about hourly, 8am to 6pm, from Chavchavadziz gamziri.

Around Telavi

The villages and lovely countryside around Telavi are full of fascinating wineries and old castles, palaces, monasteries and churches. Public transport reaches most of them, but you can pack a lot more into your day by taking a taxi tour or hiring your own vehicle. Most Telavi accommodation options either have their own vehicles or can organise one to take you to several destinations in a trip for 70 GEL to 80 GEL. Knowledgeable, English-speaking David Luashvili (p126) is a recommended driver-guide.

★**Chavchavadze Estate**   PALACE
(☑ 570-701212; www.tsinandali.ge; Tsinandali; gardens 3 GEL, museum & park 5 GEL, incl tasting 1/ several wines 7/20 GEL; ⊙10am-7pm; ℗) Prince Alexander Chavchavadze (1786–1846) was one of the most colourful and influential characters in Georgian history, and the palace and gardens he created at Tsinandali are a don't-miss stop on any Kakheti tour. The palace tour takes you around half a dozen rooms restored in 19th-century style and relates interesting episodes from the family story. The park is beautifully laid out in the English style, with venerable trees and exotic plants such as ginkgo, sequoia and yucca.

★**Alaverdi Cathedral**   CATHEDRAL
(Kvemo Alvani; ⊙8am-6pm) At the beginning of the 11th century, when Georgia was entering its cultural and political golden age, King Kvirike of Kakheti had this majestic cathedral built. At 50m tall, Alaverdi Cathedral remained the tallest church in Georgia for nearly a millennium. Situated 20km northwest of Telavi, its exterior is classically proportioned with majestic rounded arches but minimal decoration. Inside, the church has a beautiful spacious harmony, with light entering from 25 high slit windows.

Schuchmann   WINERY
(☑ 790-557045; www.schuchmann-wines.com; Kisiskhevi; tour & tasting per person incl 3/5/7 wines 15/25/35 GEL; ⊙10am-8pm; ℗) A very professional modern operation 7km southeast of

MARSHRUTKY FROM TELAVI

DESTINATION	BUS STATION	COST (GEL)	TIME	FREQUENCY
Alaverdi	Old	2	40min	every 15-20min, 8.45am-5.15pm
Alvani	Old	2	45min	every 15-20min, 9am-5.30pm
Dedoplis Tskaro	New	7	2hr	3.30pm
Kvareli	Old	3	1½hr	every 40min, 9.30am-5.30pm
Lagodekhi	New	6	1¾hr	7.30am, 8.30am, 8.40am, 1.30pm
Lagodekhi	Old	6	1¾hr	3pm
Sighnaghi	Old	5	1½hr	3.15pm Mon-Fri
Tbilisi	New	7	1¾hr	every 40min, 7.40am-1pm
Tbilisi	Roki	8	1¾hr	every 30-45min, 6am-6pm
Tsinandali	Old	0.80	20min	every 30min, 9am-5pm

central Telavi, producing 1.5 million bottles a year – 30% is *qvevri* wine (under the Vinoterra label) and the rest 'European' wine, fermented and aged in stainless-steel tanks, under the Schuchmann label.

Twins Old Cellar WINERY

(☑ 557-148282, 551-747474; www.cellar.ge; Napareuli; tour & tasting from 17 GEL; ⊘ 9am-10pm; P) A family-run operation making *qvevri* and European wine, 23km north of Telavi. Visits include its comprehensive *qvevri* wine museum and a tasting of three wines and one *chacha* (a powerful Georgian grappa). It also has a very fancy new hotel overlooking the vineyards, and a restaurant.

Shumi WINERY

(☑ 32-2381137, 598-503501; www.shumi.ge; Tsinandali; tour per person 7 GEL. 2-wine tasting free, 4-wine tasting & snacks per person 20 GEL; ⊘ 10am-6pm; P) This interesting smallish winery produces wines of numerous appellations under the Shumi and Iberiuli labels, and has a vineyard of 432 vine varieties, along with a museum housing some astonishingly old wine-related objects. Tastings take place in a pretty garden.

Winery Khareba WINERY

(☑ 32-2497770; www.winery-khareba.com; Kvareli; tour incl 2-wine tasting European/qvevri wines 12/15 GEL, without tasting 5 GEL; ⊘ 10am-8pm May–mid-Nov, to 6pm mid-Nov–Apr; P) What's special here is the 7.7km of wine tunnels, dug out of a hillside in the early 1960s for storing and ageing wine at constant temperatures. Today the tunnels store over 25,000 bottles of the Khareba company's European and *qvevri* wines. Tours go into part of the tunnels (where tastings also take place) then up to the viewing tower and restaurant.

Nekresi Monastery MONASTERY

Nekresi's early Georgian architecture and the views across the Alazani valley from its hillside-woodland site are marvellous. The monastery is 4km off the Kvareli road from a turning 10km past Gremi (Kvareli-bound *marshrutky* will drop you at the turn-off). Vehicles must park 1.5km before the monastery; from there *marshrutky* (1 GEL return trip) shuttle up and down the hill from about 9am to 5pm, from approximately mid-April to mid-December.

Ikalto Monastery MONASTERY

(Ikalto; ⊘ 9am-6pm; P) This monastery, beautifully situated in a cypress grove, was one of two famous medieval Georgian Neoplatonist academies, the other being Gelati near Kutaisi. Shota Rustaveli, the national poet, is thought to have studied here. The main Transfiguration Church was built in the 8th and 9th centuries. The roofless building along the south side of the compound was the Academy; an 8th-century stone wine press survives to its left (Georgian monasteries have always been enthusiastic winemakers).

The monastery is 2km uphill from the Telavi–Akhmeta road: turn off just after the 54/19 Km post. *Marshrutky* from Telavi terminate in Ikalto village, leaving you with a pleasant-enough 1.5km road-walk up to the monastery.

Gremi Fortress FORTRESS

(Eniseli; admission to tower 3 GEL; ⊘ 9am-6pm Tue-Sun) From 1466 to 1672, Gremi was the capital of Kakheti, but the town down to the west of the citadel was totally devastated by Shah Abbas in 1616. Within the citadel, the Church of the Archangels was built in 1565 by King Levan (who is buried inside) and contains frescoes from 1577. You can climb up inside the adjacent 15th-century tower-palace and a small museum contains explanatory panels on old Gremi, plus artefacts from the site.

☞ Tours

David Luashvili DRIVING

(☑ 593-761216, 551-300620; purgatorium@rambler.ru) Knowledgeable, English-speaking David Luashvili is a recommended Telavi-based driver-guide for trips around Kakheti. He charges 100 GEL per car for a Kakheti day tour (itineraries are flexible), and 150 GEL for a day trip from Telavi to David Gareja.

🛏 Sleeping

Twins Old Cellar HOTEL $$

(☑ 557-148282, 551-747474; www.cellar.ge; Napareuli; r incl breakfast 160-250 GEL; P ❊) The once-small hotel at Twins Old Cellar winery had completed a brand-new building at research time with very sleek and spacious rooms surrounding a large pool. The older, wood-beamed rooms overlooking vineyards are much cheaper, however. There's a museum of wine on the premises and a good restaurant offering pairing meals.

★ Villa Alazani GUESTHOUSE $$$

(☑ 577-414842; www.villaalazani.com; Kisiskhevi; r/whole house incl breakfast 250/820 GEL; P)

PANKISI VALLEY

Visiting this remote slice of Kakheti between the region's fertile wine-producing lowlands and the inhospitable mountains of Tusheti is a fascinating cultural experience. The local population, who refer to themselves as Kists after the village in nearby Chechnya from where their ancestors once came, are Sunni Muslims, speak a dialect of Chechen as well as Georgian and normally Russian, and live a traditional agrarian lifestyle in a series of five small villages strung along the Alazni River, all linked by one road.

Unfairly accused of being a hotbed of Islamic fundamentalism during the Second Chechen War (1999–2009), the area was considered dangerous for years, but in recent years a group of women in the area have formed the Pankisi Valley Tourism and Development Association, which seeks to change the image of the area by promoting the region to visitors and encouraging homestays and cultural tourism. The founder of the association, Nazy Dakishvili, also runs **Nazy's Guesthouse** (☑599-145209; www.nazysguest house.com; per person 45 GEL; P🛜) in the village of Jokolo, and this makes an excellent place to stay, not least as Nazy speaks good English, a rarity here.

There are now some eight different guesthouses in Pankisi and travellers curious to discover the people and traditions of the area will enjoy spending a few days here. Every Friday at midday local women perform a devotional Sufi ceremony of singing and chanting known as Zikr at the mosque in Duisi, which is the area's main cultural attraction. Other popular activities include cooking classes, visiting the Khodori Waterfall and the Batsara Nature Reserve, where you can see 2000-year-old yew trees, and horse riding or mountain biking along eight marked trails through the thickly forested rolling country-side of the valley.

This ample village house in Kisiskhevi, 7km southeast of Telavi, is a wonderful rural hideaway. It has been beautifully restored by its owners (a group of international journalists and film-makers) with wooden pillars, lovely spacious common areas, a marvellous collection of antique carpets, four good-sized bedrooms and a spacious kitchen.

Schuchmann Hotel　　　　　　　　HOTEL $$$
(☑790-557045; www.schuchmann-wines.com; Kisiskhevi; r incl breakfast from 250 GEL; P🛜🏊) A smart hotel at one of Georgia's top wineries, with spacious, balconied rooms in an attractive stone, wood and brick building, plus ample dining areas and excellent Georgian food. A range of Kakheti tours is also on offer.

Sighnaghi

☑355 / POP 3000

Sighnaghi is perhaps Georgia's single most attractive town, with an amazing position perched on a lofty hilltop facing the snow-capped Caucasus looming in the distance across the vast Alazani valley. Full of 18th- and 19th-century architecture and with a vaguely Tuscan feel, Sighnaghi has undergone a comprehensive renovation program in recent years that has seen scores of hotels open as the local population reorients itself towards the tourist dollar. The good news is that despite the tour groups and quad bikes, the town has retained its easy charm and is still a lovely place to spend a couple of days.

◉ Sights

★**Sighnaghi Museum**　　　　　　　MUSEUM
(Rustavelis chikhi 8; adult/student 7/1 GEL; ☉10am-6pm Tue-Sun) This well-displayed, modern museum has good exhibits on Kakheti archaeology and history downstairs, and a room of 13 paintings by Kakheti-born artist Niko Pirosmani (1862–1918) upstairs. This is the biggest collection of the self-taught painter's work outside the National Gallery in Tbilisi, and includes several famous canvases including *Vintage* and *Feast in a Grape Gazebo*.

Walls　　　　　　　　　　　ARCHITECTURE
Most of Erekle II's 4km defensive wall still stands, with 23 towers and each of its six gates named after a local village. Part of the wall runs along Chavchavadze on the hilltop on the northwest side of town, where you can enter the tiny Stepan Tsminda Church inside a tower. The best stretch to explore runs down beside Gorgasali on the northeast side of town. Here you can climb up one tower and walk along the walls down to two more.

Bodbe Convent CONVENT

(☺10am-7pm) Bodbe Convent, the revered final resting place of St Nino, is set among tall cypresses 2km south of Sighnaghi, a pleasant walk on country roads. The little church was originally built over the saint's grave by King Mirian in the 4th century. It has been rebuilt and renovated several times since. Nino's tomb, partly silver-covered, with a bejewelled turquoise cloisonné halo, is in a small chapel in its southeast corner. Its religious significance means that it's always massively crowded.

🛏 Sleeping

Sighnaghi has a few good hotels and plenty of guesthouses, several of which are on or just off historic Gorgasali, the street leading downhill inside the town wall. Many of these guesthouses have modernised their offering, making them almost hotel-like inside, though the welcome remains as traditional as ever.

⭐**Nana's Guesthouse** GUESTHOUSE $

(☎355-231829, 599-795093; www.facebook.com/pages/nanas-guest-house/268413209818; Sarajishvili 2; s/d/tr/q 35/75/90/120 GEL; 🛜) English-speaking Nana Kokiashvili certainly runs one of the most atmospheric guesthouses in town, with four spotless, spacious rooms sharing a wonderful wraparound balcony covered in grapevines running the length of her 18th-century house overlooking central Bebris Park. Nana provides home-cooked, organic breakfasts (10 GEL), and provides help organising transport and excursions.

Central Guest House GUESTHOUSE $

(☎592-404031; www.facebook.com/Sighnaghi CentralGuesthouse; 9 Apri No 30; dm/s/d/tr 15/40/60/75 GEL, breakfast 10 GEL; 🅿❄🛜📶) Just off Erekle II moedani and overlooking a deep, green valley, the Central offers a wide choice of neat, clean, wood-floored rooms with private bathroom, in a pleasantly converted 200-year-old house. The brick-walled dining room is decked out with historical photos and artefacts, which friendly English-speaking hostess Ana likes to explain to guests. Camping is also available (20 GEL per tent).

Hotel Brigitte HOTEL $$

(☎355-238080; www.brigitte.ge; Tamar Mepe 13; r incl breakfast from 150 GEL; ❄🛜📶) The best midrange option in town, Brigitte is an attractively converted house with spotless and comfortable rooms, pleasantly designed communal areas and a series of terraces out the back with stellar valley views. Staff are helpful and courteous, and breakfast is good.

Kusika Guest House GUESTHOUSE $$

(☎599-099813, 599-099812; kusikashvili.ilia@mail.ru; Gorgasali 15; d 80 GEL, breakfast 10 GEL; 🅿❄🛜📶) This friendly little place has a vine-shaded courtyard with superb views over the Alazani valley to the distant Caucasus. There are three cosy, clean rooms, two of them enjoying the same panoramas. The breakfasts are great and it's altogether a very nice find.

Zandarashvili Family Hotel GUESTHOUSE $$

(☎355-231029, 599-750510; davidzandarashvili@yahoo.com; Tsminda Giorgi 11; s/d/tr/q 50/60/75/100 GEL, s/d/tr without bathroom 15/30/45 GEL, breakfast/dinner 10/20 GEL; ❄🛜) The hospitable Zandarashvili family provide good rooms, great food and homemade wine, and their house is deservedly a travellers' favourite. Top-floor rooms are particularly attractive and bright, especially those with balconies overlooking the valley. All rooms have private bathrooms, except three downstairs that are a great bargain. Transfers from the bus station and wine tasting are complimentary, and English is spoken.

Guesthouse MATE GUESTHOUSE $$

(☎355-232036, 598-899799; m.axmeteli@mail.ru; Gorgasali 20; s/d/tr 50/60/70 GEL, breakfast/dinner 10/15 GEL; 🅿❄🛜) MATE is a very good-value guesthouse with a lovely garden out the back and big meals with homemade wine served by the welcoming owner Manana. Rooms, for up to five people, are carpeted, comfy and only slightly frilly (the best are the newer ones on the upper floor).

🍴 Eating

⭐**Pancho Villa** MEXICAN $$

(☎599-192356; Tamar Mepe 9; mains 7-18 GEL; ☺noon-10pm; 🍴) Perhaps one of Georgia's most surprising finds is this excellent and authentic Mexican restaurant in a tiny East Georgian mountain town. Owner-chef Shalva has lived in California, where he honed his skills, and now runs this impressive one-man show in a rustic but charming wooden house with just three tables and extraordinary valley views.

Sighnaghi to Dedoplis Tskaro

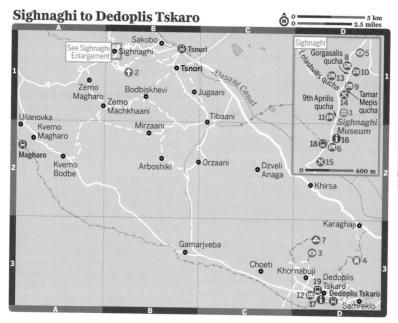

GEORGIA KAKHETI

Sighnaghi to Dedoplis Tskaro

◎ Top Sights
1 Sighnaghi Museum D1

◎ Sights
2 Bodbe Convent B1
3 Eagles Canyon D3
4 Khornabuji Fortress D3
5 Walls D1

◎ Sleeping
6 Central Guest House D2
7 Eagles Canyon Camping D3
8 Guesthouse MATE D1
9 Hotel Brigitte D1
10 Kusika Guest House D1

11 Nana's Guesthouse D1
12 Savanna Guesthouse D3
13 Zandarashvili Family Hotel D1

✕ Eating
14 Pancho Villa D1
15 Pheasant's Tears D2

ⓘ Information
16 Tourism Information Centre D2
17 Visitors Centre D3

ⓘ Transport
18 Bus Station D2
19 Bus Stop D3

★ **Pheasant's Tears**   GEORGIAN $$$
(☏ 355-231556; www.pheasantstears.com; Baratashvili 18; mains 15-35 GEL; ⊙ 11am-11pm; ☏ ✐)
✐ This Georgian-American joint venture makes top-class natural wines by the traditional *qvevri* method at its vineyards in the nearby village of Tibaani. Here in Sighnaghi it offers wine tastings and delicious Georgian meals prepared from fresh, organic and local produce, which you can enjoy in a pretty garden-courtyard. Sample dishes include grilled pork in white-wine sauce and mushrooms with tarragon.

ⓘ Information

Tourism Information Centre (☏ 355-232414; Kostava 10; ⊙ 9am-6pm Jun-Sep, from 10am Oct-May) Just off Erekle II moedani.

ⓘ Getting There & Away

Despite its popularity with travellers, Sighnaghi is a small town and is poorly connected to other towns in the region. *Marshrutky* to Tbilisi (7 GEL, 1¾ hours, six daily, 7am to 6pm) and Telavi (6 GEL, 1½ hours, 9am only Monday to Saturday) depart from the bus station, which can be found behind the police station on Erekle II moedani.

For *marshrutky* to Lagodekhi and Dedoplis Tskaro, and further services to Telavi, head 7km east down the hill to the town of Tsnori (by *marshrutka* 1 GEL, half-hourly, 9.45am to 5.15pm Monday to Friday; by taxi 5 GEL) and pick up *marshrutky* there.

Davit Gareja

The ancient monastery complex of Davit Gareja is one of the most remarkable of Georgia's historic sites. Its uniqueness is heightened by its remote setting on the border with Azerbaijan and the surrounding semidesert landscape. Add to this the total lack of provision for visitors, the absence of any efforts to restore or protect the frescoes, the frequent tensions with Azerbaijan, and visiting Davit Gareja remains a real adventure.

In July and August it can get fearfully hot here by the middle of the day, so an early start, getting here by 10am, is ideal. Bring sunscreen, water and sensible shoes as you'll have to scramble up the hillside with no shade. Also be sure to have your passport or ID card with you, as you're in border area and could potentially be stopped by both Georgian and Azerbaijani military patrols.

◉ Sights

Davit Gareja comprises about 15 monasteries spread over a wide area, but visitors usually just see two – Lavra, which has been restored since Soviet times and is now again inhabited by monks, and, just over the hill above it, Udabno, a series of caves painted with beautiful frescoes. It takes two to three hours and a lot of walking to explore Lavra and Udabno.

★**Udabno Monastery**　　　MONASTERY
Less of a monastery than a series of cavehewn chapels, Udabno runs along a steep escarpment looking down to grassy plains in Azerbaijan. While many caves are ruins, some contain fascinating frescoes painted in the 10th to 13th centuries, though the neglect is shocking with many centuries-old paintings covered in graffiti.

The exact line of the Georgia–Azerbaijan border up here has not yet been finally demarcated, and you may find Azerbaijan border guards patrolling here; they are not normally any hindrance to visiting the caves unless there is a flare-up of border tensions.

To reach Udabno, take the path uphill beside the church shop outside Lavra monastery. Watch out for poisonous vipers, including in the caves and especially from April to June. At a watchtower overlooking Lavra, take the path straight up the hill. In about 10 minutes you reach a metal railing. Follow this to the top of the ridge, then to the left along the far side of the ridge (where the railing deteriorates to a series of posts). The caves above the path here are the Udabno monastery.

The most outstanding frescoes are about halfway along the hillside. Walk along until you reach some caves numbered with green paint. Seventy metres past cave 50, a side path heads up and back to cave 36, the monastery's **refectory**, where the monks had to kneel to eat at low stone tables. It's decorated with beautiful light-toned frescoes, the principal one being an 11th-century Last Supper. Further up above here are the **Annunciation Church** (cave 42), with very striking frescoes showing Christ and his disciples (you need some agility to get inside it), and **St George's Church** (cave 41).

Return to the main path and continue 25m to the left to Udabno's **main church**. Paintings here show Davit Gareja and his disciple Lukiane surrounded by deer, depicting the story that deer gave them milk when they were wandering hungry in this remote wilderness. Below them are Kakhetian princes.

The path eventually climbs to a stone chapel on the clifftop, then heads down back to where you began.

Peristsvaleba　　　CHURCH
(Transfiguration Church) The 6th-century cave church Peristsvaleba contains Davit Gareja's tomb, to the right of the icon screen.

Lavra　　　MONASTERY
This restored monastery is on three levels, with buildings from many periods. You enter by a gateway decorated with reliefs illustrating stories of the monks' harmony with the natural world. Inside you descend to a courtyard with the caves of Davit and his Kakhetian disciple Lukiane along one side, and the 6th-century cave church Peristsvaleba on the other side. Davit's tomb sits to the right of the church's icon screen.

🛌 Sleeping & Eating

There are dozens of homestays and guesthouses in the nearby village of Udabno, which make for the best options if you plan

VASHLOVANI PROTECTED AREAS

Down in remote far southeast Kakheti, Georgia's ever-changing landscapes take yet another twist. Beyond the town of Dedoplis Tskaro, expanses of wheat fields give way to a strange semi-desert zone where eroded badlands alternate with steppe grasslands, canyons, savannah, ancient pistachio forests and woodlands along the Alazani River, which makes up the border with Azerbaijan. The 370-sq-km Vashlovani Protected Areas harbour a very high concentration of species including 46 mammals, 135 birds, 30 reptiles and 600 plants. The mammals include brown bear, wolf, otter, hyenas and goitered gazelles recently reintroduced from Azerbaijan. The best times to visit, with moderate temperatures, plants in bloom and wildlife more active, are from April to mid-June and September to mid-November. July and August are excruciatingly hot.

Also worth visiting near Dedoplis Tskaro are **Eagles Canyon** (Artsivis Kheoba), home to enormous vultures and black storks, and the ancient crag-top ruin of **Khornabuji Fortress**.

The excellent **Visitors Centre** (☎577-101849; nseturidze13@gmail.com; Baratashvili 5; ⊗9am-6pm), with helpful, English-speaking staff, an interesting little museum, good rooms (single/double 40/50 GEL) and a guest kitchen, is also in the town of Dedoplis Tskaro. Visitors must register here before entering the Vashlovani Protected Areas and should book in advance to stay here. Vashlovani hiking maps are also on sale (3 GEL).

Sleeping

The town of Dedoplis Tskaro has a couple of sleeping options, including **Savanna Guesthouse** (☎555-150835, 555-540474; welcomesavanna@gmail.com; Mosulishvili 54, Dedoplis Tskaro; s/d from 35/60 GEL, breakfast/dinner 15/20 GEL; ❀🛜). There are also clean rooms at the visitors centre and a rustic but beautifully set **campsite** (☎599-313957, 577-797400; per person with/without own tent 10/15 GEL, breakfast/dinner 20/30 GEL) in Eagles Canyon. If you have time, stay overnight in one of the six **Mijnis Kure Bungalows** (Vashlovani Protected Areas; r 50 GEL; 🅿) on the banks of the Alazani River deep within the Protected Areas. Each has three single beds, electricity and a bathroom with a hot shower. You're a long way from civilisation here, and while there's a drinking-water well, you'll need to bring mosquito repellent as well as food. Make reservations at the Visitors Centre in Dedoplis Tskaro.

Getting There & Away

The Visitors Centre can help arrange jeep trips in the reserve (day trip around 300 GEL). If you're driving yourself, you'll need a 4WD and a good GPS to navigate the labyrinthine, often very rough tracks.

Marshrutky run from Dedoplis Tskaro to Telavi (7 GEL, two hours) at 7.30am and 8.30am daily, and to Tbilisi (7 GEL, three hours) about hourly from 7.30am to 4.30pm, where they drop you at Isani metro station. Buses leave from the bus stop on a big roundabout in the middle of Dedoplis Tskaro.

---

to stay overnight. The arty and international Oasis Club is definitely the pick of the bunch, however.

⭐**Oasis Club**　　　　　　　　HOSTEL **$**
(☎574-805563; www.oasisclubudabno.com; Udabno village; dm 25 GEL, s/d/tr/q 100/120/150/180 GEL; 🅿🛜) This unlikely Polish-run hostel-hotel-restaurant is indeed an oasis of relaxation, musical performances, outdoor cinema and the occasional wild party. It can be found in the semi-abandoned village of Udabno (not to be confused with Udabno monastery), 14km before Davit

Gareja on the road from Sagarejo. The restaurant is excellent, and it makes for a great lunch stop.

For sleeping, you have a choice between the 20-bed hostel or cosy wooden hotel rooms with private bathroom. Breakfast costs an extra 12 GEL. At the restaurant-bar (dishes 10 GEL to 15 GEL), cheerful staff serve good salads, soups, *khachapuri* and other dishes. The walking distance to Lavra cross-country is 8km, and Oasis can arrange for a horse and guide to take you there (100 GEL).

ⓘ Getting There & Away

From about mid-April to mid-October **Gareji Line** (Map p46; ☑ 551-951447; www.facebook. com/gareji.line; return 30 GEL; ⊙ Apr-Nov) runs a daily minibus between Tbilisi and Davit Gareja, departing at 11am from Pushkinis skver, just off Tavisuplebis moedani, and getting back there about 7pm. You get 2½ to three hours at Lavra and Udabno monasteries, plus a stop at Oasis Club on the way back. The ticket allows you to come back any day, so you can stay over at Oasis Club if you wish.

Many hostels and agencies also run day tours from Tbilisi, or you can do the trip alone if you have your own wheels. If you're driving yourself, take the main road to Sagarejo and then the road through Udabno to the monastery.

From Sighnaghi, a taxi day trip to Davit Gareja costs around 100 GEL, or you could take a Tbilisi-bound *marshrutka* as far as Sagarejo and a taxi from there.

Lagodekhi Protected Areas

The 244-sq-km **Lagodekhi Protected Areas** (☑ 577-101834; www.visitlagodekhi.com), above the small east Kakhetian town of the same name, climb to heights of over 3000m in the soaring Caucasus. The protected areas, which date from 1913 and are Georgia's oldest, feature deep river valleys, glacial lakes and some of Georgia's best-preserved forests. They're also home to several hundred East Caucasian tur, deer and chamois. Few travellers make it out here to the remote border with Dagestan (Russia) and Azerbaijan, but those who do find some fantastic hiking and nature-watching opportunities and an enthusiastic Visitors Centre determined to help travellers make the most of this magical region.

🏃 Activities

Shavi Kldeebis Tba   WALKING
(Black Rocks Lake) The most popular hike to do here is this 24km trail from Lagodekhi up to picturesque Shavi Kldeebis Tba on the Russian border (a three-day circular route with an ascent of 2200m). The path is walkable from mid-June to late October and you can sleep at two mountain shelters on the way.

🛏 Sleeping

Lagodekhi town has several decent accommodation options, many of which can be found along the main road from town to the Visitors Centre.

Kavkasioni Twins Guesthouse   GUESTHOUSE $
(Caucasus Hostel; ☑ 599-856640; irina-orujash vili@mail.ru; Vashlovani 136; s/d 30/50 GEL, breakfast/dinner 10/20 GEL; ✳🕾) There's a warm welcome here, just 100m from the reserve entrance, and the seven rooms are bright and spotless, with shiny wood floors. Two have private bathrooms, and five more were under construction at the time of research.

Wald Hotel Lagodekhi   HOTEL $$
(☑ 593-839983; www.waldhotel.ge; Vashlovani 197; d 100 GEL, ste 150-180 GEL; ✳🕾🏊) Tucked away behind the Visitors Centre, the Wald Hotel offers the most comfortable accommodation in town and makes for an excellent base for exploring the Lagodekhi Protected Areas. It has a popular canteen serving meals (3.50 GEL to 18 GEL) all day, as well as a pool table and a pool.

ⓘ Information

Visitors Centre (☑ 577-101834, 577-101890; zazats2002@yahoo.com; Vashlovani 197; ⊙ 9am-6pm) Plentiful information on the Lagodekhi Protected Areas is available at the helpful, English-speaking Visitors Centre at the main reserve entrance, 2km up from the main road in Lagodekhi. It also rents tents (per day 10 GEL), sleeping bags (5 GEL) and horses (50 GEL).

ⓘ Getting There & Away

Marshrutky leave Lagodekhi's **bus station** (Zaqatala) for Tbilisi (7 GEL, 2½ hours, about hourly 6.45am to 5.30pm) and Telavi (6 GEL, 1¾ hours, five daily, 8am to 2.15pm).

A taxi to or from the Azerbaijan border at Matsimi, 4km southeast of Lagodekhi, costs 10 GEL. From the Azerbaijan side you can take a taxi to Balakən (AZN4) or Zaqatala (around AZN10). You'll find money changers on both sides of the border and along the main road in Lagodekhi town, which also has several ATMs.

UNDERSTAND GEORGIA

Georgia Today

The past few years in Georgian politics have been fraught with power struggles on both a national and geopolitical level. The country has once again squared up against its giant northern antagonist, Russia, while simultaneously seeking an ever-closer relationship with the EU and NATO. Popular anger has often boiled over into demonstrations, and Georgians, while generally supporting the anti-Russian, pro-European line, are still polarised with regard to social issues, and in many cases remain far from European in their attitudes.

Margvelashvili to Zurabishvili

The president between 2013 and 2018, Giorgi Margvelashvili, may have originally been the candidate of the ruling Georgian Dream Party, but he quickly split with it, apparently wanting to play more the role of mediator in the country's messy politics, rather than using the presidency to consolidate power for his own party. This enraged his Georgian Dream backers, who had placed the little-known former education minister in power, and Margvelashvili became the first Georgian president not to run for a second term. In the presidential elections of 2018, Salome Zurabishvili, a French-born former diplomat, triumphed in the second-round run-off to become Georgia's first female president, though the presidency she inherited was notably pared down by a new constitution that placed more and more power in the hands of the prime minister and parliament. While Zurabishvili ran as an independent, she was strongly supported by the ruling Georgian Dream Party, who have retained a large majority in parliament since 2012.

Unrest in Tbilisi

Georgia's economic relations with Russia appeared to have been warming slightly in recent years, although diplomatic relations between the countries remained broken. That all changed in summer 2019, when a Russian politician addressed an inter-parliamentary conference of Orthodox lawmakers at Georgia's parliament from the Speaker's chair, a poorly thought-through decision by any measure. This angered the local population, a large majority of whom consider Russia to be an occupying power ('Russia is occupant' is the linguistically compromised slogan you'll see all over the country), and there was a spontaneous demonstration in Tbilisi on 20 June 2019, which ended with the attempted storming of parliament, and hundreds of people in hospital. The Speaker of parliament resigned, but demonstrations in Tbilisi continued throughout the summer of 2019, simultaneously venting popular anger against both Russia and the Georgian government, which is widely perceived to be less anti-Russian than it should be. Russia immediately sought to punish Georgia's tourist industry by cancelling all flights from Russian airports to Georgia and advising its citizens, who make up a large proportion of Georgia's annual tourist arrivals, against all travel to the country, for fear of 'Russophobia'. Ironically, the Russian embargo of Georgia introduced in 2006 forced Georgia's economy to diversify and it's now unlikely to be too badly affected by renewed sanctions.

Western, but How Western?

The Georgian Dream government did, however, continue former President Mikheil Saakashvili's pursuit of closer ties with the West, entering into a Deep and Comprehensive Free Trade Area (DCFTA) with the EU in 2016 and working towards increased political and economic integration. As part of this, Georgia is obliged to enact a raft of reforms to bring it into line with European norms in areas including human rights and democracy. The prospect of too much Western liberal influence on Georgian culture, however, alarms the country's many social traditionalists, especially the Georgian Orthodox Church, which has enjoyed a massive revival since the end of the Soviet era and is the most powerful social force in the country. Some 40% to 45% of Georgians now attend religious services at least monthly, and the church is a highly conservative body. Indeed, its clergy were involved in violently breaking up a Tbilisi rally marking the International Day against Homophobia and Transphobia in 2013, and all subsequent attempts to hold a pride march in Tbilisi since then have been unsuccessful, with the government adamant that it's unable to guarantee the safety of marchers. One demonstration was approved in 2019, but the political unrest in the country at the time led to its eventual cancellation.

Despite Georgia remaining deeply conservative and homophobic for the most part, Tbilisi's thriving techno scene has provided an important focal point for progressives of all types and has arguably done much to change local attitudes to alternative lifestyles. This was best illustrated in 2018 when a number of heavy-handed raids on Tbilisi nightclubs led to a series of notorious protests by Tbilisi youth under the banner 'We dance together. We fight together' (p63), spearheaded by techno super-club Bassiani and its various DJs in Georgia and around the world. Cannabis was legalised in Georgia the same year, but otherwise drug laws in the country remain draconian.

Where Now?

Georgia finds itself at a strange crossroads today, between its authoritarian past and democratic present, between its Orthodox and progressive values, between the EU and Russia, both of which see this small country as an important regional influencer. EU flags may fly from outside every government building in Georgia today, but the country still has a long journey ahead before it can genuinely realise its European dream.

In terms of tourism, Georgia has undergone a significant transformation over the past decade from a niche backpacker and hiker secret to a major traveller destination. In 2019 Batumi was named Europe's leading emerging tourist destination at the World Travel Awards, while an incredible eight million tourists visited Georgia in 2018, more than double its population. Guesthouses continue to go from strength to strength, while Western-style hostels are mushrooming all over the country. The Adjara Group, which now has half a dozen properties in the country, is a home-grown hotel group that has pioneered boutique hotels in Georgia and has contributed enormously to the country's reputation. The future for Georgia's tourism, at least, looks bright.

History

Georgians live and breathe their history as a vital key to their identities today. In few countries in the world will you find people so familiar with, and so proud, of their country's past.

Early Kingdoms

In classical times the two principal kingdoms on the territory were Colchis in the west (site of Greek colonies), and Kartli (also known as Iveria or Iberia) in the east and south and some areas in modern Turkey and Armenia.

When St Nino converted King Mirian and Queen Nana of Kartli to Christianity in the early 4th century, Georgia became the world's second kingdom to adopt this faith, a quarter-century after Armenia. In the 5th century, western Georgia became tied to the Byzantine Empire, while Kartli fell under Persian control. King Vakhtang Gorgasali of Kartli (c 447–502) drove the Persians out and set up his capital at Tbilisi. But the Persians soon returned, to be replaced in 654 by the Arabs, who set up an emirate at Tbilisi.

The Golden Age

Resistance to the Arabs was spearheaded by the Bagrationi dynasty of Tao-Klarjeti, a collection of Christian principalities straddling what are now southwest Georgia and northeast Turkey. They later added Kartli to their possessions, and when these were inherited by King Bagrat of Abkhazia (northwest Georgia) in the early 11th century, most of Georgia became united under one rule. King Davit Aghmashenebeli (David the Builder; 1089–1125) made Georgia the major Caucasian power and a centre of Christian culture. It reached its zenith under Davit's great-granddaughter Queen Tamar (1184–1213), whose writ extended over much of present-day Azerbaijan and Armenia, plus parts of Turkey and southern Russia. Tamar is still so revered that Georgians today call her, without irony, King Tamar.

Death, Destruction & Division

The golden age ended violently with the arrival of the Mongols in the 1220s. King Giorgi the Brilliant (1314–46) shook off the Mongol yoke, but then came the Black Death, followed by the Central Asian destroyer Timur (Tamerlane), who attacked eight times between 1386 and 1403.

Devastated Georgia split into four main kingdoms: Kartli and Kakheti in the east, Imereti in the northwest and Samtskhe in the southwest. From the 16th to 18th centuries western Georgian statelets generally fell under Ottoman Turkish dominion, while eastern ones were subject to the Persian Safavids. In 1744 a new Persian conqueror, Nader Shah, installed local Bagratid princes as kings of Kartli and Kakheti. One of these, Erekle II, ruled both kingdoms as a semi-independent state from 1762.

Russian Rule

Russian troops crossed the Caucasus for the first time in 1770 to get involved in Imereti's liberation from the Turks. At the Treaty of Georgievsk (1783), Erekle II accepted Russian suzerainty over eastern Georgia in

GEORGIA & ST GEORGE

St George (Tsminda Giorgi in Georgian) is Georgia's patron saint (as well as England's, Portugal's, Bulgaria's and Malta's) – but the legendary dragon slayer was almost certainly not responsible for the country name Georgia. Georgians know their country as Saqartvelo (land of the Kartvelebi), tracing their origins to Noah's great-great-grandson Kartlos. The English word 'Georgia' might stem from the Persian name for Georgians, *gurj*, which was picked up by medieval crusaders.

According to widely accepted accounts, St George was a senior officer in the Roman army who was executed in AD 303 in Nicomedia, Turkey, for standing up against emperor Diocletian's persecution of Christians. He soon became venerated as a Christian martyr and it was St Nino, the bringer of Christianity to Georgia in the 320s, who first popularised him among Georgians. Today Georgia celebrates two St George's Days each year – 6 May, the anniversary of his execution, and 23 November, commemorating his torture on a wheel of swords.

return for protection against his Muslim enemies. Russia went on to annex all the Georgian kingdoms and princedoms during the 19th century, and built the recognisable centres of many contemporary Georgian towns during this time.

In the wake of the 1917 Russian Revolution, Georgia was briefly independent, but was invaded by the Red Army in 1921 and incorporated into the new Union of Soviet Socialist Republics in 1922. During the 1930s, like everywhere else in the USSR, Georgia suffered from the Great Terror unleashed by Joseph Stalin, a cobbler's son from the Georgian town of Gori who had ruthlessly taken control of the largest country on earth.

Stalin died in 1953, and the 1960s and '70s are looked back on with nostalgia by older Georgians as a time of public order, peace and high living standards. Yet by the mid-1980s Mikhail Gorbachev began his policies of reform and the USSR disintegrated in just seven years.

Independence from Dream to Nightmare

Georgia's bubbling independence movement became an unstoppable force after the deaths of 19 hunger strikers when Soviet troops broke up a protest in Tbilisi on 9 April 1989. Georgia's now anti-communist government, led by the nationalist Zviad Gamsakhurdia, declared independence on 9 April 1991. Almost immediately Georgia descended into chaos and civil war. Gamsakhurdia was replaced by a military council, which gained an international respectability when Eduard Shevardnadze, the Georgian who had been Gorbachev's foreign minister, agreed to lead it.

But internal conflicts got worse. A truce in June 1992 halted a separatist conflict in the region of South Ossetia, but an even more serious separatist conflict engulfed Abkhazia, where in September 1993 Georgia suffered a comprehensive defeat, leaving Abkhazia as well as South Ossetia de facto independent. Virtually all Abkhazia's ethnic Georgian population, about 230,000 people, was driven out of the territory, becoming internally displaced people.

The Rose Revolution

For a decade after the Abkhazia disaster, Georgia oscillated between periods of relative peace and security and terrible crime waves, gang warfare, infrastructure collapse and rampant corruption. Georgians eventually lost faith in President Shevardnadze and flawed parliamentary elections in 2003 were the focus for a mass protest movement that turned into a bloodless coup, named the Rose Revolution after the flowers carried by demonstrators. Led by Mikheil 'Misha' Saakashvili, a US-educated lawyer heading the opposition United National Movement (UNM), protestors invaded the parliament building in Tbilisi on 22 November, and Shevardnadze resigned the next morning.

The 36-year-old Saakashvili won presidential elections in January 2004 by a landslide, appointed a team of young, outward-looking ministers and set about modernising the country, slashing taxes, regulations and bureaucracy, and launching 'zero-tolerance' campaigns against crime and corruption. Within months, the entire notoriously corrupt traffic police force was sacked and replaced with better paid, better trained, unbribeable officers. Within a few years crime almost disappeared and Georgia was one of the safest countries on the planet. Foreign aid and investment helped the economy, roads and railways were improved, and endemic electricity shortages ended.

But industry had died a death in the 1990s, and levels of poverty and unemployment stayed high. In response to growing protests, Saakashvili called a snap presidential election for January 2008, and won it with 53% of the vote.

War with Russia

The Saakashvili government had a strong pro-Western stance, with ambitions to join NATO and the EU. This spooked a Russia led by ex-KGB officer Vladimir Putin, who was quoted as saying he would 'hang Saakashvili by the balls'. Saakashvili began manoeuvring to bring the Russian-backed breakaway regions Abkhazia and South Ossetia back under Tbilisi's control. After a period of mounting tensions and sporadic violence in South Ossetia, Georgian forces started shelling the South Ossetian capital, Tskhinvali, on 7 August 2008, and entered the town the next day. But in two days they were driven out of South Ossetia by rapidly arriving Russian forces, which moved on to bomb or occupy Georgian military airfields and bases as well as the towns of Gori, Zugdidi, Poti and Senaki. The Russians halted just 45km short of Tbilisi. French President Nicolas Sarkozy negotiated a ceasefire, but the ethnic cleansing of most of South Ossetia's 20,000 ethnic-Georgian population continued into November. The 'Five Day War' claimed about 850 lives (half of them civilians).

Before 2008 was over, Russia recognised both South Ossetia and Abkhazia as independent states. It went on to station missile systems and thousand of troops in both territories. By 2011 Russia was providing about half of Abkhazia's budget and virtually all of South Ossetia's, and both territories were very much Russian satellites, to the anger of Georgians, who considered them illegally occupied by a foreign power.

Souring on Saakashvili

The Saakashvili government carried on with its project to transform Georgia into a modern, Westward-looking country, renovating shabby Old Town centres, building schools, opening a new parliament in the city of Kutaisi and giving the country a seaside resort, Batumi, worthy of the name. International tourists began to arrive in increasing numbers.

But more and more Georgians began to feel alienated from the government and its path. Many felt too much power was wielded by a small, autocratic circle of politicians and their allies. Protesters frequently blocked Tbilisi's main avenue, Rustaveli. Perhaps most of all, it was the inequities of the justice system that turned people away from Saakashvili. Crime had been eradicated through a draconian court system where acquittals were almost nonexistent and plea bargaining was many accused's only hope of a relatively lenient sentence, whether or not they were really guilty of the crime of which they were accused. Critics say these same tactics came to be used not just against supposed criminals but also against others who opposed Saakashvili and his circle for one reason or another, be they political protesters, opponents in the media or citizens who objected to an infrastructure project.

In September 2012, shortly before a parliamentary election, videos showing violent abuse of prisoners in a Georgian jail appeared on national TV – a disaster for Saakashvili. The election was won by the Georgian Dream coalition, an alliance of disparate groups held together chiefly by their dislike of Saakashvili, and led by Bidzina Ivanishvili, a Georgian multi-billionaire who had made his fortune in business dealings in Russia in the 1990s.

After 10 helter-skelter years of reform and modernisation, Mikheil Saakashvili and his UNM were out. Ivanishvili became prime minister in 2012, but stepped down after a year and handed the reins to his protégés, though he remained very much in power behind the scenes. Sometimes it seemed Georgian Dream's main objective was simply to reverse the things it didn't like about the Saakashvili administration. It called a halt to the spending on grand showpiece infrastructure projects, and it gave the judiciary greater independence, addressing a widespread grievance against the previously severe court system. Yet it also launched a wave of court cases against former officials from the previous administration. Saakashvili himself went into self-imposed exile in 2015, from which he has never returned. Still regarded with contempt by most Georgians today, Saakashvili nevertheless enabled Georgia to turn an important corner during his decade in power. Inheriting a country riddled with corruption, crime, gang violence and on the brink of infrastructural collapse, he left it a place vastly changed for the better, with low crime rates, massively improved transparency, a burgeoning tourist industry and an aspirant EU and NATO member.

Arts

Georgians are an incredibly expressive people. Music, dance, song, poetry and drama all play big parts in their lives.

Music & Dance

Georgian polyphonic singing is a tradition of multi-voice *a cappella* song that goes back thousands of years. It used to accompany every aspect of daily life, and the songs survive in various genres including *supruli* (songs for the table), *mushuri* (working songs) and *satrpialo* (love songs). It's still alive and well. Mostly male ensembles such as the Rustavi Choir perform in concert halls and at festivals like Art-Gene, Tushetoba and Shatiloba, but polyphonic song is most electrifying when it happens at less formal gatherings such as around the table at a *supra* (feast), when the proximity, intimacy and volume can be literally spine-tingling. There are varying regional styles but it's typical for some singers to do a bass drone while others sing melodies on top.

Sagalobeli (ethereally beautiful church chants) have been part of Georgian life for at least 1500 years. Excellent choirs accompany services in the most important churches: the best time to catch them is Sunday morning between about 9am and noon.

Polyphonic singing may or may not be accompanied by some of Georgia's numerous folk instruments, which include the *panduri* and *chonguri* (types of lute), the *garmoni* (accordion) and various bagpipes, flutes and drums. For an easy introduction to Georgian folk music check out popular folk or folk-fusion artists such as groups Bani, Gortela and 33a, and singer Mariam Elieshvili.

Georgia's exciting folk dance ranges from lyrical love stories to dramatic, leaping demonstrations of male agility. Top professional groups such as Erisioni and Sukhishvilebi often tour overseas, but don't miss them if they are performing back home.

Jazz is also popular, with young pianist Beka Gochiashvili the rising star, and Tbilisi and Batumi both hosting annual jazz festivals.

These days lots of music lovers come to Tbilisi specifically to hear Georgian techno, a genre that has thrived since the founding

---

GEORGIAN LITERATURE

For a language with only a few million speakers, Georgia has an amazingly rich literature. In the 12th century Shota Rustaveli, a member of Queen Tamar's court, wrote *The Knight* (or *Man*) *in the Tiger's* (or *Panther's*) *Skin*, an epic of chivalry that every Georgian can quote from.

Nikoloz Baratashvili (1817–45) personified the romanticism that entered Georgian literature in the early 19th century. Some later-19th-century writers turned to the mountains for inspiration – notably Alexander Kazbegi, novelist and dramatist, and Vazha Pshavela, whom many consider the greatest Georgian poet after Rustaveli.

Mikheil Javakhishvili (1880–1937) brought the Georgian novel to the fore with vivid, ironic tales of city and country, peasant and aristocrat in tsarist and Soviet times, including *Arsena Marabdeli*, based on a real-life Georgian Robin Hood figure, and the picaresque *Kvachi Kvachantiradze*. Javakhishvili was executed by the Soviet regime. Nodar Dumbadze (1928–84) portrayed post-WWII life with humour and melancholy, and is one of the most popular Georgian novelists: *The Law of Eternity* and *Granny, Iliko, Ilarion and I* are among his novels available in English.

Leading post-Soviet writers include novelist Aka Morchiladze, whose *Journey to Karabakh* (1992) tells of two young Georgian men who suddenly, bewilderingly find themselves in the midst of the Nagorno-Karabakh conflict; and novelist, playwright and travel writer David Turashvili, whose *Flight from the USSR* (2008) is based on a real-life attempt by a group of young Georgians to escape from the USSR by hijacking an Aeroflot plane.

HOW TO EAT A KHINKALI

Arguably Georgia's most beloved hunger killer, the *khinkali* is a small bag of dough twisted into a hard nexus at the top, with a filling of spiced, ground-up meat, or potatoes or mushrooms or sometimes vegetables – and plenty of juice. You'll have a plate of at least five *khinkali* in front of you (it's impossible to order fewer). Many people like to sprinkle a good dose of pepper over the *khinkali* before starting, though liquid butter, sour cream and spicy *adjika* sauce are also popular additions.

Once they're cool enough to handle, pick one up by the hard top, and bite a small hole just below it. Suck the juice out through the hole. Then eat the rest, except for the nexus, which you normally discard, although a certain number of locals like to eat the top too. Eating *khinkali* with knife and fork is perfectly acceptable, but is rarely done by Georgians.

of Bassiani (p62) in 2014, a massively significant event that has created an exciting and progressive techno scene in the capital, with DJs such as HVL, Zitto, Varg and Kancheli putting the city on the map for electronic music fans internationally.

Georgia has produced many outstanding classical artists too. Nina Ananiashvili, artistic director of the state ballet, is one of the world's top ballerinas, while leading contemporary composer Gia Kancheli, born in 1935, has been described as 'turning the sounds of silence into music'.

Visual Arts

Many Georgian churches are adorned with wonderful old frescoes. The golden age of religious art was the 11th to 13th centuries, when Georgian painters employed the Byzantine iconographic system and also portrayed local royalty and saints. There were two main, monastic fresco schools: one at the Davit Gareja and the other in Tao-Klarjeti (modern southwest Georgia and northeast Turkey). During the same period, artists and metalsmiths were creating beautiful icons and crosses with paint, jewels and precious metals that remain among Georgia's greatest treasures today. You can see them not only in churches but also in museums in Tbilisi, Kutaisi, Mestia and elsewhere.

Perhaps the last major artist in the fresco-painting tradition was one who painted scenes of everyday life in restaurants and bars in Tbilisi. The self-taught Niko Pirosmani (1862–1918) expressed the spirit of Georgian life in a direct and enchanting way. After his death in poverty and obscurity, his work was acclaimed by the leading, Paris-influenced Georgian modernists Davit Kakabadze, Lado Gudiashvili and Shalva Kikodze. Pirosmani, Kakabadze and

Gudiashvili are well represented in Tbilisi's National Gallery (p47). The Sighnaghi Museum (p127) has another good Pirosmani collection.

Georgia's contemporary art world is again blossoming after a depressed post-Soviet period. While no local artist can boast a similar profile to Zurab Tsereteli, whose bombastic and often grotesque works have made him a star internationally, some contemporary artists worth checking out today include Rusudan Petviashvili, Irakli Bugiani, Kote Jincharadze, Maka Batiashvili and Gia Edzgveradze, many of whom work and exhibit internationally.

Project ArtBeat (p50) is an excellent contemporary art gallery in Tbilisi that showcases the work of many Georgian artists and has nurtured diverse local talents. Its Moving Gallery, a single shipping container exhibiting the work of a regularly changing single artist, is specifically designed to bring art to new audiences around Georgia. Its website is a great place to start discovering the work of local artists.

Cinema

Georgian cinema enjoyed a golden age from the late 1960s to the 1980s, when Georgian directors created dozens of films distinct from the general socialist-realist run of Soviet movies. They won international awards with brilliant visual imagery, lively characters and use of allegory, fable and dreams to provide a platform for people's real concerns without upsetting the Soviet censors. Italian director Federico Fellini was a noted fan, praising Georgian cinema's ability to combine philosophy with childlike innocence.

Perhaps the greatest maestro was the Tbilisi-born Armenian Sergei Paradjanov, whose masterpiece *The Colour of Pomegranates* remains a staggering visual novelty and an extraordinary accomplishment of Soviet cinema. Tengiz Abuladze's *Repentance* (1984) was a groundbreaking opening up of the Soviet past – a black portrait of a dictatorial politician clearly based on Stalin's Georgian henchman Lavrenty Beria. Other leading directors included Otar Iosseliani (*There Lived a Songthrush;* 1970), Eldar Shengelaia (*The Blue Mountains;* 1983) and Giorgi Shengelaia (*Pirosmani;* 1969).

Today home-grown Georgian cinema is making a comeback after the grim post-Soviet years, despite still-minuscule budgets. It gets a reasonable amount of screen time among American blockbusters at Georgia's few cinemas. The tragic conflicts of the 1990s and the massive societal change in post-Soviet Georgia figure directly or indirectly in films such as *Since Otar Left* (2003), *A Trip to Karabakh* (2005), *Corn Island* (2014), *Tangerines* (a 2015 Oscar nominee) and *Dede* (2017). Meanwhile 2019's *And Then We Danced* featured the first-ever gay storyline in a Georgian film, something which caused predictable outrage at home, despite wowing audiences abroad.

Food & Drink

Eating is central to Georgian culture and identity, and Georgia's location on ancient spice routes has contributed unique flavours and textures. Many dishes are vegetarian and some are vegan. Georgians eat and drink at all times of the day, with restaurants keeping long hours. While restaurants have improved immeasurably in the past decade, some of the best Georgian food you'll eat will still be in guesthouses or private homes, where you can enjoy home-cooked fare with that genuine touch of Georgian hospitality.

Staples & Specialities

A great staple for everybody is the *khachapuri,* essentially a cheese pie or cheese bread. Equally beloved are *khinkali* – big spicy dumplings which most Georgians adore and most visitors find they like too.

A great snack on the go is *churchkhela,* a string of nuts (usually walnuts) coated in an often-pinkish caramel made from grape juice. You'll often see bunches of it hanging, sausage-like, at roadside stalls or markets.

Starters to a larger meal may include assorted salads, the delectable *badrijani nigvzit* (aubergine slices with walnut-and-garlic paste), *lobio* (bean paste or stew with herbs and spices) and *pkhali,* which are pastes combining vegetables with walnuts, garlic and herbs. The finest fresh bread to accompany a Georgian meal is *shotis* (or *tonis*) *puri* – long white loaves baked from wheat flour, water and salt (no fat or oil) in a round clay oven called a *tone.*

More substantial Georgian dishes include the *mtsvadi* (shish kebab) and a variety of chicken, pork, beef, lamb or turkey dishes in spicy, herby sauces or stews, with names like *chakapuli, chakhokhbili, kuchmachi, ojakhuri, ostri* or *shkmeruli.*

KNOW YOUR KHACHAHPURI

An excess of *khachapuri* is not for slimmers, but Georgia's ubiquitous cheese pies are the perfect keep-me-going meal, as well as playing a part in many a feast. They're sold at street stalls and bakeries as well as in cafes and restaurants. Different regions have their own varieties, but you'll find many of them all around the country:

Khachapuri acharuli The Adjaran variety is a large, boat-shaped calorie injection, overflowing with melted cheese and topped with butter and a runny egg.

Khachapuri imeruli Relatively sedate and the most common Georgia-wide, these round, flat pies originating from Imereti have melted cheese inside only.

Khachapuri megruli Round pies from Samegrelo, with cheese in the middle and more cheese melted on top. Sometimes also referred to as Khachapuri royal when topped with *sulguni* cheese.

Khachapuri penovani Square and neatly folded into four quarters, with the cheese inside the lightish crust – particularly tasty!

Khachapuri achma A large Adjaran concoction, with the dough and cheese in layers, lasagne-style.

Georgia's favourite spices and herbs include coriander, blue fenugreek, tarragon and ground-up marigold leaves.

Many dishes contain walnut, often ground as an ingredient in sauces, dressings or pastes. A sprinkling of pomegranate seeds is a tasty and pretty-looking garnish. Wild mushrooms are also a favourite, and Georgia has a wonderful variety of local cheeses.

The Supra & Toasts

While strictly speaking the word *supra* applies to any meeting where food and drink are consumed, the full works means staggering amounts to eat and drink. A selection of cold dishes and maybe soups will be followed by two or three hot courses as well as some kind of dessert, all accompanied by bottomless quantities of wine and rounds of toasts.

MENU DECODER

Georgian menus often look daunting, even if there's an English translation, but this list explains a lot of the items you'll find undefined on most menus.

adjika	a paste of chilli or paprika with garlic and herbs
ajapsandali	stew of aubergines, potatoes, tomatoes, peppers and herbs
apkhazura	spicy meatballs/sausage
badrijani nigvzit	aubergine (in slices with walnut-and-garlic paste)
bazhe	walnut sauce
chakapuli	stew of veal or lamb with tarragon and plums
chakhokhbili	stew of chicken, turkey or sometimes pork with tomatoes, onions and herbs
chakhrakuli	lamb ribs stewed with tomato, herbs and spices
chanakhi	a lamb stew with layers of potatoes, aubergine and tomatoes
chashushuli	spicy stew of meat or mushrooms with veggies
chikhirtma	chicken broth
churchkhela	string of walnuts coated in a sort of caramel made from grape juice
elarji	cornmeal mixed with *sulguni* cheese
gebzhalia	cottage cheese in a minty yoghurt sauce
kababi	doner kebab, shawarma
khachapuri	cheese pie of various types
kharcho	soup with rice, beef and spices
khinkali	dumpling with a meat, potato or mushroom filling
kuchmachi	stewed chicken/pig/calf innards with spices, herbs and usually walnuts
kupati	sausage
lobio	bean paste or stew with herbs and spices
matsoni	yoghurt
mchadi	cornflour bread
mtsvadi (ghoris/khbos)	shish kebab (from pork/beef), often just 'barbecue' on English-language menus
ojakhuri	meat goulash
ostri	spiced meat in a tomato-based sauce
pkhali	beetroot, spinach or aubergine paste with crushed walnuts, garlic and herbs
satsivi	cold turkey or chicken in a spicy walnut sauce, traditionally a New Year dish
shkmeruli	chicken in garlic sauce
soko	mushrooms
sulguni	a salty cheese, sometimes smoked
suneli	a spicy paste
tkemali	plum sauce

Bear in mind that Georgians toast only their enemies with beer. Wine or spirits are the only drinks to toast your friends with. However, at a *supra* you shouldn't drink them until someone proposes a toast. This can be a surprisingly serious, lengthy and poetic matter, even at small gatherings of a few friends. Larger gatherings will have a designated *tamada* (toastmaker), and some complex *supras* will involve an *alaverdi,* a second person whose role is to elaborate on the toast. If you are toasted, do not reply immediately but wait for others to add their wishes before simply thanking them – then wait a while before asking the *tamada* if you can make a toast in reply.

Drinks

Wine (p36) is a national passion and Georgians have been making and drinking it for at least 8000 years. The current craze is for natural and especially *qvevri* wines, which are generally organic and unfiltered and have a very distinctive taste.

Chacha is a traditional Georgian grappa made from fermented grape skins. While for years it was made by Georgians as moonshine, its production has been professionalised greatly of late, and you'll now find excellent artisanal *chachas* on sale at specialist *chacha* bars, as well as *chacha*-based cocktails elsewhere – try a *chacha* sour before you leave the country! Vodka is also common, and beer is a popular thirst quencher: standard local brands include Natakhtari, Kazbegi and Argo, but there are also a number of excellent craft beers being produced in Georgia; look out for Shavi Lomi (Black Lion), 9 Mta and NaturAle among others.

Georgia's most famous nonalcoholic drink is Borjomi, a salty mineral water that was the beverage of choice for every Soviet leader from Lenin on. It polarises opinion. Nabeghlavi is a less salty alternative. Various still waters are also available, though tap water is safe to drink throughout the country.

SURVIVAL GUIDE

ⓘ Directory A–Z

ACCESSIBLE TRAVEL

Georgia is a tough destination for travellers with access needs for the most part, with only

PRICE RANGES

Accommodation

The following price ranges refer to a double room, including taxes and breakfast.

$ less than 80 GEL

$$ 80–250 GEL

$$$ more than 250 GEL

Eating

The following price ranges refer to a main course.

$ less than 10 GEL

$$ 10–20 GEL

$$$ more than 20 GEL

hotels built in the past few years required to be fully accessible, few accommodations in public buildings, and narrow and poorly maintained pavements in most cities. Things are slowly improving, however, with the government committing in 2015 to making both Tbilisi and Mtskheta more accessible for wheelchair users. There are now several hotels and hostels in Tbilisi, such as Fabrika Hostel & Suites (p57), actively promoting themselves to mobility impaired guests. Currently about 30% of Tbilisi's buses are wheelchair-accessible, with the fleet being gradually upgraded. In August 2019 Batumi opened an adapted beach with floating wheelchairs.

Accessible Tourism Center Parsa (www.atcp. ge) Based in Tbilisi, this company is championing accessible tourism in the country and can organise accessible tours, transfers and hotel accommodation. Its website lists accessible hotels and tourist sites around the country, although there is no detailed information and 'accessible' is not defined.

Disabled Holidays (disabledholidays.com) Based in the UK, this reputable specialist accessible travel agent runs tours to Tbilisi.

ACCOMMODATION

Georgia has an increasingly wide range of sleeping options, including family-run guesthouses, Western-style hostels, midrange and boutique hotels. Peak season in most of the country is July and August, when it's often worth calling ahead to secure a room. Seasonal variations in room rates are minor (except in ski resorts), though it's sometimes possible to get a discount at quiet times.

The Georgian Alphabet

GEORGIAN	ROMAN	PRONUNCIATION
ა	a	as in 'father'
ბ	b	as in 'bet'
გ	g	as in 'go'
დ	d	as in 'do'
ე	e	as in 'get'
ვ	v	as in 'van'
ზ	z	as in 'zoo'
თ	t	as in 'to'
ი	i	as in 'police'
კ	k'	a 'k' pronounced very far back in the throat
ლ	l	as in 'let'
მ	m	as in 'met'
ნ	n	as in 'net'
ო	o	as in 'cot'
პ	p'	as in 'tip' (with a stop on the outflow of air)
ჟ	zh	as the 's' in 'pleasure'
რ	r	as in 'rub', but rolled
ს	s	as in 'see'
ტ	t'	as in 'sit' (with a stop on the outflow of air)
უ	u	as in 'put'
ფ	p	as in 'put'
ქ	q	a 'k' pronounced very far back in the throat
ღ	gh	as a French 'r'
ყ	q'	as the 'ck' in 'lick' (with a stop on the outflow of air)
შ	sh	as in 'she'
ჩ	ch	as in 'chip'
ც	ts	as in 'tsar'
ძ	dz	as the 'ds' in 'beds'
წ	ts'	as in 'its' (with a stop on the outflow of air)
ჭ	ch'	as in 'each' (with a stop on the outflow of air)
ხ	kh	as in Scottish 'loch'
ჯ	j	as in 'judge'
ჰ	h	as in 'here'

DANGERS & ANNOYANCES

Georgia is a generally safe country where people take pride in ensuring foreigners are treated well.

➽ Penalties for drug possession are draconian in Georgia, so don't carry or consume illegal drugs here; possession and consumption of cannabis were legalised in 2018.

➽ Travel to South Ossetia from Georgia wasn't possible at research time. It's possible to travel to Abkhazia, though many governments warn against this.

➽ When trekking always go with a partner, inform others of your plans and carry a first-aid kit. Avoid sheepdogs, which are bred to protect livestock from wolves and can be very dangerous to approach.

EMBASSIES & CONSULATES

Tbilisi has dozens of foreign embassies, including those listed here. Australia, Ireland and New Zealand do not have a diplomatic presence in Tbilisi. Australia covers Georgia from its embassy in Ankara, Turkey; Ireland from its embassy in Sofia, Bulgaria; and New Zealand from its embassy in Warsaw, Poland.

Armenian Embassy (Map p44; ☎ 32-2950977; www.georgia.mfa.am; Tetelashvili 4; ⏰ consular section 10am-1pm Mon-Fri)

Azerbaijan Embassy (Map p44; ☎ 32-2242220; www.tbilisi.mfa.gov.az; Gorgasali 4; ⏰ consular section 10am-12.30pm Mon-Fri)

British Embassy (☎ 32-2274747; www.gov.uk/government/world/georgia; Krtsanisi 51; ⏰ 9am-5pm Mon-Fri)

Canadian Consulate (Map p48; ☎ 32-2982072; ccogeorgia@gmail.com; 3rd fl, Rustaveli 34; ⏰ 9am-5pm Mon-Fri)

Dutch Embassy (Map p44; ☎ 32-2276200; tbi@minbuza.nl; Chavchavadze 34, Vake; ⏰ consular department 9am-1pm & 2-5.30pm Mon-Thu, to 2pm Fri)

French Embassy (☎ 32-2721490; www.ge.ambafrance.org; Krtsanisi 49; ⏰ 9am-1pm & 2-6pm Mon-Thu, to 4.30pm Fri)

German Embassy (Map p44; ☎ 32-2443700; www.tiflis.diplo.de; David Aghmeshenebeli 166; ⏰ 8.30am-5.30pm Mon-Thu, to 2.30pm Fri)

Iranian Consulate (Map p44; ☎ 32-2913656; http://en.tbilisi.mfa.ir; Chavchavadze 80, Vake; ⏰ 10am-1pm Mon-Wed & Fri)

Kazakhstan Embassy (Map p44; ☎ 32-2552000; www.kazembassy.ge; Lvovi 77; ⏰ consular section 10.30am-12.30pm Mon, Wed & Thu)

Russian Interests Section of Swiss Embassy (Map p44; ☎ consular service 32-2912645; www.georgia.mid.ru; Chavchavadze 53, Vake; ⏰ 9am-1.30pm & 3-7pm Mon-Thu, 9am-3pm Fri)

US Embassy (☎ 32-2277000; https://ge.us embassy.gov; 29 Georgian-American Friendship Ave, Didi Dighomi; ⏰ 8.30am-5.30pm Mon-Fri)

LEGAL MATTERS

After years of suffering from corrupt officials and a police force with almost unchecked powers, the government of Mikheil Saakashvili cracked down heavily, dissolved entire agencies, sacked thousands of officers and rebuilt the Georgian police force for the 21st century. Today the force is very highly regarded by locals, and corruption is largely a thing of the past.

→ It's extremely unlikely you'll be asked for a bribe, but if it happens, politely decline to pay.

→ If you are arrested, remain calm and respectful and ask to speak to someone at your embassy.

→ There is a presumption of innocence and a right to due process in Georgia.

→ Cannabis possession and consumption was legalised in Georgia in 2018, but its cultivation and sale remains illegal.

LGBTQ+ TRAVELLERS

Despite great strides in visibility in recent years, homophobia is rife in Georgia. LGBTQ+ travellers should exercise caution when meeting other LGBTQ+ people and should be discreet when travelling with partners. In most cases, same-sex partners sharing a room or a bed is unlikely to be a problem, as in Georgia it's not considered particularly unusual for people of the same sex to share a bed anyway. Tbilisi is the only city with a well-developed gay scene and a smattering of gay bars and parties. Sex acts between people of the same sex are legal, but same-sex relationships are still a long way from being accepted by wider Georgian society.

MONEY

→ Georgia's currency is the lari (GEL). One lari is divided into 100 tetri. Banknotes come in denominations of five, 10, 20, 50, 100 and 200 lari; coins run from one tetri to two lari.

→ ATMs, generally accepting MasterCard, Visa, Cirrus and Maestro cards, are plentiful in cities and towns throughout Georgia.

→ There are plenty of banks and small money-exchange offices in most towns and cities where you can exchange US dollars, euros and sometimes pounds sterling and the currencies of Georgia's neighbouring countries, though the latter is usually at poor rates.

→ You can make purchases with credit cards at most hotels, restaurants and shops, though less frequently outside Tbilisi.

→ Tipping has caught on all over Georgia with the arrival of huge numbers of international travellers. In Tbilisi restaurants, a standard 10% is often added to the bill. Don't mistake the 18% VAT on some bills for a service charge.

PUBLIC HOLIDAYS

New Year 1 and 2 January
Orthodox Christmas Day 7 January

HOW TO DIAL GEORGIAN NUMBERS

CALLING TO	FROM LANDLINE	FROM MOBILE	FROM OTHER COUNTRIES
landline	0 + area code + number	0 + area code + number	IAC* + 995 + area code + number
mobile	0 + number	number	IAC* + 995 + number

* IAC: International access code

Epiphany 19 January
Mother's Day 3 March
Women's Day 8 March
Orthodox Easter Sunday April or May
National Unity Day 9 April
Victory Day 9 May
St Andria's Day 12 May
Independence Day 26 May
Mariamoba (Assumption) 28 August
Svetitskhovloba (Day of Svetitskhoveli Cathedral, Mtskheta) 14 October
Giorgoba (St George's Day) 23 November

TELEPHONE

Telephone offices no longer exist in Georgia, with everyone using mobile phones. Even the use of landlines is relatively limited in Georgia. Landline numbers appear as seven digits in Tbilisi, six digits elsewhere; starting with 2. Mobile phone numbers appear as nine digits, starting with 5.

Mobile Phones

→ You can easily obtain a Georgian SIM card for 5 GEL, sometimes free, from the main networks. Take your passport when you go to get a SIM. The networks have 24-hour booths at Tbilisi and Kutaisi airports where you can get one on arrival.

→ Call rates are low and there are bargain packages for international calls.

→ Internet packages are cheap: around 8 GEL to 12 GEL for 5GB, for example.

→ An easy way to top up your credit is with cash in orange 'Express Pay' machines or yellow-and-blue 'Pay Box' machines, widespread on the streets of all towns. Easy-to-follow instructions are available in English.

Armenia

Best Places to Eat

➡ Cherkezi Dzor (p178)

➡ Lavash (p160)

➡ Herbs & Honey (p178)

➡ Kchuch (p193)

➡ The Club (p161)

Best Places to Stay

➡ Villa Kars (p177)

➡ 3Gs B&B and Camping (p170)

➡ Green Stone B&B (p202)

➡ Toon Armeni (p191)

➡ Azoyan Guest House (p157)

Why Go?

Few nations have histories as ancient, complex and laced with tragedy as Armenia. And even fewer have a culture that is as rich and resilient. This is a destination where you will be intrigued by history, awed by monuments, amazed by the landscape and charmed by down-to-earth locals. It's not an easy place to explore – roads are rough, transport is often hard to navigate and those who don't speak Armenian or Russian may find communication difficult – but travelling here is as rewarding as it is revelatory.

The simply extraordinary collection of medieval monasteries scattered across the country is the number-one attraction, closely followed by a dramatically beautiful landscape that is perfectly suited to hiking and other outdoor activities. And then there's the unexpected delight of Yerevan – one of the region's most exuberant and endearing cities. Put together, they offer an enticing and tremendously enjoyable travel experience.

When to Go

➡ Most of Armenia has a dry, high-altitude climate, though there are some verdant rainy pockets in the Lori, Tavush and Syunik regions. These receive most rain in early spring.

➡ In spring temperatures are mild and the countryside is covered in wildflowers, making it a perfect time to go hiking.

➡ Autumn has long, warm days and stable weather conditions.

➡ Summer in Yerevan can be 40°C with little or no breeze for days at a time; weather in the north is cooler.

➡ Conditions in winter can be bleak, with temperatures falling to -10°C or even lower in many areas. Roads are often closed due to snow and ice.

Map Labels

Lake Paravani
▲ Mt Didi Abuli (3300m)
GEORGIA
Tbilisi (10km)

⊗ Noyemberyan
Tashir
Shamlugh
⊗ Mt Leili (3157m)
Alaverdi
Akhtala
TAVUSH
LORI
7 Debed Canyon
Stepanavan
Tumanyan
6
Yenokavan
Iljevan
Berd
Spitak
Vanadzor
Mt Maymekh (3081m)
Mt Tekhenik (3101m)
3 Dilijan National Park
Mt Mrkhuz Range (2993m)
AZERBAIJAN
Gəncə
Gyumri
Artik
Maralik
Aparan
Pambak Range
Dilijan
Sevan Pass (2114m)
4 Sevan
Ttjur
Chambarak
Mt Aragats (4090m)
ARAGATSOTN
Hrazdan
Tsakhkadzor
Chkalovka
Hayravank
Getik
Mastara
Kasagh Gorge
Byurakan
Yegvard
Charentsavan
Nor Hachyn
Gavar
Noratus
Tsapatagh
Talin
Aghtsk
Ashtarak
Abovyan
Geghard Monastery
GEGHARKUNIK
Ozero Sevan
Karchaghbyur
Vagharshapat (Etchmiadzin)
Metsamor
Yerevan 1
4
Artsvanist
Lchavan
Makenis
Kelbajar (Karvachar)
Armavir
ARMAVIR
Araks River
Masis
Khosrov Nature Reserve
ARARAT
Martuni
Makenyats Monastery
NAGORNO-KARABAKH
Iğdır
Mt Kotuts (2061m)
Selim Pass (2410m)
Istisu (Vaykunik)
Vedi
Yeghegis Valley
Jermuk
Mt Ararat (Ağrı Dağı) (5165m)
Ararat
Yaraskh
Getap
Arpi
Yeghegnadzor
Malishka
Vorotan Pass (2344m)
Sev Lich Nature Reserve
TURKEY
Küçük Ağrı Dağı (3925m)
Doğubayazıt
Sədərək
Areni 5
2
Vayk
Arpa Chay
Mt Mets Ishkhanasar (3548m)
Sisian
Aghitu
Khndzoresk 6
Noravank
VAYOTS DZOR
Vayk Range
Mt Gogi (3120m)
Aravus
Harzhis
Goris
Halidzor
8 Tatev
AZERBAIJAN (NAXÇIVAN)
Mt Shahaponk (3204m)
Dastaker
Naxçıvan City
Mt Aramazd (3392m)
Kapan
Mt Kaputjugh (3904m)
SYUNIK
Kajaran
Araks River
Meghri Range
Shikahogh Nature Reserve
IRAN
Agarak
Meghri
⊗ Noordoz

GEGHAMA RANGE

Armenia Highlights

1 **Yerevan** (p146) Lazing away a few days in the welcoming cafes, wine bars and restaurants of the capital.

2 **Noravank** (p201) Watching the sun slowly set over the dramatic reddish-gold cliffs surrounding picture-perfect church buildings.

3 **Dilijan National Park** (p194) Hiking through millions of springtime wildflowers.

4 **Geghard Monastery** (p168) Marvelling at the ancient rock-hewn churches.

5 **Areni** (p200) Winery hopping in a region that's been producing wine for 6100 years.

6 **Goris** (p209) Exploring an abandoned cave city carved out of soft volcanic rock.

7 **Debed Canyon** (p185) Visiting magnificent medieval monasteries and fresco-covered churches.

8 **Tatev** (p211) Floating to the fortified monastery on the world's longest cable car.

YEREVAN

📷 10 / POP 1.1 MILLION

Leave your preconceptions at home, because Yerevan will almost certainly confound them. This is a city of contradictions – top-of-the-line Mercedes sedans share the roads with Ladas so old they should be in museum collections; traditional *pandoks* (taverns) serving *khoravats* (barbecue meats) and *oghee* (fruit vodka) sit next to chic European-style wine bars; and street fashions range from hipster to babushka with many weird and wonderful variations in between. In summer, locals take to the streets every night, claiming tables at the city's many outdoor cafes, sauntering along its tree-filled boulevards and congregating at the beloved musical fountain in Republic Sq. Few traces of the city's ancient past remain, usurped by Soviet-era buildings and modern structures with little regard for history. But wander into any *dalan* (archway) and enter a portal into a different world – you may find a gorgeous 19th-century balcony or beautiful church beyond.

History

Yerevan's history dates back to 782 BC, when the Erebuni fortress was built by King Argishti I of Urartu at the place where the Hrazdan River widened onto the fertile Ararat Plains. It was a regional capital of Muslim khanates and Persian governors until the Russian annexation in 1828.

The Soviet rebuilding of the tsarist city removed most of its mosques and some of its churches, and hid others away in residential backwaters, but it kept some of the 19th-century buildings on Abovyan St and left the old neighbourhood of Kond more or less alone.

Alexander Tamanyan developed the current grid plan in the 1920s with the idea that main boulevards (Mashtots, Abovyan and Nalbandyan) should point in the direction of Mt Ararat.

⊙ Sights

Most of Yerevan's sights are located in the city centre and can be easily reached on foot.

★ **Cafesjian Center
for the Arts** ARTS CENTRE
(The Cascade; Map p150; 📞 010-567262; www.cmf. am; 10 Tamanyan St; ⊙ escalators 8am-8pm, museum store & visitor centre 10am-8pm Fri-Sun) **FREE**
Housed in a vast flight of stone steps known as the Cascade, this arts centre is one of the city's major cultural attractions. Originally conceived in the 1920s by Soviet architect Alexander Tamanyan as part of his plan to modernise Yerevan, work on the monumental structure finally commenced in the 1980s but stalled after the 1988 earthquake. Eventually, Armenian-American philanthropist Gerard Cafesjian came to the rescue, funding its completion and transformation into a multi-level contemporary arts space.

The centre's two external garden galleries and five exhibition halls are accessed via an internal escalator. Next to the escalator are platforms where artworks from **Cafesjian's personal collection** of 20th-century and contemporary sculpture and furniture are displayed. There's a decidedly quirky theme at work here, with pieces such as Studio 65 for Gufram's *Marilyn 'Bocca' Lip Sofa*, Giorgio

---

YEREVAN IN ONE DAY

Start off with a freshly ground *soorch* (coffee) at **Gemini** (p162) and then walk around the **Opera Theatre** (p163) to the **Cafesjian Center for the Arts** (p146). Wander through the sculpture garden in front of the centre, take a trip up and down the art-edged escalator, and consider purchasing a souvenir or two in the gift shop. Next, marvel at the illuminated manuscripts at the **Matenadaran** (p149) or make a quick visit to the **Centre of Popular Creation** (p153) to see the best folk-art collection in the country. After lunch, head to the **History Museum of Armenia** (p148), where the Bronze Age collection is sure to impress. After all of that culture, a relaxing drink or two is in order – wine aficionados should head to **In Vino** (p162), while beer drinkers should head to **Dargett** (p162). For dinner, make sure you reserve in advance and head to **Lavash** (p160) for a *ghapama* (stuffed pumpkin) with nuts, dried fruit and crispy lavash (thin unleavened bread) sliced right at your table. Or, go to **The Club** (p161) for French-Armenian fusion food and relaxing live music. After dinner, stroll to **Republic Square** (p149) to watch the sound-and-light fountain show (8pm to 10pm in summer) or kick back at one of the mega-fashionable lounge cafes around Isahakyan St.

Laveri's *Lipstick* and Richard Cresswell's *Butterfly Seat* three of many works catching the eye on the trip up and down. These and the garden galleries, which feature recessed fountains, modern *khachkars* (stone steles featuring carved crosses) and contemporary sculptures, can be visited free of charge. Internal exhibits are free, except for one temporary exhibition which costs AMD1000.

On the ground floor, the large **gift shop** is one of the best places in the city to source quality souvenirs. There's also a welcoming and well-stocked art library with a small children's section.

In front of the Cascade, a **sculpture garden** features three huge bronze works by Colombian-Italian sculptor Fernando Botero: *Cat, Roman Warrior* and *Woman Smoking a Cigarette*. These sit alongside a whimsical wrought-iron teapot by Joana Vasconcelos, a bright blue kiwi by Peter Woytuk and plenty of other works. The two streets edging the park are home to cafes, bars and restaurants with plenty of outdoor seating. The steps themselves make for a popular place to catch a sunset while (discreetly) swigging a bottle of wine.

★**Armenian Genocide Memorial & Museum** MEMORIAL
(Tsitsernakaberd; Map p148; ☑010-390981; www.genocide-museum.am; Tsitsernakaberd Hill; ☺11am-5pm Tue-Sun) **FREE** Commemorating the massacre of Armenians in the Ottoman Empire from 1915 to 1922, this institution uses photographs, documents, reports and films to deliver a powerful museum experience similar to that of Israel's Yad Vashem (Holocaust Museum). Free tours are available for five or more. On the hill above is a 44m-high spire memorial next to a circle of 12 basalt slabs leaning over to guard an eternal flame.

Built in 1967, the memorial's 12 tilted slabs represent the lost provinces of western Armenia, land lost to Turkey in a post-WWI peace deal between Ataturk and Lenin, while the spire has a fine split dividing it into larger and smaller needles, the smaller one representing western Armenia. From the museum, a broad pathway flanked by a 100m-long wall engraved with the names of massacred communities leads to the memorial.

In the grounds, there is a stand of trees planted by foreign leaders who use the term genocide to describe the events that occurred.

FAST FACTS

Currency
Dram (AMD)

Languages
Armenian, Russian

Emergencies
☑112 or 911

Visas
Visitors from the US and EU can stay for up to 180 days without a visa; citizens from most other countries can obtain a visa on entry.

Resources
Armenia Travel (www.armenia.travel)

Armeniapedia (www.armeniapedia.org)

Hetq (www.hetq.am/en)

Hike Armenia (www.hikearmenia.org)

My Armenia (https://myarmenia.si.edu)

Exchange Rates

Australia	A$1	AMD365.29
Canada	C$1	AMD363.33
Euro zone	€1	AMD544.65
Japan	¥100	AMD443.25
NZ	NZ$1	AMD323.87
UK	UK£1	AMD745.69
US	US$1	AMD482.45

For current exchange rates, see www.xe.com.

Daily Costs
➡ B&B or guesthouse room: AMD7000–35,000

➡ Two-course evening meal: AMD3500–7500

➡ Museum entrance: AMD500–1000

➡ Cheap draught beer: AMD500–800

➡ 100km minibus ride: AMD1200

The complex is on Tsitsernakaberd Hill (Fortress of Swallows) across the Hrazdan Gorge from central Yerevan. The easiest way to get here is via a ride-hailing app (about AMD600) or taxi (AMD800 to AMD1200 from the city centre). There won't be any taxis waiting when you leave unless you prearrange one, so having the GG or Yandex

ARMENIA YEREVAN

app is a good idea. Alternatively, take *marshrutka* (minivan) 46 from Mesrop Mashtots Ave and alight at the steps of Hamalir (the sports and concert complex). From here you can walk up the steps to the end of the park where the memorial and the museum are located. If driving, head towards the Hrazdan stadium, turn right onto Athena St and look for a blue sign with white lettering signalling the route.

★ **History Museum of Armenia**   MUSEUM
(Map p150;   ☎ 010-520691;   www.history museum.am;   Republic Sq;   adult/student/child AMD2000/500/300, tour AMD5000;   ⏰ 11am-6pm Tue-Sat, to 5pm Sun) Its simply extraordinary collection of Bronze Age artefacts make this museum Armenia's pre-eminent cultural institution and an essential stop on every visitor's itinerary. Many of the items were excavated at the Necropolis of Lchashen near Lake Sevan in the 1950s, and it's hard to do them justice in words. The collection includes bronze sculptures, four-wheeled wooden chariots with metal decoration, carved stone fertility symbols, and a magnificent array of weapons and armour (arrows, quivers, helmets and shields).

Other exhibits of note include medieval *khachkars*, 18th- and 19th-century Arme-

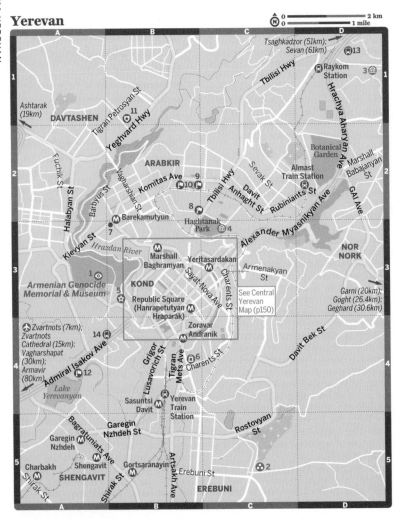

Yerevan

nian costumes, a 5500-year-old leather shoe discovered in a cave in the Vayots Dzor region in 2008, carpets and embroidered amices (liturgical vestments). The only disappointing section is the one concentrating on Soviet Armenia, which ostentatiously eschews English-language labelling (all other exhibits have Armenian, Russian and English labels). The National Gallery of Armenia (p153) is on the top floors.

Matenadaran MUSEUM
(Map p150; ☎010-562578; www.matenadaran. am; 53 Mesrop Mashtots Ave; adult/student AMD1500/300, tour AMD3000; ⊘10am-5pm Tue-Sat) Standing at the top of Yerevan's grandest avenue, this cathedral-like manuscript library is a source of enormous pride to all Armenians. The first *matenadaran* (book depository) for Armenian texts was built by Mesrop Mashtots, the inventor of the Armenian alphabet, at Etchmiadzin in the 5th century and held thousands of manuscripts. Invasions over the centuries led to enormous losses through looting and burning, but 1800 exquisitely illustrated and bound manuscripts survived. These form the basis of the stunning collection here.

At the base of the purpose-designed building, which dates from 1957, is a **statue of Mashtots** teaching his alphabet to a disciple. Six other statues of great scholars and writers stand by the door. The **outdoor gallery** has carved rock tombs and *khachkars* brought here from ancient sites around Armenia.

Inside, there are more than 23,000 manuscripts, fragments, documents and maps, although only a small number are on display. The **central hall** focuses on the development of Armenian medieval sciences, literature and arts throughout the centuries. Other halls showcase Greek and Roman scientific and philosophical works, Iranian and Arabic manuscripts, and singular items such as the 13th-century **Homilies of Mush**, so heavy that it was ripped in half to be carried away to safety by two women after the 1915 massacres. The book was not put back together until years later, as one saviour had emigrated to America and taken it with her for safekeeping.

Republic Square SQUARE
(Hanrapetutyan Hraparak; Map p150) From dawn till late into the night, Republic Sq is Yerevan's focal point and beating heart. Designed by architect Alexander Tamanyan as part of his 1924 urban plan for the city and originally named after Vladimir Lenin until 1991, the square is enclosed by a few current and former government buildings, the Armenia Marriott Hotel (p158) and the History Museum and National Gallery (p153). Its famous musical fountains (8pm to 10pm in summer) are the city's most endearing attraction and a popular meeting point.

Underneath the square is a large bunker constructed during the Cold War to protect high-ranking officials in the event of a nuclear attack. This is closed to the public.

Sergei Parajanov Museum MUSEUM
(Map p150; ☎010-538473; www.parajanov.com/museum; 15/16 Dzoragyugh St; AMD1000, tour AMD2500; ⊘10.30am-5pm) For something totally unique, head to this museum near Hrazdan Gorge. Crammed with collages, drawings, photographs and assemblages created by the experimental film-maker best known for his 1969 film *Sayat Nova* (aka *The Colour of Pomegranates*), it is as eccentric as it is engaging. Housed in an attractive 19th-century timber house, the collection manages to evoke

Yerevan

◉ **Top Sights**
1 Armenian Genocide Memorial & Museum..A3

◉ **Sights**
2 Erebuni Historical & Archaeological Museum-Reserve..C5
3 Levon's Divine Underground.................D1
4 Mother Armenia Military Museum........C3

✪ **Entertainment**
5 Hrazdan Stadium...................................B3

🛍 **Shopping**
6 G.U.M Market..B4

ℹ **Information**
7 Bogema Land..B3
8 Georgian Embassy.................................B2
9 Iranian Embassy.....................................B2
10 Nagorno-Karabakh Embassy...............B2
11 Passport and Visa Office.......................B1
12 US Embassy...A4

ℹ **Transport**
13 Hyusisayin Avtokayan...........................D1
14 Kilikya Avtokayan..................................A4

Central Yerevan

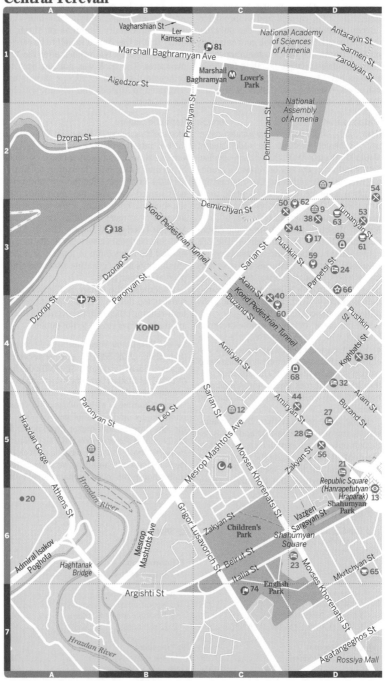

Vagharshian St
Ler Kamsar St
Marshall Baghramyan Ave
National Academy of Sciences of Armenia
Antarayin St
Sarmen St
Zarobyan St
81
Aigedzor St
Marshall Baghramyan
Lover's Park
Proshyan St
Demirchyan St
National Assembly of Armenia
Dzorap St
Demirchyan St
7
54
Kond Pedestrian Tunnel
50 62
9
Tumanyan St
53
63
38
18
41
17
69
61
Dzorap St
Sarian St
Pushkin St
59
Paronyan St
Parpetsi St
24
Aram St
Dzorap St
79
Kond Pedestrian Tunnel
40
66
Buzand St
60
Pushkin St
KOND
Amiryan St
68
Koghbatsi St
36
Sarian St
32
44
Amiryan St
27
Buzand St
64
Leo St
12
Aram St
Mesrop Mashtots Ave
28
56
Movses Khorenatsi St
Zakyan St
21
14
4
Republic Square (Hanrapetutyan Hraparak) 13
Shahumyan Park
20
Hrazdan Gorge
Athens St
Hrazdan River
Grigor Lusavorich St
Zakyan St
Children's Park
Vazgen Sargsyan St
Shahumyan Square
Mesrop Mashtots Ave
Beirut St
23
Mkrtchyan St
65
Admiral Isakov Poghota
Haghtanak Bridge
Italia St
English Park
Movses Khorenatsi St
Argishti St
74
Agatangeghos St
Hrazdan River
Rossiya Mall

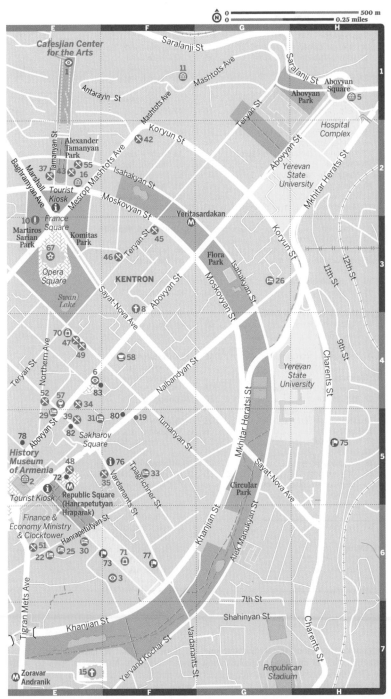

Central Yerevan

Parajanov's prodigious talent, humour and humanity while at the same time illustrating the difficulties faced by artists, film-makers and writers living in the USSR.

Born in 1924 in Tiflis (Tbilisi), Parajanov moved to Moscow in 1945 to study film-making. His early career was blighted when he was convicted of homosexuality (then illegal) in 1948, a charge that many of his friends and supporters considered bogus. After being released from jail and living in Ukraine for a few years, he moved to Yerevan in the late 1960s. Two more criminal charges were levied against him in 1973 (for rape and producing pornography) and he was sentenced to five years of hard labour in a Siberian jail.

While in prison, he used his fingernails to make faces in aluminium milk-bottle lids and called them 'thalers'. One of these can be found in the museum and a silver replica is given as an award at the Golden Apricot Yerevan International Film Festival.

Parajanov was eventually released after a high-profile international campaign for his freedom, supported by artists including Françoise Sagan, Jean-Luc Godard, François Truffaut, Luis Buñuel, Federico Fellini, Michelangelo Antonioni, Andrei Tarkovsky, Louis Aragon and John Updike. Parajanov died in Yerevan in 1990.

Centre of Popular Creation MUSEUM
(Map p150; 010-569380; www.cpc.am/en; 64 Abovyan St; AMD1000, tour AMD3000; 11am-5pm Tue-Sat, to 4pm Sun) Its somewhat esoteric name means that many visitors to Yerevan overlook this museum. This is a great shame, as it is home to the best folk-art collection in the country and is well worth a visit. Spread over two floors, the collection of woodcarving, silverwork, embroidery, carpets, lace and costumes is in mint condition and attractively displayed, with good lighting and English-language labels. The 19th- and 20th-century carpets and the intricate woodwork (some inlaid) are particularly impressive.

Katoghike CHURCH
(Map p150; cnr Sayat-Nova Ave & Abovyan St) The tiny 13th-century chapel incongruously known as the Katoghike (Cathedral) nestles beside the recently constructed Surp Anna Church. It has a fascinating history: the only Yerevan church to survive a devastating earthquake in 1679, it was incorporated into a new basilica in the 17th century and narrowly escaped being demolished when the Soviets pulled that building down in 1936. A public outcry – highly unusual for that time – led to its preservation.

Yervand Kochar Museum MUSEUM
(Map p150; 010-529326; www.kochar.am; 39/12 Mesrop Mashtots Ave; AMD800, tour AMD3000; 11am-5pm Tue-Sat, to 4pm Sun) Though small,

this fascinating museum does a great job of documenting the life and work of the prolific Armenian painter and sculptor. The museum showcases works created throughout Kochar's career, including *Lonely Woman* (1913) painted when he was only 13. Labels are in English and there's a short film about his most famous piece, the *Guernica*-like *Disaster of War* (1962).

Martiros Sarian Museum MUSEUM
(Map p150; 010-580568; www.sarian.am; 3 Sarian St; AMD1000, tour AMD4000; 11am-4pm) This museum preserves the studio and some of the works of 20th-century painter Martiros Sarian, known for his vibrant colour-saturated canvases. On the 3rd floor, Sarian's work portrays his travels to Egypt, Constantinople and Iran – trips he said ignited his creativity like school never could. The next floor down covers paintings he did in Armenia following independence in the 1920s. Finally, on the ground floor are photos and personal belongings. Staff don't speak English, but the museum is well signed.

National Gallery of Armenia GALLERY
(Map p150; 010-567472; www.gallery.am; Republic Sq; adult/student/child AMD1500/400/300, tour AMD5000; 11am-5pm Tue-Sat, to 4pm Sun) Housed on the top floors of the History Museum (p148), Armenia's foremost art gallery holds a large but somewhat underwhelming collection of European and Russian art. Its major draw is the collection of Armenian art displayed on the 4th and 5th floors.

OFF THE BEATEN TRACK

HOLY CAVES

All Tosya Arakelyan wanted was for her husband Levon to build her a potato cellar. What she got in return was an extremely intricate seven-level underground cave network built over 23 years with only simple tools. When Levon died in 2008 (he worked the last day of his life) his strange and impressive creation was opened to the public, as **Levon's Divine Underground** (Map p148; 077-178850; https://levonsdivineunderground.com; 9 Fifth St, Arinj; adult/child AMD1500/500; 10am-6pm). Don't miss the beautiful stone garden designed by Levon. Ask to speak to the couple's granddaughter for an explanation in English.

Highlights include works by Hakob Hov-natanian (1806–81), Martiros Sarian (1880–1972) and Vardges Surenyants (1860–1921). Of these, the paintings by Surenyants are the most impressive. Depicting scenes from Armenian fairy tales and various historical events, they are colourful and delicately detailed, with an Orientalist feel. Don't miss them.

Modern Art Museum of Yerevan GALLERY
(Map p150; ✆010-535359; www.mamy.am; 7 Mesrop Mashtots Ave; AMD500, tour AMD2500; ⊙11am-6pm Tue-Sun) When it opened in 1972, this was the first specialised museum of contemporary and modern art in the Soviet Union, and a source of enormous pride for the Armenian avant-garde. Many prominent local artists of the time donated works, and these form the core of the collection along with further artist donations from the 1980s. Recent acquisitions include impressive works by Karen Petrosyan, Armen Gevorgyan and Laura Avetisyan.

The museum is accessed via a narrow lane running off Movses Khorenatsi St, parallel to Mesrop Mashtots Ave.

Zoravor Church CHURCH
(Map p150; 9a Parpetsi St) Through a *dalan* on Parpetsi St tucked between Soviet apartment blocks is a late-17th-century church on the site of a 9th- to 13th-century monastery. Renovations were performed as recently as the 1990s and the church is beautifully lit up at night. Beneath the small chapel is a mausoleum dedicated to St Anania.

Erebuni Historical & Archaeological Museum-Reserve ARCHAEOLOGICAL SITE
(Map p148; ✆010-432661; www.erebuni.am; 38 Erebuni St; adult/child & student AMD1000/300, guide AMD2500; ⊙10am-4pm Tue-Sun) This archaeological site dates from 782 BC, three decades before Rome was established. It gives insight into daily life in the palace of Argishti I, one of the greatest kings of Urartu. At the foot of the hill, a poorly maintained Soviet-era **museum** displays artefacts from the palace excavations including some extraordinary silver rhytons (drinking horns), as well as objects found when an Urartian tomb was uncovered in Yerevan in 1984 during construction of a factory.

Blue Mosque MOSQUE
(Geok Jami; Map p150; 12 Mesrop Mashtots Ave; ⊙10am-1pm & 3-6pm) There has been a mosque on this site since 1765, but like the other eight or so mosques that operated in Yerevan at the beginning of the 20th century it was closed during the Soviet era. Reconstructed in the late 1990s with Iranian funds, it is now the only functioning mosque in the city. Decorated with exterior tiles, it has a modest interior, graceful tiled dome, small minaret, and shady garden with fountains and flowerbeds.

Visitors should dress appropriately – no bare legs or shoulders, and women should wear a headscarf when entering the prayer hall.

Mother Armenia Military Museum MUSEUM
(Mayr Hayastan; Map p148; Haghtanak Park; ⊙10am-5pm Tue, to 3pm Sat & Sun) **FREE** There's symbolism aplenty in this huge 22m-high memorial above the Cascade. *Mother Armenia's* stern visage, military stance and massive sword project a clear message: Armenia has had its fill of invasions, massacres and repression, and will fight to preserve its nationhood. Inside the pedestal is a somewhat dull military museum of photos and dioramas documenting Armenian involvement in WWII (150,000 to 250,000 Armenians died, half of those sent to fight) as well as the bloody 1989–94 Karabakh War.

SOVIET RAILWAY TIME MACHINE

During Soviet times, the small **Children's Railway** (Map p150; ✆010-527263; Hrazdan Gorge; AMD300; ⊙10.30am-11.30pm May-Oct) taught kids about train engineering by allowing them to take over the duties, including by playing driver, attendant and director (under adult supervision). Though no longer role-playing, local kids still ride the train when full or play in the adjacent amusement park.

The railway also makes for a great hike alongside the tracks, past the **Bidzu Get** natural pool (meaning River of Old Men for the old lads that hang out there) and ending at a hill which conveniently takes you up to the Sergei Parajanov Museum (p149).

To get here, walk through the long, somewhat creepy pedestrian tunnel from Mesrop Mashtots Ave.

Surp Grigor
Lusavorich Cathedral CATHEDRAL
(St Gregory the Illuminator Cathedral; Map p150; cnr Khandjian & Tigran Mets Aves) Built to celebrate 1700 years of Christianity in Armenia and consecrated in 2001, this is the largest cathedral of the Armenian Apostolic Church. The complex, which has a prominent location atop a hill on the eastern edge of the city centre, consists of three churches: the cathedral, the Chapel of St Tiridates the King, and the Chapel of St Ashkhen the Queen. These two royal figures supported St Gregory in converting Armenia to Christianity.

Armenian Centre for Contemporary
Experimental Art ARTS CENTRE
(Map p150; ☑010-568225; www.accea.info; 1/3 Pavstos Buzand St; ⊙11am-5pm Tue-Sat) FREE In a central location facing the popular Vernissage Market, this slightly down-at-heel arts centre is the hub of the city's avant-garde, hosting concerts, performances and talks. Experimental art in a variety of media is exhibited in four exhibition spaces and often has political overtones. Yervand Kochar's 1959 figure *Melancholy* pines at the entrance.

Hovhannes Tumanyan Museum MUSEUM
(Map p150; ☑010-560021; www.toumanian.am; 40 Moscovyan St; adult/child AMD500/300, tour AMD2500; ⊙11am-4.30pm Tue-Sat, to 3.30pm Sun) This museum celebrates the life and work of the extraordinary writer, translator and humanist who is often described as Armenia's greatest poet. The museum includes exhibits about his works, photographs and letters documenting his life, as well as a six-room reconstruction of his apartment in Tbilisi. Armenians clearly find the museum intriguing, but those that don't speak the language may struggle to get the same impression due to a lack of English or foreign-language signage.

⌒₣ Tours

Envoy Hostel TOURS
(Map p150; ☑010-530369; www.envoyhostel. com; 54 Pushkin St; per person AMD9900) For something a bit different, sign up for the informative and enjoyable minibus tour of Soviet-era Yerevan run by this hostel on Monday, Wednesday and Saturday between 11am and 3pm. It visits Republic Sq, the Yerevan train station, moribund factories, apartment blocks and other legacies of the USSR. Guides enjoy poking good-natured fun at their former Soviet masters.

WORTH A TRIP

SIGHTS AROUND YEREVAN

A number of high-profile sites can be visited on day trips from Yerevan. Garni (p169) and Geghard (p168) are east of the city and can easily be combined in one itinerary; the same applies to Zvartnots Cathedral (p172), the Mother See of Holy Etchmiadzin (p171) and Sardarapat (p170) to the west of the city. You can visit by public transport (*marshrutka*, bus or taxi) or sign up for a guided tour operated by Hyur Service (p157) or Envoy Hostel (p157).

The hostel also offers a walking tour of Yerevan (per person AMD2000), a range of guided tours to destinations around Armenia, airport transfers, and a popular hybrid tour/transfer between Yerevan and Tbilisi stopping at Sanahin (p187), Haghpat (p190) and Akhtala (p190) monasteries en route (per person AMD29,900, 11 hours, Friday).

Yerevan Free Walking Tour TOURS
(☑093-498985; www.yerevanfreewalkingtours. com; ⊙5pm) FREE Since 2015, the charismatic Armenian globetrotter Vako Khakhamian has been leading daily 'free' walking tours from Republic Sq. The tours cover Yerevan and Armenian history essentials and culminate with a beer at Calumet (p162). Tips are encouraged. Vako also leads Soviet and 'alternative' tours (up to five people AMD10,000, per additional person AMD2000) and does a free weekend pub crawl (June to September).

Yerevan Brandy Company DISTILLERY
(ArArAt; Map p150; ☑010-540000; www.ararat brandy.com; 2 Admiral Isakov Ave; 65min tour & tasting AMD4500-10,000; ⊙daily tours by appointment 9am-8pm) Occupying a commanding position on a hill, the fortress-like distillery producing ArArAt brandy offers daily guided tours and generous tastings. The cellars are full of barrels dating back to the 19th century, including one that won't be opened until a Karabakh peace deal appears. The distillery originally began in 1887 but was sold to France's Pernod Ricard in 1999. Tours last about an hour and cost AMD4500 if two recent vintages are tasted, AMD10,000 for three aged vintages.

To get here from the city centre, walk across the Haghtanak Bridge, hop aboard

ARMENIA YEREVAN

Walking Tour
Yerevan City Centre

START REPUBLIC SQUARE
END CAFESJIAN CENTER FOR THE ARTS
LENGTH 45 MINS, 2KM

Start with a sip from a water *pulpulak* (drinking fountain) and a spin around the towering tuff masterpieces in bustling ❶ **Republic Square** (p149). To the left of the ❷ **History Museum of Armenia** (p148) building, stroll up Abovyan St past the city's few remaining 19th-century black tuff buildings. You'll soon reach ❸ **Charles Aznavour Square**, named after the French-Armenian singer commonly known as Paris' Frank Sinatra. There, you'll find the Moscow Cinema, built in 1936 on the remains of an old church, and a friendly-looking spider sculpted in 2008.

Make a left on Tumanyan St to ❹ **Swan Lake**, the location of a 2015 free show by American rapper Kanye West (he surprised the crowd by diving into the lake, prompting the oh-so-perfect name Swanye Lake). Continuing ahead you'll reach the beating heart of Yerevan, ❺ **Opera Square**, where locals go to see a show, walk their dog or simply to hang out.

Circling the opera on the left and crossing the roundabout will bring you to an art market centred on a statue of Armenian painter ❻ **Martiros Sarian**. Perhaps with a painting under your arm, cross the roundabout to a row of open-air cafes that lead to a ❼ **statue of Alexander Tamanyan**, Yerevan's lead architect (though the statue makes him look more like a DJ than a city planner).

In the Cafesjian Center ❽ **sculpture garden**, stop and gander at the disproportionate *Roman Warrior* and *Cat* made by Colombia's Fernando Botero, the seated human made of Latin letters by Spaniard Jaume Plensa and various hares by British artist Barry Flanagan. Finally, you'll reach the city's most celebrated monument, the 572-step ❾ **Cafesjian Center for the Arts** (p146) aka the Cascade, which was left unfinished when the Soviet Union collapsed. Note the 15 small fountains jutting out of the base – these were initially meant to symbolise the republics of the USSR but after independence in 1991 were conveniently switched to signify Armenia's 15 ancient provinces.

marshrutka 5 or 259 on Mesrop Mashtots Ave (AMD100) or take a taxi (AMD600). Book your tour at least one day in advance.

Hyur Service TOURS
(Map p150; ☏ 010-529808; www.hyurservice.com; 96 Nalbandyan St; tour AMD11,000) This reputable company offers a five- to six-hour tour around the city centre on Thursday at 10am (March to January). The tour takes groups to out-of-the-way sights including Erebuni, the Megerian Carpet Museum and the Yerevan Brandy Company. Hyur also offers private tours around the country and to Nagorno-Karabakh, known to Armenians as Artsakh, does airport transfers and offers apartment rentals.

✦ Festivals & Events

Vardavar CULTURAL
(☉ Jun/Jul) Celebrated on a Sunday in high summer 98 days (14 weeks) after Easter, this festival sees marauding gangs of bucket-equipped young people drenching bystanders with water. Sensible people stay indoors for the day.

Golden Apricot Yerevan International Film Festival FILM
(www.gaiff.am; ☉ Jul) This high-profile film festival has been held every year since 2004 and is always hosted at the Moscow Cinema in Charles Aznavour Sq (p164).

Yerevan Jazz Fest MUSIC
(☉ Oct/Nov) Every autumn, a lineup of local and international acts grace some of Yerevan's most spectacular venues, including Aram Khachaturian Concert Hall in the opera house and Karen Demirchyan Complex near the Genocide Museum. Previous acts have included Grammy winners Dee Dee Bridgewater, Marcus Miller, Arturo Sandoval, Gonzalo Rubalcaba and Arto Tuncboyaciyan.

⌔ Sleeping

Yerevan has plenty of accommodation options to choose from for all budgets and many apartment buildings feature well-priced Airbnb rentals. Low-season rates for all accommodation usually apply between November and March; rates are highest from June to October.

Envoy Hostel HOSTEL $
(Map p150; ☏ 010-530369; www.envoyhostel.com; 54 Pushkin St; dm AMD5900-8000, s with bathroom AMD17,000-23,000, without bathroom

AMD12,000-20,000, d with bathroom AMD20,000-23,000, without bathroom AMD17,000-20,000; ☏❋@☎) An excellent location and helpful staff make this long-time backpacker hub a popular choice. There are plenty of private rooms, plus nine mixed dorms with lockers (BYO padlock), hard beds and reading lights; we suggest avoiding those in the basement. Shared bathrooms are clean and well-maintained, though in short supply. The communal lounge and kitchen are major draws.

Umba HOSTEL $
(Map p150; ☏ 010-542131; www.umbastay.com; 5 Belyakov St; dm/d AMD3000/9000; ☎) A clean, affordable and rather characterless hostel in a quiet courtyard close to the Abovyan strip. There are three dorms – a four-bed and two with eight beds – as well as a few privates. Serious drawbacks include a lack of natural light in most of the hostel, just two toilets and no air-conditioning. Overall, Umba is a decent budget option.

Yerevan Hostel HOSTEL $
(Map p150; ☏ 010-547757; www.hostelinyerevan.com; 5 Tpagrichner St; dm AMD4000, d without bathroom AMD14,000-17,000, with bathroom AMD18,000-22,000; ❋☎) In the basement of a run-down apartment block, this hostel offers two dorms (an eight-bed and four-bed female) and nine private rooms split between two buildings. The rooms have recently been renovated, although when we visited the pipes in the bathrooms had an off smell. Staff are very helpful and offer tours and transfers around the country.

★ Azoyan Guest House GUESTHOUSE $$
(Map p150; ☏ 098-566640, 010-566649; www.azoyanguesthouse.am; 32 Hanrapetutyan St; s/d/tr AMD27,000/32,000/34,000; ☏❋☎) B&Bs aren't often described as being elegant and stylish, but both terms certainly apply here. In a fantastic location between Republic Sq and the Vernissage Market, Azoyan offers three attractively decorated rooms with large beds, satellite TV and work desk. There's no lounge or outdoor area, but the generous organic breakfast just might make up for it.

Villa Delenda B&B $$
(Map p150; ☏ 010-561156; www.familycarearmenia.org/en/hotels; 22 Koghbatsi St; s/d AMD25,000/35,000) Few historic homes survived the Soviet years in Yerevan, but thanks to the honorary Italian consul, Antonio Montalto, this beautifully restored 1906

home remains intact as a charming bed and breakfast in a prime location. The rooms are finely decorated with period furniture and have comfortable beds. Downstairs, a shop sells handmade ceramics crafted by artisans in Gyumri.

Tufenkian Historic
Yerevan Hotel   HOTEL $$
(Map p150; ☑ 010-60501010; www.tufenkianher itage.com; 48 Hanrapetutyan St; s AMD35,000-91,000, d AMD47,000-105,000; ❁❋@☎☎) Though it calls itself a historic hotel, the Tufenkian was purpose-built and opened in 2012. Rooms are spacious, with excellent bathrooms and comfortable beds. The hand-made carpets and wool blankets in each room are a nice touch; watch women making the carpets in the showroom downstairs. Tufenkian also has a swimming pool, the excellent Kharpert Restaurant (p160) and a foyer cafe.

Republica Hotel   HOTEL $$
(Map p150; ☑ 011-990000; www.republica hotel.am; 7 Amiryan St; s AMD46,000-85,000, d AMD51,000-95,000, ste AMD64,000-128,000; ❁❋☎) The Republica offers 56 slightly cramped standard rooms and an array of deluxe rooms and suites that are worth the upgrade. Rooms are fashionable with beautiful designs above the bed – some feature stellar views of Mt Ararat. Downstairs, there's a stylish ground-floor restaurant (mains AMD2900 to AMD7500) and chic outdoor bar with Dargett beer on tap.

My Hotel Yerevan   HOTEL $$
(Map p150; ☑ 010-600708; www.myhotel. am; 47 Nalbandyan St; s AMD23,000-34,000, d AMD26,500-37,500; P❋@☎) Tucked into a corner of a residential courtyard on the city edge, this small hotel offers 12 attractively presented rooms with satellite TV and tea and coffee facilities. Standard rooms are on the small side, so it's worth paying extra for a deluxe. A buffet breakfast is served in the basement and there's a pleasant courtyard with a resident cat.

Paris Hotel   HOTEL $$
(Map p150; ☑ 060-600060; www.parishotel. am; 4-6 Amiryan St; r AMD39,000-79,000, ste AMD135,000-169,000; P❁❋@☎) It may not be the most stylish of the recently opened hotels in the city centre, but the Paris Hotel has a lot going for it. The great location near Republic Sq, helpful staff, fitness centre and beautiful rooftop restaurant (mains

AMD3200 to AMD7400) are all assets, as are the spacious rooms with satellite TV, coffee and tea facilities and work desk.

Best Western Congress   HOTEL $$
(Map p150; ☑ 010-591199; www.congresshotel yerevan.com; 1 Italia St; s AMD47,000-57,000, d AMD52,000-67,000; ❁❋@☎☎) Overlooking a park close to Republic Sq, the Congress has a sparkling new lobby and bar as well as a new restaurant by Moscow-based Armenian Gayane Breiova. Although the rooms are a little tired, with the huge swimming pool and health club this hotel remains an excellent choice for business travellers and families, especially in summer.

Europe Hotel   HOTEL $$
(Map p150; ☑ 010-546060; www.europehotel. am; 32-38 Hanrapetutyan St; s AMD44,000, d AMD50,000, ste AMD75,000-90,000; P❁❋ @☎) Staff at this centrally located four-star choice are both friendly and efficient, and the hotel itself is run with an impressive degree of professionalism. Rooms are rather tight with plain and dated decor, but they're well equipped and have comfortable beds. The breakfast buffet is generous, and there's a lobby bar open until midnight.

The Alexander   LUXURY HOTEL $$$
(Map p150; ☑ 011-206000; info@thealexan deryerevan.com; 3/4 Abovyan St; d/superior/ presidential AMD150,000/175,000/1.7 million; ❁❋☎☎) Yerevan's most opulent hotel is worth witnessing even if you can't afford a night. Built with a historic 18th-century building replaced brick by brick as its facade, The Alexander is the height of luxury with gorgeous rooms accented in gold and black, a pool, gym and Finnish sauna. The classy penthouse restaurant and bar is open to nonguests (mains AMD3700 to AMD10,000).

Armenia Marriott Hotel   HOTEL $$$
(Map p150; ☑ 010-599000; www.marriott. com; 1 Amiryan St; r AMD62,000-250,000, ste AMD245,000-1 million; P❁❋@☎☎) This grand pink tuff building facing Republic Sq is a Soviet-era institution; rumour has it some rooms were bugged to spy on foreign diplomats. With the USSR in the rearview, the Marriott is a respectable hotel that's showing its age. The new swimming pool is commendable, but extra charges for breakfast (AMD7200 to AMD12,000) and wi-fi (per hour AMD1800) are frustrating.

Eating

Yerevan is crowded with excellent Armenian dining options, but good international food is tougher to find (it usually looks better than it tastes). Quick snacks include *lahmajoon* (thin pizza topped with minced meat), *shawarma* (Middle Eastern wrap), *jingalov hats* (flatbread stuffed with green herbs and vegetables) and pizza from **Tashir Pizza** (Map p150; 010-511119; www.tashirpizza.am; 37 Hanrapetutyan St; slices AMD200-420, personal pizzas AMD450-790; 10am-midnight;).

Twelve Tables   CAFE $
(Map p150; 5 Alexander Spendiaryan St; mains AMD1800-2700; noon-10pm;) Entered through an artsy handicrafts shop, this cute-as-a-button tearoom has a whimsical decor reminiscent of a grandmother's living room. The menu is well-priced and features baguettes, pasta, waffles, salads and a vegan burger. There's a huge variety of leaf tea to choose from as well as milkshakes, freshly squeezed juices and an exemplary house-made lemonade. Staff are very welcoming.

Anteb   ARMENIAN $
(Map p150; 010-530988; 30 Koghbatsi St; mezes AMD450-2500, pides AMD700-2600, kebabs AMD2500-4600; 10.30am-11.30pm;) Serving 'western Armenian' dishes similar to those enjoyed in Turkey, this is one of the most popular eateries in Yerevan. The decor and service are uninspired, but this doesn't matter – everyone's attention focuses on the tasty mezes, salads, pides (flatbread), *fatayer* (stuffed pastries), *lahmajoon* and kebabs. The baklava (honeyed pastry) is an essential finale.

Lahmajun Gaidz   MIDDLE EASTERN $
(Map p150; 077-332118; 5 Nalbandyan St; mains AMD300-1500; 10.30am-7pm;) This Syrian-Armenian restaurant feels as good for your heart as it does your stomach. The family that runs it escaped Aleppo in 2013 and brought recipes for some of the best *lahmajoon* and *za'atar* (oregano, thyme, and marjoram spice) bread in town. Family matriarch Salpy always welcomes guests with a smile and is happy to make recommendations.

The place is tricky to find. Look for the name written in chalk alongside an open doorway along Nalbandyan St and go down the staircase. Then, take a left.

A CITY WITHOUT MEMORY

Not too long ago, Yerevan's city centre was filled with handsome 19th-century office and apartment buildings, and surrounding neighbourhoods were characterised by their pretty timber houses. Now, most of those buildings and houses have been demolished to make way for ugly multistorey developments owned by local oligarchs. Since the 2018 Velvet Revolution, the local government has done well to quell any more destruction, but much of the damage has already been done; few remnants of the city's pre-Soviet past remain.

One of the few 19th-century neighbourhoods to remain relatively intact is Kond in the southwestern corner of the city centre. Its ramshackle timber housing stock is – for now – almost exactly as it was a century ago. To explore its winding alleyways, enter up one of the steep cobbled slopes from Paronian or Sarian Sts.

Jingalov Hats   VEGETARIAN $
(Map p150; 010-582205; 62 Teryan St; AMD700; 10am-10pm;) If you're stumped on what to eat, you can't go wrong with a *jingalov hats*, the only item served at this small restaurant. *Jingalov hats* is a soft flatbread stuffed with a dozen or more greens best washed down with a *tan* (sour yogurt drink). The vegetarian snack originates in Nagorno-Karabakh, which is well represented here with a wall-sized mural.

Khinkali   GEORGIAN $
(Map p150; 010-521940; 21/3 Tumanyan; khinkali AMD330-640; 9.30am-midnight;) This is the best place in Yerevan to try boiled or fried *khinkali* (Georgian ravioli-like dumplings). To eat a boiled-beef one the traditional way, grab the knob like a handle and as you bite, suck out the soupy goodness. Discard the knob when finished. You can also try *khinkali* stuffed with catfish, chicken, or egg and tarragon.

Grand Candy   DESSERTS $
(Map p150; www.grandcandy.am; 54 Mesrop Mashtots Ave; sweets from AMD100; 10am-8pm;) Ask any Armenian child to name their favourite place, and they're likely to excitedly shout 'Grand Candy!' This sweets shop and cafe is painted in candy colours

(of course) and features a toy train running along tracks suspended from the ceiling. Candy, chocolate and ice cream are available, but don't miss the *ponchik* (Armenian doughnut with custard filling) for AMD100.

Green Bean
VEGETARIAN $

(Map p150; ☎ 010-529279; www.thegreenbean.am; 30 Isahakyan St; salads AMD1100-2800, bagels & sandwiches AMD1400-2700; ☺ 8.30am-midnight; ☏ ☞) Its heart is in the right place, so we wish that the coffee and food served at this modern cafe beneath the Cascade were better. Plenty of vegetarian and vegan salads and sandwiches are on offer (many produced using organically sourced produce), as well as organic teas and coffee (filtered and espresso). There's a second branch on **Amiryan St** (Map p150; 10 Amiryan St; ☺ 8.30am-11pm; ☏ ☞).

★ Lavash
ARMENIAN $$

(Map p150; ☎ 010-608800; 21 Tumanyan St; mains AMD1200-6000; ☺ 8.30am-midnight; ☏) It's tough to land a table without a reservation, but Lavash is worth the hype. The menu is fresh and highly Instagrammable, from the *ghapama* (stuffed pumpkin) overflowing with dried fruit, nuts and lavash bread to the humongous 'Guinness World Record' *gata* (sweet cake) you must see to believe (but never finish). Despite the top-notch experience, prices are reasonable.

At Gayane's
ARMENIAN $$

(Map p150; ☎ 010-530320; 35b Tumanyan St; mains AMD1200-5500; ☺ 11am-11pm) If you can't experience a home-cooked Armenian dinner, this hidden restaurant is the next best thing. The food is cooked with soul and the setting parallels a grandmother's living room. Sadly, the restaurant's resident grandmother, the beloved Gayane, died in 2019, but a long-time customer bought it and is continuing her legacy.

To find it, go through the alley beside the Jazzve, past the fence and look for the sign on your right.

Eat & Fit
HEALTH FOOD $$

(Map p150; ☎ 011-588080; 80 Aram St; mains AMD1800-5500; ☺ 8.30am-midnight; ☏ ☞) For a quinoa bowl, avocado toast or 'detox' juice, Yerevan's hip and health-conscious come to this trendy cafe which faces the park. The large menu has plenty of fresh, vegan and vegetarian options with the nutritional details attached and there's a daily lunch special. The terrace is great for people-watching and the interior is perfect for working on a laptop.

Gouroo
HEALTH FOOD $$

(Map p150; ☎ 011-222040; 13 Sarian St; mains AMD3300-5900; ☺ 8.30am-midnight; ☞) A local architect's house has been transformed into this excellent casual fine-dining restaurant, which features light meals free from added sugar, refined oil and preservatives. There's a good selection of local wines and drinks, too, but Gouroo's shining highlight is its shady backyard garden, perfect for a lazy afternoon drink or to enjoy the occasional live jazz show.

Kharpert Restaurant
ARMENIAN $$

(Map p150; ☎ 060-501030; www.tufenkianheritage.com; 48 Hanrapetutyan St; mains AMD2000-4600; ❀ ☞) Inside Yerevan's Tufenkian Hotel is this elegant room centred on a fireplace. Kharpert serves a seasonally driven menu including modern rifts on traditional western Armenian dishes not commonly found elsewhere. You'll also find some universal favourites such as burgers and steaks. Portions are small, but the quality is excellent.

Karma
INDIAN $$

(Map p150; ☎ 010-589215; www.karmarestaurantarmenia.com; 65 Teryan St; mains AMD2560-6560; ☺ 11am-11pm; ❀ ☞) The South Indian chef who runs Karma cooks up incredibly tasty curries, tikkas and biryanis as well as a delectable nutty korma. However, meals come with a price tag far heftier than virtually anywhere on the Subcontinent. The setting is dim and intimate with only a handful of tables and the staff are friendly. Cash only.

Aperitivo
CAFE $$

(Map p150; ☎ 010-586584; 1a Tamanyan St; mains AMD2000-6000; ☺ 7am-2am; ❀ ☞) This excellent cafe lining the Cafesjian Center's sculpture garden is an understandably popular place to sip a colourful cocktail from a skull-shaped glass or to have a bite to eat. The international menu includes salads, sandwiches, pasta, pizzas and meats, all well presented. The Armenian salad with goat cheese, strawberries and nuts is a wonderful summer treat.

Yerevan Tavern
ARMENIAN $$

(Pandok Yerevan; Map p150; ☎ 010-545545; www.pandokyerevan.com; 5 Amiryan St; mains AMD1100-3800; ☺ 9.30am-midnight; ❀ ☞ ♿) You'll need a big appetite and a willingness to be noisily entertained to make the most of this

KHACHKARS

Listed by Unesco on its register of intangible cultural heritage, Armenian *khachkars* are outdoor steles carved from stone by craftspeople in Armenia and communities in the Armenian diaspora. Acting as memorial stones and focal points for worship, they are ornamented with carved crosses that are often depicted resting on the symbol of a sun or wheel of eternity. Other details can include geometric motifs, flowers, saints and animals. Carved using chisel, die, sharp pens and hammers, they can reach up to 1.5m in height and are believed by many Armenians to possess holy powers. There are thought to be more than 50,000 *khachkars* in Armenia.

In Yerevan, it's possible to watch *khachkars* being carved at a traditional stonemasons yard in Aram St between Teryan and Koghbatsi Sts. Medieval monasteries around the country all have an array of *khachkars*; there are particularly fine examples at Makara-vank, Haghartsin (p193) and Goshavank (p196). Most stunning of all is the windswept cemetery filled with *khachkars* at Noratus (p197), near Lake Sevan.

traditional Armenian dining experience. Popular with large groups of local families, it features a huge *khoravats* menu, hearty sharing platters, brisk service and live music Tuesdays to Saturdays starting at 7.30pm.

Abovyan 12   ARMENIAN $$
(Map p150; ☑010-580658; 12 Abovyan St; dishes AMD1200-6500; ☺10am-midnight; 🛜👶) Enter through the tempting Dalan Handicrafts Shop and venture into the lush courtyard lined with artwork, cute tables and a central stage that occasionally plays live music. The menu is typical Armenian and the food is fresh, decent and not too pricey. Upstairs is an elegant dining room and a small gallery with temporary exhibitions.

Wine Republic   INTERNATIONAL $$
(Map p150; ☑055-001100; 2 Tamanyan St; mains AMD3300-12,900, pan-Asian AMD3500-6200; ☺noon-midnight; 🌐🛜) Wine Republic is well aware of Armenia's geography straddling Asia and Europe. It has one menu dedicated to pan-Asian cuisine and another featuring international options including cheeses, pasta, burgers and salads. True to its name, the waiters know their wines and will guide you through the huge selection (though there's no physical wine menu). The entrance is on Isahakyan St.

There's another location on Northern Ave called **Thaiwine Repubic** (Map p150; ☑055-001001; 10/1 Northern Ave; mains AMD3500-6200, dim sum AMD2000-5800; ☺7am-midnight; 🛜) which features a more pan-Asian–focused menu.

Tapastan Yerevan   TAPAS $$
(Map p150; ☑010-521932; 6 Sarian St; small plates AMD2500-9900; ☺noon-midnight; 🛜) Graze on sliders, prince fish or Armenian *tzhvzhik*

(chopped beef liver) at this popular place specialising in wine and tapas-style small plates. The food – served individually or in trios – is acceptable rather than inspired, but the international and Armenian wine list, friendly staff and attractive terrace make it worth a visit, especially during a warm summer evening.

★The Club   INTERNATIONAL $$$
(Map p150; ☑010-531361; www.theclub.am; 40 Tumanyan St; mains AMD3300-9600; ☺noon-midnight; 🌐🛜) Fusing western Armenian and French cuisine, the seasonal menu at this fashionable basement restaurant includes salads, traditional village dishes such as *dolma* (stuffed vine leaves) and *manti* (meat ravioli topped with yogurt), oven-baked fish and steaks sizzled on hot stones at the table. It's worth saving room for dessert, as these are particularly good. There's live music most nights.

The Club has two additional spaces to enjoy – a lounge with beanbag seating and a cafe serving pizzas (AMD1900 to AMD2500), burgers (AMD2500) and wraps (AMD800 to AMD950). These are accessed from a second entrance on Alexander Spendiaryan St.

★Ankyun   ITALIAN $$$
(Map p150; ☑010-544606; www.ankyun.am; 4 Vardanants St; pizzas AMD4000-5200, pastas AMD3600-6200, mains AMD4200-8200; ☺noon-11pm; 🌐) Ask local foodies to nominate the best Italian food in town, and they inevitably choose this place. The chef uses seasonal ingredients to create pizzas, antipasti, pasta, grills and excellent versions of classic desserts such as tiramisu and panna cotta. The decor nods towards Tuscany, and the staff are both professional and friendly.

Dolmama's ARMENIAN $$$

(Map p150; ☑010-561354; www.dolmama.am; 10 Pushkin St; mains AMD6500-13,000; ⊙11am-11pm) Often described as Yerevan's best restaurant, Dolmama's is housed in a rustic 19th-century dwelling. The menu focuses on eastern Armenian dishes with additional flare including *dolma*, *khashlama* (meat stewed in wine) and *khoravats* with mulberry sauce. Its wine selection is excellent and strictly Armenian. Esteemed guests have included Hillary Clinton, Vladimir Putin and George Clooney.

 Drinking & Nightlife

The sun doesn't go down until late during summer and the fun doesn't stop until much, much later. Nightlife rumbles across the city and there are sometimes pop-up shows in abandoned Soviet-era structures. It's a good idea to check Facebook for events before heading out.

★**Mirzoyan Library** CAFE

(Map p150; ☑096-888320; www.facebook.com/mirzoyanphotolibrary; 10 Mher Mkrtchyan St; ⊙noon-midnight, photo library Tue-Sun; ☜) Through an archway of a 19th-century building that once housed Soviet literati, Mirzoyan Library is much more than a cafe. It's also a photo book library (South Caucasus' first), cultural hub and bar where artists sketch, write or debate – latte or cocktail in hand – on one of Yerevan's most stunning wooden balconies. DJs occasionally play in the courtyard below.

★**Gemini** CAFE

(Map p150; ☑010-538814; 31 Tumanyan St; ⊙9am-midnight; ☜) With the look and feel of a Parisian boulevard cafe, Gemini keeps its band of regulars happy with the city's best

OUTDOOR CAFES LIVIN' THE GOOD LIFE

Cafe-hopping is something of a freestyle sport in Yerevan, particularly in summer. The most popular open-air cafes are located around Opera Sq, Isahakyan St, Tamanyan St in front of the Cascade (p146) and the park southwest of Republic Sq (p149). Grab coffee to go at one of the many stands or trucks around town. There's even a cafe bus on Parpetsi St.

coffee (we love both the Armenian and iced varieties) as well as a variety of crepes (the Nutella is legendary). Beans are roasted and can be purchased at its shop next door.

★**In Vino** WINE BAR

(Map p150; ☑010-521931; www.invino.am; 6 Sarian St; ⊙11am-midnight; ☜) A favourite Yerevan wine bar, In Vino features a great selection of new-world and old-world wines from France, Italy, Portugal, South Africa and, proudly, Armenia. Glasses or bottles may be accompanied by platters of cheese and/or *salume* (pork cold cuts), *basturma* (cured beef in ground red pepper) and olives. The bar stools inside and streetside terrace make for a terrific ambience.

Calumet BAR

(Map p150; ☑099-881173; 56a Pushkin St; ⊙5pm-2am; ☜) A favourite among diaspora Armenians, the always-busy Calumet (French for 'peace pipe') is a great place to hang out on cushions and chat over a Kilikia beer. The friendly staff keep the bar lively with great playlists and even hop around to liven up the crowd. Late-night dance parties are a likely possibility any night of the week.

Enter through the wooden door on the street and head down the dimly lit stairs.

2nd Floor COCKTAIL BAR

(Map p150; ☑044-202223; 3/1 Abovyan St; ⊙noon-2am; ☜) Sharing a floor with a vinyl store and carpet shop, this bar is one of Yerevan's funkiest places to grab a drink. The vintage-vinyl theme is evidenced throughout its several rooms and balconies as well as with the disc on the menu you spin to pick your cocktail. Some international food is available including woks, sliders and salads.

Find it through the archway that reads 'Carpets' and go up the stairs with the 'Vinyl Store' neon sign above them.

Dargett BREWERY

(Map p150; ☑060-757473; www.dargett.com; 72 Aram St; ⊙11am-midnight; ☜) The craft beer revolution has finally arrived in Yerevan. Over 20 different flavours are on tap at Dargett's massive brewery, including a great pilsener and apricot beer (of course). The place is usually packed inside and out with Yerevantsis swigging away at tasting flights or munching on pub grub. Bottles are available at several bars and restaurants across Armenia.

Simona
COCKTAIL BAR

(Map p150; ☑ 095-426619; 80 Aram St; ⊙ 7pm-
2am; ☎) The Velvet Revolution is alive and
well at this underground cocktail bar and
vinyl club. Illuminated in a red hue cast by
Victorian lampshades, Yerevan's hip and
classy sit on velvet chairs and drink inventive cocktails such as brandy with apricot
jam or whisky and wild thyme. Despite the
small space, dancing is likely after midnight.

Kond House
BAR

(Map p150; ☑ 091-013801; 46 Leo St; ⊙ 6pm-
2am; ☎) Housed in a mansion once owned
by a Soviet oligarch, the Kond House feels
a lot like an underground house party. You
can chug beer by the kitchen bar, play table
football or sip homemade vodka distilled in
the basement. The patio upstairs hosts pool
parties during summer with market-fresh
barbecued meats. You can even sleep over
if you ask.

Artbridge Bookstore Café
CAFE

(Map p150; ☑ 010-521239; www.artbridge.am; 20
Abovyan St; ⊙ 8.30am-midnight; ☎) Nothing
fancy here – just good French-press coffee,
books to read (there's a decent English selection) and a tranquil atmosphere. The food is
bland and pricey, which is a shame because
the staff and ambience are quite friendly.

Jazzve
CAFE

(Map p150; ☑ 095-559903; 35 Tumanyan St;
⊙ 10am-midnight; ☎) A *jazzve* is a long-han-
dled coffee pot in which rich Armenian
coffee is brewed, and this popular chain of
cafes specialises in coffee made this way. It
also offers espresso coffees, a huge range of
tea, snacks, ice-cream sundaes, smoothies
and cocktails. There are other branches scattered around town.

☆ Entertainment

The Opera House consistently presents
high-quality spectacles at a highly affordable price tag. Tickets often start at just
AMD1000 to AMD2000 and are available
west of the venue. Jazz has been popular
in Yerevan for decades and continues to
be played nightly at clubs and restaurants
around the city.

Malkhas Jazz Club
JAZZ

(Map p150; ☑ 010-535350; 52 Pushkin St;
AMD2000; ⊙ 11am-1am) Let's start by saying
that the Kardashian sisters spent an evening
at Malkhas in 2015. This could be a recommendation, but could also be a warning –

DON'T MISS

ARMENIA'S ARTISTIC HERITAGE

Armenia's artistic, literary and musical
heritage is long, diverse and greatly
revered by both locals and members of
the diaspora. In Yerevan, a number of
small museums memorialise the lives
and work of famous artists and are well
worth a visit. Prior familiarity with the
work of these writers, painters, film-
makers and musicians isn't necessary
because their personal stories closely
reflect the tumultuous events of the past
century and offer museum experiences
that are as rich in history as they are in
art. The most interesting are the Yervand
Kochar Museum (p153), the Martiros
Sarian Museum (p153) and the Sergei
Parajanov Museum (p149).

we'll leave it for you to decide. Armenia's
most famous jazz club is popular with oligarchs and its prices reflect this fact. Expect
plenty of smoke, loud clients, good food and
excellent live jazz.

Live sets start at 9pm, and the owner, Levon Malkhasyan, goes on at midnight. Dress
to impress.

Yerevan Opera Theatre
CONCERT VENUE

(Map p150; ☑ 010-533391; www.opera.am; 54
Tumanyan St; ⊙ 10am-8pm) The city's main
entertainment venue was built in the 1930s
and has two main halls: the Aram Khachaturian Concert Hall and the National Academ-
ic Theatre of Opera & Ballet. Performance
information is displayed on billboards outside, near Mesrop Mahtots Ave. There's also
a ticket office there.

Shopping

Cognac is a popular item to bring home, and
there's a decent selection available in the
duty-free store at Zvartnots Airport (p165).
Other popular buys include woven stuffed
animals, jewellery made with real wildflowers and handmade chess boards.

For premium carpets, the Tufenkian Hotel (p158) and Magerian Carpet Museum
south of the city are your best bets.

Vernissage Market
MARKET

(Map p150; ⊙ 10am-6pm) An open-air market
running between Hanrapetutyun and Khan-
jyan Sts, the Vernissage is where you should

TAP WATER

Pulpulak (drinking fountains) are located all over Yerevan and frequently used by locals and travellers alike. Bottled water is widely available for those not keen on sharing a spout with the mouths of potentially thousands of others.

come to source locally produced handicrafts including traditional dolls, brass pots, ceramics, wooden chess boards and pretty necklaces or bracelets with wildflowers clamped inside. Quality varies, and bargaining is only occasionally successful.

Homeland   ARTS & CRAFTS
(Map p150; ☑ 077-473335; www.hdif.org; Parpetsi 13/6; ⊘ 11am-7pm) ⚘ An official member of the World Free Trade Organization, Homeland sells delightful handicrafts made by women in 10 Armenian villages. Their products are of terrific quality and include pillowcases, ornaments, oven mitts, scarves, and irresistibly cute children's toys. Each product comes with a tag showing a picture and description of the artist who created it.

Nairian   COSMETICS
(Map p150; ☑ 060-445445; www.nairian.com; 34 Tumanyan St; ⊘ 10am-10pm) ⚘ All of Nairian's hair- and body-care products are organic, sulphate-free and made in Armenia, often using beloved local ingredients such as tarragon, thyme, apricot and beeswax. The staff are happy to make recommendations and if you need a refill, Nairian ships worldwide. You can also find its products at some shops and hotels around Armenia.

G.U.M Market   MARKET
(Gumi Shuka, Armenian Market; Map p148; 35 Movses Khorenatsi St; ⊘ 6am-8pm) The displays of fresh and dried fruits at this covered market are pretty as a picture. In summer, radiant peaches, cherries, apricots and berries decorate the stalls. Dried fruits and nuts are found year-round, including strings of syrup-coated walnuts known as sweet *sujuk*. There are also veggies, herbs, *basturma* and blocks of cheese. Come hungry as vendors give samples.

Bookinist   BOOKS
(Map p150; ☑ 010-537413; 20 Mesrop Mashtots Ave; ⊘ 10am-9pm Mon-Sat, to 7pm Sun) The city's best range of guidebooks, maps and

novels in English and other languages. There's a small cafe downstairs with a few drinks and snacks.

Information

DANGERS & ANNOYANCES
➡ Taxi drivers at Zvartnots Airport tend to hassle and even grab passengers on their way out of the terminal.

➡ Unofficial taxis should be avoided. Look for the ones with phone numbers printed on the sides of the vehicle or simply hail a GG or Yandex.

➡ Uncomfortable staring directed at women is an everyday occurrence. Catcalling can also be a issue.

EMERGENCIES

Ambulance	☑ 103
Fire	☑ 101
General emergencies	☑ 112 or 911
Police	☑ 102

INTERNET ACCESS
Free wi-fi is offered by the vast majority of Yerevan's hotels, cafes and fast-food joints. It's also available at the **American Corner** (Map p150; ☑ 010-561383; www.americancorners.am; Yerevan City Central Library, 4 Nalbandyan St; ⊘ 9am-5pm Mon-Fri, 10am-4pm Sat).

LGBT TRAVELLERS
While homosexuality was decriminalised in Armenia in 2003, discrimination is rampant and attacks are frequent. Those who are visually perceived as of a different orientation may be in danger, even in progressive Yerevan. LGBT-friendly nightlife venues include Calumet (p162), Hemingway Pub and Embassy.

MEDICAL SERVICES
Pharmacies are marked by the Russian word *apteka;* there's one open late in every neighbourhood.

Nairi Clinic (Map p150; ☑ 010-537500; www.nairimed.com; 21 Paronyan St) has an emergency department and English-speaking staff.

MONEY
There are ATMs all over the city, including in the arrivals hall at Zvartnots Airport. Euros, US dollars and roubles can be changed nearly everywhere; the British pound and Georgian lari are less commonly traded.

TELEPHONE SERVICES
Beeline, VivaCell/MTS and Ucom have offices all over the city.

TRAVEL AGENCIES

Bogema Land (Map p148; ☑ 091-005150; www.bogematravel.am; Apartment 55, 18 Hrachya Qochar St) A trusted tour agency offering trips around Armenia, Georgia and Nagorno-Karabakh.

Tatev Travel (Map p150; ☑ 010-524401; www. tatev.com; 19 Nalbandyan St; ☺9.30am-6pm Mon-Fri, to 3pm Sat) Specialises in travel to Iran, including arranging visas. It can also arrange bus and air tickets to Tehran.

TOURIST INFORMATION

Yerevan has two helpful tourist kiosks; one on **Nalbandyan** (Map p150; www.facebook.com/yerevaninfocenter; 2/1 Nalbandyan St; ☺9am-9pm Mon-Sat), the other on **Baghramyan** (Map p150; www.facebook.com/yerevaninfocenter; 2/5 Baghramyan St; ☺10am-10pm Sun-Fri), and the My Yerevan (www.myyerevan.am) and Yerevan Municipality (www.yerevan.am) websites carry some tourism-related content.

Not-for-profit ONEArmenia produces a cute crowd-sourced guide to Yerevan that is available online (https://onearmenia.org/inside-yerevan) and in printed brochures around town.

Funded with American-Armenian coin and opened in 2018, **HIKEArmenia** (Map p150; ☑ 011-445326; www.hikearmenia.org; 5 Vardanants St; ☺10am-7pm Mon-Sat) has an interactive touch-screen map and free paper ones to pre-plan your treks. It also has gear to rent and free swag. Friendly staff speak English, Armenian, Russian, French, Dutch, German and Swedish. Make sure to download the helpful HIKEArmenia app which features maps, recommends guides and lists accommodation.

ⓘ Getting There & Away

AIR

Zvartnots Airport (☑ 010-493000; www. zvartnots.aero), 11km from Yerevan, is Armenia's major airport. There are regular flights to and from Georgia (Tbilisi), Russia (Moscow, St Petersburg, Sochi, Krasnodar, Min Vody, Rostov and Stavropol), Ukraine (Odessa and Kyev), Iran (Tehran), Belarus (Minsk), France (Paris), Austria (Vienna), Belgium (Brussels), Poland (Warsaw), Romania (Bucharest), Turkey (İstanbul), Qatar (Doha), Israel (Tel Aviv), Iraq (Erbil) and the UAE (Dubai and Abu Dhabi).

In summer there are also flights to/from Batumi (Georgia), Lyon and Nice (France), Nur-Sultan (Kazakhstan), Seoul (South Korea), Greece (Athens), Cyprus (Larnaca), Lebanon (Beirut), Varna (Bulgaria) and Egypt (Cairo, Hurghada and Sharm El Sheikh). European airlines Ryanair and Wizz Air were in discussions with the government about launching low-cost flights at the time of writing. The hold-up is due to departure taxes being included in the price of a ticket.

The airport's arrivals hall has ATMs, a money exchange, booths for all the major mobile phone providers, a post office and several car-hire desks.

BUS

The main bus station is the **Kilikya Avtokayan** (Main Bus Station; Map p148; ☑ 010-565370; 6 Admiral Isakov Ave), past the Yerevan Brandy Company on the road to Vagharshapat/Etchmiadzin, which also leads to Zvartnots Airport. To get here from the city centre, take *marshrutka* 5 or 259 from Mesrop Mashtots Ave.

ARMENIA YEREVAN

INTERNATIONAL BUS & MARSHRUTKA

The following services all originate and terminate at the Kilikya Avtokayan.

Batumi (Georgia) One daily *marshrutka* (AMD10,000, 10 hours) departing at 8pm between mid-June and August only.

İstanbul (Turkey) Weekly buses (US$50, 32 hours) depart Saturday mornings.

Stepanakert (Nagorno-Karabakh, known to Armenians as Artsakh) A *marshrutka* (AMD5000, seven to eight hours), departs at 7am. Shared taxis depart at the same time (AMD8000, six to seven hours).

Tbilisi (Georgia) Daily *marshrutky* (AMD6500, six hours) departing once per hour between 8am and 11am. In addition, most of the hostels and hotels in town can organise seats in shared taxis (minivans) departing at 10.30am, 1pm, 3pm and 5pm daily (AMD7000, 5½ hours). These can pick up passengers at their hostel/hotel. The Envoy Hostel (p155) offers a hybrid tour/transfer between Yerevan and Tbilisi stopping at Sanahin, Haghpat and Akhtala monasteries en route (per person AMD29,500, 11 hours, Friday).

Tehran (via Tabriz; Iran) One daily bus (AMD25,000, 24 hours), departing at noon. A second service departs at the same time from Shahoumyan Sq near the Best Western Congress Hotel. It is essential to book seats in advance through Iranian travel specialist Tatev Travel (p165). Note that the Tabriz stop is near the train station rather than in the centre of town.

There are three types of transport operating from the bus station: large, often clapped-out, buses; the small minibuses known as *marshrutky;* and faster, more comfortable and slightly more expensive shared taxis (sometimes a car, often a minivan).

From Kilikya, there are services to many parts of the country as well as to international destinations.

Other services depart from the **Hyusisayin Avtokayan** (Northern Bus Station; Map p148; 010-621670; Tbilisian Mayrughi; 9am-5pm Mon-Sat), for Sevan and Dilijan, on the Tbilisi Hwy, 4km from the city centre; from a stand near the Sasuntsi Davit metro station; from Sevan St behind the Yerevan train station; from a stand next to the Gortsaranayin metro station; and from the Raykom bus stand in Azatutyan Ave.

CAR & MOTORCYCLE

A number of agencies rent out cars in Yerevan, including big names such as **Europcar** (Map p150; 010-544905; www.europcar.am; 8 Abovyan St; 10am-6pm Mon-Fri, 11am-3pm Sat), Sixt at the **airport** (091-373366, 060-373366; www.sixt.am; arrivals hall, Zvartnots Airport; 24hr) and in **town** (Map p150; 010-505055; www.sixt.am; Foyer, North Avenue Hotel, 10 Northern Ave), and **Hertz** (Map p150; 091-480685; www.hertz.am; 18 Abovyan St;

10am-6pm Mon-Fri, 11am-3pm Sat). A three-day rental costs AMD57,000 to AMD210,000 depending on the make and model of the car. Many of the roads in Armenia are unsealed and in poor condition, so driving can be slow and challenging. Those looking to get to off-the-beaten-path villages and monasteries might consider hiring a 4WD vehicle.

Policies on taking rented vehicles over the border to Georgia vary between companies, so be sure to clarify what is allowed. If you do take a car over, you'll need to pay for insurance (15 days 30 GEL, 30 days 50 GEL). Some agencies allow customers to pick up the car in Yerevan and drop off in Tbilisi (or vice versa).

MARSHRUTKA

Yerevan is the hub of the national network, and *marshrutky* leave from spots around the city. Try to arrive about 30 minutes before departure if you are heading out of town to ensure you get a seat. If you have a bag or pack, you'll probably have to carry it on your lap.

TRAIN

Train services to Georgia and Gyumri depart from the atmospheric Soviet-era **Yerevan train station** (Sasuntsi Davit Hraparak) off Tigran Mets Ave south of the city centre; the Sasuntsi Davit metro station is underneath the station building. If you are travelling to Georgia you should book your ticket at least one day ahead, and take food and drinks with you for the trip.

Services to Sevan depart from Almast train station northeast of the city centre.

❶ Getting Around

TO/FROM ZVARTNOTS AIRPORT

Zvartnots Airport *Marshrutky* leave from a bus park near the main terminal. Exit the arrivals hall, turn right and walk up the stairs to find it. Yerevan minibus 18 (AMD300, every hour, 8am to 8pm) runs between the airport and Abovyan St in the city centre, stopping at both Sasuntsi Davit metro station and Rossiya Mall en route. You'll be charged an additional AMD100 for your luggage. A taxi from the airport to the city centre should cost AMD3500 to AMD4000; agree on the price before getting into the taxi. Taxis from the city centre to the airport should only cost AMD3000. It's roughly half the price, and far less of an annoyance, to order a GG or Yandex taxi-hailing service – download the app before you arrive. Either way, the trip takes about 20 minutes.

PUBLIC TRANSPORT

The main way around Yerevan is by *marshrutka*. There are hundreds of routes, shown by a number in the van's front window. They stop at bus stops but you can flag one down anywhere on

---

TRAIN SERVICES FROM YEREVAN

Batumi (Georgia) Daily service between 15 June and 30 September at 3.30pm (per person bunk AMD10,790, four-bed wagon compartment AMD17,010, 1st class AMD25,850, 15½ hours). Stops in Tbilisi (open wagon bunk AMD7570, four-bed wagon compartment AMD11,780, 1st class two-person wagon AMD18,140, 10½ hours) en route.

Gyumri Daily services at 7.55am, 2.25pm and 6.25pm (AMD1000, 3½ hours). A new express train Thursday to Sunday also adds an extra service at 10am (AMD2500, two hours).

Sevan Departs 8.30am daily between 15 June and 1 October (AMD600 to AMD1000, two hours). Travels to Shorzha on Friday, Saturday and Sunday.

Tbilisi (Georgia) See Batumi listing above for details of summer service. Between October and 14 June, trains leave on even days of the month at 7.50pm (AMD8600 to AMD14,000, 10½ hours).

CURING THE CURSED

Located 32km south of Yerevan at the foot of Mt Ararat, Khor Virap Monastery (⊙9am-6pm) has been repeatedly rebuilt since the 5th century. Legend says the pagan King Trdat III imprisoned St Gregory the Illuminator (Surp Grigor Lusavorich) here for 12 years. These days, pilgrims climb down a metal ladder into the well where the saint was incarcerated. To join them, wear sturdy shoes and head to the small church in the compound's southwestern corner (the well is right of the altar).

After his cruel treatment of the saint, the king was cursed by madness (or, in a more colourful version of the tale, cursed to roam the forest with the behaviour of a wild boar) and was miraculously cured by St Gregory. Historians contend that Trdat may have switched allegiances to tap into the strength of Armenia's growing Christian community in the face of Roman aggression. In any case, the king converted to Christianity and St Gregory became the first Catholicos of the Armenian Apostolic Church. He set about building churches on top of pagan temples and teaching the faith.

The main Surp Astvatsatsin Church dates from the 17th century. Look for the carving of the saint curing the possessed King Trdat on its eastern facade, facing visitors as they enter the compound.

Just outside the monastery walls are some excavations on the site of Artashat, Trdat's capital, founded in the 2nd century BC.

The monastery is on a hillock close to the Araks River at the border with Turkey and overlooks river pastures, stork nests and vineyards. Mt Ararat towers above and is visible even on a hazy day. There are stalls below selling drinks and snacks.

Khor Virap is reached via a 4km road off the main highway, which passes through Pokr Vedi (sometimes also called Khor Virap). *Marshrutky* bound for Ararat village depart from Yerevan at the Sasuntsi David metro stop on Sevan St at 9am, 11am, and 2pm (AMD400, 40 minutes). Ask to be let off at Khor Virap, but if the driver is only willing to stop at Pokr Vedi, you'll need to walk or hitch a lift the rest of the way.

the street. Trips cost AMD100; pay the driver as you leave. Ask to stop by saying *'kangnek'*.

There are also buses and electric trolleybuses following numbered routes. Tickets cost AMD100.

The Yerevan metro is clean, safe and efficient. It runs north–south through the city, stopping at these underground stations: Barekamutyun, Marshall Baghramyan, Yeritasardakan, Republic Square (Hanrapetutyan Hraparak), Zoravar Andranik near Surp Grigor Lusavorich Cathedral/Rossiya Mall and Sasuntsi Davit at the Yerevan train station. The line continues west and south on ground level to stations in the industrial suburbs. Trains run every five to 10 minutes between 7.30am and 11pm and one-way tickets cost AMD100.

TAXI

Taxis are cheap and plentiful, and range from well-loved Ladas to late-model Benzes. Hail ones with numbers on the sides to be sure they're legitimate. Prices are AMD600 for the first 5km and then AMD100 per kilometre. Make sure the driver switches the meter on or you may be overcharged.

Alternatively, ride-hailing services GG and Yandex are safe, reliable and an increasingly popular option among Yerevantsis. Rides cost AMD600 for virtually anywhere in the city centre and about AMD1600 to Zvartnots Airport (p165). GG also offers shared 'shuttles' to Gyumri (AMD1600, 1½ hours).

CAR & MOTORCYCLE

Rental agencies have branches in Yerevan, but you'll likely be charged a transport fee if you don't pick the vehicle up at the airport.

WESTERN ARMENIA

Those looking to break out of Yerevan for a short trip will be ecstatic to know that some of Armenia's best sights are a short drive from the capital. Three Unesco World Heritage sites are less than an hour's drive, including Armenia's Vatican, Mother See of Etchmiadzin (p171); the 7th-century Zvartnots Cathedral (p172) ruins; and Geghard Monastery carved out of a rock face.

Armenia's second-largest city, Gyumri, which is soaring from the ashes following its devastating recent past, is also found here. Gorgeous hikes abound, you can zigzag up and around Armenia's largest

Western Armenia

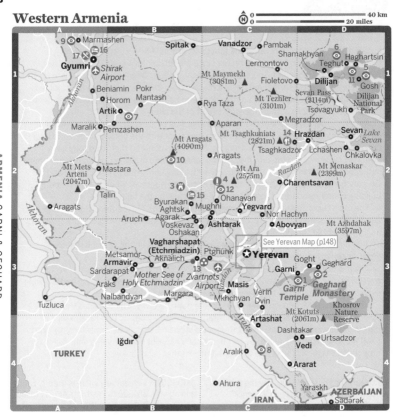

mountain, Mt Aragats (p175), or church hop along the Kasagh Gorge near Ashtarak. In winter, the Tsaghkadzor ski resort continues to be popular well after Soviet athletes trained there in the 1960s. While we recommend exploring the entire country, of course, you'll get a healthy taste of Armenia in this region.

Garni & Geghard

Less than an hour's drive from Yerevan are two of Armenia's most precious gems – the Parthenon-like Garni Temple originally built in the 1st century as well as the 12th-century Geghard Monastery, which is carved out of a rock face. The two sites make up the most popular day trip from the capital and can get extremely busy in summer.

Staying the night isn't necessary, but doing so will give visitors ample time to see the beautiful World Heritage–listed Azat Valley, which is coupled with Unesco's Geghard listing and includes the Symphony of Stones rock formation.

◉ Sights

★**Geghard Monastery**   MONASTERY
(www.garnigeghard.com; parking AMD200; ⊙8am-8pm Jun-Aug, 9am-7pm Sep-May) FREE
Named after the lance that pierced Christ's side at the crucifixion (a shard is now on display at the museum (p171) in Etchmiadzin), this World Heritage–listed monastery is carved out of a cliff alongside the Azat River Gorge. Founded in the 4th century, the monastery's oldest chapel dates back to the 12th century and its tremendously atmospheric **Surp Astvatsatsin** (Holy Mother of God Church) dates from 1215. The cathedral features wonderful carvings and its surrounding chapels make for terrific exploring.

Western Armenia

Outside Surp Astvatsatsin, above the south door, is a coat of arms of the family of the Zakarian prince who built it. The theme is a common Near Eastern one, with the lion symbolising royal might.

On the left-hand side of the *gavit* (antechamber) are two entrances to **chapels** hewn from the rock in the 13th century. One contains a basin with spring water, *khachkars* and stalactite decoration. The second includes the four-column burial chamber of Prince Papaq Proshian and his wife, Hruzakan. The family's coat of arms, carved in the rock above, features two lions chained together and an eagle.

Outside, steps to the left of the entrance lead up the hill to a 10m passageway with carved *khachkars*. This gives access to a 13th-century **burial vault** that was carved out of the raw rock. Its proportions and acoustics are quite amazing. In the far corner is an opening looking down on the church below.

Behind the church are steps that lead to some interesting monastic cells and more *khachkars*. Outside the monastery, next to the stream, is a **matagh** (sacrifice) site that is used on Sundays after the morning service. A choir usually sings at that service, too.

As you approach the monastery, look to the left up the hill for caves housing **monastic cells** built by monks. Trees here are often dotted with strips of cloth, as are trees on the other side of the monastery near the river. It is said a person can say a prayer or make a wish and tie a strip of cloth to a tree near the monastery to make it come true.

During summer, the ramp to the monastery is crammed with vendors selling souvenirs and food; you should be able to grab a snack of sweet *sujuk* or dove-shaped *gata*.

★ **Garni Temple** TEMPLE
(www.garnigeghard.com; adult/student AMD1500/250, guide AMD4000, parking AMD200; ☉ 9am-7pm, to 11pm summer) Built by Armenia's King Trdat I in the 1st century AD, this Hellenic-style temple set on the edge of a gorge overlooking the Azat River was dedicated to the sun god, Mitra. Largely destroyed by an earthquake in 1679, the Parthenon-like structure was rebuilt between 1969 and 1975. It features a monumental staircase and Ionic columns topped by a frieze. Next to the temple are the ruins of a Roman-era **bathhouse** (closed to the public) and a 7th-century **church**.

Archaeologists have found Urartian cuneiform inscriptions dating back to the 8th century BC in the area around the temple, indicating that it has been inhabited since Neolithic times. The high promontory site is protected on three of four sides by a deep valley with rock cliffs, with a wall of massive blocks on the fourth side.

In the ruins of the church, look for the *vishap* (carved dragon stone). This is a marker to show the location of water. Some marks on the middle of the stone are in fact writing from King Argishti from the 8th century BC, which reads 'Argishti, son of Menua, took people and cattle from Garni to Erebuni [the original site of Yerevan] to create a new community.'

Below the ruins is the **Symphony of Stones** rock formation visible with binoculars from the temple or along a terribly bumpy 4WD road (easier access is near Garni Fish Restaurant).

🛏 Sleeping

There are several hotels and B&Bs along the highway and in Garni. You'll find a few more in Goght including the stellar 3Gs B&B and Camping.

ARMENIA GARNI & GEGHARD

A NATION REBORN

Set on a hill, the stunning orange tuff memorial at **Sardarapat Memorial & Museum** (museum adult/child AMD700/300, guide AMD5000, war museum AMD400, guide AMD3000, parking AMD100; ☉9.30am-5.45pm Tue-Sun) commemorates the battle in May 1918 when forces of the first Armenian republic turned back the Turkish army and saved the country from a likely annihilation. Built in 1968 by Russian architect Rafael Israelyan, it's a popular pilgrimage destination for Armenians. About 1km along a flower-laden path is the State Ethnographic Museum, which includes a well-presented ethnographic collection and a hall with battle paraphernalia that's only signed in Armenian.

Sardarapat is about 10km southwest of Armavir, signposted near the village of Araks. *Marshrutky* leave from Yerevan's Kilikiya Avtokayan (p165) for Armavir (AMD400, 50 minutes, every 15 minutes from 7.30am to 8pm), from where you will need to negotiate with a taxi driver to take you to Sardarapat and return you to Armavir after two to three hours at the site. This should cost approximately AMD6000. There's a restaurant at the complex if you wish to have lunch or a coffee.

★ **3Gs B&B and Camping**　　　B&B $
(☎094-496094; www.bedandbreakfast3gs.com; Geghard Hwy, 3rd impasse, house 4, Goght; s/d/deluxe AMD19,500/22,000/27,000, tent per person AMD6500, camping per person AMD3500; 🅿🛜🏊) In between Garni Temple and Geghard Monastery, with epic 360-degree views, this B&B and campground is an oasis. The Dutch couple who run it are lovely and maintain high-quality facilities – the campground bathrooms and showers are amazing. The B&B has four rooms and two tents are available. Guests can also pitch their own tent or park a camper (hookups available).

🍴 Eating

There are a number of decent restaurants outside the Garni Temple and an excellent fishery down the road. There aren't any restaurants near Geghard. Both sights have stands outside in summer and on weekends with vendors selling *gata,* sweet *sujuk* and ice cream.

Garni Fish Restaurant　　　SEAFOOD $$
(☎093-923464; Garni; trout per kg AMD4000; ☉noon-midnight) At the bottom of a rough road near Garni Temple is this highly enjoyable pond-to-table restaurant. Trout swimming in private ponds are caught fresh and served barbecued or as a soup. Sides include salad, bread and *matsoon* (sour yogurt). Private gazebos along the river are most popular with families. Just up the road is the Symphony of Stones rock formation.

❶ Getting There & Away

To reach Garni from Yerevan on public transport, you will need to make your way to GAI St, from where buses and *marshrutky* travel to Goght via Garni. To get there from the city centre, take bus 25, trolleybus 1 or *marshrutka* 44 from Mesrop Mashtots St, or *marshrutka* 5 from Opera Sq. Look out for a large park with an equestrian statue on the right-hand side of the road and then alight at the next stop, a Mercedes-Benz showroom. *Marshrutka* 266 and bus 204 (AMD250, 35 minutes) depart for Goght when full and operate every 20 to 30 minutes between 9am and 6pm. They leave from a car park to the right of the showroom, opposite the fresh produce market.

In Garni, alight at the crossroads with a bus shelter opposite a butcher shop and then walk south to the temple.

Buses and *marshrutky* don't service Geghard. Take a *marshrutka* to Goght as described above and hire a taxi to take you the 4.2km from the bus stop to the monastery, drop you off and then collect you an hour later to return to the bus stop. This should cost AMD3000 to AMD3500.

If visiting both Geghard and Garni Temple, it makes sense to head to Geghard first and organise for the taxi driver to drop you back to Garni rather than Goght (AMD4000). After visiting the temple you can then return to Yerevan by bus or *marshrutka*.

Vagharshapat

📞 231 / POP 46,200

Armenia's fourth-largest city, Vagharshapat (commonly referred to as Etchmiadzin) is largely known for its religious sites. Primarily, the Mother See of Holy Etchmiadzin, which is ground zero for the Armenian

Apostolic Church and home to the current Catholicos, Karekin II. It's also near to the Unesco-recognised Zvartnots Cathedral ruins. Teeming with tour groups in summer, Vagharshapat is nice to stroll through, with a plethora of attractive parks and churches around the Etchmiadzin quarter and the city's central Komitas Sq, but it's better as a day trip from Yerevan than as a destination in itself.

◉ Sights

Mother See of Holy Etchmiadzin
MONASTERY

(Mayrator; ☑ 010-517234; www.armenianchurch.org; Movses Khorenatsi St) Etchmiadzin is the Vatican of the Armenian Apostolic Church, the place where Surp Grigor Lusavorich saw a beam of light in a divine vision, and where he built the first Mayr Tachar (Mother Church of Armenia). Though its rich history and symbolic importance make it a revered destination for Armenian Christians, the compound's churches and museums are underwhelming. Those who only have time for one day trip from Yerevan should consider visiting Geghard Monastery and Garni Temple instead.

The main cathedral, Mayr Tachar, stands in a quadrangle of hedges and lawn surrounded by 19th-century buildings. The original church was consecrated between AD 301 and 303 when Christianity was first adopted by the Armenian nation, but later fell into ruin and was rebuilt in 480–83. More work and expansion occurred in the 600s, 1600s and 1700s, and a major restoration of the interior was being undertaken at the time of writing. The three-tiered bell tower at the entrance of the church is richly carved and dates from 1654. Inside, the church is modest in scale, about 20m by 20m, but the roof gleams with frescoes. At the centre is an altar at the place where St Gregory saw the divine light strike the ground. Divine Liturgy is celebrated every Sunday starting at 11am (10.30am on feast days). Morning services are generally conducted at 7.30am from Monday to Saturday and 8am on Sunday. Evening services are generally conducted at 5.30pm daily.

The grounds include the Palace of the Catholicos (aka the Veharan), the home of the present Catholicos, Karekin II, who was enthroned in 1999. He is the supreme prelate of the 1700-year-old Armenian Apostolic faith. There's also the Cathedral Museum containing precious items obtained by the Church, and the disappointing Rouben Sevak Museum (AMD500; ◷10.30am-5pm Tue-Sun).

The gardens of Mayr Tachar have a 1915–23 Genocide Monument and many fine *khachkars* assembled from around the country. There are also a number of contemporary churches, seminaries and libraries in the compound, the most notable of which is the Holy Archangels Church next to the main gate. This was designed by Jim Torosyan and consecrated in 2011.

Cathedral Museum
MUSEUM

(admission & guide AMD1500; ◷10.30am-5pm Tue-Sun) Etchmiadzin's main museum houses precious objects and relics, including the Holy Lance (Surp Geghard), the weapon allegedly used by a Roman soldier to pierce

Vagharshapat

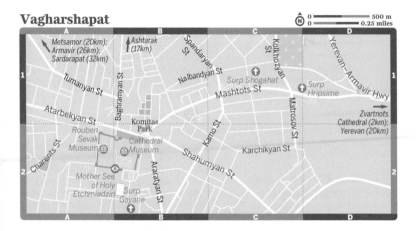

WORTH A TRIP

WORLD HERITAGE RUINS

Catholicos Nerses III (known as 'the Builder') sponsored construction of the 'Celestial Angels Cathedral' in the 7th century. Destroyed in the 10th century, the evocative ruins of **Zvartnots Cathedral** (AMD1300, tour AMD4000, parking AMD100; ⊙ 10am-6pm Tue-Sun) now stand in a semi-industrial landscape near Zvartnots Airport and were included on Unesco's World Heritage List in 2000. It was originally dedicated to – and housed relics of – Surp Grigor Lusavorich, the first Catholicos of the Armenian Church. A model in the on-site museum shows what it may have originally looked like.

The ruins lay buried until the 20th century when they were excavated and the cathedral was partially reconstructed in a polygonal form with plenty of columns supporting carved arches. There are interesting sculptural remnants surrounding the main structure – look out for the carved eagle capital in particular.

The museum in the southwest corner of the site displays artefacts found during the excavation. It also has a series of informative panels about medieval Armenian architecture. Entry is included in the overall ticket price.

Around the cathedral are the ruins of the palace of the Catholicos and the wine press and stone tanks of a medieval winery.

Zvartnots is on the Vagharshapat–Yerevan Hwy, near the delightfully named village of Ptghunk, 17km from Yerevan and 4km from Vagharshapat. To get here, take bus 111 (AMD200, 30 minutes) from Yerevan's Kilikya Avtokayan (p165) and look out for a pillar topped with an eagle on the left-hand side of the highway. This was created by noted Armenian sculptor Ervand Kochar and marks the entrance to the site.

the side of Christ while he was nailed to the cross. The spearhead is set into an ornate gold-and-silver casing. There are also clerical vestments and crowns, illuminated manuscripts, processional crosses, a reliquary of St John the Baptist, and a beautiful beaten-gold reliquary from 1300 that is said to contain a relic of the True Cross. Buy your ticket from the office behind Mayr Tachar church (look for the 'Museums' sign).

Surp Hripsime   CHURCH
(85 Mesrop Mashtots St) Constructed in 618, this church is on the site where St Hripsime was slain after she refused to marry the pagan King Trdat III, choosing instead to stay true to her faith (she was a Roman nun who had earlier fled here to escape marriage to the Roman emperor Diocletian). The small chamber at the back of this church has a niche that contains a few of the rocks purportedly used to stone Hripsime to death.

🛏 Sleeping

There are only a few guesthouses and B&Bs in town. It's better to stay in Yerevan if possible.

❶ Getting There & Away

Take bus 111 (AMD200, 30 minutes) from Yerevan's Kilikya Avtokayan (p165) to Vagharshapat and alight at Komitas Sq, a big roundabout linking Mesrop Mashtots Ave and Movses Khorenatsi St (there's a statue in the middle of the roundabout, so it's hard to miss). There's also a bus from Yerevan's Mesrop Mashtots Ave (AMD300).

Ashtarak

📞 232 / POP 16,900

Ashtarak is a midsized regional town on the **Kasagh Gorge**, 22km northwest of Yerevan. It has an array of black-tuff, 19th-century buildings, pleasant streets lined with fruit trees, a 17th-century stone bridge (sadly dwarfed by a modern replacement) and four medieval churches, two of which command epic views over the gorge. Spillover from Yerevan promises to attract more restaurants and accommodation in the future, but for now, Ashtarak remains a quiet town worth meandering through for a few hours or as a kick-off point to sights around the region.

⊙ Sights

Saghmosavank   MONASTERY
(Saghmosavank; ⊙ 9am-7pm) Surrounded by a fortified wall and commanding wonderful views over the Kasagh Gorge and to Mt Aragats, Saghmosavank (Monastery of Palms) is located in the village of the same name. The monastery is comprised of two main church buildings: the **Church of Zion**

and the smaller **Church of Karapet**; both date from the 13th century. The monastery's *gavit* and L-shaped library date from the same period. A 7.5km trail connects Saghmosavank with Hovhannavank along the Kasagh Gorge (five to six hours return).

Hovhannavank
MONASTERY
(Monastery of John; Ohanavan; ⊙9am-7pm) Perched on the edge of the Kasagh Gorge, this monastery in the village of Ohanavan was once an important educational and theological centre where manuscripts were written and illuminated. It has two adjoining churches: a **basilica** dating from the 5th century and the 13th-century **Church of St John**. The church has an altar decorated with frescoes, as well as unusual cantilevered staircases, detailed engravings and beautiful hanging chandeliers. The entrance to both buildings is via a splendid 13th-century *gavit*.

Surp Gevorg
MONASTERY
(Monastery of St George; Mughni; ⊙8.30am-7.30pm) This handsome 17th-century church is located in the neighbourhood of Mughni, on the northern edge of Ashtarak. It features striped bands of stone around its central drum, a classic half-folded umbrella cupola, an arched exterior arcade, and elaborate carvings on and over its west and south doors. Inside, there are fresco fragments. The surrounding fortress walls have small towers, monks' cells and a refectory built into them.

Mughni is an easy turn-off from the main highway that runs north to Spitak. Opposite the monastery is **Nakanak bakery** (⊙9am-7.30pm), where you can purchase savoury and sweet pastries straight from the oven. These can be enjoyed in the charming garden behind the church.

🛏 Sleeping

My Family B&B
B&B $
(☑077-126200; 3 Tamazyan St; s/d AMD8000/12,000; 🅿🛜) The owners of this guesthouse really do make you feel like one of the family. The rooms are small and simple with tiny bathrooms, but windows look out onto a lush garden with apricot, peach, nut and grape trees. Breakfast and dinner (AMD4000) are made from the heart with plenty of fresh produce.

🍴 Eating

Pascal & Diodato
CAFE $
(☑098-996903; 19 Abovyan St; mains AMD1000-2300; ⊙10am-10pm; 🅿) Named after Armeni-

ans Harutyan Pascal and Johannes Diodato, who opened the first coffee shops in London (1652), Paris (1672) and Vienna (1683), this cafe across from Karmravor Church serves traditional coffee and snacks including Levantine eats *lahmajoon, za'atar* and *shawarma*. Next door is a sweets shop. Note: no wi-fi.

Old Ashtarak
SYRIAN $
(☑094-992232; Grigor Ghapantsyan St; AMD800-2000; ⊙10am-11pm; 🛜🛝) Owned by Syrian-Armenian engineer and architect Habib Haroyan, Old Ashtarak is housed in a century-old, black-tuff building with gorgeous balconies and a welcoming stone-laden backyard terrace. The inside has a rustic feel with two wide arches leading into an attractive dining hall. The menu is tasty and affordable, featuring traditional Levantine dips, salads, kebabs and *lahmajoon.*

🍷 Drinking & Nightlife

As a fertile ground for grapes, Ashtarak is budding as another wine country, though much of the production remains in private homes. Ask at restaurants and accommodation to try some local homemade wines.

❶ Getting There & Away

You need a car to explore this region properly. Getting from Yerevan to Ashtarak is no problem as regular *marshrutky* leave from Kilikya Avtokayan (AMD250, 40 minutes, every 20 minutes from 8am to 8pm). However, once here, you'll need to hitch, walk or hire a taxi/GG/Yandex to visit surrounding sites.

Byurakan

The landscape around the village of Byurakan, about 14km northwest of Ashtarak on the southern slopes of Mt Aragats, includes an astronomical observatory and the impressive remains of Amberd, 15km up the mountain.

◉ Sights

Amberd
FORTRESS
Constructed on a ridge above the confluence of the little gorges of the Amberd and Arkashen streams, this majestic stone fortress dates back to the 7th century but its current buildings date from the 12th century. It's easy to see why the site was chosen – at 2300m above sea level it commands a

position above the farms and trade routes of the Ararat Plain. The ruins of a chapel, 13th-century bathhouse and cistern stand downhill from the fortress.

Armenian
Alphabet Monument   MONUMENT
Thirty-nine giant Armenian letters are haphazardly clustered alongside the highway, 20km northeast of Byurakan and 15km from Ashtarak. The letters were erected in 2005 to honour the 1600th anniversary of Mesrop Mashtots inventing the Armenian alphabet. Mashtots, who is also memorialised with a statue on the site, created the alphabet to give the recently established Christian kingdom its own Bible.

Byurakan Astrophysical
Observatory   OBSERVATORY
(Byurakan; ☑ 091-195901; www.bao.am; day/night tour AMD2100/3000; ◷ 9am-6pm) A large research staff observes and studies the stars through five observational instruments at this Soviet-era observatory complex, focusing on research into instability phenomena. Contact the observatory in advance to take a guided tour.

🛏 Sleeping & Eating

The best restaurant in the area is at the Amberd Hotel. There's also a small restaurant at Amberd.

Amberd Hotel   LUXURY HOTEL **$$**
(☑ 099-902802; www.amberdhotel.am; 1/36 Antarut; s AMD27,000, d AMD37,000-40,000, ste AMD70,000-80,000; 🅿⊖❄@🛜❄) This recently opened 37-room hotel on a hilltop is a popular retreat for Yerevantsis. Rooms are spacious with balconies that deliver breathtaking views over the valley and of Mt Ararat on a clear day. Amenities include indoor and outdoor pools, a tennis and basketball court, a spa (massages from AMD10,000) and a **restaurant** (mains from AMD1500) that's open to nonguests.

❶ Getting There & Away

There are four buses per day from Yerevan to Byurakan, departing at 10.30am, 12.45pm, 3.45pm and 5.30pm from the bus stand on Grigor Lusavorich St in Yerevan (AMD400). If you don't catch one of these there are also a few buses to Agarak, 6km south of Byurakan on the Ashtarak–Gyumri Hwy. From Agarak you could

---

ARMENIA'S MEDIEVAL MONASTERIES

Armenia's tourism industry has two major assets: the country's spectacular natural scenery and its extraordinary array of medieval monasteries. Fortunately, most of these monasteries are set in extremely scenic surrounds, meaning that any travel itinerary based on monastery visits will most definitely live up to a 'Best of Armenia' description.

The unique architecture of Armenia's medieval monasteries developed when elements of Byzantine ecclesiastical architecture were combined with the traditional vernacular architecture and building styles of the Caucasus. Spanning the period from the 10th to 13th centuries, many of these monasteries were built in elevated locations and were heavily fortified to protect them from marauding armies. Locally sourced stone – often tuff – was a logical and widely used building material.

The various architectural forms utilised in the churches within the monasteries – basilica, domed basilica and cruciform – are common throughout the Christian world, but Armenian monasteries have a number of distinctive elements, including conical 'umbrellastyle' domes and cupolas mounted on a cylindrical drum. Another common feature is the *gavit*, a grand space built as the narthex (entrance room) to a major church; these sometimes doubled as a mausoleum. Most distinctive of all is the profusion of ornately carved stone decoration, including the carved memorial stones known as *khachkars* (p161).

Of the 60-plus medieval monasteries in the country, the complexes at Haghpat (p190), Sanahin (p187), Geghard (p168) and Etchmiadzin (p171) are all inscribed on Unesco's World Heritage list as representatives of the highest flowering of Armenian religious architecture. Other outstanding examples include Noravank (p201), Saghmosavank (p172), Hovhannavank (p173), Haghartsin (p193), Goshavank (p196), Akhtala (p190) and Tatev (p211).

When visiting an Armenian monastery it is respectful to dress modestly (no shorts, short skirts or bare shoulders); women should consider covering their heads but this isn't essential. Members of the Armenian Orthodox faith tend to exit church backwards so as not to turn their back on God; you may wish to do the same.

MODERN ARMENIA'S TALLEST PEAK

Snow covers the top of **Mt Aragats** (parking AMD200), the highest mountain in modern Armenia, almost year-round, so climbing is best from July through September. Be careful, though – even in August, clouds can gather in the crater by 10am, so many start walking as early as possible (hikers commonly start mountain ascents at 5am). The southernmost of its four peaks (3893m) is easy enough for inexperienced climbers, but the northern peak (4090m) is more challenging and requires crossing a snowfield (experienced hikers only).

There is no public transport to Kari Lich (Kari Lake), the starting point for Mt Aragats walks. Hitchhikers usually take a bus to Byurakan and then try to thumb a lift, which is more likely on weekends. Hitchhiking back is easier, especially on weekends, as the lakeside *khoravats* (barbecue meats) **restaurant** (grills AMD500-1000) is a popular spot during summer. If driving, note that the road may be closed from January to May.

The hotel at Kari Lake costs AMD15,000 without breakfast or AMD20,000 with breakfast for two.

walk, hitch or hire a taxi (AMD100 per 1km). The four buses return to Yerevan at 7.30am, 9am, noon and 4pm.

Gyumri

📞 312 / POP 114,000

Armenia's second-largest city is on an upswing three decades after the devastating 1988 Spitak earthquake levelled most of Gyumri. Thanks in part to foreign contributions (French-Armenian singer Charles Aznavour and the European Bank are among the donors), Gyumri is being rebuilt with the addition of pretty cobblestone and lamp-lit streets. Restoration is still a work in progress though, as many art-nouveau buildings remain largely rubble and nearly 2000 people still live in shipping containers – a post-earthquake plan that was far from temporary. But there's excitement in the air. Pedestrian-friendly Rizhkov St is lined with trendy cafes and nightlife venues are starting to pop up in the traditionally sleepy city. Artists from Yerevan are coming and more importantly, young Gyumritsis are staying when they were previously known to flock to the capital or flee to Russia. Unlike ever before, Gyumri is proving Armenia has more than one city worth visiting.

History

First human settlement here dates back 2500 years and the town was named Kumayri during the Urartu period in the 8th century BC. Inhabited periodically for centuries, the Russians moved in during the early 19th century and built a large military garrison. The town even received a visit from Tsar Nicolas I who, in 1837, renamed it Alexandropol after his wife Alexandra. As the third-largest city in the South Caucasus, after Tbilisi and Baku, Gyumri was an important trading post between the Ottoman Empire and the rest of Asia and Russia. As a transport hub, it was a stop on the rail journey from Tbilisi to Tabriz.

In 1920 the Turkish-Armenian war ended here with the signing of the Treaty of Alexandropol, an event that ceased the Turkish advance on Yerevan and solidified communist control. In Soviet times the border was shut and Alexandropol became known as Leninakan.

The Spitak earthquake on 7 December 1988 crushed much of Gyumri's historic splendour and also destroyed the many factories established here by the Soviets. Besides levelling large parts of the city and surrounding villages, it killed 50,000 people and made many more homeless. The botched recovery effort would haunt the city for years as successive winters passed without heating or electricity and thousands were subjected to life in 'temporary' shipping containers. Things are better now, even though many still live in containers and there's still plenty of reconstruction work to complete.

◉ Sights

Stretching from Vardanants Sq to Central Park, Gyumri's historic **Kumayri** neighbourhood is worth meandering through, as is the area just north of the square, which includes freshly added cobblestone streets funded by the European Bank. The most charming stretch is Abovyan St.

Gyumri

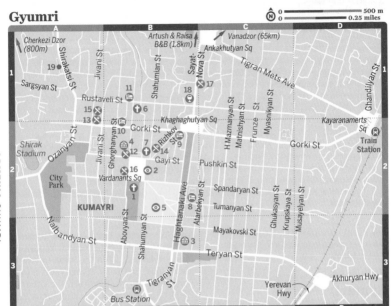

Amenaprkich Church CHURCH
(All Saviours; Vardanants Sq) Towering over Vardanants Sq, the black and apricot Amenaprkich Church was constructed between 1858 and 1872 and consecrated in 1873. It survived the 1926 earthquake, but was badly damaged in the 1988 tremor and is in the process of being rebuilt. The outside is mostly finished, but the inside is a long way away from opening to visitors.

Museum of the Aslamazyan Sisters MUSEUM
(☑ 0312-48205; www.aslamazyanmuseum.com; 242 Abovyan St; adult/child AMD300/150, English, French or Russian tour AMD2000; ◷ 10am-5pm Tue-Sat, 11am-4pm Sun) Artists Mariam (1907–2006) and Yeranuhi (1910–98) Aslamazyan were born in Bash-Shirak village near Gyumri and two floors of this handsome 19th-century building showcase a large collection of their brightly coloured canvasses and ceramics. The sisters were huge travellers and painted scenes of their trips in many parts of the world, something that was extremely unusual for any Soviet artist of the time, let alone women.

Yot Verk CHURCH
(Seven Wounds of the Holy Mother of God; ◷ 9am-6pm) The 19th-century Cathedral of the Holy Mother of God, also known as Yot Verk or the Seven Wounds of the Holy Mother of

God, is the seat of the Diocese of Shirak of the Armenian Apostolic Church. Damaged during the 1988 earthquake, the church has been rebuilt and bustles with activity all day long. The baby-blue drapes are a bright and refreshing twist.

Museum of National Architecture and Urban Life of Gyumri MUSEUM
(☑ 0312-23600; 47 Haghtanak St; adult/child AMD1000/300, sculpture museum AMD500, guide AMD2000; ◷ 11am-5pm Tue-Sat, to 4pm Sun) Though burdened with an unwieldy name and meagre budget, Gyumri's major cultural institution tries hard to provide a satisfying visitor experience. Set in a grand but crumbling 1872 mansion, its collection focuses on the traditional trades and crafts of Alexandropol, with displays on woodworking, blacksmithing, tinwork, lace, embroidery, shoemaking, hatmaking and silversmithing. An attached gallery of sculptures by Sergei Merkurov contains more Lenins and Stalins than you can shake a sickle at.

Shuka MARKET
(◷ 9am-6pm) Gyumri's historic *pak shuka* (covered market) once occupied the land now occupied by Vardanants Sq. Levelled during the Soviet era, the stallholders moved their businesses a few blocks northeast, between Shahumian and Haghtanak Sts,

Gyumri

where they remain today. The now uncovered *shuka* is one of the largest in Armenia, crammed with stalls selling fruit and vegetables, freshly ground coffee, pungent cheeses and *basturma,* bread, bottles of cognac and much more.

🛏 Sleeping

Gyumri has several excellent sleeping options at prices that tend to be far cheaper than Yerevan.

Artush & Raisa B&B   B&B **$**
(☏094-612345; www.gyumribnb.com; 1-2 Ayvazovski St; s/d AMD5000/7000; 🅿🛜) Unbelievably good value, this comfortable homestay is run by English-speaking local guide Artush Davtyan along with his wife Raisa and adult son Martin. Seven spacious guestrooms are available; five in purpose-built blocks in the garden, two in the main house which offer less privacy. Meals (breakfast AMD2000, dinner AMD4000) are enjoyed in the elegant piano room or flower-filled garden.

Hostel #1   HOSTEL **$**
(☏094-115599; 11 Rizhkov St; dm AMD1500, with breakfast for 2 AMD4000; 🛜) This sparkling-new hostel has a terrific location, spacious dorms with comfy bunk beds and privacy curtains, clean bathrooms and lightning-fast wi-fi. Sadly, the atmosphere is nonexistent as there is no common area and the staff are not especially helpful. Breakfast comes in the form of a voucher to Ponchik Monchik (p178).

⭐**Villa Kars**   HERITAGE HOTEL **$$**
(☏010-541156; www.familycarearmenia.org; cnr Rustaveli & Abovyan Sts; s/d AMD25,000/35,000;

🛜) Italian owner Antonio Montalto came to Armenia as a doctor following the 1988 earthquake and has since built his third guesthouse (following Villa Delenda and Villa Ayghedzor in Yerevan) in three historic art-nouveau homes adjoined by a charming courtyard. Rooms are impeccable re-enactments of an upper-class dwelling at the turn of the 19th century and feature wonderful Gyumri-made ceramics.

Berlin Art Hotel   HOTEL **$$**
(☏0312-23148; 25 Haghtanaki Ave; s/d AMD27,000/32,000; 🅿🌀🛜) This hotel was built as an accommodation wing for the German hospital that shares the same premises. It has a charming garden, cheerful dining area (dinner AMD4000 to AMD5000) and simple rooms that feel a tad too much like hospital rooms but have good beds and satellite TV. Paintings and sculptures by local artists adorn every wall.

The staff here are extremely helpful and can answer any question about travel within and around the city. **Shirak Tours** (☏0312-53148, 0312-50386; shiraktours@gyumri.am), a respected local tour operator, is also based here.

Hotel Araks   HOTEL **$$$**
(☏0312-51199; www.arakshotel.am; 25 Gorki St; s AMD23,000-40,000, d AMD26,000-45,000; 🅿@🌀) High ceilings, frilly drapes and a huge staircase create an old-world feel at this decent hotel. Renovations have brought the rooms up to a respectable standard and the street out front has recently been fixed up. Amenities include a sauna and an indoor pool; rare sights anywhere in Armenia. Hotel Araks also has an Italian restaurant and a bar.

✕ Eating

Gyumri's food scene has erupted in the last few years, especially along Rizhkov St where there are a number of trendy cafes and restaurants. Local specialities include *qyalla* (sheep's head), *khash* (cow or sheep feet, head and/or stomach stew) and *tatar boraki* (pasta with sautéed onions and yogurt).

Cheap street snacks are available from shops and stalls at the *shuka*.

★ Herbs & Honey   CAFE $

(☑ 093-644645; www.herbsandhoney.am; 5 Rizhkov St; mains AMD1400-2800; ⊙ 8.30am-midnight; 🕿 🔌) 🍽 This highly Instagrammable cafe is owned by Artush Yeghiazaryan, an Armenian who spent 18 years in Switzerland before returning home. Besides offering herbs and honey made by Armenian producers, the menu includes wholesome salads, vegan *dolma,* 'detox' cocktails and tea concoctions for every ailment. Try the carrot cake for dessert – you won't regret it.

Emili Aregak   BAKERY $

(☑ 077-725037; www.emiliaregak.am; 242 Abovyan St; ⊙ 8am-7.30pm Mon-Fri, from 9am Sat & Sun; 🕿) This small heartwarming bakery run by the Emili Aregak support and resource centre employs Gyumri youth with disabilities and their mothers. The European-style pastries and loaves of bread here are irresistible and there's a great selection of flavourful teas and coffees. Handicrafts produced by beneficiaries of the centre, including dolls, cards and ornaments, are also available for purchase.

Ponchik Monchik   CAFE $

(☑ 098-665577; 7/9 Sayat Nova St; mains AMD1200-2000; ⊙ 10am-11pm; 🕿) *Ponchki* (oval pastries injected with vanilla custard; AMD200) and *monchik* (with Nutella or blueberry; AMD240) are the dangerously addictive namesakes of this Gyumri mainstay. The rest of the menu includes good pizzas, *shawarmas,* breakfasts, speciality coffees and ice cream. There are two locations; this beautifully renovated one and a weathered branch on **Vardanants Square** (☑ 077-073535; 248 Abovyan St; ⊙ 10am-10.30pm).

Poloz Mukuch   ARMENIAN $

(☑ 094-909038; 75 Jivani St; mains AMD2500; ⊙ 10am-10pm) In a historic building opposite the old beer factory, this popular place prepares *khash, khinkali* and kebabs. The most famous dish is *qyalla.* Seating is in wooden cubicles, but many locals prefer to sit around the bar swilling beer (Gyumri, of course) chased with potent shots of *oghee.*

★ Cherkezi Dzor   ARMENIAN $$

(Fish Farm; ☑ 0312-65559; www.cherkezidzor. am; 1st Karmir Berd; fish per kg AMD3500-5600; ⊙ 10.30am-11pm) This fish restaurant is so popular some Russians have been known to fly here to try the fish and fly back the next day. Seating is in open pavilions surrounding the fish pools where your dinner will be caught fresh to order. Trout and sturgeon are available along with delicious salads and sides. Bread is freshly baked in on-site ovens.

The restaurant is on the western side of town near a Russian army base and a little hard to find. From the stadium, cross the opposite bank and walk north up the canyon for 1.3km. Alternatively, a taxi or GG should cost AMD500 each way from the city centre.

Florence   FUSION $$

(☑ 098-339988; 5/7 Jivani St; mains AMD1600-6500; ⊙ 11am-midnight; 🕿) Florence's funky interior (the flower wallpaper in the bathroom is a trip), as well as its atmospheric courtyard, make for a trendy casual fine-dining experience previously unheard of in Gyumri. The menu is Armenian-Italian done well; the artful eggplant rolls and *tatar boraki* are extremely tasty. Staff are eager to please.

🍷 Drinking & Nightlife

Gyumri has just a couple of nightlife options, but due to the influx of Yerevantsis coming to visit as well as foreign travellers, more are expected to pop up in the future.

Amigo Pub   PUB

(☑ 055-090988; www.facebook.com/amigopub24; 9a Sayat Nova St; ⊙ 4.30pm-2am; 🕿) Conservative Gyumri is slim on nightlife options, so this basement pub opened in 2018 is a welcome sight. Dimly lit with wooden crate seating, funky decor and Armenian carpets, Amigo is great for a drink, pub grub or to while away a few hours puffing on a hookah pipe. The bar is at its liveliest when DJs from Yerevan visit.

ℹ Information

American Corner (☑ 0312-52153; http://gyumri. americancorners.am; 68 Shirakatsi St; ⊙ 9am-5pm Mon-Fri) Internet facilities at American Corner, located next to the police department.

WORTH A TRIP

MONASTERIES AROUND GYUMRI

Once the summer residence of the Catholicos of Etchmiadzin, the still-functioning Harichavank (☺8am-7pm) is located in the old town of Harich, about 4km from the town of Artik. Its chapel dates from the 7th or 8th century but was dramatically expanded with the addition of a *gavit* (antechamber) and domes in the 13th century. There is some beautiful geometric stonework over the main church door and around the dome of the *gavit*.

If you ask, the church's caretaker can point out the anteroom/storeroom with a hole in the ceiling leading to a secret upstairs room. During times of invasion, the room was used to house women and children and sometimes even important local officials. A stone would be fitted exactly into the ceiling hole once everyone had climbed to safety.

Direct buses depart Gyumri's bus station for Harichavank (AMD400, 50 minutes) a few times daily. If you have your own vehicle, the monastery is about 15km off the main Yerevan–Gyumri road.

When you are in the area, consider checking out the well-preserved 7th-century Lmbatavank (☺10am-6.30pm) church on a hilltop southwest of Artik; it contains important early frescoes.

The location of Marmashen (☺9am-9pm), deep in a river valley 10km northwest of Gyumri, is unusual – medieval monasteries in Armenia were almost always constructed in elevated locations. There are three churches hewn from lovely apricot-coloured tuff clustered together here, the most impressive of which is the 10th-century Surp Stepanos. A ruined 13th-century *gavit* is next to the church, and beautiful carved tombs and *khachkars* dot the surrounding landscape. The monastery is a popular picnic spot in summer.

To get here, take the main road north from Gyumri, follow the signs to Vahramaberd and pass through the village of Marmashen. When you arrive at Vahramaberd, turn left onto an unsealed road leading through farmland down into the valley. The monastery is near a lake and a small hydroelectric plant. A return taxi from Gyumri should cost around AMD5000 including 30 minutes at the monastery. Make sure the driver understands that you want to see the monastery and not the nearby village of the same name.

Tourist Information Office (✆ 094-174719; www.travelgyumri.com; 1 Vardanants Sq; ☺9am-7pm) English-speaking local Armen Hovsepyan runs this info office inside City Hall and will go out of his way to help travellers. It's best to call or Whatsapp in advance before showing up.

❶ Getting There & Away

AIR

Shirak Airport, 5km southeast of town, only has regular flights to Moscow. Seasonal flights are available to other Russian cities: Krasnodar, Rostov-on-Don, Samara and Volgograd.

There are plenty of ticket agencies in town. A GG or Yandex to the airport should cost AMD1000, taxis AMD1500.

BUS, SHARED TAXI & MARSHRUTKA

From Yerevan, regular *marshrutky* (AMD1500, two hours, every 20 minutes between 8am and 8pm) depart from beside the statue of a man sitting on a horse (David of Sassoun) outside the Sasuntsi David metro station.

In Gyumri, buses, shared taxis and *marshrutky* leave from the **bus station** (Avtokayan; Sha-humyan St) south of Vardanants Sq. Services include *marshrutky* to Yerevan (AMD1500, two hours, every 20 minutes between 7am and 7pm) and Vanadzor (AMD800, one hour, on the hour between 10am and 2pm), as well as one service per day to Stepanavan (AMD1500, 1½ hours, 9am). There's also a daily bus to Vanadzor (AMD500, 90 minutes, 4pm). A seat in a GG shuttle costs AMD1600 to Yerevan, while shared taxis cost AMD2500 to Yerevan and AMD1500 to Vanadzor.

To Georgia, there is one daily *marshrutka* to Tbilisi (AMD5200, 3½ hours, 10.30am) and another for Akhaltsikhe (AMD4000, four hours, 10am). These will only depart if there is a minimum of five passengers.

TRAIN

The **train station** (✆ 031-251002; Kayaranamerts Sq) is at the eastern edge of the city centre. A dedicated train service travels between Gyumri and Yerevan three times daily. From Gyumri the trains depart at 7.45am, 11.55am and 6.40pm (AMD1000, three hours). A new express train runs Thursday to Sunday (AMD2500, two hours). The service from Yerevan to Georgia also stops in Gyumri. Call or visit the train station to confirm schedules and ticket prices.

Tsaghkadzor

 223 / POP 1200

Back when Armenia was part of the USSR, Soviet athletes came to Tsaghkadzor (Gorge of Flowers) to train for the Winter Olympics and other sporting competitions. The ski centre on the slope of Mt Teghenis is still here, and during the ski season (December to March) the village is hugely popular with wealthy Armenians keen to take to the slopes by day and relax in one of the luxury hotels at night. In summer, Tsaghkadzor is delightfully cool and makes an excellent base for those wanting to explore Lake Sevan, which is only 25km away.

The forests around the base and at the top of the mountain provide some nice walks, especially in late spring and early summer when the wildflowers are blooming.

Activities

Tsaghkadzor Ski Resort　　　SNOW SPORTS
(Ropeway; 0223-60030; per section AMD2000, parking AMD200; ⊙9.30am-5.30pm) Located on the eastern slope of Mt Teghenis (2819m), the Tsaghkadzor Ski Resort's chairlift started running in 1967. Repaired in 2004, the chairlift now has five stations and takes skiers and snowboarders up to more than a dozen runs. The lift runs year-round and equipment is available for rent at the base of the mountain or from Kecharis Hotel.

The road straight up from the **Kecharis Monastery** (⊙9am-6pm) leads to the ski base.

Sleeping

As a resort town, Tsaghkadzor isn't short on accommodation. Three- to five-star hotels are spotted everywhere, virtually outnumbering residential homes.

Kecharis Hotel & Resort　　　HOTEL $$
(060-577040; www.kecharis.am; 20 Orbeli St; d AMD34,000, f AMD44,000;) This is the type of place where local families return year after year. It offers 35 stylish rooms (12 of which are family duplexes), a gym, a restaurant serving buffet meals (AMD5000), two coffee shops, and a busy basement entertainment complex featuring a bowling alley and pool tables (both charged), a bar and two extra restaurants.

The location is convenient, being on the central square close to the town's shops.

Guests can take advantage of free minibus transfers to the ropeway.

Marriott Tsaghkadzor　　　HOTEL $$$
(010-294111; www.tsaghkadzormarriott.com; 2 Tsandzaghbyuri St; s/d AMD63,000/88,000, ste AMD213,000;) This impressive Marriott opened in 2012 on the northern edge of town. It offers spacious rooms in the main building and in seven free-standing villas. There are plenty of facilities for the whole family: huge indoor pool, sauna, spa, gym, tennis courts, tearoom, terrace restaurant (mains AMD4900 to AMD7500), two lounge bars, business centre and children's playroom with arcade games.

Eating

Tsaghkadzor has a bunch of fashionable cafes and restaurants serving Russian, Georgian and Armenian cuisine. There's also a sushi place. The majority of dining options are clustered around the main square.

Getting There & Away

Tsaghkadzor is only about 40 minutes' drive northeast of Yerevan. From the Yerevan Hwy, the access road goes through the town of Hrazdan and continues up to the village's central square. There is no *marshrutky* service; a taxi from Yerevan costs about AMD7000.

There are frequent buses and *marshrutky* between Yerevan's Raykom station and Hrazdan (AMD500), 6km down the valley – a taxi up to Tsaghkadzor from here will cost AMD1000.

NORTHERN ARMENIA

Armenia's northern region is decorated with verdant mountain ranges and ancient monasteries, many of which are in the process of being consumed by their lush natural surroundings. As with the rest of Armenia, crumbling Soviet buildings populate the cities and towns, save for the pretty resort town of Dilijan, which now boasts several superb restaurants and B&Bs.

The north is better explored outside the cities. Hiking is terrific here, and you can dip your toes into the Transcaucasian Trail (TCT), bounce along the rapids of the Debed Canyon or soar through the air on a zipline (p196) over Ijevan. This is a region nature lovers won't want to miss.

PICNIC PROVISIONS

During the warmer months, Armenia's network of roads and highways serve a dual purpose. Setting up stalls by the roadside, local farmers sell fruit, vegetables and other products to commuters keen on sourcing produce fresh from the field – it's the local version of a farmers market, and a sensational source of picnic provisions. Each town and region tends to specialise in one crop or product, including the following:

Dilijan Freshly picked corn on the cob is cooked and sold on the stretch of road between the town and the Sevan Pass, on the road to Lake Sevan.

Vanadzor Bunches of crunchy carrots are a popular purchase when driving between Vanadzor and Dilijan.

Voratan Pass Beekeepers tend their hives and sell jars of the golden bounty by the side of the highway between the Voratan Pass and the turn-off to Tatev Monastery (p211).

Areni Bottles of locally produced red wine and juicy apricots grown in orchards on the river plain are sold at highway stalls in this wine-growing region.

Debed Canyon Freshly picked berries (raspberries, mulberries and strawberries) tempt drivers around the town of Alaverdi.

There are wonderful picnic spots in rural settings throughout the country. Some of our favourites include the caravanserai on the Selim Pass between Lake Sevan and Yeghegnadzor; the stream alongside the road to Haghartsin Monastery (p193) outside Dilijan; the garden in the grounds of the Surp Gevorg Church (p173) in Mughni in the Kasagh Gorge; and the stony beach at Wishup Shore (p197) on the eastern side of Lake Sevan.

Stepanavan

📞 256 / POP 12,500

Sitting on a plateau above the steep-sided gorge of the Dzoragets River, Stepanavan is known throughout the former Soviet Union as one of the birthplaces of Armenian communism. An early cell of the Bolsheviks led by local lad Stepan Shahumian operated from hideouts and caves in this region before the revolution. Shahumian died in a lonely corner of the Turkmenistan desert with the other 26 'Baku Commissars' in 1918, and all 26 were later sanctified in countless memorials across the region. (The Baku Commissars were Bolshevik leaders in the Caucasus in the early days of the revolution.)

The town museum dedicated to Shahumian may be interesting to students of Soviet history, but there is no cogent reason for other visitors to head this way.

Outside of town, the Lori Berd ruins, however, are well worth exploring.

👁 Sights

Lori Berd   FORTRESS

(Lori Fortress) FREE On a promontory between the gorges of the Dzoragets and Miskhana Rivers, this ruined fortress has huge towers and massive stone blocks along its exposed side. Originally the base of David Anhogin, who ruled the region of Tashir-Dzoraget from 989 to 1048, it eventually became a base for the Orbelians and Zakarians, powerful Armenian noble families. There are ruined buildings worth exploring, an ancient cemetery and hillocks that are actually Bronze Age tumulus tombs. A 14th-century bridge is in the gorge below.

To reach the fortress, head out of town across the bridge and veer right at the roundabout, following the course of the river past the Lori Berd village and then veering right again at a sign. The remaining 2km is on a poor-quality road. A taxi from Stepanavan takes about 15 minutes and should cost around AMD1000; a Yandex will cost AMD500 to AMD600. From the fort, you can walk back to Stepanavan along a 4.5km trail in the steep-sided gorge; this starts on the north side of the fort.

Stepanavan Dendropark   FOREST

(Sojut; AMD200; ⊙10am-7pm) This cool and tranquil 35-hectare arboretum 11km south of Stepanavan was established in the 1930s and has a vast array of conifers and deciduous trees. It's especially popular in May when locals with respiratory problems come to inhale the pollen (not recommended for allergy sufferers!). You'll need a car to get

Northern Armenia

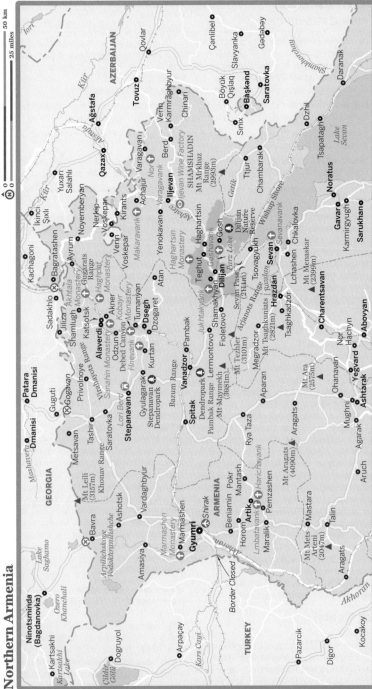

here. The Cinderella-style carriage beside the road signals the **Hekyat Restaurant** (Fairytale Restaurant; ☑ 093-303100; Gyulagarak; mains AMD600-4000; ⊙9am-7pm), which is popular with locals.

To reach the Dendropark, head towards Vanadzor until you reach the village of Gyulagarak. Cross the bridge here, pass the ruined village church and then take the first street right onto the dirt road. A taxi will cost you AMD1000.

Stepan Shahumian Museum   MUSEUM
(☑0256-22191; Garegin Nzhdehi St; admission & guide AMD400; ⊙9am-5pm) This Soviet-era edifice was constructed in 1978 on the site of the modest timber home of Stepan Shahumian and his wife Ekaterina Ter-Grigoryan, and the architects chose to preserve and display the house in the central atrium of the new building; it looks like a slightly sad dollhouse. Inside, there are some of the Shahumians' original furnishings plus documents and photographs. There's also an upstairs gallery featuring works by local artists and a downstairs exhibit about the town.

🛏 Sleeping & Eating

Lori Hotel   HOTEL $
(☑0256-22323; www.lorihotel.am; 11 Nzhdeh St; s/d/ste AMD10,000/12,000/15,000; 🕸) The best option in town only for lack of any better options. This simple centrally located hotel feels very Soviet, but it's kept reasonably clean and the rooms are brightly painted. Staff don't speak English and breakfast (AMD2000) is served in the cafe next door. Light sleepers beware: rooms with balconies onto the street can get annoyingly loud at night.

★**Carahunge**   CAFE $
(☑099-324300; www.carahunge-cafe.com; 64 Sos Sargsyan St; mains AMD1400-4000; ⊙11am-11pm; 🕸) Why the owners of this excellent cafe and bookshop chose to open in sleepy Stepanavan is a mystery, but it's a welcome sight for travellers passing through. The menu is a mix of Armenian and international with pizzas, wings and *za'atar*. Beautiful handicrafts are for sale, including unique pottery. Carahunge has a second location in Dilijan (p196).

Slobodka Restaurant   ARMENIAN $
(☑0256-21772; 44 Sos Sargsyan St; mains AMD1800-2700; ⊙noon-8pm; 🕸) The women at this charming restaurant near the museum don't speak any English, but they're happy to show guests what's in the refrig-

A MONASTERY LESS TRAVELLED

Travelling between Stepanavan and the Debed Canyon, one of two possible routes passes the monastery of **Hnevank**, located on a winding road 7km from Kurtan and 12km from Dzoraget. Standing inside the gorge on the southern side of the canyon, near the confluence of the Gargar and Dzoragets Rivers, the complex has been ruined and rebuilt several times; most of what is visible today dates from the 12th century. It is particularly attractive in spring and summer when it is surrounded by wildflowers.

erator and on the stove. *Khoravats* and *dolma* are the staples, and they're both extremely tasty.

ⓘ Getting There & Away

From Yerevan, *marshrutky* (AMD1500, three hours, 9am, 11am, 1.30pm, 2.30pm and 3.30pm) depart from Kilikya Avtokayan (p165).

In Stepanavan, all transport departs from a parking lot below the Stepan Shahumian statue. Services depart when full, and so there are no official departure times. *Marshrutky* leave for Yerevan (AMD1500, three hours) between 8am and 3pm. For Vanadzor (AMD500, one hour) there are usually five buses daily. Two *marshrutky* a day go to Tbilisi (AMD3000). A taxi anywhere in town from the main square costs AMD400.

Vanadzor
☑ 322 / POP 78,400

In a way, Vanadzor (formerly Kirovakan) is Armenia's Detroit. Its industry, chemical factories, has mostly shut down, leaving the city poor and in a shambles (and potentially toxic). Meanwhile, young people and artists are making the most of it – a few of the country's most popular bands are from here and a hip cafe and speakeasy recently opened up. Still, Vanadzor remains, on the whole, a grey post-industrial former Soviet city.

It's a good idea to stay here as a base to explore Debed Canyon.

◉ Sights

Vanadzor's **shuka** (⊙8am-8pm) is one of Armenia's busiest regional markets and its fine arts museum has a decent collection. The centre of town was almost totally rebuilt

Vanadzor

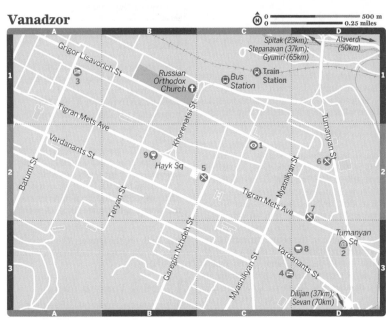

Vanadzor

◉ Sights
1 Shuka...C2
2 Vanadzor Museum of Fine Arts..........D3

🛏 Sleeping
3 Hotel Argishti.....................................A1
4 Maghay B&B.......................................C3

✖ Eating
5 Jazz Cafe..C2
6 Madera..D2
7 Tashir Pizza..D2

🍷 Drinking & Nightlife
8 Anticafe Teynik...................................D3
9 Solenoid...B2

during the Soviet era, but some elegant stone villas and country houses dating from the 19th century can be found south along Myasnikyan St.

Vanadzor Museum of Fine Arts　MUSEUM
(☎ 0322-43938; www.vanart.org; Tumanyan Sq; AMD500, guide AMD2000; ⊙ 10am-6pm Tue-Sat) There are nearly 2000 works of art on display at this three-floor branch of the National Gallery of Armenia, including paintings, sculptures, drawings, prints and decorative arts. Most are the work of artists from the Lori region.

🛏 Sleeping

⭐ **Maghay B&B**　　　　　　　　　　　B&B **$**
(☎ 091-380305; marined61@rambler.ru; 21 Azatamartikneri St; s AMD9000, d AMD16,000-35,000; P@🖥) Ashot and Marine run Vanadzor's best accommodation, so you'll need to book ahead to score one of their nine rooms. The rooms are all different sizes, ranging from a tad too cosy to extremely spacious. There's a communal kitchen where a delicious organic breakfast is served (the jams are homemade with berries from the garden). Dinner is also available (AMD4000 to AMD5000).

Hotel Argishti　　　　　　　　　　　HOTEL **$**
(☎ 095-442556; 1 Batumi St; s/d AMD18,000/22,500; P🖥) Argishti was recently completely overhauled with new furniture and freshly painted rooms. Rooms all now have a minibar and glass wardrobes. The wi-fi has also been revamped recently. Staff could be friendlier. Note that no English is spoken here. Dinner will run you AMD2500.

✖ Eating & Drinking

The best meals in town are available at Maghay B&B. Nonguests are welcome, but should call ahead to make a reservation. There are plenty of cafes and fast-food joints on the main street, Tigran Mets Ave, including a branch of the popular **Tashir Pizza** (☑0322-44401; www.tashirpizza.am; 65 Tigran Mets Ave; slices from AMD270; ☺10am-midnight; 🛜🅰️).

Madera ARMENIAN $

(☑098-822234; 56 Grigor Lusavorich St; mains AMD400-1400; ☺10am-10pm; 🛜) With very affordable Armenian and Russian food as well as friendly (non-English-speaking) service, Madera manages to be one of Vanadzor's best eateries. The *borscht* (beet soup) and dumplings are particularly tasty.

Jazz Cafe CAFE $

(☑098-117282; 1st fl, 34 Tigran Mets Ave; mains AMD1500-3000; ☺10.30am-10.30pm; 🛜) This modern cafe with a stylish rooftop balcony is where locals go to celebrate (it closes at 10.30pm, which shows just how vibrant the local nightlife is). The menu is massive, though the food is nothing special. Live music is played occasionally. Enter through the side door on Artsakh Sq.

Anticafe Teynik CAFE

(Anticafe; ☑099-522009; 41a Varadants St; per hr AMD500; ☺11am-10pm; 🛜) Popular with Vanadzor's youth, Teynik is an anticafe, meaning you pay per hour to get unlimited tea or coffee and snacks. It's a great deal considering the excellent tea flavours and freshly baked sweets that arrive at your table. There's a good selection of board games and instruments to play. Events such as screenings are often held.

Solenoid PUB

(☑055-771701; www.facebook.com/Solenoid.lV; 20 Tigran Mets Ave; ☺7am-11pm; 🛜) The sign says it's a refrigerator shop and you have to ring the doorbell to get in, but there's a good reason for that – Vanadzor's reputation for homophobia and sexism means its coolest speakeasy needs to be selective. Owned by the lead singer of a local rock band, Solenoid serves beer, wine and booze.

ℹ️ Getting There & Away

From Yerevan, *marshrutky* (AMD1200, two hours, departing when full between 8.30am and 7pm) depart from Kilikya Avtokayan.

In Vanadzor, the bus and train stations are at the bottom of Khorenatsi St, opposite the Russian Orthodox Church. *Marshrutky* to Yerevan (AMD1200, two hours from 7am to 5pm) take a 132km route via Spitak and Aparan. There are two morning *marshrutky* to Dilijan (AMD500, up to one hour), two daily *marshrutky* to Gyumri

(AMD800, one hour) and two daily *marshrutky* to Noyemberyan via Alaverdi (AMD500, up to one hour). A *marshrutka* to Tbilisi (AMD4000) leaves at 8.30am.

Shared taxis charge AMD2000 per person to Yerevan and AMD5000 to Tbilisi. A shared GG shuttle charges AMD1500 to Yerevan.

The Debed Canyon monasteries can be visited on a day trip by taxi for around AMD15,000 to AMD20,000. This can be organised directly with drivers or through Maghay B&B.

The train service (p166) between Yerevan and Georgia makes a five-minute stop at Vanadzor. You should check the schedule and purchase your ticket from Vanadzor's train station at least one day in advance.

DEBED CANYON

This canyon manages to pack in more history and culture than anywhere else in the country. Nearly every village along the Debed River has a church, a chapel, an old fort and a sprinkling of *khachkars* somewhere nearby. Two World Heritage–listed monasteries, Haghpat (p190) and Sanahin (p187), are the main attractions, but there's much more to see. Derelict Soviet-era environmentally disastrous infrastructure is sadly noticeable along the riverbank, but the dramatic scenery is quite idyllic elsewhere and worth driving, or rafting (p186), through.

Dsegh

POP 2700

Nestled on a wildflower-strewn plateau high above the gorge, this agricultural village is known throughout the southern Caucasus as the birthplace of Armenia's national poet, Hovhannes Tumanyan. Dsegh also has a 7th-century church and five trails popular with birdwatchers. The town itself is little more than a roundabout.

Fifteen minutes back along the highway is the excellent Tufenkian Avan Dzoraget Hotel near the confluence of the Debed, Pambak and Dzoraget Rivers. This hotel offers the best accommodation and eating in the area.

◉ Sights

Hovhannes Tumanyan House Museum MUSEUM

(AMD500; ☺10am-6pm Tue-Sun) Those who have already visited the Hovhannes Tumanyan Museum (p155) in Yerevan will find this

ARMENIA DSEGH

timber house where he grew up interesting, but those unfamiliar with his life and work will find the lack of English-language labelling frustrating. The house itself gives an interesting glimpse into local life during the tsarist era.

The museum is located near Dsegh's central square, which sports a statue of Tumanyan, a sculpture garden and a shop.

🛏 Sleeping

**Tufenkian Avan
Dzoraget Hotel** HOTEL $$$
(☎ 093-947889; www.tufenkianheritage.com; Dzoraget; s AMD30,000-100,000, d AMD38,000-108,000; 🅿❄@🛜🖥) Prepare to be impressed by this hotel right on the river's edge. There are 54 rooms spread over two buildings – opt for one with a river view if at all possible. Rooms are large and well equipped, and hotel facilities are excellent: indoor swimming pool, sauna, hot tub, gym, table tennis (per hour AMD1400) and a **terrace restaurant** (salads AMD1200-3300; mains AMD1800-10,000; ⊘8am-10pm; 🅿🛜✍👶).

ℹ Information

Visitor Centre (www.facebook.com/dsegh center.info; ⊘10am-6pm) Freshly built visitor centre with information about hikes and birdwatching in the area.

ℹ Getting There & Away

The 7.6km road to Dsegh is clearly signed off the main highway 30km north of Vanadzor. A clapped-out bus travels between Vanadzor and the village daily (AMD400). There are a couple of signed B&Bs if you are stranded here overnight.

RAFTING IN ARMENIA

The best way to see Debed Canyon is to bounce, bob and fly right through the river. **Visit Lori** (☎096-129013; rafting@visitlori.com; per person AMD12,000; ⊘Mar-Oct) organises rafting with brandnew, eight-person rafts and goodquality gear. English-speaking guides are excellent; Armin from Iran is hysterical. The river itself is 12km of mostly Class III rapids. Winter rafting down a snowy hill can be arranged (AMD5000, November to February).

To get to Tufenkian, *marshrutky* (AMD500) travel between Vanadzor to Noyemberyan via Alaverdi twice daily and can drop you on the highway next to the bridge leading to the hotel. A taxi ride from Vanadzor will cost you AMD5000 to AMD7000.

Odzun
POP 4000

Perched on a broad shelf that terminates at a sheer plunge down to the Debed River, Odzun is a substantial settlement of about 4000 residents that is best known for its magnificent church of St Astvatsatsin.

◎ Sights

St Astvatsatsin Church CHURCH
(Odzun Church; ⊘9am-7pm) Built on the site where legend tells us St Thomas buried Christ's swaddling clothes in the 1st century, the core of St Astvatsatsin dates from the 5th century but had considerable additions in the 8th century. The current building features plenty of carved bas reliefs, a central cupola, a handsome external pillared arcade on its southern side and two 19th-century belfries. The unusual funerary monument next to it is thought to date from the 6th century.

🛏 Sleeping & Eating

There's a small cafe near the St Astvatsatsin Church serving drinks and homemade cakes, but no other restaurants in town. Meals are available at any of the guesthouses or B&Bs.

Sergo Davtyan B&B B&B $
(B&B Odzun; ☎099-081859; www.odzunbandb. am; house 4, 22 St; per person AMD10,000; 🅿🛜) French-speaking Azniv and Sergo Davtyan and their English-speaking adult son (he's only around in summer) are justifiably proud of their eight-room B&B, which is the best in Odzun. The family home is very pleasant, with an elegant loungedining room on the ground floor (dinner AMD3000). The clean bedrooms on the 1st floor have modern bathrooms.

ℹ Getting There & Away

Five *marshrutky* per day travel from Odzun to Alaverdi (AMD200) between 8am and 5.30pm. Odzun is on the road to Stepanavan, and the Alaverdi to Stepanavan bus passes through here at 10.30am and 3.30pm (AMD700).

WORTH A TRIP

MONASTERY IN THE CANYON

Perched above the hamlet of Kobayr is the 12th-century **Kobayr Monastery**. The main church has some partially restored Georgian-style frescoes and a detached 13th-century **bell tower**. There are also three chapels, one with a scenic circular balcony. Behind the main church is a beautiful slow-dripping **waterfall** that's also worth seeing.

You'll need to watch the road carefully to spot the sign leading to the hamlet of Kobayr (also spelt Khober or Kober), around 6km north of the Tufenkian Avan Dzoraget Hotel and restaurant. Leave your car in the small lot next to the railway line and clamber up the steep path, dodging chickens, pigs and other farm animals on the way. The steep climb takes 10 to 15 minutes.

Kobayr is about 18km from Alaverdi and 33km from Vanadzor. *Marshrutky* travelling the route between Vanadzor, Alaverdi and Noyemberyan can be flagged down on the highway but only pass twice daily.

Alaverdi

📞 253 / POP 12,600

Blighted by a huge smokestack belching smoke into the valley, Alaverdi is the administrative and transport hub of this area but doesn't have much else going for it. Rows of shabby Soviet-era apartment blocks are cut into the strata by the highway and the railway line, and a half-decommissioned copper smelting plant (the source of the smoke) dominates the town's northern edge.

Tamara's bridge, about 1km north of the bus stand, was built by order of Queen Tamar of Georgia in the 12th century. This humpbacked stone bridge has four kitten-faced lions carved on the stone railing and makes for a good place to relax in summer.

Cut into the canyon wall above Alaverdi, Sanahin is home to one of Armenia's World-Heritage–listed medieval monasteries. It is an essential stop for all visitors to the Debed Canyon.

◉ Sights

Sanahin Monastery   MONASTERY

(◔9am-7pm) Sanahin is a World Heritage site packed with ancient graves, darkened chapels and medieval study halls. The inner sanctum of the cross-shaped **Surp Astvatsatsin** (Holy Mother of God Church) is the oldest structure, dating back to 934. Its adjoining *gavit* was built in 1181. In its heyday, the monastery was renowned for its school of illuminators and calligraphers and also for its medical school. Its name means 'older than that one', referring to nearby Haghpat Monastery.

Sanahin's large **library** (scriptorium) was built in 1063. Square in plan and vaulted, it has 10 niches of varying sizes in which codices and books were stored. At the southeastern corner of the library is a small church dedicated to St Gregory the Illuminator. The 11th-century **Academy of Gregory Magistros** is located between the two main churches. The **cemetery**, located to the southeast of the main buildings, contains a 12th-century mausoleum housing the Zakarian princes.

Opened in 1978, a cable car was constructed to bring as many as 15 people at a time up to Sanahin. Unfortunately, it closed in 2015 and there are no plans to reopen it.

Mikoyan Museum   MUSEUM

(📞094-157137; Mikoyan St; admission & tour AMD500; ◔9.30am-5pm) This Soviet-era museum is a shrine to brothers Anastas and Artyom Mikoyan. Anastas was in charge of administering food in the USSR and survived 60 years in the Politburo, outlasting even Stalin. Artyom was the designer of the USSR's first jet fighter in WWII, the MiG. There's an early MiG jet outside the museum (no climbing allowed!) and plenty of photos, medals, uniforms and aircraft plans and drawings inside.

🛏 Sleeping & Eating

The best eating is done at B&Bs. In summer, two outdoor cafes operate next to Tamara's bridge.

Iris Guesthouse   GUESTHOUSE $

(📞091-088812, 094-894292; irinaisrayelian@gmail.com; 65 Baghramyan St; dm/d/ste AMD6000/14,000/18,000; 🅿🛜) Popular among backpackers, this guesthouse has shared rooms with a warm cottage-like feel and tidier private rooms in a separate building.

JUSTIN FOULKES/LONELY PLANET ©

1. Cafesjian Center for the Arts (p146)

This premier arts centre in Yerevan has two external garden galleries and is dramatically housed in a flight of stone steps.

2. Khor Virap Monastery (p167)

Close to the Araks River at the border with Turkey, Khor Virap boasts a magnificent Mt Ararat backdrop.

3. Armenian Genocide Memorial & Museum (p147)

Designed by Artur Tarkhanyan, this powerful memorial and museum commemorates the massacre of Armenians in the Ottoman Empire from 1915 to 1922.

4. Sanahin Monastery (p187)

Parts of this atmospheric monastery, which is cut into the canyon wall above Alaverdi, date back to the 10th century.

English-speaking owner Irina Israeliyan is an enthusiastic host who's eager to provide information, organise transport or prepare organic meals upon request (dinner AMD4000). Tent camping is available in the garden (BYO tent per person AMD2000, tent rental AMD3000).

ArmBee   B&B **$**
(☏091-333743; armbee@inbox.ru; 27/5 Jravazan St; cabin s/d AMD8000/10,000; P🖥) 🍽 The beekeeper owner of this B&B built cabins where live bees tend to hives beneath the mattresses. Don't panic, they can't get inside the sleeping area. While we can't confirm that sleeping over bees does what the owner says it does – treat anxiety, depression, tiredness and even hangovers – this is a unique experience you won't *bee*-lieve.

❶ Getting There & Away

From Yerevan, *marshrutky* (AMD1700, three hours) depart from Kilikya Avtokayan (p165) at 9.30am, 1pm, 2pm, 3pm and 4pm. Shared taxis from Kilikya charge AMD3000 per passenger and depart when full.

In Alaverdi, buses and *marshrutky* leave from a parking bay next to shops on the main road – taxis wait here too. A bus ticket and information window is located in the back of the lot. There's one *marshrutka* to Akhtala at noon (AMD300), *marshrutky* to Yerevan at 8am, 9am, 11.30pm and 2pm (AMD1500, four hours), 10 daily *marshrutky* to Vanadzor leaving between 7.30am and 3.45pm (AMD800, one hour), and eight *marshrutky* to Haghpat on weekdays and three on weekends (AMD200, 25 minutes). The Haghpat service operates between 8.30am and 5pm Monday to Friday and at 9.30am, 1pm and 5pm on weekends.

A seat in a shared taxi costs AMD3000 to Yerevan. A private taxi will cost AMD5000 to the Georgian border, AMD15,000 to AMD18,000 to Tbilisi and AMD23,000 to Yerevan.

The Yerevan–Georgia train passes through Sanahin station and stops for one minute; you'll need to inform staff if you wish to get on. Buy your ticket in Yerevan, Tbilisi or Vanadzor (Yerevan–Tbilisi AMD5000 to AMD8000).

Haghpat

One of Debed Canyon's World Heritage-listed monastery complexes is found in this picturesque village east of Alaverdi. Views of rolling hills down from the village are spectacular and the monastery is one of the most handsome in Armenia. In summer, Haghpat gets crammed with tour groups, many of which dip down from Georgia.

◉ Sights

Haghpat Monastery   MONASTERY
(⊙8.30am-7pm) Occupying a commanding position overlooking the gorge, this monastery has atmosphere and architectural splendour in spades. Founded around 976 by Queen Khosrvanuch, who funded construction of the domed **Surp Nishan** (Church of the Holy Cross) at the centre of the complex, it saw a building boom in the 12th and 13th centuries. Surp Nishan's frescoes and the porch, *gavit,* bell tower, library and chapter house were added at this time. The monastery's name means 'huge wall', acknowledging its hefty fortifications.

WORTH A TRIP

FANTASTIC FRESCOES

Akhtala, a small village 20km northeast of Alaverdi, has one major claim to fame: the magnificent frescoes in its 13th-century church. These include a stunning Virgin Mary in the apse, and depictions of the Last Supper, Last Judgement, Crucifixion and Resurrection on other walls. Note the fresco of bearded Persians, said to have been painted so that invading armies would spare the church. To get to the church, you'll need to walk through towering 10th-century basalt fortifications.

Entering **Akhtala Monastery** (St Astavatsin) from the main gate, look left and you'll see two large **caves** that were used for smelting copper. Surrounding the church are a well-preserved **chapel** and a **graveyard** with old and new headstones – be careful where you walk, as weeds and grass hide dangerous drops into underground structures.

A daily *marshrutka* to Akhtala (AMD200, 40 minutes) departs Alaverdi at noon, but returns immediately, meaning that you will be stranded here after your visit. It's a 3km walk to the highway.

Outside the monastery is **Nurik**, a USAID-supported cafe and visitor centre established by a local women's organisation. Besides serving tasty food, Nurik offers courses in doll-, candle-, soap- and carpet-making as well as felting. Cooking classes are also available.

🛏 Sleeping

Hotel Gayane   HOTEL **$**
(☎ 093-413705; s/d AMD15,000/25,000, 4-bed
cottage AMD32,000; P⊛✻🛜🏊) An excellent choice for families visiting this region,
Gayane started as a B&B in a farmhouse but
has since expanded to include four simple
self-catering cottages and a new multistorey
building with 29 hotel-style rooms. Facilities
include an indoor and outdoor pool, billiard
table, table tennis and a cafe that's open
to nonguests. Buffet dinners are available
(AMD3000 to AMD4000).

🍴 Eating

The best eating is done at hotels and guesthouses; Hotel Qefo has a popular restaurant
that's open to nonguests. There are also a
few restaurants along the river and on the
road into town.

❶ Getting There & Away

Haghpat is 6km from the Yerevan Hwy, signed
from the northern approach but not from the
south. *Marshrutky* from Alaverdi (AMD200) run
eight times daily on weekdays between 8.30am
and 5pm and three times on weekends at
9.30am, 1pm and 5pm. It's a 7km walk to Sanahin Monastery via Akner village.

Dilijan

📞 268 / POP 17,400

It's billed as the 'Switzerland of Armenia',
and although that may be a stretch, alpine
Dilijan has undeniably attractive scenery
and an extremely pleasant climate. During
Soviet times, cinematographers, composers,
artists and writers came here to be creative;
today it's a centre for tourism with a number
of fine B&Bs and restaurants.

There's certainly enough natural beauty
to inspire creative thought: the lush oak and
hornbeam forests surrounding the town with
snow-capped peaks in the distance make for
perfect hiking territory. In summer, villagers
herd cattle down from the mountain pastures and foragers gather mushrooms and
herbs from the rich deciduous forests. The
local architecture features a lot of steep tiled
roofs and wooden beams, along with some
cute gingerbread-style structures. Even the
Soviet monuments have a touch of flair.

With the medieval churches of Haghartsin (p193) and Goshavank (p196) an easy day
trip away, Dilijan is one of Armenia's best
towns to visit.

WORTH A TRIP

PARZ LAKE

About 13km from Dilijan, Parz Lich
(meaning clear lake) is an attractive
sight that explodes with tourism during
the summer months. Lakeside attractions include an Armenian restaurant
(mains from AMD1200), boats for rent
(AMD2000 to AMD5000), a zipline
and a rope park (AMD6000 each or
AMD9000 for both). You can also stay
the night in one of the on-site cottages
(AMD12000).

A taxi from Dilijan should cost
AMD4000; on weekends you may be
able to find a cab in the parking lot for
the trip back. If there are no taxis available, the info centre in Dilijan can organise a lift for you.

◉ Sights

Dilijan Local Lore
Museum and Picture Gallery   MUSEUM
(☎ 0268-24450; 28 Myasnikyan St; AMD500, tour
AMD500; ⊙10am-5.40pm Tue-Sat, 11am-4pm
Sun) Housing an eclectic collection of European and Armenian art from the 16th to
20th centuries, this gallery is Dilijan's major cultural institution. Some of the older
works from Italian and French artists had
been housed in museums in Moscow and
St Petersburg but were moved to Dilijan
during WWII for safekeeping. The standout
Armenian work is Arpenik Nalbandyan's
Cézanne-like *Children from Khndzoresk*.
Downstairs is a thrilling ethnography and
archaeology collection featuring axes and
chain mail.

🛏 Sleeping

There are lots of hotels and sanatoriums
in and around town, which appeal mostly
to Russian and Armenian tourists. Several
great B&Bs have opened up recently, which
attract a wider clientele. There are also a
couple of hostels in Dilijan, but none worth
recommending.

★ Toon Armeni   B&B **$**
(☎ 098-787899; info@toonarmeni.am; 4 Kamarin
St; s/tw/d AMD15,000/20,000/25,000, family
AMD30,000; P🛜) This B&B in a 200-year-
old country home hits all the right notes.
Rooms on the first floor are authentic
with old furniture and modern bathrooms.

Upstairs rooms are bland, but clean. The organic restaurant overlooking the garden is outstanding and affordable (try the beet salad). Friendly English-speaking staff and superb wi-fi add to making Toon Armeni a top choice.

Old Dili
GUESTHOUSE **$**

(☑ 055-707565; 10a Sharamavyan; cottage AMD20,000, tw & d without bathroom per person AMD5000; 🛜) This guesthouse, steps from the Historic Centre, has just one A-frame cabin, but it's one of the best value accommodations in Armenia so we had to include it. The loft-style cottage is remarkably cosy with a kitchen, couches and a comfortable bed you may never want to leave. In the main house are standard clean rooms. Breakfast is AMD2000.

Daravand Guesthouse
B&B **$**

(☑ 094-420965; www.daravand.com; 46 Abovyan St; s/d AMD17,000/25,000, without bathroom AMD11,000/19,000, 6-person cottage AMD30,000; 🅿🛜) Owner Razmik is a diaspora Armenian with an Iranian upbringing and a German education, and he runs his guesthouse with great verve. Rooms are well maintained, featuring good beds and small bathrooms. The downstairs cottage with space for six is perfect for groups or families and the balconies offer great views. Dinner costs AMD5000 per person.

The guesthouse is on the road towards Jukhtakvank, 360m off the main Dilijan–Vanadzor Hwy. Head towards the railway bridge and look out for a red garage on the right-hand side of the road; the guesthouse is reached by a switchback road next to this.

Dilijan

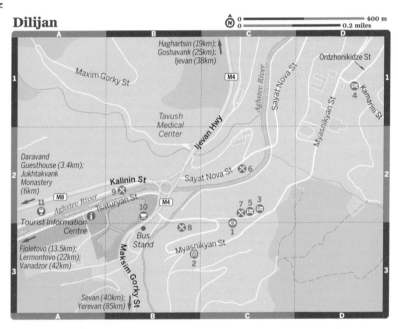

Dilijan

DANCE OF THE EAGLES

Hidden in a verdant valley 13km northeast of Dilijan is **Haghartsin Monastery** (parking AMD200; ⊙9am-8pm). Haghartsin ('Dance of the Eagles') was built between the 10th and 13th centuries and has three churches: one named for Gregory the Illuminator; another for the Virgin Mary (Surp Astvatsatsin); and the third for St Stephen (Stepanos). There are stunning *khachkars* (carved stone crosses; don't miss the one on the southern wall of Surp Astvatsatsin), a sundial on the wall of St Gregory, a ruined *gavit* (antechamber) and a refectory with a stunning arched ceiling.

The monastery was built by order of two brothers, princes of the Bagratuni kingdom, and their family seal can be seen on the back of St Stepanos.

A recent restoration of the site funded by the Sheikh of Sharjah in the UAE has seen the church buildings lose their historic patina, and many visitors find their bright and shiny appearance disconcerting. No doubt they will blend back into their surrounds in the future.

The grounds also feature a garden and a *gata* bakery (10am to 7.30pm, cakes AMD1000/1500) from the same owner as Kchuch and Losh.

The monastery is 4km off the main Dilijan–Ijevan Hwy. There is no *marshrutka* service, but it's an extremely pleasant walk from the highway, with plenty of picnic spots and look-outs along the way.

If you're travelling by public transport, the local bus starts and ends its journey from the highway turn-off.

Tufenkian

Old Dilijan Complex   HOTEL $$
(☑094-030883; www.tufenkianheritage.com; Sharambeyan St; s AMD20,000-48,000, d AMD26,000-64,000, ste AMD46,000; ☎) Re-creating the feel of 19th-century Dilijan with modern amenities, this Tufenkian Hotel features somewhat bland rooms with modern bathrooms housed in historic-looking buildings. The two Ananov guesthouse suites feel so authentic you'll regret not bringing your cloak and top hat. Breakfast is served in the disappointing **Haykanoush Restaurant** (mains AMD1500-5000; ⊙9am-10pm; ☎).

Horseback riding and hiking tours are available as well as bicycles.

✗ Eating & Drinking

Losh   ARMENIAN $
(☑042-886018; 1/2 Kalinini St; mains AMD1100-3200; ⊙10am-10pm; ✗) This restaurant is split into two. Downstairs there's Losh, serving mainly lavash, dips and starters. Upstairs is Tava (meaning pan in Armenian), a more upscale option featuring Armenian classic dishes served mostly in pans. Both are excellent, have funky decor and serve food that's a refreshing twist on what you usually come across in Armenia. Losh and Tava have the same ownership as Kchuch and the *gata* bakery at Haghartsin.

★Kchuch   ARMENIAN $$
(☑041-886010; 47 Myasnikyan St; clay-pot dishes AMD1800-3500, pizzas AMD2500-3200; ⊙10am-10pm; ☎) One of the best restaurants in Armenia, Kchuch is located in the middle of a lush park in the heart of Dilijan. Most of the food is baked inside brick ovens in *kchuch* (clay pots), and includes tasty meats like osso buco and chicken with dried apricots. Pizzas come in inventive flavours like the 'revolutionary pizza' loaded with grilled veggies.

Flying Ostrich By Dolmama   ARMENIAN $$
(☑060-655080; 6 Sayat Nova St; mains AMD3500-6000; ⊙10am-11pm; ☷) There was great excitement in Dilijan when this branch of Yerevan's upmarket Dolmama Restaurant (p162) opened next to the Aghstev River in 2014. Serving what it describes as 'traditional Armenian food with a twist', it offers indoor seating in a restored barn and outdoor seating in an attractive cobbled courtyard.

Cafe #2   CAFE
(☑060-700805; 17/1 Maksim Gorky St; ⊙9am-10pm; ☎☷) Established to give local teens a place to hang out, study, work on social initiatives and/or make a few bucks serving tables, this cafe is an excellent place to while away an afternoon. Overlooking Dilijan's central lake, the cafe has an intriguing menu of drinks and healthy food served in big portions. Staff are happy to help with tourist inquiries.

HIKING IN DILIJAN

DILIJAN TO PARZ LAKE

START DILIJAN TOURIST
INFORMATION CENTRE
END PARZ LAKE
LENGTH 14.5KM; FOUR–FIVE HOURS
DIFFICULTY MODERATELY DIFFICULT

This section of what will soon become the 3000km Transcaucasian Trail (TCT) is a tried, tested and true hike that takes you from the centre of Dilijan up to Parz Lake or vice versa. Along the way are beautiful vistas, dense forests offering respite from the sun and meadows which filled with millions of wildflowers during springtime. Wear pants and good hiking shoes as the grasses get thick and the terrain mucky.

From the Tourist Information Centre (p196), walk over the bridge to the **Dilijan Historic Centre** (p192) and up to Myasnikyan St. You'll find the trailhead across from the amphitheatre. Following the red-and-white trail markings, go up the stairs, along the 4WD road and make a left onto a narrow path until you end up in a **wooded area** with phe-

nomenal views over Dilijan. The trail crosses a small meadow before re-entering the forest and rising up to a **picnic area** with a freshwater spring. Along the roads of a Dilijan suburb, the trail eventually narrows back into a dirt path through a stretch of fields. Following the stream, you'll get to an uphill slog through a **grassy patch** with vegetation that can slice or cause a rash on bare skin. Fortunately, the reward in late spring and early summer is a huge alpine meadow known locally as **Gyolort** flooded with white, yellow and purple flowers. Prance on through the wildflowers and follow the signposts to a **forest** with plenty of switchbacks. Finally, you'll hit the home stretch; a 4WD road that can get nasty with mud and puddles, until you reach **Parz Lake** (p191). You can stay the night in one of the cottages or hail a cab in the parking lot back to Dilijan (AMD4000). If there are no taxis available, the info centre in Dilijan can organise one for you.

Those still keen on hiking can continue along the TCT to Goshavank (7.1km) and then to Gosh Lake (4.2km).

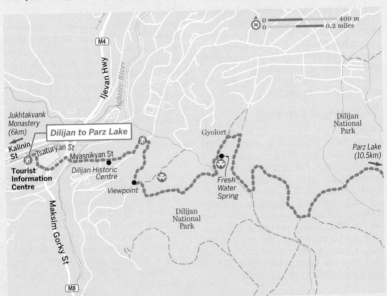

Dilijan National Park is a hiking paradise, with plenty of terrific trails that feature ancient monasteries and wonderful springtime wildflowers. Hiking accessories can be rented from the Tourist Information Centre (p196).

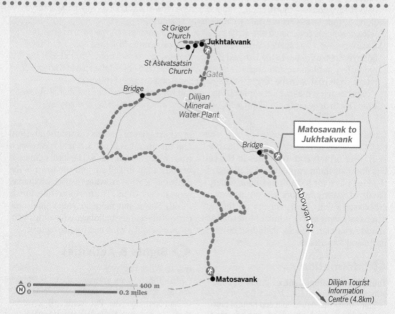

MATOSAVANK TO JUKHTAKVANK

START ABOVYAN STREET INFO SIGN
END JUKHTAKVANK
LENGTH 3.8KM; 1¼ HOURS
DIFFICULTY MODERATELY DIFFICULT

This short loop takes you through thick forest to the 11th- and 13th-century monasteries Jukhtakvank and Matosavank, both of which have nearly been consumed by the green tentacles of their natural surroundings. It's easiest to drive or hire a taxi to the trailhead by the info sign on the road, but it's also possible to start from near the Dilijan mineral-water plant, 3.2km east along the Vanadzor road and about 3.5km up to the right. Another way is to walk from the Dilijan Information Centre. If you're keen to cycle rather than walk, mountain bikes can be hired at the info centre.

Entering the **trailhead** on Abovyan St, go straight to avoid the muddy terrain and cross the bridge on your left. After about 10 minutes, make a left off the 4WD path, which will take you straight to **Matosavank**, a church built in 1247 with a grass-covered roof and a tree statue that looks like a dancing boy.

Turning back the same way, cross over the 4WD track and continue through a field until you reach another track. Following that road, go right at the mouth of a stream and then right again along a trail. When you reach the river, look for the **bridge** (looking further right you'll see the Dilijan mineral-water plant). Over the bridge, go up past a gate and left up a steep hill speckled with chamomile wildflowers in late June and early July. You'll arrive at the rear of St Astvatsatsin church in **Jukhtakvank**. The other, St Grigor, was probably built in the 11th or 12th century and has lost its domed roof over the years.

To get back to where you started, hang a right along the 4WD track until it reaches Abovyan St and walk down until you reach the info sign.

WORTH A TRIP

OH MY GOSHAVANK

Founded in 1188 by the saintly Armenian cleric Mkhitar Gosh, who was buried in a little chapel overlooking the main monastery complex, **Goshavank** (parking AMD200; ☺8am-8pm) features a main church (Surp Astvatsatsin), smaller churches to St Gregory of Narek and St Gregory the Illuminator, and a *matenadaran* (library) that is said to have held 15,000 books. A fourth church topped by a bell tower was built on top of the library in 1291; entrance was via the external cantilevered staircase.

Goshavank is considered one of the principal cultural centres of Armenia of its time; historians believe it was abandoned after the Mongol invasion in 1375. It then appears to have been reoccupied between the 17th and 19th centuries and restored from 1957 to 1963. The monastery has been restored again recently. When here, take note of the splendid *khachkar* (stone cross) between the second St Gregory chapel and the *gavit* (antechamber).

Goshavank is 6.5km off the main Dilijan–Ijevan Hwy, on the road to Chambarak. A taxi from Dilijan or Ijevan (both 23km away) should cost around AMD4500 one-way.

Carahunge   BAR
(☑043-220003; 33 Kalinini St; ☺10am-11pm; ☎)
With beer on tap and 670 wines in the cellar, many of them Armenian, Carahunge is the best place for a drink in Dilijan. There's plenty of seating indoors and out as well as a bookstore with lounge chairs up top. An extensive menu serves a mix of international and Armenian classics, including burgers, pasta and *khoravats*.

ℹ Information

Tourist Information Centre (☑094-399336; www.visitdilijan.com; 15/2 Maxim Gorky; ☺9am-8pm) This newly built and helpful tourist information centre has maps and can assist with planning hikes. Gear is available to rent at affordable prices including walking poles, sleeping bags, snowshoes and bikes.

ℹ Getting There & Away

From Yerevan, *marshrutky* (AMD1000, two hours) depart when full from Hyusisayin Avtokayan (p166) between 9am and 6pm.

The bus stand is in front of Cafe #2 near the main roundabout in the lower town. *Marshrutky* between Ijevan and Yerevan stop here en route five times per day between 8am and 4pm (to Ijevan AMD500, to Yerevan AMD1000). A private taxi costs AMD5000 to Ijevan and AMD20,000 to the Georgian border. Enquire about *marshrutky* to Tbilisi (AMD6000, three hours) at the extremely helpful Tourist Information Centre.

Ijevan

☑263 / POP 20,400

Surrounded by forested mountains and with the Aghstev River running through its centre, Ijevan is the bustling capital of Tavush province. Ijevan means caravanserai (inn) and the town has been on a major east–west trade route for millennia. The local climate is warmer than in Dilijan, and the town is the centre of a wine-growing district producing some decent wines. The town's architecture is mostly Soviet, but there are some handsome early-20th-century buildings, a bustling open-air *shuka* and a wine and cognac factory.

◉ Sights & Activities

Ijevan Wine Factory   WINERY
(☑011-919999; www.ijevangroup.com; 9 Yerevanyan St; tour AMD2000, tasting AMD2500-5000; ☺9am-5pm Mon-Sat) Put aside all expectations of a picturesque winery, because Ijevan's wine factory is just that – a large industrial complex where the local grape harvest is transformed into dry white and sparkling wines under the Haghartsin, Gayane and Makaravank labels. The tour explains how the factory's wine and cognac is produced, and the tasting includes three wines and one or two types of cognac. Tasty jams, juices and compotes are available in the shop.

The factory is about 1.5km from the town centre, on the road to Dilijan.

Yell Extreme Park   ADVENTURE SPORTS
(☑041-010030;   weekday/weekend   zipline AMD11,000/15,000, multiple activities AMD17,000-25,000; ☺10am-7pm Jun-Sep, to 6pm Oct-May) Hundreds of metres up in the lush mountains of Ijevan State Sanctuary, Yell Extreme Park has six well-maintained ziplines which take an hour or two to soar through. Via Ferrata, rock climbing, a rope park, paintball, zorbing and horseback riding are also available. Staff are excellent and the course delivers epic views of Ijevan below. Ziplining is offered year-round. If you wish to

stay the night, simple huts are available for AMD14,000 including breakfast. The extreme park is connected to the Apaga Hotel and wellness retreat, so it is also possible to stay there (single/double AMD31,700/33,700, deluxe AMD41,700). Note that neither of these accommodations have wi-fi. The park and hotel are located 2km from the town of Yenokavan and 13km from Ijevan along a bumpy mountain road.

🛏 Sleeping & Eating

The best meals in town are at Anakhit Guesthouse (reserve ahead). Some snacks are available at one of the cafes on Aboyyan St next to the river or Ankahutyan St opposite the sculpture park.

★ Anakhit Guesthouse　　　　　B&B $

(☑ 077-012274, 077-292979; 4 Tavrizyan St; s/d AMD7500/15,000; ℗🛜) Travellers rave about this family-run B&B near the *marshrutka* stand, describing it as a real home away from home. Owner Anakhit offers a warm welcome and is known for her home-cooking – her Armenian suppers are a highlight (AMD2500 to AMD5000). Rooms are cute and cosy, and there's a lovely terrace with a view. Daughter-in-law Anna speaks English and French.

❶ Getting There & Away

From Yerevan, *marshrutky* (AMD1500, three hours) depart when full from Hyusisayin bus station (p166) between 9am and 6pm.

In Ijevan, *marshrutky* leave from the wooden bus shelter next to the Dan Garden Cafe on the highway. Departure information is displayed in a window of the ticket office set back from the street.

Marshrutky to Yerevan (AMD1500, three hours) leave five times daily from 7.30am to 3.30pm; these stop in Dilijan (AMD500, 40 minutes) en route. There are also a few daily *marshrutky* to Vanadzor (AMD1000, 90 minutes). A bus leaves for Georgia at 10am (AMD1000); a private taxi to the border should cost AMD10,000. GG rideshare service goes to Tbilisi for AMD12,000.

LAKE SEVAN & AROUND

Lake Sevan

Set 1900m above sea level and covering 1240 sq km, the vast expanse of Sevana Lich (Lake Sevan) is the largest lake in the Caucasus and one of the largest freshwater high-altitude lakes in the world. Its colours and shades change with the weather, forming dazzling azure to dark blue hues, and a thousand shades in between. Fish populations include the endangered *ishkhan* (prince trout) as well as introduced crayfish and *sig* (whitefish).

In the 1950s, Soviet planners irrigated the nearby Hrazdan River, causing Lake Sevan's water level to drop 20m. The drop uncovered forts, houses and artefacts dating back 2000 years, but combined with overfishing and sewage dumping, also led environmentalists to declare the lake is on the brink of destruction.

Lake Sevan's beaches are very popular with Russian tourists and noisy day-trippers. For some tranquillity, head to the eastern side to visit Wishup Shore or the Tufenkian Avan Marak Tsapatagh Hotel.

Noratus　　　　　　　　　　CEMETERY
Approximately 900 *khachkars* dating from as far back as the 10th-century dot this breathtaking cemetery on the western edge of Lake Sevan. Legend has it that an invading army was forced to take cover as their commander mistook the field of *khachkars* for a battalion of enemy soldiers. All *khachkars* face west and thus are better photographed in the afternoon. Watch out for the ladies who propose guided tours – for a price.

A laminated paper detailing the most noteworthy *khachkars* in 10 languages is available outside the souvenir shop.

🛏 Sleeping

Sevan's beach resorts start to fill up – and raise their prices – around late May. Prices may jump by 40% in the high season. The season slows down again in early September. In spring and autumn, resorts remain open with reduced rates and in winter most are shut entirely.

Wishup Shore　　　　　CAMPGROUND $
(☑ 093-412002; Shorzha; admission AMD1000, tent per person AMD2000, shelter AMD10,000, cottage AMD30,000; � mid-Jun–mid-Sep; 🛜) On the wilder eastern side of Lake Sevan, you'll find groups of hip Yerevantsis escaping the scorching summer heat. Stony Wishup Shore hosts events and has a fun bar and restaurant (mains AMD1000 to AMD2000). The vibe is free-flowing and visitors can pitch their own tent or rent a hexagonal shelter. Cottages are also available for groups.

SEVANAVANK PENINSULA

A pagan temple once occupied the elevated site of **Sevanavank** (parking AMD200) overlooking the lake, but was replaced by a now-ruined church in 305. Two further churches, **Surp Astvatsatsin** and **Surp Arakelots** (aka Surp Karapet), were built in the 9th century. A *gavit* (antechamber) was added to Surp Astvatsatsin at a later date; now ruined, it is filled with handsome *khachkars* (stone crosses). Accessed via a long flight of steps, the monastery is one of Armenia's most popular tourist sites and is horrendously overcrowded in summer.

The main beach strip is along the sandy south side of this peninsula, crowned by the much-photographed churches on the hill at the end. Don't expect clean water or a tranquil beach experience – bars pump out loud music and beachgoers play beach volleyball, waterski, ride jetskis and have fun on paddleboats. You'll need to pay a fee to use any of the beaches (AMD2000 to AMD3000 per person depending on the beach).

A taxi between Sevan and Sevanavank costs AMD1000 each way. You'll be charged AMD2500 for a return trip with a 30-minute stop at the monastery.

Lavash HOTEL $

(☎098-727521; Chkalovka; s/d/tr AMD16,000/20,000/23,000; 📶) Built to look like a rustic village, Lavash (named after the bread) is the best option on the west side of Lake Sevan. The cabin-style rooms overlook two beaches, are spacious and have cute lake-facing tables. Much of the complex is dedicated to its Armenian restaurant and tearoom. Kids will enjoy the games room with table football and table tennis.

The hotel is located 8km from Sevan just off the highway. A taxi from Sevan city should cost about AMD2000.

Tufenkian Avan Marak Tsapatagh Hotel HOTEL $$

(☎093-947891; www.tufenkianheritage.com; Tsapatagh; s AMD22,000-30,000, d AMD38,000-46,000, ste AMD62,000; P📶🏊) The windswept eastern edge of Lake Sevan is light on tourism infrastructure, meaning that the noisy crowds so ubiquitous on the opposite shore are blissfully absent. This resort was the first of the Tufenkian hotel chain and one of the few sleeping options on the eastern side. Rooms are comfortable and there's a large swimming pool (May to September).

Eating

Roadside vendors along the highway will nearly stand in front of your vehicle in an attempt to sell you fish. Picking up a snack or lunch at the lively Tsovagyugh supermarket and bakery is a good idea, as quality restaurants are a rarity around the lake.

Tsovagyugh SUPERMARKET $

(pastries from AMD100; ⏱24hr; 📶) On the road in between Sevan and Dilijan is this immensely popular supermarket and bakery. Incandescent doughnuts, baklava, wraps, pizzas and *khoravats* are on offer. Dargett draught beers, in 2L bottles, are available to take away and there's live fish. It's a great place for lunch or to take snacks with you on the road.

Zanazan Restaurant ARMENIAN $$$

(☎093-947891; www.tufenkianheritage.com; Tsapatagh; mains AMD1600-7500; ⏱9am-10pm; P🌶👪) Housed in a huge barn-like building constructed with local stone, this restaurant serves good-quality food, yet it's pricey considering the small portions. The menu includes Armenian specialities with an added twist; the barbecue *ishkhan* is particularly delicious. The patio outside has fabulous views over the lake.

Getting There & Away

Transport options all run through Sevan. The only way to get to the eastern side is with your own vehicle or to pay for a private taxi. If hitchhiking or taking a taxi one way, be warned that the eastern side sees little traffic and you may have to wait a while. Note that if you're driving, the Sevan highway speed limit is 90km/h rather than the usual 70km/h.

Sevan

☎261 / POP 19,000

This bustling town is 6km inland from the lake's western shore and is the administrative centre for the region. It was founded in 1842 as the Russian village of Elenovka, named after the wife of Czar Nicholas I, but there are few reminders of the past. There is almost nothing to see or do in the city itself, and Sevan is not worth visiting except as a transport hub for the beaches, resorts and monasteries surrounding the lake. Taxis to Yerevan, the peninsula and lakeshore hotels leave from the main street, which also has shops, ATMs and a *shuka*.

There are some hotels in the city as well as resorts along the water. This side of the lake is most commonly visited by Russian tourists. There are only a couple restaurants in town as well as a popular teahouse.

ⓘ Information

Tourist Information Centre (☑ 099-199555, 077-023385; davidtorosyan09@yahoo.fr; 164 Nairyan St; ☺9am-6pm) The info centre is found inside the Qaghaqapetaran (city municipality building). Staff speak English, French, Armenian and Russian, and provide maps and information about the area. There are no signs in the building or out front, so just keep asking until you find the room.

ⓘ Getting There & Away

Yerevan is only 67km away by freeway. *Marshrutky* (AMD600, one hour) depart from Yerevan's Hyusisayin Avtokayan bus station (p166) when full between 8am and 6pm. *Marshrutky* pick up passengers going to Yerevan at the **bus stop** (cnr Nairyan & Sayat-Nova Sts) in Sevan. There are no *marshrutky* that go to Dilijan.

From the **taxi stand** (cnr Nairyan & Sargis Sevanetsi Sts) taxis can be hired for AMD100 per kilometre and cost between AMD7000 and AMD9000 depending on where you're going in Yerevan. For Dilijan, taxis cost about AMD5000 and AMD4000 to Tsaghkadzor. A taxi to one of the hotels on or near the peninsula is usually AMD1000, but if you want to get to Tufenkian Avan Marak Tsapatagh Hotel on the eastern side it may cost up to AMD18,000. A four- or five-hour tour of Sevanavank, Hayravank and the *khachkars* of Noratus should cost around AMD7000 plus AMD1000 per hour of waiting time.

A train leaves Yerevan's Almast train station (p166) at 8.30am daily between 15 June and 1 October travelling to Shorzha on Fridays, Saturdays and Sundays (AMD600 to AMD1000, two hours).

SOUTHERN ARMENIA

Armenia's southern regions stretch from Karabakh to the east and the Azerbaijani enclave of Naxçivan to the west. **Vayots Dzor** (Gorge of Woes) centres on the headwaters of the wine-growing Arpa valley. The name comes from a histo-

ry of ruinous earthquakes across these mountainous valleys and cliffs. It's a great area to winery hop or explore off-the-beaten-track trails by foot, horse or 4WD – just keep an eye out for snakes.

The province of **Syunik**, in the extreme south of the country, is accessed via the high-altitude **Voratan Pass**. The landscape here is surrounded by epic mountain ranges, high pastures that are home to grazing animals, drifts of wildflowers and clusters of beehives. Its main settlement, Goris, is populated with charming 19th-century buildings and is next to a mysterious ghost town of abandoned caves carved out of volcanic rock. Travellers must cut through Syunik when visiting Karabakh or Iran.

Areni

☑ 281 / POP 1800

Grapes for wine have been grown in this region for oh, not too long, just 6100 years, according to the 2007 discovery of the world's oldest-known winery at Areni-1 Cave (p200). Unlike other regions, the grapes here manage to handle Armenia's climatic extremes and locals have seized the opportunity to grow them. During the Soviet era, winemaking was done strictly in private, but traditions have been passed down and excellent wineries have popped up all over, especially along the Areni–Yeghegnadzor highway. The best include Old Bridge (p203), Momik Wine Cube, Zorah and Trinity Canyon Vineyards. Tack on some charming B&Bs and it's easy to foresee the Areni area becoming Armenia's Napa Valley.

When you drive into the village you'll see roadside stalls selling large bottles that look like they're filled with cola. These are in fact filled with red wine, camouflaged so that Iranian truck drivers can smuggle the bottles over the border.

🛏 Sleeping & Eating

The few B&Bs and restaurants in this area seem to think travellers want set menus, so that's much of what you'll get. There are a couple of restaurants at the entrance to Noravank and one at the monastery itself. Summer fruits (especially apricots) are sold from food stalls along the highway.

Areni Wine Art   B&B **$**

(☑ 094-536329; areniwineart@yahoo.com; 2nd St; s/d AMD14,000/22,000; ❄🛜) Just off Areni's main road (house 20), this family-run B&B

ARMENIA ARENI

WORLD'S OLDEST SHOE & WINERY

In 2008 an archaeologist exploring a cave in Vayots Dzor found an ancient leather shoe buried under a pile of sheep dung. She estimated that the shoe was around 700 years old and dated from the Mongol period. But once the shoe reached the laboratory a new story began to unfold. Testing dated the shoe to around 3500 BC, thus making it the world's oldest leather shoe (300 years older than a shoe found on a frozen mummy in the Alps in 1991).

The shoe is about a women's size 37 (EU), designed for the right foot and is made from leather sewn together like a moccasin. It was found stuffed with grass as if its owner wanted to maintain the shape of the shoe. (The whereabouts of the left shoe are unknown.) The shoe is now on display at the History Museum of Armenia (p148).

The cave where the shoe was found is known as **Areni-1** (Noravank Monastery Rd; AMD1000; ⊙10am-7pm) and is located not on some distant mountaintop, but rather just behind the Edem restaurant, where the main southern highway intersects with the road to Noravank. The same cave was also where archaeologists found the world's oldest known winemaking facility, which can be visited for AMD1000.

Areni-1 is just one of thousands of caves around Areni and Arpi, some of which contain a kilometre or more of chambers. About 1km up the canyon from Areni-1 is **Magili Karandzav**, one of the deepest caves in the area and significant as the home of a large colony of fruit bats; Neolithic-era stone tools have also been found here.

Some caves are filled with a wonderful collection of stalactites and stalagmites, including the **Arjeri**, **Mozrovi** and **Jerovank** caverns. These caves are not for the inexperienced, so it's best to visit on a guided tour (the caves are also locked to casual visitors).

has clean no-frills rooms built by the owner and a cute outdoor dining area. Dinner (AMD4000) includes a choice of *khoravats* with *matsoon*, two salads, hot *aveluk* (sorrel), lavash and tea or coffee. A not-so-great homemade red wine is available, as is homemade vodka. Breakfast is typical for Armenia.

Drinking & Nightlife

The Areni area has several terrific wineries that offer tastings. Trinity Canyon has some of Armenia's best wines, but be aware that staff don't speak English and the snacks it serves – refrigerated lavash and salty cheese – are underwhelming.

Hin Areni Wine Factory　　　　　WINERY
(☑041-234111; www.hinareniwine.am; Yerevan Hwy; tour & tasting AMD1000; ⊙9am-8pm) Prominently located on the main highway, Hin Areni is a professional outfit that produces a quaffable red using Areni grapes and a dry white using *voskehat* (golden seed) grapes; both varieties are grown in nearby vineyards. The factory can be visited on a short tour that is best taken in late September and early October during the grape harvest. The tasting includes three different wines and vintages. Set-menu meals are available (AMD3000 to AMD5000).

Getting There & Away

Marshrutky leave Yerevan from the Gortsaranayin subway stop between 8am and 6pm (AMD2000, one hour and 40 minutes), and continue on to Yeghegnadzor. Ask to get off at the crossroads just past the Hin Areni Winery. You can catch *marshrutky* going the other direction at the same crossroads, but times are erratic. Ask Areni Wine Art to call the Yeghegnadzor bus station to find out about times and seat availability.

Taxis cost AMD15,000 to or from Yerevan and AMD3500 to Yeghegnadzor.

Yeghegnadzor

☑281 / POP 7500

An overgrown country town built on twisting lanes that wind into the hills, Yeghegnadzor (yeh-*heg*-nadzor) is the peaceful administrative centre of Vayots Dzor *marz* (province). The town is mainly a Soviet-era confection of wide civic spaces and tuff apartment blocks, with few local industries or businesses; most locals rely on remittances or agriculture for their income. But in recent years, Yeghegnadzor has blossomed with an abundance of excellent B&Bs and guesthouses making it an ideal base from which to explore the region – you could easily spend a couple of days here while visiting Noravank and the Yeghegis Valley.

◉ Sights

There is a good walk from town down to the river and a 13th-century stone bridge, which was used during the Silk Road and designed by the same architect that built Noravank. To get there, walk down the highway, turn right and walk for 400m, then turn left down a dirt track (just before the 256 Km post) and follow it for 1.3km to the bridge.

Yeghegnadzor Regional Museum of Vayots Dzor   MUSEUM

(☑ 0281-23392; 4 Shahumian St; adult/child AMD700/100; ⊘ 9am-5pm Mon-Fri, 1-4pm Sat) This freshly renovated museum with its horseshoe-shaped entrance holds an intriguing collection of archaeological and ethnographic artefacts encased in professional-looking glass casings. The most notable item is the 14th-century *khachkar* near the entrance featuring intricate carving.

Tanahati Monastery   MONASTERY

The impressive main church at this monastery was dedicated to St Stepanos (Stephen) and was built in the 13th century on the site of a ruined 8th-century monastery. There are significant stone reliefs of animals on the exterior of the church, including the crest of the powerful Orbelian family (a bull and a lion) on the tambour and one of the Proshian family (an eagle holding a lamb in its talons) above the door.

To get here take the road to the right at the T-junction past the Museum of Gladzor University (☑ 0281-23705; Vernashen; AMD1000; ⊘ 9am-5pm Tue-Sun). It's 5km to Tanahati Monastery.

🛏 Sleeping

It's too bad Yeghegnadzor can't share its wonderful family-run B&Bs, guesthouses and campground with the rest of the country as there are an unfair amount here.

Crossway Camping   CAMPGROUND $

(☑ 094-789391; www.armcamping.am; Yerevan Hwy; sites AMD3000, sleeping platform AMD3700, bus AMD5000, d AMD6500; P 🛜 🌊) This family-owned campground near the entrance to town is set against a dramatic backdrop of pink mountains and is surrounded by farmland. There are two private rooms, sleeping platforms (mattresses and sleeping bags provided), campsites (BYO tent) and a Soviet bus with psychedelic decor. Facilities

ARMENIA YEGHEGNADZOR

DON'T MISS

SUNSET-KISSED NORAVANK

Founded by Bishop Hovhannes in 1205 and sensitively renovated in the 1990s, **Noravank** (New Monastery; Noravank Monastery Rd; parking AMD200; ⊘ 7am-9pm) is one of the most spectacular sites in Armenia and should be included on every visitor's itinerary. Around sunset, the reddish hues of the dramatic cliffs surrounding the monastery are accentuated by the setting sun, and the reddish-gold stone of its churches acquire a luminous sheen – it's a totally magnificent sight.

The complex includes the 13th-century **Surp Karapet Church**, built next to the ruins of an earlier church also dedicated to St John the Baptist. Attached to this is a small 13th-century chapel dedicated to **Surp Gregor**; it's home to a carved lion-human tombstone dated to 1300.

The main, much-photographed, structure is the 14th-century **Surp Astvatsatsin Church** (1339), built on top of the mausoleum of Burtel Orbelian, who is buried here with his family. Historians say the church is reminiscent of tower-like burial structures created in the early years of Christianity. There's a wonderful carving of Christ flanked by Sts Peter and Paul above the door.

An unimpressive **museum** (AMD500; ⊘ 9am-9pm) featuring prints, as well as some old coins and books, is found to the right of the entrance.

There are picnic spots and springs around Noravank, as well as an excellent on-site **restaurant** (set menu AMD3500-4500; ⊘ 7.30am-8pm). The valley really warms up in the middle of a summer's day, so come early, or late in the afternoon.

Noravank features on many travel-agency tours from Yerevan, which is about 90 minutes away by road – many combine a visit with a stop at Khor Virap (p167) and a winery. *Marshrutky* from Yerevan or Yeghegnadzor can drop you at the turn-off on the highway near the Edem restaurant. From here, it's 7.5km to Noravank. Hitching is a fairly easy process, especially on weekends.

include a communal kitchen, dining pavilion, washing machine (per load AMD500) and swimming pool.

Gohar's Guest House
B&B $

(☑ 094-332993; sargisyan@hotmail.com; 44 Spandaryan St; s AMD10,000-12,000, d AMD18,000-20,000, f AMD25,000; @ 🛜 🛎) This friendly B&B is owned by Gohar Gevorgyan, who keeps a clean and tidy house and uses organic home-grown produce to cook delicious meals (dinner AMD5000). Rooms are spread into two buildings. There's a communal kitchen, washing machine, vine-covered terrace and small swimming pool. Gohar speaks Armenian and Russian and her daughter and granddaughter speak English and French.

★ Green Stone B&B
B&B $$

(☑ 094-555222; www.greenstone.am; 5 Gladzoryan St, 2nd lane; s/d AMD20,000/30,000; 🛜 🛎) ⌀ Mornings at this spectacular B&B go something like this: arise to roosters cooing and step onto the balcony overlooking the garden. Take a shower using organic soaps and float down to the pool in a bathrobe for a dip before tucking into a sumptuous breakfast – homemade jams, organic produce, eggs, it's all there. Dinner (with wine AMD7500) is similarly outstanding. Green Stone is one of the few accommodations that not only uses solar power for water and electricity but also recycles and composts.

🍴 Eating

Along the highway, there are several riverside restaurants that set a good Armenian table including kebabs, *khoravats* and salads. Most also serve a regional speciality of 'buried' cheese made from goat's milk and herbs and aged in clay pots. Look out for street stands selling watermelon and other fruits, honey, nuts and homemade wines and conserves between Areni and Yeghegnadzor.

Vayots Dzor & Syunik

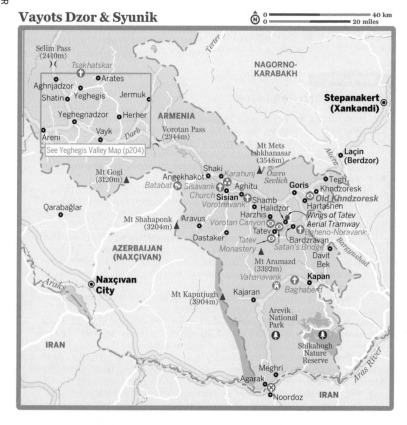

SPITAKAVOR

Only accessible by foot or 4WD, 14th-century Spitakavor Monastery was built on the site of a 5th-century basilica and has a church, *gavit* (antechamber) and bell tower. The exterior of the church features some unusual carving. The 20th-century Armenian military commander Garegin Nzhdeh is buried in the graveyard. Nzhdeh fought in the Balkan Wars against the Ottoman Empire and commanded a force of Armenian volunteer fighters in WWI. In 1921 he was prime minister of the short-lived Republic of Mountainous Armenia.

To get here, head past the Museum of Gladzor University (p201) to a T-junction. The road to the left leads to the monastery; it's about 8.4km along a winding dirt track for vehicles or 6km along a more direct walking path. Walk past the museum and through the village, cross the stream and carry on straight up the western bank of the gorge, keeping the stream and small dam on your right (ignore the vehicle road, which switches back). Continue up the track, veer left into grazing pasture and then head right. You'll then see the monastery above you.

Drinking & Nightlife

This is wine country and so enjoying a glass of red with Areni noir grapes is a must.

★**Old Bridge Winery**   WINERY
(☏093-800240; www.oldbridgewinery.com; 1 Yerevanyan Ave; tasting AMD4000; ⊙noon-3pm & 4-7pm; ☎) Named after the nearby 13th-century Silk Road bridge, this terrific winery offers the region's best wine-tasting experience. Reds (the speciality) derive from the dark-skinned Areni noir grape and are aged in oak barrels. Tastings are done in a gorgeous room facing snow-capped mountains and come with three wines as well as a generous platter of cheeses, olives and walnuts.

Getting There & Away

Marshrutky depart from the stand next to the Gortsaranayin metro in Yerevan between 8am and 6pm. From Yeghegnadzor *marshrutky* (AMD1200, two hours) leave when full for Yerevan from the bus station (p200) at the crossroad on the main highway and can stop at Areni along the way.

Hourly *marshrutky* to Vayk (AMD200) and one 2pm bus to Jermuk (AMD700) also depart from the crossroad.

Marshrutky and taxis from local village destinations arrive at the bus and taxi stop at the top end of Narekatsky St in the morning, carrying people from the region who work in town. They return to their destinations in the late afternoon. Taxis cost AMD3000 to Noravank, AMD7000 to Yeghegis, AMD12,000 to Jermuk and AMD20,000 to Tatev or Goris.

Yeghegis Valley

The beautiful Yeghegis Valley is surrounded by towering peaks and is home to many picturesque villages with medieval churches. It and the surrounding valleys are well worth exploring for a day or two, but you'll need a car and/or solid hiking boots. Beware of venomous snakes frequently encountered in this region.

Sights

Tsakhatskar Monastery & Smbataberd

About 1km from the village of Artabuynk a sign points to the left for the 10th-century Tsakhatskar Monastery, a crumbling agglomeration of churches and old *khachkars* only reachable via 4WD or on foot (keep an eye out for snakes). From the stream, continue up the main track to the right (the side of the valley with the power poles); the monastery eventually comes into view on the left. Walking from the stream to the monastery should take about an hour and a half.

From the monastery, head back down the way you came and at the fork in the path head left up the slope to Smbataberd. The stretch up to the fort takes about 30 minutes and is also best accessed with 4WD. Hiking from Tsakhatskar to Smbataberd should take about 45 minutes and then 30 minutes to get back to the stream. On the other side of Smbataberd there's a beautiful view looking down on the valley.

ARMENIA YEGHEGIS VALLEY

Yeghegis Valley

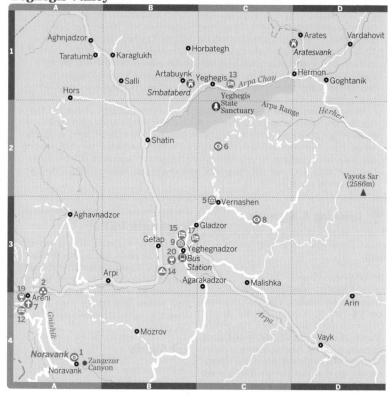

ARMENIA YEGHEGIS VALLEY

⊙ Yeghegis Village

Yeghegis (yer-ghiz) village is reached by taking the right fork after Shatin. It has three overgrown churches in the village on the left-hand side of the main road: the 18th-century **St Astvatsatsin** with its grass-covered roof; the 13th-century **Surp Karapet Church**; and the very unusual 14th-century **Surp Zorats**, where worshippers gathered before an outdoor altar. It's believed this courtyard was created so that horses and soldiers could be blessed before going off to battle. Surp Karapet and Surp Zorats are difficult to find: start at St Astvatsatsin and walk uphill, then turn right, veer left and then turn right again when you see some *khachkars*. Surp Karapet is down another road to the right; Surp Zorats is straight ahead, around a corner (left) and then in a field on the right.

Along the main road on the northeastern edge of the village, look for a blue sign saying 'Arates 9.7km'. Park here and walk down a switchback dirt road to find a rickety metal footbridge crossing the river. Cross the bridge (if you dare) to find an 800-year-old **Jewish cemetery** – Hebrew inscriptions are clearly visible on some of the grave markers. The engravings are biblical verses and the names of the deceased. Prior to the discovery of the cemetery there had been no evidence of Jews inhabiting Armenia. The cemetery was in use for about 80 years – the oldest tombstone is dated 1266 and the newest is dated 1346. Researchers theorise that this community of Jews arrived from Persia, having travelled up the Silk Road. The reason for their disappearance remains a mystery.

🛏 Sleeping

Arevi   HOTEL $

(☎ 093-306556; www.arevi.am; Yeghegis; s/d AMD22,000/25,000; ☜☏) 🍴 Set beneath a dramatic cliff face, Arevi is made entirely

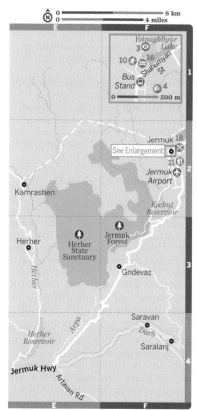

Yeghegis Valley

◎ Top Sights
1 Noravank A4

◎ Sights
2 Areni-1 Cave A3
3 Gallery of Waters F1
4 Mermaid's Hair F1
5 Museum of Gladzor University C3
6 Spitakavor Monastery C2
7 Surp Astvatsatsin Church A4
8 Tanahat (Tanahat Monastery) C3
9 Yeghegnadzor Regional
    Museum of Vayots Dzor B3

◎ Activities, Courses & Tours
10 Armenia Wellness & Spa
    Hotel, Jermuk F1
11 Jermuk Ski Resort F2

◎ Sleeping
12 Areni Wine Art A4
13 Arevi C1
14 Crossway Camping B3
15 Gohar's Guest House B3
16 Grand Resort Jermuk F1
17 Green Stone B&B B3

◎ Eating
18 Gndevank Restaurant F2

◎ Drinking & Nightlife
19 Hin Areni Wine Factory A4
20 Old Bridge Winery B3

of recycled shipping containers and is solar-powered. Rooms are modern with bright colours and sharp angles. The owner is also a trekking guide who leads trips around Armenia including up the snow-capped peaks of Mt Aragats (p175) and Mt Ararat (in Turkey). Breakfast is included and hearty dinners are available (AMD5000).

❶ Getting There & Away

To reach the area, turn north off the Yerevan–Goris Hwy at Getap and after 12km turn right (east) towards Shatin village. The sights are well signposted off the road. About 2km up from Shatin village, a road branches up the valley to the west towards Artabuynk.

Public transport to the area is limited. *Marshrutky* and taxis travel from the villages to Yeghegnadzor in the morning and return in the late afternoon. Taxis from Yeghegnadzor cost AMD7000 or the standard AMD100 per kilometre; you'll need to negotiate waiting times with the driver.

Jermuk

📞 287 / POP 4200

Since Soviet times, the upmarket spa town of Jermuk has been a popular vacation spot due to its precious mineral water treatment sanitoriums. In the old days, people would sign up for 18-day courses with medically supervised immersions in Jermuk's waters. The town is also attractive for its blissfully cool summer temperatures, its modest ski slope and its breathtaking verdant landscape, visible on the drive into town.

Outside of high season in July and August, the town morphs into a ghost town and is eerily quiet at night.

◎ Sights

Gallery of Waters SPRING

FREE This collonaded structure built in 1956 contains five flowing stone urns fed with mineral water by pipes set in the wall. Temperatures of the water range

THE SELIM PASS

Linking the provinces of Gegharkunik and Vayots Dzor, this road over the Vardenis mountain range is one of the most spectacular driving routes in the country. Climbing to an elevation of 2410m, it is covered with heavy snow in winter.

Just below the highest point of the pass on the Vayots Dzor side is the **Selim Caravanserai**, built in 1332 by order of Prince Chesar Orbelian to offer shelter to caravans following the ancient Dvin–Partav trading route. A sturdy basalt building on a windswept plateau, it comprises a three-nave hall, vestibule, domed chapel and small rooms where travellers once slept. The facade features two bas-relief statues with Orbelian dynasty insignia. Destroyed sometime between the 15th and 16th centuries, it was reconstructed in the 1950s and is open to the elements. Picnic tables outside command wonderful views over the Yeghegis Valley.

No public transport travels this road. A taxi between Yeghegnadzor and Martuni on the edge of Lake Sevan will cost around AMD20,000.

from 30°C to 53°C, each said to hold different healing properties, including treating stomach and liver problems, heart disease and cancer.

Mermaid's Hair WATERFALL
(parking AMD200) According to local legend, the beautiful daughter of an Armenian nobleman was highly sought after, but she only had eyes for the handsome shepherd's son. Every day she'd throw a rope into the gorge so he could climb up to her castle. When the nobleman saw this, he cursed her, saying she'd become a mermaid if she met the shepherd's son. Of course they met, and the curse came true – she became a mermaid and her hair is this waterfall.

Take the road opposite the town at the **statue** of Armenian diplomat Israel Ori (1659–1711) and turn down the windy road past a Symphony of Stones–like **rock formation**. You'll quickly reach the parking lot.

 Activities

The spa business gets most of its customers in the July and August holidays.

It's possible to take a 4WD from beside Armenia Wellness & Spa to a **natural geyser**. The return trip costs AMD15,000 and takes about two hours.

**Armenia Wellness
& Spa Hotel, Jermuk** SPA
(☏ 093-155555; www.jermukarmenia.com; 2 Miasnikyan St; s/d AMD35,000/60,000, ste AMD80,000-110,000; ⊙ 9am-5pm, spa Mon-Sat) This Soviet-era institution has hot baths,

mud treatments, sauna, hydrotherapy rooms and various other rooms for a long list of treatments ranging from oxygen cocktails to prostate massages and gynaecological cleansings. Yep, you read that right. Treatments cost AMD500 to AMD10,000 and massages go for AMD7000. The attached hotel is full board.

Jermuk Ski Resort SNOW SPORTS
(ski lift return AMD1500; ⊙ 10am-7pm) Jermuk's ski slopes are small (there's just one 2.6km run) but the facilities are modern and the equipment is in good condition. The chairlift runs year-round, offering beautiful panoramic views from the top. There's a cafe at the summit and a steakhouse at the base. Ski and snowboard rentals cost AMD6000 and are available from November to March.

🛏 Sleeping & Eating

There are lots of informal guesthouses and spas open in July and August, but options thin out the rest of the year. In July and August prices can double based on demand.

There aren't many decent options outside of the hotels and resorts.

Grand Resort Jermuk HOTEL $$
(☏ 060-740000; www.grandresortjermuk.com; 7 Shahumyan St; s/d with breakfast AMD54,000/59,000, full board AMD61,000/71,000; P ⊛ ❋ @ 🛜 🖭 🐾) This pink monolith on the lake opposite the Gallery of Waters is the most luxurious hotel in Southern Armenia. It was once a Hyatt, but now is independently owned. Facilities include a large indoor pool, sauna, gym, billiards table, medical

centre and spa (massages AMD15,000 to AMD30,000). There's also a restaurant with international food (mains from AMD1600).

Gndevank Restaurant   ARMENIAN $$

(☑ 0287-21690; 24 Shahumyan St; mains AMD1000-3500; ☺ 9am-11pm; ☎) This octagonal *khoravats* restaurant with medieval chairs and a chandelier is one of the most popular eateries in town, though the service can be lacklustre and the food is nothing special. Coming across the main bridge, turn right (away from the town centre); it's about 400m straight ahead in a wood-fronted building.

ⓘ Getting There & Away

Jermuk is 177km from Yerevan, about two hours by the main highway and then 26km off the main highway on a spur road. Enter via a bridge spanning a deep gorge high above the Arpa River; turn left at the end of the bridge, and then right at the small lake to reach the Grand Resort Jermuk, Gallery of Waters and Armenia Wellness & Spa Hotel.

In the high season, *marshrutky* (AMD2000, 2½ hours) depart from Yerevan's Kilikya Avtokayan (p165) at 1pm and 4pm. Services leave Jermuk for Yerevan at 8am and 11am. There's also one bus per day to Yeghegnadzor (AMD700, one hour) and to Vayk (AMD700). The bus stand is next to the bank near the Grand Resort Jermuk. Private taxis bound for Yerevan cost AMD25,000.

Sisian

☑ 283 / POP 14,800

Sisian sits on a high plateau where it snows as late as March or April. The autumn ends early here too. It has a core of decrepit early-20th-century buildings and is divided into two districts by the wide Vorotan River. The town's buildings are falling apart, unemployment is high and the river is often full of rubbish – a sad fate for a place that was prosperous and proud in the Soviet era.

The region was inhabited long before the town was built, evidenced by nearby Neolithic observatories and animal petroglyphs. These days, the only compelling reason to visit is to see the petroglyphs at Karahunj (aka Zorats Karer) and Ughtasar (Pilgrimage Mountain). Stays should aim to be as short as possible as the tourist infrastructure in Sisian is underdeveloped.

◉ Sights

Sisavank Church   CHURCH

Originally built in the 7th century, Sisavank Church was restored as recently as the 20th century. It combines an elegant square-cross floor with some striking sculptures of royal and ecclesiastical patrons inside and out. The pretty cemetery next to the church is worth meandering through.

Sisian History Museum   MUSEUM

(☑ 0283-23331; www.sisianmuseum.am; 1 Adonts St; AMD500, tours AMD2000; ☺ 11am-6pm Tue-Sun) Townsfolk are very proud of their museum, which showcases a modest array of carpets, archaeological artefacts and ethnographic displays. .

The **sculpture park** in front of the museum displays *khachkars* as well as some stones in the shape of rams. There are also a couple of stones bearing petroglyphs which were taken from Ughtasar.

⌷ Sleeping & Eating

Accommodation options in Sisian are generally lacklustre. It's ideal to stay elsewhere if possible. There are no restaurants worth recommending.

Hotel Dina   HOTEL $

(☑ 093-334392; www.dinahotel.am; 35 Sisakan St; s/d AMD8000/14,000, without bathroom or breakfast AMD3000; ☑ ☎) Its handsome exterior and pretty front garden raise hopes that are dashed when the dowdy brown rooms at this centrally located hotel are inspected. They're reasonably clean, but not particularly comfortable. That said, it's generally acknowledged to be the best sleeping option in town. The managers speak some English and can help with tours and onward transport.

ⓘ Getting There & Away

The taxi and *marshrutka* stand is on Israeliyan St, near the bridge. There is one daily *marshrutka* from Yerevan's Kilikya Avtokayan (AMD3000, four hours) at 9am; you'll need to check with the driver about its departure time from Sisian.

Semi-regular *marshrutky* travel to and from Goris (AMD1000, 30 minutes). *Marshrutky* travel to Stepanakert (AMD3000, three hours) via Goris and Shushi at 10.30am on Monday, Wednesday and Friday.

SIGHTS AROUND SISIAN

Two hundred and twenty upright basalt stones up to 3m high set along sweeping lines and loops, some punctured with sight holes aligned with stars, make up the ancient site often referred to as Armenia's Stonehenge, **Karahunj** (also called Carahunge or Zorats Karer). The site, situated on a rise above the river plains ringed by mountains, is dotted with tombs dated to before 2000 BC. The astronomical design of Karahunj is most evident at the solstices and equinoxes. Lines of stones define an egg-shaped area with a burial tumulus in the centre, with a northern arm stretching 170m and a southern alley 160m long. About 70 stones are pierced with finger-sized holes. The builders had a deep knowledge of astronomy, including the zodiac and the lunar phases, combined perhaps with worship for stars such as Sirius.

The site won't blow you away (there are no balancing stones like you'd see at Stonehenge) but the pleasant 45-minute walk here from town and excellent panoramas make it a worthwhile trip. Karahunj is 6km north of Sisian, signposted on the left about 700m before the main highway. The stones are in the fields about 400m from the turn-off.

The **Shaki Waterfall** lies about 4km from Sisian near the village of the same name. About 18m high, it gushes down a line of trees and a wide expanse of stones above the Shaki River. Locals picnic along the 10-minute walk from the parking lot. The water is used for Shaki's hydroelectric power station, so the waterfall is only 'on' from 11am to 6pm.

About 6km down the Vorotan River from Sisian in **Aghitu** (Aghudi) village is a distinctive 7th-century **tower-tomb**. There are dragon stones nearby from the 2nd to 3rd century BC. The road continues as the canyon deepens past Vaghatin to **Vorotnavank**, 12km from Sisian on the south side of the Vorotan. The first church in the Vorotnavank fortress complex was built by Queen Shahandukht in 1000. In 1007, her son Sevada built a second church.

The petroglyphs of **Ughtasar** (Pilgrimage Mountain) in the mountains north of Sisian are even older than Karahunj. They lie at an altitude of 3300m around a lake on Mt Tsghuk, accessible between June and September – and even then only if it's not a cold summer. Carvings of leaping, dancing animals and hunters adorn rocks and boulders everywhere around the small lake. It's a haunting place surrounded by isolated peaks, and you can only wonder why ancient people would hike to such an inhospitable place to leave their mark on stone. The tracks are steep, rocky and hopeless without a jeep and a guide. A guide for up to four can be hired for AMD30,000 per person. Enquire at Hotel Dina (p207) in Sisian about this.

The ruins of **Tanahat Vank** (not to be confused with the better-known monastery near Yeghegnadzor; p201) are 17km southwest of Sisian past the Tolors Reservoir. A university was established here in 1280. Called Karmir (Red) Vank by locals, Tanahat Monastery is on a high promontory by a gorge. The monks here were so pious and ascetic they refused soup, cheese and oil, eating only vegetables, hence the name Tanahat, meaning 'deprived of soup'.

Local tours can be negotiated directly with the taxi drivers or through Hotel Dina.

Goris

📱 284 / POP 20,300

The endlessly winding roads that leap through the gorges over the mountains of Syunik come to a major junction at Goris, making this an inevitable stop between Yerevan and Stepanakert or the Iranian border. The town's tree-lined avenues and grand 19th-century stone houses are a precious rarity in a country largely swept of its past by mundane Soviet-era structures. The town is run-down in parts, especially at its decrepit central **Parc de Vienne**, but Goris is an underrated base to spend a couple of days enjoying quality guesthouses and exploring the volcanic pinnacle clusters in the area. Don't miss the abandoned cave city at Old Khndzoresk, 10km east of town.

Great times to visit are in June for the town's sheep-shearing festival or for in July for the *oghee* festival.

Sights

★ Old Khndzoresk
CAVE

Dug into volcanic sandstone on the slopes of Khor Dzor (Deep Gorge), the village of Old Khndzoresk was inhabited as far back as the 13th century. By the late 19th century, the town was the largest in eastern Armenia, but after being devastated by the 1931 earthquake it was abandoned (save for a brief stint during the Karabakh War when caves were used as shelter). Now Old Khndzoresk stands a ghost town of caves and 17th-century churches worth spending several hours exploring.

Take the highway from Goris about 6km and make a right on a dirt road located about 3km before the town of Khndzoresk. The bumpy road will take you to a viewpoint and a cafe (open May to October) as well as a squeaky 160m suspension bridge over the gorge. Alternatively, drive to the end of Khndzoresk and follow the paved road to the right down the hill.

Medieval Goris Cave Dwellings
CAVE

Locals say the cave shelters of Old Goris carved into the hillside on the east side of town were built and inhabited in the 5th century. Several trails lead up over a saddle where there are epic views over Goris and volcanic pinnacle clusters similar to the 'fairy chimneys' seen in Turkey. It's worth exploring the cave rooms, many of which are linked together and feature arched 'shelve' walls. Nowadays, some caves are used to house cattle or as churches.

HIKEArmenia (p165) has a 1½-hour marked hike on its app that goes up the mountain and leaves the cemetery. The hike is rather easy, but trails can be slippery at parts – wear good shoes and watch your step.

Museum of Axel Bakounts
MUSEUM

(☑ 0284-22966; 41 Mesrop Mashtots St; AMD500; ☺ 10am-5pm Tue-Sun) This pretty villa with its stone walls, timber veranda and lovely courtyard garden was the home of writer Axel Bakounts (or Bakunts), who died in Stalin's 1937 purges. It features his personal effects and furnishings from the late 19th and early 20th centuries. The surrounding neighbourhood sports plenty of 19th-century houses.

Sleeping

Hotel Zanger
HOTEL $

(☑ 098-778977; zangerhotel@yahoo.com; 13 Bakunci St; s/d AMD12,000/18,000, without bathroom AMD10,000/14,000; P ☎) The bright-pink exterior is slightly off-putting and extremely unsympathetic to its historic surrounds, but this budget hotel on a quiet street offers well-priced, clean and comfortable rooms with satellite TV, so is worthy of recommendation. Service is friendly and there's a rear courtyard where breakfast can be enjoyed during summer.

Hostel Lovely Goris
HOSTEL $

(☑ 093-287902; jirmar28@yandex.ru; 55 Khorenatsi St; dm AMD3500, d with/without bathroom AMD10,000/8000; ☎) Operated by local artist Jirayr Martirosyan and his family, this shabby yet friendly hostel has long been the number-one backpacker pick in Goris, though it's in dire need of renovation. Three double rooms share a grubby bathroom on the 1st floor and there are two basic dorms downstairs. Dusty outdoor lounge areas feature a couple of hammocks. Dinner costs AMD4000.

Mirhav Hotel
HOTEL $$

(☑ 0284-24612; hotelmirav@yahoo.com; 100 Mesrop Mashtots St; s/d/tr AMD25,000/30,000/36,000; P ☎) It claims boutique hotel status, but the regular presence of tour groups and large extended families means that the label isn't deserved. That said, this is the best sleeping option in Goris, offering attractively decorated common areas, a range of room types in two buildings, a pretty rear garden and a top-notch restaurant.

Eating

Tur Baza Cafe
CAFE $

(☑ 0284-30078; 1 Tatevatci; mains from AMD600; ☺ 9am-midnight) With a charming flower-filled terrace, tables overlooking the river, cold beer on tap and a large menu of cheap Armenian eats, this cafe is the most happening place in Goris. Staff speak little English, but they're friendly and the terrace is warmly lit at night. Overall, it's a pleasant place to relax after a full day of cave exploring.

Mirhav Restaurant
ARMENIAN $$

(☑ 0284-24612; Mirhav Hotel, 100 Mesrop Mashtots St; mains AMD3200) The menu at the restaurant in the Mirhav Hotel is more interesting than the average Armenian eatery, featuring stews, pilafs and tasty salads. Service tends to be slow and food can take a while to arrive. Tables are in a pleasant indoor dining space or rear garden.

Goris

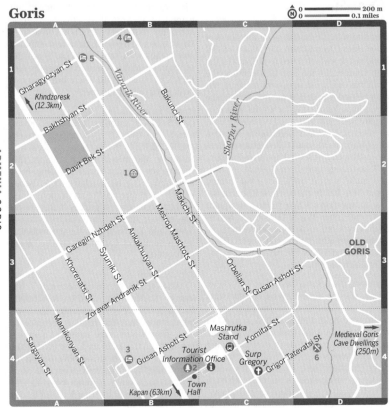

Goris

◎ Sights
1 Museum of Axel Bakounts	B2
2 Parc de Vienne	B4

🛏 Sleeping
3 Hostel Lovely Goris	B4
4 Hotel Zanger	B1
5 Mirhav Hotel	A1

🍴 Eating
Mirhav Restaurant	(see 5)
6 Tur Baza Cafe	D4

🍷 Drinking & Nightlife

Locals are skilled at making fruit *oghee*, including the deliciously potent mulberry and Cornelian cherry *(hone)* vodka. You should be able to source some at the *shuka* on Syuniki St.

ℹ Information

Tourist Information Office (☎ 093-189923; goristourism@gmail.com; 7 Komitas St; ☺ 9.30am-5.30pm Mon-Fri, 10am-5pm Sat & Sun) This helpful tourist office facing Parc de Vienne can offer assistance in English, French, Russian and Armenian.

ℹ Getting There & Away

There are two *marshrutka* per day between Yerevan and Goris (AMD2500, six hours), which leave Yerevan's Sasuntsi Davit metro station at 9am and 4pm. *Marshrutky* return from the **stand** (26 Komitas St) on Komitas St shortly after they arrive. Shared taxis cost AMD4500 per person from Yerevan and take 4½ hours. Drivers pick up around the city, so you'll need to coordinate with one ahead of time – ask at your accommodation.

Marshrutky leave from Goris to Tatev at 8.30am and 3.30pm and return at 7.30am and 2.30pm (AMD700, one hour). A private taxi will cost you AMD8000.

One daily *marshrutka* departs from Goris at 10.30am en route to Stepanakert (AMD2000). It departs from the intersection of the highway and Mesrop Mashtots St (AMD2000). You'll be able to obtain a visa at the Nagorno-Karabakh border or at the embassy (p223) in Yerevan. If you miss this one, you can wait at the same spot for a *marshrutka* to pass through from Yerevan (four or five pass through every afternoon); they'll pick you up if there is space. A *marshrutka* to Kapan costs AMD1500 (1½ hours, 11am).

Tatev

 284 / POP 900

The tiny rural village of Tatev is perched on a plateau overlooking the Vorotan River and has jaw-dropping views over the peaks to Karabakh. In the 13th century, the town was the political centre of the region, controlling 680 villages. These days, it's known for its famous medieval monastery and the Wings of Tatev Aerial Tramway (p212), the longest nonstop reversible cable car in the world.

Sights

Tatev Monastery MONASTERY
(☉10am-7pm) The bishops of Syunik built the main church, **Surp Poghos-Petros** (St Paul and St Peter), in the 9th century to house important relics. There are faint signs of frescoes, intricate carvings and portraits of the main donors on the northern side. On most days, the faithful line up to be blessed. The **Surp Grigor Church**, built in 1295 in the place of a 9th-century building, nestles next to the main church, and there's a minia-turised chapel above the gatehouse.

At the monastery's peak some 600 monks lived and worked in the complex, and na-tional icon Surp Grigor Tatevatsi (St Gregory of Tatev; 1346–1409) is buried here.

In the courtyard, look for the 8m oc-tagonal pillar topped by a *khachkar*. The 9th-century monument is said to have pre-dicted seismic activity (or the roar of hooves by approaching armies) by shifting.

The fortifications, added in the 17th cen-tury, have been restored and are full of din-ing halls, towers and libraries. Outside the main gate there is an **oil press exhibit** with a display of seeds, tools and ancient machin-ery used in the process of oil extraction.

Satan's Bridge BRIDGE
(Halidzor-Tatev Rd) If you're hiking or driving to Tatev rather than taking the aerial tramway, stop off to see Satan's Bridge, located on the

road halfway between the cable car and Ta-tev village. Legend tells that centuries ago, villagers fleeing a rebel army were blocked by the raging river. Before the invaders at-tacked, a bridge was magically created by a huge falling rock and the people were saved.

Activities

The dramatic mountainous landscape is great for short hikes, including to the ham-let of **Svarants** (20 minutes). Another trail heads north to the top of **Petroskhatch mountain** (3½ hours return).

Other popular hikes from Tatev include trekking to the overgrown 17th-century church **Mets Anapad** (2½ hours), **Harjis** (six hours), **Ltsen** (five or six hours), Satan's Bridge (one hour) and **Tanzatap** (one hour).

Enquire about maps, info and guides at the Information Centre. The Wings of Tatev Aerial Tramway ticket office also has guides.

Sleeping

There are at least four B&Bs in tiny Tatev. They are not well signed, but the hamlet is small so just ask around or contact the In-formation Centre to book.

Harsnadzor LODGE $
(☎099-007171; harsnadzor@gmail.com; Halid-zor; s/d without bathroom AMD8000/15,000, s/d AMD20,000/25,000, family cabins AMD35,000-70,000;) Thirteen kilometres from Tatev near the Wings of Tatev Aerial Tram-way is this decidedly popular eco-lodge. Accommodation is in rustic cabins on the edge of the gorge offering epic views. The so-lar-powered showers with transparent roofs are a nice touch. Breakfast is simple and the on-site restaurant specialises in *khoravats*.

Eating

Snacks are available outside the monastery, including *gata* and sweet *sujuk*. The cafe at the Information Centre serves delicious home-cooked food for breakfast, lunch and dinner (mains AMD1300 to AMD5000), and includes vegetarian options.

Information

Tatev Tourism Information Centre & Cafe
(☎093-880230; www.tatevinfo.com; ☉10am-9pm) Just uphill from the monastery is an info centre and cafe run by the exuberant Anna Arshakyan who speaks Armenian, English, Italian and Russian. This is the place to ask about hikes in the area, obtain maps and find out about B&Bs.

SCALING THE SOUTH

Travellers going from Goris to Meghri on the Iranian border will need to steel their stomach against approximately 160km of nonstop hairpin turns as the road climbs and dips through the mountains of southern Syunik. Most people coming this way are overlanders heading to Iran or curious road-trippers wanting to cover every centimetre of Armenian soil, but the drive itself is probably Armenia's best.

The first stretch is a 68km drive from Goris to Kapan. The most interesting sight along this route is Bgheno-Noravank, a monastery that was lost to the world until 1920 when writer Axel Bakounts happened upon it in the forest. The main church dates to 1062 and contains intricately carved biblical reliefs. It's a great camping spot or a logical break for cycle tourists. The turn-off from the highway has a sign directing you towards Bardzravan, a nearby village. After 3.1km on a bumpy road, turn off the road to the right and the church is visible after 150m.

Further down the highway, there is a military base (Karmerkar) and a turn-off for the 3km access road to the village of Davit Bek. The village is another pleasant stopover and sports a couple of old churches. The village borders a pristine river with cascades and swimming holes, but you'll need good shoes to get down to them. From the village there is a pleasant 40-minute walk to a pagan temple.

On the final plunge towards Kapan a bizarre turquoise lake comes into view. This is an artificial lake created by the tailings of a nearby copper mine so while it might look like the Caribbean Sea, swimming is not recommended.

Kapan marks the halfway point to Meghri and is thus a logical place to spend the night. From Kapan there are two roads to Meghri: a 75km road via Kajaran; and a newer, more scenic 94km route through the Shikahogh Nature Reserve. The most attractive part of the reserve is the valley of the Tsav River, where at the hamlet of Nerkin Hand there's an ancient grove of massive plane trees. The oak and hornbeam forests either side of the Tsav comprise the nature reserve, though you'll need a Niva or Villis 4WD to explore the 100 sq km of gorges and forests.

ⓘ Getting There & Away

Wings of Tatev Aerial Tramway (☑ 060-463333; www.tatever.am; Halidzor; one-way/return fixed time AMD5500/7000, return not-fixed AMD9000, child AMD100; ⊙10am-6pm Tue-Sun Oct-Apr, to 7pm May, 9am-8pm Jun, 9am-8pm daily Jul-Sep) The world's longest nonstop reversible cable car floats from Halidzor over the gaping Vorotan River Gorge to the Tatev Monastery. The 5.7km trip (12 minutes each way) soars over breathtaking scenery, but the price seems exorbitant (Armenians pay less, AMD500). The station at the top is sparkling new and features a good restaurant with a great view (mains from AMD1600).

Cars leave every 15 minutes and each car has a capacity of 30 people.

Marshrutky from Goris to Tatev leave at 8.30am and 3.30pm from the bus stop (p210) on Komitas St, and go to Goris from Tatev at 7.30am and 2.30pm (AMD700, one hour). The *marshrutka* in Tatev will drive around to pick people up starting at the scheduled time. Wait at the turn-off to the road leading to Halidzor. A private taxi to Goris will cost AMD8000. Shared taxis from Yerevan to Halidzor leave from various places around the city and should cost

AMD6000. You'll need to prearrange pick-up – ask at your accommodation. Note that there is no taxi stand at Halidzor, so you'll need to hop on the *marshrutka* or get a taxi the rest of the way to Tatev. Ask at the Information Centre if you need help with any of this.

Kapan

☑ 285 / POP 42,300

The largest city in Syunik *marz*, Kapan is wedged between high mountains and splintered by numerous valleys. The name itself is derived from the Armenian word *kapel* (to lock), a reference to the interlocking mountain chains that converge here.

During the 18th century, Kapan was a base for Davit Bek, an Armenian freedom fighter who took on Muslim invaders encroaching on Armenia's southern border. The village grew rapidly during the Soviet era when Russian geologists, seeing the potential for mineral extraction, arrived with blueprints for a massive mining complex. There is so much unrefined metal underground that compasses won't work in some parts of town.

Kapan is as big of a hub as you're going to get in southern Armenia. It's home to plenty of shops, several hotels and cafes, making it a useful stop when driving to the Iranian border.

Sights

Mighty **Mt Khustup** (3210m) is visible high above the town. The approach to the peak is via the village of Verin Vachagan, about 3km southwest of Kapan. It's approximately 7km to the base, where you'll find a small church. You can get fine views from here; another three hours of hiking is required to reach the top.

Vahanavank   CHURCH
The main sight in the immediate area around Kapan is the remains of 10th-century Vahanavank, about 7km from Kapan just off the Kajaran road. The monastery was once the religious centre for Syunik's kings. An attempt to restore the monastery in 1978 was later abandoned and the church was roofless until 2006 when a jarringly modern-looking red roof was added.

Sleeping

The best hotels share the same building. Visitors in search of a rustic camping experience can try ARK Armenia campground (www.arkarmenia.com) about 1km up Azatamartikneri St.

Hotel Mi & Max   HOTEL $
(0285-20300; mimaxhotel@rambler.ru; 8th & 9th fl, 2 Demirchyan St; d/deluxe AMD12,000/20,000; ❄️🛜) This hotel within a hotel proves the old adage that it's not always wise to judge by initial appearances. Occupying the top floors of the worn Soviet-era Hotel Lernagorts, Mi & Max offers affordable modern, light-filled rooms with good beds, unbelievably soft sheets, satellite TV and a stylish decor. The deluxe versions have a sitting area and larger-than-usual bathroom.

Eating

There's a cluster of cafes surrounding Demirchyan Sq across from Hotel Lernagorts. Grocery stores, supermarkets and bakeries are found on Shahumian St.

Elegant Restaurant   ARMENIAN $
(077-499934; 32 Shahumian St; mains AMD600-3200; ⏰11am-midnight; ❄️🛜) As classy as

Kapan gets, this large restaurant functions as a cafe, bar and restaurant and is popular with locals wanting to enjoy a night out on the town. The menu is different than the usual, with a good choice of salads and pizzas. Try the pizza with *dolma* for a quintessentially Armenian experience.

Xacmeruk Cafe   CAFE $
(Demirchyan Sq; salads AMD650-1300, pizzas AMD2200-3000; ⏰noon-midnight; 🛜) In the middle of the park at Demirchyan Sq is this friendly cafe perfect for whiling away an afternoon or taking a break in the midst of a road trip. The menu includes smoothies, juices, booze, ice cream, salads, pizzas and pasta.

Getting There & Away

From Yerevan, a daily *marshrutka* departs from the stand near Sasunti Davit metro station (AMD5000, eight hours) at 7am.

From Kapan, one daily *marshrutka* to Yerevan (AMD5000, six to eight hours) leaves from the stop in front of Hotel Lernagorts at 9am. Shared taxis depart when full from the same location for AMD6000.

There's usually at least one daily *marshrutka* to Goris (AMD1500, 1½ hours) leaving from the bus stand on the main highway near the Davit Bek statue.

If you're heading to Iran, one daily *marshrutka* to Agarak (AMD2000) departs from the same spot between 2pm and 3pm, travelling via Meghri (AMD1500).

Meghri

286 / POP 4500

Strategic Meghri, Armenia's toehold on Iran, is worth exploring for its fine stone houses and stark beautiful scenery. The town sits deep in the lushly irrigated gorge of the Meghri River surrounded by sawtooth peaks. The 24-hour border crossing is at the Araks bridge near Agarak (population 4200), 8km from Meghri.

In Iran, just across the river from Agarak, is the ancient village of Noordoz (also spelt Noghdoz or Norduz) – the minarets of the local mosque are visible in the distance. This is a sensitive border area so be careful where you point your camera.

Travellers coming from Iran will be pleased to know Meghri restaurants serve booze, but there are no proper drinking holes to speak of.

◉ Sights

The Meghri town monastery is the brick domed 17th-century Surp Hovannes. In the centre of town is the fine Surp Astvatsatsin Church with a distinctive octagonal dome built in the 17th century with later frescoes. There's also the Surp Sargis Church across the river in Pokr Tagh with two rows of columns and some delicately restored frescoes.

🛏 Sleeping & Eating

There are a few simple B&Bs in town as well as Hotel Meghri close to the border. There are a couple of cafes and restaurants as well as a supermarket where the highway meets the main road leading up into town.

ℹ Getting There & Away

One daily *marshrutka* leaves from the stand at Yerevan's Sasuntsi Davit metro station at 7am travelling to Agarak via Meghri (AMD7000, nine hours in summer and 11 hours in winter).

From Meghri, a Yerevan service departs at 7am from Hotel Meghri, just off the central square, on Block 2. One bus to Kapan (AMD1500) also departs in the morning. A taxi to Kapan should cost AMD15,000 (90 minutes) from Agarak or Meghri. A taxi between Meghri and Agarak costs AMD1000 to AMD2000.

On the other side of the border, buses are rare or nonexistent; a taxi to Jolfa (one hour) should cost US$15. A shop just outside Iranian immigration exchanges currencies.

UNDERSTAND ARMENIA

Armenia Today

Armenia certainly *feels* different from before 2018's Velvet Revolution. The country kicked out the old guard that held the leadership for most of the years since independence and the break up of the Soviet Union. In its place is a popular centrist government with an anti-corruption agenda. The excitement is palpable and morale hasn't been this high in recent memory, but it's unclear how much tangible change will occur in a country that struggles with growth, unemployment, poverty and a declining population.

Viva la Revolución

One of the most significant events in recent Armenian history kicked off on 31 March 2018 when a member of parliament and former journalist named Nikol Pashinyan started a protest walk from Gyumri to Yerevan. His goal was to prevent two-term president Serzh Sargsyan from accepting the newly formed office of prime minister, which would virtually give him a third term in power.

Over the weeks that followed, fed-up Armenians joined Pashinyan in Yerevan and around the country demanding #MerzhirSerzhin (#RejectSerzh). Crowds swelled to hundreds of thousands, but the demonstrations were largely peaceful, prompting the name 'Velvet Revolution'. On 23 April, Sargsyan gave up his post.

Roughly a week later, a general strike ground the country to a halt and 150,000 people gathered in Republic Sq demanding Pashinyan be named prime minister. On 8 May, they got their wish and seven months after that, his My Step political alliance won 70.4% of the vote in snap elections.

A Tough Road Ahead

The Pashinyan regime has vowed to crush corruption and tackle abysmal unemployment and poverty rates, but it's too soon to gauge how much impact their policies will have. Armenia posted 5.5% GNP in 2018, which is well and good until you consider it's gone down from 7.5% growth in 2017 and it's plummeted from the 30% it hit between 1960 and 1988. The World Bank estimates growth will remain slow as investors feel out the new government.

The unemployment rate hit 15.7% in 2018, the lowest number in a decade, but compared to its regional neighbours that rate is still very high. Post-revolution stats on poverty aren't yet available, but the rate dropped to 25.7% in 2017, down from 29.4% in 2016. Of those individuals, 12.3% live on less than US$3.20 per day.

When strolling around downtown Yerevan this type of poverty might seem implausible, but when travelling in rural regions it's clear that Armenians trying to make a living are struggling to make ends meet.

With Friends Like These

Pashinyan has no plans to bungle the country's relationships with the USA, Russia and Iran – a trifecta of friendships few governments share. The US has a huge embassy in Yerevan (on 8.9 hectares of land) and USAID and the State Department fund a range of economic and cultural assistance programs.

THE DIASPORA

For nearly 2000 years, an Armenian diaspora has spread across the world, establishing communities in over 85 countries – but the 1915–22 mass killings in the Ottoman Empire caused the most dramatic exodus. Today, there are an estimated eight million Armenians living outside of the current country's borders, and just three million inside.

Out there in the world, Armenians continue to make names for themselves. In Ethiopia, Armenian Kevork Nalbandian composed the country's national anthem. In France, Charles Aznavour and his smooth tenor voice became that country's equivalent to Frank Sinatra. In the USA, where approximately 460,000 people claim Armenian heritage, Armenian-Americans invented the automated teller machine (ATM) and magnetic resonance imaging, aka MRI (Luther George Simjian and Raymond Vahan Damadian). They have also become tennis superstars (Andre Agassi), pop goddesses (Cher) and California lawyers whose kids are perhaps the world's most famous people for being famous (Robert Kardashian and his children Kim, Rob, Khloé and Kourtney).

On any given day in Yerevan, you might overhear diaspora Armenians chatting in English over a Kilikia beer. Many of them come to participate in Birthright Armenia, inspired by the Israeli program of the same name, which invites young members of the diaspora aged 21 to 32 to spend at least nine weeks volunteering in the country. A high percentage stay longer, to grow businesses, start families and to help build the nation their ancestors were forced to abandon.

Pashinyan has vowed to improve trade on the southern border with Iran and has no plans to leave the Russia-led Eurasian Economic Union, which Armenia joined in 2015 instead of vying to enter the EU. The new prime minister also plans to keep open the Russian base of 3000 soldiers in Gyumri as a safeguard against Turkey, which all but cancels out any chances of joining NATO.

Ceaseless Conflict

Despite the Karabakh War officially ending in 1994, relations with Azerbaijan remain hotter than a bonfire. Sniper fire across the border is a near daily occurrence with casualties faced by armed forces on both sides. Borders with Azerbaijan and Turkey are officially closed due to the ongoing dispute and aren't expected to open anytime soon.

Since taking office, Pashinyan has pushed for an internationally brokered peace deal with Azerbaijan over the disputed territory of Nagorno-Karabakh (known to Armenians as Artsakh), but has in no way hinted at plans to give up land for peace – a prerequisite from Azerbaijan's perspective. We're not going out on a limb here in saying the conflict isn't likely to reach its conclusion on this government's watch.

Gone But Never Forgotten

Armenians have far from forgotten Medz Yeghern (the Great Crime) committed by the Ottoman Empire between 1915 and 1922. Virtually every Armenian still wants the international community to label the mass killings a genocide. To date, 31 states including Canada, France, Germany and Russia, as well as 49 US states, have heeded Armenia's call. Turkey is not one of them and there's little hope President Recep Tayyip Erdogan will shift his country's stance.

Pashinyan says he'd love for relations to improve with Turkey and the border to be opened, but without resolution to the Karabakh conflict nor a statement on Medz Yeghern to Armenia's liking, it's hard to see any change happening on that front either.

History

In the Beginning...

Like many countries, ancient Armenia has a murky origin. According to Bible lore, Armenians are the descendants of Hayk, great-great-grandson of Noah, whose ark grounded on Mt Ararat after the flood. In recognition of their legendary ancestry, Armenians have since referred to their country as Hayastan, land of the Hayk tribe. Greek and Persian records first mention Armenians in the 6th century BC as a tribe living in the area of Lake Van (now in Turkey).

The Armenian highlands north of the Fertile Crescent had long been inhabited, and historians believe that local advances

A SURNAME PRIMER

The vast majority of Armenian surnames end in '-ian' or '-yan'. The suffix means 'from' or 'of', either from a town (Marashlian from Marash; Vanetsian from Van), from a parent (Davidian, son of David), from an occupation (Najarian, son of a carpenter; Boyajian, from the Turkish word 'boyaj' for someone who dyes fabrics), or from status or personal traits (Melikyan, son of a king; Sinanian, from a Turkish term for a well-endowed gent). Names with the prefix 'Ter' mean that a married priest (Ter Hayr) was an ancestor, eg ex-president Levon Ter-Petrossian. Western Armenian names may spell it 'Der', as in Der-Bedrossian. There are also families with the suffix '-runi', such as Siruni and Artsruni. These families were once aristocrats.

in mining, chemical and metallurgical technologies were major contributions to civilisation. With invasion routes open in four directions, the early Armenian kings fought intermittent wars against Persia and the Mediterranean powers. Greek and Roman cultures mixed with Persian angel-worship and Zoroastrianism.

In the 1st century BC the borders of Armenia reached their greatest extent under Tigranes II, whose victories over the Persian Seleucids gave him land from modern Lebanon and Syria to Azerbaijan.

Christianity & the Written Word

The local religious scene in Armenian villages attracted Christian missionaries as early as AD 40, including the apostles Bartholomew and Thaddeus. According to lore, King Trdat III declared Christianity the state religion in 301. His moment of epiphany came after being cured of madness by St Gregory the Illuminator, who had spent 12 years imprisoned in a snake-infested pit, now located under Khor Virap Monastery. A version preferred by historians suggests that Trdat was striving to create national unity while fending off Zoroastrian Persia and pagan Rome. Whatever the cause, the church has been a pillar of Armenian identity ever since.

Another pillar of nationhood arrived in 405 with Mesrop Mashtots' revolutionary Armenian alphabet. His original 36 letters

were also designed as a number system. Armenian traders found the script indispensable in business. Meanwhile, medieval scholars translated scientific and medical texts from Greek and Latin.

Kingdoms & Conquerors

Roman and Persian political influence gave way to new authority when western Armenia fell to Constantinople in 387 and eastern Armenia to the Sassanids in 428. The Arabs arrived around 645 and pressure slowly mounted from Baghdad to convert to Islam. When the Armenians resisted they were taxed to the point where many left for Roman-ruled territories, joining Armenian communities in a growing diaspora.

Better conditions emerged in the 9th century when the caliph (Muslim ruler) approved the resurrection of an Armenian monarch in King Ashot I, the first head of the Bagratuni dynasty. Ani (now in Turkey) served as capital for a stint. Various invaders including the Seljuk Turks and Mongols took turns plundering and at times ruling and splitting Armenia.

By the 17th century Armenians were scattered across the empires of Ottoman Turkey and Persia, with diaspora colonies from India to Poland. The Armenians rarely lived in a unified empire, but stayed in distant mountain provinces where some would thrive while others were depopulated. The seat of the Armenian Church wandered from Etchmiadzin to Lake Van and further west for centuries.

The Armenian Question

The Russian victory over the Persian Empire, which occurred around 1828, brought the territory of the modern-day Armenian republic under Christian rule and saw Armenians begin to return to the region. The tsarist authorities tried to break the Armenian Church's independence, but conditions were still preferable to those in Ottoman Turkey, where many Armenians still lived. When these Ottoman Armenians pushed for more rights, Sultan Abdulhamid II responded in 1896 by massacring between 80,000 and 300,000 of them.

The European powers had talked often about the 'Armenian Question', considering the Armenians a fellow Christian people living within the Ottoman Empire. During WWI some Ottoman Armenians sided with Russia in the hope of establishing their own nation state. Viewing this as disloyal to the empire and still smarting from their 1915 defeat at the hands of Russia, the ruling Committee of Union and Progress (CUP) party, also known as the Young Turks, immediately ordered the dispossession and forced deportation of all Armenian subjects from the empire in an action variously labelled genocide, mass murder or Medz Yeghern (the Great Crime). What is less certain – and remains contentious to this day – is whether the Young Turks also ordered pogroms and issued a decree for all Armenians to be exterminated. Armenians today claim that there was a specific order to commit genocide; Turks strenuously deny this. Putting this argument aside, one fact is inescapable – between 1915 and 1922 around 1.5 million Ottoman Armenians were murdered in Ottoman Turkey or forced into the Syrian desert where they subsequently died.

The first independent Armenian republic emerged in 1918, after the November 1917 Russian Revolution saw the departure of Russian troops from the parts of Ottoman Armenia that it had occupied. The republic immediately faced a wave of starving refugees, the 1918 influenza epidemic, and wars with surrounding Turkish, Azerbaijani and Georgian forces. It fought off the invading Turks in 1918, and left the final demarcation of the frontier to Woodrow Wilson, the US president. Meanwhile, the Turks regrouped under Mustafa Kemal (later Atatürk) and overran parts of the South Caucasus. Wilson's map eventually arrived without troops or any international support, while Atatürk offered Lenin peace in exchange for half of the new Armenian republic. Beset by many other enemies, Lenin agreed.

The Armenian government, led by the Dashnaks, a party of Armenian independence fighters, capitulated to the Bolsheviks in 1921. They surrendered in order to preserve the last provinces of ancient Armenia. The Soviet regime hived off Karabakh and Naxçivan (Nakhchivan) for Azerbaijan and absorbed both it and Armenia into its empire. Yerevan was largely rebuilt in the 1920s and in ensuing decades Armenia became an important Soviet centre of manufacturing and technology. There were also many research institutes here.

Independence

The debate over the Armenian-majority region of Nagorno-Karabakh inside Azerbaijan brought a new wave of leaders to the fore under Soviet leader Gorbachev's *glasnost* (openness) reforms. Armenians voted for independence on 21 September 1991, and Levon Ter-Petrossian, a 40-year-old scholar and leader of the Karabakh Committee, became president. The war with Azerbaijan over Karabakh exploded just as the economy went into free-fall.

KOMITAS & SOGHOMIAN TEHLIRIAN

Two figures from the Medz Yeghern (the Great Crime) are particularly well remembered by Armenians. Soghomon Soghomonian, more commonly known as Komitas, represents the losses. A *vardapet* (monk) of the Armenian Church, Komitas travelled through Armenian villages collecting folk songs and also worked on deciphering the mysteries of medieval Armenian liturgical music. He moved to İstanbul in 1910 to introduce Armenian folk music to wider audiences and it was there, on 24 April 1915, that he was rounded up with 250 other Armenian community leaders and intellectuals. Komitas was one of possibly two of the 250 to survive – his life was literally bought from the Young Turks by a benefactor and he was smuggled to France. Sadly, the atrocities he witnessed had a terrible effect, and he died in an asylum in Paris in 1937 having never spoken again. His ideas for breathing life into the ancient harmonies and chorales were lost with him.

Soghomian Tehlirian represents a different face of the Medz Yeghern. After losing his family to the killings, he ended up in Berlin in the early 1920s, where, on 15 March 1921, he assassinated the man considered by many to have been most responsible for the mass killings, Mehmet Talaat Pasha. At Tehlirian's trial, survivors and witnesses gave testimony on the marches, massacres, tortures and rapes, as well as Talaat Pasha's prime role in orchestrating events. After two days the German jury found Tehlirian not guilty and released him. He later settled in America. Other senior Turkish officials were killed in the early 1920s in Operation Nemesis, a secret Dashnak (Armenian Revolutionary Federation) plan to execute their own justice.

After the war, rumours of coups and assassination attempts prompted Ter-Petrossian to reverse civil rights and throw Dashnak leaders and fighters from the Karabakh War into jail, where some spent three years as political prisoners. Ter-Petrossian was re-elected for another five-year term in 1996 but resigned in 1998, isolated and unpopular.

He was replaced in March 1998 by Robert Kocharian, a war hero from southern Karabakh. Kocharian quickly moved to woo back the diaspora, especially the influential Dashnak faction.

By the end of the 1990s the new class of wealthy import barons stood out in shocking contrast to the country's poverty. Anger over this disparity was at least partly responsible for the terrible 1999 massacre in the national assembly, when gunmen, screaming that the barons were drinking the blood of the nation, murdered eight members of parliament and wounded six others. The event sparked a wave of emigration and endless recriminations, but the 1700th anniversary of the founding of the Armenian Church in 2001 marked something of a turning point in the country's fortunes. Memories of the suffering and upheaval since independence linger on with Mt Ararat a constant reminder of what they lost, but since 2018's Velvet Revolution most Armenians are now firmly focused on the 21st century.

Arts

Cinema

The best-known name in Armenian cinema is Sergei Parajanov, known for the avant-garde films he made between 1951 and 1990. These include the internationally acclaimed *Sayat Nova* (aka *The Colour of Pomegranates*), made in 1969; *The Legend of Souram Fortress* (1985); and *Ashik Kerib* (1988). His final masterpiece, *The Confession*, was unfinished when he died in 1990; part of the original camera negative survived and is included in Mikhail Vartanov's *Parajanov: The Last Spring* (1992).

Canadian-Armenian art-house director Atom Egoyan has made several films on Armenian themes, including *Calendar* (1993), a story of a disintegrating marriage partly shot on location in Armenia; and *Ararat* (2002), a film within a film dealing with the hefty subject of the Medz Yeghern. Egoyan's

2015 film *Remember* also deals with the themes of historical memory, justice and accountability through its story of a Jewish Holocaust survivor who determines to exact revenge on the Nazi officer who killed his family in a concentration camp.

There was great anticipation and controversy ahead of 2016's *The Promise* starring Oscar Isaac, Charlotte Le Bon and Christian Bale, which would be the first big-budget film to deal with Medz Yeghern. In the days following the $100 million film's debut at the Toronto Film Festival (it was funded entirely by Armenian-American billionaire Kirk Kerkorian), tens of thousands of one-star ratings flooded online review sites Rotten Tomatoes and IMDB – a coordinated strike by those in opposition to calling the massacres a genocide, according to director Terry George. Armenians responded with a flood of 10/10 reviews. In the end, the movie was a box office bomb losing the studio that released it $102 million.

Spitak (2018) was Armenia's submission to the 91st Academy Awards, but it didn't get nominated. It's a dramatisation of the devastating events of 1988 when an earthquake virtually wiped the town of Spitak off the map. The music was scored by Serj Tankian of Armenian-American heavy metal band System of a Down.

Music

Armenian religious music's mythically complex harmonies are partly lost, though there are many fine, melancholy choirs of the Armenian liturgy.

The 18th-century poet, musician and composer Sayat Nova, often considered the greatest singer-songwriter in the South Caucasus, began his career in the court of Erekle II of Georgia but was exiled for his forbidden love of the king's daughter and became an itinerant troubadour. The majority of his surviving ballads are in Azerbaijani, as it was the lingua franca of the South Caucasus at the time.

The great composers of the 19th and 20th centuries include Komitas, whose works for choir and orchestra put Armenian music on an international stage, and Armen Tigranyan for his operas *Anoush* (1912) and *Davit Bek* (1950). Aram Khachaturian is best known for two ballet scores: *Gayane* (1942), which includes the well-known 'Sabre Dance'; and *Spartacus* (1954).

RABIZ MUSIC

Rabiz is a contraction of the Russian words *'rabochee iskustvo'* (workers' art). It's entertainment and it's also a lifestyle – the guys in the silk shirts and gold chains driving too fast while smoking and talking on their cellphones. If you ask a hip student, they'll say that Armenian popular culture is divided between loud, showy, raucous *rabiz* culture on one hand, and everything of good taste on the other. *Rabiz* also covers a lot of highly inventive slang. *Rabiz* music is *marshrutka*-driver music, a mix of brainless pop and over-the-top tragic ballads (girl has cancer, boy says he'll kill himself before she dies) that strike a sentimental Middle Eastern chord in Armenian hearts. Fans want music that will make them cry, as well as impassioned love songs and arms-aloft dancing music. This kind of music booms from taxis in Greek, Russian, Turkish and Arabic. The Armenian variety comes from Los Angeles, Beirut and Moscow as well as Yerevan, where it plays in neighbourhood bars, clubs and *khoravats* (barbecued food) joints late into the night.

Folk music is alive and well in town troupes, late-night clubs and *khoravats* palaces. The *duduk*, a double-reed instrument made from apricot wood, will become the soundtrack to your journey in Armenia. Its inescapable trill features in traditional music and many modern pop tunes blaring from the speakers of taxi cabs.

For good traditional music try the Real-World label, which has albums by *duduk* master Djivan Gasparian. Also try Parik Nazarian, Gevorg Dabagian and the album *Minstrels and Folk Songs of Armenia* by Parseghian Records.

Current Armenian chart toppers include Eurovision contestants Iveta Mukuchyan and Aram Mp3.

Visual Arts

Of the many notable Armenian visual artists of the 19th and 20th centuries, three stand out: Vardges Surenyants (1860–1921), Martiros Sarian (1880–1972) and Yervand Kochar (1899–1979). All were known for their paintings, and Kochar was also a notable sculptor. Many of Surenyants' works are in the collection of the National Gallery of Armenia, and both Kochar and Sarian have Yerevan museums dedicated to their lives and works.

Sarian Park behind the Opera House features a grandiose statue of the great man. Suitably, this same park is the venue for Yerevan's art market, where painters gather to offer a critique of each other's work and sell their paintings. Most of the paintings have religious iconography or capture familiar Armenian landscapes.

Contemporary artists of note include Arthur Sarkissian, Karen Petrosyan, Armen Gevorgyan and Laura Avetisyan. All have work in the collection of the Modern Art Museum of Yerevan.

Theatre & Dance

Theatre runs deep in Armenian culture – a 10th-century fortress at Saimbeyli in Cilicia had three storeys of theatres and two storeys of libraries.

The Hellenic kings of Armenia patronised theatre in the 3rd century BC, and Greek dramas played to King Tigran the Great. There are about half a dozen active theatre houses in Yerevan specialising in musical comedy, contemporary plays and drama revivals.

Armenia has a rich tradition of folk dancing, and you may be lucky enough to stumble across a performance in a public square. Revellers at country weddings might not be so professional, but then again, it is the real deal. Armenia has a rich diversity of dances and costumes, straight out of a medieval spring festival. There are also dance and ballet companies in Yerevan.

Food & Drink

The Armenian kitchen is hundreds if not thousands of years in the making, combining fresh flavours and spices from its own fertile soil along with borrowed flavours retrieved by its expansive diaspora. If invited in for dinner, accept; it could very well be the best memory from your trip.

Staples & Specialities

Armenian cuisine combines elements of the foods of all its historic neighbours – Arabic, Russian, Greek and Persian – but remains distinctive. The quality of local produce is high, and the fruits and vegetables on offer are fresh and packed with flavour. This is because crops are often grown on a small scale

MENU DECODER

abour	soup
basturma	cured beef or ham
biber	capsicum (pepper)
bourek	flaky stuffed pastry
dolma	vine or cabbage leaves stuffed with rice or meat
eetch	bulgur salad
gala	sweet bun or bread
ghapama	baked pumpkin stuffed with rice and dried fruits
harissa	porridge made of wheat and meat cooked together for a long time
hats	bread
hav	chicken
hummus	ground chickpea paste with oil
ishkhan	Sevan trout
kadayif	crunchy dessert pastry
kebab	ground meat cooked on a skewer
khaghogh	grapes
khamaju	a meat pie similar to Georgian cheese pie
khash	winter stew of animal parts including the foot of a cow or ox
khashlama	lamb stew cooked in beer or wine
khoravats	barbecue, usually pork, lamb or beef, also vegetables and fish, does not include kebab
khoz	pork
kyufta	meatballs mixed with onion and egg
lahmajo (lahmajoon)	thin pizza topped with tomato, minced-lamb and spices
lavash	thin, unleavened bread
loleek	tomato (also *pomidor*)
matsoon	yogurt
oghee	fruit vodkas
paneer	cheese
patlijan	eggplant (aubergine)
pomidor	tomato (also *loleek*)
shaker	sugar
siga	river trout
spas	yogurt soup
sujuk	cured sausage
sweet sujuk	plum and walnut sweet
tabouleh	diced green salad with semolina
tan	yogurt drink
tavar	beef
tsiran	apricot
vochkhar	lamb

in villages and backyards across the country without the use of greenhouses or pesticides. Meat isn't factory farmed, as evidenced by highway cow and sheep traffic jams.

If there's one word for dining, it's *khoravats* (barbecued meat). Pork is the favourite, though lamb, beef and sometimes chicken are usually available too. *Ishkhan khora-*

vats is grilled trout from Lake Sevan. *Siga* is another good grilled-fish dish. Kebabs are also very common. The signature herb is dill – Armenians use it in innumerable dishes but especially in salads.

Broadly speaking, western Armenian cuisine has a Levantine influence, while eastern Armenian cuisine incorporates Russian and Georgian influences. Besides *khoravats,* staples include *dolma* (rice wrapped in vine leaves), *spas* (yogurt soup) and lavash fresh from the oven. *Khash* is a thick winter stew made from animal parts. Starters include cold salads, farmyard-smelling cheese and dips such as *matsoon* (sour yogurt) and *jajik* (yogurt with cucumbers and fennel). Cured meats include *sujuk* (dark, cured spicy sausage) and *basturma* (finely cured ham).

There are few strictly vegetarian restaurants in Armenia but many restaurants offer beet salads and veggie stews made with tomatoes, rice, eggplants (aubergines), zucchinis (courgettes) and a profusion of herbs and spices. Western Armenian cuisine features hummus, tabouleh, labneh, *fatayer* (cheese or spinach pastries) and other vegetarian dishes associated with Lebanese cuisine.

Drinks

The most popular drink is *soorch* (Armenian coffee), also claimed by Georgians, Greeks and Arabs. It's a potent, finely ground cup of lusciously rich coffee, with thick sediment at the bottom. It goes well with honeyed pastries such as baklava. Tea is also popular. There is an interesting array of mineral and table waters, ranging from salty, volcanic Jermuk to lighter Noy and Dilijan waters. Fruit juices are cheap and delicious.

The two main lagers are Kilikia and Kotayk, widely available and quite refreshing on a hot summer afternoon. Kilikia is a typical middle European lager, very good when cold. Its main rival, Kotayk, is sold everywhere and is a little more reliable, if bland. Other popular brands include Erebuni, made by Kotayk; Gyumri and Ararat, made by the Gyumri Beer Company; and Aleksandrapol. Fresh on the scene is Dargett craft beer, which makes over 20 flavours and is available at select places around the country.

The country's national liquor is *konyak* (cognac), which is around 40% alcohol. There are several other producers, such as Great Valley, but the Yerevan Brandy Company's ArArAt label is the real deal, a

PUNCH DRUNK

Oghee (pronounced something like 'orh-ee') are delicious fruit vodkas, sometimes called *vatsun* or *aragh,* made in village orchards everywhere. Around 60% alcohol, *oghee* is made from apples, pears, apricots, pomegranates, grapes, cherries, Cornelian cherries or cornels, mulberries and figs. The best mulberry (*t'te*) and Cornelian cherry (*hone*) *oghee* are intense, lingering liqueurs. Vedi Alco makes some *oghee* commercially, weaker than the village stuff. You won't need to go far to try some; it's a usual accompaniment to a *khoravats* dinner and sometimes offered after a meal. The drink tastes best in autumn when homes turn into distilleries after the harvest.

smooth, intense liquor with a smoky aroma similar to whisky. Armenian *konyak* has a huge following in Russia and Ukraine. Even Winston Churchill favoured it over the French stuff and Stalin used to send him cases of ArArAt cognac.

Armenia is going through something of a wine revolution of late with many of Yerevan's top restaurants and bars leaning heavily towards local. Most locally produced red wines are made from the Areni noir grape, which is well suited to the hot summers and harsh winters. White wines are produced by vineyards in Tavush, Lori and Karabakh. Look out for wines by Trinity Canyon, Zorah, Malishka, Maran, ArmAs, Kataro, Noravank, Bagratuni and Karas. Tariri's dry white is particularly quaffable, as is the ever-reliable Karas red from Armavir.

SURVIVAL GUIDE

ℹ️ Directory A–Z

ACCESSIBLE TRAVEL

Armenia has much work to do to improve accessibility, especially outside Yerevan. Zvartnots Airport (p165) has facilities for wheelchair users, including accessible toilets, but elsewhere cracked and potholed pavements make life difficult for wheelchair users and people with a visual impairment. Only about 1% of buses in Yerevan are accessible, and metro stations lack elevators. The cost of renting a car and driver-helper isn't extortionate, so that might be a better transport option. On the plus side, at least a dozen hotels in Yerevan have facilities for disabled guests. The most visited monasteries have information written in braille.

Wheels on Wheels (☏091-016565) has a wheelchair-accessible taxi and wheelchairs for hire in Yerevan.

Arara (☏098-110138; araratour.com) runs tours to the country for wheelchair users.

Download Lonely Planet's free Accessible Travel guides from http://lptravel.to/Accessible Travel.

ACCOMMODATION

Peak-season accommodation rates apply from July to August, but may also reach the shoulder seasons from May to June and September to October. Even outside these months it's a good idea to book your room ahead of time, particularly in Yerevan. This is especially true for B&Bs so the hosts can organise food and be available for your arrival. Discounts are usually available in the low season (November to April).

ACTIVITIES

Birdwatching Armenia has quite a reputation among birdwatchers – about 350 species have been recorded here, including one-third of Europe's threatened species, and 240 species breed here. Two books on the topic include *A Field Guide to Birds of Armenia* and *Handbook of the Birds of Armenia,* which are both by Martin S Adamian and D Klem Jr.

Caving There are *karst* (limestone) caves in Vayots Dzor, largely unexplored and for experienced spelunkers only. The cave villages, such as Old Khndzoresk (p209), around Goris are an easier challenge.

Cycling Armenia is an excellent biking destination, as long as you don't mind pothole-ridden roads. A useful resource is Cycling Armenia (www.cyclingarmenia.com), a volunteer-run site that recommends routes and offers tips.

Hiking It's possible to hike to the top of Mt Aragats (p175) in summer, and there are great walking trails in the forests and mountains around Dilijan and the Yeghegis Valley. The HIKEArmenia (p165) office in Yerevan is very helpful and its app is a seriously useful tool.

Horseback riding Available mostly in the Lori and Vayots Dzor regions.

Rafting The best way to explore the Debed Canyon. Inquire with Rafting in Armenia (p186).

Ziplining Soar high over the verdant hills near Ijevan (p196).

BORDER CROSSINGS

The closed border with both Turkey to the west and Azerbaijan to the east means that connections to Armenia are somewhat limited. Land borders are open with both Georgia and Iran. As a result, many overlanders regard Armenia as something of a side trip from Georgia, heading south from Tbilisi for a week or two before returning to Georgia. Minibus transfers between Georgia and Armenia are fast and frequent, making it easy to pop between the two republics. Organise one with your accommodation.

Only a handful of travellers travel to or from Iran (given the visa restrictions of that country), but there are daily bus connections between Yerevan and Tehran and *marshrutky* to the border.

If driving across the Georgian border in an Armenian hire car, make sure you've cleared it with your rental agency. Once across the Georgian border, you'll need to buy insurance at the office 300m past the crossing in a strip of shops on the left (15 days for 30 GEL, 30 days for 50 GEL).

CUSTOMS REGULATIONS

The usual restrictions apply (200 cigarettes, two bottles of alcohol, other goods up to the value of US$5000) and there's no currency declaration. If you plan to take something out of the country considered to be of cultural, historical or national value that's 50 years old or more (eg a rug, a samovar or similar), a certificate is required from the **Ministry of Culture** (Map p150; ☏011-234702; www.mincult.am; 51 Komitas St, Yerevan). You'll find it's much easier if the shop you bought the item from arranges the permit for you, or if you can speak Armenian. Otherwise the bureaucracy can be quite baffling.

DANGERS & ANNOYANCES

➡ Armenia is considered safe, but rare earthquakes have caused devastating aftermaths and war with surrounding neighbours remains possible, although unlikely.

PRICE RANGES

Accommodation

The following price ranges are based on high-season accommodation for two people including breakfast and taxes:

$ less than AMD25,000

$$ AMD25,000–AMD70,000

$$$ more than AMD70,000

Eating

The following price ranges are based on one main course:

$ less than AMD3000

$$ AMD3000–AMD5000

$$$ more than AMD5000

→ Many Armenians drive erratically, overtaking in the face of oncoming traffic and on blind corners, speeding and taking no notice of delineated road lanes. When driving, stay alert and drive extremely defensively.

→ Uncomfortable staring is an issue, especially aimed at women.

→ Be careful when hiking around the border with Azerbaijan since as of 2017 there are nearly 10 sq km of confirmed or suspected landmine areas, but stay on well-trotted routes or paths and you'll have nothing to fear.

EMBASSIES & CONSULATES

A full list of Armenian embassies and consulates can be found at www.embassy.am.

Canadian (Map p150; ☎ 010-567990; yerevan@international.gc.ca; 17 Buzand St, Yerevan; ☺10am-2pm Mon-Fri)

French (Map p150; ☎ 060-651950; www.ambafrance-am.org; 8 Grigor Lusavorich St, Yerevan; ☺9am-1pm & 2-5.30pm Mon-Fri)

Georgian (Map p148; ☎ 010-200738; www.armenia.mfa.gov.ge; 2/10 Babayan St, Yerevan; ☺10am-6pm Mon-Fri)

German (Map p150; ☎ 010-523279; www.eriwan.diplo.de; 29 Charents St, Yerevan; ☺8am-3.30pm Mon-Fri)

Iranian (Map p148; ☎ 010-280457; www.hy.yerevan.mfa.ir; 1 Budaghyan St, Arabkir Park, Yerevan; ☺9am-6pm Mon-Fri)

Irish (Map p150; ☎ 010-526330; 18/1 Vardanants St; ☺11am-5pm Mon-Fri)

Nagorno-Karabakh (Map p148; ☎ 010-249705; www.nkr.am; 17/2 Zaryan St, Yerevan; ☺9am-6pm Mon-Fri)

UK (Map p150; ☎ 010-264301; www.gov.uk/world/armenia; 34 Marshall Baghramian Ave, Yerevan; ☺9am-5pm Mon-Fri)

US (Map p148; ☎ 010-464700; https://am.usembassy.gov; 1 American Ave, Yerevan; ☺9am-6pm Mon-Fri)

ETIQUETTE

Church Some locals choose to leave churches walking backwards as they face the altar, but they won't chastise foreigners who don't.

Photos Ask before taking photos – most Armenians won't mind.

Invitations If invited to dinner, it is customary to accept. Bring a small gift if you can.

Flowers If buying flowers it is customary to give an odd number as even numbers are meant for funerals.

Toasts If you want to propose a toast, it's polite to ask the permission of the *tamada* (main toastmaker). There's a custom in clinking glasses of holding your glass lower than the next person's, as a sign of deference. This can develop into a game until the glasses are at

table level. If you empty a bottle into someone's glass, it obliges them to buy the next bottle – it's polite to put the last drops into your own glass.

HEALTH

Medical facilities can be excellent in Yerevan, but in remote areas they may be very basic. A doctor's visit usually costs a minimum fee of

The Armenian Alphabet

ARMENIAN	ROMAN	PRONUNCIATION
Ա ա	a	as in 'hat'
Բ բ	b	as in 'bet'
Գ գ	g	as in 'get'
Դ դ	d	as in 'do'
Ե ե	ye-/-e-	as the 'ye' or 'e' in 'yet'
Զ զ	z	as in 'zoo'
Է է	e	long, as in 'there'
Ը ը	e	neutral vowel; as the 'a' in 'ago'
Թ թ	t	as in 'tip'
Ժ ժ	zh	as the 's' in 'measure'
Ի ի	ee	as in 'meet'
Լ լ	l	as in 'let'
Խ խ	kh	as 'ch' in Scottish 'loch'
Ծ ծ	ts	as in 'bits'
Կ կ	k	as in 'kit'
Հ հ	h	as in 'here'
Ձ ձ	dz	as in 'adze'
Ղ ղ	gh	as French 'r'
Ճ ճ	ch	as in 'each'
Մ մ	m	as in 'met'
Յ յ	y	as in 'yet'
Ն ն	n	as in 'no'
Շ շ	sh	as in 'shoe'
Ո ո	vo-/-o-	as in 'vote'
Չ չ	ch	as in 'chair'
Պ պ	p	as in 'pet'
Ջ ջ	j	as in 'judge'
Ռ ռ	r	a rolled 'r'
Ս ս	s	as in 'sit'
Վ վ	v	as in 'van'
Տ տ	t	as in 'ten'
Ր ր	r	as in 'run'
Ց g	ts	as in 'tsar'
Ու ու	u	as in 'rule'
Փ փ	p	as in 'pit'
Ք ք	k	similar to the 'c' in 'cat'
Օ o	o	long, as in 'wore'
Ֆ ֆ	f	as in 'fit'

The original 36 letters also have a numerical value, meaning any number can be represented using combinations of letters. Ա (a) to Թ (t) is 1 to 9, Ժ (zh) to Ղ (gh) is 10 to 90, Ճ (ch) to Ջ (j) is 100 to 900, and Ռ (r) to Ք (k) is 1000 to 9000.

AMD10,000. Communication with doctors or nurses can be challenging if you don't speak Armenian or Russian.

Health Insurance

Not all insurers cover Armenia as part of Europe and very few will cover you along the borders with Iran and Azerbaijan or if you visit Nagorno-Karabakh. While simple medical procedures may be cheap, if you get insurance it's ideal to get a policy that pays the medical facility directly rather than you having to pay on the spot and claim later, although these policies are rare. If you have to claim later, make sure you keep all documentation and get a medical report from the doctor. Carry proof of your insurance with you; this can be vital for avoiding any delays to treatment in emergency situations.

Find out which private medical service your insurer uses in Armenia so that you can call them directly in the event of an emergency. Your policy should ideally cover emergency air evacuation home, which may be essential in the case of an earthquake or war.

INTERNET ACCESS

Armenia has great 4G coverage for the most part, though it may be difficult to find a signal when hiking in forests or mountains or on the road in between towns. Free wi-fi is offered in the vast majority of accommodation.

LGBT TRAVELLERS

On 5 April 2019, trans woman Lilit Martirosyan spoke at the National Assembly in Yerevan about torture, rape, assault and discrimination committed against her community. The heavy backlash she received, particularly from politicians, proves how far this country needs to come on LGBTQ+ issues.

While homosexuality was decriminalised in 2003, discrimination remains widespread and those who openly display their orientation continue to face danger. In general, LGBTQ+ travellers won't encounter discrimination as long as they are discreet. Two men or women booking a hotel room or sharing a bed is not automatically construed as a sexual relationship and indeed

ⓘ CAGED BROWN BEARS

Caged brown bears are sometimes used as tourist attractions at hotels and restaurants in Armenia, and activist groups such as International Animal Rescue campaign against supporting such businesses. Lonely Planet does not recommend businesses that keep caged bears due to the animal cruelty concerns it raises.

will often be considered far less scandalous than an unmarried mixed couple doing the same. Same-sex marriage ceremonies are not carried out in the country, but are recognised when performed abroad.

Websites and advocacy or support groups include:

Gay and Lesbian Armenian Society (www.galasla.org)

Pink Armenia (www.pinkarmenia.org)

Unzipped: Gay Armenia (www.gayarmenia.blogspot.com)

MAPS

The full-colour foldout *Armenia & Mountainous Karabakh* and *Yerevan* maps are up-to-date and easy to use. Both are available at Bookinist (p164) and HIKEArmenia (p165) in Yerevan.

MONEY

Every city and most towns have ATMs. Credit cards are widely accepted in Yerevan, but you'll need cash outside the capital.

Bargaining

Taxi drivers won't complain if you set the price when getting in and stick to it when getting out (though ordering with taxi-hailing apps GG and Yandex will save you the trouble). Shops have set prices, but *shukas* (markets) and outdoor fruit and vegetable stands are more negotiable, especially when buying more than one item.

Exchanging Money

The best cash currencies are US dollars, euros and Russian roubles, roughly in that order. Georgian lari can also be changed in Yerevan and border towns. Other currencies are hard to change except at a handful of major banks in Yerevan. There are moneychanging signs waving flags and rates at customers everywhere in Yerevan and around *shukas* in all major towns. Virtually any shop can change money legally, and many food stores and smallgoods vendors do. Scams seem to be rare, and transactions straightforward. Avoid exchanging dram in Georgia as vendors there offer terrible rates. Western Union money transfer is not available in Armenia.

Tipping

Restaurants The usual tipping rule is 10% on top of the 10% service fee that may be charged on some bills, especially in Yerevan.

Taxis It's acceptable but not necessary to give your driver an extra 10%.

POST

National postal service Haypost has offices in every major town. A letter might take anything from three to six weeks to reach North America or Australia, but the service is fairly reliable.

PUBLIC HOLIDAYS

Annual public holidays in Armenia:

New Year's Day 1 January

Christmas Day 6 January

International Women's Day 8 March

Good Friday Varies, from mid-March to late April

Genocide Memorial Day 24 April

Victory and Peace Day 9 May

Republic Day 28 May

Constitution Day 5 July

Independence Day 21 September

Earthquake Memorial Day 7 December

SMOKING

Most hotels have dedicated nonsmoking floors or rooms and a few have outlawed smoking altogether. A growing number of cafes and restaurants have dedicated nonsmoking sections. There has been talk about restrictions on smoking coming to Yerevan, but nothing has come to fruition as yet.

TELEPHONE

➡ The country code is ✆ 374, while Yerevan's area code is ✆ 10.

➡ For calls within Armenia, dial ✆ 0 + city code + local number.

➡ For mobile numbers dial the prefix first (this varies according to the mobile phone company used), then the number. Note that the '0' is not dialled when calling from overseas.

➡ For international calls, dial ✆ 00 first.

Mobile Phones

➡ Local SIM cards are affordable, simple to get and work with most unlocked mobile phones, so it's ideal to buy a prepaid plan and plug a SIM into your own device. Don't forget to bring your passport when buying a SIM card.

➡ Mobile-phone services, operated by Viva-Cell, Ucom and Beeline, are fairly priced and wide-ranging. There is little difference between the providers, although there seem to be more subscribers to VivaCell (and calling other VivaCell phones is a little cheaper).

➡ You can get mobile-phone service just about anywhere in the country these days, unless you are hiking in the backcountry.

➡ SIM cards are easily purchased from Vi-vaCell (www.mts.am), Ucom (www.ucom. am) and Beeline (http://beeline.am) shops; bring your passport. Ten GB of data for 30 days costs around AMD6000; calls and texts average AMD5 to numbers from the same company and AMD15 to numbers from competition companies. An international text averages AMD20.

➡ SIM cards can be recharged at phone company offices.

ⓘ HITCHING

Due to the unreliability of *marshrutky* and relative costliness of taxis, many travellers and locals alike stick out their thumbs and request lifts around the country. Popularity aside, hitching is never entirely safe, and we don't recommend it. Travellers who hitch should understand that they are taking a small but potentially serious risk.

TIME

Time in Armenia is GMT/UTC plus four hours. The country does not observe daylight saving time.

TOILETS

➡ Toilets in newer buildings and most of Yerevan are the typical sit-down kind, but squat toilets remain common, especially in the countryside.

➡ It's often fine to flush toilet paper, but some older toilets may require tossing used paper in a bin.

➡ Public toilets (where attendants charge a small fee) are rare and only large bus and train stations have them.

TRAVEL WITH CHILDREN

Armenia is a child-friendly country – you'll often see kids playing in the streets. Baby change facilities in restaurants are rare, as Armenians don't usually take their children to dine with them except on special occasions. Roads are potholed and bumpy, so driving prams around might be a challenge. Children love the musical fountains at Yerevan's Republic Square (p149), playing at the Soviet-era Children's Railway (p154) and teens will get a kick out of Yell Extreme Park (p196) near Ijevan.

VISAS

Visitors from the US and EU can stay for up to 180 days without a visa; citizens from most other countries can obtain a visa on entry.

Visa Options

While they don't need a visa for short trips, visitors from the US and EU countries will need to present a passport at entry points. See www. mfa.am/en/visa for a list of eligible nationalities, and also for a list of nationalities whose citizens must obtain an invitation from an Armenian embassy or consulate overseas before visiting Armenia.

Many countries who require a tourist visa can purchase one upon entry. A 21-day tourist visa will cost AMD3000 and a 120-day visa will cost AMD15,000. Visas are free for eligible children under 18 years of age. You'll need one empty page in your passport for the visa and you must also pay in dram (money changers are available at border points and next to the visas booth at the airport, which is in the hall before the immigration booths). Some nationalities, like Canada for instance, are instructed to purchase an e-visa (https://evisa.mfa.am) in advance of arrival which costs US$6 for a 21-day visa and US$31 for 120 days. Most visas are single-entry unless prearranged with an embassy.

Don't overstay your visa – a fine of AMD50,000 to AMD100,000 will be levied at your exit point if you do, and you will be unable to re-enter the country for one year.

Visa Extensions

You can get a visa extension for as long as 60 days at the **Passport and Visa Office** (Map p148; ☑ 010-370264; www.police.am) in the district of Davtashen, northwest of Yerevan's city centre.

Visas for Onward Travel

Georgia Citizens of more than 90 countries and territories, listed at www.geoconsul.gov.ge, can enter Georgia without a visa for stays of up to one year. Non-visa-free nationalities should organise a visa through Georgia's e-visa portal (www.evisa.gov.ge).

Iran It is possible to obtain 15-day tourist visas on arrival at the airports in Tehran, Esfahan, Shiraz, Tabriz and Mashad (the visas are not available at the land border). However, there are 10 countries whose nationals are not eligible for this; the US, UK, Canada, Afghanistan, Bangladesh, Colombia, Iraq, Jordan, Pakistan and Somalia. Israeli passport holders or anyone with an Israeli stamp within 365 days will be refused entry. The Iranian embassy (p223) in Yerevan provides visas only after you have received approval from the Iranian Ministry of Foreign Affairs, and for this you'll need to go through a travel agent. Allow at least a month to complete the whole process and the embassy will charge AMD20,000 for a reference code on top of the visa charge. Tatev Travel (p165) in Yerevan can assist you with the process and with onward travel.

Nagorno-Karabakh If in Armenia it is rather easy to visit the occupied territory known locally as Artsakh, despite it being internationally recognised as part of Azerbaijan. Visas can be obtained at the border crossing or at the embassy in Yerevan (p223); you'll need a passport, 3cm x 4cm photo and to fill in the visa application. Tourist visas are free for 21 days and rise to AMD20,000 for multi-entry over three months.

Turkey Though the land border between Armenia and Turkey is not open, it is possible to fly between Yerevan and İstanbul. Turkish visas must be obtained before arrival; see www.evisa.gov.tr.

VOLUNTEERING

Armenian Volunteer Corps (www.armenian-volunteer.org)

Birthright Armenia (www.birthrightarmenia.org)

US Peace Corps (www.peacecorps.gov/armenia)

Workaway (www.workaway.info)

WWOOF (www.wwoof.net)

Azerbaijan

☑ 994 / POP 9,981,457

Best Places to Eat

➡ Şirvanşah Muzey-Restoran (p244)

➡ Calğalıq Restoranı (p282)

➡ Saat Meydanı (p297)

➡ Qafqaz Karavansaray (p271)

➡ Paris Bistro (p242)

Best Places to Stay

➡ Karavansaray Hotel (p275)

➡ Sultan Inn (p240)

➡ Quba Palace Hotel (p259)

➡ MinAli Boutique Hotel (p276)

➡ Xan Lənkəran (p291)

Why Go?

Billing itself as the 'Land of Fire', Azerbaijan (Azərbaycan) is a tangle of contradictions and contrasts. Neither Europe nor Asia, it's a nexus of ancient historical empires, but also a 'new' nation which has undergone an extraordinary transformation from the war-ravaged post-Soviet 1990s to an oil-enriched host of Formula 1 and Europa League football. The cosmopolitan capital counterpoints a Unesco-listed ancient core with dazzling 21st-century architecture on a balmy bay of the Caspian Sea. In the surrounding semi-desert are mud volcanoes and curious fire phenomena. Yet barely three hours' drive away, timeless rural villages lie amid lush orchards backed by the soaring Great Caucasus Mountains. Come quickly. Having long been overlooked by visitors, Azerbaijan's new easy visas, bargain-value hotels and close-packed range of beautiful landscapes are starting to attract significant flows of tourists, though, as yet, few of them from Western countries.

When to Go

➡ Lowland Azerbaijan is especially lovely from April to June as showers interspersed by clear skies enliven bright-green, flower-dappled fields.

➡ October is very pleasant in Baku, though much of the rural countryside is parched brown.

➡ Summer gets oppressively hot and humid in low-lying areas but late July is the best hiking season in the higher mountains.

➡ Although winters are relatively mild around the Caspian shores, you'll probably need a warm coat in Baku, adding extra sweaters inland.

➡ January to February is the top ski season, a frigid time of year in Xınalıq or Lahıc.

Azerbaijan Highlights

1 Baku (p230)
Contrasting the medieval stone core with the modernist skyline in Azerbaijan's buzzingly dynamic capital.

2 Şəki (p272)
Delving into 18th-century palaces and an unforgettable caravanserai-hotel in a Unesco-listed Old Town that's beautifully backed by wooded mountains.

3 Alinja Castle (p298) Climbing Azerbaijan's Machu Picchu

4 Xınalıq (p262)
Making repeated roadside photo stops amid the forests, canyons and passes that lead to this fabled mountain settlement with a language all of its own.

5 Qobustan (p251) Taking in Stone- and Bronze-Age petroglyphs and a nearby 'family' of wonderfully weird mud volcanoes.

6 Lahıc (p268)
Listening to sounds of copper-beaters resonating down the roughly stone-flagged main street of this picturesque ancient village.

7 Ateşgah (p252)
Learning about the spiritual imagery of flame in a still-burning historic fire temple.

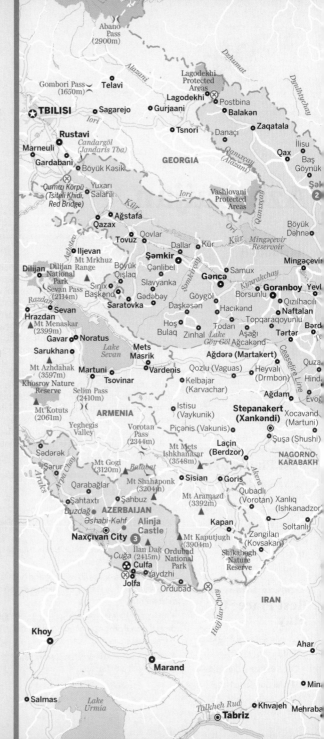

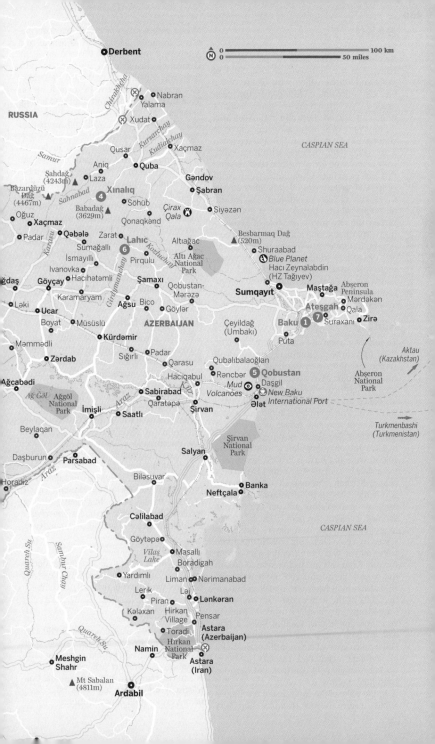

BAKU

♪ 012 / POP 2.26 MILLION

Azerbaijan's capital Baku (or Bakı in Azerbaijani) is the architectural love child of Paris and Dubai...albeit with plenty of Soviet genes floating half-hidden in the background. Few cities in the world are changing as quickly and nowhere else in the Caucasus do East and West blend as seamlessly or as chaotically. At its heart, the Unesco-listed İçəri Şəhər (Old City) lies within an exotically crenellated arc of fortress wall. Around this are gracefully illuminated stone mansions and pedestrianised tree-lined streets filled with exclusive boutiques. The second oil boom, which started around 2006, has turned the city into a crucible of architectural experimentation and some of the finest new buildings are jaw-dropping masterpieces. Meanwhile romantic couples canoodle their way around wooded parks and hold hands on the Caspian-front bulvar (promenade), where greens and opal blues make a mockery of Baku's desert-ringed location.

History

Though by then it was already ancient, Baku first came to prominence after an 1191 earthquake destroyed the region's previous capital, Şamaxı. Wrecked by Mongol attacks then vassal to the Timurids, it returned to brilliance under Shirvanshah Khalilullah I (1417–65), who completed his father's construction of a major palace complex. Yet, when Peter the Great captured the place in 1723, the city's population was less than 10,000 with any further growth hamstrung by a lack of drinking water. Everything changed when commercial oil extraction was deregulated in 1872. Workers and entrepreneurs arrived from all over the Russian Empire, swelling the population by 1200% in under 30 years, and Baku's thirst was slaked by a canal bringing potable mountain water all the way from the Russian border. By 1905 Baku was producing around 50% of the world's petroleum and immensely rich 'oil barons' built luxurious mansions outside the walls of the increasingly irrelevant Old City. Meanwhile, most oil workers lived in appalling conditions, making Baku a hotbed of labour unrest and revolutionary talk. Following a general strike in 1904, the Baku oil workers negotiated Russia's first-ever worker-management contract. But tensions continued to grow.

In the wake of the two Russian revolutions Baku's history became complex and very bloody with a series of brutal massacres between formerly neighbourly Armenian and Azerbaijani communities. When Azerbaijan's Democratic Republic was declared in 1918, Baku was initially still controlled by Bolsheviks, a position bolstered by a small British force that secretly sailed in from Iran hoping to defend the oilfields against the Turks (Britain's WWI enemies). Turkish and Azerbaijani troops eventually stormed the city as the British ignominiously withdrew by sea under cover of darkness. In the end game of WWI, the Turks were forced to evacuate, too. Baku became capital of independent Azerbaijan until 28 April 1920 when the Red Army marched in.

The Soviets subdivided the grand oil-boom villas into smaller flats while Stalin's anti-religion drive of the 1930s saw majestic mosques and a superb cathedral destroyed. In WWII, Baku escaped capture despite being top of Hitler's wish list but post-war oil investment dwindled, only resuming in earnest after independence. A second oil boom started around 2006 and is still playing out.

Religion in Baku

Although predominantly Muslim, Baku is a cosmopolitan city where pubs outnumber mosques. Some local women do wear headscarfs, but many more follow a beauty regime that is more inspired by Instagram fads and Russian glamour. Those dressed in head-to-toe black hijab will almost certainly be tourists from the Arabian Gulf countries. The influx of Middle Eastern visitors has also encouraged a few top hotels to offer female-only bathing slots in their swimming pool timetables.

Well-attended mosques include Təzə Pir (p235) and Əjdərbəy Məscidi (north of Təzə Bazar; p248) but there are also incense-filled Russian Orthodox churches, a Catholic chapel, and two active synagogues.

◉ Sights

A great Baku delight is simply wandering the streets, delving into Old City alleys and strolling the Bulvar in the cool of evening.

◉ Old City

İçəri Şəhər, Baku's Unesco-listed Old City, is photogenically ringed with stone walls and contains medieval caravanserais, tiny mosques, plentiful art galleries and dozens of eateries that brim with atmosphere. Contrastingly quiet back alleyways offer fascinating exploration opportunities.

The hefty 'double gates' pierce the Old City fortifications at their northeast corner with an **information centre** (Map p236; www.icherisheher.gov.az; Qüllə küç; ⊙10am-7pm) just inside. Here or at the ticket booth of the iconic Maiden's Tower, ask about walking tours and self-guided audio tours.

★**Maiden's Tower**   HISTORIC BUILDING
(Qız Qalası; Map p236; adult/student AZN15/6; ⊙10am-6.30pm mid-Apr–mid-Oct, 9am-5.30pm mid-Oct–mid-Apr) This tapering 29m stone tower is Baku's foremost historical icon, with rooftop views surveying Baku Bay and the Old City. Possibly millennia old, its construction date is the subject of much debate, though much of the present structure appears to be 12th century. The Azerbaijani name, Qız Qalası, is usually rendered 'Maiden's Tower' in English, leading to plenty of patently fictitious fairy tales. Various versions are considered in the imaginative little **multimedia installations** that adorn several floors of the tower's interior.

A better translation of Qız Qalası would be 'Virgin Tower', alluding to military impenetrability rather than any association with tragic females. It was certainly an incredibly massive structure for its era, with walls 5m thick at the base and an unusual projecting spine-buttress.

Set back from the tower is a small, former Medieval Market Square area now displaying a selection of historic stones. Some consider this to be the site where Jesus' disciple St Bartholomew was martyred.

★**Palace of the Shirvanshahs**   PALACE
(Şirvanşahlar Saray Kompleksi; Map p236; ☑012-4921073; http://shirvanshah.az/?lang=3; Qəsr küç 76; adult/student/child AZN15/5/0.20, guided tour/audio guide AZN20/15; ⊙10am-6.30pm mid-Apr–mid-Oct, to 5.30pm mid-Oct–mid-May) This splendid confection of sandstone walls and domes was the seat of northeastern Azerbaijan's ruling dynasty during the Middle Ages. Mostly 15th century, it was painstakingly (over)restored in 2003 with artefacts adding interest plus one or two entertaining audiovisual surprises. Enter via the main ceremonial courtyard. A small gateway on the left leads into the courtyard of the 1428 Divanxanə, an open-sided, octagonal rotunda where Shirvanshah Khalilullah I once assembled his court: a decidedly small court it would seem, judging from the structure's diminutive size.

To survey the whole palace complex without paying for entrance, buy a drink on the rooftop at Floors (p245).

Central Baku

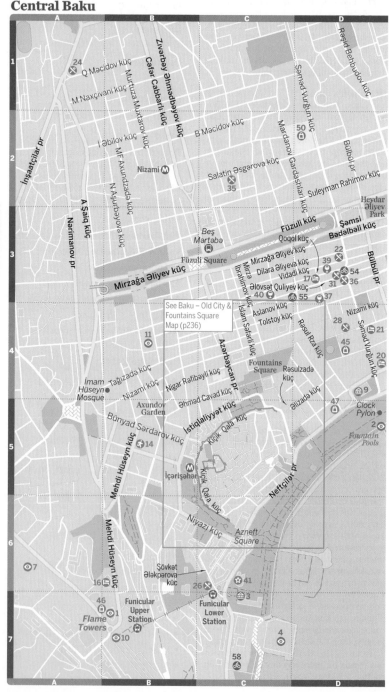

Ziverbəy Əhmədbəyov küç
Cəfər Cabbarlı küç
Q Məcidov küç
M Naxçivani küç
Murtuza Muxtarov küç
B Məcidov küç
İ Əbilov küç
MF Axundzadə küç
N Aşurbəyova küç
İnşaatçılar pr
A Şaiq küç
Nərimanov pr
Nizami
Mardanov Gardashlar küç
Salatin Əsgərova küç
Samed Vurğun küç
Bülbül pr
Suleyman Rahimov küç
Rəşid Behbudov küç
Heydar Əliyev Park
Beş Mərtəbə
Füzuli küç
Şəmsi Bədəlbəli küç
Qoqol küç
Mirzağa Əliyeva küç
Dilara Əliyeva küç
Vidadi küç
Ələvsət Quliyev küç
Füzuli Square
Mirzağa Əliyev küç
Mirza İbrahimov küç
Bülbül pr
22
39
54
31
36
17
40
55
37
Aslanov küç
Tolstoy küç
Nizami küç
Samed Vurğun küç
28
21
45
20
11
Tağızadə küç
Nizami küç
Nigar Rəfibəyli küç
Azərbaycan pr
İslam Səfərli küç
Rəsul Rza küç
Fountains Square
Rəsulzadə küç
Əlizadə küç
9
Imam Hüseyn Mosque
Axundov Garden
Əhməd Cavad küç
İstiqlaliyyat küç
Clock Pylon
47
2
Fountain Pools
Bünyad Sərdarov küç
Kiçik Qala küç
Mehdi Hüseyn küç
14
İçərişəhər
Kiçik Qala küç
Neftçilar pr
Mehdi Hüseyn küç
Niyazı küç
Azneft Square
7
Şövkət Ələkpərova küç
16
26
41
3
46
1
Flame Towers
Funicular Upper Station
Funicular Lower Station
4
10
58

See Baku – Old City & Fountains Square Map (p236)

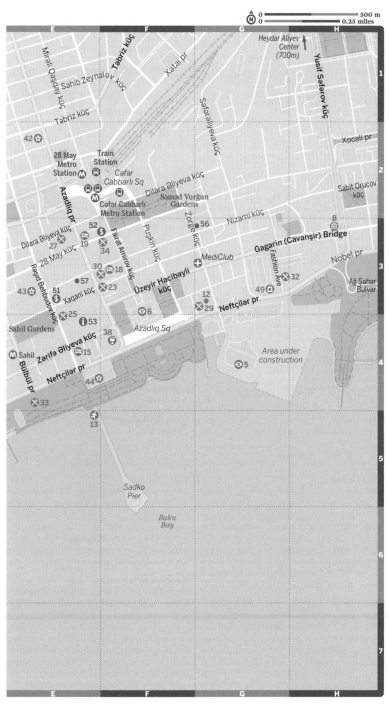

Central Baku

Cümə Mosque   MOSQUE
(Cümə məscidi; Map p236; Zeynallı küç) Though it appears relatively squat seen from outside, the interior of the Old City's carving-festooned 'Friday' mosque contains beautifully patterned interior vaults around a central dome and chandelier. The current structure dates from 1899, albeit built on the site of a 12th-century original with a minaret from 1437.

QGallery   GALLERY
(Map p236; ☑012-4927481; www.qgallery.net; Qüllə küç 6; ⊙10am-7pm Sun-Fri, 11am-7pm Sat) Of all the free-to-enter commercial galleries in Baku's atmospheric Old City, Q has the finest collection of 20th-century Azerbaijani art. It often stocks works by some of the nation's top names, including revered neo-impressionist Səttar Bəhlulzadə (1909–74).

Vahid Gardens   SQUARE
(Əliağa Vahid bağı; Map p236) An arched gateway in the Old City wall leads from İçerişəhər metro station to a pretty handkerchief of garden. It's dominated by the superbly imaginative bust of **poet Aliagha Vahid** (1895–1965), subtly incorporating characters from his works into the lines of his hair.

Museum of Miniature Books   MUSEUM
(Map p236; İçeri Şəhər; ⊙11am-5pm, closed Mon & Thu) **FREE** One of Baku's charming oddities, this small museum presents books that are so small you'd need a magnifying glass to read the print. The fact that so many minuscule publications have been printed at all is a surprise, and amassing the thousands shown here has been a lifetime's passion for collector Zərifə Salahova who started the place in 2002.

Sınıq Qala Mosque MOSQUE
(Məhəmməd Məscidi; Map p236) Partly dating from at least 1079, this little mosque is considered the the oldest still standing in Baku. Its nickname, 'Sınıq Qala' (Broken Tower), was gained when its typical local-style minaret was left damaged by a 1723 Russian naval bombardment. It was repaired around a century later but the name stuck.

Artım GALLERY
(Map p236; Kiçik Qala küç 5; ⊘ noon-8pm Tue-Sun) FREE Changing exhibitions are necessarily a little hit-and-miss at this experimental art space, which gives a platform to young or emerging new Azerbaijani artists. Don't miss sneaking up to the top floor to snap a perfectly framed photo of the Shirvanshahs' palace.

⊙ Central Baku

★ **Fountains Square** SQUARE
(Fəvvarəlör meydani; Map p236) Ever-popular with strollers, this leafy piazza forms Central Baku's natural focus. The fountains for which it is named include one topped by shiny silvered spheres giving fish-eye reflections of the trees and stone facades.

Historical Museum MUSEUM
(Map p236; ☑ 012-4933648; www.azhistory museum.az; HZ Tağiyev küç 4; foreigner/local AZN10/5; ⊘ 10am-6pm Tue-Sun, last entry 5pm) Well-presented exhibits on Azerbaijan's history and culture might miss the odd century here and there, but there's more than enough to fill several hours if you're really interested. If not, it's still worth a brief trot through to admire the opulent 1895–1901 mansion of HZ Tağiyev, one of Baku's greatest late-19th-century oil barons.

Don't miss the dazzling neo-Moorish 'Oriental Hall' and Tağiyev's rebuilt art-nouveau bedroom. Entry is free for university students on the first Wednesday of the month.

Museum Centre MUSEUM
(Map p232; Neftçilər pr 123; ⊘ 10am-5.30pm Tue-Sun) Once a Lenin Museum, this neoclassical building has a sternly photogenic facade that looks best seen from across the Bulvar. Inside, the top floor holds changing exhibitions, often good and usually free. The somewhat sparse 2nd-floor **Museum of Musical Culture** (AZN1) will teach you what it means to be a Tarzan in Azerbaijan. The 3rd-floor **Museum of Independence** (AZN5) gives a somewhat dry, if unashamedly partisan, political history of the nation.

Təzə Pir Mosque ARCHITECTURE
(Təzəpir Məscidi; Map p232; ☑ 012-4923855; http://qafqazislam.com; Sübhi küç) The grandest historic mosque in central Baku, Təzə Pir was built between 1903 and 1914, funded by a female philanthropist. More-recent renovations added gilding to its minaret tips and stone cladding to the surrounding buildings, which house the Centre for Islam in the Caucasus.

BAKU'S ART SCENE

Baku is buzzing with artistic energy. While the **State Art Museum** (Milli İncəsənət Muzeyi; Map p236; www.nationalartmuseum.az; Niyazi küç 9-11; adult/youth/student AZN10/5/2; ⊘ 10am-6pm Tue-Sun) is very competent and splendidly endowed, it's arguably more interesting (and cheaper) to flit between the Old City's excellent commercial minigalleries. The most imaginative include QGallery, **Kiçik Qalart** (Map p236; Qəsr Gardens; ⊘ 3-9pm Tue-Sun), **Bakı Gallery** ('Bakı' Rəsm Qalereyası; Map p236; Qəsr, 1st Lane 84; ⊘ 11am-7pm), Artım, the **Center of Contemporary Art** (Müasir İncəsənət Mərkəzi; Map p236; https://club-artcenter.blogspot.com; Qüllə küç 15; ⊘ 11am-8pm Tue-Sun) and **Ali Şamsi's studio** (Map p236; ☑ 055-7129894; www.ali-shamsi.com; Kiçik Qala küç 84; ⊘ vary), whose psychedelic exterior is a popular selfie spot even for those who don't venture inside.

Meanwhile the family home of Azerbaijan's greatest living painter, Tahir Salahov, has been converted into a **museum** (Map p236; www.facebook.com/TahirSalahovmuseum; İlyas Əfəndiyev küç 55/3; adult/student AZN2/0.60; ⊘ 9am-5.30pm) celebrating his work and featuring many of his later (if not classic) paintings, plus photos of him meeting everyone from Leonid Brezhnev to Michael Jackson.

Inspirationally wacky restaurant Mayak 13 (p244) reflects much of the feel you'll get at the city's superb modern-art gallery MOMA (p238). But for cutting-edge installations it's hard to beat the art collective Yarat – its Contemporary Art Centre on the Bulvar trumps the lot in terms of thoughtful provocation.

Baku – Old City & Fountains Square

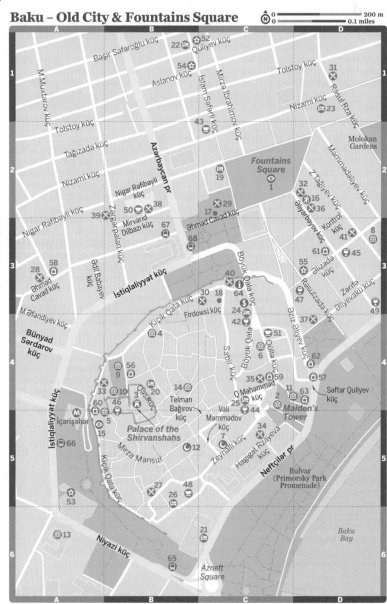

☉ Baku Bulvar

Fountains and fairground rides plus a growing selection of striking modernist buildings make Baku's long sweep of **bayfront park** (Map p232) eternally popular with families,

amateur musicians and courting couples. The Bulvar's liveliest section is behind **Park Bulvar Mall** (Map p232; www.parkbulvar.az; Neftçilər pr 78; ☉ 9am-midnight; ⊛ ⊞) with rare trees, cacti, fairground rides and cafes. Near the Carpet Museum there's even a **little**

Baku – Old City & Fountains Square

AZERBAIJAN BAKU

Venice, a compact parkland area of canals where you can rent your own gondola.

Nearby, the five storey Caspian Waterfront Mall (p247) – nearing completion at the time of research – is strikingly designed like a gigantic flower. From here, the Yeni Bulvar (new promenade) lacks shade so to save sweat, continue by renting a bicycle from **Velopark** (Map p232; Yeni Bulvar; city/mountain bike per hour AZN3/5). Then glide past the **Baku Eye** (Şeytan çarxı; ☑050-2956370; Bulvar; adult/child (6-12)/child under 6 AZN5/3/free; ⊙noon-10pm, closed in windy weather), a 60m ferris wheel, and **National Flag Square** (Dövlət Bayrağı meydanı) which was

briefly (2010) the site of the world's tallest flagmast. Beyond is a repurposed former naval dockyard now home to several upmarket restaurants, a steam engine and the cutting-edge contemporary gallery, Yarat.

Note that reaching the Bulvar requires getting across busy Neftçilər pr using relatively rare underpasses (at Flag Sq, the Carpet Museum or the Puppet Theatre), or at the traffic lights near Park Bulvar Mall.

★**Yarat Contemporary Art Centre** GALLERY
(www.yarat.az; Europa Park; ⊙11am-8pm Tue-Fri & Sun, 11am-11pm Sat; ☐5) **FREE** Yarat means

'create', a spirit that's in ample evidence in this centre's many thought-provoking installations that don't shy away from sociopolitical commentary. Even the cafe is inspired, set around a repurposed metal-press rescued as part of the revamping of this former naval-factory building.

Carpet Museum
MUSEUM

(Xalça Muzeyi; Map p232; www.azcarpetmuseum. az; Bulvar; adult/student AZN7/3, audio/human guide AZN3/8; ⊙10am-6pm Tue-Fri, to 8pm Sat & Sun) From historic flatweaves to modernist picture-rugs, this tailor-made museum displays and explains a superb collection of Azerbaijani carpets. It's housed in a 2014 building by Austrian architect Franz Janz, designed like a stylised roll of carpet. The idea probably looked great on paper but does create certain presentation difficulties, with some exhibits awkwardly placed on sloping or curving surfaces.

There's a carpet shop here, too, and this is where to come to secure the export permit if you've purchased any carpet over 2 sq metres (permit service closed Sundays).

Dom Soviet
ARCHITECTURE

(Government House; Map p232; Azadlıq Sq) Baku's most striking Soviet-era building is a gigantic stone construction fronted by an impressive series of layered stone arches and topped by rows of mini obelisks. It's at its most photogenic when uplit in the early evening, seen either from the upper floors of the JW Marriott Hotel or from the fountain pools across the Bulvar.

Crescent Moon Building
ARCHITECTURE

(Map p232; Bulvar) Several gleaming towers are under construction at Crescent Bay opposite Port Baku, including a potentially phenomenal architectural attention-grabber in the form of a gigantic upside-down crescent moon. That building remains unfinished – construction is reportedly stalled due to technical problems with the upper curve – but once finished it should be yet another great architectural legacy for the city.

⊙ Flame Towers Area

For a fine view over the bay and city centre it's worth climbing onto the ridge that's unmistakably marked by Baku's iconic Flame Towers. Access is possible by funicular (Funikulyor; Şövkət Ələkpərova küç; AZN1; ⊙10am-1pm & 2-10pm Tue-Sun), by a 15-minute stairway climb from the Bulvar, or by bus 18 from the Monolit stop (Map p236; Ahmad Cavad küç) just west of Fountains Sq.

★ Flame Towers
ARCHITECTURE

(Alov Qüllələri; Map p232; Mehdi Hüseyn küç; light show dusk-midnight; ☐6, 18) Completed in 2012, this trio of sinuous blue-glass skyscrapers forms contemporary Baku's architectural signature. The three towers range from 28 to 33 storeys – so huge that they're most impressive seen from a considerable distance, especially at night when they form a vast palette for a light show which interchanges between fire effects, pouring water and the national flag.

Şəhidlər Xiyabanı
CEMETERY

(Martyr's Lane; Map p232; Gülüstü Park; ⊙24hr) The most notable feature of the 'Highland Park' that stretches south from the Flame Towers is this sombre row of grave memorials – Bakuvian victims of the Red Army's 1990 attack, along with early martyrs of the Karabakh conflict.

Fəxri Xiyaban
CEMETERY

(Alley of Honour; Map p232; Parlament pr 7; ⊙10am-7pm; ☐6) Since 1948 this attractively tree-shaded graveyard has been set aside as the last resting place for Azerbaijan's foremost public figures. Many of the memorials are impressive works of statuary. Former president Heydar Əliyev's tomb, located here, is the first place that any dignitary is likely to be taken during an official visit to Baku.

⊙ East of the Centre

By public transport, bus 1 from the train station gets you to MOMA then on to the Heydar Aliyev Center. From a block north of there, bus 5 takes you back to the Old City area via the train station.

★ Heydar Aliyev Center
ARCHITECTURE

(Heydər Əliyev Mərkəzi; www.heydaraliyevcenter.az; Heydər Əliyev pr 1; adult/student AZN15/2; ⊙11am-6pm Mon-Fri, to 5pm Sat & Sun; ☐1, 2, 5) Vast and jaw-droppingly original, this Zaha Hadid building is a majestic statement of fluid 21st-century architecture forming waves and peaks that seem to melt together. The real delight is simply pondering and photographing the extraordinary exterior from ever-changing angles. The interior is impressive, too, and hosts concerts and exhibition spaces. Arguably the best part of the permanent collection is 'Treasures of Azerbaijan', which walks you through the nation's cultural highlights.

MOMA
GALLERY

(Baku Museum of Modern Art, Bakı Müasir İncəsənət Muzeyi, MIM; Map p232; ☎012-4908404; www. moma.az/en; Yusif Səfərov küç 5; adult/student/child

AZN5/2/free; ⊘11am-9pm Tue-Sun, last entry 8pm; ▣1, 2) This joyous tailor-made gallery uses struts and tubing to create a wide variety of intimate viewing spaces, in many of which you can recline on bean-bag sofas as you contemplate the extensive collection of mind-bending, predominantly post-1980 Azerbaijani art. Upstairs, some earlier 20th-century canvases also appear, along with three original Picassos, a Dalí and a Chagal.

Eastbound buses 1 and 2 from the train station stop directly across a thundering 12-lane road from the gallery. To find the returning buses, however, you'll need to walk two blocks north.

Azər-İlmə   WORKSHOP
(☑012-4659036, 050-2509607; http://azerilme. az/en; Şəmsi Rəhimov küç 2; ⊘9am-1pm & 2-6pm; ▣88) Hand-woven carpets using wool coloured with vegetable dyes are created before your eyes in this amazingly grand, suburban gallery-workshop that includes a museum-like selection of traditional handicrafts. Tours are free and in English with no sales pressure. Ideally call ahead.

🏃 Activities

Tazə Bəy Hamamı   BATHHOUSE
(Map p232; ☑012-4373444, 012-4926440; www. tazebey.az; Şeyk Şamil küç 30; bathing AZN23; ⊘10am-midnight) This 1886 stone-vaulted bathhouse (men only) is merrily overloaded with knick-knacks and kitschy statuettes but as the bar areas are more evocative than the sauna and small modern pool, you might prefer to simply come for a beer to soak up the atmosphere. Three doors down, the equivalent for women is **İncə Kaprizlər**, albeit not quite as wacky.

Mirvari   BOATING
(Map p232; Sadko Pier; standard/deluxe AZN3/ 10; ⊘typically 7-11pm, during fine weather May-Oct) If the weather is encouraging, you can take a 30-minute pleasure-boat cruise around Baku Bay on a sleek three-level motor yacht. You don't go far out to sea and the main attraction is watching the city lights, so many departures are at night.

☞ Tours

A couple of youthful guides run 'free' city walking tours, though naturally you're expected to tip. Probably the best is led by **Gani** (Map p236; https://bakufreetour.com; ⊘11am): his English is good and he carries a file of historical maps and pictures to add context (tour 2½ hours). Sign up online.

If you want a similar tour that goes inside the main monuments, consider the very professional outfit **Baku Sightseeing** (Map p232; ☑050-2911103; www.bakusightseeing.com; Azadlıq Sq 674; ⊘phone bookings 24hr, office 9am-8pm Mon-Fri, 10am-7pm Sat & Sun). It also offers some quirky private tours including one on the metro, another visiting teahouses and – best of all – a 'Hello Comrades' tour giving insights into Soviet-era Baku.

There are dozens of tour outfits that offer group and tailored excursions to a range of destinations around Azerbaijan. These can prove worthwhile for visiting Qobustan (p251) and the Abşeron Peninsula (p252) but the value of punishingly long day trips to Qəbələ or Xınalıq is less clear. For those places, organising your own trip and staying overnight is likely to be more satisfying and generally cheaper, if more fiddly. A great alternative is to join highly recommended Camping Azerbaijan (p303) for one of its fixed-departure group hiking trips. These provide transport to and from trailheads along with a walking guide and, usually, a meal in a rustic village home en route. Several other copycat groups offer much the same formula, including MountainHost (www.facebook.com/moun tainhost.az) and BagBaku (p303).

🎊 Festivals & Events

Azerbaijan Grand Prix   SPORTS
(www.bakucitycircuit.com; ⊘late Apr) One of the Caucasus' biggest sporting events, this Formula One race uses a city circuit which shows off Baku's beautiful streetscapes to world cameras but causes residents plenty of traffic chaos for several weeks around the main event. The pits area is on Azadlıq meydanı, the large square in front of Dom Soviet.

Baku Jazz Festival   MUSIC
(www.bakujazzfestival.com; ⊘Oct) In past years, headline acts at Baku's world-class jazz festival have included Herbie Hancock and Aziza Mustafa Zadeh. See website for venues.

🛏 Sleeping

🛏 Old City

★**Buta Hotel**   GUESTHOUSE $
(Map p236; ☑050-3181439, 012-4923475; www. butahotel.com; Qəsr küç 16; prebooked s/d AZN76/85, walk-in AZN60/70; ❋🔊) This well-kept nine-room gem is entered via a lounge decked with cushions and traditional copperwork. Climb the stairs past etchings and a few antiques to well-presented if unfussy

rooms with well-functioning showers, assorted art and clean, wood-effect floors. Breakfast is on the 4th floor in a glass-walled, rooftop dining room with superb views but no lift. Room 7 is particularly spacious with fine views from its bathroom window.

★**Sultan Inn** BOUTIQUE HOTEL $$
(Map p236; ☑055-4040029, 012-4372305; www. sultaninn.com; Böyük Qala küç 20; s/d AZN160/180; ✸🛜) This luxurious 11-room boutique hotel hits a fine balance between opulent elegance and cosy comfort, with superhigh ceilings, gilt-edged doors and highly obliging service. The perfectly central Old City location is a great plus.

Sweet House Boutique Hotel GUESTHOUSE $$
(Map p236; ☑050-5560504; info.sweethouse hotel@gmail.com; Vali Məmmədov küç 6; r AZN80-100; ✸🛜) Sweet is a fair description for this little warren of rooms and courtyards, recycling a couple of small houses and including some ivy-covered half-built 'ruins' to create a lovable boutique guesthouse. Owners speak good English and the Old City location is a joy. Walk-in prices can be as low as AZN50.

Shah Palace Hotel HERITAGE HOTEL $$$
(Map p236; ☑012-4970405; www.shahpalace hotel.com; Böyük Qala küç 47; r AZN200; ✸🛜) Entering this upmarket charmer gives a little of the frisson of arriving in a fairy-tale Middle Eastern palace. The four-storey colonnaded courtyard is filled with birdsong and retains historic well-shafts from which archaeological finds have been kept. Rooms are liable to overload the senses with all the gilt and brocade, but if it's glitz you want, this place is hard to pass up. There's a small sauna and splendid *hamman* (bathhouse). Paying by credit card costs 18% extra.

Four Seasons Baku LUXURY HOTEL $$$
(Map p236; ☑012-4042424; www.fourseasons. com/baku; Neftçilər pr; d/ste from AZN421/799; ✸@🛜🏊) This majestic flower-filled beaux arts palace fits perfectly with central Baku's nouveau-Parisian self-image, while the indulgent pool and spa feel more Roman. Of the city's numerous swanky addresses the Four Seasons' combination of comfort, location and timeless style are unbeatable, assuming your budget will stretch this far.

🛏 City Centre

★**Sahil Hostel** HOSTEL $
(Map p232; ☑050-8882101; www.sahilhostel.com; 4th fl, Zərifə Əliyeva küç 61; dm/s/d AZN12/48/52;

✸@🛜) Large, modern and sparkling clean, this central hostel is hard to fault, from the excellent bunks to the helpful, multilingual staff to the chilled bar-lounge area. The private en suite rooms are a great budget option for couples.

Kaha Hostel HOSTEL $
(Map p232; ☑050-4741555; www.facebook.com/ kahahostel; Qoqol/Mardanov küç 13; dm AZN12-19, d without bathroom AZN43; ⊙24hr; ✸🛜) Kaha is a well-appointed, high-ceilinged hostel run by switched-on, multilingual, eco-aware folks who seem more interested in creating a convivial social atmosphere than on making money. With its big, single table, the lounge becomes a popular cross-cultural conversation space. Some dorms are slightly cramped and the bunks a little squeaky but each has a lamp and power point. Decent sized lockers, tiny kitchen, 24-hour staff and fun location handy for Baku's cheapest and most-alternative bars and cafes.

Travel Inn Hostel HOSTEL $
(Map p232; ☑012-4981008; info@travelinnhostel. com; 3rd fl, Xaqani küç 20; dm AZN10-12; ⊙24hr; ✸🛜) This hostel is slick, comfortable and comes with ample safe storage and plentiful bathrooms. High ceilings, good air-con, kitchen, TV room and 24-hour reception are all benefits.

Royal Palace Hotel HOTEL $
(Baku Palace Hotel; Map p236; ☑070-3961071, 012-5961071; www.instagram.com/royalpalace baku; İslam Səfərli küç 23; r from AZN50, Jun-Aug from AZN80; ✸🛜) Converted from a luxury apartment, the Royal (ex 'Baku') Palace has expansive, totally renovated rooms with flamboyant flourishes, kettles and brand-new bathrooms. Rooms are accessed from marble hallways and a spiral of staircase wrapped around a long, crystal chandelier.

Sapphire City Hotel LUXURY HOTEL $$
(Map p236; ☑012-4988006; www.sapphire.az; Nizami küç 64; r from AZN180; ✸🛜) The lobby's chandeliers, fresh orchids, gilt-legged rococo furniture and elegantly attired staff set the scene for similarly indulgent guestrooms. The location is superbly central, a block from Fountains Sq.

Azcot Hotel GUESTHOUSE $$
(Map p236; ☑012-4972507; www.azcothotel.com; Nigar Rəfibəyli küç 38b; s/d from AZN80/100; ✸🛜) In a fabulously central 1885 mansion, period settees, large Chinese vases and tasteful landscape paintings give character to the

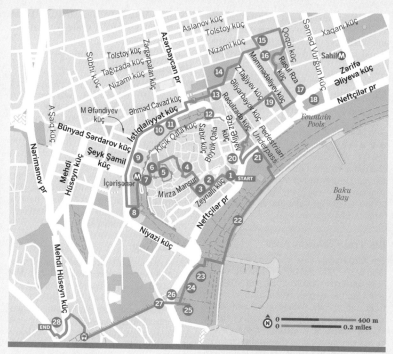

🏃 City Walk
Exploring Central Baku

START MAIDEN'S TOWER
END FLAME TOWERS
LENGTH 4KM; AT LEAST THREE HOURS

From ❶ **Maiden's Tower** (p231) wander colourfully touristy ❷ **Zeynallı küç** to the ❸ **Cümə Mosque** (p234), then pick your way through the Old City's most lived-in ❹ **backstreets** to the ❺ **Palace of the Shirvanshahs** (p231). Peep into a few art galleries, the free ❻ **Museum of Miniature Books** (p234) and the curious shop-cave ❼ **Ovdan** (p247). Exit İçəri Şəhər onto grand İstiqlaliyyət küç near the handsomely renovated ❽ **Filarmoniya** (p247) concert hall. Curving northeast you'll pass the noble, late-19th-century ❾ **Baku City Hall**, the equally grand ❿ **Institute of Manuscripts** and ⓫ **İsmailiyya Palace**.

Beyond lies the Old City's sturdy, castle-style ⓬ **Double Gateway**, while on your left is the ⓭ **Nizami Literature Museum**, its facade inset with statues of revered poets. Behind that, ⓮ **Fountains Square** (p235)

is a great place for people-watching and cafe life. Wander pedestrianised shopping street ⓯ **Nizami küç**, cross ⓰ **Molokan Gardens**, pass the boutiques of ⓱ **Rəsul Rza küç** and spy the Soviet-acropolis-style ⓲ **Museum Centre** (p235), a former Lenin museum. The tree-lined streets to the northwest are full of pubs, restaurants and century-old 'oil-boom' mansions, including one that houses the ⓳ **Historical Museum** (p235).

Peruse more ⓴ **boutiques** on Əziz Əliyev küç then use the pedestrian underpass, emerging beside the dinky 1910 ㉑ **Puppet Theatre**. Stroll along the ㉒ **Bulvar** (p236), gazing across the Caspian's oil-rainbowed waters and passing ㉓ **Veneziya** (little Venice), where gondolas punt on a small loop of artificial canals. Admire the ㉔ **International Muğam Centre** (p247) and visit the major ㉕ **Carpet Museum** (p238). Cross back to the ㉖ **Bahram Gur** dragon-slaying statue-fountain and take the ㉗ **funicular** to Highland Park for city panoramas and close-up views of the huge and impressive ㉘ **Flame Towers** (p238).

corridors, but don't expect a big business hotel. The 48 rooms are spacious with kettles and minibars but the furniture is functional and with the odd sign of wear here and there.

🛏 Flame Towers Area

Fairmont Flame Towers LUXURY HOTEL **$$$**
(Map p232; ☑012-5654848; www.fairmont.com/baku; Mehdi Hüseyn küç 1a; r from AZN268; ✷🛜�) Occupying one of the iconic Flame Towers, this is the spectacular hotel whose 'thousand diamond necklace' atrium wowed Joanna Lumley in her 2019 TV tour of the Caucasus. No, you don't have to take the €5000-a-night presidential suite that featured in that episode.

🛏 Train Station Area

Old Yard Hotel GUESTHOUSE **$**
(Map p232; ☑012-4934167, 077-5312121; oldyardhotel@gmail.com; Azadlıq pr 28; s/d AZN45/55; ✷🛜) Simple inexpensive rooms close to the train station come with good AC and decent wi-fi. There is a small but well-equipped shared kitchenette–sitting room where guests can meet each other and help themselves to drinking water, tea and instant coffee. Follow the signs off Azadıq pr into an inner courtyard marked '16/21' to find the little reception booth.

★Landmark Hotel BUSINESS HOTEL **$$$**
(Map p232; ☑012-4652000; www.thelandmarkhotel.az; Nizami küç 90a; d/ste AZN192/299; ✷@🛜🚺) Stunning views complement suave decor softened with patchwork headboards and cobble-tiled bathrooms with giant rain-shower heads. All rooms count as 'executive', allowing access to the top floor self-service bar, while the bay views are superb from the breakfast room with its excellent buffet spread. There's also a sizeable gym, long-if-narrow swimming pool and sauna. The entrance is oddly hard to spot: pass what seems to be just a security desk then a series of very bold murals and take the lift to the 19th floor for check-in.

Dinamo Hotel DESIGN HOTEL **$$$**
(Map p232; ☑012-3772000; www.dinamohotelbaku.com; Zərifə Əliyeva küç 32; r from AZN250, ste AZN380; ✷🛜🚺) No expense has been spared in converting this former Soviet sports centre into a 28-room art deco hotel. It's full of triumphalist sporting references, hi-tech gadgets (like electronic window blinds), a retractable roof over the gorgeous

swimming pool and a Michelin-starred chef running the kitchen. A white Bentley provides guest transport.

🛏 Bus Station

Crossway Hotel HOTEL **$**
(☑055-2247171, 012-4060133; www.crossway.az; 5th fl, Main Bus Station, Sumqayıt Hwy; s/d/ste AZN20/40/50; ✷🛜; 🚌14, 37, 96) The bus station is miles from town so it's worth considering sleeping at this bargain-value place if you have an early-morning bus to catch. Apart from some old carpeting, standards are good for the price. Rooms aren't luxurious, but they have comfy beds and bathrooms with toiletries. Reception speaks English, there's a 24-hour cafe-restaurant and the central atrium-lounge looks rather smart.

🍴 Eating

Baku is a culinary treat and many good midrange restaurants offer weekday lunch-deal menus for AZN10 or less. Some budget restaurants have full meals for AZN5. Always check before ordering tea: in some lounge-style places a tea-and-jams set might cost AZN30 or more. Many restaurants are halal, at least one is kosher (p245).

🍴 Old City & Fountains Square

An enticing cluster of tourist-friendly restaurants hug the northern Old City wall along Kiçik Qala street, with plenty more in the streets around Fountains Sq. There's a **Bravo supermarket** (Map p236; Əhməd Cavad küç 3; ⊘24hr) near Axundov Sq and **Elxanoğlu** (Map p236; Rəsul Rza küç 28g; qutab AZN0.5-1; ⊘24hr) has hot bread fresh from the *təndir* (clay oven) for 50q.

Firuzə AZERBAIJANI **$**
(Map p236; ☑012-4934934; Əliyarbəyov küç 28a; mains AZN5-15, steak/fish AZN19/22, beer/fresh juice from AZN3/6; ⊘noon-1am) Fountains Sq's long-lasting subterranean favourite is an attractive stone-walled basement draped in local carpets with tablecloths embroidered in a similar style. Good air-con and a non-smoking section add further appeal to a phenomenally wide-ranging Azerbaijani menu. It includes some vegetarian options: try the garlic-rich *badımcan sırdağı* (an eggplant-potato-tomato dish). Service adds 10%.

★Paris Bistro FRENCH **$$**
(Map p236; ☑012-4048215; www.facebook.com/ParisBistroAz; Zərifə Əliyeva pr 1/4; mains AZN10-

19, snacks AZN6-15, coffee/beer/wine/bubbles from AZN3.50/4/7.50/9; ⊙24hr; 🛜) It's hard to believe there are more than a few metres from the Champs-Élysées in this perfectly pitched French masterpiece. It hits all the right Parisian notes down to the plane trees which curve out from an appealing park-facing street terrace. Waiters in claret aprons busy themselves delivering garlic escargots, duck breast with tapenade or flaming crème brûlée.

Passage 1901 — MULTICUISINE $$

(Map p236; ✆012-5555556; www.facebook.com/Passage-1901-396317184089820; Mirvarid Dilbazı küç; mains AZN7-16; ⊙9am-11pm; 🛜) For good, fair-priced Azerbaijani food in an unusual setting, visit the main restaurant section in this cavernous former market hall, which uses many mid-20th-century elements to conjure up nostalgic memories of Soviet-style bazaars.

Qaynana — AZERBAIJANI $$

(Map p236; ✆070-4340013; www.facebook.com/qaynanarestaurant; Kiçik Qala 126; mains AZN8-16, qutab AZN1, beer AZN4.40; ⊙8am-11pm; 🛜) Big glass windows illuminate a plethora of pickle jars and hanging rugs, festive musical rhythms create further atmosphere and at the back, big *tandir* (clay ovens) ensure a supply of fresh baked bread to accompany a range of Azerbaijani specialities.

CafeCity — INTERNATIONAL $$

(Map p236; www.cafecity.az; İslam Səfərli küç 1a; mains AZN9-17, beer from AZN3; ⊙9am-midnight Sun-Thu, to 1am Fri & Sat; 🛜) Picture menus offer mouthwatering arrays of both Azerbaijani and international cuisine and there's a special section of *sağlam həyat* (healthy-eating) options. The decor is fashion-conscious without undue pretensions, adding tasteful carved screenwork to three elegant old-Baku buildings. The original location has an in-demand summer terrace just off Fountains Sq, but there's also an immensely popular branch at **Statistika** (Map p232; İnşaatçılar pr 112a; mains AZN5-25; ⊙9am-midnight; 🛜) and a wine-bar version at **Sahil Gardens** (Map p232; Rəşid Behbudov küç 8; mains AZN8-24; ⊙9am-1am; 🛜).

Cizz-Bizz — AZERBAIJANI, INTERNATIONAL $$

(Map p236; ✆012-5055001; www.facebook.com/cizzbizzoldcity; Kiçik Qala küç 114; mains AZN8.80-17.60 plus AZN3.30 garnish, coffee/beer/wine/cocktail from AZN4/4/6/6; ⊙8am-2am) Stone floors, hanging flower baskets, a shady terrace and contrived but well-thought-out attempts at old-world decor all combine to

make spaciously open Cizz-Bizz an understandable magnet for Old City tourists. The food covers a range of Azerbaijani bases and adds alternatives including trout (AZN11), and chicken in white-wine sauce (AZN16.50).

Museum Inn — INTERNATIONAL $$

(Map p236; ✆012-4971522; www.museuminn.az; Q Məhəmməd küç 3; mains AZN8-30, beer from AZN4; ⊙noon-11pm; 🛜) The eight-room hotel is a tad kitschy but the front two tables of the upstairs restaurant have the best view of the Maiden's Tower (p231) of any Old City eatery. Decent pastas are reasonably priced and there's a range of other international and local dishes.

Namaste — INDIAN $$

(Adams Curries; Map p236; http://namastebaku.com; Əliyarbəyov küç 12; mains AZN9-20, rice AZN4; ⊙1-11.30pm; 🛜) There is now a plethora of more-exotic Indian options in the main nightlife area but Namaste (formerly Adams) is a reliable, family-owned place for genuine curries and it's a long-standing stalwart of the Baku expat scene.

Zakura — JAPANESE $$

(Map p236; ✆012-4981818; www.zakura.az; Əlizadə küç 9; mains from AZN8; ⊙11.30am-10.30pm; 🛜) While Baku has more-upmarket Japanese options, Zakura combines stylish modernist decor with great-value food. The weekday lunch deal is one of Baku's foremost dining bargains.

★ Paul's — STEAK $$$

(Map p236; ✆055-5200092; www.pauls-baku.com; Zərgəpalan küç; steak AZN25.50-63, sides/dips AZN6/2, beer AZN4.50-9.90; ⊙6-10pm Mon-Sat; 🛜) It's inconspicuous, comfortably unpretentious and the menu is short. But if you want perfectly cooked, top-quality steak, this German-Austrian yard-garden can't be bettered. Pork shashlik, Bratwurst and Thüringer sausages are also specialities. For winter there's a wooden cottage area inside; in summer much seating is outdoors, shaded by plane trees. Reservations advised at weekends.

Art Club — AZERBAIJANI $$$

(Map p236; ✆050-4442013, 012-4922013; www.artgroup.az; Zeynallı küç 9; kebabs AZN10-17, mains AZN25-60; ⊙noon-11pm; 🛜) A flight of silver doves over the doorway welcome diners into what is as much a gallery as a restaurant with canvases on the walls and artefacts beneath glass floor circles. Food prices are high but so is the quality and the ambience is soothingly calm.

AZERBAIJAN BAKU

Mayak 13 — FUSION $$$

(Map p236; ☎077-5050304, 012-5050304; https://instagram.com/mayak_13; Kiçik Qala 54; mains AZN14-35; ⊗noon-10.30pm; 🙊) If you liked Altay Sadikhzade's cartoon-esque work at Baku MOMA, you'll adore the interior of his eccentric Mayak 13 Cafe. Marvellously absurd rope-tied abstracts represent ripped sails and intersperse a gamut of nautical bric-a-brac. Merrily naive lighthouses, landscapes and portraits splatter bare stone walls. The small selection of beautifully prepared Azer-Euro fusion dishes are classily served, but the portions are nouvelle-cuisine petite. The place is rarely crowded; indeed you might get it all to yourself some evenings, which adds to the surreal experience.

Muğam Club — AZERBAIJANI $$$

(Map p236; ☎012-4924085; Həqiqət Rzayeva küç 9; meals/kebabs from AZN20/15; ⊗11am-11pm) This historic two-storey caravanserai wraps its alcoved stone walls around a coverable courtyard featuring two dwarf fig trees and a trickling fountain. It's a quintessential Baku experience that's very photogenic, and the Azerbaijani food is good. However, prices are steep and this is a place that's squarely aimed at feasting groups rather than individuals or couples.

🍴 Central Baku

There are concentrations of high-quality eateries in the **JW Marriott Absheron Hotel** (Map p232; www.facebook.com/JWMarriott AbsheronBaku; Azadlıq Sq 674; ⊗vary per venue; 🙊) at the southern end of the Bulvar, with plenty more in the fashionable (if rather soulless) wind tunnel of the **Port Baku dining strip** (Map p232; Fashion Ave; ⊗9am-11pm; 🙊) and at **Park Bulvar Mall** (Map p232; www. parkbulvar.az; Bulvar; ⊗10am-midnight). A trio of East Asian restaurants in the **Landmark Building** (Map p232; Nizami küç; ⊗vary per restaurant; 🙊) offer excellent midweek lunch deals aimed at local office workers.

Central 24-hour supermarkets include **Spar** (Map p232; Səməd Vurğun küç 59; ⊗24hr) and **Bravo** (Map p232; Xaqanı küç; ⊗24hr).

Samik Cafe & Restaurant — AZERBAIJANI $

(Map p232; ☎012-4983933; 28 May küç 76a; mains AZN2.20-6.50, fish AZN4-11, garnish AZN1-2.50, tea glass/pot AZN0.60/2.50; ⊗24hr; 🙊) Though it's one of the cheapest central places around, Samik has a certain degree of elegance with touches of gilding on its arched vaulting and attractive embroidery for tablecloths. Open all night, its unsophisticated Caucasian food is a godsend for those arriving in Baku on a dawn train.

★ Şirvanşah Muzey-Restoran — AZERBAIJANI $$

(Map p232; ☎050-2420903, 012-5950901; www. facebook.com/shirvanshahmuzeyrestoran; Salatın Əsgərova küç 86; mains AZN5-15; ⊗noon-11pm) On an unassuming backstreet, this enticing place started life as a 19th-century bathhouse but is now a veritable ethnographic museum of handicrafts and knick-knacks that's sometimes used as a film set. Reliable Azerbaijani food covers a similarly wide range, but really you come here for the atmosphere. Over a dozen rooms are themed to different historical eras, from rustic craftsman's workshops to Soviet *aparachik*'s office.

Partizan — RUSSIAN $$

(Map p232; ☎077-6194145; www.instagram.com/ partizanrestaurant; Bəşir Səfiroğlu küç; mains AZN8-21; ⊗11am-11pm) Fun, full of character and not as kitschy as it might sound, this theatre-dining experience has waiters dressed as Soviet soldiers who demand a password (your booking) and might bark orders at guests or break into a gun-toting dance while an accordionist plays 'Kalinka'. The menu of mostly Russian and Azerbaijani favourites comes dressed as Pravda.

Partizan has no sign but is easy enough to spot, opposite the Lucky 13 Pub on the short lane that links Bəşir Səfiroğlu küç to Əlövsət Quliyev küç. Getting in without prebooking is hit-and-miss.

Entrée — CAFE, BAKERY $$

(Map p232; www.facebook.com/Entree.az; Dilarə Əliyeva küç; snacks/meals from AZN2.50/8; ⊗9am-10pm; ❄🙊) Entrée is an appealing bakery-cafe chain whose Baku flagship is this big, suave branch with a glass-walled kitchen, comfy seating and excellent coffee.

Imereti — GEORGIAN $$

(Map p232; ☎012-4934181; Xaqani küç; mains AZN8-12, xacapuri 8; ⊗10am-11pm) There are several fancier places with similar menus, but this unpretentious little basement remains our long-term favourite in central Baku for genuine Georgian food with a cosy atmosphere and homemade wine by the litre (AZN15).

SAHiL — AZERBAIJANI $$$

(Map p232; ☎012-4048212, 050-2850022; www. sahilbaku.az; Neftçilər pr 34, Bulvar; mains AZN12-28, sturgeon AZN40-250; ⊗noon-midnight; 🙊) Faultless Azerbaijani and Persian cuisine in a suave-but-relaxed setting right on the Bulvar. It's one of few places to offer *shah plov* (a giant ball of mixed-ingredient rice pilaf) by portion, and to offer *mirzaghassemi* (a delicious South Caspian eggplant and garlic mash). If money is no option it also has real caviar and stuffed sturgeon.

7/40
KOSHER $$$

(Map p232; ☎ 051-2500784, 012-4048224; www. facebook.com/7_40_baku_kosher; Səməd Vurğun küç; meze dishes AZN5-11, mains AZN14-27, falafel AZN7; ☺ 11am-11pm Sun-Thu, to 4pm Fri; ☎) The 100% kosher food is the main draw of this relaxed, upper-market restaurant, but whatever your diet or religion, the menu offers a lot of tempting creativity. Selections include lamb-stuffed quince (AZN15) and roast chicken with vodka and clementine (tangerine). Full bar.

Chinar
ASIAN $$$

(Map p232; ☎ 012-4048211, 051-4048211; www. chinar-dining.az; Şövkət Ələkpərova küc 1; snacks AZN8-21, mains AZN14-44, cocktails from AZN10; ☺ noon-1am Sun-Thu, to 2am Fri & Sat, reduced kitchen after 11pm; ☎) This fashion-conscious lounge-restaurant sports a 'theatre kitchen' producing sophisticated East Asian and Asian-fusion dishes, plus steaks and real caviar (AZN250). After 11pm it morphs into a bar with sushi available till closing time.

Click the QR code on the menu for pictures of the dishes. Service charge 5%.

✕ Batamdar

Teleqüllə
INTERNATIONAL $$$

(☎ 070-7707070, 012-5370808; www.telequlle. az; Ak Abbaszadə küç 2; kebabs AZN10-25, mains AZN20-50, beer/wine/cocktails from AZN6/8/15; ☺ 10.30am-11pm) Dining at this revolving restaurant is the only way to gain access to Baku's iconic Soviet-era TV tower. Views are stupendous and the upscale menu includes interesting options like sturgeon in pomegranate (AZN40) and tenderloin in cognac-gorgonzola sauce (AZN30). Reservations are usually required. There is an AZN20 'deposit' (ie minimum per-person charge) that can be recouped against purchases of drinks or food.

Take bus 3 from the Flame Towers to the Zoological Institute stop, then walk seven minutes steeply down to the entrance portal. From here a surreal tunnel of lights and gilding lead 85m to the tower's elevator.

If you don't want to pay the deposit, you could have a drink at the outdoor ground-floor terrace section which has excellent views of its own.

🍷 Drinking & Nightlife

Expat-style bars are concentrated to the southeast of Fountains Sq towards Əlizadə küç. There's even a **Hard Rock Cafe** (Map p236; ☎ 012-4048228; www.hardrockcafe.com/location/baku; Əziz Əliyev küç 8; beer/cocktails from AZN16/11, burgers AZN16-24; ☺ noon-1am; ☎). For much cheaper beer (from AZN1) try the bars and quirky cafes on Qoqol küç and half hidden along nearby streets, notably Aslanov and Tolstoy. Plush new lounge bars and tea parlours are scattered far more widely. Polish up a platinum credit card to join the city's glam-set clubbers at **Enerji** (☎ 050-7007057; www.enerji.az; National Flag Sq; ☺ noon-midnight Sun-Thu, to 4am Fri & Sat) or pass a stringent dress code to get into the ever-shifting hipster rave-club **iN** (https://inclubbaku.com; Ceyhun Səlimov küç 18a; ☺ see website).

Pubs & Bars

★ Old School Cafe
BAR

(Map p232; www.facebook.com/oldschool.cafe andshop; Topçubaşov küç; ☺ noon-2am; ☎) Old School is a wonderfully off-beat hang-out for intellectual young Bakuvians. The sign is a typewriter and the interior decked with clocks, cameras and old-school chairs – hence the name. Although there are occasional live concerts, this is more a place for conversation over a slowly sipped beer or herbal tea.

Floors
BAR

(Map p236; ☎ 070-4920117; www.facebook.com/floorsbaku; Qəsr dongəsi 1; dry/sweet wine from AZN9/7, shots AZN5, beer AZN4; ☺ 4pm-2am; ☎) Each storey of this enticing Old City bar has its own character, including a gallery lounge on floor 2, but the most spectacular feature is the rooftop terrace. Its late-afternoon view of the Shirvanshahs' palace (p231) is alone worth the price of a drink.

Avto Stop
PUB

(Map p232; Qoqol küç 21c; ☺ noon-11pm) A certain graffiti chic makes Avto Stop the funkiest of a whole series of inexpensive yet welcoming (if smoky) bars on Qoqol (Mardanov) küç, with beers from just AZN1.20. Nearby bars stay open later.

Finnegans
PUB

(Map p236; www.facebook.com/finnegansbaku; Əlizadə küç 8; beer from AZN5/7; ☺ 11am-1am; ☎) Baku's old faithful Anglo-Irish pub has big wrought-iron lamps in high vaults and some of the best live blues-rock music in town. If things aren't hopping or you want a cheaper beer, there are numerous alternatives within stumbling distance.

Crazzy Bear PUB

(Map p232; www.facebook.com/crazzybear.az; Bəşir Səfəroğlu küç 197; ⏰5pm-2am; 🛜) Popular with local 20-somethings, this self-declared 'concept pub' welcomes potential revellers with a disembodied car-end and invocations to 'Eat, drink and rock'. It's a good place to find a dancey late-night vibe that is neither sleazy nor excessively glitzy.

Barfly BAR

(Map p236; www.facebook.com/barfly.baku; Böyük Qala küç 41; ⏰3pm-late) In the afternoon you might come for a quiet wine tasting (five Azerbaijani varieties with cheeses for AZN30). But after 10pm expect a hip crowd, bottle-spinning mixologists and very likely a DJ getting the buzz going.

Bar 360 BAR

(Map p232; 25th fl, Hilton Hotel, Azadlıq pr 1b; ⏰5pm-2am; 🛜) Upmarket rotating bar with ever-changing views across the city. Check for changing happy-hour deals.

Wine Bars

⭐**Kefli Local Wine & Snacks** WINE BAR

(Map p236; ☎051-3089909; www.facebook.com/kefliwinebar; Əliyarbəyov küç 4a; ⏰3pm-1am Sun-Thu, to 3am Fri & Sat) Kefli can take you on a full oenological tour of Azerbaijan with a book-thick menu of bottled vintages organised by grape (or pomegranate) type, and some 20 options available by the glass.

Enoteca Meydan WINE BAR

(Map p236; ☎070-4977414; www.facebook.com/enotecaMeydan; Böyük Qala küç; ⏰11am-1am; 🛜) Small and wonderfully understated, this wine shop with tasting bar is run by real experts who know all there is to know about Azerbaijani vintages.

Coffee & Tea

İçərişəhər Bookhouse Cafe CAFE

(Map p236; Vali Məmmədov küç; tea AZN2-5; ⏰3-10pm; 🛜) Cute, quiet and quirky, the atmosphere here is like sitting in a friend's front room, albeit an intellectual friend who has covered the walls with trippy murals and squiggle portraiture. Female-run and couple-friendly, it's a relaxing place for earnest conversation over a pot of herbal tea (plus books most Anglo travellers won't be able to read).

Coffee Moffie CAFE

(Map p236; ☎050-9641880; www.facebook.com/coffeemoffiebaku; İslam Səfərli küç 9; ⏰9am-midnight; 🛜) Beloved by the laptop brigade but also great for a quiet chat over a flat white or glass of local pomegranate wine, Coffee Moffie finds that sweet spot between offbeat alternative and relaxed comfort with film art, footprint murals and a battered old upright piano.

Kofetearea COFFEE

(Map p236; Passage 1901, Mirvari Dilbazı küç; coffee AZN3.5-7; ⏰10am-8pm Mon-Fri, noon-8pm Sat & Sun; 🛜) Made using a La Marzocca espresso machine with beans that are freshly roasted on-site, it's hardly surprising that Kofetearea's coffees are among the best in town. The cafe is within the large yet easily overlooked Passage 1901 (p243) building. It's five minutes' walk from Fountains Sq using the underpass.

Qadım Bakı TEAHOUSE

(Old Baku Tea House; Map p236; ☎012-4370818; Qüllə küç 22; tea pot/samovar AZN5/15; ⏰1pm-1am; 🛜) This cosy stone cavern is smothered in carpets and lit by colourful Moroccan lamps plus daylight filtered through a few *şəbəkə* (stained-glass) windows. Food is served but the main point is to linger over a classic spread of tea plus jams and *paxlava* (baklava). Shisha (waterpipes) cost AZN25 for up to two hours' smoking. No alcohol.

☆ Entertainment

Baku has a vibrant arts scene. The theatre season runs from mid-September to late May. Tickets for various venues are sold at a **ticket booth** (Teatri və Konsert Biletləri; Map p236; Əlizadə küç 4; ⏰11am-3pm & 4-8pm) in the pedestrianised area south of Fountains Sq or online through iTicket (https://iticket.az).

The Muğam Club (p244) restaurant often provides a dinner-show of traditional music and Caucasian dancing. Several restaurants beside the Old City's north walls are serenaded by singers of various genres.

For what's-on listings see http://salamba ku.travel or, in Azerbaijani, https://citylife.az.

Etud LIVE MUSIC

(Map p236; ☎050-7666690; www.facebook.com/etudbaku; İslam Səfərli küç 23; ⏰3pm-2am) There's no sign on the stairs that lead down into this very modest cellar place, but if you hit the right night you can hear some of Baku's most experimental and eclectic music here. No cover, cheap drinks.

Le Château LIVE MUSIC

(Map p236; www.facebook.com/lechateaubaku; İslam Səfərli küç; ⏰5pm-2am) This is one of the city's most unapologetically grungy dives. Its live jams (typically weekends 9pm to 11pm) form a wonderfully nonchalant backdrop to the lively wave of conversation. No admission fee, beer from AZN2.

Filarmoniya CONCERT VENUE
(Azərbaycan Dövlət Filarmoniyası; Map p236; 012-4972901, box office 012-4973609; www.instagram.com/filarmoniya_baku; İstiglaliyyat küç 10; box office 11am-7pm) With its twin Mediterranean-style towers, this 1910 Baku landmark was originally built as an oil-boom-era casino. The interior is as impressive as its architecture, making a fine venue for a very varied roster of concerts.

International Muğam Centre CONCERT VENUE
(Beynəlxalq Muğam Mərkəzi; Map p232; 012-4978972; www.mugamradio.az; Neftçilər pr 9) This stylish concert hall, designed to resemble stylised musical instruments, hosts a sparse schedule of concerts in an eclectic variety of styles.

Mime Theatre LIVE PERFORMANCE
(Dövlət Pantomima Teatrı; Map p232; 012-4414756; http://pantomima.az; Azadlıq pr 75/49; tickets from AZN5) Superbly creative mime performances in a tiny theatre fashioned from a 1900 former chapel. Generally weekends only.

Opera & Ballet Theatre OPERA, BALLET
(Azərbaycan Dövlət Akademik Opera və Balet Teatrı; Map p232; 012-4931651; www.tob.az; Nizami küç 113; mid-Sep–May) This 1910 theatre has very distinctive twin-spired facade and a classically grand interior, though the place could do with some refreshing. It produces a mixed bag of shows, some grandiose, other more mundane repertory performances but most are easy enough to follow without speaking the show's language.

Park Bulvar Cinema CINEMA
(Map p232; 012-5987414; https://parkcinema.az/kinoteatrlar/park-bulvar?lang=en; Park Bulvar Mall, 4th fl, Neftçilər pr 78) High-quality multiplex cinema showing some films in 3D.

Shopping
Pedestrianised Nizami küç, still known by its Soviet-era moniker of Torgovaya (Trade St), is a popular strolling/shopping area. More-exclusive boutiques are found on southern Rəsul Rza küç, Əziz Əliyev küç, western 28 May küç and on the northern side of the Bulvar. Big 21st-century shopping centres include Park Bulvar Mall (p236), 28 Mall, Ganjlik Mall, **Port Baku Mall** (Map p232; www.portbakumall.az; Neftçilər pr 151; 10am-10pm;) and – nearing completion at the time of writing – **Caspian Waterfront Mall** (Map p232; Yeni Bulvar).

Ovdan FOOD & DRINKS
(Map p236; 050-4434443; İçəri Şəhər; 8am-10pm) A selection of very genuine regional sweets, preserves and variants on halva/*paxlava* are sold in this delightful little shop. It's in a stone-lined cavern entered through the tunnel that was an underground water-collection point in medieval times. It's immediately on the left as you enter the Old City from İçərişəhər metro station.

Baku Book Center BOOKS
(Map p232; 012-5059999; http://bakubookcenter.az; Üzeyir Hacıbəyli küç 5; 10am-9pm;) A marvel in this age of closing bookstores,

AZERBAIJAN BAKU

BAKU BLING

Catering to the ostentation of Baku's oil nouveau riche, but also to the recent flood of high-end tourists from Gulf State countries, there is a wealth of upmarket boutiques. A selection are at the southern end of Əziz Əliyev küç, where you'll find **Tiffany** (Map p236; 050-2919970; Əziz Əliyev küç 1c; 11am-8pm Mon-Sat) and **Bvlgari** (Map p236; Əziz Əliyev küç 1a; 11am-8pm). Around the corner, the **Tom Ford** (Map p236; www.tomford.com/men; Neftçilər pr 23a; 11am-8pm Mon-Sat) men's couture store occupies a classic carving-encrusted mansion that once hosted Charles de Gaulle during a secret 1944 stopover en route to Moscow. Several other prominent boutiques, including **Dolce & Gabbana** (Map p232; Neftçilər pr 45b; 11am-8pm) and Gucci, line the Bulvar near the Museum Centre.

A **Rolls Royce** (Map p236; www.rolls-roycemotorcars-baku.az; Əlizadə küç 5; 9am-6pm Mon-Fri, 10am-4pm Sat) dealership fills the 1901 former Gorodskoi Bank building with its splendid 'dripping face' stonework. **Baku Lamborghini** (Map p232; 012-4048410; www.facebook.com/lamborghiniStoreBaku; Parlament pr 4; 10am-7pm Mon-Sat) sits at the base of the Flame Towers, while Ferrari and Bentley have showrooms close to Port Baku Mall, where you'll find boutiques by Alexander McQueen and Stella McCartney, among others.

this impressive palace of reading opened in 2018 and holds regular book signings and exhibitions.

Çiraq Books
BOOKS

(Map p236; ☑012-4923289; www.facebook. com/chiraqbookstore; Yusifbəy İbrahimli küç 2a; ⊙10am-8pm Tue-Sat, to 5pm Mon) For two decades, Çiraq has been Baku's leading English-language bookshop. It has a decent range of classics, bestsellers, travel guides and locally relevant titles, plus a good souvenir section.

Karavansara Bazarı
GIFTS & SOUVENIRS

(Map p236; Qüllə küç; ⊙9am-9pm) While the majority of the wares on sale here are a little tacky, it's worth taking a quick look inside if only to admire the architecture of one of Baku's most photogenic caravanserais.

Təzə Bazar
MARKET

(Map p232; Səməd Vurğun küç; ⊙approx 7am-6pm; ☐88a) For everything from caviar (sometimes with tastings) and photogenically piled fruit to assorted homewares and Lənkəran tea, head to this fairly central, workaday market.

ℹ️ Information

MONEY

ATMs are ubiquitous. Many hotels and some restaurants accept credit cards. For great US-dollar or euro exchange rates try **Kapital Bank** (Map p232; Zərifə Əliyeva küç 63; ⊙9am-5pm Mon-Fri), near the Museum Centre, or **Amrah Bank** (Map p232; 28 May küç 74; ⊙10am-5pm Mon-Fri) branches near the train station or at **Sahil Gardens** (Map p232; Xaqanı küç 59; ⊙9am-5pm Mon-Fri). Around Fountains Sq or in the Old City, rates are typically at least 2% worse but some booths open late, notably **Günay Bank** (Map p236; Qüllə küç; ⊙9am-10pm), which also changes UAE dirhams.

TOURIST INFORMATION

Tourist Information Center (Map p232; ☑012-4981244; www.facebook.com/Baku TourismInformationCenter; Üzeyir Hacıbəyli küç 70; ⊙9am-6pm Mon-Fri, 11am-4pm Sat & Sun)

ℹ️ Getting There & Away

AIR

Baku's **Heydar Aliyev International Airport** (GYD; www.airport.az; Bina; ☐H1) has flights to/from plenty of European, Russian and Central Asian cities, plus Dubai, New York, Qatar, Tehran, Tel Aviv, and Batumi and Tbilisi in Georgia. AZAL (www.azal.az) also offers fixed-price domestic flights to Gənca (AZN61; three weekly) and Naxçivan (AZN70; at least four daily) sold online or through **SW Travel** (Map p232; ☑012-598880; www.swtravel.az; Nizami küç 126c; ⊙9am-8pm).

Terminal 1 (T1), for most long-haul destinations, is a very impressive modernist tricorn with lots of photogenic design features, notably the use of 'cocoon' spaces for cafes and bars. Domestic services and budget international flights using Buta Airways and WizzAir use Terminal 2, a four-minute, unsheltered walk across the car park. T2 is wrapped in filigree that looks intriguing from outside when lit at night but is basic within.

Airport Transport

The Airport Shuttle Bus (www.aeroexpress.az) to Baku train station departs from outside T1 half-hourly from 6am to 7pm, every 40 minutes till 9pm then hourly through the night. Cost is AZN1.30, which must be loaded onto a BakıKart (p250). These are available from a vending machine just outside the exit doors of the Terminal 1 and within the northern entrance hall of Terminal 2. The bus picks up briefly outside T2, from a slightly hard-to-spot stop beyond the covered drop-off lane.

Metered London-style taxis waiting outside T1 are likely to cost from AZN25, depending on the

TRAINS DEPARTING BAKU

DESTINATION	VIA	DEPARTS	ARRIVES	FARE (AZN)
Astara	Lənkəran	11.50pm	8am	p/k 7/11
Balakən	Şəki	11.20pm	10am	p/k 9/14
Gənca		9am	1pm	seat 10**
Kiev (Ukraine)	Xaçmaz	1.35am Sat	11.35 Mon	p/k 185/263
Moscow Kurskaya (Russia)	Xaçmaz	1.35am Thu	4.15am Sat	p/k 208/278
Qazax	Gənca	11pm	11.50am	p/k 9/14
Tbilisi (Georgia)	Gənca	8.40pm	12.15pm	p/k 25/35

p/k = *platskart/kupe* (open-bunk accommodation/2nd-class compartment accommodation)

** = travels by day; for a sleeper to Gənca use the Qazax train

Baku Metro

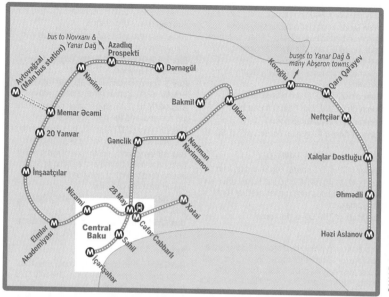

destination – Baku is big. Heading to the airport, a prebooked **Taxi189** (☏ 189; www.189taxi.az; ⊙ 24hr; 🐾) might charge less than AZN20.

BOAT

The **Caspian Shipping Company** (☏ 012-4043900, Kazakhstan boat info 055-9999124, Turkmenistan boat info 055-9999061; https:// asco.az/en; 🖳) operates services to Turkmenbashi, Turkmenistan, and to Kyruk, 30km from Aktau, Kazakhstan. While passengers are accepted and each boat has a few cabins, be very aware that these are mostly cargo ships without luxury nor any set timetable. They could run several times weekly, or not at all. Journey times could also extend to several days if there's a queue at the arrival dock. For Aktau, flying on **SCAT** (Map p232; ☏ 050-4693379, 051-3447777; www.scat.kz/en/; Rixard Zorge küç 13c) or AZAL is often cheaper overall – even with a bicycle.

Buying the ferry tickets is a dark art. Start by phoning every morning and again around 3pm until a sailing is confirmed. Get your name on the passenger list for a scheduled boat. Then, at an arranged time, you'll need to get yourself to the **New Baku International Seaport** (https:// portofbaku.com; Ələt) near Ələt, a massive 75km south of Baku. If you don't have your own wheels, a taxi to/from Baku should cost around AZN30 (one hour). Alternatively take bus 195 (AZN1, 80 minutes) from **Lökbatan Dairəsi** (Salyan Highway; 🚌 125, 195) or nearby Binə Ba-

zar (at the western terminus of Baku bus route 125). Get off the 195 after passing through Baş Ələt, by a big roundabout from where waiting taxis charge AZN5 for the last 3km to backtrack to the port.

BUS & SHARED TAXI

Almost all long-distance services start from the **main bus station** (Avtovağzal; Bakı Beynəlxalq Avtovağzal Kompleksi; ☏ 012-4060158; https:// avtovagzal.az; Sumqayıt Hwy; 🚌 14, 37, 96, Ⓜ Avtovağzal). That's around 8km north of central Baku, most conveniently accessed by metro using the one-stop Avtovağal spur line from metro Memar Əcəmi.

To buy tickets find the relevant sales window (kassa). For destinations in Turkey and Iran look on floor 1 (and prebook days ahead). For Georgia and domestic buses head to the departures level (floor 3), where kassa 1 to kassa 10 are beside platform A3, kassa 11 to kassa 19 by platform B11. Screens display the number of seats still available for each departure. If you've prebooked online, collect a physical ticket at kassa 16.

International services include the following:

İstanbul (Turkey, US$70, 32 to 40 hours, many daily at around 11am). Compare companies with offices fronting floor 1 and check whether the route is direct or via Ankara (this can add several hours).

Tbilisi (Georgia, AZN15, overnight at 9pm, 11pm and midnight) Kassa 19.

Tehran (Iran, AZN40, around 16 hours, 3pm) and Tabriz (AZN30, around 11 hours, 10pm daily plus 9am Fridays) Floor 1, units 1309A&B

For Tabriz you could alternatively take a Naxçivan-bound bus (AZN25, 14 hours, 9am or 9pm, *kassa* 19) and change to a cheap shared taxi at Iranian Julfa.

Domestic services run roughly hourly to the following:

Gəncə (AZN8.40, seven hours) *Kassa* 1.

İsmayıllı (AZN4, four hours) *Kassa* 15.

Lənkəran (AZN5, three hours)

Qırmızı Körpü (Georgian border; AZN11.90, 10 hours) *Kassa* 1.

Quba (AZN4, 2½ hours) *Kassa* 7.

Qusar (AZN4, 3¼ hours) For Shahdag, *kassa* 6.

Şəki (AZN8.40, 5½-6½ hours) Buses drive via Ağdaş, minibuses take the far prettier route via Şamaxı.

Zaqatala (AZN8.50, eight hours)

Shared Taxi

Shared taxis typically cost around 2.5 times the bus fare (or 10 times for the whole car). For most major destinations drivers wait at one of two points in the car park directly north of the bus station. However, for Şamaxı and İsmayıllı you'll need to go to **Şamaxinka** (Moskva pr; 🚌 65), a large chaotic roundabout 1km nearer to central Baku (accessed by bus 14 or by bus 65 from Azneft Sq).

TRAIN

All overnight trains give you a sleeping berth, with sheets included in the modest fare. You'll need your passport both to buy a ticket and to board the train. To buy an international ticket for a date more than 14 days after your arrival in Azerbaijan, also bring proof of visa registration.

❶ Getting Around

PUBLIC TRANSPORT

The metro links the Old City (İçərişəhər) via the train station (28 May) to a series of suburban stations, most usefully Koroğlu, Qara Qarayev

---

and Neftçilər, each with bus connections to certain Abşeron towns. All metro rides and most buses require a prepaid BakıKart and cost a flat 30q regardless of distance.

Routes are mapped on www.gomap.az and many on www.bakubus.az, including:

Bus 1 & 2 (Map p232) To the Heydar Aliyev Center and beyond.

Bus 5 Approximately links Flag Sq with the Heydar Aliyev Center (after a short walk).

Bus 14 (Map p232) Bus station to train station via Yasamal and the Hyatt Hotel area.

Bus 21 (Map p232) From Vurğun Bağı south of the train station, runs east along the coast.

Bus 88 Very handy north–south route using Behbudov northbound and Azadlıq pr southbound then swinging along or parallel to the Bulvar past the Old City.

Bus 88a Heads north on Səməd Vurğun küç passing Təzə Bazar.

Bus 125 From the train station to Binə Bazar via Şıxov Beach and Bibi-Heybət Mosque.

TAXI

BakıTaksi (📞 9000; http://btx.az) runs the deep-purple London-style cabs, the only taxis to use a meter. Pre-phoning services such as Taxi189 (p249) is often cheaper. From AZN1.60 for the shortest ride, Bolt is generally more popular than Uber as an app-based taxi-hailing service and has a 'cash' option so you don't need a local credit card. For a fuller listing (with reviews in Russian) see www.bakutaxi.info.

BICYCLE

RentaSport (Map p232; 📞 051-8518011; Rəsul Rza küç 59; per day AZN20-30; ⏰10am-11pm) has mountain bikes for rent, and if you need to get your own bicycle mended **2Təkər** (Map p232; Səməd Vurğun küç 61c; ⏰11am-8pm Mon-Sat, to 7pm Sun) can help. If you just want to glide down the Yeni Bulvar to Yarat, you might prefer a short-rent city bike from Velopark (p237). You'll need to leave ID as a deposit.

> ### BAKIKART
> ....
> To use the metro and most city-centre buses you'll need to buy a BakıKart, a rechargable electronic purse. It works much like London's Oyster card except that you only tap in, no need to tap out.
>
> Cards are sold from vending machines at metro stations and at bigger bus stops. A plastic one (AZN2) can be reused indefinitely. A disposable paper one (20q) allows just one or two ride-credits to be loaded.

AROUND BAKU

The most popular day-tours from Baku drive south to Qobustan's petroglyph reserve and the isolated mud volcanoes above Ələt. Many then head east to see Abşeron highlights like Yanar Dağ and Suraxanı's fire temple, returning via the Heydar Aliyev Center. Many companies offer slightly different variants and prices, with/without entry fees or meals. Transport-only deals by **TES Tour** (Map p236; 📞 055-6991040, 012-4925506, Whatsapp 050-4925506; www.testour.az; Sabir küç 21) cost only AZN50 per head and are often sold through hostels.

South of Baku

South of Baku, the city peters out into semidesert hiding petroglyphs and mud volcanoes, fringed by an opal-blue sea that is peppered with oil derricks.

◉ Sights

Qobustan

Petroglyph Reserve   ARCHAEOLOGICAL SITE
(☎ 012-5446627; foreigner/local/student AZN10/4/1; ⏱10am-6pm, last entry 5pm) The Unesco-listed Qobustan Petroglyph Reserve protects thousands of stick-figure stone engravings dating back up to 12,000 years. Themes include livestock, wild animals and shamans. The images were carved into what were probably caves but over time they have crumbled into a craggy chaos of boulders. Even if you have no particular interest in ancient doodles, Qobustan's eerie landscape and the hilltop views towards distant oil-workings in the turquoise-blue Caspian are still fascinating.

A visit starts 3km west of Qobustan Town at a state-of-the-art museum, which gives context to what you will see on the mountain ridge 2km above. English-speaking staff offer guided tours (AZN15) to assist you in spotting and deciphering the petroglyphs, but alone you'll still be able to spot the key scratchings. Don't miss the spindly reed boat sailing towards the sunset. Comparing this with similar ancient designs in Norway led ethnologist Thor Heyerdahl to speculate that Scandinavians might have originated in what is now Azerbaijan.

Mud Volcanoes   VOLCANO
(Palçıq Vulkanları) **FREE** On top of utterly unpromising little Daşgil Hill is a weird collection of baby mud volcanoes, a whole family of 'geologically flatulent' little conical mounds that gurgle, ooze, spit and sometimes erupt with thick, cold, grey mud. It's more entertaining than it sounds – even when activity is at a low ebb, you get the eerie feeling that the volcanoes are alive.

From Qobustan, the 10km unpaved direct route follows the west side of the rail tracks but is rough and dusty. A longer but easier drive turns right off the main Qazax highway at Km 69 (Ələt). Take the first left (sign says 'Şpal Zavodu') then turn right immediately after crossing the rail tracks. Follow this unpaved track for 3km, forking right en route. The mud volcano area is 300m up a steep, well-worn slope. There's a parking area up top but in wet conditions these last 300m are dangerously slippery.

Around Baku ◎

Bibi-Heybət Mosque   MOSQUE
(Bibiheybət Məscidi; Salyan Hwy) Worth a quick stop en route to Qobustan, this 1998 neo-Ottoman-style mosque replaced a 13th-century original demolished by the Soviets 'for road widening' in September 1937. The interior is impressive and the rear terrace has curious views across an oil-rig port, 5km south of central Baku. The 1281 original was built to honour the Ukeyma, a daughter of Musa Al Kazim, the seventh Shi'ite Imam, and sister to Rahima (buried at Nardaran on the Abşeron Peninsula) and Fatima (at Qom, Iran).

Şixov Beach   BEACH
(Şıx çimərliyi; 🚌125) The nearest beach to central Baku, Şixov is most fascinating for photographers who want to snap bathers gambolling on the 'sand' with a romantic backdrop of giant offshore oil rigs.

❶ Getting There & Away

Tours are easiest. By bus, the 125 from Baku train station passes Bibi-Heybət Mosque and Şixov Beach en route to the vast Binə Bazar wholesale market. Change there or at nearby Lökbatan dairəsi (p249) for the 195 to Qobustan (AZN1, 45 minutes). At the south end of Qobustan Town hop off in front of a few lacklustre shops where waiting taxi drivers typically ask between AZN30 and AZN40 to combine visits to the petroglyphs and mud volcanoes (price per car, return including waiting time). Few speak any English.

Abşeron Peninsula

Stretching north and east from Baku, the Abşeron Peninsula confounds easy definition. Until the 1990s this was a semibarren expanse of degraded agricultural land, blanched by salt lakes and sodden with petroleum run-off. While some areas of rusty oil derricks remain (mostly hidden from view behind tall walls), former villages are rapidly merging into one gigantic urban sprawl. Yet amid this bewildering formlessness, you can seek out several historic castle towers along with ever-burning fires that inspired Zoroastrian and Hindu pilgrims. And beneath the cultural surface, a traditionally conservative population retains some of Azerbaijan's oddest folk beliefs. It's a perversely fascinating area.

Atmospheric if tourist-oriented dining choices on the peninsula include the impressive **pseudo-medieval cafe-restaurant** within the outer precincts of Suraxanı's Ateşgah, and memorable Gala Bazaar between Qala and Mərdəkən. There's plenty more in choice Mərdəkən and both hotels and restaurants lie along the Abşeron's north-coast

beaches, though these rarely lure foreign visitors. With patience, it's possible to get fairly close to most of the main sights using public buses starting from Baku's metro stations Ulduz or Koroğlu (south exit).

Suraxanı

The unique **Ateşgah** (Atəşgah Məbədi; ☑ 012-4524407; http://unesco.preslib.az/az/page/TNkh 1GCDYE; Atamoğlan Rzayev küç; foreigner/local adult AZN4/2, student AZN1; ☉ 9am-6pm; ☐ 184) is an 18th-century fire temple, a fortified complex whose centrepiece is a flaming hearth beneath a four-pillared stone dome with side flues. This sits in a roughly triangular courtyard surrounded by simple stone cell-rooms originally built for Indian Shivaite devotees and now hosting a well-explained museum. It's in the otherwise forgettable township of Suraxanı. Until train service is reinstated, the easiest access is by bus 184 from Baku's Ulduz metro. This terminates at the north concourse of Suraxanı train station. To find the fire temple, cross the rail tracks through that station, turn left, go through a grandiose stone gateway then walk another three minutes passing a baronial hall-style cafe-restaurant (closes by 6pm).

To continue east from Suraxanı train station, take bus 104 for 15 minutes, getting off

Abşeron Peninsula

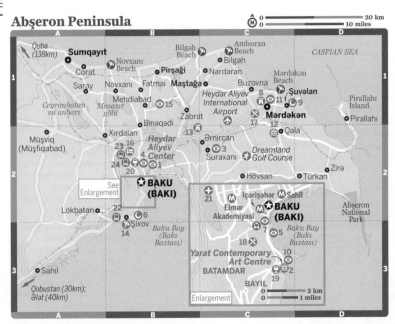

where it turns a right angle to the south. Walk one minute north to an obvious highway bus stop (Heydar Əliyev pr 402). From there bus 136 continues to Mərdəkən, bus 101 to Qala.

Qala

The historic little village of Qala is dominated by a reconstructed fortress tower fronted by a fearsome warrior statue. It's near the entrance to the **Qala Ethnographic Complex** (☑012-4593714; Qala Village; complex/tour/fortress AZN2/8/2; ⏱9am-6pm; 🚌136), an impressive open-air park-museum featuring several furnished, traditional-style Abşeron buildings – houses, a blacksmith's forge, a potters' workshop etc – set amid a wide range of archaeological finds and petroglyphs (not all original). In a building across the road, don't miss the free indoor art exhibition made from recycled garbage. And leave time to stroll into the windswept villagescape beyond where several rustic buildings are in various stages of restoration.

Note that there's minimal shade so visiting in midsummer can be exhausting.

The easiest way to reach Qala from Baku is on a three-hour excursion (AZN15, daily 3pm) sold from the ticket booth of the Maiden's Tower (p231). By public transport, take Türkan-bound bus 101 from Baku's Ulduz metro station then walk 300m west along Sülh street to find the ethnographic complex. Bus 182 links Qala with Mərdəkən.

Gala Bazaar AZERBAIJANI **$$**
(www.galabazaar.az/en/restaurant; Qala yolu; kebabs AZN8-10, fish AZN35, salads AZN2-5; ⏱9am-11pm; 🅿🛜♿) Packed with imaginative decor that incorporates elements from Moorish stone arches to southern French shutters, this place really does base itself on the model of an antique market-place cum caravanserai. The enclosed yard is vast with trees, *hamman* and fire-pit, as well as well-spaced tables, a kids play area and a stage for live violin music.

Mərdəkən & Şüvəlan

Together forming one extensive semi-urban sprawl, neither Mərdəkən nor Şüvəlan are particularly attractive towns but they are well off most of the tour-bus routes and hide some of the Abşeron Peninsula's more intriguing places of legend and superstition.

Bus 136 from Baku's mtero station Koroğlu gets you close to the three main sights.

Mir Mövsüm Ağa Ziyarətgahı ISLAMIC SHRINE
(⏱vary; 🚌136) One of Azerbaijan's most intriguing shrines, this complex is topped with a beautifully patterned Central Asian–style dome and has an interior spangled with polished-mirror mosaic facets. Most Azerbaijanis firmly believe that a wish made here will come true – and when it does they return in droves, offering suitable donations to show their gratitude. The holy man entombed here was not a scholar or a warrior but a 20th-century invalid whose 'blessing' was having bones so soft that he couldn't stand.

Abşeron Peninsula

◎ **Top Sights**

◎ **Sights**

🛏 **Sleeping**

🍴 **Eating**

🍷 **Drinking & Nightlife**

ℹ **Information**

ℹ **Transport**

AZERBAIJAN ABŞERON PENINSULA

At the back of the complex is a cemetery with a fascinating mix of Islamic, Soviet-atheist and Christian graves. It's at the east end of Şüvəlan, around 4km east of central Mərdəkən. Bus 136 stops outside.

Pir Həsən   SHRINE
Pir Həsən is a shrine area where you can come to have a bottle smashed over your head. Honestly. It's considered a cure for nervousness of spirit. The smashing occurs at the back of a pretty view-garden whose focus is the grave of oil-baron Zeynalabdin Tağıyev beneath an egg-shaped stone pavilion, surrounded by archaeological fragments. To find Pir Həsən turn north at the traffic light directly west of central Mərdəkən's arboretum ('Dendroloji Parki'). Swing west again on Ramin Qazımov küç and then turn north once more.

Mardakan Castle   FORTRESS
(Böyük Mərdəkan Qəsri; by donation; ☺ 8am-8pm) This 22m square-plan tower is a very dramatic construction yet it somehow manages to lie almost entirely hidden in a series of old village-style backstreets. Some sources claim it was first built in the 12th century for the Shirvanshah, Ahistan I, though much of its grandeur comes from two 20th-century restorations. There's very little inside but if you want to get in and climb the five flights of unlit, rather unsafe steps to the rooftop, seek out the key-holder who lives in one of the closest houses.

The tower is accessed off Kolxoz küç, about 1.5km west of Pir Həsən following Ramin Qazımov küç. Bus 136 to Baku picks up from Yesenin küç around three minutes' walk to the south.

Yanar Dağ
A 10m-long strip of 'eternal' fire burns gently in a raised gully at a place called Yanar Dağ (Fire Mountain; http://yanardag.az; Məmmədli Village; foreigner/local AZN9/2, student AZN1; ☺ 9am-8pm or later; P ♿). Some say that the flames have gone unquenched for millennia, others that the naturally escaping gas was accidentally ignited by a shepherd's discarded cigarette back in the 1950s. The site's name means 'Fire Mountain', rather misleading for what is actually a very modest hillock, but an inspired 2019 makeover has parlayed this minor curiosity into a satisfying tourist attraction by adding an exhibition space, children's activities, a viewing-amphitheatre and explanations of some ancient stones nearby.

Bus 217 (50q, 40 minutes) from Koroğlu metro station and bus 147 (50q, 30 minutes) from Azadliq Prospekti metro station both terminate opposite the site.

Ramana
On a rocky outcrop above an eponymous village, Ramana Fortress (🚌 204 from Koroğlu metro station) is one of the Abşeron's most dramatic castles. Adding to the interest of a visit is the view across many grungy old oil workings, nodding donkeys and run-off pools.

NORTHERN AZERBAIJAN
Of Azerbaijan's many splendours, few can beat the powerful grandeur of the north's towering mountainscapes, the intrigue of its timeless highland villages and the contrasting comforts of the Shahdag ski resort. The region also boasts a remarkably wide range of lowland sceneries, from the colourfully painted semideserts towards Xızı to the abrupt crags of Çirax Castle and Beşbarmaq Dağ and the apple orchards and golf greens of Quba.

Baku to Quba
While the region's highlights are clustered in the far north, there are several interesting discoveries en route for those with wheels.

⊙ Sights & Activities

Candycane Mountains   NATURAL FEATURE
(Giləzi–Xızı road) An eye-catching area of vivid pink-and-white striped hills is commonly nicknamed the 'Candycane Mountains' by Baku expats. Look carefully and you find that the colourful landscape is littered with little fossils. The area is around 15km east of the Baku–Quba Hwy: turn at Giləzi taking the Xızı road that leads eventually to the gently attractive woodlands of the Altıağac National Park.

Beşbarmaq Dağ   MOUNTAIN
(Five Finger Mountain; Siyəzən spur road, Km 3.5; AZN2) Atop a supersteep grassy ridge, Beşbarmaq Dağ is a distinctive split crag whose mystical crown of phallic rocks attracts (mostly female) pilgrims. They climb a steep, partially laddered trail from a ridgetop car park, taking around 20 minutes. Pilgrims kiss the stones and sometimes

Northern & Northwestern Azerbaijan

30 km
15 miles

CASPIAN SEA

Sumqayıt
Baku (28km)
Blue Planet
Shuraabad
Gilazi
Samur-Abşeron kanalı
(Samur-Abşeron Canal)
Beşbarmaq Dağ
Candycane
Mountains
Xızı
Altıağac
Altı Ağac
National Park
Visitors Centre
4WD Only
Qızmeydan
Qobustan
(Maraza)
Qala
Qala (Davaçı)
Çıraq Qala
Şabran (Davaçı)
Gondov
Xaçmaz
Nabran
Xanoba
Yalama
Xudat
Qusar
Qırız
Quba
Quba Palace
Hotel
Alpan
Qəçrəş
Susay
Qızılqaya (3726m)
Tengəaltı
Çiçi
Zeyvə
Qonaqkənd
Gilgilçay
Şahnəzərdağ
Babadağ
Lahic
Niyal Qalası
Fit Dağ Castle
Pirqulu
Şamaxı
Kalaxana
Ağsu
Padar (20km)
Baku (235km)
Sulut
Başqal
İsmayıllı
İvanovka
Hacıhatamlı
Qaramaryam
Göyçay
Ağdaş
Yevlax
Bərdə
Tərtər
Aşağı Ağcakənd
Naftalan
Goranboy
Mingəçevir
Xaldan
Kür River
Yuxarı Şirvan Canal
Mingəçevir
Reservoir
Kür
Göygöl
Ganca
Airport
Hacıkənd
Çaykənd
Göy Göl
Daşkəsən (11km)
Xoş Bulaq (20.5km)
Tbilisi (185km)
Tbilisi (140km)
Lagodekhi
Qudurdağ (3401m)
Balakən
Zaqatala Train Station
Zaqatala
Əlibad
Lakit
İlisu
Qum
New Qax Train Station
Qax
Old Qax Train Station
Kiş
Şəki
Şəki Train Station
Marxal Resort
Gələrsən Görəsən Fortress Ruins
Qaradağ (3620m)
Car
Lazzat İstirahat Zonası
Oğuz
Fazlı
Aydınbulaq
Niç
Lake Ajnohur
Karimli
Mirzəbəyli
Old Gabala
Vəndam
Yengicə
Qəbələ
Laza
Durca
Tufandağ Ski Fields
Salavat Pass (2915m)
Tufandağ (4191m)
Bazardüzü (4466m)
Şahdağ (4243m)
Shahdag Mountain Resort
Zukul
Sudur
Zindanmuruq
Kuzun
Laza
Xınalıq
Qarxun
Onq
Cek
Rük
Söhüb
Budug
Qaraçay
Babaçay
Qalacıq
Sumağallı
Gurbangah
Babadağ (3629m)
Qrız
Dahna
Çay
Çayqovşan
Aniq
Hil
Hazra
SDK (Samur)
Quşençay
Qusarçay
Ağçay
RUSSIA
(DAGESTAN)
GEORGIA
Dağbilici
Axtıçay
Quanıx
Kiş çay
Qurmux
Tala çay
Katex çay
Balakənçay
Qumuq çay
Atazan
Kür

speak in tongues en route, hoping to score spiritual merit, good fortune and/or divine assistance in getting pregnant. Holy men lurk in rocky nooks ready to help out – but only with prayers.

The peak's looming 520m silhouette flips the bird at passing traffic high, high above Km 88 of the Baku–Quba Hwy. At that point, Baku–Xaçmaz and Baku–Quba buses stop outside a stone mosque surrounded by food stalls. From the mosque there is a path to the top, but it's a strenuous multihour climb and requires finding the one single point at which the possible paths cross a concrete-boxed canal.

It's much easier to drive to the ridgetop car park. The 6km access track is unpaved and steep but passable by most cars in dry weather, though the upper section gets very tough after rain. The track starts 10km south of Siyəzən on the 'old road'. Turn beside the long-defunct Karabağ Kafesi where a green sign reads 'Xıdır Zində Piri'.

Blue Planet Kitesurfing   WINDSURFING
(☑ 050-2770730; www.kitesurfing.az; Shuraabad Beach; weekday/weekend beach access AZN20/25, kiteboard set per hour/day AZN90/180, paddleboard AZN10/30; ☺ 9am-7pm May–late Sep by appt) Azerbaijan's kitesurfing centre offers a unique opportunity to go skimming across a Caspian lagoon with glorious sunsets, and reliable wind yet relatively calm shallow water. Private lessons available (from AZN320). Consider booking a few days ahead. Along with its Italian cafe-restaurant, the centre is set on an isolated headland beach, 16km off the main Baku–Quba Hwy via Shuraabad. The 'day-pass' ticket allows beach and pool access with towel, sunshade and lounger.

🍴 Sleeping & Eating

Qalaaltı Hotel & Spa   SPA HOTEL $$$
(☑ 051-2252800; https://qalaalti.az; Qalaaltı Village; d/ste AZN149/179; P ❄ 🤖 🐶) For locals, Qalaaltı's drawcard is the sickeningly sulphurous mineral water: drinking it is a prescribed health cure. However, the resort also accepts hotel guests in luxuriously huge rooms which gaze out across the Caspian for magnificent sunrises. The views are bettered only by those from the extraordinary infinity pool. An added bonus of staying here is that one of rural Azerbaijan's best-preserved castle ruins, Çirax Qala, is accessible by an uphill forest walk from the complex. Nonguests need to take a more circuitous route – a muddy 4km off-road drive plus 15 minutes' walk.

Qalaaltı is accessed by a mostly paved Siyəzən–Şabran back road.

Quba
☑ 023 / POP 38,000 / ELEV 580M

Famous for apples and carpet-making, Quba is a town in three parts. Old Quba is a grid of low-rise streets raised above the deep-cut Qudiyalçay River. This had been the 18th-century capital of local potentate Fatali Khan, but later became a provincial backwater once the khanate had been absorbed into the Russian Empire (1806). North across the river is Qırmızı Qəsəbə, a unique Jewish settlement. And to the east, the new town stretches 3km to Flag Sq, where a monumental trio of 21st-century public buldings boast proud stone facades and pediments. Quba is a popular getaway in itself but more particularly a gateway to Azerbaijan's most interesting and remote mountain villages.

ℹ HIKING IN NORTHERN AZERBAIJAN

Azerbaijan's new tourist board plans to waymark a series of hiking trails over the coming years, to facilitate independent trekking. Until then, Northern Azerbaijan's extensive networks of beautiful footpaths and shepherd tracks are best appreciated by joining one of the low-key tours run by mini-agencies like Camping Azerbaijan (p303) and BagBaku (p303). They offer a changing menu of hikes in the region at very reasonable prices (including transport to and from Baku). Sign up online for the option you want. Most are at weekends and some include overnight stays in archetypal homestays. One of the most popular village bases for such adventures is timeless Qrız (p262), a place that's otherwise well off the tourist circuit and with minimal facilities. The hike to reach Qrız from Cek is a classic canyon-crossing trail, and from Qrız a popular walk takes visitors to a waterfall which is particularly photogenic when frozen in winter. Lovely Laza (p266) is also excellent for short waterfall hikes, but, like the fabled ancient village of Xınalıq (p262), the village is hamstrung as a base for many longer walks by bureaucratic rules preventing easy entry to the upland sections of the Shahdag National Park (www.eco.gov.az/index.php?pg=86; from AZN2). This should improve in coming years.

⊙ Sights

Quba's main attraction is just wandering the quiet leafy streets of the Old Town. That's centred on **Meydan**, the central grassy square backed by Quba's distinctive pointy-roofed main mosque – the **Cümə Məscid** (Fətəli Xan küç). **Ərdəbil küç** has several typical old-Quba houses with rounded door shields and overhanging upper windows and features **Hacı Cəfər Məscid** (Ərdəbil küç 60), a colourfully painted brick mosque that was originally a square-plan 19th-century church. There's also a historic beehive-domed **hamam building** (070-5955981; Ərdəbil küç 33). The **history museum** (Tarix-diyarşünaslıq Muzeyi; Nizami Park; AZN2; ⊙9am-1pm & 2-6pm) is most interesting for its collection of local carpet styles and its castle-styled building overlooking pretty **Nizami Park** where old chaps in flat caps slap dominoes beneath the shady chestnut and plane trees. Statues of poets, peasants and sportswomen give a nostalgic sense of Soviet optimism to a stairway that leads down to a pedestrianised old stone bridge. Across the river is Qırmızı Qəsəbə.

Qırmızı Qəsəbə
AREA

(Krasnaya Sloboda) Across the river from central Quba, Qırmızı Qəsəbə is a much-celebrated Jewish village with two active synagogues, including the **Grand Synagogue** (Altı Günbəz sinaqoqu). Its comfortable existence is often cited as proof of Azerbaijan's history of religious tolerance, though to the casual observer the townscape's biggest difference from the rest of Quba is that of conspicuous wealth.

Quba 1918 Genocide Memorial Complex
MEMORIAL

(Quba Soyqırımı Memorial Kompleksi; Yusif Qazimov küç; ⊙9am-6pm Mon-Fri, 10am-5pm Sat & Sun) FREE A startling pair of concrete spike-pyramids rise dramatically above a subterranean museum that very powerfully commemorates the massacres of April and May 1918. In the then-larger Quba district, 122 villages were ravaged by predominantly Armenian Bolshevik forces. Some 16,782 mostly unarmed civilians died – Azerbaijanis, Jews, Avars and Lezghins. Many were dumped in a mass grave that was uncovered on this site in 2007. Captions and the free audio guide both have English versions.

For great, early morning views of the museum's architectural shards counterpointed against a backdrop of distant snowy mountains, approach from N Nərimanov küç (partly pedestrianised).

XAÇMAZ

The rarely visited town of Xaçmaz sports a comical plethora of **bizarre monuments** – gigantic lanterns, a two-storey clothes peg, three biblical magi and kitschy ornamental spring-houses that light up in rainbow colours. A reduced scale Tower Bridge built in sandstone spans the main road junction. Visiting is easy with twice-hourly minibuses from Quba and three good-value hotels lie within a short walk of Xaçmaz bus station.

Qədim Quba
WORKSHOP

(023-3353270; Heydar Əliyev pr 132; ⊙8am-noon & 1-5pm Mon-Sat) Quba is famous for its handmade carpets and this workshop is one accessible place where visitors can see the process in action.

🏃 Activities

Azerbaijan National Golf Course
GOLF

(050-2189621; www.qubapalace.com; Amsar–Ispik Rd; 9/18 holes from AZN77/102, shoes/clubs/trolley/buggy rental AZN15/30/15/40; ⊙starting time 9am-4pm) Azerbaijan's leading golf course is up to international PGA standards and open to nonmembers. The best seasons are March–April and October.

🛏 Sleeping

Two modern hostels are planned but, for now, Quba's budget options are pretty grim and thoroughly male-oriented. Hidden within the bazaar, **Xınalıq Hotel** (023-3354445; xinaliqotel@mail.ru; 22-ci Məhəllə 22; s/tw/tr/q AZN15/25/40/50, without bath dm/tw/tr/q AZN10/20/30/40) is no worse than the price might predict. Noisy little **Oskar Hotel** (077-6276888; Heydar Əliyev pr 200; tw AZN25) crams in ropey en suite bathrooms. Spirit-sapping **Hostel Bey** (Hostel Bai Guba; dm AZN20) has only its location and ebullient owner in its favour while newer, nearer **Motel Alfa-M** (dm AZN20) at the old bus station is not really a place for women.

The only midrange hotel in central Quba, **Şahdağ Quba Hotel & Spa** (050-6666033, 050-6666044; http://shahdaghotel.az; Nizami Park; s/d/ste AZN95/120/150; ❄🖳🏊), is new and acceptable but rooms are disappointingly lacklustre. Better options lie in the suburbs and countryside beyond.

Quba

N

0   400 m
0   0.2 miles

G1

@(1.6km);
Qusar (13km)

Vaqif küç

Gənclər küç

Cəfər Cabbarlı küç

Aslanov küç

Sane Hotel (800m);
@(2.5km);
Golf Course (8km);
Quba Palace Hotel
& Chalette (8km);
Xaçmaz (27km)

Flag Sq (1.7km);

Natavan küç

Heydər Əliyev pr

9

11
Bazaar

Qarabağ küç

Shared
taxis to
Qusar

12

17

Qusar (13km)

14

N Ibrahimov küç

Axundov küç

15

Azizbəyov küç

Heydər Əliyev pr

Qudiyalçay River

M Assadov küç

Xatai küç

Fətəlixan küç

Azadliq

N Nərimanov küç

**QIRMIZI
Qəsəbə**

Maarif küç

8

Samed Vurğun küç

Fatalixan küç

Bakıxanov

1

The
Fatali Xan Meydan

Ərdəbil küç

3

Rəsulzadə

13

istiqlal

7

DAĞLI

Krasnaya
Sloboda

2

Hikmat Hüseynov

5

Musabayev

Samed Vurğun

M Asadov küç

6   4

Ə Əliyev

10

Hüseynzada

Orucov küç

20 Yanvar

Qarimov küç

N Narimanov küç

Walking Route to
Quba 1918
Genocide Memorial
Complex (250m)

16

Quba 1918
Genocide Memorial
Complex (550m);
Qəçrəş (5km);
Xinaliq (50km)

Quba

Şane Hotel   HOTEL **$$**
(☑023-3356171; www.shane.az; Heydar Əliyev
pr 227t; d/tr/ste AZN70/80/100; P❋🛜; 🖳1)
Quality pure-white sheets, chestnut furniture and comfortable beds at a decent price mean it's easy to forgive Şane the occasional elements of kitsch and the edge-of-town, main-road location.

The restaurant menu makes valiant if sometimes comical attempts to give English translations.

★Quba Palace Hotel   RESORT **$$$**
(☑050-2818150; https://qubapalace.com/en;
Amsar–Ispiq road; r from AZN270; P❋🛜🏊)
Preening above the Azerbaijan National Golf Course (p257), this sumptuous 21st-century palace has all the five-star trappings yet midweek in the low season you can often score a room for a bargain AZN150.

It's 8km south of central Quba.

✗ Eating

A handful of eateries are scattered between the bazaar and the Meydan, a few more urban options lie near Flag Sq and kebab barbecues dot the forest for several kilometres along the Qəçrəş road towards Xınalıq. Some restaurants charge foreigners higher prices with double sets of menus. A local speciality sweet-snack is *bükmə*, like shredded wheat filled with syrupy nut fragments.

Şah Plov   CAFETERIA **$**
(Əlqulu Nərimənov küç; mains AZN3-7; ⊙9am-10pm) Point to choose your cheap but hearty precooked meal and wash it down with a pint of ice-cold NZS beer (AZN1).

Mahir Fastfood   CAFE **$**
(☑070-3649413; Meydan; snacks AZN2.60-6, tea/coffee AZN0.80/1.5; ⊙9am-11pm; 🛜) The name undersells this log-cabin cafe with its big glass-sided terrace stretching onto the chestnut- and willow-framed central square.

It does sell burgers, pizzas and 'free' (chips) but there's also a small range of cakes to accompany espressos made on a simple but competent machine.

Mahir also has a cake shop and a lahmacun (☑070-3579413; Heydar Əliyev pr 182; lahmacun/dönər from AZN1.50/1.70; ⊙8.30am-8pm) specialist outlet nearer the bazaar.

Sərin   AZERBAIJANI **$$**
(☑Anar 050-8814141; mains AZN12, sac AZN26, kebabs AZN5-8; ⊙8am-11pm) The speciality here is a slow-cooked local stew that includes *bozport* (lamb with *kəvər* greens) or *buzdamac* (beef with carrots and garlic), served in small portions at tables dotted widely through a pretty (but poorly lit) woodland garden. The place has been popular for years and manager Anar speaks some English.

🍷 Drinking & Nightlife

Teahouses in Nizami Park charge locals AZN1 a pot but foreigners are sometimes asked vastly more: check before ordering. AZN1 beers are also served here and at several places near the bazaar, including garden-style Çay Evi 004 (Sahil küç; ⊙10am-11pm). A more stylish if pricey place for shisha sets (AZN35) is Lucky (☑050-7770609; www.facebook.com/luckyquba; Heydar Əliyev pr; mains AZN6-12; ⊙8am-1am) – no alcohol.

❶ Getting There & Away

Quba's cylindrical **bus station** (Yeni Avtovağzal; 🚌1) is on the Qusar-bound bypass, 800m north of Flag Sq. Destinations include the following:

Baku (AZN4, 2½ hours) At least hourly buses till 5.30pm.

Qusar (for Laza) Buses (0.50AZN, 25 minutes, three hourly till 6pm) plus shared taxis (per person/car AZN1/4) usually collect passengers at a stop near the bazaar roundabout, saving the hassle of going first to the bus station.

260

JUAN CARLOS MUNOZ/GETTY IMAGES ©

SAXSAGAN/SHUTTERSTOCK ©

CHRISTIAAN VAN HEIJST/500PX ©

ELNUR/SHUTTERSTOCK ©

1. Palace of the Shirvanshahs (p231)

Dating from the 15th century, this palace in Baku's Old City was once home to northeastern Azerbaijan's ruling dynasty.

2. Quba (p256)

Postcard-perfect mountainscapes and remote villages characterise this region.

3. Carpet Museum (p238), Baku

This fascinating museum's exterior, which resembles a roll of carpet, is by Austrian architect Franz Janz.

4. Baku (p230)

The Flame Towers (p238), by architects HOK, present a striking backdrop in this architecturally eclectic city.

Xaçmaz Twice-hourly minibuses (AZN1, 35 minutes).

Xınalıq (via Cek) Shared jeeps (per person/car AZN10/40, 1¾ hours) depart from opposite Xınalıq Hotel if there's custom. That's most likely between 2pm and 4pm. To pay the whole vehicle typically costs AZN40/50 one way/return, though we found prices AZN10 cheaper in older vehicles.

ⓘ Getting Around

By day, bus 1 (0.30AZN) runs regularly from the bus station via Flag Sq, Heydar Əliyev pr, the bazaar and through the Old Town, turning around just short of the main access lane to the Genocide Memorial. It returns along Əliqulu Nərimanov küç then restarts the route.

Quba to Xınalıq

Taking less than two hours each way, the drive from Quba to Xınalıq is magical and ever varied. At first the road tunnels through thick woodlands full of picnic spots. After Qəçrəş, grassy knolls provide viewpoints overlooking riverside orchards and looming foothills. At Minarə, a lonely teahouse clings precariously to a rocky pillar as the road enters the first of two impressive canyons. The second of these emerges at an uninhabited grassy picnic spot called Çaygoşan (Quba–Xınalıq Rd, Km 37-39) in an achingly beautiful bowl-valley backed by towering cliffs. The road then climbs high above the treeline passing a fabulous viewpoint at Km83.3 and at the minuscule village of Cek (Quba–Xınalıq road, Km 43), pronounced 'Jek'.

From a point around 1.5km beyond Cek, a hiking trail descends into the canyon, crosses a seasonal bridge then climbs straight up the far side to the clifftop plateau-village of Qrız. This makes a wonderful half-day trek, but some years the bridge at the canyon bottom gets washed away and without that (or a horse to carry you across the river), you might have to return the way you came. There's a very rough 4km jeep-road from Qrız back down to the Quba road near Çaygoşan.

🛏️ Sleeping & Eating

Between Quba and Qəçrəş, plus halfway along the Xınalıq–Quba road, there are many roadside kebab-barbeque places, often with bungalow accommodation. Tour groups tend to eat lunch at busy MəstDərgah whose summer tables are balanced across a trickling stream that runs off a waterfall pool.

MəstDərgah RESORT $$

(☏077-7324040; www.facebook.com/Mastdargah; Quba–Xınalıq road, Km 32; d/q/cottages AZN80/150/250; ❋ ☎) The high-quality, all-wooden cottages of this boutique resort constitute the most comfortable accommodation option on the Quba–Xınalıq road, with a particularly superb setting in the cliff-backed village of Qrız Dəhnə (not Qrız).

Xınalıq

☏ 023 / POP 700 / ELEV 2335M

Xınalıq, often transliterated as Khinalug, sits at 2335m - by some definitions, that makes it Europe's highest village. The settlement's upper half retains many ancient stone houses that form distinctively austere, stepped terraces up a steep highland ridge. The whole scene is often magically wrapped in spooky clouds that part sporadically to reveal 360-degree views of the surrounding Caucasus.

Apart from gazing at the hypnotic views, and enjoying the fabulous journey to get here, the main attraction is meeting and staying with Xınalıq's hardy shepherd folk who have their own language (Ketsh) and culture. Bring warm clothes - outside midsummer, nights here can be icy cold.

◉ Sights & Activities

The village has two little museums but guests at Hajibala's Homestay (p266) will get to see his private collection of historical and cultural curiosities which is arguably more interesting than either. The village's most important potential attraction is the Ateshgah, a mountainside shrine containing a spontaneously burning natural flame overlooking a glorious valleyscape. Currently, perplexing bureaucracy means that the five-hour return hike to get there is impossible without a series of permits that take at least a month to procure. English-speaking Xeyraddin Gabbarov of ME Travel (Mountain Eagle Travel; ☏ Whatsapp 050-2259250; www.xinaliq.com) can organise these and other walks that are otherwise blocked by the permit impasse. Tourist authorities hope that the situation will soon be simplified. Till then, an alternative for an easy, permit-free round-trip day-hike starts by following the Quba road back down 8km to Km 48.5 (finding a ride should be fairly easy). Take the 2km side-lane that climbs north to the attractive little village of Qalay Xudat, then follow the unpaved upper track back to Xınalıq, high above the valley.

Around Babadağ & Quba

Qusar – Laza

Qusarçay

Qusar
(13km)

⊙ **Quba**

Qudyalçay

Quba Palace
Hotel

connection
hard to find

Qəçrəş ○

Birinji Njugedi ○
(Nügədi I)

Nügədi II ○

Çənlibel

Qımıl ○

Qımılqazma ○

Dakhna ○

Minarə
Teahouse

Qımılqazma
Viewpoint

Aşağı
Tülakəran ○

Noydun ○

Alıc ○

Suduq ○

Rustov

Qrız ○
Dəhnə ○

MəstDərgah

Qrız ○

Cağacuçay

Qalay
Xudat ○

Çaygoşan ○

Quba-Xınalıq yolu

Xanagah ○

Təngəəlti ○

Cek ○

Buduq ○

Klab ○

Afurca ○

○ Bostankeş

Əlik ○

Zəyid ○

Qaraçay

Zixir ○

Gurdah ○

Afurca
Waterfall

Xınalıq
(6km)

Daliqaya ○

Haput ○

Rük ○

Söhüb ○

Adur ○

Qarxun ○

Yerfi ○

Qonaqkənd ○

Path to Babadağ

Valvala çayı

Xaltan-
Şamaxı yolu

Amanevi ○

Babadağ
(3629m) ▲

See Babadağ Hiking Route
Map (p264)

Şeitan
Daştan
(3361m) ▲

Göyçay

Gurbangah
Camp

Summer only
4WD Track

Girdimançay

Burovadal ○

Zarat ○

Chandakhar ○

Duvaryan ○

Odiyanar (tiny
natural flame)

Haftəsov ○

Qoydan ○

very steep
road

Müdrü ○

Vasha ○

Bağəli ○

Arakit ○

Əhən ○

Dəmirçi ○

Namazgah ○

Lahic

Qəndov ○

Şamaxı
(22km)

Pirqulu ○

CLIMBING MT BABADAĞ

HOLY BABADAĞ

START GURBANGAH
END GURBANGAH
LENGTH 14KM, EIGHT HOURS
DIFFICULTY MODERATE
SEASON JULY & AUGUST ONLY

The bald, 3629m peak of Mt Babadağ is not Azerbaijan's most spectacular mountain but it is by far the easiest high summit to climb, offers 360-degree panoramas and has the added cachet of being holy to locals. That means that fellow hikers on this route are far more likely to be pilgrims than sports-folk.

The mountain's 'holy' status is related to the mythical disappearance of Həzərət Baba, a 12th-century hermit who, faced by enemies pressuring him to give up his faith, retreated into the mountains. In a story with Biblical parallels, as he climbed ever higher he fought off temptation by throwing stones at a demon who attempted to trick him into returning. On reaching the summit he simply vanished: probably a metaphorical representation of his achieving a kind of Sufi-nirvana. These days, pilgrims believe that reaching the top once means that they'll be granted a wish, while climbing seven times is seen to achieve as much merit as making the hajj to Mecca.

☆ Planning

Although you'll find tour companies offering climbing packages (such as https://tours.cbtazerbaijan.com), the ascent is not much more than a steep walk and it is entirely possible in good weather to do the up-and-back route on your own by following everyone else (July and August only).

Reaching the Gurbangah trailhead requires a very bumpy, two-hour jeep ride from Lahıc (one-way AZN100, return within 24 hours around AZN140) on a track that's generally impassable until mid-June when it gets bulldozed into an approximate road.

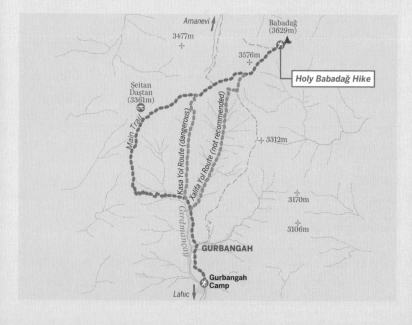

Climbing Azerbaijan's 'holy mountain' is a tiring but non-technical midsumer hike, great for sweeping views and curious cultural insights. It's possible as a very long day trip leaving Lahıc well before dawn.

Gurbangah is just a huddle of tea shacks (with sleeping spaces) and a camping area. The vast majority of climbers rest for a few hours here, then commence the hike well before dawn to avoid the worst of the heat – there is no shade on the slopes. Thus the most popular weeks for climbing are the third of each lunar month when there's a strong moon that rises late. Bringing a head torch is also highly advised. As you ascend, don't be surprised to find discarded sweaters here and there beside the trail: as people warm up they leave layers and collect them on the way back down.

☆ Routes Up

There are three variants for the Gurbangah–Babadağ walk, but two are dangerously steep, heading almost straight up an amphitheatre of scree. The far easier **main path** crosses the **Gırdmançay River** then makes a large semicircle to the west. It passes a couple of seasonal tea stalls, and accesses one of the mountain's unique highlights, **Şeitan Daştan** (Stone the Devil). A gorgeous viewpoint, this is where pilgrims very literally play out the Həzərət Baba story by launching rocks into the air, figuratively rejecting Satan.

After around four hours' climb, keep ahead where there is a small metal sign reading 'Quba' in Cyrillic letters, pointing obliquely north and down. This is the route to take on the way back should you wish to continue to Amanevi. From here, continuing east on the steadily rising path takes just over an hour more to the summit, where, as well as the panoramic view, there is a tiny, half-collapsed **shrine**. Beside this you'll normally find a queue of the pious waiting to share prayers with a *mollah* (holy man) who dots their foreheads with holy mud in a simple ritual that looks more Hindu than Muslim.

☆ Alternative Descent

Most walkers return the same way to Gurbangah. However, it's also possible to descend in around six hours northward to Amanevi (17km total one way from Gurbangah), a small shepherds camp area at the riverside where there is the chance of shelter but neither beds nor toilets. If you continue to Amanevi, you're much more likely to need linguistic assistance, as the north route down the mountain is far less frequented; you might arrive at the camp to find it unoccupied, in which case you'll need your own tent and sleeping gear. The northbound descent offers many fine views of the deep-cut river valley spreading out its tentacles into the mountain massif and there are a couple of attractive meadow stopping-places each with a seasonal shepherds camp. Beware of dogs. A third meadow below offers a good camping spot if it's getting too late to continue.

From Amanevi to the nearest village, Qarxun, is around 13km up the river. Occasionally there is a six-wheel truck-bus but you will probably need to take a second day to walk it. At 6am most days there's a shared jeep-taxi from Qarxun to Quba.

🛏 Sleeping & Eating

In Xınalıq village, one place misleadingly calls itself an 'Otel' and several options are bookable online, but all are simply local houses with basic beds and outdoor toilets, usually of the squat variety. Most are unmarked. Rates of around AZN20 to AZN25 per person usually include breakfast and plenty of tea, dinner might cost extra. Foodwise, the only in-village alternative to eating at your homestay is a tiny shop and a seasonal *qutab* (pancake) stall.

Hajibala's Homestay　　　　HOMESTAY $
(☎ 023-3349051, 051-8500142; Xınalıq; incl breakfast AZN20-25, half-board AZN35) Xınalıq's affable village historian speaks good Russian and has a comparatively comfortable Old Town house decorated with local historical curiosities. The guest bedroom has a novelty light that changes colour by remote control. You'll dream in vain of an indoor toilet but this is Xınalıq, after all.

ℹ Getting There & Away

To get back to Quba, ask your host to find you a space in a shared jeep (early morning).

Laza & Shahdag Ski Area

☎ 023 / POP 250

On a clear day, as you drive west from Qusar (13km north of Quba), the noble bulk of Şahdağ (4243m) is visible for kilometres ahead. It looks especially impressive when viewed from near the historic village of Əniğ with its distinctively metal-domed old mosque. Around 10km later, just after Aladaş, is Azerbaijan's foremost ski resort with seasonal cable cars, ultraluxurious hotels and gourmet restaurants. Some 5km further via a much rougher road is the contrastingly modest village of Laza, which has what is arguably the most spectacular setting of any village in Azerbaijan.

Just beyond Laza, exploration is hindered by the strict visiting requirements of Shahdag National Park (p256), but with permits, the hiking and mountaineering is superb.

👁 Sights & Activities

Hiking groups including Camping Azerbaijan (p303) occasionally offer the Sudur–Elik–Kuzun walk, which offers superb, little-seen vistas of the Shahdag Massif's north face, but can't be done alone due to permit worries. Permit-free walks include explorations along the river canyon, some routes towards the craggy tops of Qızıl Qaya, and a climb up beside the main Laza waterfall onto sheep pastures that could lead you (in a very long day) to Qrız (p262).

Once the most popular hike in Azerbaijan, the one-day walk to Xınalıq via the Ateshgah has been out of bounds for several years due to bureaucratic issues, but it is hoped that in 2020 or 2021 the route will reopen. Till then, guide Mevlud Azizov might be able to organise the necessary paperwork for you given a few weeks' notice (and AZN50 per person plus guide fee).

Laza　　　　VILLAGE
Laza is a diffuse scattering of houses encircled by soaring mountains with grass-clad slopes and ribbon waterfalls cascading over perilous cliff edges. A rocky pinnacle beside the little metal-roofed mosque adds foreground for photos of the mind-blowing panorama.

Shahdag Mountain Resort　　　　SKIING
(Şahdag Turizm Kompleksi; http://shahdag.az; Qusar–Laza road, Km 39; 1-day ski pass AZN30; ☺ ski lifts mid-Jun–Sep & mid-Dec–late Mar, weather dependent) Azerbaijan's top ski resort has a lower base (1435m) beside the Zirve Hotel and an upper 'resort village' (1650m) which is essentially a trio of very snazzy five-star hotels. Four chairlifts and a gondola service the 17km of pistes, mostly blues and reds, which descend a very attractive amphitheatre of slopes from a high ridge at 2525m.

In summer there is a selection of outdoor activities, including quad-bike rides and organised hikes.

🛏 Sleeping & Eating

Azizov Family Homestay　　　　HOMESTAY $
(☎ Khaled 051-4172600; Laza; per person from AZN20) Near the entrance to Laza there's a small shop. The houses facing and behind it are homestays of the Azizov family, who also own self-contained bungalows at the other end of the village (AZN30 to AZN50) close to the waterfalls en route to Suvar.

Park Qusar　　　　RESORT $$
(☎ 055-4243333; www.facebook.com/parkqusar; Qusar–Laza Rd, Km 30.2, Əniq; d/q from AZN90/160; 🅿🛜) Offering spectacular panoramic views of the whole Şahdağ Massif, this quality rural resort offers fully equipped pine bungalows, a range of sports, and a restaurant that is remarkably well priced.

It's across the valley from Əniq village, 10km short of the Shahdag ski lifts and a 1.4km drive off the Qusar–Laza road after Km 30. Taxis cost AZN10 from Qusar. Open year-round.

Shahdag Hotel & Spa
HOTEL $$$

(☎ 012-3101110, from local mobile 1110; s/d from AZN179/195, low season AZN119/135; ⓟ 🛜 🐾) Şəbəkə panels and lamps like upturned oriental parasols create a warm-yet-stylish ambience in the suave Shahdag Hotel. It's an upper-market resort with over 170 rooms, an Ovdan-branded spa and good-sized indoor pool. It is the only one of three five-star hotels in the ski area that stays open year-round.

ℹ Information

Mevlud Azizov (☎ Whatsapp 070-9014048; misha_971@mail.ru; Laza) Mevlud, aka Misha, speaks some English and has years of experience as a licensed mountain guide around Laza.

Contact him a month or more in advance for the latest details about permits for mountaineering and treks such as the Laza–Xınalıq trek. He charges AZN50 per person plus guide fee to arrange the paperwork for hard-to-organise Shahdag National Park trekking permits, using scanned copies of your passport etc.

ℹ Getting There & Away

Once or twice hourly there are buses from Baku (AZN4, three hours) and Quba (0.50AZN, 25 minutes) to the Lezghin town of Qusar. From there the ski resort is around 40 minutes' drive. Taxis cost as little as AZN15 in summer, rather more in ski season.

NORTHWESTERN AZERBAIJAN

The most appealing route between Baku and Tbilisi (Georgia) is the scenic odyssey that sets off across semi-desert, passes the vineyard hills of once-powerful Şamaxı then continues into leafy northwestern Azerbaijan with its pretty meadows, woodland foreslopes and glimpses of high peaks. Don't miss the quaint coppersmith village of Lahıc, the glitzy resorts of Qəbələ or the Unesco-lauded historical core of Şəki. As you continue, little Qax and hazelnut city Zaqatala are also charming. With your own wheels, there's a scattering of ancient archaeological ruins to discover in offbeat villages.

Şamaxı

📍 020 / POP 36,800 / ELEV 745M

For centuries, Şamaxı (Shemakha), not Baku, was northern Azerbaijan's foremost city. However, apart from some ancient graves, essentially nothing of antiquity has survived the ravages of earthquakes and invasions. The one must-see sight is Şamaxı Grand Mosque (Şamaxı Cümə Məscidi; Şirvani küç; ⊙ 3am-midnight), the Caucasus' 'second-oldest mosque'. It's a very impressive structure but essentially rebuilt within the last decade. On the moorland hills some 20km north of the town, the Rəsədxana (Şamaxı Astrofizika Rəsədxanası; ☑ Sabahaddin 055-2513644; http://shao.az; ⊙ museum 8am-6pm, stargazing 10pm & 2am) is Azerbaijan's foremost place for scientific astronomy and a photogenic sight if you're driving the newly paved backcountry route to Lahıc via the Şamaxı Safari Park and Dəmirçi village, which has a small 8th-century mosque and a newly opened archaeological museum (Dəmirçi village; ⊙ 8am-6pm) FREE.

İsmayıllı

📍 020 / POP 21,700 / ELEV 660M

Mainly useful as a transport hub for Lahıc, İsmayıllı has a gently attractive central square shaded by beautiful mature trees and is intriguing for its long stretches of newly built fortress-style wall: amusingly these have absolutely no historical context. On the hilltops 15km to the south lies İvanovka, partly populated by Molokans (Russian nonconformists) and the last place in the country to maintain its Soviet-style collective farm. Continuing from there, a gloriously panoramic skyline drive brings you to the lonely Chabiant Winery (Şato Monolit, Chateau Monolith; ☑ Tilly 055-5459001, Xalid 051-2504393; Hacıhətəmli village; ⊙ phone ahead, closed Jan) with hotel, swimming pool, hefty stone cellars and a sweeping vine-framed panorama.

ℹ Getting There & Away

The **bus station** (Avtovağzal) is at the northeastern edge of the town centre just behind an area of small shops built into one of the corners of the 'castle'-style walls. Services include Baku (12 daily), Gəncə (8am and 2pm) and Bərdə (noon and 2.30pm). For Lahıc (AZN1.50, 1½ hours) the minibus starts instead from the roundabout 100m further northeast, departing at 7am, 11am, 2pm and 4pm.

For Şəki or Oğuz via Qəbələ, minibuses originating in Baku pass through İsmayıllı and, if not full, should pick up passengers at the Heydər Əliyev pr junction, 2km west of the bus station. If seeking a shared car here, note that 55 number plates are from Şəki. Alternatively take a Bərdə bus from the bus station for Qəbələ.

Lahıc

⏰ 020 / POP 950 / ELEV 1200M

Lahıc is a pretty, highland village that's locally famous for its Persian-based dialect and traditional coppersmiths. It can feel just a little touristy at weekends when Bakuvians arrive to get photographed in vaguely preposterous sheepskin costumes. But stay a day or two and listen to the mellifluous mosques as mists swirl around the partly forested crags and you'll find it a delightful starting point for hiking and meeting locals who, more than in almost any other village in Azerbaijan, speak a smattering of English.

◉ Sights

Zərnava Bridge   LANDMARK
(Girdimançay Asma Körpü; Lahıc Yolu, Km 9) This spindly suspension footbridge was designed to help villagers reach the hamlet of Zərnava but these days its users are mostly selfie-snapping tourists challenging their senses of vertigo. It's around halfway between Lahıc and the main Baku–Qəbələ road.

Hüseynov Küç   STREET
(Coppersmith Street) Lahıc's pedestrianised main street is unevenly paved with smooth pale river-stones and lined with older houses built traditionally with interleaving stone and timber layers plus box windows. Even though it's an unashamed tourist trap by day, it remains a delight to stroll amid the copper boutiques, ice-cream sellers and snack vendors. The simple workshop at number 82 remains an active forge and number 43–45 is a superbly photogenic coppersmithy with a dusty, museum-like antique section and an Ali Baba's cavern-like shop.

Lahıc History Museum   MUSEUM
(Nizami küç; donation expected; ⏰9am-1pm & 2-6pm Tue-Sat) This quaint little one-room collection of cultural artefacts is housed in a 1902 former mosque next door to the tourist office. Posted opening times are very approximate.

🏃 Activities

There are many great walks around Lahıc and neighbouring villages. Horse riding is also possible and in midsummer, quad bikes are available for rent from the Evim Hotel, ideal for zigzagging up to Müdrü.

Hiking up the steep wooded hillsides, you emerge on bare mountaintop sheep meadows *(qaylağ)* with views towards snow-topped Caucasus peaks that are majestic on clear days. For easy access you could cross the Girdmançay Bridge, climb 4km up the muddy jeep track towards Müdrü then walk along the upper ridge roads.

There is a tiny fire vent on a mountainside above Həftəsov village. Or with a horse and guide you could make a full-day excursion via the Fit Dağ castle ruins emerging at Sulut or Mucu, from where there's a drivable 4WD route back to the main İsmayıllı road via Basqal. Two hours' drive north of Lahıc is the Gurbangah camp from which pilgrims make predawn climbs of 'holy mountain' Babadağ (p264) in July and August: bring a head torch. The tourist office offers many more suggestions and can help you find guides and horses.

Niyal Qalası   HIKING
(Girdaman Qalası) This utterly ruined castle site is a barely recognisable heap of stones, but for a half-day hike (1½ hours up, less back) it is arguably more interesting than heading up the riverbed to a 4m waterfall. Both are relatively easy-to-follow walks that start up the Kişçay valley beside Cənnət Bağı Guest House. For Niyal, cross then climb and stay high.

🛏 Sleeping

Cənnət Bağı Guest House   HOMESTAY $
(Garden of Paradise; ⏰070-2870140, 050-5870140; pgjessylahic@gmail.com; camping per tent AZN10, per person homestay AZN15-20, cottages AZN40-60; ⏰closed Dec-Feb; 🅿🛜) This large, simple homestay is set in lovely landscaped cherry and apple orchards right at the entrance to the village. Four cottages come with private bathroom. The attractive house has shared toilets and shower on the yard but its private *hammam* (bathhouse) is a popular bonus (free for homestayers, extra for campers).

English-speaking Cəsarət İsmailov ('Jessy') is almost always in residence and can rustle up guides and horses at relatively short notice. Reliable quality meals (dolma AZN6, beer AZN4) are available in the very pretty garden.

Rustam Rustamov's Guesthouse HOMESTAY $$
(☑ 050-3658049; http://lahijguesthouse.com; Aracit; s/d AZN80/90; P ⊜ ☏) With the comfort of a midrange hotel but the personal charm of a great homestay, this is far and away the most appealing choice in Lahıc, with verandah seating, a pretty orchard garden, great private bar-lounge and a dining room lavished with local handicrafts and swords. Affable English-speaking host Rustam can help with hiking suggestions.

The best room has a big balcony with rocking chairs. Delicious dinners from locally sourced produce are available by advance arrangement. To find Rustam's place, follow the main street to Əracit Sq, then turn right.

Evim Otel HOTEL $$
(☑ 051-8800010; www.evimotel.az; s/d/tr/apt AZN60/80/90/140; P☏) Built in semi-traditional style, this family-friendly place has pleasant, pine-floored rooms with kilims and semi-style-conscious bathroom fittings. Several pairs of rooms share bathroom and kitchenette to form mini-apartments. Hidden to one side there's a garden play area for children. It's just south of the central crossroads. To find it by vehicle, take the riverside road to the big bridge then turn into the village and cross the main street beside the old bridge.

✖ Eating

Though you'd never guess it from the somewhat forbidding exterior wall, **Lahıc Restaurant** (☑ 055-4211242; mains AZN6; ⊙8am-9pm; P) near the school has an appealing interior and a tree-shaded garden with fine mountain views. Alternatively, a very pretty spot to eat is the orchard garden of Cənnət Baği Guest House, which makes a local 'sugar bread' (*şəkər çörəyi*). **Lahıc Riverside** (☑ 050-6761444; Bridge Approach; mains AZN3-6; ⊙7am-10.30pm) stays open later than most places.

ℹ Information

Tourist office (☑ 055-6777517, 050-6777517; lahij.tourizm@mail.ru; Nizami küç; ⊙ call) A helpful little office beside the Lahıc History Museum and a good first call if you're thinking of hiring guides or horses, or need a homestay recommendation. English spoken.

ℹ Getting There & Away

Lahıc is 20km off the main Baku–İsmayıllı road turning north opposite the Səhih-M/M Petrol Station.

Transport departures leave from the little bridge on Hüseynov küç, halfway to Əragit.

Baku A minibus leaves most days at 8am (AZN8, four hours), book ahead.

İsmayıllı Minibuses (AZN1.50, 1½ hours) at 8.30am, 11am, 1pm and 4pm (AZN1.50, 1½ hours). Taxi AZN15, worth considering for photo stops.

Şəki/Şamaxı Hosts can arrange informal taxis to Şəki with photo stops and a side trip to Old Qəbələ (around AZN70). Or to Şamaxı using the super-steep new lane via Dəmirçi (AZN50)

Qəbələ

☑ 024 / POP 18,600 / ELEV 785M

Azerbaijan's top provincial holiday centre, Qəbələ is backed by high mountains and equipped with a year-round network of four cable-car rides that whisk visitors up into the wooded foothills where skiing is popular in winter. Qəbələ is enormously popular with Gulf tourists who savour the unfamiliarity of forests and seasonal snow from the comfort of several high-quality resort hotels, most of which come with fine spas and great swimming pools yet charge affordable rates, especially in low season. A series of events and meetings hosted here also attracts a wider audience.

◉ Sights

The central area is pleasant but all major sights require driving out of town. Popular excursions include the excellent **Savalan Winery** (☑ 077-339-6007; www.savalan.az; Ağdaş Yolu; per person AZN15-25; ⊙call ahead) 30km south, the Old Gabala archaeological site 20km southwest and the pretty but often tourist-packed **Seven Beauties Waterfall** (Yeddi Gözəl Şəlaləsi; Rusiyan village; ⊙cafes May-Sep only) 12km east, typically combined with a boat ride on **Nohur Lake**.

Durca VILLAGE
(Duruja) This photogenic village was built for semi-nomadic shepherds whose families only live here during the summer. Get off the ropeway between the third and fourth rides to take a stroll around. Despite some newer holiday homes, the upper village remains essentially unspoilt with several older stone houses and plenty of walking opportunities in the valley behind.

Old Gabala Site ARCHAEOLOGICAL SITE
(☑ 024-2021257; qebele_qoruq@inbox.ru; Çuxur Qəbələ; admission/guide AZN2/10; ⊙9am-6pm) Today's Qəbələ was renamed for an ancient

---

DON'T MISS

BATHING IN OIL

The curative properties of special oils from Naftalan in central Azerbaijan have been known for centuries and were reported by Marco Polo. In the Soviet era, the idea of bathing in such oil was developed into a potent treatment for a range of maladies, and health-seekers from across the USSR flew to Azerbaijan to recuperate. Today Naftalan remains a very popular spa town for Russians and Central Asians but if you just want to try the experience, there's no need to go all that way: you can take a Naftalan oil bath in the appealing **Qafqaz Thermal Resort** (☏ 024-2054393; info@qafqazthermalhotel. com; Yengicə village; s/d/ste from AZN110/140/195; P ❀ 🛜 🌊) spa hotel at Yengicə, 17km from Qəbələ.

One catch is that, 'for your protection', before you take the bath (AZN15) you must pass a medical exam to check that your heart is strong enough for the experience... and the doctor isn't always available.

Note to gain any real medical advantage, you're supposed to do at least a week-long course of treatment so taking a single bath is just for the novelty.

---

city mentioned in Pliny the Elder's *Natural History* (AD 77), and forgotten after it was destroyed by the 18th-century invader Nader Shah. Rediscovered in 1959, Old Gabala is now a serene rural archaeological site 20km west of town. What you see is mainly a large grassy field, containing a couple of interesting excavations plus the stumpy remains of two massive gate-towers. A brand-new museum shows off numerous finds and adds some context.

The site is 4km off the Qəbələ–Şəki road, turning south at Mirzəbəyli. There's no public transport. Consider chartering a taxi between Qəbələ and Oğuz, seeing Old Gabala as a side trip, and possibly adding a visit to the Albanian church at the ethnically Udi village of Nic.

🏃 Activities

Winter skiing and summer hikes are joined by lots of other activities. Try skidoo or quad-bike rides (according to season) from behind the Tufandağ Hotel; tandem paragliding with **Canfly** (☏ Whatsapp 050-4999191; www. facebook.com/canflyaz; tandem flight AZN200; ☉ Jun-Aug, call ahead); pistol and clay-pigeon shooting in **Bum** (Qəbələ atıcılıq klubu; www. facebook.com/gabalashooting; Bum; ☉ 10am-7pm; 🖥 2); bowling at the Qafqaz Resort; skating, karting and electronic paintball at Qabaland; or swimming at excellent pools in half a dozen resorts.

Tufandağ Ropeways   CABLE CAR
(http://tufandag.az; non-skier return ticket AZN10-20, ski pass half-/full day AZN16/25, card deposit AZN10; ☉ 9am-5.30pm or later) Riding these four cable cars takes you up, down, along

then back up different mountain slopes between appealing cafe-restaurants and, in winter, ski-pistes. Allow at least a couple of hours to make the most of it; if you're in a rush, just use the Riverside lift (L2) which is the the most thrilling.

For those not carrying skis, tickets cost AZN20 allowing one out-and-back ride on all four cable cars. Or pay AZN10 for either half of the system. Buy tickets at the **Riverside** (☉ 9am-5.30pm, last return 6pm) or Tufandağ ropeway stations behind the hotels of the same names.

Qabaland   AMUSEMENT PARK
(www.facebook.com/Qabaland; admission AZN3, plus per attraction AZN1-4; ☉ noon-midnight Jun-Aug, 9am-8pm Sep-Jan & Mar-May, weekends only Feb; 🅿) It's not quite Disneyland, but Azerbaijan's top theme park is a godsend for local families and has something for all ages. All rides are paid through a pre-charged cash card.

It's 3km north of central Qəbələ, 300m east of the grand congress-centre building.

Skiing

The ski season is generally mid-December to February on 10 pistes totalling 17km, including an easy, wide 1.2km blue-green run and a couple of killer reds that feel pretty much black. Good-quality ski rental is available from beside the Riverside Ropeway Station and from the Qafqaz Tufandağ Hotel. Either charges AZN25 for boots, poles and skis/snowboard. Helmet (AZN5) and ski-wear are also available to rent but you'll need your own goggles or sunglasses (available for sale).

Private ski lessons cost AZN35/50 for one/ two hours, less per person in a group or for children.

 Festivals & Events

Gabala International Music Festival
MUSIC

(www.gabalamusicfestival.com; ☉ Jul) Qəbələ's highbrow music festival is certainly not Glastonbury. Collared shirts trump tie-dyes here and the focus is on classical music. Concerts are mostly held at the Heydar Aliyev Congress Centre in the Riverside resort area.

🛏 Sleeping

Six impressive hotel-resort complexes in and around Qəbələ are all part of the Qafqaz chain (https://qafqazhotels.com). Apart from the luxurious Tufandağ Hotel, whose guests share use of a giant sports complex with the Qafqaz Resort Hotel, 2km away, all have superb swimming pools and indulgent spas. There are two cheaper hotels in the town centre, simple guesthouses dotted all around the area and a hostel near the Riverside ropeway station.

Kahran Hostel
HOSTEL $

(Kəhran Hostel; ☎ 070-3032920; www.insta gram.com/kahranhostel; İsmayıl bəy Qutqaşınlı pr; dm AZN10-15) One of the best hostels in rural Azerbaijan. Dorm beds come with drawer lockers, there's a large shared kitchen and one of the shop-units downstairs has a coffeeshop-cafe. The youthful owners speak excellent English. Kahran sits above the co-owned RaJa Indian Restaurant, around 600m southwest of the Riverside Ropeway.

Tufandağ Hotel
LUXURY HOTEL $$$

(☎ 024-2054383; https://qafqazhotels.com; Durca Yolu; s/d/ste from AZN201/222/332) An excellent base if you're skiing, Tufandağ is Qəbələ's most tastefully upmarket property (other than the absurdly exclusive Chenot Palace) and provides one of the best breakfast buffets in Azerbaijan. It's 2km up the road towards Duruca from the Qafqaz Resort Hotel, whose extensive sports facilities guests here can use without charge.

You can alternatively get here across the mountain from Riverside by a pair of cable-car rides.

Qafqaz Karavansaray
HERITAGE HOTEL $$$

(☎ 024-2054455; https://qafqazhotels.com/en/ hotels/qafqaz-karvansaray-hotel; Elçin Kərimov küç; s/d from AZN110/125, peak season d/ste from AZN175/260) The best value of Qəbələ's design hotels, the courtyards here are stylised to evoke a caravanserai while the excellent, if sometimes compact rooms have more neo-art-deco touches.

The restaurant here tends to be somewhat more experimental than those of the other big resorts and the little cafe serves fine coffee and excellent chestnut halva.

Qafqaz Riverside
RESORT $$$

(☎ 024-2054330; www.qafqazriversidehotel.com; d/ste/cottages from AZN190/250/360) Glitzy but not over the top, Qəbələ's luxurious seven-storey flagship hotel stares up the valley towards a lovely mountain panorama. There are indoor and outdoor pools, a spa with classic marble *hammam* rooms, shisha lounges, a billiard hall and plenty of summer activities for families. It's beside an area of pretty woodland, ideally placed for accessing the steepest cable car.

The resort is located some 4km north of central Qəbələ, 6km from the bus station.

🍴 Eating

Qəbələ's classic, if greasy, local speciality is *daş arası*, a way of cooking kebabs between hot stones. More tempting is *qəbələ aş*, a rich rice dish incorporating chicken and chestnuts, available cheaply at Kafe #1. Of the hotel restaurants, the one at Qafqaz Karavansaray has the most imaginative cuisine. Chalet is the top choice on the mountaintops.

Kafe #1
AZERBAIJANI $

(28 May küç; mains AZN4-8; ☉ 11am-11pm) The best-value local food is served in an attractive antique-styled wooden interior at this rather hidden place off 28 May küç in the town centre. The only sign says 'Təndir', reminding customers that even the bread here is deliciously fresh-baked. Cheap draught beer.

Qəbələ Xanlar
AZERBAIJANI $$

(☎ 050-5363634; www.facebook.com/qabalax anlar; Qutqaşınlı küç; mains from AZN6; ☉ 10am-11pm) Various differently designed thatched dining platforms are set behind a series of amusing water-powered mobiles at one of Qəbələ's longest-running and best-respected rustic kebab restaurants. The extensive menu includes assorted pre-bookable group feasts that might feature *shah plov, sac* (meat, veggies and potatoes on a sizzling hotplate) or *səbət* (roasted rack of sheep-ribs).

★ **Chalet** INTERNATIONAL $$$

(📱 050-290-2832; Yatmish Gozal; mains AZN10-22, steaks AZN25-90; ⏱1-6pm Tue-Sun) At the top of the Yatmish Gozal cable car (L6), Chalet is not just a great place to sit amid the mountain scenery, but also serves the best-quality Western food in Qəbələ, notably sizzlers and great pasta along with some exclusive imported steaks. Downstairs there's a rather hidden barrel-decor wine-bar.

Some weekends the restaurant stays open till 11pm, as does the ropeway to get you back down afterwards.

🍷 Drinking & Nightlife

All of the Qafqaz hotels have bar-cafes, often opening all night. There are several places to smoke shisha and the Riverside Hotel has a (guests-only) nightclub. For a glass of wine with great views take the ropeway to **Qəbələ Restaurant** (Tufandağ Ropeway; ⏱10am-6pm; 📷). For cheap, town-centre beers with the locals, **Beer Bros** (Heydər Əliyev pr) is fun and quirky, if male-dominated, with a friendly, English-speaking owner.

☆ Entertainment

Gabala FC FOOTBALL

(FK Qəbələ; http://gabalafc.az/eng) Although FK Qəbələ is one of the nation's top football teams, winning the Azerbaijan Cup in 2019, attending its home games is usually entirely free. The stadium is on the western edge of town with the entrance on the north side.

The team was once managed by ex-Arsenal and England star Tony Adams.

ℹ Information

There's a small **tourist office** (📱024-2052256; Mədəniyyət Evi, Heydər Əliyev pr; ⏱10am-6pm) in the west side of the Culture Centre building. English-speaking Anar at **Travel Center** (📱070-3384301; www.travel-center.az; Qutqaşınlı pr 24; ⏱10am-1pm & 2-6pm Mon-Fri, or call) is a mine of local information and organises a range of culturally relevant experiences including horse riding, village dinners, day-with-a-shepherd and cow-milking.

Some hiking routes behind Qəbələ fall within the Shahdag National Park and need permits (AZN2), a guide and in some cases military clearance. You can try to organise these for yourself through the **park office** (Şahdağ Milli Parkı Qəbələ Rayon Şöbəsi; 📱Səməd 050-3476588; cnr Heydər Əliyev pr & Aslanov küç; ⏱9am-1pm & 2-6pm Mon-Fri) in the city centre, but nobody there speaks English. Javid and Rahul at Kahran Hostel (p271) can help their guests with hiking and permit information.

ℹ Getting There & Away

The only flight from **Gabala International Airport** (GBB; Ağdaş Yolu) is a good-value Tuesday service to Moscow–Vnukovo (AZN256).

The **bus station** (Avtovağzal; Qutqaşınli pr) is 2km south of the town centre, beyond the splendid 21st-century stone mosque. Useful services:

Baku Buses (AZN6, 3½ hours) around twice hourly 7am to 6pm, fewer in afternoons. For İsmayıllı pay the full Baku fare or risk being refused a seat. Shared taxis to Baku (AZN12, three hours) start from a point just across the main river bridge east of the centre.

Gəncə Buses (AZN5, three hours) at 8.15am, 8.40am, 10am and 3pm.

Şəki Buses (AZN2, two hours) via Oğuz at 9am, 11am, noon and 3pm. Alternatively try to find a space on a Baku–Oğuz bus. Oğuz has two small, inexpensive hotels near its bus station and onward services to Şəki (AZN1, 40 minutes) running hourly 8am to 3pm plus 5pm. Beautiful scenery.

ℹ Getting Around

A few times per hour, bus 2 (30q) runs east from Bum village to central Qəbələ then turns south down Qutqaşınlı küç to Zarağan (the junction for the road to Oğuz), passing the bazaar and bus station. If you're in a hurry you could jump into a shared taxi from near the **Qutqaşınlı–Heydər Əliyev küç junction** (Qutqaşınlı küç): these run all the way to Hacıalılı via Zarağan and the airport (AZN1).

Şəki

📱024 / POP 68,400 / ELEV 630M

Snoozing amid green pillows of beautifully forested mountains, Şəki (Sheki) is Azerbaijan's loveliest town, dappled with tiled-roof old houses and topped off with a glittering little khan's palace. In 2019 its old core was declared a Unesco World Heritage Site.

History

Historic Şəki was originally higher up the valley around the site now occupied by Kiş. That town was ruined by floods in 1716 but rebuilt by rebellious Khan Haci Çələbi, who set up a defiantly independent khanate there in the 1740s. He also built a second fortress at Nukha (today's Şəki). When the original Şəki was obliterated by a second, even more catastrophic flood in 1772, Nukha became the new royal capital.

After 1805, when the khanate was ceded to Russia, Nukha continued to flourish as a silk-weaving town and was a trading junction between caravan routes to Baku, Tbilisi and Derbent (Dagestan), with five working caravanserais at its peak. Nukha was re-named Şəki in the 1960s.

◉ Sights

◉ Within the Fortress Walls

The sturdy stone perimeter wall of Haci Çələbi's Nukha Fortress today encloses an 18th-century palace, tourist office, craft workshops and a decent cafe-restaurant, all set in patches of sheep-mown grass. There are also two largely forgettable museums (each AZN2), one of them in a circular for-mer 'Albanian' church (Museum of National Applied Art; foreigner/local AZN2/1; ⊙10am-6.30pm) with a photogenic exterior.

★ **Xan Sarayı** PALACE
(Fortress grounds; foreigner/local AZN5/2, guide AZN5; ⊙10am-6pm) This ornate 1762 palace building features vivid murals and dazzling coloured light streaming through *şəbəkə*, making it Şəki's foremost sight and one of the South Caucasus' most iconic buildings. It was originally the Şəki Khan's adminis-trative building, just one of around 40 now-lost royal structures within the fortress compound.

You don't have to pay the entrance fee to enter the walled rose garden in which the palace is set behind two huge plane trees, planted in 1530. The facade combines sil-vered stalactite vaulting with strong ge-ometric patterns in dark blue, turquoise and ochre. The petite interior is only one room deep, but lavished with intricate designs. Most are floral but in the central upper chamber you'll find heroic scenes of Haci Çələbi's 1743 battle with Persian emperor Nader Shah complete with requisite swords, guns and severed heads. No photos are al-lowed inside.

Şəbəkə Workshop WORKSHOP
(Şəbəkə Şənət Evi; ☑050-6483015; Fortress grounds; ⊙9am-8pm) FREE The *şəbəkə* fea-tured at Xan Sarayı are laboriously made by slotting together hundreds of hand-carved wooden pieces to create intricate wooden frames without metal fastenings. You can see them being produced at this no-hassle family workshop where young apprentices are learning the trade in the back room be-hind an unmarked little shop where exam-ples are sold and explained.

◉ Beyond the Fortress Walls

Beyond the fortress walls, a canalised stream parallels MF Axundzadə pr from the fortress area to the new town's main square, passing two 19th-century mosques, two great caravanserais and numerous shops selling distinctive Şəki sweets. Away from this road, it's fun to delve into the maze of residential Old Town alleys full of typical tiled-roof homes.

Xanların Evi PALACE
(House of Sheki Khans; Hikmət Ələkbərzadə küç, Otağ Eşiye; foreigner/local AZN5/2, guide AZN5; ⊙8am-8pm) The Şəki Khans' little-publicised 'other' palace is a slightly small-er, older version of the Xan Sarayı set in its own rose garden. While five of the six rooms are essentially plain, the sixth has a stunning series of original 1765 murals depicting scenes from Nizami classics. The English-speaking guide, Rumella, lives next door. She and her family protected the monument for years, long before it was restored.

Karavansaray Hotel NOTABLE BUILDING
(MF Axundzadə pr 185) FREE Even if you don't stay (p275) here, do peep inside this his-toric caravanserai whose twin-level arcade of sturdy arches enclose a sizeable central courtyard. Stride through the imposing wooden gateway door and if questioned say you're heading for the restaurant in the gar-den behind. Groups are permitted to visit between 11am and 7pm.

Dili Qala FORT
There's nothing historic about this curious castle-like folly, an intriguing landmark on the ridge above town. It was designed to be a hotel but so poorly constructed that it was never finished. Foliage growing through the remnants adds a photogenic touch and there are great city views from here.

◉ Kiş & Beyond

Kiş Albanian Church CHURCH
(Kiş Alban Məbadi; Kiş village; foreigner/local/ student/child AZN4/2/1/0.20, guide AZN10; ⊙8am-8pm; ☑15) The brilliantly renovat-ed round-towered 'temple' in pretty Kiş village has been lovingly converted into a very well-presented trilingual muse-um. It's the best place anywhere to learn about mysterious Caucasian Albania, the Christian nation that once covered most of northern Azerbaijan. In fact, the church

AZERBAIJAN ŞƏKI

Şəki (Sheki)

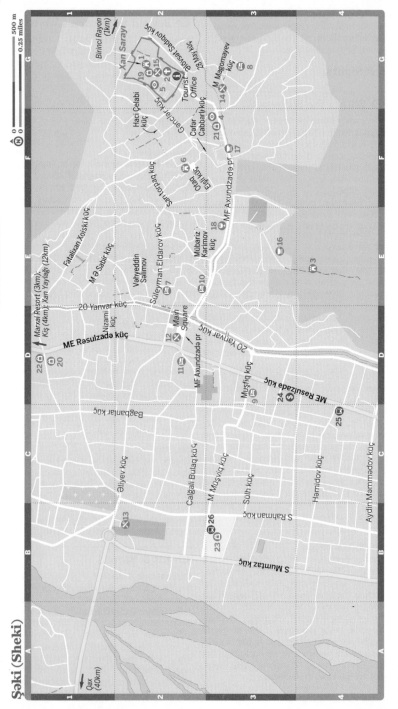

site goes back well beyond the Christian era and glass-covered grave excavations allow visitors to peer down onto Bronze Age skeletons.

To find the church, take the first climbing lane that doubles back to the right after Kiş' main street becomes cobbled and climb an 800m loop (there are signs). At a charming cafe opposite the entrance you might meet site director İlhamə Hüseynova, who organises homestays in the village and at her own little **guesthouse** (☑024-2498833, 050-6310246; ilhame633@mail.ru; Kiş village; homestay per person AZN15, with full board AZN30).

Xan Yaylağı   VIEWPOINT
High above the city, a plateau of summer pastures known as Xan Yaylağı offers truly superb viewpoints back over the valley and northwards towards high Caucasian peaks.

The easiest access is by 4WD using a 7km switchback forest track that zigzags up from Marxal Resort. If you'd prefer to walk, there's an alternative path that starts from the terminus of *marshrutka* 17 in Şəki's Birinci Rayon district, taking around 3½ hours up, two hours back. However, at the time of writing, this route was officially closed, if not actually guarded. Even if/when it does reopen, note that bears live in the forest so hiking alone isn't recommended, especially in spring.

Activities

Xan Yaylağı Offroad   SCENIC DRIVE
(☑055-5003633; Marxal Resort; per person AZN22; ⏱10am-6.30pm) The easy way to the scenic mountaintop pastures of Xan Yaylağı is to sign up for a 4WD ride (minimum four people) starting from the rear section of Marxal Resort.

Sleeping

You're spoilt for choice in Şəki, which has several impressive boutique options, homestays, a new but growing handful of hostels and the chance to sleep in a genuine caravanserai. And at least 10 more hotels are under construction. Around Kiş there are several rural alternatives including a major resort, Marxal (p276).

★Karavansaray Hotel   INN $
(☑055-7555570, 024-2444814; MF Axundzadə pr 185; s/d/tr/q AZN20/30/36/48, ste AZN50-80) Staying in this converted genuine caravanserai is justification enough to visit Şəki. Rooms have arched brickwork ceilings and while they're certainly not luxurious, all have sitting areas and Western toilets in the humorously dated little bathrooms.

Booking ahead can be wise, especially if you want a single room, of which there are only two. Or ask the tourist office to make reservations on your behalf.

AZERBAIJAN Şəki

Şəki (Sheki)

Canal Hostel HOSTEL **$**

(☑ 077-3112017; www.facebook.com/canalhostel; Eldarov küç 2; dm without/with AC AZN7/12, d AZN25; P ❀ 🛜) One of Şəki's very first hostels, Canal is a sprawling courtyard house in an obscure yet relatively central location down a highly improbable back lane. Conditions are fairly rudimentary but host Asim speaks English and claims he can organise activities from bicycle hire to paragliding. It can squeeze in up to 50 backpackers with plenty of space for bicycles.

Ilgar's Homestay HOMESTAY **$**

(☑ 055-6238295; www.facebook.com/ilgar.azerbaiajanhostels; M Magomayev 20; beds AZN20) If you'd prefer a simple homestay to a hostel, contact pious, English-speaking İlqar Ağayev, whose family place has a great location in a quiet corner of the Old Town. There's a hot shower and, unlike many traditional homestays, an indoor toilet. İlqar is an obliging guide who can help with local hikes and organising horse riding.

★ **MinAli**
Boutique Hotel HERITAGE HOTEL **$$**

(☑ 050-4920044, 055-4831155; www.facebook.com/MuzeyHotel; MF Axundzadə küç 11/15; d/q/ste AZN95/160/120) The 12-room MinAli is built around an 1896 house with a museum of a lobby guarded by a warrior statue. Opened in 2019, standards are top notch and manager Araz speaks good English. Original bare stone walls and brick window arches show between antique hung carpets in rooms 102, 103, 203 and 204. Other rooms are contrastingly plush modern affairs. The top-floor breakfast room continues the museum-like feel with its collection of old samovars and a mirror wall of other treasures.

İnci Design Hotel
& Hostel BOUTIQUE HOTEL **$$**

(☑ 055-4700052; www.facebook.com/InciDesign Hotel; Mikayıl Müşfiq küçəsi 47a; dm/ste AZN9/70) In a curious rich-man/poor-man combination, İnci has three huge suites which go over the top to impress yet cost less than many standard rooms in other hotels. Meanwhile, sex-segregated dorms come with good-sized lockers, free towels and air-conditioning (male-dorm only) but more toilets, lights and power points would be helpful. There's a kitchen, cute little garden area and staff speak good English. To get here from the bus station walk four blocks north then one west.

Şəki Saray Hotel BOUTIQUE HOTEL **$$**

(☑ 055-2382724, 024-2448181; www.shekisaray.az; ME Rəsulzadə küç 187; s/d/ste AZN90/100/250; ❀ 🛜) Local, oriental and modernist touches combine with original photography, Moroccan-style lamps and spacious, business-like rooms to make this 21st-century hotel a fine choice right in the centre of town. Staff speak English, the restaurant offers some European options and there's an inviting female-friendly bar.

Marxal Resort RESORT **$$$**

(☑ 055-5003585; www.marxalresort.az; d without/with balcony AZN150/170; P 🛜 ⛱) The region's most glamorous resort is a huge new affair with particularly impressive expanses of lounge, indoor and outdoor pools, games rooms, activities and a memorable spa accessed by tram or a psychedelically colourful tunnel-way. It's 6km north of central Şəki set in vast, forest-edged grounds across the river from Kiş and with glorious mountain peaks on the horizon. Being over 300m higher, the air is noticeably cooler here than in Şəki.

🍴 **Eating**

Piti (a soupy meat stew with chickpeas and saffron) is a popular main course here and Şəki also specialises in miniature vine-leaf dolma. There are many pleasantly rural restaurants on the road continuing north from

---

AZERBAIJAN Şəki

LOCAL KNOWLEDGE

EATING PITI

So you've taken our suggestion and ordered *piti*. But all you can see in the conical earthenware *dobu* (pot) is a lump of lamb fat floating lugubriously in broth. Don't panic! Before eating anything, start by tearing up pieces of bread into a separate bowl. Sprinkle with sumac (the purplish-red condiment you'll see on the table) and then pour the *piti* broth over the top. Eat the resultant soup as a first course. Then transfer the remaining *piti* solids to the dish and mash together using spoon and fork. Yes. Including that lump of fat. Without it the dish just won't taste right. Another sprinkling of sumac and your 'second course' is ready to eat. Delicious.

Marxal plus several much cheaper if mostly forgettable places dotted around Təzə Bazaar.

Ləziz
AZERBAIJANI $

(☑ 055-6416424, 024-2448783; Axundov Park; mains AZN4-6, salads AZN1-2.50, draught beer AZN1; ⊙ 9am-11.30pm) Off the tourist trail, this sprawling parkland restaurant is far from refined but the food quality is excellent at genuine local prices, there's outdoor seating under the trees and service comes with huge smiles. Service charge 10%.

Çələbi Xan Restoran
AZERBAIJANI $$

(Main Sq; mains/kebabs from AZN4/5; ⊙ 9am-11pm; ✳) This ever-popular restaurant has a pine interior that's as eccentric as a cuckoo clock while its striking exterior combines classic *şəbəkə* with modern smoked glass. It's fronted by al fresco tables around a tree-framed water feature. Prices are sensible and while the *piti* (AZN6) is excellent, for just AZN3 you could fill up on bread and borscht. Beer AZN4, shisha AZN10, 5% service charge.

Xan Bağı
AZERBAIJANI $$

(Fortress Grounds; mains AZN5-8; ⊙ 9am-10pm) Although it's the only restaurant within the fortress, prices are reasonable and the Azerbaijani food is reliable. Summer tables are almost lost in the foliage while in winter there's a small interior dominated by a large model boat. A good place for local-style mini-dolma.

Qaqarin Restoranı
AZERBAIJANI $$

(☑ 024-2448313; Qazimov küç; most mains AZN4-7, beer AZN2; ⊙ 8am-11pm) Hugely popular with local diners, Qaqarin – named for the cosmonaut Yuri Gagarin – has mostly simple outdoor seating but it's a fine place to dine with sunset views across the city as the sky burns golden over the western ridges. The menu of typical local fare has no listed costs but prices are sensible.

🍷 Drinking & Nightlife

The **Buta Bar** (Şəki Saray Hotel, ME Rəsulzadə küç 187; beer/cocktails from AZN4/8; ⊙ 7am-midnight) at the Şəki Saray Hotel is the most female-friendly spot for alcoholic drinks. It also makes good coffee, which is also available at cosy **Illy Espresso House** (MF Axundzadə pr; espresso/cappuccino AZN2.50/4.50; ⊙ 9am-8.30pm) or you can get a truly excellent Julius Meinl at Marxal.

There are male-only teahouses in Füzüli Park with cheap NZS beer, or climb to **Abidə Çayxana** (beer AZN1; ⊙ 10am-midnight) for AZN1 draft Xırdalan with a great view.

More central **Ovuçlar Məkanı** (MF Axundzadə pr 43; local/imported beers from AZN1.50/3; ⊙ 9am-2am; ☎) is a relatively comfortable, late-night place to sink beers if you're not put off by the hunting trophies. Refreshingly air-conditioned **Art Club** (☑ 051-7692624; www.instagram.com/Sheki_Art_Club; MF Axundzadə küç; ⊙ 9am-11pm) serves local candies as part of its AZN3 *çay dəsgahı* (tea set) and hosts occasional workshops, music, wine tasting and other events.

🛍 Shopping

Şəki is famous for its confectionery. Shops along MF Axundzadə pr flog lurid *nöğul* (sugar-coated beans) and much more palatable *mindal* (nuts in a crisp caramel coating). But by far their best-known offering is *Şəki halvası*, a misnomer for a syrupy local kind of *paxlava* (baklava). **Halvaçı Yəhyə** (MF Axundzadə pr 185/20; ⊙ 10am-11pm) is a particularly celebrated halva outlet having received a double presidential visit in 2015. It's one of many small souvenir-oriented shop-units tucked into the arched sides of the Karavansaray Hotel.

Abad
CERAMICS

(Fortress grounds; ⊙ 9.30am-6pm) In a newly restored 19th-century building, this centre is predominantly a community project to support local potters in their craft. You can watch artisans at work and peruse a selection of ceramics, glassware and mini-carpets. In the yard there's an 18th-century *anbar* (stairway to underground water source).

Təzə Bazar
MARKET

(🚌 5, 8, 11, 16) The big, bustling bazaar sells everything from pottery, metalwork and carpets to masses of fresh food. Saffron comes in a wide variety of qualities, the cheapest just AZN1 a cupful.

Şəki İpek
SILK

(ME Rəsulzadə küç; ⊙ 9am-6pm; 🚌 2, 8) The showroom of Şəki's *kombinat* (silk factory) stocks high-quality carpets and some attractively simple silk scarves.

ℹ Information

Several banks directly south of Şəki Saray Hotel have ATMs and currency exchange. **Bank of Baku** (ME Rəsulzadə küç 149b; ⊙ 9am-1pm &

2-5pm Mon-Fri, to 6pm Sat) near the bus station has reasonable rates for US$.

A helpful, English-speaking **Tourist Office** (2nd fl, Sənətkarlar Evi; ☺ 9am-6pm Mon-Fri, from 10am Sat & Sun) is upstairs in the **Crafts House** (Şəki Şənətkarlar Evi; Fortress grounds; ☺ 10am-dusk) within the walls of the old citadel.

ℹ Getting There & Away

BUS & TAXI

The well-organised **bus station** (☏ 024-244617; ME Rəsulzadə küç) is around 700m south of the central square. Useful services:

Baku Over 20 services daily, last 6pm (AZN9). Big buses drive via Xaldan and Kürdamir (6½ hours), while 'Ford' minibuses (5½ hours) and shared taxis (AZN15, five hours) go via İsmayıllı.

Balakən (AZN3.50, three hours) 10.10am and 2pm.

Gəncə (AZN4, 2½ hours) 8am, 9.10am, 11.50am and 1.30pm. Alternatively, head first to Mingəçevir (AZN2.20, 1½ hours, eight daily, last 5pm) and change there. The journey should get faster once the new Şəki–Xaldan highway is finished.

Qax (AZN1, 45 minutes) 8am, 10am, 11.30am, 1pm, 3pm, 4.45pm, 5.30pm.

Qəbələ (AZN2.50, 1½ hours) 6.50am, noon, 2pm.

Zaqatala (AZN3, two hours) 7.15am, 9am, 11am, noon, 3pm, 4.30pm, 5pm.

TRAIN

Due to the ease of buying tickets in Baku, taking the overnight Baku–Şəki train – *platskart/kupe* (open-bunk accommodation/2nd-class compartment accommodation) AZN7/12, eight hours – is much easier westbound than in reverse. From Şəki it departs at 11.20pm but you can't always count on getting a ticket for same-day departures. Although some Şəki agencies offer to book train tickets for you, they are not able to print them so typically you'll still need to pick up the physical ticket at the station at least one hour before departure.

There is a **train ticket booth** (Dəmir Yol Kassası; ☏ Coşqun 050-6621361; ☺ call) on the southeast corner of Təzə Bazaar, but it is often unmanned: call ahead, bring a photocopy of your passport and apply at least by lunchtime, ideally much earlier.

Şəki train station is a whopping 17km south of town. On arrival it's easy to find a shared taxi into town, but should you dawdle off the train too slowly, you could alternatively walk 700m east to the AzPetrol roundabout then flag down any northbound vehicle.

ℹ Getting Around

Marshrutky (30q) run till around 8pm. Routes 8 and 11 both connect Təzə Bazaar to the town centre. *Marshrutka* 11 continues via the Karavansaray Hotel to the Xan Sarayı area: the nearest **route 11 stop** (Hämidov küç) to the bus station is on the corner half a block north up ME Rəsulzadə küç. Route 17 does the same as route 11 but continues into Birinci Rayon. Route 8 goes on past the Silk Factory. Route 15 heads from the bazaar to Kiş. Route 7 runs to Marxal.

Taxis charge AZN2 for short rides within town, around AZN6 to the train station.

Qax & İlisu

☏ 024 / POP 14,300 / ELEV 630M

Qax (pronounced 'gakh') has a partly Georgian-speaking population and three historic churches, one right beside the quaintly old-fashioned museum. From its gently attractive centre, the town straggles up through beautiful landscapes towards İlisu (15km north), former capital of a historic sultanate and touted, somewhat overgrandly, as a 'mini-Switzerland'.

◉ Sights

If you arrive from Zaqatala, hop off the bus at BOil Petrol Station, walk three blocks southeast to the interesting His-tory Museum (Qax Tarix Diyarşünaslıq Muzeyi; Üzeyir Hacıbəli küç 1; AZN1; ☺10am-1pm & 2-6pm Mon-Sat) which is tucked into the garden-courtyard of a fine Georgian Church. Continue east via pleasantly tree-shaded Mustafayev küç to find İçəri Bazar. Then grab a taxi and zip up to historic, mountain-framed İlisu village, perhaps stopping en route for food or tea at absurdly eccentric Səngər Qala.

İçəri Bazar   AREA

Old Town Qax is centred on cobbled İçəri Bazar, a streetscape where older houses have been given a faux-antique look on a lane guarded by castle-style gateways and verdigris-green warrior statues. The centrepiece is a small open-air theatre that's especially attractive on summer evenings when colonised by tea tables whose dim lights twinkle amid the trees.

İlisu Village   VILLAGE

Two beautiful high-altitude valleys meet at charming little İlisu. Amazingly this diminutive village of photogenic old homes was once the capital of a short-lived

18th-century sultanate. Many houses retain box windows, arched doorways and red-tiled roofs, there's an antique mosque and several remnant fortifications. At the very southwestern end of the village, the square-plan, five-storey Summaqala Tower is rather over-restored but it commands a picture-perfect valley view towards distant snow-topped peaks.

At the northernmost end of İlisu there are more fine views from the Uludağ restaurant-resort. Turn right and hike 40 minutes uphill to find a locally famous **waterfall** (*şəlalə*). Walking up the main valley towards Russia isn't allowed (closed border zone). Reaching the curious hamlet of **Sarıbaş** is possible by any 4WD that is capable of fording the river en route.

🛏 Sleeping & Eating

Although there is a cheap and cheerful little hotel close to central Qax, the vast majority of the accommodation and dining options are along the road to İlisu.

Hotel Qax
HOTEL $

(Mehmanxana; ☎055-9682832; Nərimanov küç 3; tw/tr with AC AZN30/40, dm/s/tw without bathroom AZN5/10/20; 🌀) Friendly and good value, simple little Hotel Qax' rooms mostly share clean squat toilets, with showers costing AZN2 extra. En suite rooms come with air-conditioning, a sitting area and ample power points. It's in central Qax just north of the Heydər Əliyev statue between İçəri Bazaar and the Kiş road. The cafe next door serves cheap but very edible meals.

İlisu Pansionat
COTTAGE $

(☎050-3285615; per person with breakfast/3 meals AZN24/40) The attraction of this little resort is its mixture of outdoor facilities (hiking trails, flora-and-fauna identification boards, assault course, short zip line) and the relatively quiet location amid trees. It offers a potluck mixed bag of new and older rooms and cottages with private bathroom. Many rooms sleep four or six people but outside peak weekends, individuals and couples usually get a whole unit at the same per-person rate. In summer you might find English speakers. The Pansionat is on a rise set back from the meadow area around the 17th-century Ulu Bridge (3km south of İlisu village).

El Resort
HOTEL $$$

(☎024-2555202; www.elresort.az; Heydər Əliyev pr; s/d/ste AZN150/160/190; 🅿🌀🌐🏊) Qax's most fashion-conscious accommodation offering has well-equipped, high-quality rooms, curious formed-wood lamps and an array of facilities including saunas, an 18m indoor swimming pool, a large gym, games rooms, billiards and a conference centre. It's 5km north of central Qax on the road towards İlisu.

Səngər Qala
Restaurant & Hotel
AZERBAIJANI $$

(☎024-2593505, 070-9305505; www.facebook.com/pg/Sangarqala; İlisu Yolu; salads AZN3, kebabs AZN4-7, mains AZN6-9, shah plov AZN40; ⏰9am-11pm) Even if you don't eat here, it's worth a quick stop to photograph this restaurant, which takes the form of a fantasy castle built within crenellated dark stone walls and full of quirky oddities. The menu is mostly kebabs but also offers trout, stroganoff, and some pre-orderable specials like wild boar (AZN18). Beer from AZN3. The new **hotel** (s/d AZN70/98) section continues the pseudo-medieval theme and has a pretty good indoor pool and spa. Səngər Qala is 1km south of İlisu.

ℹ Getting There & Away

The Baku–Balakən train stops at both of Qax's stations, but neither are close to the city. A taxi to Şəki or Zaqatala costs only AZN15. Add a little more for stops and side trips en route.

The **bus station** (Avtovağzal; 🚌1) is on the main street (Heydər Əliyev pr) at the far southwestern edge of town. Useful services:

Gəncə (AZN6, four hours) 8am.

Şəki (AZN1, one hour) 9.30am, 12.15pm, 4.30pm, 6.30pm.

Tbilisi (AZN8, five hours) 8.30am, 10.30am and 1pm. It's worth booking at least a few hours ahead.

Zaqatala (AZN1, 1¼ hours) 7.40am, 8.30am, 10.05am, 12.20pm, 2pm, 3.30pm and 5.10pm. There are also three services that use a larger loop road. Arriving from Zaqatala you can hop off at the amusingly named **BOil Petrol Station** (Eyvazov küç) then walk three blocks east to find the History Museum.

ℹ Getting Around

Sporadic *marshrutka* 1 drives from the bus station to the Flag Roundabout (1.5km), loops through the Old Town then continues north as far as El Resort, but it can be a long wait.

For İlisu, minibuses (50q, 20 minutes) depart the bus station at 7.20am, 9.30am, noon, 2pm and 5pm, returning almost immediately. A Qax–İlisu taxi costs around AZN6, or AZN15 return with an hour or two's sightseeing.

Zaqatala

♪ 024 / POP 32,000

Azerbaijan's hazelnut capital sits at the confluence of two wide mountain rivers with the peaks of the Greater Caucasus as a dramatic backdrop. The town's small but picturesque old core is backed by an extensive if somewhat formless fortress and a large, semi-wooded park on the slope that climbs steadily to the pretty village of Car (pronounced 'jar') from which a shepherds' trail leads steeply up to glorious highland pastures. Zaqatala's lower town, where the bazaar and bus station are located, 2km downhill from the centre, is unremarkable but a useful place to stay and organise transport.

⊙ Sights

Old Town Square   GARDENS

(Old Town Sq) Zaqatala's Old Town is centred on a pretty garden-square, above which rise two 30m tall *çınar* (plane trees) planted in the 1780s. To the south, there are numerous old-style house facades on the upper reaches of Heydər Əliyev pr. Follow a path past the maudlin shell of a drum-towered Orthodox **church** to find a minor fortress entrance.

Around 300m southwest is the charmingly old-fashioned little **Historical Museum** (Heydər Əliyev pr 30; AZN2; ⊙9am-1pm & 2-6pm).

Car Village   VILLAGE

Car is a chocolate-box village half-hidden in blossoms and greenery. Picturesque houses are tucked away behind mossy dry-stone walls in abundant orchards. Several rustic restaurants are nestled in its woodland fringes.

Fortress   FORTRESS

(AZN1; ⊙9am-1pm & 2-6pm Mon-Fri) Zaqatala's Russian fortress is a sprawling affair whose grey stone walls are sturdy but not

Zaqatala

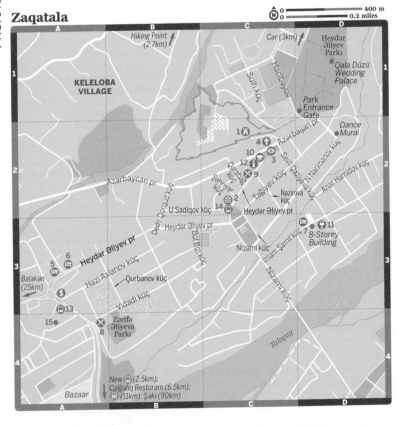

really imposing. Built between 1830 and 1860, it originally guarded against attacks from the Dagestan-based guerrilla army of Shamil and later imprisoned sailors from the battleship *Potëmkin,* whose famous 1905 mutiny at Odessa foreshadowed the Russian revolution. The walls look more appealing from the outside. Despite posted opening times, you can usually stroll inside at any time.

 ## Activities

High alpine pastures above Zaqatala's treeline offer some of the loveliest vistas in Azerbaijan. The only way up is on foot or by horse. A fine day-hike heads for the **Şamilovka Yaylağı** upland meadows via a sheep track that climbs a fairly obvious forest ridge from the western side of Car. The route is easily discernible from a Google Earth image.

To get to the starting point, get off the Car *marshrutka* at **Amin Market** (Car Yolu), cross the metal-plate bridge and walk 900m west, turning left at each of the two main junctions. The sheep trail should be on your right before a small stream starts to cut away a valley beside you.

The tourist office can arrange a hiking guide for this (AZN50) or other walks. Pay AZN300 to AZN500 per group for the popular three-day return camping trip to **Xalaxı Göl**, a mountain lake at around 2000m.

Sleeping

Hotel Zaqatala HOTEL $
(☑ 050-5173859, 070-9138324; Heydər Əliyev pr 92; dm/tw/tr/ste AZN5/20/30/35, with breakfast AZN8/25/35/40; ❄ 🛜) This sensibly pitched, no-nonsense budget hotel has good standards for the price and there are well-maintained private bathrooms even in the men-only dorm, though you'll need your own toilet paper. Only the 'suites' have air-conditioning.

Turqut Motel INN $
(☑ 024-2256229, 050-8550353; Imam Şamil küç; tw without/with bathroom AZN15/20) Good-value, basic-but-clean rooms mostly come with air-conditioning, functioning bathrooms and toiletries; simpler rooms share a seatless sit-down toilet in the corridor. If reception is dormant, seek out a waiter in the fountain beer-garden out back. No English.

Grata Hotel HOTEL $$
(☑ 024-2253353, 050-2163636; Grata-hotel@mail.ru; Heydər Əliyev pr 100; s/d/tr/ste AZN40/60/90/140; ❄ 🛜) The best choice in town with European-standard rooms featuring high ceilings, enclosed shower booths and effective air-conditioning. At the back there's a large yard-garden with dining. It's very close to the old bus station on the road that climbs to the town centre.

Eating & Drinking

Spilling onto the Old Town Square, **Meydan Kafesi** (Old Town Sq; tea/coffee from AZN2/1; ⊙ 11am-11pm) does a great Turkish coffee while nearby **Meydan Dönər** (Heydər Əliyev pr 10; kebabs AZN2) serves some of the best fast-food kebabs in Azerbaijan. By day, the top teahouses are in Heydər Əliyev Park, but by night, more compact Zərifa Əliyeva Park is easier to reach.

Berkli Restoran AZERBAIJANI $
(Vidadi küç; mains AZN2.50-4; ⊙ 9am-10.30pm) A large black-and-white portrait poster of a suave young Alain Delon dominates this lovably old-fashioned restaurant otherwise decorated with wing flagons and Russian

AZERBAIJAN ZAQATALA

LOCAL KNOWLEDGE

BLESSED BREAD

If you look carefully behind any apartment block, you're likely to see bags of discarded stale bread hanging on trees or hooks, separate from the domestic trash. That's because bread is considered holy and can't simply be binned or even placed on the ground, leaving superstitious Azerbaijanis with a disposal problem.

Eating bread with someone is considered to seal a bond of friendship. If you drop a piece of bread on the ground, it's good form to kiss it as an apology!

winter landscapes. The short, handwritten menu typically includes *piti, bozbaş* (stew usually featuring a meatball formed around a central plum), *xinqal* (meaty chunks served with lasagne-like leaves of pasta) and other Azerbaijani classics. NZS beer AZN1.

★ **Calğalıq Restoranı**　　AZERBAIJANI $$
(☎ 050-4147998, 024-2267700; www.facebook.com/calgaliq; Aşağı Tala; mains AZN4-15) The most characterful restaurant for miles around, Calğalıq is packed with more antique handicrafts than the average museum and the enchanted garden is all a-croak with frogs. There are some Georgian options and very local seasonal specialities like *maxara* (*sac*-cooked savoury pancakes). The location is utterly improbable: around 2.5km east of the flag roundabout/old bus station, take the Aşağı Tala turn-off and drive 4km south.

Ləzzət İstirahət Zonası　　CAUCASIAN $$
(☎ 070-8872299, 050-3761160; Car village; mains AZN4.50-6.50, trout AZN9) In a pretty corner of Car, Ləzzət is interesting for the chance to drink or eat Dagestani food in a treehouse or rustic pavilions in the woods. But the unique feature is encountering the highly eccentric owner Hacibey Zakatalinski. Typically sporting a cowboy hat and grey goatee, he likes to rant humourously about his self-proclaimed status as King of Zaqatala.

Behind the restaurant, set around a central lawn, is a ring of stone-and-wattle cottages (single/double AZN25/30). They have somewhat gone to seed of late but remain fair value with functional en suite bathrooms.

Qaqaş　　AZERBAIJANI
(İmam Şamil küç; beer AZN1; ⊙10am-11pm) Original if a bit ageing, this inexpensive little bar-restaurant has a facade of bottle-ends, an interior of quirky timber rooms and a series of roughly fashioned log perches behind as dining platforms. The local creamy-headed Helles draught beer costs only AZN1, and the food comes in generous portions.

❶ Information

Tourist office (Zaqatala Turizm və İnformasiya Mərkəzi; ☎ 024-2254143, WhatsApp 055-3228123; www.facebook.com/zagatalatic; Heydər Əliyev pr 2; ⊙8am-6pm Mon-Fri or by appointment) Can help organise hiking guides for mountain adventures.

Bank Respublika (F Əmirov 4; ⊙9am-5.30pm Mon-Fri) Has an ATM and changes US dollars at good rates. So-so rates for euros.

❶ Getting There & Away

From outside the old bus station *marshrutky* to Balakən (70q, 35 minutes) depart approximately every 40 minutes or when almost full. After 5pm you can usually find a shared taxi (per seat/car AZN1.20/5). Some buses for Qax (AZN1, 1¼ hours) start here around 15 minutes before arriving at the new bus station.

Longer-distance services leave from the **new bus station** (Yeni Avtovağzal; Zaqatala Beynəlxalq Avtovağzalı) at the far eastern end of town including to the following destinations:

Gəncə (AZN5.30, 4½ hours) 8.30am, 11am, 3pm and 4.30pm.

Mingəçevir (AZN3.60, 2½ hours) 9am, 9.50am, 2pm and 5.10pm.

Qəbələ (AZN4.50, four hours) 9.30am.

Qax (AZN1, one hour) 7.40am, 8.30am, 10.15am, 11.40am, 12.30pm, 2pm, 3.30pm, 4pm, 5.10pm (90q) plus slower 'new road' services at 8am, 11.10am and 3pm (AZN1.40, two hours).

Şəki (AZN1.80, 2½ hours) 8.30am, 9.15am, 10.30am, noon, 1.30pm, 3pm and 5pm), plus a bus via Qax at 4pm (AZN2.60, 3½ hours).

For Baku (AZN10) buses travel via Kürdamir. For the more scenic route go first to Şəki. If travelling overnight the train is more comfortable.

The overnight train to Baku (*platskart/kupe* AZN8/13, 10 hours) departs at 9.10pm from Zaqatala train station, 8km southeast of town. When arriving you might prefer to copy other passengers and get off at the Naib Bulaq (Zaqatala Yolu) stop, which has no ticket office or station building but is on the Baku road:

Aliabad- and Mosul-bound minibuses pass by. To buy train tickets in advance, find the **Dəmir Yol Kassa booth** (Dəmir Yolu Kassası; ☑ 050-3006665, 070-3128942; old bus station; ⊙ 9am-1pm & 2-9pm) which is tucked almost invisibly into the rear courtyard of the old bus station.

⓲ Getting Around

Marshrutky marked 'Qala Düzü' go from the bazaar to the old bus station roundabout then through the Old Town area to Heydər Əliyev Parkı (30q). Three or four times an hour (7am to 6.30pm) a minibus does the same route then continues to Car (50q).

Returning from the Old Town area to the Grata Hotel, a good place to wait for the *marshrutka* is on the corner of U Sadıqov küç.

A variety of small buses link the two bus stations, but waits can be painfully long; a taxi costs AZN3.

Balakən

☑ 024 / POP 12,700

Balakən is the first town you'll reach on arrival from Georgia via Kakheti. A large flagpole marks the central junction near the bazaar. Comfortable Hotel Qubek (☑ 055-4929272, 050-4929272; www.facebook.com/qubekhotel; Səttar Gözəlov küç; s/d/ste/tr AZN55/60/70/75; P ❄ ☎ ✉) is a short walk north of here beside a large park with an entertainingly pointless cable car sometimes running to a low, statue-topped hillock. Hidden away in the older centre, a fine mosque (Balakən Şəhər Mərkəzi Məscidi; Əsədov küç) with a beautiful brick-faceted minaret is the only real 'sight'.

Two blocks northeast, ABB (International Bank of Azerbaijan; Əsədov küç 1; ⊙ 10am-5pm Mon-Fri) offers exchange and an ATM near the northwestern end of Balakən's long main street.

⓲ Getting There & Away

For Georgia start from the forecourt of **MMOil** petrol station at the flagpole roundabout. Minibuses to Qubali via Lagodekhi (AZN2) depart from here at 11am, noon and 1.30pm. Otherwise use a shared/private taxi to the border (AZN1/4) then walk across. If you arrived by train, taxis at the station ask AZN5 to the border ('*tamozhna*').

For Şəki, minibuses (AZN3.10, three hours) depart at 8.30am and 2pm from the **avtovağzal** (main bus station; Heydər Əliyev pr 96), beside the big hospital.

For Zaqatala *marshrutky* (70q, 35 minutes) leave roughly every 40 minutes from a stand at the northeast corner of Culture Centre Park, 700m west of the flagpole roundabout. Vehicles also pick up at the bazaar and bus station but might already be full by then. Last at 5.30pm. Change in Zaqatala for Qax.

⓲ Getting Around

Various *marshrutky* labelled 'şəhər arası' pass close to the central mosque, then run around 2.5km along the main east–west thoroughfare passing the Zaqatala *marshrutka* stop, flagpole and bus station. Around 600m further east they turn around beside the **AzPetrol Motel** (Heydər Əliyev pr) where there's an ATM.

CENTRAL AZERBAIJAN

Beyond the rapidly gentrifying city of Gəncə, making the most of Central Azerbaijan really requires you to venture south into the attractive foothills of the Lesser Caucasus Mountains. Here, there are some picturesque highland lakes and impressive views of beak-shaped Mt Kyapaz (Kəpəz Dağı). Several towns, of which Göygöl is best known, have a Germanic heritage dating back to the early 19th century. However, the monotonous main Baku–Ələt–Gəncə–Qazax highway traverses a seemingly endless agricultural plain giving little sense of the region's charms except on exceptionally clear days when high mountains rise very distantly like ghostly apparitions on both the north and south horizons.

Gəncə

☑ 022 / POP 335,000

Several years of restoration and reimagining are starting to bear fruit in Azerbaijan's second city. Century-old brickwork has been spruced up, there's a quirky art cafe plus some appealing new eateries and even a couple of hostels.

The fanciful new Filarmoniya concert hall (Fikrət Əmirov adına Gəncə Dövlət Filarmoniyası; ☑ 022-2565321; Cavadxan küç) brings a grand flourish to the already impressive central square, while on the city fringes lie a superb Islamic shrine and one of Azerbaijan's biggest parks – Heydar Əliyev Park – sporting Gəncə's own Arc de Triomphe.

Central Azerbaijan

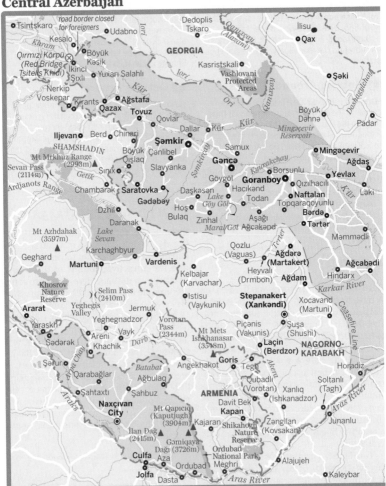

◉ Sights

Gəncə's top attractions are out of town but the city centre has been extensively gentrified in recent years and is well worth a stroll (p287). Dusk is an excellent time, when the lighting is especially attractive.

If driving into Gəncə from the east, notice **Gəncə Darvazası**, a pair of gigantic brick gateways at the M2 bypass junction. Though built in 2014 they are designed to evoke a long-lost ancient citadel portal whose iron gates were plundered in an 1139 Georgian attack and removed to Gelati (p87). The long avenue into town then passes 2km of mock fortress walls and literature mosaics, tunnelling beneath the space-shuttle-shaped **Nizami Mausoleum** commemorating the city's great 12th-century poet.

★ **İmamzadə**　　　ISLAMIC SITE
(Tatlı Yolu; 🚌 33) One of Azerbaijan's most impressive Islamic structures, the İmamzadə is a masterpiece of brickwork and Central Asian–style blue majolica tiles on the northern edge of Gəncə. Though evidence seems sketchy, the site is considered to be the grave of Maulana Ibrahim, son of the fifth Shiite Imam, Muhammad Al Baqir.

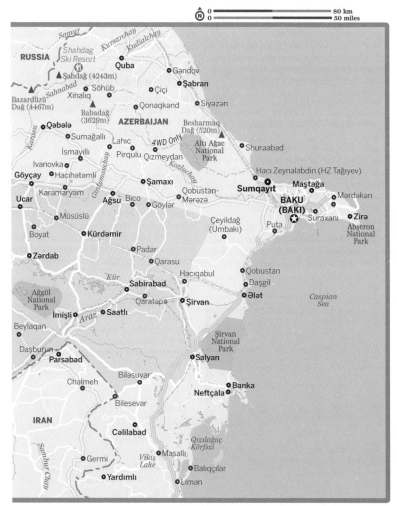

0 | 80 km
0 | 50 miles

AZERBAIJAN Gəncə

The vast majority of today's structure dates from 2016, curiously encasing a far more modest 19th-century equivalent within a soaring dome. Access takes around 25 minutes by minibus 33 that picks up at Univermaq or by very rare bus (not minibus) 18 from outside Gəncə train station. Consider paying a taxi (AZN5 return from the train station).

Heydər Əliyev Park   PARK
(P; 📱11) In the unofficial 'Top Park' competition between Azerbaijani cities, Gəncə's vast Heydər Əliyev Park wins hands down. Along with a fairground, modern-art mu-

seum, culture centre and amphitheatre for occasional free concerts, there's what looks like a full-sized Arc de Triomphe. It's off Rte 50 at the western edge of town.

🛏 Sleeping

Ganja Homestay   HOMESTAY $
(📲 050-2310121; www.facebook.com/GanjaHome Stay; Aydın Məmmədov küç 23; tw without bath US$15; 🛜; 📱4, 14, 25) The great advantage of this very genuine homestay is the real family setting, a yard beneath grapevines or orchard garden and, weekends only, the company of thoughtful, ever-obliging host Afgan

Mehtikhanov. Afgan speaks excellent English and can help you get a really personal insight into this underestimated city.

The homestay is a short bus hop south of the central area on a street whose old name, Qacaq Nabi küç, still appears on most maps. Phone ahead to arrange arrival times.

Cinema Boutique Hotel
HOTEL $$
(☑ 050-5607001, 022-2566999; Cavadxan küç 2; s/d from AZN50/70) Some fittings show signs of minor wear and decor isn't especially tasteful, but the good-sized rooms are comfortable and the location is very handy. It is near the riverside at the top of Gəncə's most appealing commercial street. It's located above the hip Kolorit Coffeeshop, where a fairly basic breakfast is provided.

Vego Hotel
BOUTIQUE HOTEL $$$
(☑ 050-2711448, 022-2640182; www.vegohotel.com; Cavadxan küç 50; s/d AZN100/120; ❊ ☎) Gəncə's best central choice has the comfort-

able standards of a business hotel but adds some 1960s retro features. Guests pay half price (only AZN15) to use the large, genuine 17th-century *hamman* to which the hotel is connected by a mural-covered tunnel.

✕ Eating & Drinking

There's a fairly modest choice of dining in central Gəncə. In summer, almost anyone with a vehicle drives out of town to dine at one of the woodland eateries along the way to Hacikənd.

Zeqa
INTERNATIONAL $
(☑ 055-5217172; Həsənli Qardəşləri küç; mains AZN3.50-7.50, steak AZN13.50, espresso AZN1.50; ☎) Colourfully decorated with window frames, alarm clocks and painted keys, this youthful place offers pizzas, salads and a selection of Russian, Turkish and local semi-fast food. The *lahmacun* (skinny Turkish pizza-wrap, from AZN1.70) is excellent.

Epikur Bağı
INTERNATIONAL $$
(☑ 022-2662070, 070-6439090; www.facebook.com/epikurbagi; Heydar Əliyev pr 157; mains AZN5-13, sushi from AZN4; ⊙ 11am-11pm) Gəncə's widest selection of non-local cuisine is served in a cutesy snow-queen palace setting with a huge Michaelangelo reproduction on the ceiling. Enter from Şeyx Bahəddin küç.

Gəncə
Ⓝ 0 ————— 500 m
0 ————— 0.25 miles

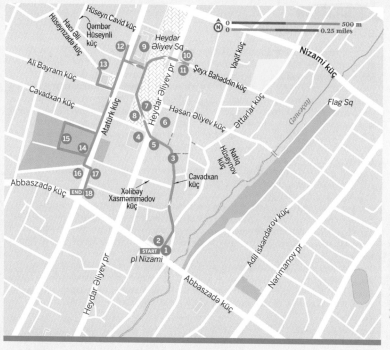

🏃 Walking Tour
A Stroll around Central Gəncə

START: NIZAMI STATUE
END: ART GARDEN
LENGTH: 2KM, AROUND 90 MINUTES

Gəncə's extensively revamped central area looks especially attractive at dusk as the monumental streetlamps start to glow. Start a short wander at the ① **statue of Nizami**, Azerbaijan's locally born 'national' poet, behind which rises the fascinatingly hideous ② **Kəpəz Hotel**, a 1970s monstrosity of Soviet architectural miserabilism. Contrastingly majestic stone buildings descend Əttarlar küç to the north while lots of cute statuary adds interest to the buzz of coffee shops and teahouses on pedestrianised ③ **Cavadxan küç**. Notice the widespread use of classic Azerbaijani symbol, the *buta* (a paisley-Arabesque flame shape) forming the basis for Cavadxan küç's street furniture. At that road's northern end, use the underpass to reach a point from which you can take in the grandly statue-fronted ④ **Filarmoniya**, the more modestly domed ⑤ **Ziraat Bank building**, the 21st-century ⑥ **Gəncə Mall** and the

17th-century ⑦ **Cümə Mosque**. Nearby there's a similarly aged working ⑧ **hamman** and the heavily restored little tomb-tower of Cavad Xan, the last man to rule Gəncə as an independent khanate (1786–1804).

Walk north from here to admire the imposing Stalinist bulk of the ⑨ **City Hall** and the pillar-fronted ⑩ **Hotel Gəncə**. Next, peep inside the as-yet unfinished ⑪ **Karvansaray hotel**. Looping back southwest, pass the old-fashioned but richly endowed ⑫ **History Museum** and the active ⑬ **Nevski Russian Orthodox Church**. Enjoy the deep shade of the densely wooded ⑭ **Xan Bağı** park, where a 15m section of ⑮ **brick wall** is all that remains of what was, in 1588, a 13.7km rampart encircling the whole city. Walking further south down Atatürk küç you'll pass the brick facade of the ⑯ **Agricultural University**. Back in 1918, that building briefly hosted Azerbaijan's very first independent parliament, a history recalled by a small ⑰ **parliament museum** across the road (Atatürk küç 521). Finish your walk with a well-deserved coffee or beer at the city's most alternative cafe, ⑱ **Art Garden** (p288).

WORTH A TRIP

GÖYGÖL – TOWN & LAKE

For a surreal slice of transplanted Teutonic history, drive around half an hour south of Gəncə to Göygöl, an agreeable small town founded as Helenendorf by German winemakers in the 1830s. Stalin bundled the Germans' descendants off to permanent exile in Kazakhstan during WWII, but the tree-lined centre still retains dozens of older German houses. A very ill-conceived 'restoration' campaign in 2015 added inauthentic-looking varnished wooden fronts to many buildings, but the overall scene retains a quaintly timeless feel. From Göygöl's little bus station, walk up Heydar Əliyev küç past a museum house (No 22) and particularly fine frontages at No 36 and No 38, then turn left through the small park to find the spired, red-stone Lutheran Church. Outside it, there's a map of further sites. Printed information is in German and Azerbaijani, but with a QR code reader this and other signboards offer background in English and Russian, too.

Driving south from Göygöl you'll find numerous woodland restaurants, then after Hacikənd the road emerges onto a ridge with magnificent views of the Lesser Caucasus range, crowned by the beaklike peak of Mt Kyapaz (Kəpəz Dağı). Further still, edged with forests and a few hotels, lies the much vaunted mountain lake for which Göygöl is named. Maral Göl, a smaller, higher and arguably lovelier lake is around 7km further.

To reach Göygöl from Gəncə take a shared taxi (AZN1, 20 minutes) from Nərimanov küç, located just south of the Nizami pr junction. Alternatively take minibus 14 from opposite the Nizami Statue (or bus 4 from near the Cümə Mosque) and swap minibuses at the **Gülüstan bus stop** (Vazeh pr 50; ☒4, 5, minibus 14), each ride 0.30AZN, around 20 minutes.

A taxi from Göygöl (the town) to Göy Göl (the lake) costs around AZN30 return (an hour each way) or AZN40 if including Maral Göl.

★ **Art Garden** CAFE
(Xoyski Cafe & Brasserie; ☒ 055-991 0290, 050-341 9504; www.facebook.com/xoyskicafe; Atatürk küç 553; espresso/Turkish coffee/beer AZN2.4/2/1.8; ☺12.30-9.30pm; ☎) Grafitti and hanging plants, a battered old piano and plenty of offbeat paintings combine to bring a fun, alternative vibe to Gəncə's quirkiest cafe in a barely marked old house. Enter through the little 'Art Garden' by which the place is also known. Local wine and draught beer available, as well as good coffee. Music-wise, think Portishead.

ℹ Information

There are several money-changing banks on Cavadxan küç but you'll get better rates at **Amrahbank** (Abbaszadə küç 49; ☺9am-6pm Mon-Fri). The **Tourist office** (☒022-2662383; Hasan Əliyev küç; ☺9am-6pm) has good free city maps and travel-agency services.

ℹ Getting There & Away

AIR

Globus Travel (☒022-2521121, 070-2562240; www.safar.az; Cavadxan küç 63e; ☺9am-6pm) sells air tickets. Gəncə's **airport** (KVD;

Gəncə Beynəlxalq Hava Limanı) is 8km northwest of the city centre, around 15 minutes by taxi (AZN7).

Flights include the following:

Baku Three weekly services (AZN61) on **AZAL** (☒044-2220325, 022-2665800; www.azal.az; Atatürk küç 420; ☺9am-6pm).

İstanbul Flights with **Turkish Airlines** (www.thy.com; Abbaszadə küç 55; ☺9.30am-5.30pm Mon-Fri), some days via Naxçivan.

Moscow Four weekly on AZAL, three with Ural Airlines.

BUS

Buses to Baku and all destinations east use the Yeni (or 'Yevlax') **Avtovağzal** (Yevlax Avtovağzal, Gəncə Beynəlxalq Avtovağzal; Nizami pr), accessible by bus 2, 17, 23 or 29 from central Gəncə. Also from this station are minibuses to the following destinations:

Lənkəran (AZN10) 8am and 9.30am.

Qəbələ (AZN4.10, three hours) 10.30am, 1pm and 3.30pm.

Şəki (AZN4, 2½ hours) 8.20am, noon, 4.30pm and 5.30pm.

Tbilisi (AZN10, five hours) 9am, call ☒055-3648611 for bookings.

Buses to Krasny Most (Red Bridge, the Georgian border; 2½ hours) pick up at the New Ganja junction opposite the Ramada Plaza hotel.

The **New Shamkir Bus Station** (28 May küç), 300m southwest of the Ramada Plaza by bus 4, handles minivans to Daşkəsən (AZN1, last 6.30pm), Şəmkir, Gadabey and Qazax (AZN2, last 7.30pm).

TRAIN

The train station is 4km north of the city centre by bus 1 or 4 . To Baku the seat-only express service (AZN10) departs at 6pm, arriving 10.15pm. There are also three sleeper trains (*platskart/ kupe* AZN8/13) – the best option is train 97 originating in Qazax, departing around midnight (6½ hours). Try to avoid the service originating in Böyük-Kəsik (train 665, departs 11.22pm) which has older carriages and malfunctioning AC.

ⓘ Getting Around

There's an efficient public-transport system (rides 0.30AZN) but routes can be confusing due to the one-way system and the strange numbering system. Here, minibus and (small) bus routes with apparently the same number can use entirely different roads.

SOUTHERN AZERBAIJAN

Southern Azerbaijan's coastal strip is the lush breadbasket of the country, where tea plantations line the roadsides and trees are heavy with citrus fruit. Inland, bucolic mountain valleys offer tempting streamside getaways, there's hiking potential in the mossy forests of the Hirkan National Park and further exploration potential on the grassy uplands beyond. The area is home to the Talysh people, famed for their hospitality, distinctive cuisine and for living to great ages. Apart from a few seaside and spa hotels (around hub city Lənkəran) and country retreats (along the roads to Lerik and Yardımlı), this is mostly untouched territory for tourists, especially foreigners.

Southern Azerbaijan

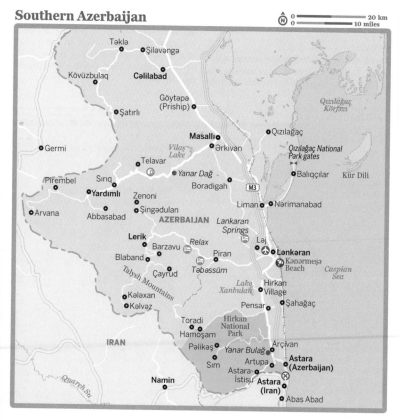

Lənkəran

🎵 025 / POP 52,530

The southern region's biggest town, likeable Lənkəran (Lenkoran) is famous for flowers, tea and its trademark *ləvəngi* cuisine. The city is short on must-see attractions but exudes a laid-back charm, has some fine-value accommodation, is full of relentlessly hospitable people, and serves as a springboard for visiting the Talysh Mountains.

👁 Sights

A distinctive if heavily restored mansion built in 1913 for the grandson of Talysh khan Mir Mustafa now houses a local **history museum** (Tarix Diyarşünaslıq Muzeyi; Ş Axundov küç; AZN5; ◷10am-1pm & 2-6pm Tue-Sun). It overlooks well-tended Dosa Park, home to a powerful WWII monument and the refreshingly air-conditioned **Heydar Əliyev Mərkəzi** (Dosa Park; ◷10am-1pm & 2-6pm Mon-Sat) FREE with photos celebrating the life and times of Azerbaijan's 'National Leader'. The nearest (somewhat scraggy) beach is accessed via the train-station footbridge.

⭐ Bazaar   MARKET
(Mir Mustafaxan küç; ◷6am-6pm, reduced activity Sun) Lənkəran's sprawling bazaar area is centred on an architecturally drab concrete hangar, but it's loaded with colourful produce and equally colourful local characters. Remarkably friendly.

Imam Ali Məscidi   MOSQUE
(Koroğlu küç 102) Dating from 1876, this tile-roofed brick mosque is archetypal of the region with its coloured-glass windows set within large pointed arches. Its pair of slightly off-line buildings form two sides of a peaceful open courtyard, just south of the contrastingly frenetic bazaar.

It's a place of active worship but sensitive visitors are welcome.

Fisherman's Beach   BEACH
Lənkəran's grey-sand beaches aren't a big attraction if you want to swim and many are dotted with debris. Nonetheless, the coastal area around 1km north of the train station is a fascinating place to drink tea at one of many simple cafes while watching local fishers cast their lines.

Stalin's Prison   LANDMARK
(Dairəvi Qala; Fikrət Məmmədov küç) This sturdy brick-barrel tower once imprisoned Joseph Stalin during his early revolutionary days. However, there's no attempt to commemorate the fact and the building is essentially derelict, with the tiled roof in a state of partial collapse.

Lənkəran

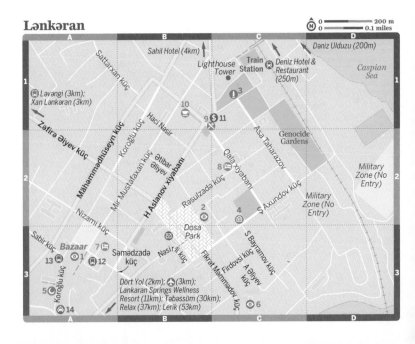

Həzi Aslanov Statue
STATUE

(H Aslanov xiyabanı) The figure standing proudly in front of the train station is local WWII hero Həzi Aslanov, whose plinth rises from a stylised concrete tank.

🛏 Sleeping

Central Lənkəran has half-a-dozen budget accommodation options including **Hostel Forrest** (📞055-5090511, 025-2550511; forrest042@gmail.com; Səmədzadə küç 54a; dm/tw/tr AZN12/24/36; ⊗24hr; ❄🛜), which is aimed at market traders but a reasonable bet for male backpackers. A few posher coastal places are several kilometres out of town. Not really 'beach hotels', most of these are across the rail tracks from the Caspian, and in summer, high-volume music is often provided as an inexplicable form of guest torture.

Luxe Lankaran
HOTEL $

(📞025-2551663, 051-4914196; www.luxelankaran.az/lang; Qala xiyabanı 11; s/d AZN35/55; P❄🛜) Supercentral on Lənkəran's main strollstreet, this well-appointed hotel has fully equipped rooms with kettle, fridge, basic toiletries and big-headed shower that does run hot if you're patient enough. A honey-and-cream breakfast is included and it's only AZN10 to use the spa (closed June to August). Wi-fi doesn't reach all rooms.

★ Xan Lənkəran
HERITAGE HOTEL $$

(📞070-3905446, 050-3905446; www.xanlankaran.com; Ləvəngi bus station; s/tw/d from AZN40/60/70; P❄🛜) Oh, for more hotels like this. If you don't mind staying out by the bus station, this handicraft-filled complex combines an air of well-contrived antiquity with all modern conveniences, including Grohe bathroom fittings, fluffy dressing gowns and underfloor heating. There's a village-style dining room, a Tolkienesque garden and a reception desk fashioned from two vast tree trunks. Some walls are made of traditional mud-wattle, and in one sitting area you can lounge like a khan on piles of carpets and *mutəkə* (elbow cushions). Shelves are hewn from logs and 'hung' from chains, lamps are designed like 19th-century lanterns and even the cleaners wear traditional village costumes. The **restaurant** (📞050-6323430; mains/snacks from AZN5/1, beer AZN1.50; ⊗8am-11.30pm) offers excellent-value meals.

Lankaran Springs Wellness Resort
SPA HOTEL $$$

(📞051-235 9600; www.lankaransprings.az; Sultan Aliyev küç 1, Haftoni; s/d AZN150/165, weekend AZN170/185; P❄🛜🏊) Lənkəran's most stylish, contemporary hotel uses naturally heated, salt-rich spring water to offer medically focused wellness getaways, with free childcare available to parents using the spa. All rooms have big boxed balconies, specially commissioned art and pillows piled high on super-comfy beds. There's an excellent gym and fine views of İbadi Ridge from the 9th-floor Sky Lounge bar. Staff speak excellent English and Southeast Asian experts provide Thai or Balinese massages (per hour AZN70). From Lənkəran bazaar, take the İstisu bus (30q) or pay AZN5 for a taxi (around 20 minutes).

🍴 Eating

★ Borani
CAFE $$

(Qala xiyabanı; mains AZN5-12; ⊗9am-midnight; 🛜♿) Borani brings Lənkəran an urban vibe with contemporary beats, good-looking hipster waitstaff and an airy modern sense of 21st-century style. Their thin-crust pizzas are creditable (especially when served as calzone) but there are also various kebabs, Russian dishes, Georgian *khachapuri* (cheese bread) and salads. Soups start at just AZN2, including the delicious fresh bread.

Deniz Hotel & Restaurant   AZERBAIJANI **$$**
(☑ 051-4220101, 025-2550101; Sahil küç; mains AZN4-14, fish AZN10-40, duck AZN18; 🅿✳🔊📶🐾) Deniz offers, and partly delivers, a phenomenal menu that includes a wide range of different *ləvəngi* dishes (local stuffed fowl), Caspian fish, salads, roast mushrooms and countless kebabs. It's the only seaside restaurant within easy walking distance of central Lənkəran, with tables ranged around a colourfully lit (if questionably cleaned) beach-facing swimming pool. It's excellent value and portions are huge but sadly, loud music can drown out the crashing waves.

🍷 Drinking & Nightlife

Dəniz Ulduzu (Lənkəran Beach; beer AZN1; ⊙ 9am-11.30pm) is a cheap if very basic place for pints right on the beach. In the tree-shaded area around the train station there's an overpriced pub plus half a dozen male-dominated teahouses, some serving the light, yeasty local beer. For women, **a'love** (Qala xiyabanı 17; tea/cakes from 0.20/0.60AZN; ⊙ 9am-midnight; 🔊) is more welcoming for tea, or try very contemporary Borani (p291) for Illy espressos and fresh juices.

🔒 Shopping

Lənkəran region is famous for its tea, which can be purchased at several shops along Hazı Aslanov xiyabanı.

ℹ️ Information

Several banks in the central area change money. **Bank of Baku** (H Aslanov xiyabanı; ⊙ 9am-5pm Mon-Fri) has decent rates for US dollars and surprisingly acceptable ones for UK pounds.

ℹ️ Getting There & Away

Long-distance services start from Ləvəngi Bus Station, 3km northwest of the town centre. A 'Dairəsi' bus connects from here to the city centre/bazaar.

Useful destinations include the following:

Baku (AZN7, four hours) At least hourly until 5.30pm.

Biləsuvar (AZN4, 2½ hours) and/or **Masallı** (AZN3, one hour) Twice hourly till 5pm.

Gəncə (AZN10, seven hours) 7am and 9am.

Mingəçevir (AZN8, 6½ hours) 8.30am. Take this bus and change at Xaldan junction for Şəki.

The departure point for minibuses to **Astara** (AZN1, one hour) is the junction of Koroğlu and Sabir streets.

For Lerik, taxis (per person/car AZN5/20, 1¼ hours) start from **Dört Yol** (Old M3 Hwy Km 203/40), the road junction near the airport. Getting to Dört Yol costs AZN2 by taxi, taking less than 10 minutes from a **stand** (Koroğlu küç) near the Imam Ali mosque. Or, take a Ləj-bound minibus from the bazaar.

The overnight train to Baku (*platskart/kupe* AZN6.65/10.20, 7½ hours, departs 10.15pm) is far slower than buses but takes long enough to allow a decent sleep.

Other than a weekly flight to Moscow, the airport is essentially dormant.

ℹ️ Getting Around

From the local bus stand within the bazaar area, minibuses marked Dairəsi run to the bus station and Xan Lənkəran hotel; those marked Ləj pass Dört Yol where you can find shared vehicles to Lerik; Liman buses pass Fisherman's Beach; İstisu buses go to the Lankaran Springs spa resort.

The Talysh Mountains

There are several appealing ways to drive inland from the coastal strip following pretty streamsides as you rise through thick woodlands to sheep-mown uplands. Rustic getaways for Bakuvian families are scattered along some of the roadsides but otherwise there's minimal tourism infrastructure and finding English speakers is very rare. Ideally keep a distance of several kilometres between yourself and the Iranian border.

Lənkəran–Lerik

The 55km Lənkəran–Lerik road leads up through extensive deciduous forests then continues into the bare, rolling Talysh Mountains. Especially beyond Piran there's plenty of idyllic greenery with a wide variety of rest areas which, for most Azerbaijani tourists, are the Lerik region's main attraction. They range from very basic dining areas to rustic getaways to full-blown family resorts. While some can be used as the starting point for random strolls or longer hikes, most are seen as relaxation destinations in and of themselves. Addresses are kilometre-marker post readings from central Lənkəran.

🛏️ Sleeping & Eating

Cənub Resort   RESORT **$$**
(☑ 050-4333636, 050-4093535; www.cenub.com. az; Lənkəran–Lerik road, Km 36; d/q AZN80/100; ✳🔊) Cənub's well-built pine cottages are

OTHER TALYSH EXCURSIONS

As well as the Lerik road, three other paved routes can lead you through glorious woodland scenery into the little-visited Talysh Mountains.

Yardımlı

Relatively easy and satisfying is the Masallı–Yardımlı–Arvana road. It has hot springs after 13km, a little fire pool at Yanar Dağ (Km 15), a waterfall at Km 27. There is a simple but great-value en suite hotel in little Yardımlı and some miniresorts at the Masallı end of the route.

Sım

The fabled village of Sım has its own very impressive waterfall, small watermill and assorted mystery stones that reputedly date back to a period of cultural importance around the 7th century. If you can find a guide, there's a fabulous hike between Astara Istisu and Sım through the shaggy forests of the Hirkan National Park, home to Azerbaijan's last Persian leopards.

Toradi

Starting near the historic village of Pensar, with its two archetypal Talysh mosques, a new road to Toradi was built in 2017 through villages where you might still be one of the first foreigners in a generation. The asphalt stops near Toradi with a minor if locally famous shrine, but if you can find a local driver with an indestructible 4WD, it's worth continuing 7km up a mountain track to Gəlindaşları. This high hilltop has fabulous views from a rocky outcrop, claimed by folk myth to be a wedding party turned to stone by a rocky dragon.

a definite notch above most of the competition along the Lənkəran–Lerik road, with little stone patios or raised miniterraces shaded by trees, if a little tightly packed.

Relax RESORT $$
(☑ 050-2508464; www.relax.az; Lənkəran–Lerik road, Km 34; ☺ d/ste AZN100/130, cottages AZN120-300; ❄ ☎ ☒) Almost a whole village in its own right, Relax provides holidaying Bakuvian families with suitably plush rooms and a vast waterpark (mid-June to mid-September, nonguest adult/child AZN20/10) in what was once an idyllic rural valley.

For some tastes the place is too big and brash, with electric buggies shuttling guests around the site, but most cottages are tastefully built with local materials and traditional tiled roofs. Some English is spoken.

Təbəssüm RESTAURANT $
(☑ 050-2263027; Lənkəran–Lerik road, Km 27; kebabs/tea from AZN4/3; ☎) Təbəssüm is a particularly appealing small-scale rural restaurant-resort that prides itself on not cutting down any trees. Indeed some foliage grows right 'through' the kitchen buildings. Long footbridges link dining pavilions that nestle into the mossy rocks, overlooking a rear fork and minor waterfall. Kebabs and tea are sensibly priced.

There are also several pine-fragrant **huts** (from AZN30 to AZN80 according to size). These are attractive, though not luxurious, with en suite toilet (but no paper) and a shower that might never run hot. Wi-fi is a possibility in the restaurant area.

Lerik

♫ 025 / POP 7100 / ELEV 1096M

The overgrown mountainside village of Lerik, known for the longevity of its inhabitants, also offers many panoramic viewpoints. For the most central, climb the long stairway behind Flag Sq onto the main suburban ridge. For still wider views, hike/drive up to the TV tower across the valley. Driving further west takes you through a beautiful area of crags and gorge viewpoints to flower-filled valley villages set between rolling high fields that are often sunny when Lerik hides in fog.

Lerik is refreshingly cool in summer, seriously cold in winter. The town has two very basic if super-central places to stay: the hidden garden stalwart of **Gussein Baba's Cafe** (☑ 050-5387474; Heydar Əliyev Sq 4; dm/tw/tr AZN5/14/21; ☎), and some soulless rooms at easier-to-find **Nur** (☑ Balarzar 055-6761211; Heydar Əliyev Sq 8/14; tw without bath AZN14). There are summer-only rural retreats at Kalaxan and Qosmalion on the Kəlvəz Road.

◉ Sights

Centenarians Museum   MUSEUM
(Uzunömürlülər Muzeyi; foreigner/local AZN2/1; ☉8am-5pm) This modest museum celebrates the statistically high proportion of centenarians among Talysh mountain people. Most famous was Şirəli Müslümov (aka Shirali Muslimov), cited as the world's oldest man when he died in 1973, supposedly aged 168. And there were plenty more. The museum is hidden away on the short but circuitous route that leads from Flag Sq to the culture house. A little of the information is in French.

❶ Getting There & Away

Between 3am and 9am minibuses to Baku (AZN12, five hours) leave the *avtovağzal*, an area of shops and teahouses 800m steeply downhill from Lerik bazaar (Km 55).

Early morning shared taxis to Lənkəran (per person/car AZN5/20, 1¼ hours) also leave from here but after around 11am, passengers wait at the small shelter close to the eastern city gate ('*arka*').

Astara

◪ 025 / POP 16,800

Relatively wide beaches give Astara a semblance of seaside-resort potential and there are some lovely forest areas in the **Hirkan National Park**, several kilometres to the west of town. However, travellers mostly use Astara as a transit point for Iran.

The **pedestrian border crossing** (Azərbaycan küç; ☉24hr) is a somewhat intimidating series of unmarked grey metal gratings, five minutes' walk south from Astara's central square. On that square, semi-smart **Hotel Şindan** (◪050-4257282; Azərbaycan küç 11; d/ste AZN30/50; ❉ 🛜) has the town's best rooms. Two minutes' walk further northeast the **Hotel Xəzər** (◪070-7976373, 055-7976373; 1st fl, Heydar Əliyev pr 69; tw without bathroom AZN10; ❉) is a simple budget alternative opposite **Kapital Bank**, which has a 24-hour international ATM.

Around 9km north of Astara beside the old road to Lənkəran is **Yanar Bulağ** (Burning Spring; Km 234.6, Old Hwy M3, Arçıvan Village), where you can watch water burn. The water that bubbles out of this drinking fountain is made 'flammable' by partly dissolved methane. Bring your own matches!

❶ Getting There & Away

If you arrive on the sleeper train from Baku (*platskart/kupe* AZN7/11, 8½ hours), don't linger getting off – the isolated little station is several kilometres north of Astara's centre and there's a limited supply of waiting taxis. These charge AZN1 per head to the *gömrük* (border crossing).

If you want to head to Baku by train, it's worth going first to Lənkəran as the train station there is contrastingly central. Minibuses to Lənkəran (AZN1, 50 minutes) depart regularly till 3pm from a point that's two minutes' walk north of Astara's Hotel Şindan. Some others start from Oğur petrol, one block north of the border exit. An Astara–Lənkəran taxi (30 minutes) should charge AZN10 using the new road. Drivers will ask more if you want to use the old road and make a brief stop at Yanar Bulağ.

NAXÇIVAN

Naxçivan (pronounced Nakhchivan) is one of the most fascinating places you've probably never heard of. It's home to Noah's tomb, the 'Machu Picchu of Eurasia' (Alinja Castle), a Soviet salt mine you can sleep in (Duzdağ), and a surreally neat, clean yet historical capital (Naxçivan City) where all of the countless museums are free. Ancient if heavily restored monuments and oasis villages are all relatively accessible in a fascinatingly diverse landscape of deserts and melon fields, craggy mountains and upland grass-rimmed lakes. A historic cradle of cultures, the area was once a major trade crossroads – but by geopolitical chance it has ended up as a disconnected lozenge of Azerbaijani territory wedged uncomfortably between hostile Armenia and ambivalent Iran. That impedes trade for Naxçivan, but for travellers, it creates a fine opportunity to visit a chunk of Azerbaijan from Turkey, perhaps as a transit route to Iran. From Baku, however, you have to fly.

History

The Bible relates that post-flood, Noah grew vines, got drunk and lived on for a further 350 years while his progeny multiplied. According to local legend, all this happened in Naxçivan. Having been its own kingdom in the 10th century, the region blossomed – especially after 1139, when it briefly became the capital of the post-Seljuk Atabey dynasty. Naxçivan re-emerged as an independent khanate in 1747 and was the last such entity to be absorbed into the Russian empire in the 19th century. It was not until the 1920s, however, that the proto-USSR gave Armenia the province of Zangezur, causing Naxçivan to become geopolitically disconnected from the rest of Azerbaijan. Following independence in 1991, Armenia started a blockade of the exclave, cutting rail links from Baku. Support and supplies from Turkey kept it going, however, and helped prevent the Karabakh War from spreading into Naxçivan.

ℹ️ Getting There & Away

AZAL (www.azal.az) flights between Baku and Naxçivan (AZN70) operate several times daily with frequency varying by demand. In some years, connections to Gəncə have also operated but these were suspended at the time of writing.

Turkish Airlines flies Naxçivan–İstanbul twice weekly for around US$150. UTAir flies weekly to Moscow.

Buses run several times daily between Naxçivan and Iğdır (Turkey, AZN5, four hours), continuing to destinations as far afield as İstanbul. Coming from Iğdır, a good alternative is using one of the comfortable eight-person vans that usually pick up from outside the Iğdırli Turizm office on the *meydan* (central square).

There are overnight Naxçivan–Baku buses (AZN25, 13 hours), but to take those most foreigners will need both an Iranian transit visa and a double-entry visa for Azerbaijan.

Naxçivan City

📱 036 / POP 92,100

Naxçivan's eponymous city is the exclave's capital, main transport hub and home to virtually all of its accommodation. Other than Azerbaijan's finest tomb-tower – the 1186 MömInə Xatun – the architecture here gives few hints of the site's very ancient history. However, the wide, quiet boulevards are highly manicured and set with gleaming new administrative buildings creating an almost surreal sense of otherworldliness. The feeling is accentuated by the ghostly white apparition of Mt Ararat (Ağrı Dağı) which, on clear days, seems to float on the distant northwestern horizon. Nearer and more dramatic is the looming presence of İlan Dağ, a very photogenic rocky pinnacle that dominates the landscape east of town. Locals believe that its cleft peak was cut during the Biblical flood by the passage of the ark; its captain, Noah, was reputedly buried in what would later become Naxçivan City. His supposed tomb was rebuilt in 2013.

◎ Sights & Activities

The city has plenty of small, free museums featuring historical themes and Azerbaijani celebrities who were born or once lived here, notably 'national leader' Heydər Əli-

yev (www.aliyev-museum.nakhchivan.az; Bektaşi küç; ⊙10am-1pm & 2-5pm) FREE.

★ Mömİnə Xatun   MONUMENT

(İstirahət Parkı; ⊙park 24hr, interior 9am-1pm & 2-6pm Tue-Sun) FREE Perfectly proportioned, if gently leaning, Naxçivan's architectural icon is a 26m brick tower dating from 1186. It's decorated with geometric patterns and Kufic script (a stylised, angular form of Arabic) picked out in turquoise glaze. Views of it are more interesting than going inside, and the surrounding park is a veritable open-air museum of historic stone rams and grave markers.

A short stroll south, the Xan Sarayı (Mömİnə Xatun Parkı; ⊙10am-1pm & 2-6pm Tue-Sun) FREE is the enthusiastically restored former palace of the Naxçivan khans.

Carpet Museum   MUSEUM

(Xalça Muzey; 2nd fl, Heydər Əliyev pr 21; ⊙10am-1pm & 2-6pm Tue-Sun) FREE A superb collection of carpets from the Naxçivan region are clearly labelled, illustrating a remarkable range of styles. The rugs are interspersed by old spinning, carding and weaving paraphernalia.

Noah's Tomb   MONUMENT

(Nuh Peyğəmbər türbəsi) An octagonal tomb-tower with gilded roof-point stands just outside the small gate at Naxçivanqala's south tip. It was built in 2008 but the brickwork is antique styled and it stands on far-older foundations. Whether the site is really the grave of Biblical Noah, however, is a matter of faith. Walk towards the a gigantic new multidomed mosque that rises behind, then turn around. If the weather is exceptionally clear, you can see the triangular form of Mt Ararat (Ağrı Dağı) on the horizon beside the tomb-tower...which feels suitably symbolic.

Naxçivanqala   FORTRESS

(Cəlil Məmmədquluzadə küç, 1st lane 4; ⊙fortress dawn-dusk, museum 10am-1pm & 2-5pm Tue-Sun) FREE Before 2006, the site of Naxçivan's 7th-century citadel was just a series of muddy undulations, almost indistinguishable from the nearby graveyard. It has since been 'reconstructed' as a large square 'fortress', surrounded by crenellated walls which look better suited to a funfair than a historical site. Still, they provide many fine viewpoints and the circular building in the middle displays some fascinating archaeological discoveries.

Yeni Şərq Hamamı   HAMAM

(📱036-550 8446; Azadlıq pr; AZN4; ⊙9am-11pm) This large, attractive Turkish-style bath

Naxçivan City Centre

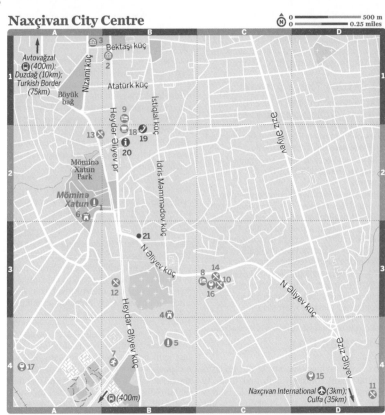

complex is great value, as the fee includes use of a sauna and the option of a private room. It's not a historic complex but its form is traditional.

🛏 Sleeping & Eating

The city has a limited range of accommodation. The central **Hotel Tabriz** (Mehmanxana Təbriz; ☑ 036-5447701; Təbriz meydanı; s/d/tr/ste AZN80/120/160/180; ❄ ⬛ ⬛) is a business-style place with English-speaking reception and fine views from the 13th-floor restaurant. At roughly half the price, **Hotel Qrand** (Grand Hotel Nakhchivan; ☑ 036-544 5930; grandhotel@neqsicahan.az; Cəlil Məmmədquluzadə küç; P ❄ ⬛) is great value despite some stained carpets and is fairly well located beyond Naxcivanqala. A new luxury hotel at nearby Saat Meydanı had opened just as we went to press.

That's also the top place for international dining though the Əyləncə Adası fun-park area at the southern end of town also has

two barista coffee shops and several eateries in a green-glass building designed like an cubist's sketch of a helicopter. A fine choice there is the eccentric **Bullet Steakhouse** (www.facebook.com/bulletsteakhouse; Goruş Yeri, Əyləncə Adası Parkı; kebab sets AZN3.50-8, steak meals AZN10-25; ⏱ 9am-11pm; ☎; ⬛ 6).

City-centre choices include two eateries on Nizami küç, cafes around a boating pond opposite the Jame Mosque and restaurants both beside and atop the Hotel Tabriz. Steeply below Naxcivanqala you can eat beside another artificial pond or in an ancient icehouse at curious **Buzxana** (Milli Yeməklər; Azadlıq pr; mains AZN5; ⏱ 9am-10.30pm).

Qədim Dunya   BARBECUE $
(Nizami küç 29a; kebabs AZN3.5-5, salad AZN1.5, beer AZN1.4; ⏱ 9.30am-midnight) This modestly enticing, very central kebab shop plays at historical-themed decor and serves local beer at reasonable prices.

Naxçivan City Centre

AZERBAIJAN NAXÇIVAN CITY

For something more contemporary, go to Park Kafe on the top floor of the next-door shopping centre.

★ **Saat Meydanı**   MULTICUISINE **$$**
(www.facebook.com/saatmeydani; Cəlil Məmmədquluzadə küç; mains AZN5-20; ⊙vary per venue) Brand new in 2019, this multi-restaurant complex is ranged around a large stone courtyard featuring central fountains and the photogenic mechanical clocktower for which it is named. Within shady arcades are all of Naxçivan's top international eateries, with cuisines including Turkish-Anatolian, at **Köşebaşı**; upmarket east-Asian, at **Jasmine**; and Georgian, at **Batum** (Saat Meydanı, Cəlil Məmmədquluzadə küç; mains AZN5-15; ⊙8am-10pm; 🤖).

The complex also houses a cinema and upmarket **hotel** (room from AZN140).

Drinking & Nightlife

Naxçivan's brewery uses mountain water and Czech equipment to create light, highly quaffable Prestij. The beer is served cheaply at out-of-centre beer gardens like low-key **Dost Qapısı** (Lifan Zavodu dongası; ⊙9am-midnight) or more whacky **Naxış Nərgiz** (Qəmküsər küç; ⊙noon-11pm) which features a dragon's-mouth folly. Saat Meydanı has a contrastingly indulgent **English Pub** (Saat Meydanı, Cəlil Məmmədquluzadə küç; ⊙10am-11pm).

Şərq Hamamı Çay Evi   TEAHOUSE
(İsmayılxan Hamamı; Təbriz meydanı; ⊙9am-11pm) This charming teahouse hides within an 18th-century bathhouse building, whose interior is more atmospheric than the peeling faux-gilt on the domed roof might suggest. It's refreshingly cool and usually very peaceful, yet a whole pot of tea with lemon costs only AZN2.

It's on the leafy square right in front of Hotel Tabriz. No toilet.

ℹ Information

Nar Merkezi (www.nar.az; Cəlilov küç; ⊙9am-6pm) One of very few phone shops in Naxçivan that will issue a local SIM card to foreign tourists. It is diagonally across the road from the tourist office.

Tourist Information Office (📞036-5457755; http://turizm.nakhchivan.az; Cəlilov küç; ⊙9am-4pm Mon-Sat) English is spoken but no city maps are available. It's a block south of the Hotel Tabriz in an onion-domed brick structure that is supposedly 'historic'.

ℹ Getting There & Away

Buy air tickets online or at the often-crowded **Aviakassa** (Cəlil Məmmədquluzadə küç 1; ⊙8am-8pm).

Buses to most destinations, including those in Turkey, start from the **Avtovağzal** (Bayraq meydanı) at the northern edge of town, with a new bus station under construction across the same junction. Useful services include Culfa (AZN1, one hour) and Ordubad (AZN2, two hours) both approximately hourly (9am to around 4pm) and a 1pm bus to Qarabağlar (AZN1) returning around 20 minutes after arrival.

A return taxi ride to Ordubad is likely to cost around AZN35 depending on waiting time, and considerably more if you add extra stops en route.

Trains to Culfa (80q, 90 minutes) leave at 10.30am, returning at 12.15pm, and at 3pm, returning next morning. The fascinating route passes right along the Araz River – picturesque and offering a chance to look across the border into Iran. If you have an Iranian visa, Culfa is the easiest crossing point.

ℹ Getting Around

Bus 2 runs south from the bus station to the train station, bus 3 does a similar route in reverse. Bus 6 continues to the airport which is 4km east of central Naxçivan City, around 10 minutes by taxi (AZN7).

Around Naxçivan

Roads are good and distances modest. For a satisfying taxi day trip combine climbing Alinca Castle with visits to Əshabi-Kəhf and Ordubad. If you want an English-speaking driver/guide consider using the reliable agency **Nakhchivan Travel** (Natig Travel; ☏ 070-5672506; www.nakhchivantravel.com), which also offers specialist bird-watching and climbing trips.

◉ Sights & Activities

In winter, snow makes it impractical to visit Batabat or to climb Alinja Castle but will prove an attraction at Ağbulaq where a small new ski centre is under development. Summers can be contrastingly sweaty. March, April and October are ideal times to explore.

★ **Alinja Castle**   VIEWPOINT
(Əlincəqala) For those prepared to climb over 1500 steps up a mountain crag, one of Naxçivan's great highlights is the magnificent view from the sparse medieval ruins of Alinja Castle, sometimes nicknamed 'Azerbaijan's Machu Picchu'.

Historic wall-stubs have been partly built up to outline how the site might have been laid out in its 12th-century heyday. The main fortifications date from the 1140s when Naxçivan was at its most powerful, under a leader known as Eldegyz (Eldəniz). They were so secure that Alinja managed to hold out for 14 years against a siege that started in 1386. Other than a mosque-like museum at the base, there are no complete buildings and no shade, so bring a hat and plenty of drinking water. To avoid exhausting heat, climb early in the morning or a couple of hours before sunset.

The stairs up start from the Qazançı road, 33km northeast of Naxçivan City. Rare minibuses to Xanəgah pass within 1km of the spot. Taxis ask AZN30 to AZN50 depending on waiting time.

Duzdağ   MINE
(☏ 036-544 4901; www.duzdag.com; Duzdağ şaxtası yolu; entry/overnight stay free/AZN30; P) **FREE** In decades past, being sent to a Soviet salt mine was a synonym for horror. At Duzdağ, however, a former mine site has been converted into a curative retreat for asthma sufferers. In daytime hours, the curious are free to walk 300m down the prettily lit rock-salt access tunnel with its twinkling ceiling and little cavern teahouse. It's 10km northwest of Naxçivan City, AZN8 by taxi. If you want to stay overnight, apply through the Duzdağ Resort Hotel 1.3km further back towards the city. That also has a free salt museum and a small aquapark with swimming pool and water slide that nonguests can use for AZN10 (2pm to 7pm only).

Cahan Kudi Xatun   MONUMENT
(Qarabağlar Türbəsi; Qarabağlar Village) Second only to the Mömina Xatun (p295) as Azerbaijan's most impressive medieval tomb-tower, the main 1320 mausoleum is a ribbed cylinder inlaid with ample 'Allah Allah' calligraphy in blue glaze. Extensively restored in 2018, it's fronted by a double minaret and a small museum. The complex is hidden away in Qarabağlar, a small, largely forgotten agricultural village 40km northwest of Naxçivan City. It's 7km off the main highway to Turkey: turn beside the NP3 petrol station. A minibus from Naxçivan City bus station leaves at 1pm (AZN1) but you'll be quite rushed to see the tower before it returns around 20 minutes later: ask the driver to wait or be prepared to walk back to the main highway to Qıvraq/Kəngirli and flag down a passing vehicle.

Ordubad   VILLAGE
Naxçivan's most attractive settlement appears like an oasis amid craggy desert landscapes. Its central square features a classic old-men's teahouse beneath giant *çinar* and its narrow streets hide many an older building behind mud-brick walls. There are a couple of small museums to seek out, one of them opposite a distinctive brick mosque in a former *zorkhana* (venue for a distinctive Persian strength-meditation martial art).

The last returning minibus to Naxçivan City (AZN2, 90 minutes) departs around 4pm from a bus station around 400m south of the central area.

Batabat   BIRD SANCTUARY
FREE In stark contrast to lowland Naxçivan's arid semideserts, the upland lakes of Batabat are set in high, rolling grasslands. They make for cooling family picnic spots in sum-

mer and are known for the novelty of their 'floating islands'. For twitchers, however, it's the birdlife (golden oriole, Radde's accentor etc) that form the sanctuary's main attraction. Never venture beyond the upper lake: although there are no signs, that's a military zone and your presence could cause an international incident. The site is 60km north of Naxçivan City, around AZN35 return by taxi.

Əshabi-Kəhf
ISLAMIC SITE

(www.ashabikahf.nakhchivan.az) Əshabi-Kəhf is a series of holy caves, locally believed to be the scene of a Koranic miracle in which seven pious men managed to evade their enemies by falling asleep for three centuries. For some Muslim visitors it is Naxçivan's top attraction, but the attractive rocky cleft setting has a quiet charm whatever your faith.

Əshabi-Kəhf is 20km east of Naxçivan City, reached by turning northeast off the main highway to Ordubad some 5km southeast of the airport. Buses (AZN2) depart from Naxçivan City bus station at 8.30am and 2pm, returning at noon and 5pm.

Several other countries have counterclaims as being site of the same legend.

UNDERSTAND AZERBAIJAN

Azerbaijan Today

Between 2014 and 2016, the collapse of oil prices punched a gaping hole in Azerbaijan's budget plans and two devaluations saw the value of the Manat tumble to barely half its former value. However, the government was able to raid the piggy bank of its reserve oil fund to paper over short-term fiscal cracks and prevent wide-scale discontent. Indeed the crisis ultimately proved galvanising in speeding up a much-touted economic diversification to move Azerbaijan away from its severe oil dependency.

One major new focus would be tourism: visas were radically simplified and the newly weakened Manat meant that glitzy hotels and spas built with rich oil-folk in mind were now affordable enough to entice a wave of visitors, especially those from the Gulf Cooperation Council (GCC) countries escaping from searing hot Arabian summers. The influx of visitors has continued to snowball since, while rebounding oil prices during 2018 allowed stalled building projects to restart, giving Baku a palpable sense of bustling optimism.

In June 2019 Baku hosted the finals of the Europa League, one of the biggest matches in European club soccer, just the latest of several high-profile sporting events that is crowned by the spectacular Azerbaijan Grand Prix, a remarkable annual showcase for Baku's charms.

History

Early History

From the 6th century BC (and indeed for much of its later history) proto-Azerbaijan was part of the Persian Empire, with Zoroastrianism developing as the predominant religion. Around the 4th century BC the ill-defined state of Arran emerged, also known as 'Caucasian Albania' (no link to the present-day Balkan republic). From about AD 325 these Albanians adopted Christianity, building many churches, the ruins of some of which still remain today. The history of the Caucasian Albanians is of great political importance to modern-day Azerbaijanis, largely for the disputed 'fact' that they weren't Armenian.

The Muslim Era

Islam became the major religion, starting with the Arabs' 7th-century advance into Caucasian Albania. For later waves of Turkic herder-horsemen, proto-Azerbaijan's grassland plains presented ideal grazing lands. So it was here that the Caucasus' Turkic ethnicity became concentrated while original Caucasian Christians tended to retreat into the mountain foothills.

A classic cultural era bloomed in the 12th-century cities of (old) Qəbələ, Bərdə and Naxçıvan. Şamaxı emerged as the capital of Şirvan and Gəncə's regional preeminence was symbolised by the classical 'national' poet Nizami Gəncəvi. However, from the 13th century these cities were pummelled into dust by the Mongols, Timur (Tamerlane) and assorted earthquakes.

After two centuries and an improving caravan trade, Şirvan had revived. Its rulers, the Shirvanshahs, scored an important home victory in a 1462 battle against Arbadil (southern Azerbaijan, now in Iran), only to lose in the 1501 rematch. Subsequently converted to Shia Islam, Şirvan bonded with (south) Azerbaijan under the originally

Azerbaijani Safavid shahs who came to rule the whole Persian Empire.

In the early 18th century, a collection of autonomous Muslim khanates emerged across Azerbaijan. However, to preserve their independence against a rebounding Persia, several khanates united and asked Russia for assistance. They got more than they bargained for. The Russian Empire swiftly annexed several northerly khanates. Persia's bungled attempts to grab them back ended with the further Russian annexation of the Şirvan, Karabakh, Naxçıvan, Talysh and Yerevan khanates, recognised under the humiliating treaties of Gulistan (1813) and Turkmenchay (1828).

The Russian Era

To consolidate their rule over their new conquests the Russians encouraged the immigration of Christians, particularly members of non-Orthodox religious sects from Russia, Germans from Würtemburg and Armenians from the Ottoman-Turkish Empire. This indirectly sowed the seeds of ethnic conflicts that would break out in 1905, 1918 and 1989.

In the 1870s, new uses for petroleum suddenly turned little Baku into a boom town. By 1905 it was supplying half the world's oil, creating immense wealth and a cultural renaissance, but also an underclass of workers suffering appalling conditions. Exploited by a young Stalin, their grievances ballooned into a decade of revolutionary chaos that resulted in several horrific interethnic clashes.

Independence & Soviet Conquest

Following the Russian revolution of 1917, and with WWI still undecided, Azerbaijan declared itself the Muslim world's first 'democracy'. Baku only became part of this formulation once its pro-Russian socialist revolutionary leaders were driven out, helped by an invading Turkish army. The Turks rapidly withdrew, leaving the Azerbaijan Democratic Republic (ADR; Azərbaycan Xaiq Cümhuriyyəti) independent. This forward-thinking secular entity, of which Azerbaijanis remain intensely proud, lasted barely two years as the Bolshevik Red Army invaded in 1920. The short-lived Transcaucasian Soviet Socialist Republic (SSR) was formed with Georgia and Armenia as a prelude to the USSR.

Border changes diminished Azerbaijan's area in favour of Armenia, leaving Naxçıvan entirely cut off from the rest of the Azerbaijan SSR. The passionate insistence of Azerbaijan's 'father of communism', Nəriman Nərimanov,

kept Nagorno-Karabakh within the nation, but for his pains Nərimanov was poisoned in 1925. His replacement, Mir Jafar Bağirov, oversaw Stalin's brutal purges in which over 100,000 Azerbaijanis were shot or sent to prison camps, never to return. Following the Khrushchev 'thaw', Bağirov was himself arrested and shot.

During WWII, one of Hitler's priorities was grabbing Baku's oil wealth for energy-poor Germany. Luckily for Baku, the German army became divided and bogged down trying to take Stalingrad on the way. Nonetheless, realisation of Baku's potential vulnerability later encouraged Soviet engineers to develop new oil fields in distant Siberia.

Perestroika (Soviet restructuring) in the late 1980s was also a time of increasing tension with Armenia. Tit-for-tat ethnic squabbles between Armenians and Azerbaijanis over the status of Nagorno-Karabakh bubbled over into virtual ethnic cleansing, as minorities in both republics fled escalating violence. On 20 January 1990, the Red Army made a heavy-handed intervention in Baku, killing dozens of civilians and turning public opinion squarely against the USSR. Azerbaijan declared its independence from the Soviet Union in 1991.

Independent Again

The Karabakh War reached its nadir with the massacre of over 600 Azerbaijani civilians by Armenian forces at Xocalı (26 February 1992). Dithering post-independence president Ayaz Mütəllibov was thereupon ousted. His replacement, Əbülfəz Elçibəy, himself fled a year later in the face of an internal military rebellion. This was comeback time for Heydər Əliyev, an ex-USSR politburo member who had been Azerbaijan's Communist Party chairman in the 1970s. Əliyev stabilised the fractious country, kick-started international investment in the oil industry and signed a ceasefire agreement with Armenia and Nagorno-Karabakh in May 1994. However, around 16% of Azerbaijan's territory remained (and remains) disputed. The 'frozen conflict' left around 800,000 Azerbaijanis displaced. Azerbaijan's 21st-century oil boom belatedly allowed funds for many rehousing projects, but also led to a vast spurt of military spending sending a barely disguised message that the nation is one day intent on getting back at least part of the 'lost territories'.

Azerbaijan's new oil boom really got started in earnest when the US$4-billion

Baku–Tbilisi–Ceyhan (BTC) pipeline began pumping Caspian oil to Turkey in 2006. A resultant building bonanza started in Baku and is now evident in regional centres nationwide. Heydər Əliyev is still unblinkingly referred to as Azerbaijan's 'National Leader', even though he died in 2003. His photos appear everywhere and each town has a cultural centre and park named in his honour. Meanwhile, the dynasty continues under his son İlham.

Arts

Azerbaijan's cultural greats are revered across the country. Their busts adorn Baku's finest buildings, their names are commemorated as streets and their homes are often maintained as shrine-like 'house-museums' (ev-muzeyi), where fans can pay homage.

Literature

Azerbaijan has a long and distinguished literary tradition. Best known among its authors is the Azerbaijani 'Shakespeare', Nizami Gəncəvi (1141–1209), whose ubiquitous statues almost outnumber those of Heydər Əliyev. Nizami wrote in Persian rhyming couplets, but Mehmed bin Suleyman Füzuli (1495–1556) was the first to write extensively in Azerbaijani-Turkish. His sensitive rendition of Nizami's classic 'Leyli and Majnun' (a Sufi parable wrapped up as a tale of mad, all-engrossing love) influenced many later writers, including poet Khurshudbanu Natavan (1830–97), playwright Mirza Fatali Axundov (1812–78) and satirist Mirza Sabir (1862–1911), as well as inspiring Eric Clapton's hit song 'Layla'. Azerbaijan's 20th-century star writer was Səmət Vurğun, who remains especially popular in his native Qazax district. For more recent fiction, a great read is Ella Leya's 2015 novel The Orphan Sky set in Soviet-era Baku.

Music

Azerbaijan's muğam music is recognised by Unesco as being one of the world's great forms of intangible cultural heritage. To some Western ears it sounds more like pained wailing than singing, but at its best it's intensely emotional, an almost primal release of the spirit. The greatest living muğam superstar is Alim Qazimov. Traditional music was also performed by aşıqlar (wandering minstrels; singular aşıq), some of whom would compete in contests similar to the bardic competitions of the Celtic world. A more upbeat, light-hearted latter-day form known as meyxana has bantering lyrics and cantering synthesiser accompaniment.

In Baku, jazz grew popular in the 1950s and '60s and took on an original local flavour under Vaqif Mustafazadeh (1940–79), who fused American jazz with traditional Azerbaijani muğam improvisation. His multitalented daughter Aziza Mustafazadeh (b 1969) has further blended muğam jazz with classical music. Other contemporary jazz-muğam pianist sensations include Shahin Novrasli and Isfar Sarabski, both Montreux Jazz Festival champions.

Much of Azerbaijani pop is based firmly on the Turkish mould. There is also a minor rap, R & B and rock scene, and many up-and-coming DJs.

Painting & Sculpture

Azerbaijani art blossomed in the later Soviet era and today the works of neo-impressionist superstar Səttar Bəhlulzadə cost hundreds of thousands of dollars. Similarly admired, Tahir Salaxov's work ranges from thoughtful Soviet realism to densely coloured portraiture and semi-cubist landscapes. Much of the expressive pre-Independence public statuary has been removed of late in favour of fountains or replaced by images of Heydər Əliyev, but great works remain, notably by Omar Eldarov, whose swirlingly creative statue of Hüseyn Cavid dominates the square fronting Baku's Elmlər Akademiyası. In the 21st century there's been an explosion of interest in contemporary art as well as a rediscovery of modern painting genres, with Baku full of exciting conceptual galleries.

Food & Drink

Azerbaijani cuisine's strengths are in fruity sauces, wonderful fresh vegetables and mutton-based soups. Barbecued meat often takes centre stage while various rice pilaf dishes feature mainly at banquets.

Many rural restaurants lack a menu. Almost all charge AZN5 to AZN7 for a kebab, but sizes and quality vary considerably – in many places you'll want two portions per person. Bread, salad, cheese and other side plates can easily double the bill.

Staples & Specialities

Baku restaurants offer a wide range of cuisines but beyond the capital, Azerbaijani

MENU DECODER

antreqot	lamb ribs
aş	fruity rice-pilaf meal generally served on huge multi-person platters; also known as *plov*
badımcan	aubergine
balıq	fish, sturgeon
borş	hearty cabbage-based soup
bozbaş	stew-soup usually featuring a meatball formed around a central plum
buğlama	mutton-and-potato stew slow-cooked to condense the flavour
çığırtma	soft omelette incorporating chicken, tomato and garlic (not a soup as in Georgia)
cız-bız	fried tripe and potato
çörək	bread
dograma	a cold soup made with sour milk, potato, onion and cucumber
dolma	various mince-stuffed vegetables
dovğa	a hot, thick yoghurt-based soup
düşbərə	lightly minted broth containing tiny bean-sized ravioli and typically served with sour cream and garlic
düyü	rice
Gürcü xingalı	Georgian-style spiced dumplings
kabab(lar)	kebab(s)
kotlet	meat patties
küftə	meatballs
kükü	thick omelette cut into chunks
lahmajun	Turkish wafer-thin version of *pide* that you should fill with salad then squeeze on lemon juice
lavaş	very thin bread-sheets
ləvəngi	Talysh-style *toyuq* (chicken) or *balıq* (fish) stuffed with a paste of herbs and crushed walnuts
qızıl balıq	salmon
qovurma	mutton fried in butter with various fruits
qreçka	boiled buckwheat or a meal served with such buckwheat as the main filler
qutab	thin, pancake turnover filled with spinach *(göyərti)* or meat *(ətlə)*
pide	long Turkish 'pizza' but not necessarily with cheese
piti	two-part soupy stew: you'll need to mash the solids yourself
püre	mashed potato
sac	sizzler hot-plate meal, usually served for multiple diners
sosiska	frankfurter-style sausage
tabaka	pricey, flattened whole chicken
xama	sour cream
xaş	heavily garlic-charged soup made from bits of sheep that many Westerners prefer to avoid; wash down with a hair-of-the-dog vodka
xinqal, xəngəl	meaty chunks served with lasagne-like leaves of pasta
yağ	butter

and Turkish food is almost all you'll find. Many rustic dining areas, commonly known as *istirahət güşəsi* or *istirahət mərkəzi*, focus almost entirely on flame-grilled kebabs. A standard *tikə kəbab* consists of skewered meaty chunks, often including a cube of tail fat that locals consider a special delicacy. *Lülə kəbab* is minced lamb with herbs and spices. Pricier kebab types include *antreqot* (ribs) and *dana bastırma* (marinated beef strips).

Barbecued vegetables are often available, too, though vegetarians might be alarmed to find lurking morsels of lamb fat inserted into aubergines to make them more succulent.

Whatever you order, don't be surprised if a series of fresh vegetables, fruits, salads, cheese and bread arrive. In most cases, each costs extra, so refuse anything you don't want to pay for. In towns, for a cheap, unpretentious non-kebab meal, look for a *yeməkxana*, which is likely to serve *qazan-yeməkləri* (plate foods) including various potato-and-mutton stews, such as *buğlama*, *bozbaş* (with *küftə* meatballs plus the odd cherry) and *piti* (with chickpeas, requiring mashing). But the classic non-kebab dish is dolma. A common dolma meal is a baked-vegetable trio (tomato, pepper and mini-aubergine) stuffed with a herb-infused mixture of rice and minced lamb. You can also find *kələm* (cabbage-leaf) or *yarpaq* (vine-leaf) dolma with similar fillings. 'Şəki dolma' means a pot full of mini vine-leaf dolma.

Fish like *sudak* (pike-perch) or *farel* (trout) are sporadically available, tasting best when smeared with tangy sauces made from sour-plum *(alça)* or pomegranate juice *(narşərab)*. Typical of southern Azerbaijan, deliciously fruity Talysh cuisine is best known for *ləvəngi* (chicken or fish stuffed with walnuts and herbs). *Çoban* (shepherd) salad comprising chopped tomato, cucumber, raw onion, dill and coriander leaves is served as a preamble to most meals.

Azerbaijani breakfast foods *(səhər yeməkləri)* are bread *(çörək)*, butter *(yağ)* and cheese *(pendir)*, maybe with some honey *(bal)* or sour cream *(xama)*, all washed down with plentiful sweet tea *(çay)*. Scrambled eggs *(qayğana)* or fried eggs *(qlazok)* might be available on request.

Drinks

The national drink is *çay* (tea), usually served in pear-shaped *armudi* glasses and sucked through a sugar lump for sweetness, or accompanied by jams and candies. Barista coffee shops are as much a fad in Baku as in any international city but they are much rarer in the provinces and in small towns the best hope of an espresso machine is likely to be in the swankiest hotel.

Azerbaijan has long made decent *konjak* (brandy) but its *şərab* (wines) are improving in leaps and bounds. The Savalan, Chabiant and Fireland brands are all reliably good, but for excellent value it's hard to beat Az-Granata's deep, rich Qaragöz Saperavi black label at under AZN5 a bottle. Be aware that many locals prefer their wine *kəmşirin* (semi-sweet) or *şirin* (very sweet). *Kəmturş* (semi-dry) or *turş* (dry) options are generally closer to Western tastes. A particular local speciality is wine made from pomegranates. An increasing number of wineries are opening their doors to visitors (see www.azer baijanwine.com) and since 2019 there's a wine festival (www.winefest.az).

Xırdalan lager is the best known of several unsophisticated beers *(piva)* but Naxçıvan's Prestij along with Aysberq from the far north are quaffable too and Baku has a fashion-conscious brewpub and a Paulaner Germanic beer hall.

Toasting with vodka *(arak)* remains an important social ritual between older men with significant social standing (and bellies) to maintain. However, it is less formalised than in Georgia and less compulsive than in Russia.

Drinking water *(su)* from the tap is usually fine in mountain villages, but not recommended in lowland towns. Bottled water is widely available: choose from sparkling *(qazlı)* or still *(qazsız)*.

SURVIVAL GUIDE

ⓘ Directory A–Z

ACCOMMODATION

Azerbaijan's portfolio of hotels is expanding rapidly with plenty of bargains to be had, especially in upper-market resorts where prices are often remarkably reasonable for the comparatively glitzy standards. There's generally at least one or two simple but acceptable budget hotels in regional towns. Homestays and rural 'rest centres' offer cultural insights. And since around 2016, hostels have started to appear in most major cities.

ACTIVITIES

Azerbaijan offers a wealth of opportunities for hiking, bird-watching, water sports, spa retreats, golf and skiing. However, the idea of active holidays is relatively new here and many rural hotel proprietors still seem bemused by the idea that you'd want to do much more than eat, drink or soak in the pool between selfie opportunities.

Hiking & Mountaineering

There are some fabulous village-to-village hikes, especially in the Quba–Shahdag and Lahıc areas, plus shorter upland hikes from Zaqatala. Outfits like **Camping Azerbaijan** (☑ 051-8868380, 051-4009091; www.facebook.com/campingazer baijan2014) and **BagBaku** (Map p236; ☑ 051-3703111; www.facebook.com/bagbakutour;

The Azerbaijani Alphabet

AZER.	ROMAN	PRONUNCIATION
A a	a	long, as in 'far'
B b	b	as in 'bit'
C c	c	as the 'j' in 'jazz'
Ç ç	ch	as in 'chase'
D d	d	as in 'duck'
E e	e	as in 'bet'
Ə ə	a	short, as in 'apple'
F f	f	as in 'far'
G g	g	like the 'gy' in 'Magyar'
Ğ ğ	gh	a soft growl from the back of throat (like French 'r')
H h	h	as in 'here'
X x	kh	as the 'ch' in Scottish 'loch'
I ı	ı	neutral vowel; as the 'a' in 'ago'
İ i	i	as in 'police'
J j	zh	as the 's' in 'leisure'
K k	k	as in 'kit'
Q q	q	hard 'g' as in 'get'
L l	l	as in 'let'
M m	m	as in 'met'
N n	n	as in 'net'
O o	o	short as in 'got'
Ö ö	er	as in 'her', with no 'r' sound
P p	p	as in 'pet'
R r	r	a rolled 'r'
S s	s	as in 'see'
Ş ş	sh	as in 'shore'
T t	t	as in 'toe'
U u	u	as in 'chute'
Ü ü	ew	as in 'pew'
V v	v	as in 'van'
Y y	y	as in 'yet'
Z z	z	as in 'zoo'

Words in Azerbaijani are usually lightly stressed on the last syllable. Note that in many parts of the country, the hard k is pronounced more like a 'ch', so that Bakı sounds like 'ba-chuh' and Şəki becomes 'sha-chee'.

Əliyarbəyov küç 26/14) offer regular, good-value walking adventures led by English-speaking guides. For mountaineers, the most exciting opportunities fall within the Shahdag National Park. Access to the highest peaks there is hampered by bureaucracy but the system is in flux so the coming years might prove full of opportunity.

Skiing

Azerbaijan's main ski resorts are at Şahdağ/Laza and Tufandağ/Qəbələ, though seasons are short and you'll find more visitors come to be photographed than to actually ski. See https://skiazerbaijan.com for an overview. A new, smaller ski field (Ağbulaq Xizək Mərkəzi) at Ağbulaq in Naxçıvan was nearing completion at the time of writing.

Spas, Swimming & Water Sports

Oil bathing in Naftalan, sulphur-water springs at Qalaaltı (p256) and salt-mine accommodation at Duzdağ (p298) near Naxçıvan City are major attractions, especially for local, Russian and Central Asian tourists. You can also sample a medicinal petroleum bath at the Qafqaz Thermal Resort (p270) in Yengicə near Qəbələ, provided you pass the preliminary medical examination.

Pollution means that the Caspian isn't the most pristine sea for swimming, especially at Şixov where the beach has a curious offshore backdrop of oil rigs. In summer, locals flock to the somewhat better beaches at Nabran and on the northern Abşeron Peninsula where jet skis can be rented. Kitesurfing is possible at Blue Planet (p256) on a pretty lagoon southeast of Şuraabad.

Golf

There are impressive courses outside Quba (p257) and at Dreamland (www.dreamlandgolfclub.com) near Baku Airport.

Bird-Watching

Azerbaijan is an ornithologist's delight with a vast range of habitats encouraging a similarly wide range of birdlife. *Birdwatching in Azerbaijan* is a superb guidebook and online resource (http://birdingaze.blogspot.com). Birdwatching Azerbaijan (www.facebook.com/birdwatchingazerbaijan2019) offers eco-aware tours within the country while Nakhchivan Travel (p298) has specialist bird-watching trips in Naxçıvan.

CUSTOMS REGULATIONS

Importing vehicles is complex and expensive. Export restrictions include the following:

Artworks & artefacts Export can prove awkward, as you'll often need written permission from the Ministry of Culture.

Carpets Exporting carpets bigger than 2 sq metres requires a certificate from the Baku Carpet Museum (AZN46/26 to get it issued in one day/week). Baku carpet shops can usually organise this for you. Carpets more than 50 years old may not be taken out of Azerbaijan at all.

Caviar Limit of 125g per person.

MONEY

Azerbaijan's manat is denoted AZN or by a special 'M' that looks like a euro symbol rotated through 90 degrees. AZN1 equals 100 *qəpiq* (100q).

Many transactions still require cash but Visa & Mastercard usage is becoming increasingly widespread and ATMs are available in all cities and regional centres.

PUBLIC HOLIDAYS

New Year's Day 1 January

Novruz Bayramı 20–26 March

Genocide Day 31 March (mourning day for those killed in Baku, 1918)

Ramazan Bayram (April–May, date varies) Eid al-Fitr, the holiday after the end of Ramadan

Victory Day 9 May

Republic Day 28 May (founding of first Azerbaijan Democratic Republic in 1918)

National Salvation Day 15 June (parliament asked Heydər Əliyev to lead the country in 1993)

Armed Forces Day 26 June (founding of Azerbaijan's army in 1918)

Gurban Bayramı (June–July, date varies) Eid al-Adha, Festival of the Sacrifice

National Independence Day 18 October (date of Azerbaijan's breakaway from the USSR)

Flag Day 9 November (celebrates the 2010 unfurling on what was then the world's tallest flagpole)

Constitution Day 12 November (framing of constitution in 1995)

National Revival Day 17 November (first anti-Soviet uprising in 1988)

Solidarity Day 31 December (breaking down of border fences between Azerbaijan and Iran in 1989)

TELEPHONE SERVICES

➡ SIM cards typically cost from AZN5 for pay-as-you-go, with SMS messages costing 4q, calls per min 4q and data around AZN6 for a 1.5GB package. To buy a SIM card you'll need your passport and may need to go to the main office in any town of one of the three providers (AzerCell, Bakcell or Nar).

➡ Mobile phones not purchased in Azerbaijan can be used for up to 30 days but after that you'll need to register the phone's IMEI code through www.imei.az or at a post office. The cost can be anywhere between AZN5 and AZN90 depending on the value of your phone. To find its IMEI code tap *#06#.

TOURIST INFORMATION

The new Azerbaijan Tourist Board is undertaking a massive revamp of the nation's tourist information offices and is working on themed tour ideas including wine (www.azerbaijanwine.com), golf (www.golfazerbaijan.com) and skiing (www.skiazerbaijan.com).

VISAS

E-Visas

Apply online for single-entry visas for a stay of up to 30 days. You can pick the start date of validity after which the visa must be used within 90 days. As long as you use the official site (https://evisa.gov.az) the cost is US$24 with processing taking three days. Or pay US$51 and get it within three hours. Beware that there are several copycat websites by commercial agencies that have con-

fusingly similar addresses – these might charge more money, or demand that you book a tour with them. There is no tour requirement with the official site. Passports must be valid for at least three months beyond the expiry date of the visa.

Other Visas

Visas are available on arrival at international airports for around 15 nationalities, mostly those from East Asian and Arab Gulf states plus Israel.

If you are a citizen of a nation which isn't listed as part of the e-visa agreement, you will need to apply through an embassy, consulate or designated visa service agency, typically in your country of residence or, if there is no diplomatic mission there, in a specific designated country nearby. Almost all such applications require a Letter of Invitation (LOI) from a travel agency or from a contact or business in Azerbaijan.

Visa Registration

If you plan to stay more than 15 days, police registration (*müveqqəti qeydiyat*) is a legal requirement. This should not incur a cost and will be done for you automatically at many better hotels, but it's worth double-checking especially at smaller places where you might need to insist. A few hostels have been known to charge for the service.

Theoretically you can register in a regional Migration Office or online through https://eservice.migration.gov.az. The latter is now in English but you will need to upload documents and might be required to have a local mobile-phone number to receive confirmation. Staying in a hotel for at least a night might generally prove worth it to save the trouble. Not registering carries a penalty of AZN350 charged as you exit the country. One original registration currently suffices for a whole stay.

Nagorno-Karabakh

Fast Facts

➡ Largest city: Stepanakert

➡ Area code: 374

➡ Population: 147,906

➡ Currency: Dram (AMD)

➡ Official language:
Armenian

➡ Status: Disputed region in
the South Caucasus

➡ Year territorial dispute
began: 1988

Resources

Introduction

Nagorno-Karabakh (known to Armenians as Atrsakh) is one of three internationally unrecognised South Caucasus territories to have self-declared independence after the collapse of the USSR. The subject of a brutal war between 1990 and 1994, Nagorno-Karabakh is still legally part of Azerbaijan by international law. Its name sums up its myriad cultural influences: *nagorno* means mountainous in Russian, *kara* means black in Turkish and *bakh* means garden in Persian.

The Nagorno-Karabakh conflict began in 1988 and intensified after Armenia and Azerbaijan attained independence in 1991. By the time a ceasefire took effect in 1994, separatists, with Armenian support, controlled Nagorno-Karabakh. Today, while there exist many questions about Nagorno-Karabakh and its political status, the beauty and cultural richness of its remote mountain landscape are undeniable.

Travel Warning

The 1994 ceasefire continues to hold, although fighting persists along the line of contact separating the opposing forces, as well as the Azerbaijan–Armenia international border. The final position of Nagorno-Karabakh remains the subject of international mediation by the Organization for Security and Cooperation in Europe (OSCE) Minsk Group, which works to help the two countries settle the conflict peacefully. Without successful mediation efforts, renewed tensions threaten to reignite a military conflict between Armenia and Azerbaijan and destabilize the South Caucasus region once again.

The UK, US and Australian governments all advise against travel to Nagorno-Karabakh. Due to serious safety concerns in the region, Lonely Planet cannot recommend travelling to Nagorno-Karabakh at this time. If you are determined to travel to the area, be aware that by entering the entity without express permission from Baku, you will be breaking Azerbaijani law so will be banned from later visiting Azerbaijan and could possibly be subject to prosecution. Also be sure to check your own government's advice before setting off and keep an eye on local news before and during your visit.

Nagorno-Karabakh

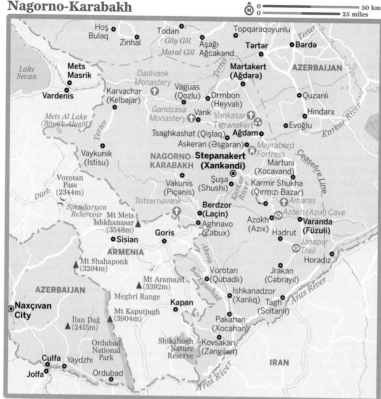

Lake Sevan

Mets Al Lake (Böyük Alagöl)

Nagorno-Karabakh Today

According to nearly all international protocols, the territory of Nagorno-Karabakh (Artsakh) is still legally part of Azerbaijan. It is not officially recognised as a sovereign state and we do not regard it as such. It is an independent state only according to the Nagorno-Karabakh Declaration of Independence and can only be visited from Armenia. Nagorno-Karabakh's biggest single problem is the lack of recognition as an independent state even by its sponsor Armenia.

Together the Karabakhi diaspora abroad and Armenia proper provide the vast majority of investment in Karabakh. The local economy is otherwise lacklustre and most people outside the few urban centres are farmers. While outside investment has brought new life to Karabakh, especially in Stepanakert, the region still faces high levels of unemployment and poverty, while occupied, depopulated former ghost cities like Ağdam remain in eerie ruins. The government believes increasing the population will stimulate development and pays large cash handouts to newlyweds and newborns.

Azerbaijan has never accepted Nagorno Karabakh's independence, let alone the loss of considerable other areas of territory lost during the war (Kelbajar, Lachin, Gubadli, Jebrail plus parts of Fuzuli and Ağdam provinces). The ceasefire line is heavily militarised and by no means completely at peace. Baku's implicit threat to reclaim these territories, if necessary by force, remains a global concern, not just because of the potential for massive human casualties but also for its potential to disrupt Caucasian oil and gas supplies.

History

In this region, names and history are as contested as the land itself. Azerbaijanis claim 'Qarabaq' as their cultural heartland, and point to the role of Şuşa (Shushi) in the growth of their literature and language. In Azerbaijani accounts, the Christian inhabitants of Karabakh are descendants of the Christian nation of Albania (unrelated to the present-day state of Albania). Caucasian Albania lost independence after the Arab invasion in the 7th century, and most Albanians converted to Islam, while the remnants of the Albanian Church were usurped by the Armenian Church.

During the Middle Ages the region was under the control of Persia, with local rule in the hands of five Armenian princes known as Meliks. The Karabakh Khanate, with Panahabad (Shushi) as its capital, passed into Russian hands in 1805. During the 19th century many native Muslims left for Iran while Armenians from the Persian and Ottoman Empires emigrated to Karabakh with Russian encouragement.

Stalin, always keen on divide and rule policies, separated Karabakh from Armenia in the 1920s and made it an autonomous region within Azerbaijan. The natural growth of the Azerbaijani population outpaced growth of the Armenian one and Azerbaijani settlers were moved to Armenian villages. By the 1980s the territory's population was down to about 75% Armenian.

Demands to join Armenia Soviet Socialist Republic (SSR) grew in 1987–88, until the local assembly voted for independence from Azerbaijan SSR in December 1989, and hostilities commenced. From 1990 to 1994 the area was racked by war, which, in its first stage, pitted the Karabakhi against Azerbaijani and Soviet forces. After the fall of the USSR, the war escalated into a heavily armed clash between Armenian troops and *fedayeen* (irregular soldier) commandos on one side and the Azerbaijani army assisted by Turkish officers on the other. A ceasefire was declared in May 1994 and the line of control has remained unchanged since then. The war cost around 30,000 lives. It also resulted in a mass emigration of Azerbaijanis: figures for those who fled Nagorno-Karabakh and surrounding war-affected areas of Azerbaijan range between 500,000 and 750,000, in addition to 150,000 other Azerbaijani refugees from Armenia.

Over the past decade, artillery shelling and minor altercations between Azerbaijani and Armenian troops have caused hundreds of deaths. In April 2016 the two sides clashed again, resulting in the most intense fighting since 1994. After four days of hostilities, the two sides announced that they had agreed on a ceasefire. In October 2017 the presidents of Armenia and Azerbaijan met in Geneva, beginning a series of talks on a possible settlement of the conflict in Nagorno-Karabakh.

Bako Sahakyan, Nagorno-Karabakh's president since 2007, was re-elected in 2012. In a constitutional referendum held in 2017, citizens of the Nagorno-Karabakh Republic voted in favor of transforming the breakaway state into a presidential system. On 19 July 2017 the National Assembly voted to elect the president until the next general election, held in 2020. The incumbent, Sahakyan, was re-elected to a third term. If it was not for the amendment to the constitution, Sahakyan would have had to step down in 2017 after serving two consecutive five-year terms.

ℹ️ Survival Guide

DANGERS & ANNOYANCES

Unexploded ordnance (UXO) does occasionally injure people and livestock and it is unwise to venture into open pastureland anywhere near the front line. Warning signs are prominently displayed in areas close to the main roads. Regarding personal safety, crimes against visitors are almost unheard of. Do be aware that due to its unrecognized status, there is no diplomatic representation in Nagorno-Karabakh; you will need to return to Armenia to seek consular services.

VISAS

To enter the Nagorno-Karabakh Republic, foreign travellers should hold a valid international passport or an equivalent document and a Nagorno-Karabakh Republic (NKR) entry visa, with a payment of the corresponding state fee.

NKR entry visas are granted to foreign travellers at the Embassy of the Nagorno-Karabakh Republic in Armenia. Entry visas can also be issued at the Consular Service Department of the NKR **Ministry of Foreign Affairs** (☑ 95 07 68, 94 14 18; www.nkr.am/en/; 28 Azatamartikneri Poghota; ⊙ 9am-1pm & 2-6pm Mon-Fri, noon-3pm Sat) in Stepanakert. All foreigners need to buy a visa on arrival. You simply need to fill out a single-page form that includes the towns you're heading to in Karabakh. A 21-day visa is issued on the spot for AMD3000. Multiple-entry visas valid for up to 90 days are also available. The entire process is fairly quick and easy, and English is spoken.

Note that you will not be permitted to enter Azerbaijan if you have a Nagorno-Karabakh visa in your passport, so if you plan to visit Azerbaijan, request that the visa be left outside the passport: this is quite normal, but also illegal and if applying for an Azerbaijani visa you will be asked to sign a declaration that you have never visited Nagorno-Karabakh. While no checks on your papers are likely to be made while travelling in Nagorno-Karabakh, the visa will be checked on departure at one of the two exit checkpoints to Armenia, so it's essential to have your paperwork in order.

Understand Georgia, Armenia & Azerbaijan

History

The Caucasian mountainous isthmus between the Black and Caspian Seas stands at the frontiers of Europe and Asia and of Islam and Christendom. An eternal crossroads of cultures and empires, the region's history is a fascinatingly complicated jigsaw of kingdoms and khanates, republics and principalities, emirates and satrapies, that have blossomed and wilted over the centuries. Beneath any facade of independence, such entities were often pawns in the grand imperial games of Romans, Persians, Byzantines, Arabs, Ottomans, Russians and others.

Early Empires

Top History Reads

....

The Caucasus
(Thomas de Waal)
....

The Ghost of Freedom
(Charles King)
....

Black Dog of Fate
(Peter Balakian)
....

The Oil and the Glory
(Steve LeVine)

The 1.8-million-year-old early human remains found in 2005 at Dmanisi, 80km southwest of Tbilisi, are among the oldest ever discovered outside Africa. Archaeologists have also found 8000-year-old evidence of viniculture in Georgia, apparently corroborating what Georgians have claimed all along – that they made the world's first wine.

Greeks, Persians and Romans brought the classical pagan faiths and philosophies to the South Caucasus in the 1000 years before Christianity took hold, helping to create rich local cultures. The Greeks established colonies in Colchis (western Georgia) perhaps as early as the 8th century BC. The Armenians trace their origins back to the Urartu kingdom of about 1000 to 600 BC centred on Lake Van in eastern Turkey. They were incorporated successively into the Persian Achaemenian Empire, the Greek Macedonian Empire and the Middle Eastern Seleucid Empire. After the Romans defeated the Seleucids, Tigranes the Great (r 95–55 BC) built an Armenian empire stretching from the Caspian Sea to the Mediterranean. But Rome moved into Armenia and Georgia after Tigranes unwisely allied against it with Mithridates of Pontus (in northern Turkey). Armenia ended up as a buffer between the Romans and the Persians, who fought long wars for control of the region.

First Christian Kingdoms

Christian apostles were already visiting the South Caucasus in the decades after the death of Jesus. In 301 Armenia's King Trdat III was converted to Christianity and Armenia became the first nation officially to

TIMELINE	1st Century BC	AD 301	642–661
	Tigranes the Great builds an Armenian empire stretching from the southwest corner of the Caspian Sea to the eastern shores of the Mediterranean, with its capital at Tigranakert.	Armenia becomes the first state officially to embrace Christianity, after King Trdat III's conversion. The eastern Georgian kingdom of Kartli (Iveria) follows suit in 327.	Muslim Arabs take over the South Caucasus, reaching Azerbaijan in 642, setting up an emirate in Tbilisi in 654 and gaining control of Armenia in 661.

embrace the religion. The eastern Georgian kingdom of Kartli (Iveria), and the state of Albania in what's now Azerbaijan (no relation to Balkan Albania), followed suit within the next 30 years or so.

As the Christian Byzantine Empire expanded eastward from Constantinople, western Armenia and western Georgia fell under its sway, while their eastern areas came under Persian control.

Islam & Asian Conquerors

After the death of the Prophet Mohammed in 632, Arabs carried Islam well beyond the Arabian peninsula, taking over the South Caucasus by 661. In the 9th century the Arabs recognised a local prince of the Bagratid family, Ashot I, as king of Armenia. By the 11th century, another Bagratid branch controlled most of Georgia.

Nomadic Turkic herders arriving from Central Asia from about the 9th century were probably the ancestors of modern Azerbaijanis. Another group of Turks from Central Asia, the Seljuks, brought death, plunder and destruction to the Caucasus region in the 11th and 12th centuries, but Georgian king Davit Aghmashenebeli (David the Builder; 1089–1125) managed to drive the Seljuks out of Georgia, initiating its medieval golden age. David's great-granddaughter, Queen Tamar (1184–1213), controlled territory from western Azerbaijan to eastern Turkey, including many Armenian-populated regions.

The whole region was floored by the next great wave from the east, the Mongols, who invaded in the 1230s. They were followed in the late 14th century by another ruthless Asian conqueror, Timur (Tamerlane). Shirvan, a long-lasting Muslim principality in what is today Azerbaijan, managed to retain some autonomy for several centuries under rulers known as 'Shirvanshahs' prospering from trade on a Caucasian branch of the pan-Asian Silk Route. In 1501 Shirvan was conquered by fellow Azerbaijanis, the Safavid dynasty of what's now northern Iran, who converted much of the Persian Empire from Sunni to Shia Islam.

Meanwhile to the west, the Ottoman Turks had taken Constantinople and swept away the Byzantine Empire in 1453. In 1514–16 the Ottomans took over nearly all of Armenia, keeping most of it for nearly 400 years. In Persia, the Safavids collapsed in 1722 to be replaced by Nader Shah, a ruthless, stunningly successful but short-lived conqueror. After his assassination in 1747, a relative power vacuum allowed the flourishing of Bagratid kingdoms in eastern Georgia, and of a patchwork of autonomous Muslim khanates in Azerbaijan.

A Hero of Our Time (1840), Mikhail Lermontov's masterpiece about a bored, cynical Russian officer in the Caucasus, was the first – and shortest – Great Russian Novel. An entirely different fictional experience, *The Girl King* (2011) is Meg Clothier's hard-to-put-down imagining of the great medieval Georgian Queen Tamar's life.

Russia Arrives & Stays

In the 1720s Peter the Great's expanding Russia grabbed much of the Caspian coast and bombarded Baku in 1723, but they swiftly retired as the Persians returned with a vengeance under Nader Shah. It wasn't

11th–13th centuries	13th & 14th centuries	16th century	1783
Georgia enjoys a golden age under rulers like Davit Aghmashenebeli (David the Builder; 1089–1125) and Tamar (1184–1213).	The South Caucasus is devastated by the Mongol invasion in the 1230s, the Black Death (1340s) and the ruthless Central Asian conqueror Timur (Tamerlane) in the late 14th century.	The Constantinople-based Ottoman Turks take over nearly all of Armenia; the Azerbaijani/Persian Safavids take control of Azerbaijan and the khanate of Yerevan; Georgia is divided between the Ottomans and Safavids.	The Treaty of Georgievsk sees east Georgian King Erekle II accept Russian control in exchange for protection from Muslim foes. Russia goes on to take over the whole South Caucasus in the 19th century.

until the 1790s that the Russians returned in force. Over the next two decades, the Georgian princedoms and many of the northern Azerbaijani khanates (including Yerevan, Karabakh and Naxçivan) were annexed by Russia one after the next. After the failure of several counter-offensives, Persia essentially accepted the status quo in 1828.

As part of a pacification process in its newly acquired Caucasian territories, Russia encouraged the influx of Christian settlers. Some were Russian nonconformists. Some came from parts of Germany that had been ravaged by the Napoleonic wars. But very many were Armenians from the Persian and Ottoman Empires who felt they would be safer under a Christian ruler. Nonetheless, a good half of historic Armenia and perhaps 2.5 million Armenians remained in the Ottoman Empire after the 1870s. Unrest among them led to massacres of Armenians in the 1890s, and in 1915 the Young Turk government in İstanbul ordered the dispossession and deportation of virtually all Armenians within the Ottoman Empire. Deportation meant walking into the Syrian deserts. In all, 1.5 million are thought to have been killed or to have died in the desert.

The Russian Revolutions of 1917 and the immensely complex endgame of WWI resulted in the South Caucasus briefly declaring itself an independent federation in 1918. National and religious differences saw this quickly split into three separate nations: Georgia, Armenia and Azerbaijan. Once Lenin had consolidated power in Moscow, however, the Red Army marched south to reclaim the Caucasus in 1920–21. In 1922 Georgia, Armenia and Azerbaijan were thrown together in the Transcaucasian Soviet Federated Socialist Republic, one of the founding republics of the Soviet Union. This in turn was split into separate Georgian, Armenian and Azerbaijani Soviet Republics in 1936.

The later Soviet period, after Stalin's death in 1953, was relatively calm, despite worsening corruption. But the wider Soviet economy stagnated, and Mikhail Gorbachev's efforts to deal with this through *glasnost* (openness) and *perestroika* (restructuring) unlocked nationalist tensions that would tear both the Caucasus region and the whole Soviet Union apart.

Independence

The three Caucasian countries regained independence in 1991, not through long-term planning but due to the USSR's implosion. By some theories, the terrible conflicts of that era were deliberately sewn as the Soviet Union's last desperate divide and rule tactic that went horribly wrong.

In Georgia, 19 hunger strikers died as Soviet troops broke up a protest in Tbilisi in 1989. This galvanised a push for independence, but celebrations were short-lived as civil war saw Abkhazia and South Ossetia break away with Russian assistance. Arguably things were even worse for

Post-Soviet Wars & Politics
....
Black Garden: Armenia and Azerbaijan through Peace and War (Thomas de Waal)
....
Azerbaijan Diary (Thomas Goltz)
....
Georgia Diary (Thomas Goltz)
....
The Guns of August 2008 (Svante E Cornell and S Frederick Starr)

1915	1918–21	1930s	1989–94
The Young Turk government in İstanbul orders the dispossession and deportation of the Ottoman Empire's Armenian population. About 1.5 million Armenians are killed or die in the Syrian desert by 1922.	Following the Russian Revolution, Georgia, Armenia and Azerbaijan exist briefly as independent nations, before being taken by the Red Army and incorporated into the new USSR in 1922.	Anti-nationalist repression, led by Georgian Bolsheviks Stalin, Beria and Ordzhonikidze, and the Great Terror see hundreds of thousands of people from the region executed or imprisoned.	Tit-for-tat killings lead to growing tensions between Armenians and Azerbaijanis and eventually to the Karabakh War. Fighting is focused on Azerbaijan's Armenian-majority region of Nagorno-Karabakh and surrounds.

A TANGLED WEB

Just how interwoven are the stories of the South Caucasus' different peoples is well illustrated by the life of the famed 18th-century poet and Armenian cultural hero Sayat Nova. Though Armenian, Sayat Nova was part of the court of the Georgian king Erekle II in Tbilisi. Exiled for his forbidden love of the king's daughter, Sayat Nova lived as a wandering troubadour and as a monk in Armenian monasteries. He wrote over 200 songs, some of them still sung today, in Armenian, Georgian, Persian and, most of all, in Azerbaijani, which was spoken by Armenia's large Muslim population of the day and was also a lingua franca (common language) for much of the South Caucasus. Sayat Nova died helping defend Tbilisi from the Persians in 1795 and his tomb stands outside the city's Armenian Cathedral of St George. His life is the subject of one of the great Soviet-era films, *The Colour of Pomegranates*, directed by another Tbilisi-born Armenian, Sergei Paradjanov.

Armenia and Azerbaijan where former neighbours were turned against each other, both communities suffering massacres, possibly initiated by agents provocateurs. An intense spiral of violence led to de facto ethnic cleansing as Armenians fled from Azerbaijan and vice versa.

A major bone of contention was (and remains) the autonomous region of Nagorno-Karabakh, officially part of Azerbaijan but, by the 1980s, having a majority Armenian population. The region's appeal for unification with Armenia was anathema to Baku and by 1990 Armenian and Azerbaijani militias were battling it out in an undeclared war. Several years of vicious fighting finally ground to a halt with a 1994 ceasefire that left Armenian and Karabakhi forces in control of Nagorno-Karabakh and also other large areas of Azerbaijan including the now-deserted city of Ağdam and the Lachin corridor (the land between Karabakh and Armenia).

The wars of the early 1990s cost around 40,000 lives and displaced over a million people, most of whom were never able to return as the various conflicts became 'frozen'.

The 21st Century

All the region's economies nosedived in the 1990s, but took an upturn in the 2000s. In Georgia, President Eduard Shevardnadze, formerly Gorbachev's Soviet foreign minister, managed to stabilise the political situation but did not quell crime or corruption. He was booted out in the peaceful Rose Revolution of 2003 led by the modernising, pro-Western Mikheil Saakashvili. The new broom effectively eradicated crime and corruption, liberalised the economy and attracted a good deal of foreign investment, which helped to modernise Georgia's infrastructure. But Saakashvili's attempt in 2008 to regain control of Russian-backed South Ossetia by military force ended disastrously in

1991	1991–93	1990s	1994
Georgia, Armenia and Azerbaijan all declare independence from the USSR, which formally dissolves itself in December. The region is already wracked by interethnic unrest.	Interethnic conflict in Georgian regions South Ossetia (1991–92) and Abkhazia (1992–93) leaves both regions de facto independent. Abkhazia ethnically cleanses its ethnic-Georgian population (about 230,000 people).	Economic collapse throughout the region due to internal wars, refugee problems, corruption, infrastructure collapse and the end of Soviet state support for industry and agriculture.	A cease-fire freezes the Karabakh War that has killed some 30,000 people. Nagorno-Karabakh becomes de facto independent but unrecognised, with many surrounding areas of Azerbaijan still under Armenian occupation.

a brief, humiliating Russian invasion of Georgia. Following this 'Five Days War', Russia went on to tighten its grip over South Ossetia and Georgia's other breakaway region, Abkhazia. Saakashvili's star waned further as his style of government became increasingly autocratic and intolerant of opposition, with Georgians especially angered by the draconian justice system where acquittals were virtually nonexistent. The Saakashvili era came to an end with the victory of the rival Georgian Dream coalition in the elections of 2012 and 2013.

In Azerbaijan, ex-communist boss Heydar Əliyev had returned to power in 1993. He helped stabilise and ultimately freeze the conflict with Armenia, and negotiated a highly lucrative deal with Western oil companies over Azerbaijan's Caspian Sea oil reserves. The oil deal sowed the seeds of an economic boom over which his son İlham Əliyev has presided following a seamless transition of power upon his father's death in 2003. Massive investment in new infrastructure was pushed through, and until 2015 Azerbaijan enjoyed a steady rise in living standards albeit guided by a regime that tolerated little opposition or dissent.

In retaliation for the Karabakh War, Azerbaijan and its ally Turkey closed their borders with Armenia, leaving Armenia economically isolated and dependent on investment and military support from Russia. Relations with Turkey were also bedevilled by a long-standing dispute over whether the Medz Yeghern (mass deaths of Armenians at Turkish hands; 1915–22) should be labelled genocide. In 2009 the two countries attempted to normalise relations, with their foreign ministers signing protocols to establish diplomatic ties and open their mutual border. But the deal was rejected by nationalists on both sides and has never been ratified by their parliaments. In 2013, under Russian pressure, Armenia decided against signing a potentially lucrative EU association agreement and instead joined the Russian-dominated Eurasian Economic Union. In summer 2015 huge 'Electric Yerevan' street protests erupted. Though triggered by a planned hike in utility prices, they reflected general anger about economic stagnation and corruption. Fed up, many Armenians have chosen emigration as the way out: the population has dropped by around 20% since 1990.

2003	2008	2016	2018
Georgia's peaceful Rose Revolution brings in a pro-Western, anti-Russian, modernising government led by Mikheil Saakashvili to replace the regime of former Soviet boss Eduard Shevardnadze.	Russia inflicts a humiliating defeat on Georgia in a brief war over South Ossetia, then recognises South Ossetian and Abkhazian independence and starts military build-ups in both territories.	Baku shows the world its charms by hosting the first-ever Formula 1 Grand Prix in the Caucasus on a circuit around the city streets.	Anti-corruption street protests lead to Armenia's Velvet Revolution ejecting Serzh Sargsyan from power after a decade as president.

People of Georgia, Armenia & Azerbaijan

The Caucasus region is home to so many peoples and languages that the Arabs called it the 'Mountain of Languages'. Kept alive by rugged terrain that divides every valley from its neighbours, over 40 mutually incomprehensible tongues are spoken between the Black and Caspian Seas. Each defines a people. The southern side of the Caucasus is home to at least 16 languages. Some number only a few thousand speakers, isolated in remote mountain valleys.

Religious Revival

For seven decades until 1991, the South Caucasus was part of an officially atheist state, the USSR. But underlying religious sentiments never died and were a major part of the national independence movements in the late Soviet years. Today Christianity in Georgia and Armenia, and Islam in Azerbaijan, are ubiquitous; very few people call themselves atheists, and religious authorities are now strong, socially conservative forces. Churches and mosques, many of them newly built or recently renovated, are busy with worshippers; monasteries and convents have been repopulated by monks and nuns. Old traditions of tying bits of cloth to wishing trees, visiting shrines and graves, and spending lavishly on funerals, remain common everywhere.

The Armenian Apostolic Church was the first legal Christian church in the world, dating back to AD 301. The Georgian Orthodox Church was the second, dating from the 320s. While the Georgian church is part of the Eastern Orthodox tradition, like the Greek and Russian Orthodox churches, the Armenian church belongs to the separate Oriental Orthodox branch of Christianity, along with the Coptic Egyptian and Ethiopian churches. The Armenians diverged from Eastern Orthodoxy back in AD 451, when they disagreed with the authorities in Constantinople over the nature of Jesus Christ: the Armenian church sees Christ's divine and human natures combined in one body (monophysite), while the Eastern Orthodox churches see each nature as separate.

Azerbaijan is the only Turkic country where a major part of the population follows Shia Islam. The country proudly proclaims its religious tolerance with minimal signs of fundamentalism and a strong relationship with Israel. Women are not obliged to cover their hair and relatively few do. Although Islamic chic is a growing trend among some younger women, those who you might see in full hijab are likely to be tourists from the Arab Gulf States, not locals. Restaurants stay open during the fasting month of Ramazan, though a few stop serving alcohol during that period.

Kurban Said's 1937 novel *Ali and Nino* is a turbulent love story between an Azerbaijani Muslim and a Georgian Christian. Set in WWI, the book gives many richly textured insights into lives lived a century ago on the Europe–Asia divide. Don't be put off by the syrupy 2016 film version.

Strained Relations

Georgians, Armenians and Azerbaijanis form more than 90% of the South Caucasus' nearly 17 million people. Differentiated by religion, language, alphabets, geography and more, these three peoples have nevertheless lived interwoven existences for centuries, which makes it all the more sad that the region today is riven by intractable ethnic and territorial quarrels.

Until the 1990s, communities of (Muslim) Azerbaijanis and (Christian) Armenians had coexisted for centuries across much of what are now Armenia and Azerbaijan, under Persian, Turkish or Russian rulers. Before WWI Muslims outnumbered Armenians in what is now Armenia's capital, Yerevan – and Armenians outnumbered Georgians in the Georgian capital, Tbilisi.

Today Armenians and Azerbaijanis are deeply divided over the Karabakh issue; Armenians and Georgians harbour a mutual distrust; while Georgians and Azerbaijanis rub along OK, without having too much to do with each other.

Origins

After centuries of emigration, many more Armenians (possibly 10 million) live outside Armenia than in it. Diaspora Armenians include Cher, Andre Agassi, the members of System of a Down, Charles Aznavour, William Saroyan, Herbert von Karajan, Kim Kardashian and US billionaire Kirk Kerkorian (a big benefactor of Armenia).

The Armenians are an ancient people who trace their origins back to the Urartu kingdom of about 1000 to 600 BC, centred on Lake Van in eastern Turkey. Historic Armenia was a much larger area than today's Armenia, encompassing sizeable expanses of what are now eastern Turkey and northwest Iran.

Georgians' origins are shrouded in the mists of distant antiquity, and they still identify strongly with their local regions (Samegrelo, Adjara, Svaneti, Kakheti and so on), but they are united by shared, or similar, languages, and a shared culture and history going back at least 1500 years.

Azerbaijanis are a Turkic people whose animal-herding ancestors probably arrived on the southwestern shores of the Caspian Sea from Central Asia from about the 9th century AD. In the Great Caucasus mountain areas live several minority nationalities including the Lezgi, Avar and, most curiously, the Udi people linked linguistically to the Caucasian Albanians who predated Turkic Azerbaijanis in the region.

Common Traditions

Despite ethnic differences, the ways of life around the region share much in common. The three large capital cities, home to a quarter of the total population, are large, cosmopolitan places (above all, oil-boom Baku) with layers of 21st-century Western lifestyle over much older traditional ways filtered through seven decades of attempted Soviet regimentation.

With their pubs, clubs and contemporary fashions, city dwellers might appear to live like Londoners or Parisians, but deeply ingrained social traditions keep the paternalistic family, and extended-family loyalties, supreme. Even in Georgia, the most socially liberal of the three countries, women are generally considered to be failures, or weird, if they are not married by the age of 26, and the concept of unmarried couples living together is unheard of.

Most city dwellers still have roots in the countryside, where life remains slow-paced and very conservative. Family homesteads often house three or more generations. Wives are expected to have food ready whenever their husband appears, and in Azerbaijan women wouldn't think to set foot in the teahouses that are the traditional hubs of male social life. Wedding and funeral customs, and rituals held 40 days after death, are similar throughout the region.

Equally strong are traditions of hospitality and toasting (wine and brandy are produced in all three countries). Throughout the region it is both a custom and a pleasure to welcome guests with food and drink. People everywhere enjoy meeting, helping and hosting foreigners: as a visitor you will see the locals' warmest side, which will undoubtedly provide some of the best memories of your trip.

Landscape

The South Caucasus is a landscape- and nature-lover's delight. Verdant and lightly populated, about a quarter of the region is still classed as natural habitat offering remarkable scenic variety. The foremost feature is the Greater Caucasus mountain range. Longer and higher than the Alps, it strides from the Black Sea to the Caspian in a spectacular sequence of snow-capped peaks, rocky crags, deep green valleys and rushing rivers. And there's plenty more highland drama in the Lesser Caucasus, further south.

The Lie of the Land

Great Caucasus

The Great Caucasus divides Russia from Georgia and Azerbaijan. Some contend that it also separates Europe from Asia, although the nations on its south flank would dispute that. Several of its peaks reach above 5000m, and in all its 700km length, the Caucasus is crossed by only three motorable roads. Its rugged topography, with valleys connected only by high, often snowbound passes, has yielded fascinating ethnic diversity. Yet feet and hooves can travel where wheels cannot: mountain peoples on both flanks of the Caucasus share cultural traits, and historically have always had contact with each other.

The Plains

The Great Caucasus' fertile lower slopes give way to broad plains running west–east along central Georgia and Azerbaijan, and it's these lower areas (along with Armenia's valleys) that are home to most of the region's all-important agriculture. Much of central Azerbaijan is monotonous steppe, semidesert and salt marsh, intensively irrigated for cultivating cotton and grain.

The Rioni River drains the western Georgian plains into the Black Sea. The Mtkvari flows eastward through Tbilisi and on into Azerbaijan where it becomes the Kür (Kura) and enters the Caspian Sea. The Araz (Araks, Araxes) River forms the western and southern borders of Armenia and Azerbaijan along much of its course from eastern Turkey, before joining the Kür in Azerbaijan.

Lesser Caucasus

South of the plains rises the Lesser Caucasus, stretching from southwest Georgia across Armenia to Karabakh. Less lofty than the main Caucasus range, the Lesser Caucasus still packs in some spectacular mountain, gorge and forest scenery, and has plenty of peaks above 3000m. Western Armenia and the Azerbaijani enclave of Naxçivan sit on the edge of the Anatolian Plateau, with the magnificent snow-topped volcanic cone of Mt Ararat (Ağrı Dağ; 5165m) sometimes visible across the border in Turkey.

Beasts of the Hills & Forests

With habitats embracing deserts and glaciers, alpine and semitropical forests, steppe and wetlands, the South Caucasus is a biodiversity hotspot. Mountain areas are home to brown bears (under 3000 in the

Semi-nomadic shepherds still move their flocks seasonally between the lowlands and mountains, but some traditional routes have been blocked, notably in Karabakh where upper and lower pastures are now on opposite sides of the ceasefire line.

GETTING OUT INTO NATURE

Hiking

For the most scenic hiking in the Great Caucasus, home in on Georgia's Svaneti, Tusheti, Khevsureti and Kazbegi areas, and the Quba and Zaqatala hinterlands in Azerbaijan. Georgia's Borjomi-Kharagauli National Park and Armenia's Mt Aragats and Dilijan, Ijevan and Tatev areas and Yeghegis Valley offer further excellent walking. Trail marking is most advanced in Borjomi-Kharagauli, Svaneti and Tusheti. If you prefer to enjoy scenery from a saddle – or at least have a horse carry your gear while you walk – horses are available in the same Georgian areas, and at places such as Lahıc (Azerbaijan), and Tsaghkadzor and the Yeghegis Valley (Armenia).

Climbing

Mt Kazbek (5047m) on the Georgia–Russia border is the most popular high summit for mountaineers – a serious challenge but technically uncomplicated, and easy enough to organise locally. Mt Chaukhi, east of Stepantsminda, presents some great technical challenges. Twin-peaked Mt Ushba in Svaneti is the most extreme and perilous challenge of all.

Skiing

Skiers have four good, up-to-date resort areas to choose from in Georgia, plus two glitzy options in Azerbaijan – Qəbələ and Shahdag – with a smaller one planned at Ağbulaq in Naxçıvan. Armenia has a minor slope in the resort town of Jermuk and a larger network of runs at Tsaghkadzor.

Other Activities

Rafting is increasingly popular on Georgia's upper Mtkvari River and on the branches of the Aragvi River north of Tbilisi, plus in the Lori region of Armenia. The best season is late April to July on most rivers. There's a specialist kitesurfing centre on a Caspian lagoon near Shuraabad an hour north of Baku. Paragliding is possible near Tbilisi or in the Caucasus around Stepantsminda. Ornithologists can seek out some 380 known bird species.

whole Caucasus region including Russia), wolves, lynx, deer, chamois and more.

Many of the most exciting species are, sadly, endangered. A small number of Persian leopards survive in places like Azerbaijan's Hirkan and Zangezur National Parks and possibly Armenia's Khosrov State Reserve. Until the turn of the 21st century, the elegant goitered gazelle (also called the Persian gazelle or *ceyran*) had its last South Caucasus refuge in Azerbaijan's Şirvan National Park. However, successful conservation has seen numbers rebound with populations reintroduced to southeast Georgia's Vashlovani Protected Areas and Azerbaijan's Ağgöl National Park.

To learn more about the Caucasus region's special species and ecological value, check http://caucasus-naturefund.org.

Parks & Reserves

National parks, nature reserves and other protected areas cover about 8% of the total land area. The degree of genuine protection these areas receive is steadily increasing. Georgia has the most visitor-friendly network, with good infrastructure (including helpful visitors centres) in places like Borjomi-Kharagauli National Park and the Tusheti, Lagodekhi and Vashlovani Protected Areas. In Azerbaijan, some national park tickets must be prepurchased before arrival, which can frustrate visitors. In some higher Caucasus areas of the Shahdag National Park, complex bureaucratic rules mean that it takes at least a couple of weeks to gain the necessary permits for a visit, effectively shutting down Azerbaijan's most popular longer-distance hike (Laza–Xınalıq–Vandəm). However, a 2020 tourism plan hopes to address these frustrations.

Architecture

The charm of the old and the shock of the new – South Caucasus builders have been putting a wow factor into their work since the 4th century AD. And they have a wonderful sense of landscape, creating structures that enhance the already-beautiful scenery they are part of. From the quaint, conical-towered, old churches perched on Georgian and Armenian hilltops to the dazzling 21st-century towers of Baku's bayfront, the region's architecture is a continuous visual feast.

Contemporary Tendencies

Over the past decade or so the skyline of oil-rich Baku has sprouted dozens of concrete, steel and glass towers, some of which are among the world's most stunning contemporary architecture. The three blue-glass Flame Towers (a hotel, offices and apartments) twist their way up to pointed tips 28 or more storeys high, and really do appear to burn at night thanks to a dazzling light show. Many other stylish new skyscrapers line the airport highway, while more earthbound yet even more remarkable is the vast Zaha Hadid–designed Heydar Aliyev Center whose sinuous contours create a form vaguely reminiscent of a gigantic white conch shell. The 21st century is also giving Azerbaijan its most impressive Islamic structure – the İmamzadə complex at Gəncə, the reconstructed ancient mosque at Şamaxı, and a huge new complex nearing completion in Naxçivan.

Much of the architectural energy of post-Soviet Georgia and Armenia has gone into building new churches and restoring old ones. Tbilisi's Tsminda Sameba (2004) and Yerevan's Surp Grigor Lusavorich (2001) are their countries' biggest cathedrals. But Georgia's modernising Saakashvili government also added spectacular new secular architecture, such as the sinuously elegant Bridge of Peace in Tbilisi, the fancifully quirky towers that make Batumi so unique, and the avant-garde Public Service Halls that have sprouted in a dozen towns around the country. The conversion of a Soviet-era publishing house into Georgia's fanciest hotel, Tbilisi's Stamba, is a breathtaking achievement.

Georgia & Armenia

Armenia and Georgia were the world's first two Christian kingdoms, and their unique churches and monasteries, often erected in the most beautiful locations, are a highlight of both countries. Until the last couple of centuries, most other buildings were constructed in perishable materials and so have not survived – the chief exceptions being defensive constructions such as the impressive fortresses at Amberd, Armenia, and Akhaltsikhe, Georgia, plus the very picturesque tower-houses that give such character to Georgia's high Caucasus valleys.

Early Christian Architecture

The earliest churches in the Caucasus were basilicas, rectangular edifices, often divided into three parallel naves based on designs originally devised by the Romans for meeting or reception halls. Basilicas usually

World Heritage Sites in Georgia & Armenia

....

Echmiadzin Cathedral and the ruins of Zvartnots (Armenia)

....

Geghard Monastery (Armenia)

....

Gelati Monastery (Georgia)

....

Haghpat and Sanahin Monasteries (Armenia)

....

Mtskheta (Georgia)

....

Ushguli (Georgia)

had vaulted stone roofs, and domes began to appear above these roofs as early as the 6th century.

Church designs soon began to transmute from the rectangular basilica to symmetrical constructions with a dome above the centre. Such churches could be square, or take the form of an equal-armed cross, or of a four-leafed clover (known as a quatrefoil or tetraconch). Tall, windowed drums supporting the domes let light into the church.

In some churches a quatrefoil inner space is enclosed within a rectangular or square exterior. Such are the very typical and architecturally influential Surp Hripsime church at Vagharshapat, Armenia, and Jvari Church at Mtskheta, Georgia, both completed in the early 7th century. Symmetrical design reached its ultimate form with Armenia's circular Zvartnots Cathedral (641–61), which was as high as it was wide (about 45m).

Almost all the key features of Armenian and Georgian church design were established before the Arab invasion of the 7th century and new churches even today still imitate these original forms.

Later Christian Architecture

Church building revived under the Bagratid dynasties of both Armenia and Georgia from the 9th century onwards. Quite a lot of this new work, especially the Armenian, took place in what's now Turkey – buildings like the Holy Cross Cathedral on Akhtamar Island in Lake Van (on the Hripsime model), and the cathedral of the ruined Armenian capital Ani.

In Georgia the old basilica form was developed into the elongated-cross church, with a drum and pointed dome rising above the crossing. Such are the beautiful tall Alaverdi, Svetitskhoveli (Mtskheta) and Bagrati (Kutaisi) Cathedrals. This was also the major era of monastery construction in Georgia and Armenia.

The Mongol and Timurid invasions brought another hiatus in Christian construction, but it revived again under Persian Safavid rule from the 16th century.

Azerbaijan

Little early architecture survives in Azerbaijan because of earthquakes and invaders like the Mongols and Timur. The few churches remaining from the early Christian Albanian culture, in places like Nic, Oğuz and Kiş, bear a strong resemblance to Georgian and Armenian churches. Outstanding among Azerbaijan's medieval Muslim buildings are some tomb towers, notably the 26m-high Möminə Xatun in Naxçivan, with its turquoise glazing, and some of old Baku's stone buildings, especially the indeterminately ancient Maiden's Tower and the 15th-century Palace of the Shirvanshahs.

The finer buildings from later centuries include Gəncə's twin-minareted Cümə Mosque, credited to Persia's Shah Abbas (17th century), and the beautiful Xan Sarayı (Khan's Palace) and Karavansaray in Şəki (18th century). Baku's first oil boom a century ago spawned numerous fine mansions in eclectic European styles. Many of these have been elegantly restored, while many newer buildings in the city have been adorned with similar mansard roofs and stonework facades, creating a Parisian effect that contrasts with the 'New Dubai' pizzazz of Baku's more cutting-edge constructions.

World Heritage Sites in Azerbaijan

....
Walled Old City (Baku)
....
Petroglyph Reserve (Qobustan)
....
Historic Centre and Xansaray (Şəki)

Survival Guide

Directory A–Z

Accessible Travel

Facilities for travellers with disabilities are limited if slowly improving. Cracked and potholed pavements, cobbles and other impediments are challenges for those with mobility issues or vision impairment. Most hotel lifts aren't planned for wheelchairs, though a few upmarket options are now promoting accessibility.

Public transport can be problematic and even those buses that are wheelchair-enabled are often too crowded for such capabilities to be genuinely useful. On the plus side, the cost of renting a car and a driver-helper isn't extortionate, with Wheels on Wheels (www.facebook.com/wheelsonwheels) in Yerevan specialising in wheelchair-accessible taxis. In August 2019 Batumi opened an adapted beach with floating wheelchairs.

Accommodation

The capital cities tend to have hotel prices that are considerably more expensive than their equivalents elsewhere, but that is counterbalanced by the ever-increasing numbers of competitively priced hostels in the bigger cities. Reservations are rarely required outside July and August.

➡ **Hotels** From budget to high end, hotels can be found in all decent-sized towns in the region.

➡ **Hostels** Now springing up all over the South Caucasus, Western-style hostels offer cheap dorms and private rooms.

➡ **Guesthouses** Often your only option in remote mountain villages.

➡ **Camping** Campsites are rare, but many places allow camping in the garden.

Sleeping Price Ranges

The following prices are for a double room.

$ under US$30

$$ US$30–70

$$$ over US$70

BOOK YOUR STAY ONLINE

For more accommodation reviews by Lonely Planet authors, check out http://lonelyplanet.com/hotels/. You'll find independent reviews, as well as recommendations on the best places to stay. Best of all, you can book online.

Children

Family is important in the South Caucasus, and children are considered treasured gifts from God. Local people love meeting children and are very relaxed with them – it's perfectly normal for strangers to strike up a conversation over kids, and for the most part people will be extremely considerate towards travellers with children.

➡ Children are only likely to enjoy travel in the region if they enjoy the things most travellers do here, such as hiking, horse riding and visiting monuments.

➡ Journeys in sweltering, crowded minivans and buses can be trying, and delays and minor inconveniences can make life difficult travelling on a budget.

➡ Resort areas like Batumi (Georgia) and Qəbələ (Azerbaijan) have some child-friendly attractions.

➡ Most Azerbaijani woodland retreats have toddler play areas.

➡ Lonely Planet's *Travel with Children* is full of practical tips on both planning and travelling with kids.

Practicalities

➡ Disposable nappies are sold in the larger towns, but may be hard to come by elsewhere.

→ Extra beds for children sharing a parents' room are often available at no, or low, cost but don't assume that cots will be an option.

→ High chairs are are available in some better restaurants.

→ Most car-rental firms are small enterprises that are unlikely to have child seats available, though some bigger chains might have them.

→ There is reportedly little stigma in Armenia or Georgia about mothers breastfeeding at train stations or airports when the situation is urgent, but such public breastfeeding is very rarely seen and in reality privacy is widely preferred.

Electricity

**Type C
220V/50Hz**

Climate

Baku

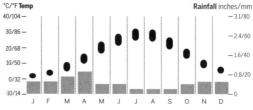

Tbilisi

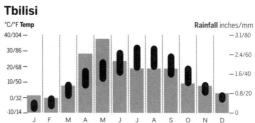

Yerevan

Embassies & Consulates

→ If you are worried that your trip could take you to areas of potential danger, it might prove reassuring to register with your home embassy, though the scope of embassies to help you in an emergency is very limited. For some nationals registration is possible online, eg for US citizens through STEP (www.travel registration.state.gov).

→ In Nagorno-Karabakh, Abkhazia and South Ossetia, you're on your own: assistance from your embassy is not possible as these unrecognised if de facto independent territories are outside the control of their nominal national governments.

→ Some countries have only one embassy in the region, or, like Australia, Canada, Ireland and South Africa, none at all. Consular responsibility might thus be handled from missions as far away as Moscow, Ankara, Sofia (Bulgaria) or Kiev (Ukraine).

Food

For information on food and drink in the South Caucasus, see p34.

Insurance

It is important to be properly insured against theft, loss and medical problems. Health insurance should cover you for emergency air evacuations in addition to visits to private clinics in the capitals. These generally provide the best medical care, but can be expensive. Check that your policy covers any activities you plan, such as horse riding, climbing, skiing and even hiking: some policies stipulate an altitude maximum, which is easy to breach in the Caucasus. Keep the contact details handy as many policies require you to inform the insurer promptly for validation before incurring a major claimable expense like hospitalisation. Worldwide travel insurance is available at www.lonelyplanet.com/travel-insurance. You can buy, extend and claim online anytime – even if you're already on the road.

Internet Access

Virtually all accommodation now provides free wi-fi for guests, as do an ever-increasing proportion of cafes and restaurants. Internet cafes are no longer common and, where they exist, generally specialise in network games for young men. Buying a SIM card for your smartphone allows inexpensive internet access with good 4G connection across much of the region. Service might drop to 3G in country areas, and remote areas have gaps in coverage but generally less so than in, say, the UK.

Legal Matters

You might be questioned by police or soldiers if you visit sensitive areas around military installations, border areas or ceasefire lines. In Azerbaijan sensitivity extends to some government buildings and economically strategic installations such as oilfields.

➡ Visiting Nagorno-Karabakh from Armenia is illegal under Azerbaijan law. Evidence that you have done so, such as a Nagorno-Karabakh visa in your passport, will prevent you from entering Azerbaijan.

➡ Entering Abkhazia or South Ossetia from Russia is illegal under Georgian law, with a maximum penalty of five years' imprisonment. If you have entered Abkhazia from Russia, don't attempt to continue across Abkhazia's southern border into undisputed Georgia.

➡ It's sensible always to carry at least a photocopy of your passport and visa. Carry the real thing, too, if you are going anywhere where you might be questioned.

➡ There is a zero limit on blood alcohol for drivers in all three countries.

➡ Consuming drugs, including cannabis, carries the risk of long prison sentences.

LGBTQ+ Travellers

Homosexuality is legal in all three countries, but social acceptance is minimal: traditional and religious values in these patriarchal societies make the subject pretty much taboo. Homophobia remains quite widespread even in comparatively tolerant Georgia, where a 2013 Tbilisi Pride march was attacked by far-right groups. An attempt to try again in 2019 received threats from Nazis/religious extremists, albeit a little more muted. Nonetheless, Tbilisi's queer progressive club culture, particularly centred on clubs Bassiani and Khidi, is starting to make a difference to young people's attitudes.

The scene in Baku remains almost entirely underground. Citizens were generally bemused more than offended by the colourful international folk who arrived briefly for the 2012 Eurovision Song Contest, but despite the best attempts of Minority Magazine (https://minorityaze.org) and others, Azerbaijan rates as the worst place in Europe to be gay. The press reported anti-LGBTQ+ crackdowns in 2017, and in 2019 a TV presenter went public on social media with a call to kill those of different sexual persuasion.

In Yerevan, there are a handful of LGBTQ+-friendly nightlife venues, and in 2017 Armenia voted to recognise same-sex marriage; however, this applies only for those who wed outside the country. Armenians still don't consider it safe to be open about their orientation on the streets or with conservative family members.

In general, LGBTQ+ travellers should encounter no problems if they are discreet. Two men or women sharing a bed is not automatically construed as having a sexual motive and indeed will often be considered far less scandalous than an unmarried mixed couple doing the same.

Maps

Google Maps and regional sites like gomap.az are great for cities but near useless for rural hamlets. Maps.me is a useful app; you can download the area you need, then use it offline. The ViewRanger app allows you to record and map your hiking exploits.

Money

ATMs, Western Union transfer offices and money-changing facilities are widely available. Credit-card acceptance remains limited outside major cities, so make sure you carry enough cash.

ATMs

The easiest way to carry money is with a Visa or MasterCard debit/credit card for use in local ATMs. These are plentiful in cities and can be found in almost every town, but overseas transaction charges often make them an expensive way to access cash. Check with your card issuer to avoid shocks.

Changing Money

Commission-free money-changing offices are common in towns and cities. For US dollars and euros, rate splits are excellent – often less than 1% except at airports and fancy hotels. Rates for Russian roubles are bearable, but changing other currencies can be more problematic outside the capitals. Where they are accepted at all, British pounds, Australian and Canadian dollars and Swiss francs will score far-poorer rate splits than US dollars, but not necessarily bad enough to warrant the comparatively huge costs you'd incur in converting those currencies to US dollars in your home country.

Before leaving any one of the Caucasian countries, it's usually wiser to change remaining local currency back into US dollars rather than trying to change large quantities of, say, Georgian lari into Armenian dram or Azerbaijani manat into lari. Changing manat into dram or vice-versa isn't possible.

Credit Cards

Credit-card acceptance is relatively low compared to other parts of Europe: you can use them at better hotels, restaurants and in some shops in the capitals, but less frequently elsewhere.

Exchange Rates

See p43 for exchange rates for Georgia, p147 for Armenia and p231 for Azerbaijan. For current exchange rates, see www.xe.com.

Tipping

Restaurants Appreciated but not expected in simpler restaurants; in fancier places 10% is appropriate. The addition of a service charge to a bill doesn't necessarily mean that you have passed on a gratuity.

Taxis For metered taxis, rounding up is polite; consider being generous to drivers using ride-hailing apps whose incomes are often very low.

Weights & Measures Georgia, Armenia and Azerbaijan use the metric system.

Discount Cards An International Student Identity Card (ISIC) card is useful to prove student status and score discounts on entertainment and museums, plus some shops, restaurants and even certain places to stay. See www.isic.org.

Smoking Tobacco smoking is extremely widespread among local men, less common among women. In 2018 legislation came into effect banning indoor smoking in public places in both Georgia and Azerbaijan. This has worked well in hotels and restaurants but less comprehensively in bars and clubs. Armenia has mooted a similar law but as yet hasn't passed it and many places remain smoky.

Opening Hours

Museums 10am–5pm or longer; many close Monday

Offices 9am or 10am–5pm or 6pm Monday to Friday; lunch breaks last an hour or more

Restaurants 8am–9pm in rural locations, 11am–11pm in big cities or even longer

Shops 10am–7pm, often much longer

Theatres Shows often start around 6pm; many close for the season from June to early September

Photography

It's wise to leave your camera in its case pretty much anywhere near a border, ceasefire line or military base. Azerbaijani police and security guards can get suspicious at anyone photographing government buildings or 'unflattering' or 'inappropriate' scenes (factories, transport infrastructure, metro stations etc). When photographing people, extend the usual courtesies – people (especially men) will often happily pose if you ask their permission to snap them, and it's a good way to break the ice. Be sensitive if photographing at religious sites.

Lonely Planet's *Travel Photography* is a comprehensive, jargon-free guide to getting the best shots of your travels.

Post

The mail services are comparatively inexpensive but don't be surprised if your postcard takes up to a month to get home.

Public Holidays

New Year's Day 1 January

Christmas 6 to 7 January (Armenia and Georgia)

Epiphany 19 January (Georgia)

Noruz Bayramı 20 to 26 March (Azerbaijan)

Genocide Memorial Day 31 Mar (Azerbaijan), 24 April (Armenia)

Good Friday/Easter* April or early May (different dates in Armenia and Georgia)

Ramazan Bayram/Eid al-Fitr* May or late April (Azerbaijan)

Gurban Bayramı/Eid al-Adha* July or late June (Azerbaijan)

Mariamoba 28 August (Georgia)

Giorgoba 23 November (Georgia)

The religious holidays marked * have variable dates.

Safe Travel

These countries have generally very low crime rates.

➡ Take normal precautions, especially in crowded or dark, lonely places.

➡ Border areas are sensitive. Especially avoid the Nagorno-Karabakh ceasefire line and Armenia–Azerbaijan frontiers. The borders of Abkhazia and South Ossetia are also tense. Conflicts might flare up at any time around these areas. Keep an ear to the ground.

➡ If climbing or hiking in the mountains, seek local advice and go with company or take a guide, especially in isolated areas. Give sheepdogs a wide berth: they're bred for fending off wolves and can be vicious.

➡ Bears live in upland forests.

Government Travel Advice

Government websites have information on potential danger areas and general safety tips. They sometimes err on the side of excessive caution

Australia (www.smartraveller. gov.au)

Canada (www.voyage.gc.ca)

Germany (www.auswaertiges -amt.de)

Netherlands (www.nederland wereldwijd.nl)

New Zealand (www.safetravel. govt.nz)

UK (www.fco.gov.uk)

USA (https://travel.state.gov)

Telephone

The use of landline phones is relatively limited in much of the region.

Time

All three countries are four hours ahead of Greenwich Mean Time (GMT plus four hours). That means that in winter they are three hours ahead of most of Western Europe, four hours ahead of the UK and nine hours ahead of New York. These gaps narrow by one hour in summer as none of the countries uses daylight saving time.

Toilets

➡ Public toilets are rare and may not have toilet paper, so it's a good idea to carry some.

➡ Except in top-end hotels, it's generally bad form to flush toilet paper into the toilet as drains block easily – use the small bin provided.

➡ Some basic homestays and guesthouses have squat toilets in an outhouse across the yard.

➡ Larger bus and train stations usually have toilets but they're often the squat variety. Although there's typically a small fee to pay to the attendant, that doesn't mean toilets are necessarily well kept.

Tourist Information

Georgia has an excellent network of tourist offices throughout the country, which is a huge asset, especially if you have language issues etc. They're always happy to call people and make arrangements for you. Armenia and Azerbaijan have more limited facilities, but things are improving with new tourist info booths in Yerevan, a new centre in Dilijan, and since 2019 a major push in Azerbaijan to relaunch several local offices with more dynamic, multilingual staff.

Visas

Simple or unnecessary for visitors to Georgia and for many to Armenia. Essential but generally painless for most visiting Azerbaijan; allow at least 24 hours.

Visas for Onward Travel

A fine up-to-date source for latest reports is www.cara vanistan.com.

Central Asia Kyrgyzstan, Kazakhstan and, since 2019, Uzbekistan can all be visited visa-free by citizens of most of the world's wealthier nations. In contrast, getting a Turkmen visa is a frustratingly labyrinthine process that's best organised through a reputable Turkmen tour agency.

Iran Most world nationalities can usually get a visa on arrival if flying into one of the major Iranian airports, though some conditions apply and it's necessary to fill out a preliminary e-visa request through http://e_visa.mfa.ir/ en and print out the application status receipt. Among the 10 nationalities that need to pre-apply for visas, well in advance, are UK, US and Canadian citizens, who may only visit as part of an approved tour. Israelis are not allowed at all. Neither, technically, is anyone who has visited Israel. See https://caravanistan. com/visa/iran.

Turkey Most nationals need to apply online at www.evisa.gov.tr/ en for an e-visa. It's a painlessly simple procedure costing US$20 and is almost instant. You don't need to print a hard copy.

Russia CIS, South African, most South American and a few Asian nationals can visit on a visa waiver, but most other citizens need a visa for which an invitation is required and for which you must usually apply in your home country.

Women Travellers

➡ The capital cities are relatively liberated, but in some provincial areas it's wise to dress modestly, keeping shoulders covered in public places. This is obligatory in mosques and churches, where you'll normally also need to wear a headscarf.

➡ Other than in mosques, covering the hair is a woman's personal choice and an expression of piety (unlike in neighbouring Iran it is certainly not a legal requirement).

➡ Moderate drinking is generally fine in the capitals but unaccompanied women ordering alcohol or smoking publicly can raise eyebrows in more conservative towns, such as Zaqatala or Şǝki.

➡ Sitting alone at cheap, male-dominated restaurants can be uncomfortable and in Azerbaijan a çayxana (teahouse) is usually an all-male preserve too. However, there are plenty of family restaurants and cafes that are female friendly.

➡ Some cheap lodgings aimed at truck drivers are uncomfortably male-dominated.

➡ In the Georgian mountain region of Tusheti, women are not permitted to approach the traditional animist shrines known as khatebi.

Transport

GETTING THERE & AWAY

Three major and several smaller international airports welcome those who fly into the region. Getting here is also possible by road from Iran, Russia and Turkey (but not Turkey–Armenia), by rail (Russia–Azerbaijan and from 2020 Turkey–Georgia–Azerbaijan) and less reliably by ferries across the Black and Caspian Seas.

Travelling to and between the South Caucasus countries is complicated by the fact that both the Armenia–Turkey and Armenia–Azerbaijan borders are completely closed. There are no Armenia–Azerbaijan flights either.

Entering the Region

Arrival procedures at airports are generally straightforward and quick. Some land borders can take an hour or two to cross, especially if you're on a through bus and must wait for fellow passengers.

Air

Airports & Airlines

Tbilisi International Airport (Georgia; www.airport-tbilisi.com) and Baku's Heydar Əliyev International Airport (Azerbaijan; www.airport.az) are busy international hubs. Yerevan's Zvartnots Airport (Armenia; www.zvartnots.aero) has more limited connections.

David the Builder Kutaisi International Airport (www.kutaisi.aero) in Kutaisi, Georgia, is the main hub for budget airlines.

Batumi International Airport (www.batumiairport.com) in Georgia is especially busy with seasonal charters.

Flag carriers are AZAL (Azerbaijan Airlines; www.azal.az) and Georgian Airways (www.georgian-airways.com).

Turkish Airlines (www.turkishairlines.com) often proves good value for quality service including luggage and on-board catering. It flies to five Caucasus airports (Baku, Batumi, Gəncə, Naxçivan and Tbilisi), offers a vast array of connections via İstanbul and good open-jaw ticketing options.

Ultra-budget airline WizzAir (www.wizzair.com) links Kutaisi to many European cities and Baku to Budapest. Wizz prices can be ultra-low but read the small print: even most carry-on baggage costs extra.

Tickets

Booking major carrier tickets to South Caucasus destinations is easy enough. But there are several ticketing alternatives that you might not have thought of.

CLIMATE CHANGE & TRAVEL

Every form of transport that relies on carbon-based fuel generates CO_2, the main cause of human-induced climate change. Modern travel is dependent on aeroplanes, which might use less fuel per kilometre per person than most cars but travel much greater distances. The altitude at which aircraft emit gases (including CO_2) and particles also contributes to their climate change impact. Many websites offer 'carbon calculators' that allow people to estimate the carbon emissions generated by their journey and, for those who wish to do so, to offset the impact of the greenhouse gases emitted with contributions to portfolios of climate-friendly initiatives throughout the world. Lonely Planet offsets the carbon footprint of all staff and author travel.

CENTRAL ASIA

There are useful links on Uzbekistan Airways (www.uzairways.com) to/via Tashkent, and to Kazakhstan with Air Astana (www.airastana.com), SCAT (www.scat.kz) and AZAL (www.azal.az). Lufthansa (www.lufthansa.com) flies Baku–Ashgabat, the only cross-Caspian flight hop to Turkmenistan.

EUROPE

There's a rapidly expanding range of European flights with Georgian Airways from Tbilisi and with budget carrier WizzAir from Kutaisi, Georgia. AZAL has many connections from Baku; Air France (www.airfrance.com) flies to Tbilisi and Yerevan; Lufthansa (www.lufthansa.com) to Baku and Tbilisi; Austrian Airlines (www.austrian.com) and Brussels Airlines (www.brusselsairlines.com) to Yerevan; and there are plenty more options to Poland, Latvia, Ukraine, Belarus and Russia. Connecting via Turkey is often a good option, especially for open-jaw returns.

GULF COUNTRIES & EAST ASIA

Choices include Qatar Airways (www.qatarairways.com), Etihad (www.etihad.com), China Southern (www.flychinasouthern.com; via Urumqi), FlyDubai (www.flydubai.com) and AirArabia (www.airarabia.com). AZAL has a direct Baku–Beijing overnight flight.

IRAN

From Tehran, Iran Air (www.iranair.com) flies to each capital. Mahan Air (www.mahan.aero) and Iran Aseman (www.iaa.ir) both serve Yerevan.

ISRAEL

From Tel Aviv, Arkia (www.arkia.com) flies to Batumi, Tbilisi and Yerevan, El Al (www.elal.com) to Batumi, Georgian Airways to Tbilisi and AZAL to Baku.

NORTH AMERICA

AZAL's Baku–New York service is the only direct transatlantic flight to the Caucasus. Various other airlines connect via European or Gulf State hubs.

RUSSIA

Numerous airlines operate, notably Aeroflot (www.aeroflot.com), S7 Airlines (www.s7.ru), Ural Airlines (www.uraluirlines.com) and UTair (www.utair.ru).

Land

Assuming you have the requisite visas, it is possible to enter the region by land from Iran, Russia or Turkey.

Border Crossings
TO/FROM IRAN
ARMENIA

The only border crossing (open 24 hours) is at Agarak near Jolfa. A single daily Yerevan–Tehran bus comes this way.

AZERBAIJAN

The most convenient 24-hour border crossings are at Astara (for Tehran, Rasht or Ardabil) and near Biləsuvar (for Tabriz). Coming from Naxçivan, use the low-key Culfa–Jolfa border. In Jolfa, shared taxis to Tabriz depart from just south of the pedestrian immigration post, but be careful not to follow the crowds and mistakenly jump into a car to Bileh Savar – most Azerbaijanis crossing the border use this route as a way to reach Baku via Biləsuvar, not to see Iran.

TO/FROM RUSSIA
AZERBAIJAN

As well as the rail crossing, two 24-hour road borders are open to foreigners if they have suitable visas. Samur-SDK is the main crossing used by buses but it can be very slow due to truck queues. Around 4km north of Yalama, Xanoba is a quieter

alternative so crossing is faster but access requires a taxi ride or your own wheels. The Zuxul border crossing is closed to non-locals. Beware, the area of Russia north of these border posts is Dagestan, for which you might need special permits. Some Western governments advise against visits to Dagestan altogether and it is one of the UK Foreign and Commonwealth Office's security 'red zones'.

GEORGIA

The road border at Verkhny Lars/Kazbegi is open 24 hours in summer but from 7am to 7pm only from October to May. It's possible to walk across no man's land but that is a distance of 3km. There's no bus from Stepantsminda (Kazbegi). A taxi from Stepantsminda to Vladikavkaz costs 150 GEL or you could use Tbilisi–Vladikavkaz vehicles including a bus leaving Didube at 5am.

TO/FROM TURKEY
AZERBAIJAN

The only border is at the northwestern nose of Naxçivan. It's open 24 hours if you're driving, but walking across the no-man's-land bridge is not allowed and the frontier posts are far from anywhere so you'd be advised to use Naxçivan–Iğdır buses, which cost only AZN5 anyway. Note: the only way to reach Baku from Naxçivan without leaving Azerbaijan is to fly.

GEORGIA

Three border posts are open. Only Sarpi–Sarp on the Batumi–Hopa road is open 24 hours a day. This is the route taken by Turkey-bound buses from Baku, Tbilisi and Batumi, but it's usually faster to cross in stages taking a Batumi–Sarpi *marshrutka* (public minivan transport), walking across then jumping onto a waiting bus to Hopa, Rize or Trabzon.

The other two border crossings, Türgözü between Vale and Posof, and Aktaş between Kartsakhi and Çıldır, are open 7am to 7pm Georgia time. Other than a thrice-weekly Kars–Akhalstikhe–Tbilisi bus via Posof, there is no public road transport to either crossing. From 2020, however, the Baku–Tbilisi–Kars railway should start operation via Aktaş.

Bus

International buses operate across several borders, but some major routes, notably Batumi–Trabzon and Baku–Ardabil, can prove quicker, cheaper and almost as easy to cross by a sequence of local bus and taxi hops.

ARMENIA–IRAN

Yerevan–Tabriz–Tehran buses (US$53/25,000AMD, 24 hours) depart daily at noon from Kilikya bus station, but book tickets in advance through **Tatev Travel** (☑010-524401; www.tatev.com; 19 Nalbandyan St; ☺9.30am-6pm Mon-Fri, to 3pm Sat). Returning, it departs from Tehran Western bus terminal at 1pm and picks up in Tabriz around 10pm, with tickets sold from agencies on Tabriz' central Imam Khomeini Ave.

AZERBAIJAN–IRAN

Several companies operate Baku–Tehran (AZN40, around 16 hours, 3pm) and Baku–Tabriz (AZN30, around 11 hours, 10pm daily plus 9am Friday) buses. For Tabriz, you could alternatively take a Naxçivan-bound bus (AZN25, 14 hours) at 9am or 9pm but get off in Julfa, Iran, and transfer to a cheap shared taxi.

AZERBAIJAN–RUSSIA

There are buses to a wide variety of destinations in

Russia from Baku's main bus station, and also from Zaqatala, or if you're only heading for Dagestan, you could take a minibus from Xaçmaz to Samur-SDK. Beware that Dagestan is on the 'Do not visit' list of many Western governments.

GEORGIA–RUSSIA

A Tbilisi–Vladikavkaz bus leaves at 5am from the Okriba section of Didube bus station, from where seven-seat minivans also depart (US$30, four hours) when full. A taxi from Stepantsminda to Vladikavkaz costs 150 GEL. Longer-distance buses link Tbilsi to a wide selection of Russian cities.

TURKEY–AZERBAIJAN

➔ İstanbul–Trabzon–Baku buses (US$60 to US$70, 32 to 40 hours) operate at least daily through several companies including Metro (www.metroturizm.com.tr) and Luxistanbul (www.luksistanbul.com), departing from the Eminiyet Otogar off Küçük Langa Caddesi in the Aksaray area of İstanbul. Some drive via Ankara and are thus slower. All go via Georgia.

➔ İstanbul–İğdır–Naxçivan buses (US$35, 30 hours) operate several times daily through İğdırıTurizm (www.igdirliturizm.com.tr). Boarding in İğdır, the short journey to Naxçivan (AZN5) can take several hours due to time-zone changes, border formalities and inter-bus-station transfers. Things are somewhat faster if you use one of the air-conditioned vans that wait outside the bus office on the *meydan* (main square) charging AZN20 per head. Be aware that if continuing from Naxçivan to Baku the only domestic route is by air.

TURKEY–GEORGIA

➔ International buses to/from various Turkish cities use the 24-hour Sarp–Sarpi border, where passengers

are usually required to get off the bus and carry their own bags through customs. At least five İstanbul–Batumi–Tbilisi buses (US$40 to US$50, around 26 hours) run daily.

➔ Trabzon–Batumi buses and minibuses run frequently almost round the clock but most so-called 'Batumi' services actually terminate at the border eastbound, leaving passengers a local bus hop or US$10 taxi ride into town. Crossing this border in hops using local transport is usually painless via Hopa.

➔ **Kars Vipturizm** (☑0474-444 9188; www.facebook.com/KarsVipTurizm; Faikbey Caddesi 72; ☺5am-6pm) has buses from Tbilisi's Ortachala bus station via Posof to Kars on Sundays, Wednesdays and Fridays, returning on Tuesdays, Thursdays and Saturdays at 9am Turkish time (₺100, six hours).

Car & Motorcycle

Drivers bringing vehicles into the region will need the vehicle's registration papers and liability insurance. Each country requires you to buy a local insurance (typically costing around US$25 for a month). You will pay this at the border when entering Georgia and Azerbaijan, with Azerbaijan charging an additional US$20 for road tax. For Armenia pre-purchasing insurance online through https://aswa.am is usually the best option.

Note: vehicles older than 2006 might be refused entry to Azerbaijan, charged an emissions tax and/or limited to a three-day stay.

Train

At the time of research, the İstanbul–Kars–Tbilisi–Baku railway line was finally due to be operating in 2020.

Otherwise, the only international trains to the South Caucasus are weekly services linking Baku to Moscow and Kiev, both taking over

50 hours. Southbound, both of these cross the Russia–Azerbaijan border around midnight. Guards can be very pedantic about changing their date stamps at the exact stroke of midnight, so ensure that your visas have a day's extra leeway.

Sea

Georgia

From Batumi to Sochi, a hydrofoil operated by Express Batumi (one way US$100) leaves Batumi at 11am on Mondays from early June to mid-September only, arriving at Sochi at 4pm. From Sochi, the boat returns on Tuesdays at 11am, arriving in Batumi at 4pm.

If you're happy to spend 50 hours on a Black Sea ferry, UkrFerry (www.ukrferry.com) and less-comfortable NaviBulgar (www.navbul.com) both operate several monthly ferries between Batumi and Chernomorsk (formerly Ilyichevsk, Ukraine) for between US$150 and $250 per person in a two-bed cabin. NaviBulgar also serves Varna in Bulgaria, taking about 2½ days Varna–Batumi, but 4½ days Batumi–Varna. Buy tickets via the websites.

Azerbaijan

Cross-Caspian Sea ships leave the port at Ələt, 75km south of Baku, to Turkmenbashi (Turkmenistan) and Aktau (Kazakhstan) as often as every couple of days, but then maybe not again for a week. The boats are primarily rail-cargo vessels for which passengers and private vehicles are a minor afterthought. So don't expect a comfortable ferry. Strict timetables don't exist: they leave when they have enough freight.

Ticket price theoretically includes a sleeping berth and basic meals, though latecomers might have to sleep in public areas on some ships. Bicycles are accepted for the standard passenger fare, motorbikes cost double and cars are charged per metre's length (ie US$500 to US$800 per standard vehicle). To start the surreal ticket-purchasing process, call **Caspian Shipping** (☎012-4043900, Kazakhstan boat info 055-9999124, Turkmenistan boat info 055-9999061; https://asco.az/en; 🖥), put your name and mobile-phone number on the departure list, then stand by and wait for a call back.

Even once you're aboard, the lack of an available dock at the destination can result in hours (or days) of further delays, so while Baku–Turkmenbashi might be as fast as 12 hours, either route could take 30 to 50 hours. Consider taking extra food and water in case delays mean that the ship's supplies run out. If you don't have a vehicle, consider flying instead.

GETTING AROUND

Air

There are very few domestic or intra-regional flights, and no direct air links between Armenia and Azerbaijan. Flying is useful to connect Baku and Naxçivan without leaving Azerbaijan. Tiny planes to Mestia (Georgia) offer superb mountain views but are often cancelled.

Intra-Regional Flights

Tbilisi and Batumi both have air connections with Baku on AZAL/Buta Airways and with Yerevan on Georgian Airways. Qatar Airways also operates a Tbilisi–Baku leg.

Domestic Flights

Georgia Georgian Airways flies Tbilisi–Batumi. In good weather, Vanilla Sky operates 19-seater turboprops to Mestia from Kutaisi and/or Tbilisi's Natakhtari Airfield, but cancellations are common.

Azerbaijan AZAL flies Baku–Naxçivan and Baku–Gəncə.

Bicycle

Cycling in the South Caucasus is becoming popular as a leg of a cross-Asia trip. Local driving styles are somewhat less predictable than in Western countries, there's lots of hilly terrain and some road surfaces are awful. However, traffic is relatively light away from the few busy highways, scenery is mostly gorgeous and wild camping is practicable in much of the region.

Bus

Almost every town and village has some sort of bus or (more commonly) minibus service, the latter being known widely as a *marshrutka* (plural *marshrutky*). Services can run hourly between larger towns, but rural villages often have just one single minibus that leaves for the regional centre in the morning, then returns from the bazaar after lunch.

Domestic fares average around US$1.50 per hour of travel. Standards can vary considerably. Local vehicles can get loaded up with freight (sacks of potatoes, crates of drinks), as well as people. It's rarely necessary (and often not possible) to book ahead except for a few international services. *Marshrutky* usually have a destination sign inside the windscreen but it will use the local alphabet. To hail a *marshrutka* out on the road, stick out your arm and wave. If you want to get off, say 'stop' in the local language, ie *kangnek* in Armenia, *sakhla* in Azerbaijan or *gaacheret* in Georgia.

Car & Motorcycle

Driving in the capital cities can be very tough due to convoluted one-way systems, rush-hour traffic jams and uncertain parking conditions. Elsewhere parking is usually uncomplicated and traffic is light, though it can prove challenging to adapt to sometimes-anarchic local driving styles.

The capital cities have branches of major international car-rental companies as well as local outfits that are typically far cheaper (from around US$20 per day), but generally, hired cars cannot be taken across borders (except Georgia–Armenia in some cases). Hiring a local driver is worth considering for intercity trips or excursions. A cost-effective way to do this is to find the shared taxi stand for your proposed destination and then offer to pay four times the regular fare plus a little extra for diversions and photo stops. Hostels can also arrange a driver at prices that can prove favourable than finding a taxi on the street.

Less-used mountain roads are often very poorly surfaced and can get blocked or washed away by landslides or flash floods. These need a 4WD, for which car-rental agents usually charge at least US$80 a day. If self-driving in such areas, it's safest to travel in a convoy of at least two vehicles with winches and tow cables for mud patches. You'll often do better finding a local driver with an old Niva or UAZ at the starting village of any off-road adventure; but without speaking local languages (or Russian), organising things can be tough.

➡ Driving is on the right-hand side of the road.

➡ The legal maximum blood-alcohol level for driving in all three countries is zero.

➡ Roundabout priority is typically reversed from European norms (give way to oncoming vehicles).

➡ It is usually acceptable to drive using a driving licence from most Western countries but it is wise to get an International Driving Permit before departure to carry in addition, especially if your license does not have a photo.

➡ Filling stations are fairly common along main roads, but if you are going into remote areas, fill up beforehand.

Hitching

In rural areas with poor public transport, local people sometimes flag down passing vehicles. If you do the same, it's customary to offer a little money (the equivalent of the bus or *marshrutka* fare). Hitching along main roads between cities is less common, though not impossible. Locals may pick you up because they're interested in talk with you.

Hitching is never entirely safe, and we don't recommend it. Travellers who hitch should understand that they are taking a small but potentially serious risk. Refusing rides from drunk drivers is crucial.

Local Transport

All three capitals have cheap, easy-to-use metro systems. Other urban transport comprises a mixture of *marshrutky* and buses. *Marshrutky* will stop to pick up or drop off passengers anywhere along their routes; buses often use fixed stops. Either can get very crowded.

Route boards are often in local script. Taxis are plentiful. Most in Yerevan and some in Baku are metered. For others, agree on the fare before you get in. A ride of 3km or so normally costs around US$3 or less. In the

capitals, the cheapest rides are usually those prebooked by phone or through app-based taxi-hailing services, notably Yandex (taxi.yandex.com; known as Uber in Azerbaijan), Bolt (bolt.eu) and GG (ggtaxi.com).

Train

Trains are slower and much less frequent than road transport. But they're cheap, and on overnight routes sleeper berths are included in the price, making the experience more comfortable than a bus ride.

You need your passport both for buying tickets and for boarding an overnight train whether domestic or international but not for a suburban/local day train (commonly known as an *elektrichka*), nor for other domestic trains in Armenia.

Overnight Trains

Overnight trains have three classes, all of them with sleeping berths:

1st class (*luks* or *SV*) Upholstered berths, two people per compartment; only available on a few trains.

2nd class (*kupe*) – four to a compartment, harder berths with fold-down upper bunks. Good value, rarely over US$10 for a domestic overnight journey.

3rd class (*platskart*) – open bunk accommodation without closable compartment door. Two of the six bunks are placed lengthways in the corridor and aren't ideal for taller individuals.

Once a night train is underway and bedtime approaches, an attendant will dole out sheets for you to make up your own bed. On better trains, a samovar provides boiling water with which to make tea or instant noodles, but bring your own food as there is usually no restaurant carriage.

Health

The South Caucasus is generally a pretty healthy region but, as you would be advised anywhere, minimise the risk of problems by avoiding dodgy food and water, and taking precautions against insect and animal bites.

BEFORE YOU GO

Insurance

EU citizens are entitled to free public medical and some dental care in Georgia, Armenia and Azerbaijan under reciprocal arrangements. However, standards of public healthcare in the region are very patchy and if you want to use far better but expensive Western-standard clinics in the major cities, good insurance coverage is essential. Ideally get a policy that will make payments directly to providers, rather than reimburse you later.

Websites

There is a wealth of travel-health advice online. The following include country-specific information:

UK Travel Health Network (https://travelhealthpro.org.uk)

US Centers for Disease Control and Prevention (wwwnc.cdc.gov/travel)

RECOMMENDED VACCINATIONS

You should be up to date with the vaccinations that you would normally have back home, such as diphtheria, tetanus, measles, mumps, rubella, polio and typhoid. Further vaccines may be advisable for children or the elderly.

Hepatitis A Classed as an intermediate risk in the region: vaccination may be recommended for those who are staying for long periods, particularly in areas with poor sanitation.

Hepatitis B Has high endemicity: vaccination may be recommended for some groups, including people who are likely to have unprotected sex.

Tuberculosis (TB) Vaccination is a good idea for young people who plan to work in high-risk areas such as refugee settlements.

Rabies Exists in all three countries. Consider vaccination if you plan a lot of activities that might bring you into contact with domestic or wild animals, such as cycling, hiking or camping, especially in remote areas where post-bite vaccine may not be available within 24 hours.

IN GEORGIA, ARMENIA & AZERBAIJAN

Availability & Cost of Health Care

The capital cities have some expensive, Western-standard clinics. Public medical care is available in all towns, though clinics and hospitals may be ill supplied, and nursing care limited (families and friends are often expected to provide this). In Georgia some formerly public hospitals have been privatised and will charge fully for treatment, although the cost is still modest by Western standards.

In past years it was typically the custom to give cash tips to nurses or doctors for hospital treatment. This is no longer common and in places where it does still happen, foreigners would usually be forgiven for not knowing about it. If you want to give a cash tip for special attention,

TAP WATER

Tap water is generally safe to drink in most of the region, though in Baku and the lowland areas of Azerbaijan, you're better off with bottled purified water, which is very widely available. If you aren't sure of your tap water's quality, boil tap water for 10 minutes, use water-purification tablets, or use a filter. The South Caucasus is also home to some regionally famous mineral waters of which Georgia's sparkling Borjomi is best known. Keep your empty bottles to refill at springs, which you'll often find beside country roads in upland areas. Most are safe and indeed positively healthy, but check with locals especially if a spring seems little used.

do it discreetly by putting money in an envelope, with a card saying something like 'for coffee and cakes in the office'.

Environmental Hazards

Altitude Sickness

Altitude sickness may develop in anyone who ascends quickly to altitudes above 2500m. It is common at 3500m and likely with rapid ascent to 5000m. The risk increases with faster ascents, higher altitudes and greater exertion. Symptoms may include headaches, nausea, vomiting, dizziness, fatigue, insomnia, undue breathlessness or loss of appetite.

Severe cases may involve fluid in the lungs (the most common cause of death from altitude sickness), or swelling of the brain. Anyone showing signs of altitude sickness should not ascend any higher until symptoms have cleared. If symptoms get worse, descend immediately.

Acclimatisation and slow ascent are essential to reduce the risk of altitude sickness: fit, fast climbers are often the most at risk – less dynamic hikers being more likely to pace themselves on steep ascents. Drink at least

4L of water a day to avoid dehydration: a practical way to monitor hydration is to check that urine is clear and plentiful. Avoid tobacco and alcohol. Some climbers credit mint, ginger and garlic as being helpful, though that is largely apocryphal. Diamox (acetazolamide) reduces the headache pain caused by altitude sickness and helps the body acclimatise to the lack of oxygen. It is normally only available by prescription and it is not usually recommended for preventative use.

Hypothermia

Hypothermia occurs when the body loses heat faster than it can produce it. Even on a hot day in the mountains the weather can change rapidly, so carry waterproof garments, warm layers and a hat, and inform others of your route. Hypothermia starts with shivering, loss of judgement and clumsiness. Unless rewarming occurs, the sufferer deteriorates into apathy, confusion and coma. Prevent further heat loss by seeking shelter, warm dry clothing, hot sweet drinks and shared bodily warmth.

Insect Bites & Stings

Mosquitoes are found in most parts of the Caucasus but while they can be an-

noying, no cases of locally acquired malaria have been reported since 2013. Repellents containing DEET are generally effective and last longer than plant-extract oils, but wash hands carefully after use as DEET can perish rubber and damage certain plastics, including many types of sunglasses.

Travellers' Diarrhoea

In general the South Caucasus countries are healthy places and stomach upsets are not noticeably more common than in other parts of Europe. If you do develop diarrhoea, however, be sure to drink plenty of fluids, preferably in the form of an oral rehydration solution such as Gastrolyte. If diarrhoea is bloody, persists for more than 72 hours or is accompanied by fever, shaking, chills or severe abdominal pain, seek medical attention.

Travelling with Children

➡ Make sure children are up to date with routine vaccinations, and discuss possible travel vaccines well before departure as some are not suitable for children.

➡ Be extra wary of contaminated food and water. If your child has vomiting or diarrhoea, lost fluid and salts must be replaced.

➡ Children should be encouraged to avoid and mistrust unfamiliar dogs or other mammals because of the potential risk of rabies and other diseases. Sheepdogs are not pets and can be dangerously fierce.

Languages

This chapter offers basic vocabulary to help you get around the South Caucasus. If you read our coloured pronunciation guides as if they were English, you'll be understood.

RUSSIAN

Russian is widely spoken in all three countries, and few people will ever object to being spoken to in it. If you speak passable Russian, you'll be able to get by. Note that kh is pronounced as in the Scottish *loch*, zh as the 's' in 'pleasure', r is rolled in Russian and the apostrophe (') indicates a slight y sound. The stressed syllables are shown in italics.

Basics

Hello.	Здравствуйте.	zdrast·vuyt·ye
Goodbye.	До свидания.	da svee·dan·ya
Excuse me./ Sorry.	Извините, пожалуйста.	eez·vee·neet·ye pa·zhal·sta
Please.	Пожалуйста.	pa·zhal·sta
Thank you.	Спасибо.	spa·see·ba
Yes./No.	Да./Нет.	da/nyet

What's your name?
Как вас зовут?   kak vaz za·vut

My name is ...
Меня зовут …   meen·ya za·vut …

Do you speak English?
Вы говорите по-английски?   vi ga·va·reet·ye pa·an·glee·skee

I don't understand.
Я не понимаю.   ya nye pa·nee·ma·yu

Accommodation

campsite	кемпинг	kyem·peeng
guesthouse	пансионат	pan·see·a·nat
hotel	гостиница	ga·stee·neet·sa
youth hostel	общежитие	ap·shee·zhi·tee·ye

Do you have a ... room?   У вас есть …?   u vas yest' …

| single | одноместный номер | ad·nam·yes·ni no·meer |
| double | номер с двуспальней кроватью | no·meer z dvu·spaln·yey kra·vat·yu |

How much is it ...?	Сколько стоит за …?	skol'·ka sto·eet za …
for two people	двоих	dva·eekh
per night	ночь	noch'

Eating & Drinking

What would you recommend?
Что вы рекомендуете?   shto vi ree·ka·meen·du·eet·ye

Do you have vegetarian food?
У вас есть овощные блюда?   u vas yest' a·vashch·ni·ye blyu·da

I'll have ...
…, пожалуйста.   … pa·zhal·sta

Cheers!
Пей до дна!   pyey da dna

I'd like the ..., please.	Я бы хотел/ хотела … (m/f)	ya bi khat·yel/ khat·ye·la …
bill	счёт	shot
menu	меню	meen·yu

(bottle of) beer	(бутылка) пива	(bu·til·ka) pee·va
(cup of) coffee/tea	(чашка) кофе/чаю	(chash·ka) kof·ye/cha·yu
water	вода	va·da
(glass of) wine	(рюмка) вина	(ryum·ka) vee·na

WANT MORE?

For in-depth language information and handy phrases, check out Lonely Planet's *Russian Phrasebook*. You'll find it at **shop.lonelyplanet.com**.

Numbers – Russian		
1	один	a·deen
2	два	dva
3	три	tree
4	четыре	chee·ti·ree
5	пять	pyat'
6	шесть	shest'
7	семь	syem'
8	восемь	vo·seem'
9	девять	dye·veet'
10	десять	dye·seet'

Emergencies

Help!	Помогите!	pa·ma·gee·tye
Go away!	Идите отсюда!	ee·deet·ye at·syu·da
Call ...!	Вызовите ...!	vi·za·veet·ye ...
a doctor	врача	vra·cha
the police	милицию	mee·leet·si·yu

I'm lost.
Я потерялся/ потерялась. (m/f) — ya pa·teer·yal·sa/ pa·teer·ya·las'

I'm ill.
Я болею. — ya bal·ye·yu

Where are the toilets?
Где здесь туалет? — gdye zdyes' tu·a·lyet

Shopping & Services

I'd like ...
Я бы хотел/ хотела ... (m/f) — ya bi khat·yel/ khat·ye·la ...

How much is it?
Сколько стоит? — skol'·ka sto·eet

That's too expensive.
Это очень дорого. — e·ta o·cheen' do·ra·ga

bank	банк	bank
market	рынок	ri·nak
post office	почта	poch·ta
tourist office	туристическое бюро	tu·rees·tee·chee·ska·ye byu·ro

Transport & Directions

Where's the ...?
Где (здесь) ...? — gdye (zdyes') ...

What's the address?
Какой адрес? — ka·koy a·drees

Can you show me (on the map)?
Покажите мне, пожалуйста (на карте)? — pa·ka·zhi·tye mnye pa·zhal·sta (na kart·ye)

One ... ticket, please.	Билет ...	beel·yet ...
one-way	в один конец	v a·deen kan·yets
return	в оба конца	v o·ba kant·sa
boat	параход	pa·ra·khot
bus	автобус	af·to·bus
plane	самолёт	sa·mal·yot
train	поезд	po·yeest

ARMENIAN

Armenian is an Indo-European language, with its own script and heavy influences from Persian evident in its vocabulary. It has also borrowed many words and phrases from Russian, Turkish, French and Hindi. The standard eastern Armenian is based on the variety spoken in Ashtarak, close to Yerevan. People from Lori *marz* (region) have a slower, more musical accent, while speakers from Gegharkunik and Karabakh have a strong accent that can be difficult for outsiders to understand, and vocabulary that is sometimes unique to one valley.

Below we've provided pronunciation guides (in red) rather than the Armenian script. Note that zh is pronounced as the 's' in 'measure', kh as the 'ch' in the Scottish *loch*, dz as the 'ds' in 'adds', gh is a throaty sound and r is rolled. See p223 for the alphabet.

Basics

Hello.	barev dzez (pol) barev (inf)
Goodbye.	tsetesutyun (pol) hajogh (inf)
Yes.	ayo/ha (pol/inf)
No.	voch/che (po/inf)
Please.	khuntrem
Thank you.	shnorhakalutyun
No problem.	problem cheeka
How are you?	vonts ek/es? (pol/inf)
I'm fine, thank you.	lav em shnorhakalutyun
And you?	eesk' duk?
What's your name?	anunut eench eh?
My name is ...	anuns ... e
Do you speak English?	khosum es angleren?
I don't understand.	chem haskanum

Accommodation

Do you have a room?	unek senyak?
guesthouse	panseeonat
hotel	hyuranots

Emergencies

Where is the toilet?	vortegh e zugarane?
I'm sick.	heevand em
doctor	bjheeshk
hospital	heevandanots
police	vosteegan

Shopping & Services

How much?	eench arjhey?
bank	bank
chemist/pharmacy	deghatun/apteka
currency exchange	dramee bokhanagum
expensive	tang
market	shuka
open	bats
post office	post
shop	khanut
telephone	herakhos

Time & Dates

When?	yerp?
yesterday	yerek
today	aysor
tomorrow	vaghe
Monday	yerkushaptee
Tuesday	yerekshaptee
Wednesday	chorekshaptee

Numbers – Armenian	
1	mek
2	yerku
3	yerek
4	chors
5	heeng
6	vets
7	yot
8	ut
9	eenuh
10	tas

Thursday	heengshaptee
Friday	urpat
Saturday	shapat
Sunday	keerakee

Transport & Directions

When does ... leave?	yerp jampa gelle ...?
When does ... arrive?	yerp gee hasne ...?
Stop!	kangnek!
airport	otanavakayan
bus	avtobus
bus station/stop	avtokayan/gankar
car	mekena
minibus	marshrutny/marshrutka
petrol	petrol/benzeen
plane	eenknateer/otanov
taxi	taksee
ticket	doms
Where?	ur/vortegh?
here	aystaeegh
left	dzakh
right	ach

AZERBAIJANI

Azerbaijani is a member of the Turkic language family, and shares its grammar and much of its vocabulary with Turkish. Originally written in a modified Arabic script, and during the Soviet rule in Russian Cyrillic script, it's now written in a modern Azerbaijani Latin alphabet (used below; see p304 for more on the alphabet).

Note that r is rolled, ğ is pronounced at the back of the throat, g as the 'gy' in 'Magyar', ç as the 'ch' in 'chase', c as the 'j' in 'jazz', x as the 'ch' in the Scottish loch, j as the 's' in 'pleasure', q as the 'g' in 'get', ş as the 'sh' in 'shore', ı as the 'a' in 'ago', ə as in 'apple' (short), ö as the 'e' in 'her', and ü as the 'ew' in 'pew'. In many parts of the country, the hard 'k' is pronounced more like a 'ch'. Words are lightly stressed on the last syllable.

Basics

Hello.	*Salam.*
Goodbye.	*Sağ olun/ol.* (pol/inf)
How are you?	*Necəsiniz?* (pol)
	Necəsən? (inf)
Yes.	*Bəli./Hə.* (pol/inf)
No.	*Xeyr./Yox.*

Please.	*Lütfən.*
Thank you.	*Təşəkkür edirəm.*
You're welcome.	*Buyurun.*
Excuse me./Sorry.	*Bağışlayın.*
Do you speak English?	*Siz ingiliscə danışırsınız?*
I don't understand.	*Mən anlamıram.*
Cheers!	*Deyilən sağlığa!*

Accommodation

hotel	*mehmanxana*
room	*otaq*
toilet	*tualet*

Emergencies

ambulance	*tacili yardım maşını*
doctor	*hakim*
hospital	*xastaxana*

Shopping & Services

How much?	*Nə qədər?*
bank	*bank*
chemist/pharmacy	*aptek*
currency exchange	*valyuta dayışma*
expensive	*baha*
market	*bazar*
open	*açıq*
post office	*poçt*
shop	*dukan/mağaza*
telephone	*telefon*

Time & Dates

When?	*Nə vaxt?*
yesterday	*dünən*
today	*bu gün*
tomorrow	*sabah*

Monday	*Bazar ertəsi*
Tuesday	*Çərşənbə axşamı*
Wednesday	*Çərşənbə*
Thursday	*Cümə axşamı*
Friday	*Cümə*
Saturday	*Şənbə*
Sunday	*Bazar*

Numbers – Azerbaijani

1	bir
2	iki
3	üç
4	dörd
5	beş
6	altı
7	yeddi
8	səkkiz
9	doqquz
10	on

Transport & Directions

When does ... leave?	*... nə zaman gedir?*
When does ... arrive?	*... nə zaman gəlir?*
Stop!	*Saxla!*
airport	*hava limanı*
bus	*avtobus*
bus station	*avtovağzal*
bus stop	*avtobus dayanacağı*
car	*maşın*
ferry	*bərə*
minibus	*mikroavtobus*
petrol	*benzin*
plane	*təyyarə*
port	*liman*
taxi	*taksi*
ticket	*bilet*
train	*qatar*
train station	*damir yolu stansiyası*
Where?	*Hara?/Harada?* (for verbs/nouns)
avenue	*prospekt*
lane/alley	*xiyaban*
square	*meydan*
street	*küçə*

GEORGIAN

Georgian belongs to the Kartvelian language family, which is related to the Caucasian languages. It is an ancient language with its own cursive script. See p142 for the alphabet.

Here we've provided pronunciation guides (in red) rather than the Georgian script. Note that q is pronounced as the 'k' in 'king' but far back in the throat, kh as the 'ch' in the Scottish *loch*, zh as the 's' in 'pleasure', dz as the 'ds' in 'beds', gh is a throaty sound (like an incipient gargle) and r is rolled. Light word stress usually falls on the first syllable.

Basics

Hello.	gamarjobat
Goodbye.	nakhvamdis
Yes.	diakh/ho (pol/inf)
No.	ara
Please.	tu sheidzleba
Thank you.	madlobt
How are you?	rogor khart?
Excuse me.	ukatsravad
It doesn't matter.	ara ushavs
Do you speak English?	inglisuri itsit?
I don't understand.	ar mesmis
Cheers!	gaumarjos!

Accommodation

hotel	sastumro
room	otakhi
toilet	tualeti

Emergencies

doctor	eqimi
hospital	saavadmq'opo
police	politsia

Shopping & Services

How much?	ramdeni?
bank	banki
chemist/pharmacy	aptiaqi
expensive	dzviri
market	bazari/bazroba

Numbers – Georgian	
1	erti
2	ori
3	sami
4	otkhi
5	khuti
6	ekvsi
7	shvidi
8	rva
9	tskhra
10	ati

open	ghiaa
post office	posta
shop	maghazia
telephone	teleponi

Time & Dates

When?	rodis?
yesterday	gushin
today	dghes
tomorrow	khval
Sunday	kvira
Monday	orshabati
Tuesday	samshabati
Wednesday	otkhshabati
Thursday	khutshabati
Friday	paraskevi
Saturday	shabati

Transport & Directions

When does it leave?	romel saatze gadis?
When does it arrive?	romel saatze chamodis?
Stop here!	gaacheret!
airport	aeroporti
boat	gemi
bus	avtobusi/troleibusi
bus station	avtosadguri
bus stop	gachereba
car	manqana
minibus	marshrutka
petrol	benzini
plane	tvitmprinavi
port	porti
taxi	taksi
ticket	bileti
train	matarebeli
train station	(rkinigzis) sadguri
Where?	sad?
avenue	gamziri
road/way	gza
square	moedani

GLOSSARY

You may encounter some of the following words during your time in Georgia (Geo), Armenia (Arm) and Azerbaijan (Az). Some Russian (Rus) and Turkish (Tur) words, including the ones below, have been widely adopted in the Caucasus.

abour (Arm) – soup

ajika (Geo) – chilli paste

alaverdi (Geo) – person appointed by the toast-master at a *supra* to elaborate on the toast

Amenaprkich (Arm) – All Saviours

aptek/apteka/aptiaqi (Az/Rus & Arm/Geo) – pharmacy

Arakelots (Arm) – the Apostles

ARF (Arm) – Armenian Revolutionary Federation; the Dashnaks

aşig (ashug) (Az) – itinerant musician

astodan (Az) – ossuary

Astvatsatsin (Arm) – Holy Mother of God

aviakassa (Rus) – shop or window selling air tickets

avtokayan (Arm) – bus station

avtosadguri (Geo) – bus station

avtovağzal (Az) – bus station

baklava – honeyed nut pastry

baliq (Az) – fish, usually sturgeon, often grilled

basturma (Arm) – cured beef in ground red pepper

berd (Arm) – fortress

bulvar (Az) – boulevard

caravanserai – historic travellers inn, usually based around a courtyard

Catholicos – patriarch of the Armenian or Georgian churches

çay (Az) – tea

çayxana (Az) – teahouse

chacha (Geo) – powerful grappa-like liquor

chakapuli (Geo) – lamb and plums in herb sauce

churchkhela (Geo) – string of nuts coated in a sort of caramel made from grape juice and flour

chvishdari (Geo) – Svanetian dish of cheese cooked inside maize bread

CIS – Commonwealth of Independent States; the loose political and economic alliance of the former republics of the USSR (except Georgia and the Baltic states)

çörək (Az) – bread

dacha (Rus) – country holiday cottage or bungalow

darbazi (Geo) – traditional home design with the roof tapering up to a central hole

doğrama (Az) – cold soup made with sour milk, potato, onion and cucumber

dolma (Arm, Az) – vine leaves with a rice filling

domik (Rus) – hut or modest bungalow accommodation

dram – Armenian unit of currency

duduk (Arm) – traditional reed instrument; also *tutak* (Az)

dzor (Arm) – gorge

elektrichka (Rus) – local train service linking a city and its suburbs or nearby towns, or groups of adjacent towns

eristavi (Geo) – duke

gavit (Arm) – entrance hall of a church

ghomi (Geo) – maize porridge

glasnost (Rus) – openness

halva (Az) – various sweet pastries, often containing nuts

hraparak (Arm) – square

IDP – internally displaced person

Intourist (Rus) – Soviet-era government tourist organisation

ishkhan (Arm) – trout from Lake Sevan

istirahət zonası (Az) – rural bungalow resort

jvari (Geo) – religious cross; spiritual site in mountain regions

kamança (Az) – stringed musical instrument

kartuli – Georgian language

Kartvelebi – Georgian people

kassa (Rus) – cash desk or ticket booth

katoghike (Arm) – cathedral

khachapuri (Geo) – savoury bread or pastry, usually with a cheese filling

khachkar (Arm) – medieval carved headstone

khamaju (Arm) – meat pie

khash/khashi (Arm/Geo) – garlic and tripe soup; also *xaş* (Az)

khashlama (Arm) – lamb or beef stew with potato

khati/khatebi (Geo) – animist shrine in Tusheti, Georgia

khevi (Geo) – gorge

khidi (Geo) – bridge

khinkali (Geo) – spicy meat, potato or mushroom dumpling

khoravats (Arm) – barbe-cued food

kişi (Az) – men (hence 'K' marks men's toilets)

köfte/kyufta/küftə (Tur/Arm/Az) – minced-beef meatballs with onion and spices

körpü (Az) – bridge

koshki/koshkebi (Geo) – defensive tower in Georgian mountain regions

kubdari (Geo) – spicy Svane-tian meat pie

küçəsi (Az) – street

kupe/kupeyny (Rus) – 2nd-class compartment accommodation on trains

kvas (Rus) – beverage made from fermented rye bread

lahmacun/lahmajoon (Tur/Arm) – small lamb and herb pizzas

lari – Georgian unit of currency

lavash/lavaş (Arm/Az) – thin bread

ləvəngi (Az) – casserole of chicken stuffed with walnuts and herbs

lich (Arm) – lake

lobio/lobiya/lobya (Geo/Rus/Az) – beans, often with herbs and spices

luks (Rus) – deluxe; used to refer to hotel suites and 1st-class accommodation on trains

manat – Azerbaijani unit of currency

marani (Geo) – wine cellar

marshrutka/marshrutky (Rus) – public minivan transport

marz (Arm) – province, region

matagh (Arm) – animal sacrifice

matenadaran (Arm) – library

matsoni (Geo) – yoghurt drink

mayrughi (Arm) – highway

mehmanxana (Az) – hotel

merikipe (Geo) – man who pours wine at a *supra*

meydan (Az) – square

mədrəsə (Az) – Islamic school

moedani (Geo) – square

most (Rus) – bridge

mtsvadi (Geo) – shish kebab, *shashlyk*

muğam (Az) – traditional musical style

mushuri (Geo) – working songs

muzhskoy (Rus) – men's toilet

nagorny (Rus) – mountainous

nard, nardi (Az/Arm) – backgammonlike board game

obshchy (Rus) – general-seating class (unreserved) on trains

oghee (Arm) – fruit vodkas; sometimes called *vatsun* or *aragh*

OSCE – Organisation for Security and Co-operation in Europe

OVIR (Rus) – Visa and Registration Department

paneer (Arm) – cheese

paxlava (Az) – honeyed nut pastry

pendir (Az) – cheese

perestroika (Rus) – restructuring

pir (Az) – shrine or holy place

piti (Az) – soupy meat stew with chickpeas and saffron

pivo (Rus) – beer

pkhali/mkhali (Geo) – beetroot, spinach or aubergine paste with crushed walnuts, garlic and herbs

platskart/platskartny (Rus) – open-bunk accommodation on trains

plov – rice dish

poghota (Arm) – avenue

poghots (Arm) – street

prospekti (Az) – avenue

qadım (Az) – woman (hence 'Q' marks womens toilets)

qala, qalasi (Az) – castle or fortress

qəpiq – Azerbaijani unit of currency (100 qəpiq equals one manat)

qucha (Geo) – street

qutab (Az) – stuffed pancake

rabiz (Rus) – Armenian workers' culture, party music

rtveli (Geo) – grape harvest

sagalobeli (Geo) – church songs

sagmiro (Geo) – epic songs

sakhachapure (Geo) – café serving *khachapuri*

sakhinkle (Geo) – café serving *khinkali*

saxlama kamera (Az) – left-luggage room(s)

satrap – Persian provincial governor

satrpialo (Geo) – love songs

satsivi (Geo) – cold turkey or chicken in walnut sauce

şəbəkə (Az) – intricately carved, wood-framed, stained-glass windows

shashlyk – shish kebab

shirvan – old Azerbaijani unit of currency, equal to two manat

shkmeruli (Geo) – chicken in garlic sauce

shuka (Arm) – market

soorch (Arm) – coffee

spalny vagon/SV (Rus) – two-berth sleeping compartment in train

suchush (Arm) – plum and walnut sweet

sulguni (Geo) – smoked cheese from Samegrelo

supra (Geo) – dinner party; literally means 'tablecloth'

supruli (Geo) – songs for the table

surp (Arm) – holy, saint

tabouleh (Arm) – diced green salad with semolina

tamada (Geo) – toastmaster at a *supra*

tan (Arm) – yoghurt

tetri – Georgian unit of currency (100 tetri equals one lari)

tikə kəbab (Az) – shish kebab; commonly called *shashlyk*

tqemali (Geo) – wild plum, wild plum sauce

tonir (Arm) – traditional bread oven

tsikhe (Geo) – fortified place

tufa – volcanic stone famous to Armenia

tur – large, endangered Caucasian ibex

tutak (Az) – traditional reed instrument; also *duduk* (Arm)

vank (Arm) – monastery

virap (Arm) – well

vishap (Arm) – carved dragon stone

xaş (Az) – garlic and tripe soup; also *khash/khashi* (Arm/Geo)

xəzri (Az) – gale-force wind in Baku

yeməkxana (Az) – food house, cheap eatery

zhensky (Rus) – womens toilets

Behind the Scenes

SEND US YOUR FEEDBACK

We love to hear from travellers – your comments keep us on our toes and help make our books better. Our well-travelled team reads every word on what you loved or loathed about this book. Although we cannot reply individually to your submissions, we always guarantee that your feedback goes straight to the appropriate authors, in time for the next edition. Each person who sends us information is thanked in the next edition – the most useful submissions are rewarded with a selection of digital PDF chapters.

Visit **lonelyplanet.com/contact** to submit your updates and suggestions or to ask for help. Our award-winning website also features inspirational travel stories, news and discussions.

Note: We may edit, reproduce and incorporate your comments in Lonely Planet products such as guidebooks, websites and digital products, so let us know if you don't want your comments reproduced or your name acknowledged. For a copy of our privacy policy visit lonelyplanet.com/privacy.

OUR READERS

Many thanks to the travellers who used the last edition and wrote to us with helpful hints, useful advice and interesting anecdotes:

Aina Margalef, Alessandra Martina, Alex Jones, Alice Jacobs, Ana Louro, Anna Schappert, Ariel Jacob, Bernard Kosto, Caroline Peters, Christian Huegel, Dave Vassar, David Haseler, Ewa Stachura, Faissal Sharif, Floor Molenaar, G Keller, JA de Roo, Jan Sebastiaan Nutma, Jan Vilis Haanes, Jennifer Armstrong, Johnny Gere, Judith Weiss, Lauren Wolfe, Lene Hansen, Leyla Rasulzade, Maggie Webb, Mary Rose-Miller, Mengzhu Wang, Michal Struk, Mireille Grosjean, Nuria Pérez Oreja, Olof Tilly, Paul Berman, Pay Cargill, Peter Geczi, Peter Voelger, Petr Kratochvíl, Quan Wen, Riccarda Kirwald, Ruth Schopenhauer, Ryan Sturgill, Suren Adamyan, Tina Tamman, Tommy Bay Smidt, Ton Trijssenaar, Torje Sunde, Victoria Bainbridge, Willem Bakker, WJ Underwood, Yuji Fujimoto

WRITER THANKS

Tom Masters

Didi madloba to my extended crew of friends in Saqartvelo, but especially: Zurab Zaalishvili, Dato Imnadze, Davit Gogshelidze and Levan Berulava. Thanks also to Moritz Estermann, Sadia Belhadi, Josa Glück and Michelle Gurevich for sharing some wonderful travel experiences with me, to Gianluca Pardelli and Emily Sherwin for useful contacts, to Gemma Graham for trusting me with Georgia and to John Noble for having worked so hard on the content over the years and leaving the text in such great shape.

Joel Balsam

Thanks to my partner and teammate Stephanie Foden, who joined me at all those churches and helped me eat endless dolma. *Merci* to my helpful contacts in Armenia: Carine Tomassian, Ardag Kosian, Ruzik Gasparyan, Armen Hovsepyan, Sashka Avanyan and Ara Arasunts. And thanks to my family and Stephanie's family for bearing with me as I spent all of July writing this book – my first, hopefully of many, for Lonely Planet.

Jenny Smith

A big thank you to the dozens of kind people who have helped make the research more thorough and enjoyable, and to much-missed Gemma Graham at Lonely Planet for giving me the chance to do this fascinating project.

ACKNOWLEDGEMENTS

Climate map data adapted from Peel MC, Finlayson BL & McMahon TA (2007) 'Updated World Map of the Köppen-Geiger Climate Classification', *Hydrology and Earth System Sciences*, 11, 1633–44.

Cover photograph: Tsminda Sameba Cathedral, Tbilisi, Georgia; Christian Kober/ AWL Images ©

THIS BOOK

This 6th edition of Lonely Planet's *Georgia, Armenia & Azerbaijan* guidebook was researched and written by Tom Masters, Joel Balsam and Jenny Smith. The previous edition was written by Alex Jones, Tom Masters, Virginia Maxwell and John Noble. This guidebook was produced by the following:

Destination Editor Gemma Graham

Senior Product Editors Sandie Kestell, Genna Patterson

Regional Senior Cartographer Valentina Kremenchutskaya

Product Editor Carolyn Boicos

Book Designer Jessica Rose

Assisting Editors Jennifer Hattam, Jodie Martire, Anne Mulvaney, Kristin Odijk, Charlotte Orr, Monique Perrin, James Smart, Amanda Williamson

Assisting Cartographer James Leversha

Cover Researcher Meri Blazevski

Thanks to William Allen, Imogen Bannister, Piotr Czajkowski, Melanie Dankel, Sasha Drew, Karen Henderson, Chris LeeAck, Jenna Myers, Zurab Zaalishvili

344

Index

Map Legend

Sights

- Beach
- Bird Sanctuary
- Buddhist
- Castle/Palace
- Christian
- Confucian
- Hindu
- Islamic
- Jain
- Jewish
- Monument
- Museum/Gallery/Historic Building
- Ruin
- Shinto
- Sikh
- Taoist
- Winery/Vineyard
- Zoo/Wildlife Sanctuary
- Other Sight

Activities, Courses & Tours

- Bodysurfing
- Diving
- Canoeing/Kayaking
- Course/Tour
- Sento Hot Baths/Onsen
- Skiing
- Snorkelling
- Surfing
- Swimming/Pool
- Walking
- Windsurfing
- Other Activity

Sleeping

- Sleeping
- Camping
- Hut/Shelter

Eating

- Eating

Drinking & Nightlife

- Drinking & Nightlife
- Cafe

Entertainment

- Entertainment

Shopping

- Shopping

Information

- Bank
- Embassy/Consulate
- Hospital/Medical
- Internet
- Police
- Post Office
- Telephone
- Toilet
- Tourist Information
- Other Information

Geographic

- Beach
- Gate
- Hut/Shelter
- Lighthouse
- Lookout
- Mountain/Volcano
- Oasis
- Park
- Pass
- Picnic Area
- Waterfall

Population

- Capital (National)
- Capital (State/Province)
- City/Large Town
- Town/Village

Transport

- Airport
- Border crossing
- Bus
- Cable car/Funicular
- Cycling
- Ferry
- Metro station
- Monorail
- Parking
- Petrol station
- Subway station
- Taxi
- Train station/Railway
- Tram
- Underground station
- Other Transport

Routes

- Tollway
- Freeway
- Primary
- Secondary
- Tertiary
- Lane
- Unsealed road
- Road under construction
- Plaza/Mall
- Steps
- Tunnel
- Pedestrian overpass
- Walking Tour
- Walking Tour detour
- Path/Walking Trail

Boundaries

- International
- State/Province
- Disputed
- Regional/Suburb
- Marine Park
- Cliff
- Wall

Hydrography

- River, Creek
- Intermittent River
- Canal
- Water
- Dry/Salt/Intermittent Lake
- Reef

Areas

- Airport/Runway
- Beach/Desert
- Cemetery (Christian)
- Cemetery (Other)
- Glacier
- Mudflat
- Park/Forest
- Sight (Building)
- Sportsground
- Swamp/Mangrove

Note: Not all symbols displayed above appear on the maps in this book

OUR STORY

A beat-up old car, a few dollars in the pocket and a sense of adventure. In 1972 that's all Tony and Maureen Wheeler needed for the trip of a lifetime – across Europe and Asia overland to Australia. It took several months, and at the end – broke but inspired – they sat at their kitchen table writing and stapling together their first travel guide, *Across Asia on the Cheap*. Within a week they'd sold 1500 copies. Lonely Planet was born.

Today, Lonely Planet has offices in Franklin, London, Melbourne, Oakland, Dublin, Beijing and Delhi, with more than 600 staff and writers. We share Tony's belief that 'a great guidebook should do three things: inform, educate and amuse'.

OUR WRITERS

Tom Masters

Georgia Dreaming since he could walk of going to the most obscure places on earth, Tom has always had a taste for the unknown. This has led to a writing career that has taken him all over the world, including North Korea, the Arctic, Congo and Siberia. Despite a childhood spent in the English countryside, as an adult Tom has always called London, Paris and Berlin home. He currently lives in Berlin and can be found online at www.tommasters.net. Tom also curated the Plan Your Trip, Understand and Survival Guide chapters.

Joel Balsam

Armenia Who's the man behind the flower beard? I'm a Canadian freelance journalist, backpacker and nomad who's been travelling the world pretty much nonstop since 2015 (50 countries and counting). My work has appeared in *National Geographic Travel, Time,* the *Guardian*, *Travel + Leisure, ESPN* and *Vice*. For Lonely Planet, I've worked on two guidebooks so far: *Georgia, Armenia & Azerbaijan*, as well as *Morocco*. Travel writing has always been a dream for me, well, since becoming an NHL goalie didn't work out (I'm Canadian after all).

Jenny Smith

Azerbaijan The Azerbaijan chapter was written and researched by an experienced Lonely Planet writer who has visited Azerbaijan and Georgia on over a dozen occasions since 1995. She has chosen to use a pseudonym due to cultural and political sensitivities in the region.

Other Contributors

Jenna Myers curated the Nagorno-Karabakh chapter.

Published by Lonely Planet Global Limited
CRN 554153
6th edition – Jun 2020
ISBN 978 1 78657 599 9
© Lonely Planet 2020   Photographs © as indicated 2020
10 9 8 7 6 5 4 3 2 1
Printed in Singapore